Ford Kuga
Owner's Workshop Manual

Euan Doig

Models covered *(6464 – 352)*

Ford Kuga 'Mk 2' SUV with front- and four-wheel-drive (2WD & 4WD)

Petrol: 1.5 litre (1499cc) EcoBoost
Turbo-diesel: 1.5 litre (1499cc) & 2.0 litre (1998cc) Duratorq

Does NOT cover models with 1.6 litre petrol engines or semi-automatic 'PowerShift' transmission
Does NOT cover 'Mk 3' Kuga introduced Spring 2020

ABCDE
FGHIJ
KLMNO
PQRST

A book in the Haynes Owners Workshop Manual Series

ISBN 978 1 78521 464 6

British Library Cataloguing in Publication Data
A catalogue record for this book is available from the British Library.

Printed in Malaysia

J H Haynes & Co Ltd
Sparkford, Yeovil, Somerset BA22 7JJ, England

Haynes North America, Inc
859 Lawrence Drive, Newbury Park, California 91320, USA

Printed using NORBRITE BOOK 48.8gsm (CODE: 40N6533) from NORPAC; procurement system certified under Sustainable Forestry Initiative standard. Paper produced is certified to the SFI Certified Fiber Sourcing Standard (CERT - 0094271)

Contents

LIVING WITH YOUR FORD KUGA

Roadside Repairs

MAINTENANCE

Routine maintenance and servicing

Contents

REPAIRS AND OVERHAUL

Building on the success of the original Ford Kuga (model name C394) introduced in July 2002, the 'MkII' Kuga (model designation C520) covered by this manual was introduced in December 2012.

The range of engines offered were Ford's own modular designed 3-, and 4-cylinder petrol and diesel engines, featuring double overhead camshafts, turbochargers, direct fuel injection and advanced emission control systems.

Over the years, the range was has been improved with minor cosmetic/mechanical revisions and variants, but the same practicality and driving fun have remained.

All models have fully-independent front and rear suspension, with anti-roll bars fitted both to the front and rear assemblies.

A wide range of standard and optional equipment is available within the Kuga range to suit most tastes, including central locking, electric windows, air conditioning, an electric sunroof, an anti-lock braking system, a traction control system, a dynamic stability control system, and numerous air bags.

Provided that regular servicing is carried out in accordance with the manufacturer's recommendations, the Kuga should prove reliable and very economical. The engine compartment is well-designed, and most of the items requiring frequent attention are easily accessible.

Your Ford Kuga manual

The aim of this manual is to help you get the best value from your vehicle. It can do so in several ways. It can help you decide what work must be done (even should you choose to get it done by a garage). It will also provide information on routine maintenance and servicing, and give a logical course of action and diagnosis when random faults occur. However, it is hoped that you will use the manual by tackling the work yourself. On simpler jobs it may even be quicker than booking the car into a garage and going there twice, to leave and collect it. Perhaps most important, a lot of money can be saved by avoiding the costs a garage must charge to cover its labour and overheads.

The manual has drawings and descriptions to show the function of the various components so that their layout can be understood. Tasks are described and photographed in a clear step-by-step sequence.

References to the 'left' and 'right' of the vehicle are in the sense of a person in the driver's seat facing forward.

Acknowledgements

Thanks are due to Draper Tools Limited, who provided some of the workshop tools, and to all those people at Sparkford who helped in the production of this manual.

We take great pride in the accuracy of information given in this manual, but vehicle manufacturers make alterations and design changes during the production run of a particular vehicle of which they do not inform us. No liability can be accepted by the authors or publishers for loss, damage or injury caused by any errors in, or omissions from, the information given.

Dimensions and weights

Note: *All figures are approximate, and may vary according to model. Refer to manufacturer's data for exact figures.*

Dimensions

Overall length:	
Standard models	4531 mm
ST and ST- Line models	4541 mm
Overall width (inc. mirrors)	2086 mm
Overall height:	
Standard models	1689 mm
With roof rails	1749 mm
Wheelbase:	2690 mm

Weights

Gross vehicle weight (depending on model)	1615 to 1815 kg

Working on your car can be dangerous. This page shows just some of the potential risks and hazards, with the aim of creating a safety-conscious attitude.

General hazards

Scalding

• Don't remove the radiator or expansion tank cap while the engine is hot.

• Engine oil, transmission fluid or power steering fluid may also be dangerously hot if the engine has recently been running.

Burning

• Beware of burns from the exhaust system and from any part of the engine. Brake discs and drums can also be extremely hot immediately after use.

Crushing

• When working under or near a raised vehicle, always supplement the jack with axle stands, or use drive-on ramps.

Never venture under a car which is only supported by a jack.

• Take care if loosening or tightening high-torque nuts when the vehicle is on stands. Initial loosening and final tightening should be done with the wheels on the ground.

Fire

• Fuel is highly flammable; fuel vapour is explosive.

• Don't let fuel spill onto a hot engine.

• Do not smoke or allow naked lights (including pilot lights) anywhere near a vehicle being worked on. Also beware of creating sparks (electrically or by use of tools).

• Fuel vapour is heavier than air, so don't work on the fuel system with the vehicle over an inspection pit.

• Another cause of fire is an electrical overload or short-circuit. Take care when repairing or modifying the vehicle wiring.

• Keep a fire extinguisher handy, of a type suitable for use on fuel and electrical fires.

Electric shock

• Ignition HT and Xenon headlight voltages can be dangerous, especially to people with heart problems or a pacemaker. Don't work on or near these systems with the engine running or the ignition switched on.

• Mains voltage is also dangerous. Make sure that any mains-operated equipment is correctly earthed. Mains power points should be protected by a residual current device (RCD) circuit breaker.

Fume or gas intoxication

• Exhaust fumes are poisonous; they can contain carbon monoxide, which is rapidly fatal if inhaled. Never run the engine in a confined space such as a garage with the doors shut.

• Fuel vapour is also poisonous, as are the vapours from some cleaning solvents and paint thinners.

Poisonous or irritant substances

• Avoid skin contact with battery acid and with any fuel, fluid or lubricant, especially antifreeze, brake hydraulic fluid and Diesel fuel. Don't syphon them by mouth. If such a substance is swallowed or gets into the eyes, seek medical advice.

• Prolonged contact with used engine oil can cause skin cancer. Wear gloves or use a barrier cream if necessary. Change out of oil-soaked clothes and do not keep oily rags in your pocket.

• Air conditioning refrigerant forms a poisonous gas if exposed to a naked flame (including a cigarette). It can also cause skin burns on contact.

Asbestos

• Asbestos dust can cause cancer if inhaled or swallowed. Asbestos may be found in gaskets and in brake and clutch linings. When dealing with such components it is safest to assume that they contain asbestos.

Special hazards

Hydrofluoric acid

• This extremely corrosive acid is formed when certain types of synthetic rubber, found in some O-rings, oil seals, fuel hoses etc, are exposed to temperatures above 4000C. The rubber changes into a charred or sticky substance containing the acid. *Once formed, the acid remains dangerous for years. If it gets onto the skin, it may be necessary to amputate the limb concerned.*

• When dealing with a vehicle which has suffered a fire, or with components salvaged from such a vehicle, wear protective gloves and discard them after use.

The battery

• Batteries contain sulphuric acid, which attacks clothing, eyes and skin. Take care when topping-up or carrying the battery.

• The hydrogen gas given off by the battery is highly explosive. Never cause a spark or allow a naked light nearby. Be careful when connecting and disconnecting battery chargers or jump leads.

Air bags

• Air bags can cause injury if they go off accidentally. Take care when removing the steering wheel and trim panels. Special storage instructions may apply.

Diesel injection equipment

• Diesel injection pumps supply fuel at very high pressure. Take care when working on the fuel injectors and fuel pipes.

Warning: Never expose the hands, face or any other part of the body to injector spray; the fuel can penetrate the skin with potentially fatal results.

Remember...

DO

• Do use eye protection when using power tools, and when working under the vehicle.

• Do wear gloves or use barrier cream to protect your hands when necessary.

• Do get someone to check periodically that all is well when working alone on the vehicle.

• Do keep loose clothing and long hair well out of the way of moving mechanical parts.

• Do remove rings, wristwatch etc, before working on the vehicle – especially the electrical system.

• Do ensure that any lifting or jacking equipment has a safe working load rating adequate for the job.

DON'T

• Don't attempt to lift a heavy component which may be beyond your capability – get assistance.

• Don't rush to finish a job, or take unverified short cuts.

• Don't use ill-fitting tools which may slip and cause injury.

• Don't leave tools or parts lying around where someone can trip over them. Mop up oil and fuel spills at once.

• Don't allow children or pets to play in or near a vehicle being worked on.

Vehicle identification

1 Modifications are a continuing and unpublicised process in vehicle manufacture, quite apart from major model changes. Spare parts manuals and lists are compiled upon a numerical basis, the individual vehicle identification numbers being essential to correct identification of the component concerned.

2 When ordering spare parts, always give as much information as possible. Quote the car model, year of manufacture, body and engine numbers as appropriate.

3 The vehicle identification plate is situated on the driver's side B-pillar. The vehicle identification number is also repeated in the form of plate visible through the windscreen on the passenger's side **(see illustrations)**.

4 The engine identification numbers are situated on the front face of the cylinder block **(see illustration)**, either on a plate, or stamped directly to the cylinder block face. On some models, the engine type is shown on a sticker affixed to the timing belt cover.

5 Other identification numbers or codes are stamped on major items such as the gearbox, etc.

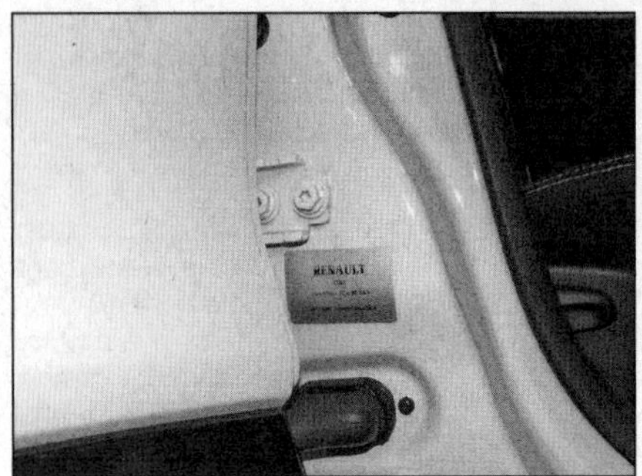

5.3a VIN plate at the base of the B-pillar ...

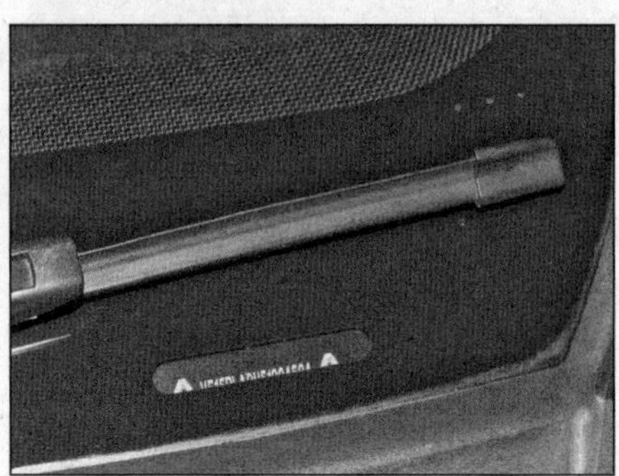

5.3b ... and on a plate on the facia (visible through the windscreen)

5.4 Engine number on cylinder block adjacent to the starter (1.5 litre petrol engine)

Buying spare parts

1 Spare parts are available from many sources, including maker's appointed garages, accessory shops, and motor factors. To be sure of obtaining the correct parts, it may sometimes be necessary to quote the vehicle identification number. If possible, it can also be useful to take the old parts along for positive identification. Items such as starter motors and alternators may be available under a service exchange scheme – any parts returned should always be clean.

2 Our advice regarding spare part sources is as follows:

Officially-appointed garages

3 This is the best source of parts which are peculiar to your car, and are not otherwise generally available (eg, badges, interior trim, certain body panels, etc). It is also the only place at which you should buy parts if the vehicle is still under warranty.

Accessory shops

4 These are very good places to buy materials and components needed for the maintenance of your car (oil, air and fuel filters, spark plugs, light bulbs, drivebelts, oils and greases, brake pads, touch-up paint, etc). Parts like this sold by a reputable shop are of the same standard as those used by the car manufacturer.

Motor factors

5 Good factors will stock all the more important components which wear out comparatively quickly and can sometimes supply individual components needed for the overhaul of a larger assembly. They may also handle work such as cylinder block reboring, crankshaft regrinding and balancing, etc.

Tyre and exhaust specialists

6 These outlets may be independent or members of a local or national chain. They frequently offer competitive prices when compared with a main dealer or local garage, but it will pay to obtain several quotes before making a decision. Also ask what 'extras' may be added to the quote – for instance, fitting a new valve and balancing the wheel are both often charged on top of the price of a new tyre.

Other sources

7 Beware of parts of materials obtained from market stalls, car boot sales or similar outlets. Such items are not always sub-standard, but there is little chance of compensation if they do prove unsatisfactory. In the case of safety-critical components such as brake pads there is the risk not only of financial loss but also of an accident causing injury or death.

8 Second-hand components or assemblies obtained from a car breaker can be a good buy in some circumstances, but this sort of purchase is best made by the experienced DIY mechanic.

Known faults and recalls

Recalls

Listed here are the official recalls issued by the manufacturer. To check that the relevant recall has been carried out on your vehicle, contact your local Ford dealer.

Recall subject	Date
B-pillar trim too close to seatbelt pretensioner	30th August 2017
Side and knee airbags can fail to deploy in collision	4th September 2017
Cylinder head may crack	8th January 2018
Sump can crack from engine overheating	12th March 2018
Clutch pressure plate may fracture	16th July 2018 and again on 22nd February 2019

Fault finding

Online assistance

1 Haynes.com provides a wealth of information about your vehicle, including repair tips and techniques; however, the specifics of diagnosing an issue on your particular vehicle is sometimes extremely specialised and intricate. If you're having difficulty diagnosing a problem, you may wish to judiciously engage in online research or request assistance from experts.

The source matters!

2 As we're all aware, information on the internet is only as reliable as the person or organisation who provides it. We suggest the following hierarchy when searching:

a) *The manufacturer or related source: Ideally, your source would be associated directly with the vehicle manufacturer or the manufacturer of the affected component(s). They are the most likely to be authoritative and generally have an interest in assuring diagnosis and repair are carried out safely and correctly.*

b) *Fee-based assistance: Some sites employ experts who assist owners with their vehicle diagnostics. Their fees are reasonable in comparison with the diagnostic charges you're likely to encounter at a dealership or repair workshop. Look for popular sites with many positive reviews.*

c) *Recommendation from an expert: Repair workshops who specialise in your vehicle type will likely be aware of online resources for your vehicle. Repair workshops may not readily divulge sources because they want to do the work for you. Nevertheless, they want positive relationships with potential customers and are unlikely to give you false information.*

d) *Owner forums: Information from online forums can be anything from first-rate to entirely wrong. The quality of information is not always obvious. Get involved with forums before you need help so you will know who you can trust. Search for confirmed fixes – If someone trustworthy shared the solution to a problem similar to yours, it might be your solution too.*

Introduction

3 The vehicle owner who does his or her own maintenance according to the recommended service schedules should not have to use this section of the manual very often. Modern component reliability is such that, provided those items subject to wear or deterioration are inspected or renewed at the specified intervals, sudden failure is comparatively rare. Faults do not usually just happen as a result of sudden failure, but develop over a period of time. Major mechanical failures in particular are usually preceded by characteristic symptoms over hundreds or even thousands of miles. Those components which do occasionally fail without warning are often small and easily carried in the vehicle.

4 With any fault finding, the first step is to decide where to begin investigations. Sometimes this is obvious, but on other occasions, a little detective work will be necessary. The owner who makes half a dozen haphazard adjustments or replacements may be successful in curing a fault (or its symptoms), but will be none the wiser if the fault recurs, and ultimately may have spent more time and money than was necessary. A calm and logical approach will be found to be more satisfactory in the long run. Always take into account any warning signs or abnormalities that may have been noticed in the period preceding the fault – power loss, high or low gauge readings, unusual smells, etc – and remember that failure of components such as fuses or spark plugs may only be pointers to some underlying fault.

5 The pages which follow provide an easy-reference guide to the more common problems which may occur during the operation of the vehicle. These problems and their possible causes are grouped under headings denoting various components or systems, such as Engine, Cooling system, etc. The Chapter which deals with the problem is also shown in brackets. Whatever the fault, certain basic principles apply. These are as follows:

Verify the fault. This is simply a matter of being sure that you know what the symptoms are before starting work. This is particularly important if you are investigating a fault for someone else, who may not have described it very accurately.

Don't overlook the obvious. For example, if the vehicle won't start, is there fuel in the tank? (Don't take anyone else's word on this particular point, and don't trust the fuel gauge either). If an electrical fault is indicated, look for loose or broken wires before digging out the test gear.

Cure the disease, not the symptom. Substituting a flat battery with a fully-charged one will get you off the hard shoulder, but if the underlying cause is not attended to, the new battery will go the same way. Similarly, changing oil-fouled spark plugs for a new set will get you moving again, but remember that the reason for the fouling (if it wasn't simply an incorrect grade of plug) will have to be established and corrected.

Don't take anything for granted. Particularly, don't forget that a 'new' component may itself be defective (especially if it's been rattling around in the boot for months), and don't leave components out of a fault diagnosis sequence just because they are new or recently-fitted. When you do finally diagnose a difficult fault, you'll probably realise that all the evidence was there from the start.

Consider what work, if any, has recently been carried out. Many faults arise through careless or hurried work. For instance, if any work has been performed under the bonnet, could some of the wiring have been dislodged or incorrectly routed, or a hose trapped? Have all the fasteners been properly tightened? Were new, genuine parts and new gaskets used? There is often a certain amount of detective work to be done in this case, as an apparently-unrelated task can have far-reaching consequences.

Engine

Engine fails to rotate when attempting to start

- ☐ Battery terminal connections loose or corroded (see Section 9)
- ☐ Battery discharged or faulty (Chapter 5 Section 3)
- ☐ Broken, loose or disconnected wiring in the starting circuit (Chapter 5 Section 2)
- ☐ Defective starter solenoid or ignition switch (Chapter 5 Section 7 or Chapter 12 Section 6)
- ☐ Defective starter motor (Chapter 5 Section 7)
- ☐ Starter pinion or flywheel ring gear teeth loose or broken (Chapter 5 Section 7 or Chapter 8 Section 6)
- ☐ Engine earth strap broken or disconnected (Chapter 5 Section 2)
- ☐ Engine suffering 'hydraulic lock' (eg, from water ingested after traversing flooded roads, or from a serious internal coolant leak) – consult a Ford dealer or specialist for advice
- ☐ Automatic transmission not in position P or N (Chapter 7B Section 1)

Engine rotates, but will not start

- ☐ Fuel tank empty
- ☐ Battery discharged (engine rotates slowly) (Chapter 5 Section 3)
- ☐ Battery terminal connections loose or corroded (Chapter 5 Section 4)
- ☐ Ignition components damp or damaged – petrol models (Chapter 6A)
- ☐ Crankshaft sensor fault (Chapter 6A Section 12 or Chapter 6B Section 10)
- ☐ Broken, loose or disconnected wiring in the ignition circuit – petrol models (Chapter 6A)
- ☐ Preheating system faulty – diesel models (Chapter 6B)
- ☐ Fuel injection system fault (Chapter 6A or Chapter 6B)
- ☐ Air in fuel system – diesel models (Chapter 4B Section 2)
- ☐ Major mechanical failure (eg, timing chain snapped) (Chapter 2D)

Engine (continued)

Engine difficult to start when cold

- ☐ Battery discharged (Chapter 5 Section 3)
- ☐ Battery terminal connections loose or corroded (Chapter 5 Section 4)
- ☐ Other ignition system fault – petrol models (Chapter 6A)
- ☐ Preheating system faulty – diesel models (Chapter 6B Section 17)
- ☐ Fuel injection system fault (Chapter 4A Section 2 or Chapter 4B Section 2)
- ☐ Wrong grade of engine oil used (Chapter 1A Section 13 or Chapter 1B Section 13)
- ☐ Low cylinder compression (Chapter 2A Section 2, Chapter 2B Section 2 or Chapter 2C Section 2)

Engine difficult to start when hot

- ☐ Air filter element dirty or clogged (Chapter 1A Section 27 or Chapter 1B Section 29)
- ☐ Fuel injection system fault (Chapter 4A Section 2 or Chapter 4B Section 2)
- ☐ Low cylinder compression (Chapter 2A Section 2, Chapter 2B Section 2 or Chapter 2C Section 2)

Starter motor noisy or excessively-rough in engagement

- ☐ Starter pinion or flywheel ring gear teeth loose or broken (Chapter 2A Section 23, Chapter 2B Section 15, Chapter 2C Section 15 or Chapter 5 Section 7)
- ☐ Starter motor mounting bolts loose or missing (Chapter 5 Section 7)
- ☐ Starter motor internal components worn or damaged (Chapter 5 Section 7)

Engine starts, but stops immediately

- ☐ Loose or faulty electrical connections in the ignition circuit – petrol models (Chapter 4A Section 2)
- ☐ Vacuum leak at the throttle body or intake manifold (Chapter 4A Section 2 or Chapter 4B Section 2)
- ☐ Blocked injectors/fuel injection system fault (Chapter 4A Section 2 or Chapter 4B Section 2)
- ☐ Air in fuel, possibly due to loose fuel line connection – diesel models (Chapter 4B Section 2)

Engine idles erratically

- ☐ Air filter element clogged (Chapter 1A Section 27 or Chapter 1B Section 29)
- ☐ Vacuum leak at the throttle body, intake manifold or associated hoses (Chapter 4A Section 2 or Chapter 4B Section 2)
- ☐ Uneven or low cylinder compression (Chapter 2A Section 2, Chapter 2B Section 2 or Chapter 2C Section 2)
- ☐ Camshaft lobes worn (Chapter 2A Section 14, Chapter 2B Section 9 or Chapter 2C Section 6)
- ☐ Blocked injectors/fuel injection system fault (Chapter 4A Section 2 or Chapter 4B Section 2)
- ☐ Air in fuel, possibly due to loose fuel line connection – diesel models (Chapter 4B Section 2)

Engine misfires at idle speed

- ☐ Vacuum leak at the throttle body, intake manifold or associated hoses (Chapter 4A Section 2 or Chapter 4B Section 2)
- ☐ Blocked injectors/fuel injection system fault (Chapter 4A Section 9 or Chapter 4B Section 2)
- ☐ Faulty injector(s) – diesel models (Chapter 4B Section 14)
- ☐ Uneven or low cylinder compression (Chapter 2A Section 2, Chapter 2B Section 2 or Chapter 2C Section 2)
- ☐ Disconnected, leaking, or perished crankcase ventilation hoses (Chapter 6B Section 18)

Engine misfires throughout the driving speed range

- ☐ Fuel filter choked (Chapter 1B Section 28 or Chapter 1B Section 28)
- ☐ Fuel pump faulty, or delivery pressure low – (Chapter 4A Section 6 or Chapter 4B Section 8)
- ☐ Fuel tank vent blocked, or fuel pipes restricted (Chapter 4A Section 5 or Chapter 4B Section 7)
- ☐ Vacuum leak at the throttle body, intake manifold or associated hoses (Chapter 4A Section 2 or Chapter 4B Section 2)
- ☐ Faulty injector(s) – diesel models (Chapter 4B Section 14)
- ☐ Faulty ignition coils – petrol models (Chapter 6A Section 7)
- ☐ Uneven or low cylinder compression (Chapter 2A Section 2, Chapter 2B Section 2 or Chapter 2C Section 2)
- ☐ Blocked injector/fuel injection system fault (Chapter 4A Section 9 or Chapter 4B Section 14)
- ☐ Blocked catalytic converter/particulate filter (Chapter 4A Section 2 or Chapter 4B Section 2)
- ☐ Engine overheating (Chapter 3 Section 2)
- ☐ Fuel tank level low

Engine hesitates on acceleration

- ☐ Vacuum leak at the throttle body, intake manifold or associated hoses (Chapter 4A Section 2 or Chapter 4B Section 2)
- ☐ Blocked injectors/fuel injection system fault (Chapter 4A Section 2 or Chapter 4B Section 2)
- ☐ Faulty injector(s) – diesel models (Chapter 4B Section 14)

Engine stalls

- ☐ Vacuum leak at the throttle body, intake manifold or associated hoses (Chapter 4A Section 2 or Chapter 4B Section 2)
- ☐ Fuel filter choked (Chapter 4A Section 2 or Chapter 1B Section 28)
- ☐ Fuel pump faulty, or delivery pressure low (Chapter 4A Section 2 or Chapter 4B Section 2)
- ☐ Fuel tank vent blocked, or fuel pipes restricted (Chapter 4A Section 2 or Chapter 4B Section 2)
- ☐ Blocked injectors/fuel injection system fault (Chapter 4A Section 9 or Chapter 4B Section 14)
- ☐ Faulty injector(s) – diesel models (Chapter 4B Section 14)

Engine lacks power

- ☐ Air filter element blocked (Chapter 1A Section 27 or Chapter 1B Section 29)
- ☐ Fuel filter choked (Chapter 4A Section 2 or Chapter 1B Section 28)
- ☐ Fuel pipes blocked or restricted (Chapter 4A Section 2 or Chapter 4B Section 2)
- ☐ Engine overheating (Chapter 3 Section 2)
- ☐ Fuel tank level low
- ☐ Accelerator position sensor faulty (Chapter 6A Section 5 or Chapter 6B Section 5)
- ☐ Vacuum leak at the throttle body, intake manifold or associated hoses (Chapter 4A Section 2 or Chapter 4B Section 2)
- ☐ Blocked injectors/fuel injection system fault (Chapter 4A Section 9 or Chapter 4B Section 14)
- ☐ Faulty injector(s) – diesel models (Chapter 4B Section 14)
- ☐ Fuel pump faulty, or delivery pressure low – petrol models (Chapter 4A Section 2)
- ☐ Uneven or low cylinder compression (Chapter 2A Section 2, Chapter 2B Section 2 or Chapter 2C Section 2)
- ☐ Blocked catalytic converter or particulate filter (Chapter 4A Section 17 or Chapter 4B Section 21)
- ☐ Brakes binding (Chapter 9 Section 2)
- ☐ Clutch slipping (Chapter 8 Section 1)
- ☐ Turbocharger fault (Chapter 4A Section 16 or Chapter 4B Section 19)

Engine (continued)

Engine backfires

- ☐ Vacuum leak at the throttle body, intake manifold or associated hoses (Chapter 4A Section 2 or Chapter 4B Section 2)
- ☐ Blocked injectors/fuel injection system fault (Chapter 4A Section 2 or Chapter 4B Section 2)
- ☐ Blocked catalytic converter or particulate filter (Chapter 4A Section 17 or Chapter 4B Section 21)
- ☐ Ignition coil faulty – petrol models (Chapter 6A Section 7)

Oil pressure warning light illuminated with engine running

- ☐ Low oil level, or incorrect oil grade (see Chapter 1A Section 13 or Chapter 1B Section 13)
- ☐ Faulty oil pressure sensor, or wiring damaged (Chapter 2A Section 20, Chapter 2B Section 14 or Chapter 2C Section 12)
- ☐ Worn engine bearings and/or oil pump (Chapter 2A Section 19, Chapter 2B Section 12, Chapter 2C Section 10 or Chapter 2D)
- ☐ High engine operating temperature (Chapter 3 Section 2)
- ☐ Oil pump pressure relief valve defective (Chapter 2A Section 19, Chapter 2B Section 12 or Chapter 2C Section 10)
- ☐ Oil pump pick-up strainer clogged (Chapter 2A Section 17, Chapter 2B Section 11 or Chapter 2C Section 9)

Engine runs-on after switching off

- ☐ Excessive carbon build-up in engine (Chapter 2D)
- ☐ High engine operating temperature (Chapter 3 Section 2)
- ☐ Fuel injection system fault (Chapter 4A Section 2 or Chapter 4B Section 2)

Engine noises

Pre-ignition (pinking) or knocking during acceleration or under load

- ☐ Ignition timing incorrect/ignition system fault – petrol models (Chapter 6A)
- ☐ Incorrect grade of spark plug – petrol models (Chapter 1A Section 26)
- ☐ Incorrect grade of fuel (Chapter 4A Section 2)
- ☐ Knock sensor faulty – petrol models (Chapter 2A Section 7)
- ☐ Vacuum leak at the throttle body, intake manifold or associated hoses – petrol models (Chapter 4A Section 2)
- ☐ Excessive carbon build-up in engine (Chapter 2D)
- ☐ Blocked injector/fuel injection system fault (Chapter 4A Section 2 or Chapter 4B Section 2)
- ☐ Faulty injector(s) – diesel models (Chapter 4B Section 14)

Whistling or wheezing noises

- ☐ Leaking intake manifold or throttle body gasket (Chapter 4A Section 2 or Chapter 4B Section 2)
- ☐ Leaking exhaust manifold gasket or pipe-to-manifold joint (Chapter 4A Section 17 or Chapter 4B Section 21)
- ☐ Blowing cylinder head gasket (Chapter 2A Section 15, Chapter 2B Section 10 or Chapter 2C Section 8)
- ☐ Leaking air/turbocharger/intercooler ducts (Chapter 4A Section 16 or Chapter 4B Section 19)

Tapping or rattling noises

- ☐ Worn valve gear or camshaft (Chapter 2A Section 14, Chapter 2B Section 3 or Chapter 2C Section 6)

Knocking or thumping noises

- ☐ Worn big-end bearings (regular heavy knocking, perhaps less under load)
- ☐ Worn main bearings (rumbling and knocking, perhaps worsening under load)
- ☐ Piston slap – most noticeable when cold, caused by piston/bore wear (Chapter 2D Section 10)
- ☐ Ancillary component fault (coolant pump, alternator, etc) (Chapter 3, Chapter 5, etc)
- ☐ Engine mountings worn or defective (Chapter 2A Section 24, Chapter 2B Section 16 or Chapter 2C Section 16)
- ☐ Front suspension or steering components worn (Chapter 10)

Cooling system

Overheating

- ☐ Insufficient coolant in system (see Chapter 1A Section 6 or Chapter 1B Section 6)
- ☐ Thermostat faulty (Chapter 3 Section 7)
- ☐ Radiator core blocked, or grille restricted (Chapter 3 Section 2)
- ☐ Cooling fan faulty (Chapter 3 Section 8)
- ☐ Inaccurate coolant temperature sender (Chapter 3 Section 9)
- ☐ Airlock in cooling system (Chapter 1A Section 34 or Chapter 1B Section 36)
- ☐ Expansion tank pressure cap faulty (Chapter 3 Section 2)
- ☐ Engine management system fault (Chapter 6A or Chapter 6B)
- ☐ Coolant pump failure (Chapter 3 Section 10)

Overcooling

- ☐ Thermostat faulty (Chapter 3 Section 7)
- ☐ Inaccurate coolant temperature sender (Chapter 3 Section 9)
- ☐ Cooling fan faulty (Chapter 3 Section 8)
- ☐ Engine management system fault (Chapter 6A or Chapter 6B)

External coolant leakage

- ☐ Deteriorated or damaged hoses or hose clips (Chapter 3 Section 3)
- ☐ Radiator core or heater matrix leaking (Chapter 3 Section 6)
- ☐ Expansion tank pressure cap faulty (Chapter 3 Section 4)
- ☐ Coolant pump internal seal leaking (Chapter 3 Section 10)
- ☐ Coolant pump gasket leaking (Chapter 3 Section 10)
- ☐ Boiling due to overheating (Chapter 3 Section 2)

Internal coolant leakage

- ☐ Leaking cylinder head gasket (Chapter 2A Section 15, Chapter 2B Section 10 or Chapter 2C Section 8)
- ☐ Cracked cylinder head or cylinder block (Chapter 2D Section 2)

Corrosion

- ☐ Infrequent draining and flushing (Chapter 1A Section 34 or Chapter 1B Section 36)
- ☐ Incorrect coolant mixture or inappropriate coolant type (Chapter 1A Section 34 or Chapter 1B Section 36)

Fuel and exhaust systems

Excessive fuel consumption

- ☐ Air filter element dirty or clogged (Chapter 1A Section 27 or Chapter 1B Section 29)
- ☐ Fuel injection system fault (Chapter 4A Section 2 or Chapter 4B Section 2)
- ☐ Engine management system fault (Chapter 6A or Chapter 6B)
- ☐ Crankcase ventilation system blocked (Chapter 2A Section 22)
- ☐ Tyres under-inflated (Chapter 1A Section 9)
- ☐ Brakes binding (Chapter 9 Section 2)
- ☐ Fuel leak, causing apparent high consumption (Chapter 4A Section 2 or Chapter 4B Section 2)

Fuel leakage and/or fuel odour

- ☐ Damaged or corroded fuel tank, pipes or connections (Chapter 4A Section 2 or Chapter 4B Section 2)
- ☐ Evaporative emissions system fault – petrol models (Chapter 6A Section 18)

Excessive noise or fumes from exhaust system

- ☐ Leaking exhaust system or manifold joints (Chapter 4A Section 17 or Chapter 4B Section 21)
- ☐ Leaking, corroded or damaged silencers or pipe (Chapter 4A Section 17 or Chapter 4B Section 21)
- ☐ Broken mountings causing body or suspension contact (Chapter 2A Section 24, Chapter 2B Section 16 or Chapter 2C Section 16)

Clutch

Pedal travels to floor – no pressure or very little resistance

- ☐ Air in hydraulic system/faulty master or slave cylinder (Chapter 8 Section 2)
- ☐ Faulty hydraulic release system (Chapter 8)
- ☐ Clutch pedal return spring detached or broken (Chapter 8 Section 5)
- ☐ Broken clutch release bearing or fork (Chapter 8 Section 6)
- ☐ Broken diaphragm spring in clutch pressure plate (Chapter 8 Section 6)

Clutch fails to disengage (unable to select gears)

- ☐ Air in hydraulic system/faulty master or slave cylinder (Chapter 8 Section 2)
- ☐ Faulty hydraulic release system (Chapter 8 Section 2)
- ☐ Clutch disc sticking on transmission input shaft splines (Chapter 8 Section 6)
- ☐ Clutch disc sticking to flywheel or pressure plate (Chapter 8 Section 6)
- ☐ Faulty pressure plate assembly (Chapter 8 Section 6)
- ☐ Clutch release mechanism worn or incorrectly assembled (Chapter 8 Section 6)

Clutch slips (engine speed increases, with no increase in vehicle speed)

- ☐ Faulty hydraulic release system (Chapter 8 Section 2)
- ☐ Clutch disc linings excessively worn (Chapter 8 Section 6)
- ☐ Clutch disc linings contaminated with oil or grease (Chapter 8 Section 6)
- ☐ Faulty pressure plate or weak diaphragm spring (Chapter 8 Section 6)

Judder as clutch is engaged

- ☐ Clutch disc linings contaminated with oil or grease (Chapter 8 Section 6)
- ☐ Clutch disc linings excessively worn (Chapter 8 Section 6)
- ☐ Faulty or distorted pressure plate or diaphragm spring (Chapter 8 Section 6)
- ☐ Worn or loose engine or transmission mountings (Chapter 2A Section 24, Chapter 2B Section 16 or Chapter 2C Section 16)
- ☐ Clutch disc hub or transmission input shaft splines worn (Chapter 8 Section 6)

Noise when depressing or releasing clutch pedal

- ☐ Worn clutch release bearing (Chapter 8 Section 6)
- ☐ Worn or dry clutch pedal bushes (Chapter 8 Section 5)
- ☐ Worn or dry clutch master cylinder piston (Chapter 8 Section 3)
- ☐ Faulty pressure plate assembly (Chapter 8 Section 6)
- ☐ Pressure plate diaphragm spring broken (Chapter 8 Section 6)
- ☐ Broken clutch disc cushioning springs (Chapter 8 Section 6)

Manual transmission

Noisy in neutral with engine running

- ☐ Lack of oil (Chapter 7A Section 2)
- ☐ Input shaft bearings worn (noise apparent with clutch pedal released, but not when depressed) (Chapter 7A Section 7)*
- ☐ Clutch release bearing worn (noise apparent with clutch pedal depressed, possibly less when released) (Chapter 8 Section 6)

Noisy in one particular gear

- ☐ Worn, damaged or chipped gear teeth (Chapter 7A Section 7)*

Difficulty engaging gears

- ☐ Clutch fault (Chapter 8 Section 6)
- ☐ Worn or damaged gearchange cables (Chapter 7A Section 3)
- ☐ Lack of oil (Chapter 7A Section 2)
- ☐ Worn synchroniser units (Chapter 7A Section 7)*

Jumps out of gear

- ☐ Worn or damaged gearchange cables (Chapter 7A Section 3)
- ☐ Worn synchroniser units (Chapter 7A Section 7)*
- ☐ Worn selector forks (Chapter 7A Section 7)*

Vibration

- ☐ Lack of oil (Chapter 7A Section 2)
- ☐ Worn bearings (Chapter 7A Section 7)*

Lubricant leaks

- ☐ Leaking driveshaft or selector shaft oil seal (Chapter 7A Section 7)
- ☐ Leaking housing joint (Chapter 7A Section 6)*
- ☐ Leaking input shaft oil seal (Chapter 7A Section 4)*

** Although the corrective action necessary to remedy the symptoms described is beyond the scope of the home mechanic, the above information should be helpful in isolating the cause of the condition, so that the owner can communicate clearly with a professional mechanic.*

Automatic transmission

Fluid leakage

Automatic transmission fluid is usually brown in colour. Fluid leaks should not be confused with engine oil, which can easily be blown onto the transmission by airflow.To determine the source of a leak, first remove all built-up dirt and grime from the transmission housing and surrounding areas using a degreasing agent, or by steam-cleaning. Drive the vehicle at low speed, so airflow will not blow the leak far from its source. Raise and support the vehicle, and determine where the leak is coming from. The following are common areas of leakage:

a) Fluid pan
b) Drain or filler plugs.
c) Transmission-to-fluid cooler unions (Chapter 7B Section 6)

Transmission fluid has burned smell

Transmission fluid level low (Chapter 7B Section 2)

General gear selection problems

Chapter 7B Section 4 deals with checking the selector cable on automatic transmissions. The following are common problems which may be caused by a faulty cable or sensor:

a) Engine starting in gears other than Park or Neutral.
b) Indicator panel indicating a gear other than the one actually being used.
c) Vehicle moves when in Park or Neutral.
d) Poor gear shift quality or erratic gear changes.

Transmission will not downshift (kickdown) with accelerator pedal fully depressed

☐ Low transmission fluid level (Chapter 7B Section 2)
☐ Engine management system fault (Chapter 6A or Chapter 6B)
☐ Faulty transmission sensor or wiring (Chapter 7B Section 1)
☐ Faulty selector cable (Chapter 7B Section 4)

Engine will not start in any gear, or starts in gears other than Park or Neutral

☐ Faulty transmission sensor or wiring (Chapter 7B Section 8)
☐ Engine management system fault (Chapter 6A or Chapter 6B)
☐ Faulty selector cable (Chapter 7B Section 4)

Transmission slips, shifts roughly, is noisy, or has no drive in forward or reverse gears

☐ Transmission fluid level low (Chapter 7B Section 2)
☐ Faulty transmission sensor or wiring (Chapter 12 Section 6)
☐ Engine management system fault (Chapter 6A or Chapter 6B)

Note: *There are many probable causes for the above problems, but diagnosing and correcting them is considered beyond the scope of this manual. Having checked the fluid level and all the wiring as far as possible, a dealer or transmission specialist should be consulted if the problem persists.*

Braking system

Vehicle pulls to one side under braking

☐ Worn, defective, damaged or contaminated brake pads on one side (Chapter 9 Section 2)
☐ Seized or partially-seized brake caliper piston (Chapter 9 Section 9)
☐ A mixture of brake pad lining materials fitted between sides (Chapter 9 Section 5 or Chapter 9 Section 6)
☐ Brake caliper mounting bolts loose (Chapter 9 Section 9 or Chapter 9 Section 10)
☐ Worn or damaged steering or suspension components (Chapter 10 Section 1)
☐ Disconnected, damaged or insecure brake servo vacuum hose (Chapter 9 Section 4)
☐ Primary or secondary hydraulic circuit failure (Chapter 9 Section 2)
☐ Seized brake caliper piston (Chapter 9 Section 9 or Chapter 9 Section 10)
☐ Brake pads incorrectly fitted (Chapter 9 Section 5 or Chapter 9 Section 6)
☐ Incorrect grade of brake pads fitted (Chapter 9 Section 5 or Chapter 9 Section 6)
☐ Brake pad linings contaminated (Chapter 9 Section 5 or Chapter 9 Section 6)

Noise (grinding or high-pitched squeal) when brakes applied

☐ Brake pad friction lining material worn down to metal backing (Chapter 9 Section 5 or Chapter 9 Section 6)
☐ Excessive corrosion of brake disc (may be apparent after the vehicle has been standing for some time (Chapter 9 Section 7 or Chapter 9 Section 8)
☐ Foreign object (stone chipping, etc) trapped between brake disc and shield

Excessive brake pedal travel

☐ Faulty master cylinder (Chapter 9 Section 11)
☐ Air in hydraulic system (Chapter 9 Section 3)
☐ Faulty vacuum servo unit (Chapter 9 Section 13)

Brake pedal feels spongy when depressed

☐ Air in hydraulic system (Chapter 9 Section 3)
☐ Deteriorated flexible rubber brake hoses (Chapter 9 Section 4)
☐ Master cylinder mounting nuts loose (Chapter 9 Section 11)
☐ Faulty master cylinder (Chapter 9 Section 11)

Excessive brake pedal effort required to stop vehicle

☐ Faulty vacuum servo unit (Chapter 9 Section 13)
☐ Faulty vacuum pump (Chapter 9 Section 20)

Judder felt through brake pedal or steering wheel when braking

Note: *Under heavy braking, vibration may be felt through the brake pedal. This is a normal feature of ABS operation, and does not constitute a fault.*

☐ Excessive run-out or distortion of discs (Chapter 9 Section 7 or Chapter 9 Section 8)
☐ Brake pad linings worn (Chapter 9 Section 5 or Chapter 9 Section 6)
☐ Brake caliper mounting bolts loose (Chapter 9 Section 9 or Chapter 9 Section 10)
☐ Wear in suspension or steering components or mountings (Chapter 10 Section 1)
☐ Front wheels out of balance

Brakes binding

☐ Seized brake caliper piston (Chapter 9 Section 9 or Chapter 9 Section 10)
☐ Incorrectly-adjusted handbrake mechanism (Chapter 9 Section 14)
☐ Faulty master cylinder (Chapter 9 Section 11)

Rear wheels locking under normal braking

☐ Rear brake pad linings contaminated or damaged (Chapter 9 Section 6)
☐ Rear brake discs warped (Chapter 9 Section 8)

Suspension and steering

Vehicle pulls to one side

- ☐ Defective tyre (Chapter 1A Section 9)
- ☐ Excessive wear in suspension or steering components (Chapter 10 Section 1)
- ☐ Incorrect front wheel alignment (Chapter 10 Section 21)
- ☐ Accident damage to steering or suspension components (Chapter 10 Section 1)

Wheel wobble and vibration

- ☐ Front wheels out of balance (vibration felt mainly through the steering wheel)
- ☐ Rear wheels out of balance (vibration felt throughout the vehicle)
- ☐ Roadwheels damaged or distorted (Chapter 1A Section 4)
- ☐ Faulty or damaged tyre (Chapter 1A Section 9)
- ☐ Worn steering or suspension joints, bushes or components (Chapter 10 Section 1)
- ☐ Wheel nuts loose (Chapter 1A Section 23)

Excessive pitching and/or rolling around corners, or during braking

- ☐ Defective shock absorbers (Chapter 10 Section 4 or Chapter 10 Section 10)
- ☐ Broken or weak spring and/or suspension component (Chapter 10 Section 4)
- ☐ Worn or damaged anti-roll bar or mountings (Chapter 10 Section 6)

Wandering or general instability

- ☐ Incorrect front wheel alignment (Chapter 10 Section 21)
- ☐ Worn steering or suspension joints, bushes or components (Chapter 1A Section 20)
- ☐ Roadwheels out of balance
- ☐ Faulty or damaged tyre (see Chapter 1A Section 9)
- ☐ Wheel nuts loose (Chapter 1A Section 23)
- ☐ Defective shock absorbers (Chapter 10 Section 4 or Chapter 10 Section 10)

Excessively-stiff steering

- ☐ Seized steering linkage balljoint or suspension balljoint (Chapter 1A Section 20)
- ☐ Incorrect front wheel alignment (Chapter 10 Section 21)
- ☐ Steering rack damaged (Chapter 10 Section 18)

Excessive play in steering

- ☐ Worn steering column/intermediate shaft joints (Chapter 10 Section 17)
- ☐ Worn track rod balljoints (Chapter 10 Section 20)
- ☐ Worn steering rack (Chapter 10 Section 18)
- ☐ Worn steering or suspension joints, bushes or components (Chapter 1A Section 20)

Lack of power assistance

- ☐ Electrical wiring fault (Chapter 12 Section 2)
- ☐ Faulty steering rack (Chapter 10 Section 18)

Tyre wear excessive

Tyres worn on inside or outside edges

- ☐ Tyres under-inflated (wear on both edges) (Chapter 1A Section 9)
- ☐ Incorrect camber or castor angles (wear on one edge only) (Chapter 10 Section 21)
- ☐ Worn steering or suspension joints, bushes or components (Chapter 1A Section 20)
- ☐ Excessively-hard cornering or braking
- ☐ Accident damage

Tyre treads exhibit feathered edges

- ☐ Incorrect toe-setting (Chapter 10 Section 21)

Tyres worn in centre of tread

- ☐ Tyres over-inflated (see Chapter 1A Section 9)

Tyres worn on inside and outside edges

- ☐ Tyres under-inflated (Chapter 1A Section 9)

Tyres worn unevenly

- ☐ Tyres/wheels out of balance
- ☐ Excessive wheel or tyre run-out
- ☐ Worn shock absorbers (Chapter 10 Section 4 or Chapter 10 Section 10)
- ☐ Faulty tyre (Chapter 1A Section 9)

Electrical system

Battery will not hold a charge for more than a few days

- ☐ Battery defective internally (Chapter 5 Section 3)
- ☐ Battery terminal connections loose or corroded (Chapter 5 Section 2)
- ☐ Auxiliary drivebelt worn or incorrectly tensioned (Chapter 1A Section 16 or Chapter 1B Section 17)
- ☐ Alternator not charging at correct output (Chapter 5 Section 2)
- ☐ Alternator or voltage regulator faulty (Chapter 5 Section 6)
- ☐ Short-circuit causing continual battery drain (Chapter 12 Section 2)

Ignition/no-charge warning light remains illuminated with engine running

- ☐ Auxiliary drivebelt broken, worn, or incorrectly tensioned (Chapter 1A Section 16 or Chapter 1B Section 17)
- ☐ Internal fault in alternator or voltage regulator (Chapter 5 Section 6)
- ☐ Broken, disconnected, or loose wiring in charging circuit (Chapter 12 Section 2)

Ignition/no-charge warning light fails to come on

- ☐ Broken, disconnected, or loose wiring in warning light circuit (Chapter 12 Section 2)
- ☐ Alternator faulty (Chapter 5 Section 6)
- ☐ Faulty instrument panel (Chapter 12 Section 12)

Lights inoperative

- ☐ Bulb blown (Chapter 12 Section 7)
- ☐ Corrosion of bulb or bulbholder contacts (Chapter 12 Section 7)
- ☐ Blown fuse (Chapter 12 Section 3)
- ☐ Faulty relay (Chapter 12 Section 3)
- ☐ Broken, loose, or disconnected wiring (Chapter 12 Section 2)
- ☐ Faulty switch (Chapter 12 Section 6)

Electrical system (continued)

Instrument readings inaccurate or erratic

Fuel or temperature gauges give no reading

- ☐ Faulty gauge sensor (Chapter 4A Section 6 or Chapter 4B Section 9)
- ☐ Wiring open-circuit (Chapter 12 Section 2)
- ☐ Faulty instrument cluster (Chapter 12 Section 12)

Fuel or temperature gauges give continuous maximum reading

- ☐ Faulty gauge sensor (Chapter 4A Section 6 or Chapter 4B Section 9)
- ☐ Wiring short-circuit (Chapter 12 Section 2)
- ☐ Faulty instrument cluster (Chapter 12 Section 12)

Horn inoperative, or unsatisfactory in operation

Horn operates all the time

- ☐ Horn push either earthed or stuck down (Chapter 10 Section 16)
- ☐ Horn cable-to-horn push earthed (Chapter 12 Section 2)

Horn fails to operate

- ☐ Blown fuse (Chapter 12 Section 3)
- ☐ Cable or connections loose, broken or disconnected (Chapter 12 Section 2)
- ☐ Faulty horn (Chapter 12 Section 13)

Horn emits intermittent or unsatisfactory sound

- ☐ Cable connections loose (Chapter 12 Section 13)
- ☐ Horn mountings loose (Chapter 12 Section 13)
- ☐ Faulty horn (Chapter 12 Section 13)

Windscreen wipers inoperative, or unsatisfactory in operation

Wipers fail to operate, or operate very slowly

- ☐ Wiper blades stuck to screen, or linkage seized or binding (Chapter 12 Section 16)
- ☐ Blown fuse (Chapter 12 Section 3)
- ☐ Battery discharged (Chapter 5 Section 3)
- ☐ Cable or connections loose, broken or disconnected (Chapter 12 Section 2)
- ☐ Faulty wiper motor (Chapter 12 Section 16)

Wiper blades sweep over too large or too small an area of the glass

- ☐ Wiper blades incorrectly fitted, or wrong size used (Chapter 1A Section 10)
- ☐ Wiper arms incorrectly positioned on spindles (Chapter 12 Section 15)
- ☐ Excessive wear of wiper linkage (Chapter 12 Section 16)
- ☐ Wiper motor or linkage mountings loose or insecure (Chapter 12 Section 16)

Wiper blades fail to clean the glass effectively

- ☐ Wiper blade rubbers dirty, worn or perished (Chapter 1A Section 10)
- ☐ Wiper blades incorrectly fitted, or wrong size used (Chapter 1A Section 10)
- ☐ Wiper arm tension springs broken, or arm pivots seized (Chapter 12 Section 15)
- ☐ Insufficient windscreen washer additive to adequately remove road film (Chapter 1A Section 8)

Windscreen washers inoperative, or unsatisfactory in operation

One or more washer jets inoperative

- ☐ Blocked washer jet
- ☐ Disconnected, kinked or restricted fluid hose (Chapter 12 Section 19)
- ☐ Insufficient fluid in washer reservoir (Chapter 1A Section 8)

Washer pump fails to operate

- ☐ Broken or disconnected wiring or connections (Chapter 12 Section 2)
- ☐ Blown fuse (Chapter 12 Section 3)
- ☐ Faulty washer switch (Chapter 12 Section 6)
- ☐ Faulty washer pump (Chapter 12 Section 19)

Washer pump runs for some time before fluid is emitted from jets

- ☐ Faulty one-way valve in fluid supply hose (Chapter 12 Section 19)

Electric windows inoperative, or unsatisfactory in operation

Window glass will only move in one direction

- ☐ Faulty switch (Chapter 12 Section 6)

Window glass slow to move

- ☐ Battery discharged (Chapter 5 Section 3)
- ☐ Regulator seized or damaged, or in need of lubrication (Chapter 11 Section 15)
- ☐ Door internal components or trim fouling regulator (Chapter 11 Section 15)
- ☐ Faulty motor (Chapter 11 Section 15)

Window glass fails to move

- ☐ Blown fuse (Chapter 12 Section 3)
- ☐ Faulty relay (Chapter 12 Section 3)
- ☐ Broken or disconnected wiring or connections (Chapter 12 Section 2)
- ☐ Faulty motor (Chapter 11 Section 15)
- ☐ Faulty control module (Chapter 12 Section 28)

Central locking system inoperative, or unsatisfactory in operation

Complete system failure

- ☐ Remote handset battery discharged, where applicable (Chapter 1A Section 33 or Chapter 1B Section 35)
- ☐ Blown fuse (Chapter 12 Section 3)
- ☐ Defective control module (Chapter 12 Section 28)
- ☐ Broken or disconnected wiring or connections (Chapter 12 Section 2)
- ☐ Faulty motor (Chapter 11 Section 29)

Latch locks but will not unlock, or unlocks but will not lock

- ☐ Remote handset battery discharged, where applicable (Chapter 1A Section 33 or Chapter 1B Section 35)
- ☐ Faulty master switch (Chapter 11 Section 29)
- ☐ Broken or disconnected latch operating rods or levers (Chapter 11 Section 16 or Chapter 11 Section 22)
- ☐ Faulty control module (Chapter 12 Section 28)
- ☐ Faulty motor (Chapter 11 Section 29)

One solenoid/motor fails to operate

- ☐ Broken or disconnected wiring or connections (Chapter 12 Section 2)
- ☐ Faulty operating assembly (Chapter 11 Section 29)
- ☐ Broken, binding or disconnected latch operating rods or levers (Chapter 11 Section 16 or Chapter 11 Section 22)
- ☐ Fault in door latch (Chapter 11 Section 16 or Chapter 11 Section 22)

The following pages are intended to help in dealing with common roadside emergencies and breakdowns. You will find more detailed fault finding information at the back of the manual, and repair information in the main chapters.

If your car won't start and the starter motor doesn't turn

- ☐ Lift the bonnet, unclip and remove the battery cover. Make sure that the battery terminals are clean and tight.
- ☐ Switch on the headlights and try to start the engine. If the headlights go very dim when you're trying to start, the battery is probably flat. Get out of trouble by jump starting (see next page) using a friend's car.

If your car won't start even though the starter motor turns as normal

- ☐ Is there fuel in the tank?
- ☐ Is there moisture on electrical components under the bonnet? Switch off the ignition, then wipe off any obvious dampness with a dry cloth. Spray a water-repellent aerosol product (WD-40 or equivalent) on ignition and fuel system electrical connectors like those shown in the photos.

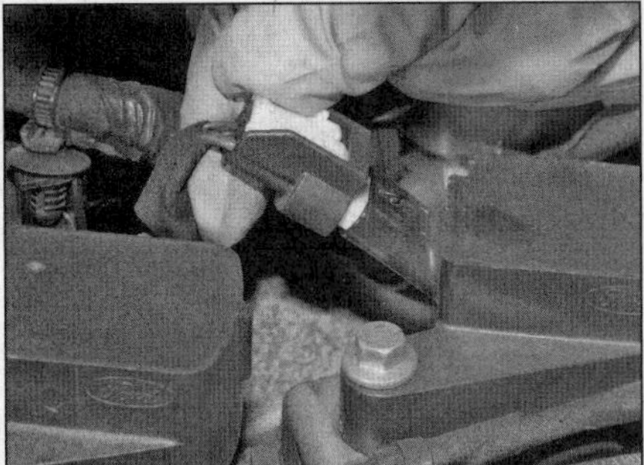

A A Check the security of the ignition coil harness connectors.

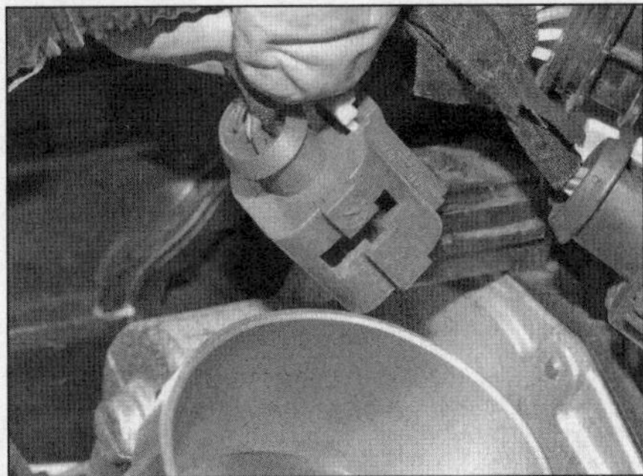

B Check the throttle body wiring connector with the ignition switched off.

C Check the security and condition of the battery terminals.

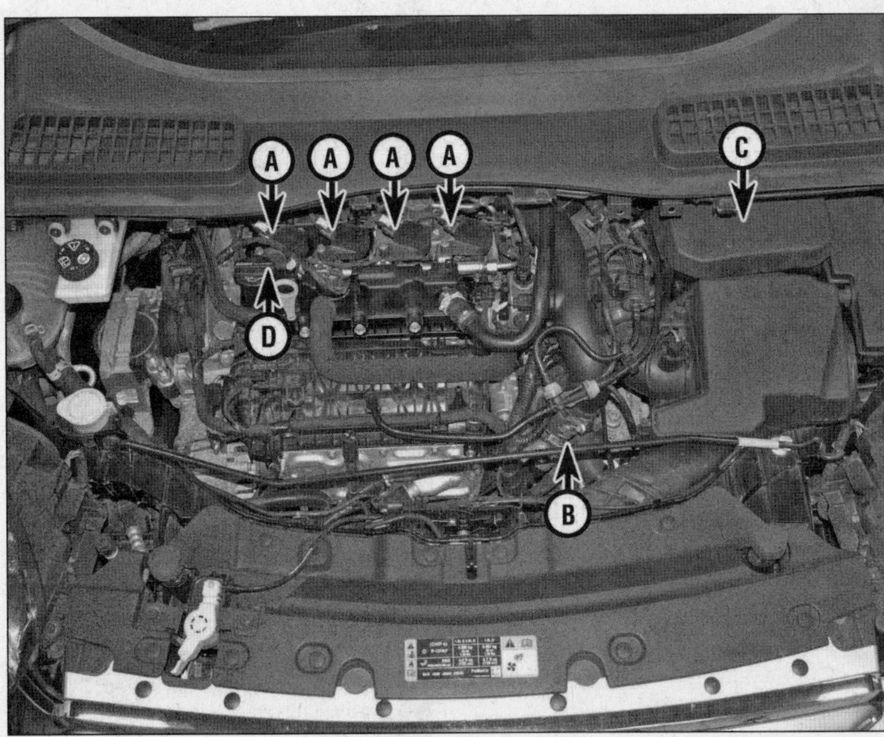

Check that electrical connections are secure (with the ignition switched off) and spray them with a water-dispersant spray like WD-40 if you suspect a problem due to damp.

D Check the security of the camshaft position sensors.

Jump starting

Jump starting will get you out of trouble, but you must correct whatever made the battery go flat in the first place. There are three possibilities:

***1** The battery has been drained by repeated attempts to start, or by leaving the lights on.*

***2** The charging system is not working properly (alternator drivebelt slack or broken, alternator wiring fault or alternator itself faulty).*

***3** The battery itself is at fault (electrolyte low, or battery worn out).*

When jump-starting a car, observe the following precautions:

✓ Before connecting the booster battery, make sure that the ignition is switched off.

Caution: Remove the key in case the central locking engages when the jump leads are connected

✓ Ensure that all electrical equipment (lights, heater, wipers, etc) is switched off.

✓ Take note of any special precautions printed on the battery case.

✓ Make sure that the booster battery is the same voltage as the discharged one in the vehicle.

✓ If the battery is being jump-started from the battery in another vehicle, the two vehicles MUST NOT TOUCH each other.

✓ Make sure that the transmission is in neutral (or PARK, in the case of automatic transmission).

Budget jump leads can be a false economy, as they often do not pass enough current to start large capacity or diesel engines. They can also get hot.

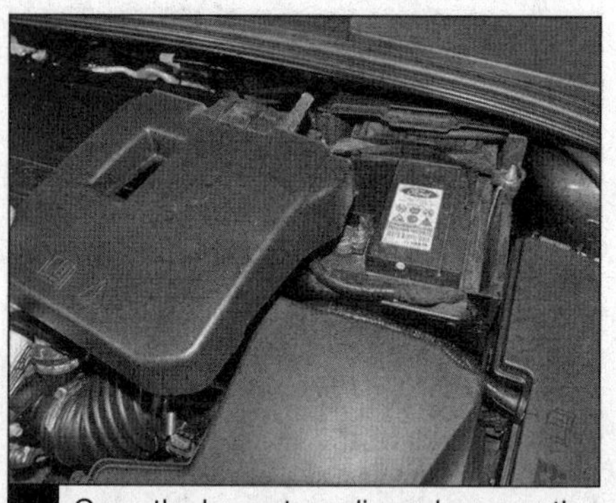

1 Open the bonnet, unclip and remove the battery cover, then connect the red jump lead to the terminal positive (+) terminal.

2 Connect the other end of the red lead to the positive (+) terminal of the booster battery.

3 Connect one end of the black jump lead to the negative (-) terminal of the booster battery.

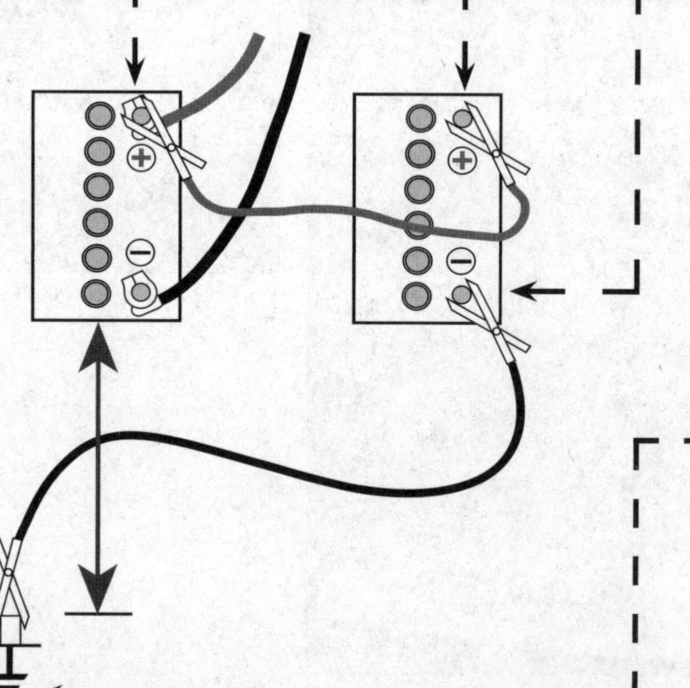

4 Connect the other end of the black jump lead to the battery negative terminal or metal bracket in the engine compartment.

5 Make sure that the jump leads will not come into contact with the fan, drive-belts or other moving parts of the engine.

6 Start the engine using the booster battery and run it at idle speed. Switch on the lights, rear window demister and heater blower motor, then disconnect the jump leads in the reverse order of connection. Turn off the lights etc.

Wheel changing

Warning: Do not change a wheel in a situation where you risk being hit by other traffic. On busy roads, try to stop in a lay-by or a gateway. Be wary of passing traffic while changing the wheel – it is easy to become distracted by the job in hand.

Preparation

- ☐ When a puncture occurs, stop as soon as it is safe to do so.
- ☐ Park on firm level ground, if possible, and well out of the way of other traffic.
- ☐ Use hazard warning lights if necessary.
- ☐ If you have one, use a warning triangle to alert other drivers of your presence.
- ☐ Apply the handbrake and engage first or reverse gear (manual transmissions) or Park (automatic transmissions).
- ☐ Chock the wheel diagonally opposite the one being removed.
- ☐ If the ground is soft, use a flat piece of wood to spread the load under the jack.

Vehicles with the Compact spare wheel

Changing the wheel

The spare wheel and tools are stored under the luggage compartment floor. Lift up the floor.

Unscrew the retaining plate from the centre of the spare wheel and lift the wheel from place

Remove the jack and tools from the boot. Ensure the handbrake is fully applied.

Using the wheel brace from the toolkit, slacken each wheel nut by a half turn.

If anti-theft wheel nuts are fitted, slacken them using the adapter supplied in the tool kit.

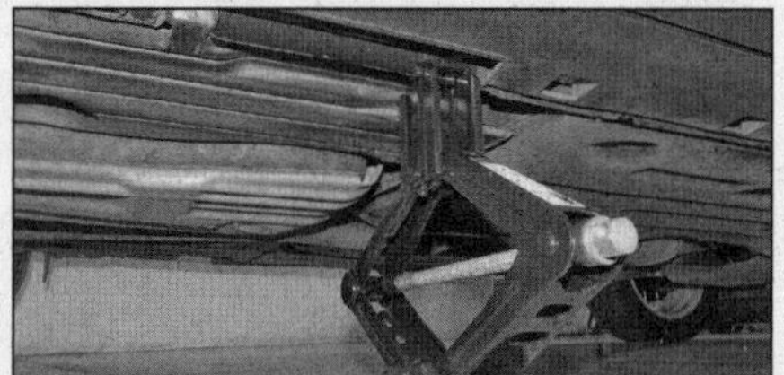

Locate the jack head under the jacking point nearest to the wheel that is to be removed. As the jack is raised, the head must enter the rectangular recess in the jacking point.

Make sure the jack is located on firm ground then turn the jack handle clockwise until the wheel is raised clear of the ground. Unscrew the wheel nuts and remove the wheel. Fit the spare wheel and screw on the wheel nuts. Lightly tighten the nuts with the wheelbrace then lower the vehicle to the ground.

Securely tighten the wheel nuts in a diagonal pattern then refit the wheel trim/hub cap (as applicable). Note that the wheel nuts should be slackened and retightened to the specified torque at the earliest possible opportunity.

Finally...

- ☐ Remove the wheel chocks.
- ☐ Stow the jack, chock and tools in the correct locations in the car.
- ☐ Check the tyre pressure on the wheel just fitted. If it is low, or if you don't have a pressure gauge with you, drive slowly to the next garage and inflate the tyre to the correct pressure.
- ☐ Have the damaged tyre or wheel repaired as soon as possible, or another puncture will leave you stranded.

Vehicles with emergency mobility system

The system comprises a bottle of puncture sealant and a compressor. Rather than change the punctured wheel, the system allows the tyre to be sealed, enabling the journey to be resumed, albeit at a reduced speed.

The system is stored beneath the floor of the luggage compartment.

Remove the sealant bottle from the luggage compartment, and shake the contents well. Attach the hose to the bottle.

Slide the bottle into place on top of the compressor until it audibly engages.

Insert the compressor's power plug into the vehicle's power outlet socket.

Connect the compressor hose to the tyre valve, and with the ignition switch turned to position I, turn the compressor on and inflate the tyre to a pressure of approximately 2.5 bar. If this pressure is not achieved within 6 minutes, turn off the compressor, disconnect it from the valve, and drive the vehicle forwards about 10 m, then reverse back to place to redistribute the sealant, and repeat the inflation process. With the correct pressure achieved, disconnect the compressor and stow it in the tool kit.

Caution: Do not allow the compressor to run for more than 10 minutes. It may overheat, causing damage.

Immediately drive the vehicle for approximately 10 minutes at a speed of between 12 and 37 mph to redistribute the sealant.

Stop the vehicle, connect the compressor, and check the tyre pressure. If the pressure is less than 2.0, it's not safe to continue your journey, and the vehicle must be recovered. If the pressure is above this, turn on the compressor and inflate the tyre to the normal pressure for the vehicle, as specified on the sticker in the driver's door aperture.

With the tyre inflated to the correct pressure, do not exceed the maximum speed of 50 mph. Have the tyre repaired or replaced at the earliest opportunity.

Towing

When all else fails, you may find yourself having to get a tow home – or of course you may be helping somebody else. Long-distance recovery should only be done by a garage or breakdown service. For shorter distances, DIY towing using another car is easy enough, but observe the following points:

- ☐Ford insists that vehicles with automatic transmission must not be towed with the front wheels on the ground. Consequently, a recovery truck cable of lifting the front of the vehicle must be used.
- ☐Use a proper tow-rope – they are not expensive. The vehicle being towed must display an ON TOW sign in its rear window.
- ☐Always turn the ignition key to the 'on' position when the vehicle is being towed, so that the steering lock is released, and that the direction indicator and brake lights work. Note that as an electrically operated steering lock is fitted, if the vehicle's electrical system fails, the vehicle cannot be towed.
- ☐Only attach the tow-rope to the towing eyes provided. The towing eye is supplied as part of the tool kit which is fitted under the luggage compartment lid or floor. To fit the eye, prise out the access cover from the front/rear bumper (as applicable). The front access cover must be pressed hard on its side nearest the foglight, and the opposite edge prised open. Screw the eye into position and tighten it securely.
- ☐Before being towed, release the parking brake and select neutral on the transmission.
- ☐Note that greater-than-usual pedal pressure will be required to operate the brakes, since the vacuum servo unit is only operational with the engine running.
- ☐The driver of the car being towed must keep the tow-rope taut at all times to avoid snatching.
- ☐Make sure that both drivers know the route before setting off.
- ☐Only drive at moderate speeds and keep the distance towed to a minimum. Drive smoothly and allow plenty of time for slowing down at junctions.

Prise off the cover to access the bolt-hole for the towing eye

Identifying leaks

Puddles on the garage floor or drive, or obvious wetness under the bonnet or underneath the car, suggest a leak that needs investigating. It can sometimes be difficult to decide where the leak is coming from, especially if an engine undershield is fitted. Leaking oil or fluid can also be blown rearwards by the passage of air under the car, giving a false impression of where the problem lies.

Warning: Most automotive oils and fluids are poisonous. Wash them off skin, and change out of contaminated clothing, without delay.

HAYNES HiNT ***The smell of a fluid leaking from the car may provide a clue to what's leaking. Some fluids are distinctively coloured. It may help to remove the engine undershield, clean the car carefully and to park it over some clean paper overnight as an aid to locating the source of the leak. Remember that some leaks may only occur while the engine is running.***

Sump oil

Engine oil may leak from the drain plug...

Oil from filter

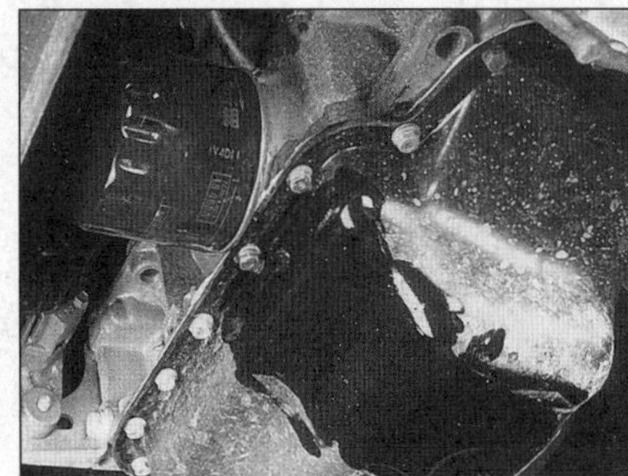

...or from the base of the oil filter.

Gearbox oil

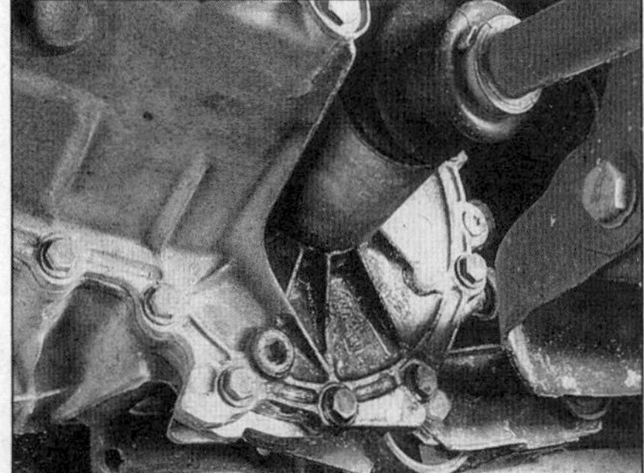

Gearbox oil can leak from the seals at the inboard ends of the driveshafts.

Antifreeze

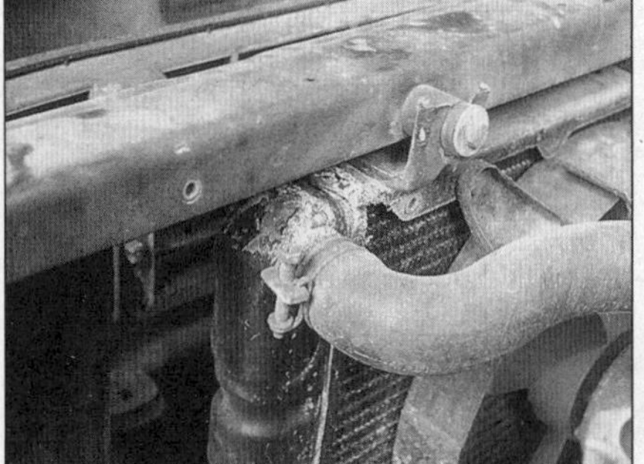

Leaking antifreeze often leaves a crystalline deposit like this.

Brake fluid

A leak occurring at a wheel is almost certainly brake fluid.

Jacking and vehicle support

The vehicle jack should **only** be used for changing the roadwheels in an emergency. When carrying out any other kind of work, raise the vehicle using a heavy-duty hydraulic ('workshop' or 'trolley') jack, and always supplement the jack with axle stands positioned under the vehicle jacking points. If the roadwheels do not have to be removed, consider using wheel ramps – if wished, these can be placed under the wheels once the vehicle has been raised using a hydraulic jack, and the vehicle lowered onto the ramps so that it is resting on its wheels.

Only ever jack the vehicle up on a solid, level surface. If there is even a slight slope, take great care that the vehicle cannot move as the wheels are lifted off the ground. Jacking up on an uneven or gravelled surface is not recommended, as the weight of the vehicle will not be evenly distributed, and the jack may slip as the vehicle is raised.

As far as possible, do not leave the vehicle unattended once it has been raised, particularly if children are playing nearby.

Before jacking up the front of the car, ensure that the handbrake is firmly applied. When jacking up the rear of the car, place wooden chocks in front of the front wheels, and engage first gear (or P).

The jack supplied with the vehicle locates in the holes provided in the sill **(see illustration)**. Ensure that the jack head is correctly engaged before attempting to raise the vehicle.

Never work under, around, or near a raised vehicle, unless it is adequately supported in at least two places.

When jacking or supporting the vehicle at these points, always use a block of wood between the jack head or axle stand, and the vehicle body. It is also considered good practice to use a large block of wood when supporting under other areas, to spread the load over a wider area, and reduce the risk of damage to the underside of the car (it also helps to prevent the underbody coating from being damaged by the jack or axle stand).

Never work under, around, or near a raised vehicle, unless it is adequately supported on stands. Do not rely on a jack alone, as even a hydraulic jack could fail under load. Makeshift methods should not be used to lift and support the car during servicing work.

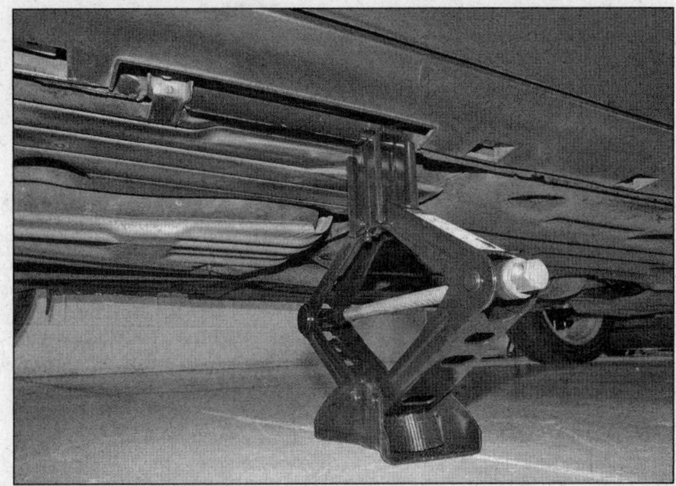

The jacking points are under the sills each side

This is a guide to getting your vehicle through the MOT test. Obviously it will not be possible to examine the vehicle to the same standard as the professional MOT tester. However, working through the following checks will enable you to identify any problem areas before submitting the vehicle for the test.

It has only been possible to summarise the test requirements here, based on the regulations in force at the time of printing. Test standards are becoming increasingly stringent, although there are some exemptions for older vehicles.

An assistant will be needed to help carry out some of these checks.

The checks have been sub-divided into four categories, as follows:

1 Checks carried out **FROM THE VEHICLE INTERIOR**

2 Checks carried out **WITH THE VEHICLE ON THE GROUND**

3 Checks carried out **WITH THE VEHICLE RAISED AND THE WHEELS FREE TO TURN**

4 Checks carried out on **YOUR VEHICLE'S EXHAUST EMISSION SYSTEM**

1 Checks carried out FROM THE VEHICLE INTERIOR

Handbrake (parking brake)

☐ Test the operation of the handbrake. Excessive travel (too many clicks) indicates incorrect brake or cable adjustment.

☐ Check that the handbrake cannot be released by tapping the lever sideways. Check the security of the lever mountings.

☐ If the parking brake is foot-operated, check that the pedal is secure and without excessive travel, and that the release mechanism operates correctly.

☐ Where applicable, test the operation of the electronic handbrake. The brake should engage and disengage without excessive delay. If the warning light does not extinguish, or a warning message is displayed when the brake is disengaged, this could indicate a fault which will need further investigation.

Footbrake

☐ Depress the brake pedal and check that it does not creep down to the floor, indicating a master cylinder fault. Release the pedal, wait a few seconds, then depress it again. If the pedal travels nearly to the floor before firm resistance is felt, brake adjustment or repair is necessary. If the pedal feels spongy, there is air in the hydraulic system which must be removed by bleeding.

☐ Check that the brake pedal is secure and in good condition. Check also for signs of fluid leaks on the pedal, floor or carpets, which would indicate failed seals in the brake master cylinder.

☐ Check the servo unit (when applicable) by operating the brake pedal several times, then keeping the pedal depressed and starting the engine. As the engine starts, the pedal will move down. If not, the vacuum hose or the servo itself may be faulty.

Steering wheel and column

☐ Examine the steering wheel for fractures or looseness of the hub, spokes or rim.

☐ Move the steering wheel from side to side and then up and down. Check that the steering wheel is not loose on the column, indicating wear or a loose retaining nut. Continue moving the steering wheel as before, but also turn it slightly from left to right.

☐ Check that the steering wheel is not loose on the column, and that there is no abnormal movement of the steering wheel, indicating wear in the column support bearings or couplings.

☐ Check that the ignition lock (where fitted) engages and disengages correctly.

☐ Steering column adjustment mechanisms (where fitted) must be able to lock the column securely in place with no play evident.

Windscreen, mirrors and sunvisor

☐ The windscreen must be free of cracks or other significant damage within the 'swept area' of the windscreen. This is the area swept by the windscreen wipers. A second test area, known as 'Zone A', is the part of the swept area 290 mm wide, centred on the steering wheel centre line. Any damage in Zone A that cannot be contained in a 10 mm diameter circle, or any damage in the remainder of the swept area that cannot be contained in a 40 mm diameter circle, may cause the vehicle to fail the test.

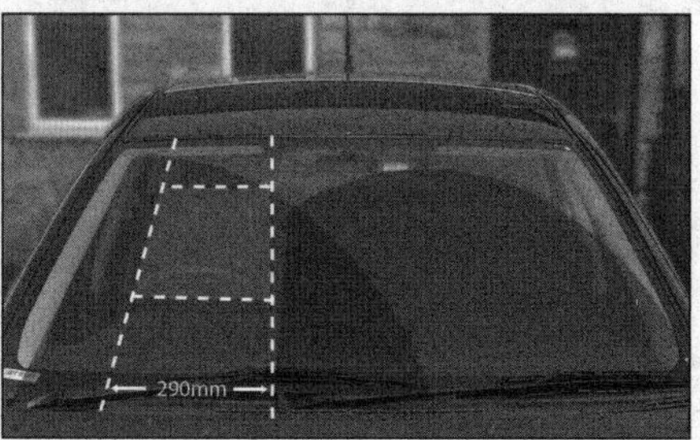

☐ Any items that may obscure the drivers view, such as stickers, sat-navs, anything hanging from the interior mirror, should be removed prior to the test.

☐ Vehicles registered after 1st August 1978 must have a drivers side mirror, and either an interior mirror, or a passenger's side mirror. Cameras (or indirect vision devices) may replace the mirrors, but they must function correctly.

☐ The driver's sunvisor must be capable of being stored in the "up" position.

Seat belts, seats and supplementary restraint systems (SRS)

Note: *The following checks are applicable to all seat belts, front and rear.*

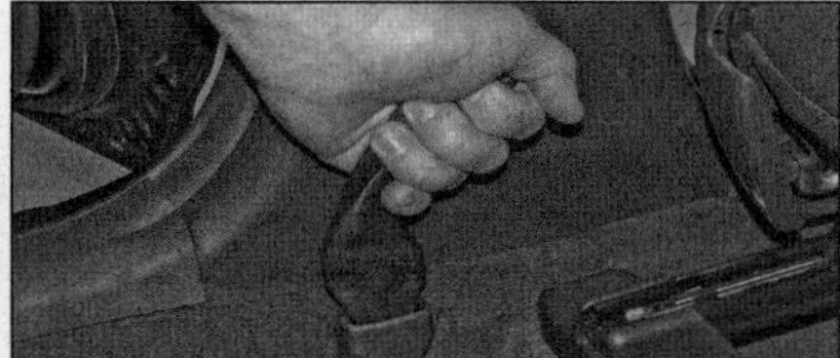

☐ Examine the webbing of all the belts (including rear belts if fitted) for cuts, serious fraying or deterioration. Fasten and unfasten each belt to check the buckles. If applicable, check the retracting mechanism. Check the security of all seat belt mountings accessible from inside the vehicle, ensuring any height adjustable mountings lock securely in place.
☐ Where the seat belt is attached to a seat, the frame and mountings of the seat form part of the belt mountings, and are to be inspected as such.
☐ Any airbag, or SRS warning light must extinguish a few seconds after the ignition is switched on. Failure to do so indicates a fault which must be investigated.
☐ Seat belts with pre-tensioners, once activated, have a "flag" or similar showing on the seat belt stalk. This, in itself, is a reason for test failure.
☐ Check that the original airbag(s) is/are present, and not obviously defective.
☐ The seats themselves must be securely attached and the backrests must lock in the upright position. The driver's seat must also be able to slide forwards/rearwards, and lock in several positions.

Doors

☐ Both front doors must be able to be opened and closed from outside and inside, and must latch securely when closed.
☐ The rear doors must open from the outside.
☐ Examine all door hinges, catches and striker plates for missing, deteriorated, or insecure parts that could effect the opening and closing of the doors.

Speedometer

☐ The vehicle speedometer must be present, and appear operative. The figures on the speedometer must be legible, and illuminated when the lights are switched on.

2 Checks carried out WITH THE VEHICLE ON THE GROUND

Vehicle identification

☐ Number plates must be in good condition, secure and legible, with letters and numbers correctly spaced – spacing at (A) should be 33 mm and at (B) 11 mm. At the front, digits must be black on a white background and at the rear

black on a yellow background. Other background designs (such as honeycomb) are not permitted.
☐ The VIN plate and/or homologation plate must be permanently displayed and legible.

Electrical equipment

☐ Switch on the ignition and check the operation of the horn.
☐ Check the windscreen washers and wipers, examining the wiper blades; renew damaged or perished blades. The wiper blades must clear a large enough area of the windscreen to provide an 'adequate' view of the road, and be able to be parked in a position where they will not affect the drivers' view.

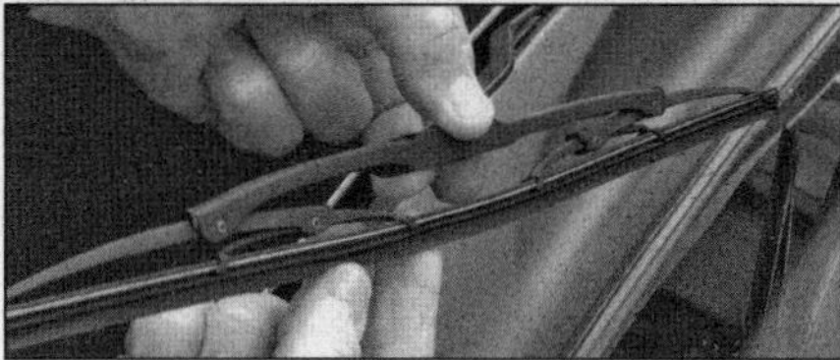

☐ On vehicles first used from 1st September 2009, the headlight washers (where fitted) must operate correctly.
☐ Check the operation of the stop-lights. This includes any lights that appear to be connected – Eg. high-level lights.
☐ Check the operation of the sidelights and number plate lights. The lenses and reflectors must be secure, clean and undamaged.
☐ Check the operation and alignment of the headlights. The headlight reflectors must not be tarnished and the lenses must be undamaged. Where plastic lenses are fitted, check they haven't deteriorated to the extent where they affect the light ouput or beam image. It's often possible to restore the plastic lens using a suitable polish or aftermarket treatment.
☐ Where HID or LED headlights are fitted, check the operation of the cleaning and self-levelling functions.
☐ The headlight main beam warning lamp must be functional.
☐ On vehicles first used from 1st March 2018, the daytime running lights (where fitted) must operate correctly.
☐ Switch on the ignition and check the operation of the direction indicators (including the instrument panel tell-tale) and the hazard warning lights. Operation of the sidelights and stop-lights must not affect the indicators – if it does, the cause is usually a bad earth at the rear light cluster. Indicators should flash at a rate of between 60 and 120 times per minute – faster or slower than this could indicate a fault with the flasher unit or a bad earth at one of the light units.
☐ The hazard warning lights must operate with the ignition on and off.
☐ Check the operation of the rear foglight(s), including the warning light on the instrument panel or in the switch. Note that the foglight must be positioned in the centre or driver's side of the vehicle. If only the passenger's side illuminates, the test will fail.
☐ The warning lights must illuminate in accordance with the manufacturers' design (this includes any warning messages). For most vehicles, the ABS and other warning lights should illuminate when the ignition is switched on, and (if the system is operating properly) extinguish after a few seconds. Refer to the owner's handbook.
☐ On vehicles first used from 1st September 2009, the reversing lights must operate correctly when reverse gear is selected.
☐ Check the vehicle battery for security and leakage.
☐ Check the visible/accessible vehicle wiring is adequately supported, with no evidence of damage or deterioration that could result in a short-circuit.

Footbrake

☐ Examine the master cylinder, brake pipes and servo unit for leaks, loose mountings, corrosion or other damage. If ABS is fitted, this unit should also be examined for signs of leaks or corrosion.
☐ The fluid reservoir must be secure and the fluid level must be between the upper (**A**) and lower (**B**) markings.

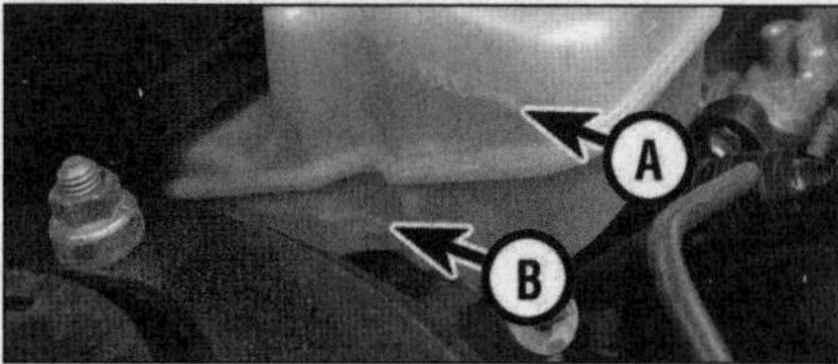

☐ Check the fluid in the reservoir for signs of contamination.
☐ Inspect both front brake flexible hoses for cracks or deterioration of the rubber. Turn the steering from lock to lock, and ensure that the hoses do not contact the wheel, tyre, or any part of the steering or suspension mechanism. With the brake pedal firmly depressed, check the hoses for bulges or leaks under pressure.

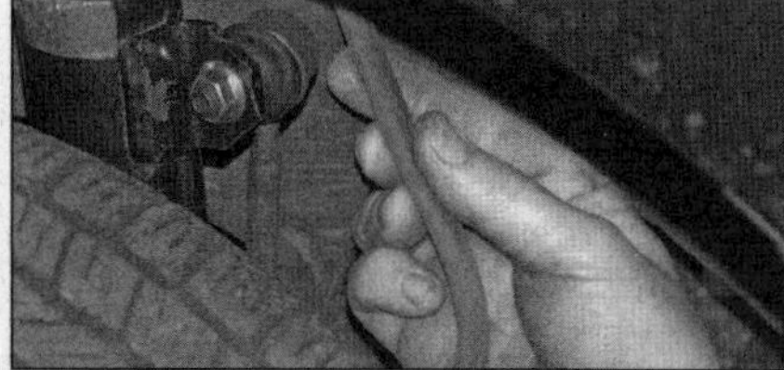

Steering and suspension

☐ Have your assistant turn the steering wheel from side to side slightly, up to the point where the steering gear just begins to transmit this movement to the roadwheels. Check for excessive free play between the steering wheel and the steering gear, indicating wear or insecurity of the steering column joints, the column-to-steering gear coupling, or the steering gear itself. With a standard (380 mm diameter) steering wheel, there should be no more than 13 mm of free play for rack-and-pinion systems, and no more than 75 mm for non-rack-and-pinion designs.
☐ Have your assistant turn the steering

wheel more vigorously in each direction, so that the roadwheels just begin to turn. As this is done, examine all the steering joints, linkages, fittings and attachments. Renew any component that shows signs of wear or damage. On vehicles with hydraulic power steering, check the security and condition of the steering pump, drivebelt and hoses.

☐ Note that all movement checks on power steering systems are carried out with the engine running.

☐ Check that the vehicle is standing level, and at approximately the correct ride height.

Exhaust system

☐ Start the engine. With your assistant holding a rag over the tailpipe, check the entire system for leaks. Repair or renew leaking sections.

3 Checks carried out WITH THE VEHICLE RAISED AND THE WHEELS FREE TO TURN

Jack up the front and rear of the vehicle, and securely support it on axle stands. Position the stands clear of the suspension assemblies. Ensure that the wheels are clear of the ground and that the steering can be turned from lock to lock.

Steering mechanism

☐ Have your assistant turn the steering from lock to lock. Check that the steering turns smoothly, and that no part of the steering mechanism, including a wheel or tyre, fouls any brake hose or pipe or any part of the body structure.

☐ Examine the steering rack rubber gaiters for damage or insecurity of the retaining clips. If power steering is fitted, check for signs of damage or leakage of the fluid hoses, pipes or connections. Also check for excessive stiffness or binding of the steering, a missing split pin or locking device, or severe corrosion of the body structure within 30 cm of any steering component attachment point.

☐ Check the track rod end ball joint dust covers. Any covers that are missing, seriously damaged, deteriorated or insecure, may fail inspection.

Front and rear suspension and wheel bearings

☐ Starting at the front right-hand side, grasp the roadwheel at the 3 o'clock and 9 o'clock positions and rock gently but firmly. Check for free play or insecurity at the wheel bearings, suspension balljoints, or suspension mountings, pivots and attachments.

☐ Now grasp the wheel at the 12 o'clock and 6 o'clock positions and repeat the previous inspection. Spin the wheel, and check for roughness or tightness of the front wheel bearing.

☐ If excess free play is suspected at a component pivot point, this can be confirmed by using a large screwdriver or similar tool and levering between the mounting and the component attachment. This will confirm whether the wear is in the pivot bush, its retaining bolt, or in the mounting itself (the bolt holes can often become elongated).

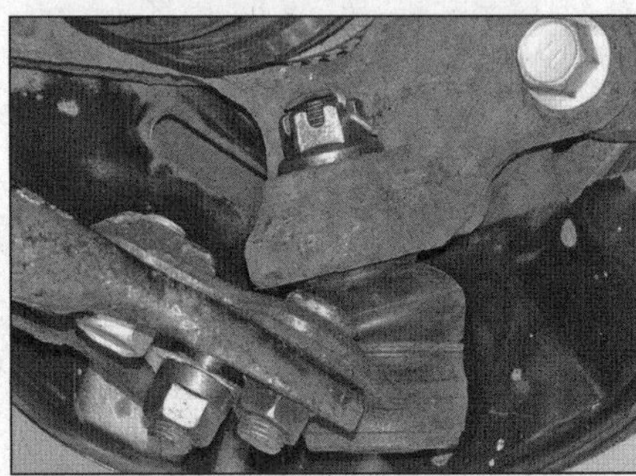

☐ Carry out all the above checks at the other front wheel, and then at both rear wheels.

Springs and shock absorbers

☐ Examine the suspension struts (when applicable) for serious fluid leakage, corrosion, or damage to the casing. Also check the security of the mounting points.

☐ If coil springs are fitted, check that the spring ends locate in their seats, and that the spring is not corroded, cracked or broken.

☐ If leaf springs are fitted, check that all leaves are intact, that the axle is securely attached to each spring, and that there is no deterioration of the spring eye mountings, bushes, and shackles.

☐ The same general checks apply to vehicles fitted with other suspension types, such as torsion bars, hydraulic displacer units, etc. Ensure that all mountings and attachments are secure, that there are no signs of excessive wear, corrosion or damage, and (on hydraulic types) that there are no fluid leaks or damaged pipes.

☐ Check any suspension and anti-roll bar link ball joint dust covers. Any covers that are missing, seriously damaged, deteriorated or insecure, may fail inspection.

☐ Examine each shock absorber for signs of leakage, corrosion of the casing, missing, detached or worn pivots and/or rubber bushes.

Driveshafts (fwd vehicles only)

☐ Rotate each front wheel in turn and inspect the inner and outer joint gaiters for splits or damage. Also check that each driveshaft is straight and undamaged.

Braking system

☐ If possible without dismantling, check brake pad wear and disc condition. Ensure that the friction lining material has not worn excessively, (A) and that the discs are not fractured, pitted, scored or badly worn (B). As a general rule, if the friction material is less than 1.5 mm thick, the inspection will fail.

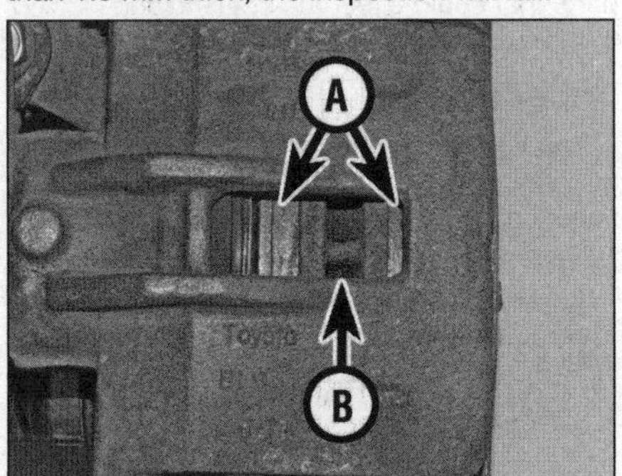

☐ Examine all the rigid brake pipes underneath the vehicle, and the flexible hose(s) at the rear. Look for corrosion, chafing or insecurity of the pipes, and for signs of bulging under pressure, chafing, splits or deterioration of the flexible hoses.

☐ Look for signs of fluid leaks at the brake calipers or on the brake backplates. Repair or renew leaking components.

☐ Slowly spin each wheel, while your assistant depresses and releases the footbrake. Ensure that each brake is operating and does not bind when the pedal is released.

□ Examine the handbrake mechanism, checking for frayed or broken cables, excessive corrosion, or wear or insecurity of the linkage. Check that the mechanism works on each relevant wheel, and releases fully, without binding.

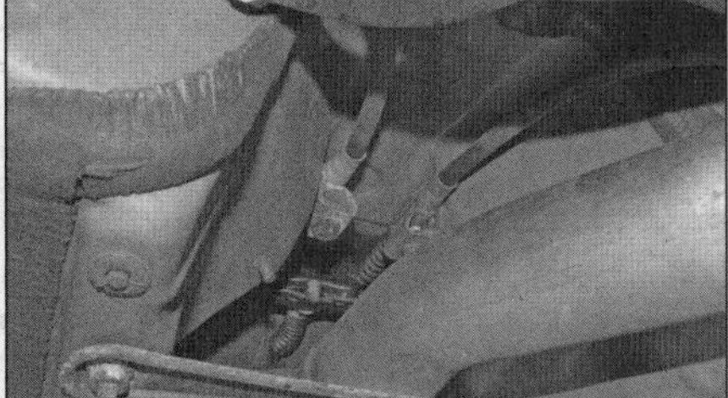

□ Check the ABS sensors' wiring for signs of damage, deterioration or insecurity.

□ It is not possible to test brake efficiency without special equipment, but a road test can be carried out later to check that the vehicle pulls up in a straight line.

Fuel and exhaust systems

□ Inspect the fuel tank (including the filler cap), fuel pipes, hoses and unions. All components must be secure and free from leaks. Locking fuel caps must lock securely and the key must be provided for the MOT test.

□ Examine the exhaust system over its entire length, checking for any damaged, broken or missing mountings, security of the retaining clamps and rust or corrosion.

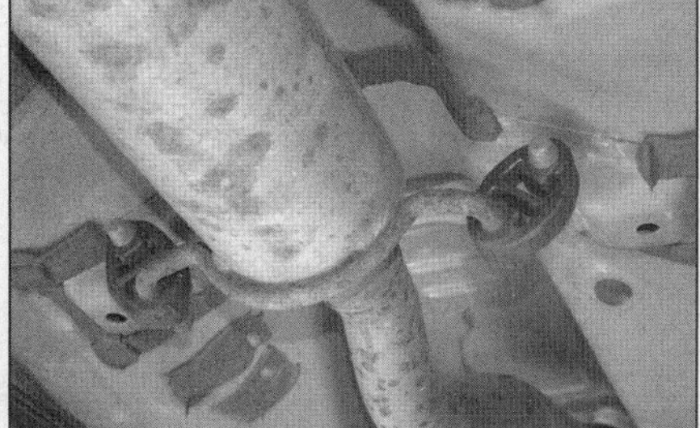

□ If the vehicle was originally equipped with a catalytic converter or particulate filter, one must be fitted.

Wheels and tyres

□ Examine the sidewalls and tread area of each tyre in turn. Check for cuts, tears, lumps, bulges, separation of the tread, and exposure of the ply or cord due to wear or damage. Check that the tyre bead is correctly seated on the wheel rim, that the valve is sound and properly seated, and that the wheel is not distorted or damaged.

□ Check that the tyres are of the correct size for the vehicle, that they are of the same size and type on each axle, and that the pressures are correct. The vehicle will fail the test if the tyres are obviously under-inflated.

□ Check the tyre tread depth. The legal minimum at the time of writing is 1.6 mm over the central three-quarters of the tread width. Abnormal tread wear may indicate incorrect front wheel alignment or wear in steering or suspension components.

□ Check that all wheel bolts/nuts are present.

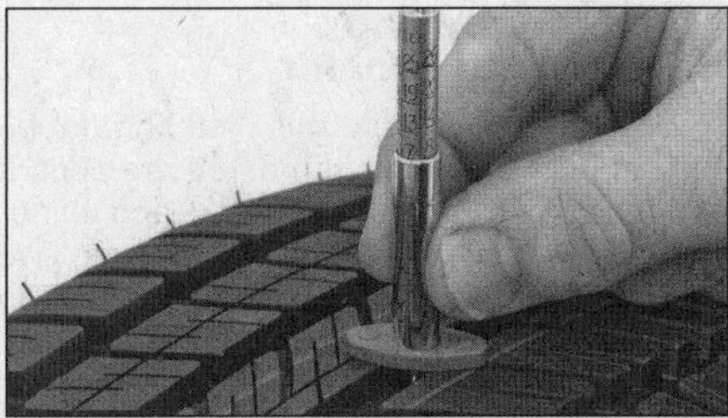

□ If the spare wheel is fitted externally or in a separate carrier beneath the vehicle, check that mountings are secure and free of excessive corrosion.

Body corrosion

□ Check the condition of the entire vehicle structure for signs of corrosion in load-bearing areas. (These include chassis box sections, side sills, cross-members, pillars, and all suspension, steering, braking system and seat belt mountings and anchorages.) Any corrosion which has seriously reduced the thickness of a load-bearing area (or is within 30 cm of safety-related components such as steering or suspension) is likely to cause the vehicle to fail. In this case professional repairs are likely to be needed.

□ Damage or corrosion which causes sharp or otherwise dangerous edges to be exposed will also cause the vehicle to fail.

Towbars

□ Check the condition of mounting points (both beneath the vehicle and within boot/hatchback areas) for signs of corrosion, ensuring that all fixings are secure and not worn or damaged. There must be no excessive play in detachable tow ball arms or quick-release mechanisms.

□ Examine the security and condition of the towbar electrics socket. If the later 13-pin socket is fitted, the MOT tester will check its' wiring functions/connections are correct.

General leaks

□ The vehicle will fail the test if there is a fluid leak of any kind that poses an environmental risk.

4 Checks carried out on
YOUR VEHICLE'S EXHAUST
EMISSION SYSTEM

Petrol models

□ The engine should be warmed up, and running well (ignition system in good order, air filter element clean, etc).

□ Before testing, run the engine at around 2500 rpm for 20 seconds. Let the engine drop to idle, and watch for smoke from the exhaust. If the idle speed is too high, or if dense blue or black smoke emerges for more than 5 seconds, the vehicle will fail. Typically, blue smoke signifies oil burning (engine wear); black smoke means unburnt fuel (dirty air cleaner element, or other fuel system fault).

□ An exhaust gas analyser for measuring carbon monoxide (CO) and hydrocarbons (HC) is now needed. If one cannot be hired or borrowed, have a local garage perform the check.

CO emissions (mixture)

□ The MOT tester has access to the CO limits for all vehicles from 1st August 1992. The CO level is measured at idle speed, and at 'fast idle' (2500 to 3000 rpm). The following limits are given as a general guide:

At idle speed – Less than 0.3% CO
At 'fast idle' – Less than 0.2% CO
Lambda reading – 0.97 to 1.03

□ If the CO level is too high, this may point to poor maintenance, a fuel injection system problem, faulty lambda (oxygen) sensor or catalytic converter. Try an injector cleaning treatment, and check the vehicle's ECU for fault codes.

HC emissions

□ The MOT tester has access to HC limits for all vehicles. The HC level is measured at 'fast idle' (2500 to 3000 rpm). The following limits are given as a general guide:

At 'fast idle' – Less than 200 ppm

□ Excessive HC emissions are typically caused by oil being burnt (worn engine), or by a blocked crankcase ventilation system ('breather'). If the engine oil is old and thin, an oil change may help. If the engine is running badly, check the vehicle's ECU for fault codes.

Diesel models

□ If the vehicle was fitted with a DPF (Diesel Particulate Filter) when it left the factory, it will fail the test if the MOT tester can see smoke of any colour emitting from the exhaust, or finds evidence that the filter has been tampered with.

□ The only emission test for diesel engines is measuring exhaust smoke density, using a calibrated smoke meter.

□ This test involves accelerating the engine to its maximum unloaded speed a minimum of once, and a maximum of 6 times. With the smoke meter connected, the engine is accelerated quickly to its maximum speed. If the smoke level is at or below the limit specified, the vehicle will pass. If the level is more than the specified limit then two further accelerations are carried out, and an average of the readings calculated. If the vehicle is still over the limit, a further three accelerations are carried out, with the average of the last three calculated after each check.

Note: *On engines with a timing belt, it is VITAL that the belt is in good condition before the test is carried out.*

Vehicles registered after 1st July 2008

Smoke level must not exceed 1.5m-1 – Turbo-charged and non-Turbocharged engines

Vehicles registered before 1st July 2008

Smoke level must not exceed 2.5m-1 – Non-turbo vehicles
Smoke level must not exceed 3.0m-1 – Turbocharged vehicles:

□ If excess smoke is produced, try fitting a new air cleaner element, or using an injector cleaning treatment. If the engine is running badly, where applicable, check the vehicle's ECU for fault codes. Also check the vehicle's EGR system, where applicable. At high mileages, the injectors may require professional attention.

Introduction

A selection of good tools is a fundamental requirement for anyone contemplating the maintenance and repair of a motor vehicle. For the owner who does not possess any, their purchase will prove a considerable expense, offsetting some of the savings made by doing-it-yourself. However, provided that the tools purchased meet the relevant national safety standards and are of good quality, they will last for many years and prove an extremely worthwhile investment.

To help the average owner to decide which tools are needed to carry out the various tasks detailed in this manual, we have compiled three lists of tools under the following headings: *Maintenance and minor repair, Repair and overhaul*, and *Special*. Newcomers to practical mechanics should start off with the *Maintenance and minor repair* tool kit, and confine themselves to the simpler jobs around the vehicle. Then, as confidence and experience grow, more difficult tasks can be undertaken, with extra tools being purchased as, and when, they are needed. In this way, a *Maintenance and minor repair* tool kit can be built up into a *Repair and overhaul* tool kit over a considerable period of time, without any major cash outlays. The experienced do-it-yourselfer will have a tool kit good enough for most repair and overhaul procedures, and will add tools from the *Special* category when it is felt that the expense is justified by the amount of use to which these tools will be put.

Maintenance and minor repair tool kit

The tools given in this list should be considered as a minimum requirement if routine maintenance, servicing and minor repair operations are to be undertaken. We recommend the purchase of combination spanners (ring one end, open-ended the other); although more expensive than open-ended ones, they do give the advantages of both types of spanner.

- ☐ *Combination spanners:*
  Metric - 8 to 19 mm inclusive
- ☐ *Adjustable spanner - 35 mm jaw (approx.)*
- ☐ *Spark plug spanner (with rubber insert) - petrol models*
- ☐ *Spark plug gap adjustment tool - petrol models*
- ☐ *Set of feeler gauges*
- ☐ *Brake bleed nipple spanner*
- ☐ *Screwdrivers:*
  Flat blade - 100 mm long x 6 mm dia
  Cross blade - 100 mm long x 6 mm dia
  Torx - various sizes (not all vehicles)
- ☐ *Combination pliers*
- ☐ *Hacksaw (junior)*
- ☐ *Tyre pump*
- ☐ *Tyre pressure gauge*
- ☐ *Oil can*
- ☐ *Oil filter removal tool (if applicable)*
- ☐ *Fine emery cloth*
- ☐ *Wire brush (small)*
- ☐ *Funnel (medium size)*
- ☐ *Sump drain plug key (not all vehicles)*

Repair and overhaul tool kit

These tools are virtually essential for anyone undertaking any major repairs to a motor vehicle, and are additional to those given in the *Maintenance and minor repair* list. Included in this list is a comprehensive set of sockets. Although these are expensive, they will be found invaluable as they are so versatile - particularly if various drives are included in the set. We recommend the half-inch square-drive type, as this can be used with most proprietary torque wrenches.

The tools in this list will sometimes need to be supplemented by tools from the *Special* list:

- ☐ *Sockets to cover range in previous list (including Torx sockets)*
- ☐ *Reversible ratchet drive (for use with sockets)*
- ☐ *Extension piece, 250 mm (for use with sockets)*
- ☐ *Universal joint (for use with sockets)*
- ☐ *Flexible handle or sliding T "breaker bar" (for use with sockets)*
- ☐ *Torque wrench (for use with sockets)*
- ☐ *Self-locking grips*
- ☐ *Ball pein hammer*
- ☐ *Soft-faced mallet (plastic or rubber)*
- ☐ *Screwdrivers:*
  Flat blade - long & sturdy, short (chubby), and narrow (electrician's) types
  Cross blade – long & sturdy, and short (chubby) types
- ☐ *Pliers:*
  Long-nosed
  Side cutters (electrician's)
  Circlip (internal and external)
- ☐ *Cold chisel - 25 mm*
- ☐ *Scriber*
- ☐ *Scraper*
- ☐ *Centre-punch*
- ☐ *Pin punch*
- ☐ *Hacksaw*
- ☐ *Brake hose clamp*
- ☐ *Brake/clutch bleeding kit*
- ☐ *Selection of twist drills*
- ☐ *Steel rule/straight-edge*
- ☐ *Allen keys (inc. splined/Torx type)*
- ☐ *Selection of files*
- ☐ *Wire brush*
- ☐ *Axle stands*
- ☐ *Jack (strong trolley or hydraulic type)*
- ☐ *Light with extension lead*
- ☐ *Universal electrical multi-meter*

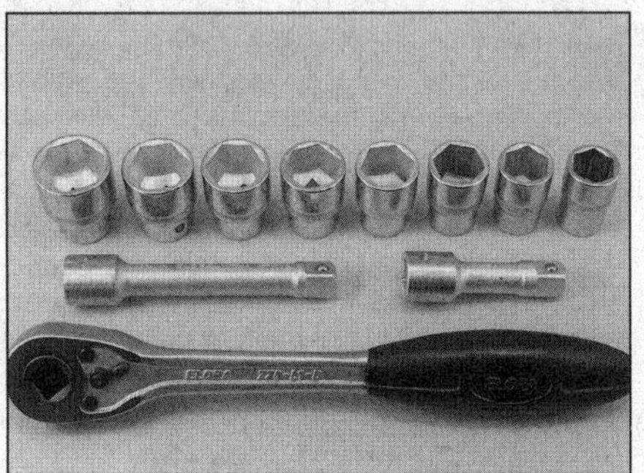

Sockets and reversible ratchet drive

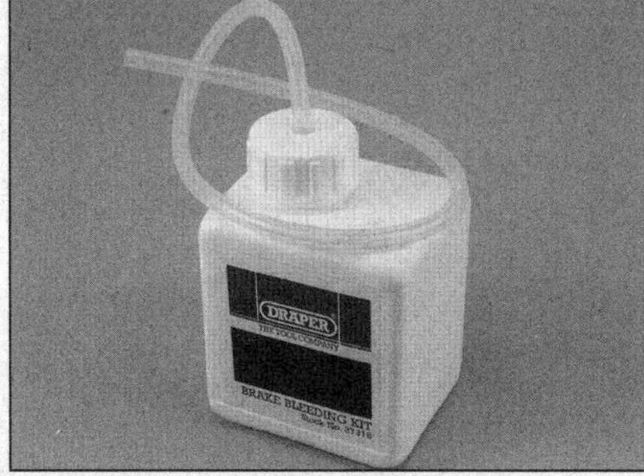

Brake bleeding kit

Torx key, socket and bit

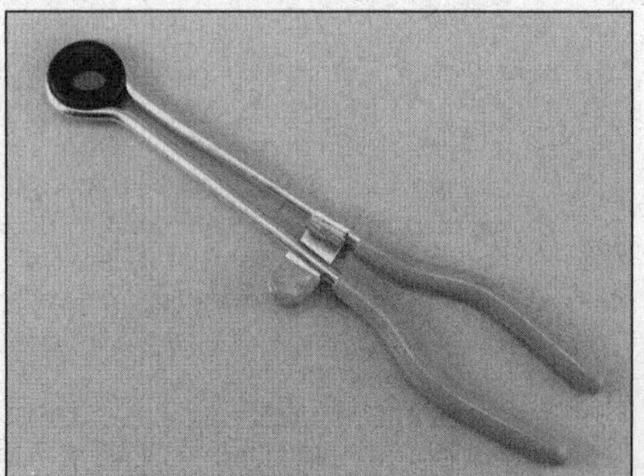

Hose clamp

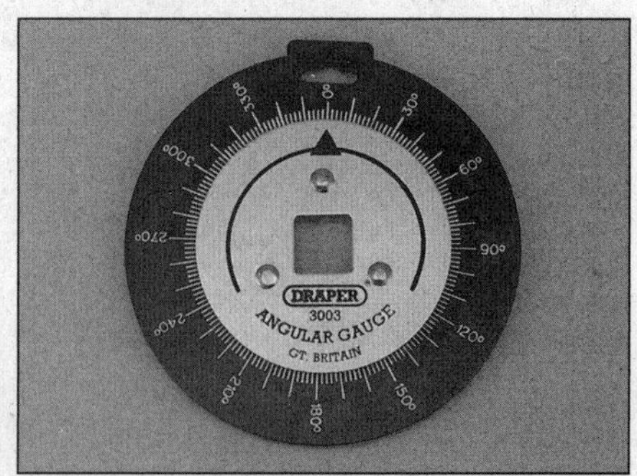

Angular-tightening gauge

Special tools

The tools in this list are those which are not used regularly, are expensive to buy, or which need to be used in accordance with their manufacturers' instructions. Unless relatively difficult mechanical jobs are undertaken frequently, it will not be economic to buy many of these tools. Where this is the case, you could consider clubbing together with friends (or joining a motorists' club) to make a joint purchase, or borrowing the tools against a deposit from a local garage or tool hire specialist.

The following list contains only those tools and instruments freely available to the public, and not those special tools produced by the vehicle manufacturer specifically for its dealer network. You will find occasional references to these manufacturers' special tools in the text of this manual. Generally, an alternative method of doing the job without the vehicle manufacturers' special tool is given. However, sometimes there is no alternative to using them. Where this is the case and the relevant tool cannot be bought or borrowed, you will have to entrust the work to a dealer.

- ☐ *Angular-tightening gauge*
- ☐ *Valve spring compressor*
- ☐ *Valve grinding tool*
- ☐ *Piston ring compressor*
- ☐ *Piston ring removal/installation tool*
- ☐ *Cylinder bore hone*
- ☐ *Balljoint separator*
- ☐ *Coil spring compressors (where applicable)*
- ☐ *Two/three-legged hub and bearing puller*
- ☐ *Impact screwdriver*
- ☐ *Micrometer and/or vernier calipers*
- ☐ *Dial gauge*
- ☐ *Tachometer*
- ☐ *Fault code reader*
- ☐ *Cylinder compression gauge*
- ☐ *Hand-operated vacuum pump and gauge*
- ☐ *Clutch plate alignment set*
- ☐ *Brake shoe steady spring cup removal tool*
- ☐ *Bush and bearing removal/installation set*
- ☐ *Stud extractors*
- ☐ *Tap and die set*
- ☐ *Lifting tackle*

Buying tools

Reputable motor accessory shops and superstores often offer excellent quality tools at discount prices, so it pays to shop around.

Remember, you don't have to buy the most expensive items on the shelf, but it is always advisable to steer clear of the very cheap tools. Beware of 'bargains' offered on market stalls, on-line or at car boot sales. There are plenty of good tools around at reasonable prices, but always aim to purchase items which meet the relevant national safety standards. If in doubt, ask the proprietor or manager of the shop for advice before making a purchase.

Care and maintenance of tools

Having purchased a reasonable tool kit, it is necessary to keep the tools in a clean and serviceable condition. After use, always wipe off any dirt, grease and metal particles using a clean, dry cloth, before putting the tools away. Never leave them lying around after they have been used. A simple tool rack on the garage or workshop wall for items such as screwdrivers and pliers is a good idea. Store all normal spanners and sockets in a metal box. Any measuring instruments, gauges, meters, etc, must be carefully stored where they cannot be damaged or become rusty.

Take a little care when tools are used. Hammer heads inevitably become marked, and screwdrivers lose the keen edge on their blades from time to time. A little timely attention with emery cloth or a file will soon restore items like this to a good finish.

Working facilities

Not to be forgotten when discussing tools is the workshop itself. If anything more than routine maintenance is to be carried out, a suitable working area becomes essential.

It is appreciated that many an owner-mechanic is forced by circumstances to remove an engine or similar item without the benefit of a garage or workshop. Having done this, any repairs should always be done under the cover of a roof.

Wherever possible, any dismantling should be done on a clean, flat workbench or table at a suitable working height.

Any workbench needs a vice; one with a jaw opening of 100 mm is suitable for most jobs. As mentioned previously, some clean dry storage space is also required for tools, as well as for any lubricants, cleaning fluids, touch-up paints etc, which become necessary.

Another item which may be required, and which has a much more general usage, is an electric drill with a chuck capacity of at least 8 mm. This, together with a good range of twist drills, is virtually essential for fitting accessories.

Last, but not least, always keep a supply of old newspapers and clean, lint-free rags available, and try to keep any working area as clean as possible.

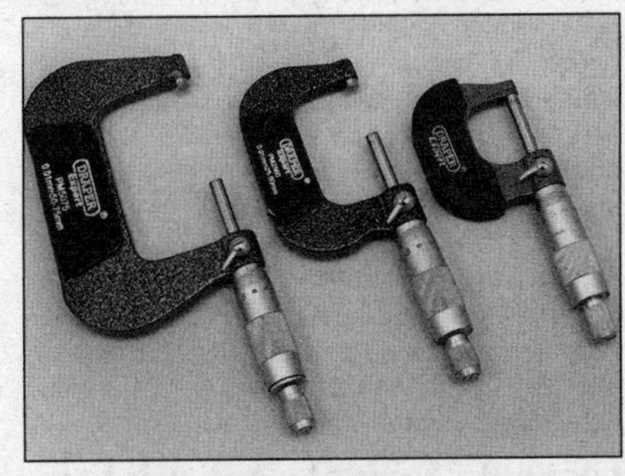

Micrometers

Dial test indicator ("dial gauge")

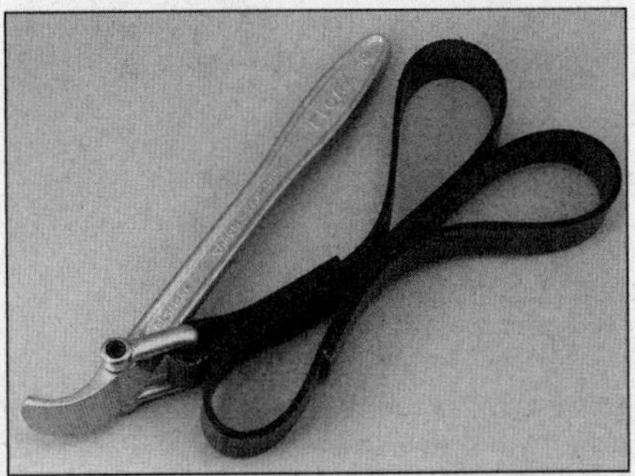

Oil filter removal tool (strap wrench type)

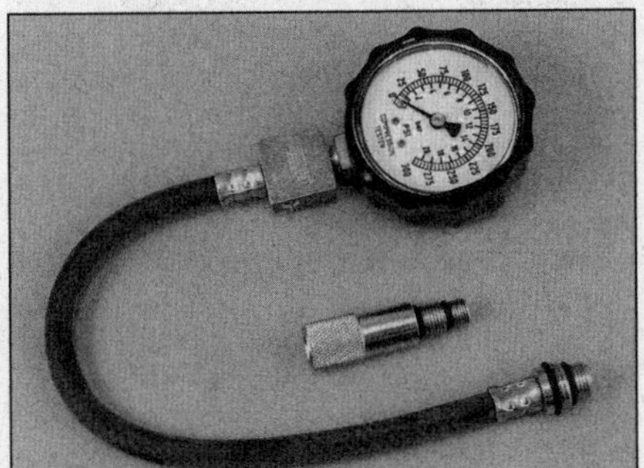

Compression tester

Bearing puller

Whenever servicing, repair or overhaul work is carried out on the car or its components, observe the following procedures and instructions. This will assist in carrying out the operation efficiently and to a professional standard of workmanship.

Joint mating faces and gaskets

When separating components at their mating faces, never insert screwdrivers or similar implements into the joint between the faces in order to prise them apart. This can cause severe damage which results in oil leaks, coolant leaks, etc upon reassembly. Separation is usually achieved by tapping along the joint with a soft-faced hammer in order to break the seal. However, note that this method may not be suitable where dowels are used for component location.

Where a gasket is used between the mating faces of two components, a new one must be fitted on reassembly; fit it dry unless otherwise stated in the repair procedure. Make sure that the mating faces are clean and dry, with all traces of old gasket removed. When cleaning a joint face, use a tool which is unlikely to score or damage the face, and remove any burrs or nicks with an oilstone or fine file.

Make sure that tapped holes are cleaned with a pipe cleaner, and keep them free of jointing compound, if this is being used, unless specifically instructed otherwise.

Ensure that all orifices, channels or pipes are clear, and blow through them, preferably using compressed air.

Oil seals

Oil seals can be removed by levering them out with a wide flat-bladed screwdriver or similar implement. Alternatively, a number of self-tapping screws may be screwed into the seal, and these used as a purchase for pliers or some similar device in order to pull the seal free.

Whenever an oil seal is removed from its working location, either individually or as part of an assembly, it should be renewed.

The very fine sealing lip of the seal is easily damaged, and will not seal if the surface it contacts is not completely clean and free from scratches, nicks or grooves. If the original sealing surface of the component cannot be restored, and the manufacturer has not made provision for slight relocation of the seal relative to the sealing surface, the component should be renewed.

Protect the lips of the seal from any surface which may damage them in the course of fitting. Use tape or a conical sleeve where possible. Where indicated, lubricate the seal lips with oil before fitting and, on dual-lipped seals, fill the space between the lips with grease.

Unless otherwise stated, oil seals must be fitted with their sealing lips toward the lubricant to be sealed.

Use a tubular drift or block of wood of the appropriate size to install the seal and, if the seal housing is shouldered, drive the seal down to the shoulder. If the seal housing is unshouldered, the seal should be fitted with its face flush with the housing top face (unless otherwise instructed).

Screw threads and fastenings

Seized nuts, bolts and screws are quite a common occurrence where corrosion has set in, and the use of penetrating oil or releasing fluid will often overcome this problem if the offending item is soaked for a while before attempting to release it. The use of an impact driver may also provide a means of releasing such stubborn fastening devices, when used in conjunction with the appropriate screwdriver bit or socket. If none of these methods works, it may be necessary to resort to the careful application of heat, or the use of a hacksaw or nut splitter device. Before resorting to extreme methods, check that you are not dealing with a left-hand thread!

Studs are usually removed by locking two nuts together on the threaded part, and then using a spanner on the lower nut to unscrew the stud. Studs or bolts which have broken off below the surface of the component in which they are mounted can sometimes be removed using a stud extractor.

Always ensure that a blind tapped hole is completely free from oil, grease, water or other fluid before installing the bolt or stud. Failure to do this could cause the housing to crack due to the hydraulic action of the bolt or stud as it is screwed in.

For some screw fastenings, notably cylinder head bolts or nuts, torque wrench settings are no longer specified for the latter stages of tightening, “angle-tightening” being called up instead. Typically, a fairly low torque wrench setting will be applied to the bolts/nuts in the correct sequence, followed by one or more stages of tightening through specified angles.

When checking or retightening a nut or bolt to a specified torque setting, slacken the nut or bolt by a quarter of a turn, and then retighten to the specified setting. However, this should not be attempted where angular tightening has been used.

Locknuts, locktabs and washers

Any fastening which will rotate against a component or housing during tightening should always have a washer between it and the relevant component or housing.

Spring or split washers should always be renewed when they are used to lock a critical component such as a big-end bearing retaining bolt or nut. Locktabs which are folded over to retain a nut or bolt should always be renewed.

Self-locking nuts can be re-used in non-critical areas, providing resistance can be felt when the locking portion passes over the bolt or stud thread. However, it should be noted that self-locking stiffnuts tend to lose their effectiveness after long periods of use, and should then be renewed as a matter of course.

Split pins must always be replaced with new ones of the correct size for the hole.

When thread-locking compound is found on the threads of a fastener which is to be re-used, it should be cleaned off with a wire brush and solvent, and fresh compound applied on reassembly.

Special tools

Some repair procedures in this manual entail the use of special tools such as a press, two or three-legged pullers, spring compressors, etc. Wherever possible, suitable readily-available alternatives to the manufacturer’s special tools are described, and are shown in use. In some instances, where no alternative is possible, it has been necessary to resort to the use of a manufacturer’s tool, and this has been done for reasons of safety as well as the efficient completion of the repair operation. Unless you are highly-skilled and have a thorough understanding of the procedures described, never attempt to bypass the use of any special tool when the procedure described specifies its use. Not only is there a very great risk of personal injury, but expensive damage could be caused to the components involved.

Environmental considerations

When disposing of used engine oil, brake fluid, antifreeze, etc, give due consideration to any detrimental environmental effects. Do not, for instance, pour any of the above liquids down drains into the general sewage system, or onto the ground to soak away, as this is likely to pollute your local environment. Many local council refuse tips provide a facility for waste oil disposal, as do some garages. You can find your nearest disposal point by calling the Environment Agency on 03708 506 506 or by visiting www.oilbankline.org.uk.

Note: It is illegal and anti-social to dump oil down the drain. To find the location of your local oil recycling bank, call 03708 506 506 or visit www.oilbankline.org.uk.

A

ABS (Anti-lock brake system) A system, usually electronically controlled, that senses incipient wheel lockup during braking and relieves hydraulic pressure at wheels that are about to skid.

Air bag An inflatable bag hidden in the steering wheel (driver's side) or the dash or glovebox (passenger side). In a head-on collision, the bags inflate, preventing the driver and front passenger from being thrown forward into the steering wheel or windscreen.

Air cleaner A metal or plastic housing, containing a filter element, which removes dust and dirt from the air being drawn into the engine.

Air filter element The actual filter in an air cleaner system, usually manufactured from pleated paper and requiring renewal at regular intervals.

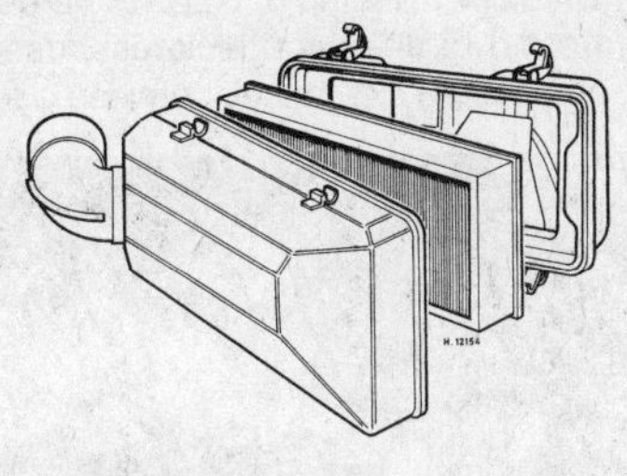

Air filter

Allen key A hexagonal wrench which fits into a recessed hexagonal hole.

Alligator clip A long-nosed spring-loaded metal clip with meshing teeth. Used to make temporary electrical connections.

Alternator A component in the electrical system which converts mechanical energy from a drivebelt into electrical energy to charge the battery and to operate the starting system, ignition system and electrical accessories.

Ampere (amp) A unit of measurement for the flow of electric current. One amp is the amount of current produced by one volt acting through a resistance of one ohm.

Anaerobic sealer A substance used to prevent bolts and screws from loosening. Anaerobic means that it does not require oxygen for activation. The Loctite brand is widely used.

Antifreeze A substance (usually ethylene glycol) mixed with water, and added to a vehicle's cooling system, to prevent freezing of the coolant in winter. Antifreeze also contains chemicals to inhibit corrosion and the formation of rust and other deposits that would tend to clog the radiator and coolant passages and reduce cooling efficiency.

Anti-seize compound A coating that reduces the risk of seizing on fasteners that are subjected to high temperatures, such as exhaust manifold bolts and nuts.

Asbestos A natural fibrous mineral with great heat resistance, commonly used in the composition of brake friction materials. Asbestos is a health hazard and the dust created by brake systems should never be inhaled or ingested.

Axle A shaft on which a wheel revolves, or which revolves with a wheel. Also, a solid beam that connects the two wheels at one end of the vehicle. An axle which also transmits power to the wheels is known as a live axle.

Axleshaft A single rotating shaft, on either side of the differential, which delivers power from the final drive assembly to the drive wheels. Also called a driveshaft or a halfshaft.

B

Ball bearing An anti-friction bearing consisting of a hardened inner and outer race with hardened steel balls between two races.

Bearing The curved surface on a shaft or in a bore, or the part assembled into either, that permits relative motion between them with minimum wear and friction.

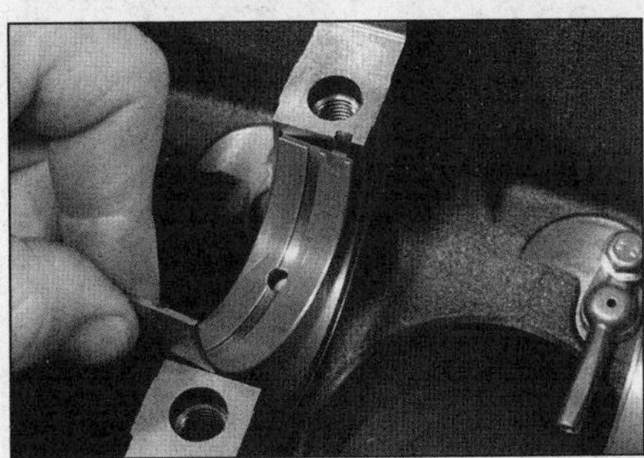

Bearing

Big-end bearing The bearing in the end of the connecting rod that's attached to the crankshaft.

Bleed nipple A valve on a brake wheel cylinder, caliper or other hydraulic component that is opened to purge the hydraulic system of air. Also called a bleed screw.

Brake bleeding Procedure for removing air from lines of a hydraulic brake system.

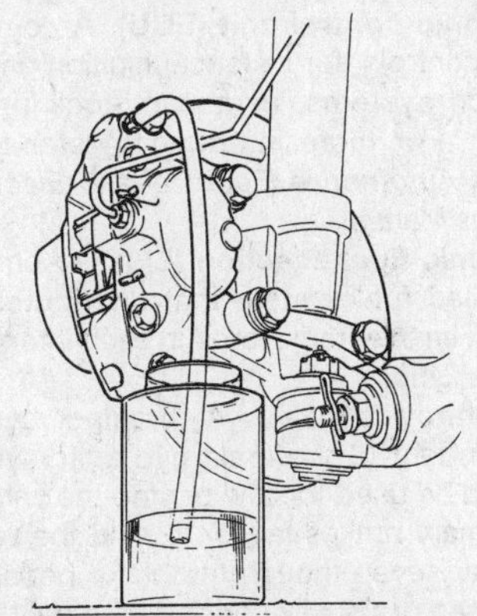

Brake bleeding

Brake disc The component of a disc brake that rotates with the wheels.

Brake drum The component of a drum brake that rotates with the wheels.

Brake linings The friction material which contacts the brake disc or drum to retard the vehicle's speed. The linings are bonded or riveted to the brake pads or shoes.

Brake pads The replaceable friction pads that pinch the brake disc when the brakes are applied. Brake pads consist of a friction material bonded or riveted to a rigid backing plate.

Brake shoe The crescent-shaped carrier to which the brake linings are mounted and which forces the lining against the rotating drum during braking.

Braking systems For more information on braking systems, consult the *Haynes Automotive Brake Manual*.

Breaker bar A long socket wrench handle providing greater leverage.

Bulkhead The insulated partition between the engine and the passenger compartment.

C

Caliper The non-rotating part of a disc-brake assembly that straddles the disc and carries the brake pads. The caliper also contains the hydraulic components that cause the pads to pinch the disc when the brakes are applied. A caliper is also a measuring tool that can be set to measure inside or outside dimensions of an object.

Camshaft A rotating shaft on which a series of cam lobes operate the valve mechanisms. The camshaft may be driven by gears, by sprockets and chain or by sprockets and a belt.

Canister A container in an evaporative emission control system; contains activated charcoal granules to trap vapours from the fuel system.

Canister

Carburettor A device which mixes fuel with air in the proper proportions to provide a desired power output from a spark ignition internal combustion engine.

Castellated Resembling the parapets along the top of a castle wall. For example, a castellated balljoint stud nut.

Castor In wheel alignment, the backward or forward tilt of the steering axis. Castor is positive when the steering axis is inclined rearward at the top.

Catalytic converter A silencer-like device in the exhaust system which converts certain pollutants in the exhaust gases into less harmful substances.

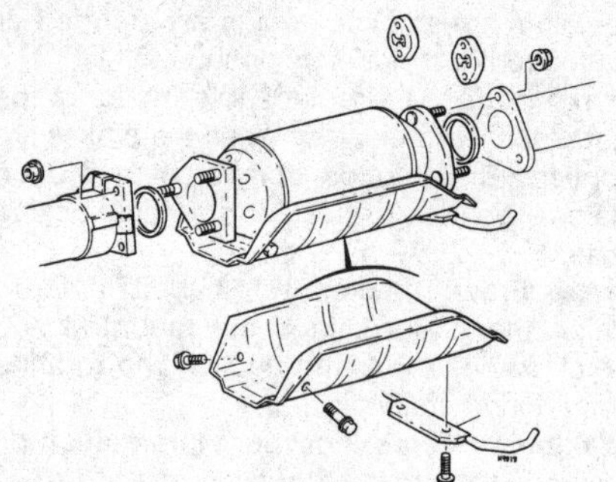

Catalytic converter

Circlip A ring-shaped clip used to prevent endwise movement of cylindrical parts and shafts. An internal circlip is installed in a groove in a housing; an external circlip fits into a groove on the outside of a cylindrical piece such as a shaft.

Clearance The amount of space between two parts. For example, between a piston and a cylinder, between a bearing and a journal, etc.

Coil spring A spiral of elastic steel found in various sizes throughout a vehicle, for example as a springing medium in the suspension and in the valve train.

Compression Reduction in volume, and increase in pressure and temperature, of a gas, caused by squeezing it into a smaller space.

Compression ratio The relationship between cylinder volume when the piston is at top dead centre and cylinder volume when the piston is at bottom dead centre.

Constant velocity (CV) joint A type of universal joint that cancels out vibrations caused by driving power being transmitted through an angle.

Core plug A disc or cup-shaped metal device inserted in a hole in a casting through which core was removed when the casting was formed. Also known as a freeze plug or expansion plug.

Crankcase The lower part of the engine block in which the crankshaft rotates.

Crankshaft The main rotating member, or shaft, running the length of the crankcase, with offset "throws" to which the connecting rods are attached.

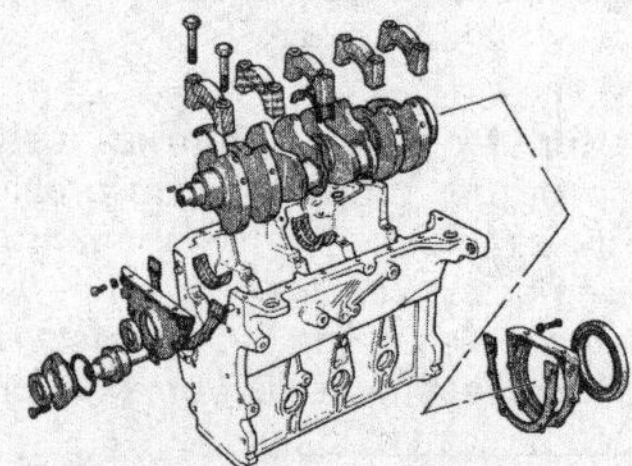

Crankshaft assembly

Crocodile clip See Alligator clip

D

Diagnostic code Code numbers obtained by accessing the diagnostic mode of an engine management computer. This code can be used to determine the area in the system where a malfunction may be located.

Disc brake A brake design incorporating a rotating disc onto which brake pads are squeezed. The resulting friction converts the energy of a moving vehicle into heat.

Double-overhead cam (DOHC) An engine that uses two overhead camshafts, usually one for the intake valves and one for the exhaust valves.

Drivebelt(s) The belt(s) used to drive accessories such as the alternator, water pump, power steering pump, air conditioning compressor, etc. off the crankshaft pulley.

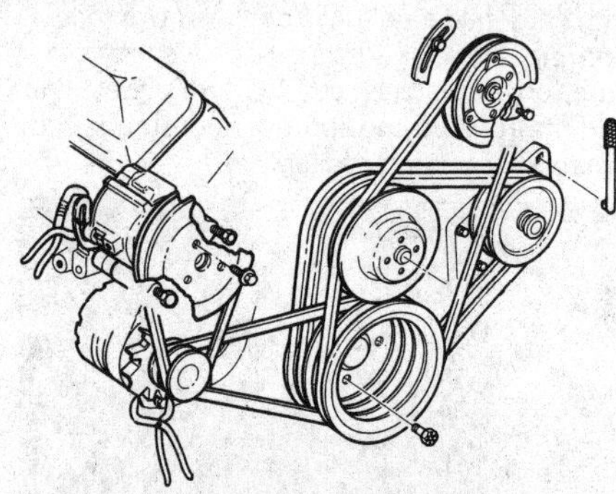

Accessory drivebelts

Driveshaft Any shaft used to transmit motion. Commonly used when referring to the axleshafts on a front wheel drive vehicle.

Drum brake A type of brake using a drum-shaped metal cylinder attached to the inner surface of the wheel. When the brake pedal is pressed, curved brake shoes with friction linings press against the inside of the drum to slow or stop the vehicle.

E

EGR valve A valve used to introduce exhaust gases into the intake air stream.

Electronic control unit (ECU) A computer which controls (for instance) ignition and fuel injection systems, or an anti-lock braking system. For more information refer to the *Haynes Automotive Electrical and Electronic Systems Manual.*

Electronic Fuel Injection (EFI) A computer controlled fuel system that distributes fuel through an injector located in each intake port of the engine.

Emergency brake A braking system, independent of the main hydraulic system, that can be used to slow or stop the vehicle if the primary brakes fail, or to hold the vehicle stationary even though the brake pedal isn't depressed. It usually consists of a hand lever that actuates either front or rear brakes mechanically through a series of cables and linkages. Also known as a handbrake or parking brake.

Endfloat The amount of lengthwise movement between two parts. As applied to a crankshaft, the distance that the crankshaft can move forward and back in the cylinder block.

Engine management system (EMS) A computer controlled system which manages the fuel injection and the ignition systems in an integrated fashion.

Exhaust manifold A part with several passages through which exhaust gases leave the engine combustion chambers and enter the exhaust pipe.

F

Fan clutch A viscous (fluid) drive coupling device which permits variable engine fan speeds in relation to engine speeds.

Feeler blade A thin strip or blade of hardened steel, ground to an exact thickness, used to check or measure clearances between parts.

Feeler blade

Firing order The order in which the engine cylinders fire, or deliver their power strokes, beginning with the number one cylinder.

Flywheel A heavy spinning wheel in which energy is absorbed and stored by means of momentum. On cars, the flywheel is attached to the crankshaft to smooth out firing impulses.

Free play The amount of travel before any action takes place. The "looseness" in a linkage, or an assembly of parts, between the initial application of force and actual movement. For example, the distance the brake pedal moves before the pistons in the master cylinder are actuated.

Fuse An electrical device which protects a circuit against accidental overload. The typical fuse contains a soft piece of metal which is calibrated to melt at a predetermined current flow (expressed as amps) and break the circuit.

Fusible link A circuit protection device consisting of a conductor surrounded by heat-resistant insulation. The conductor is smaller than the wire it protects, so it acts as the weakest link in the circuit. Unlike a blown fuse, a failed fusible link must frequently be cut from the wire for replacement.

G

Gap The distance the spark must travel in jumping from the centre electrode to the side electrode in a spark plug. Also refers to the spacing between the points in a contact breaker assembly in a conventional points-type ignition, or to the distance between the reluctor or rotor and the pickup coil in an electronic ignition.

Adjusting spark plug gap

Gasket Any thin, soft material - usually cork, cardboard, asbestos or soft metal - installed between two metal surfaces to ensure a good seal. For instance, the cylinder head gasket seals the joint between the block and the cylinder head.

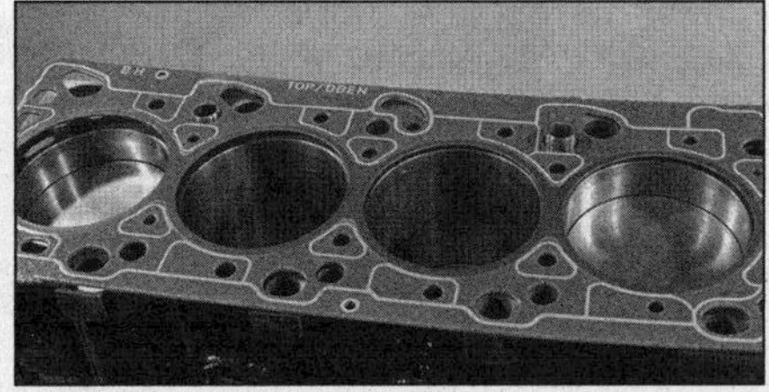

Gasket

Gauge An instrument panel display used to monitor engine conditions. A gauge with a movable pointer on a dial or a fixed scale is an analogue gauge. A gauge with a numerical readout is called a digital gauge.

H

Halfshaft A rotating shaft that transmits power from the final drive unit to a drive wheel, usually when referring to a live rear axle.

Harmonic balancer A device designed to reduce torsion or twisting vibration in the crankshaft. May be incorporated in the crankshaft pulley. Also known as a vibration damper.

Hone An abrasive tool for correcting small irregularities or differences in diameter in an engine cylinder, brake cylinder, etc.

Hydraulic tappet A tappet that utilises hydraulic pressure from the engine's lubrication system to maintain zero clearance (constant contact with both camshaft and valve stem). Automatically adjusts to variation in valve stem length. Hydraulic tappets also reduce valve noise.

I

Ignition timing The moment at which the spark plug fires, usually expressed in the number of crankshaft degrees before the piston reaches the top of its stroke.

Inlet manifold A tube or housing with passages through which flows the air-fuel mixture (carburettor vehicles and vehicles with throttle body injection) or air only (port fuel-injected vehicles) to the port openings in the cylinder head.

J

Jump start Starting the engine of a vehicle with a discharged or weak battery by attaching jump leads from the weak battery to a charged or helper battery.

L

Load Sensing Proportioning Valve (LSPV) A brake hydraulic system control valve that works like a proportioning valve, but also takes into consideration the amount of weight carried by the rear axle.

Locknut A nut used to lock an adjustment nut, or other threaded component, in place. For example, a locknut is employed to keep the adjusting nut on the rocker arm in position.

Lockwasher A form of washer designed to prevent an attaching nut from working loose.

M

MacPherson strut A type of front suspension system devised by Earle MacPherson at Ford of England. In its original form, a simple lateral link with the anti-roll bar creates the lower control arm. A long strut - an integral coil spring and shock absorber - is mounted between the body and the steering knuckle. Many modern so-called MacPherson strut systems use a conventional lower A-arm and don't rely on the anti-roll bar for location.

Multimeter An electrical test instrument with the capability to measure voltage, current and resistance.

N

NOx Oxides of Nitrogen. A common toxic pollutant emitted by petrol and diesel engines at higher temperatures.

O

Ohm The unit of electrical resistance. One volt applied to a resistance of one ohm will produce a current of one amp.

Ohmmeter An instrument for measuring electrical resistance.

O-ring A type of sealing ring made of a special rubber-like material; in use, the O-ring is compressed into a groove to provide the sealing action.

Overhead cam (ohc) engine An engine with the camshaft(s) located on top of the cylinder head(s).

Overhead valve (ohv) engine An engine with the valves located in the cylinder head, but with the camshaft located in the engine block.

Oxygen sensor A device installed in the engine exhaust manifold, which senses the oxygen content in the exhaust and converts this information into an electric current. Also called a Lambda sensor.

P

Phillips screw A type of screw head having a cross instead of a slot for a corresponding type of screwdriver.

Plastigage A thin strip of plastic thread, available in different sizes, used for measuring clearances. For example, a strip of Plastigage is laid across a bearing journal. The parts are assembled and dismantled; the width of the crushed strip indicates the clearance between journal and bearing.

Plastigage

Propeller shaft The long hollow tube with universal joints at both ends that carries power from the transmission to the differential on front-engined rear wheel drive vehicles.

Proportioning valve A hydraulic control valve which limits the amount of pressure to the rear brakes during panic stops to prevent wheel lock-up.

R

Rack-and-pinion steering A steering system with a pinion gear on the end of the steering shaft that mates with a rack (think of a geared wheel opened up and laid flat). When the steering wheel is turned, the pinion turns, moving the rack to the left or right. This movement is transmitted through the track rods to the steering arms at the wheels.

Radiator A liquid-to-air heat transfer device designed to reduce the temperature of the coolant in an internal combustion engine cooling system.

Refrigerant Any substance used as a heat transfer agent in an air-conditioning system. R-12 has been the principle refrigerant for many years; recently, however, manufacturers have begun using R-134a, a non-CFC substance that is considered less harmful to the ozone in the upper atmosphere.

Rocker arm A lever arm that rocks on a shaft or pivots on a stud. In an overhead valve engine, the rocker arm converts the upward movement of the pushrod into a downward movement to open a valve.

Rotor In a distributor, the rotating device inside the cap that connects the centre electrode and the outer terminals as it turns, distributing the high voltage from the coil secondary winding to the proper spark plug. Also, that part of an alternator which rotates inside the stator. Also, the rotating assembly of a turbocharger, including the compressor wheel, shaft and turbine wheel.
Runout The amount of wobble (in-and-out movement) of a gear or wheel as it's rotated. The amount a shaft rotates "out-of-true." The out-of-round condition of a rotating part.

S

Sealant A liquid or paste used to prevent leakage at a joint. Sometimes used in conjunction with a gasket.
Sealed beam lamp An older headlight design which integrates the reflector, lens and filaments into a hermetically-sealed one-piece unit. When a filament burns out or the lens cracks, the entire unit is simply replaced.
Serpentine drivebelt A single, long, wide accessory drivebelt that's used on some newer vehicles to drive all the accessories, instead of a series of smaller, shorter belts. Serpentine drivebelts are usually tensioned by an automatic tensioner.

Serpentine drivebelt

Shim Thin spacer, commonly used to adjust the clearance or relative positions between two parts. For example, shims inserted into or under bucket tappets control valve clearances. Clearance is adjusted by changing the thickness of the shim.
Slide hammer A special puller that screws into or hooks onto a component such as a shaft or bearing; a heavy sliding handle on the shaft bottoms against the end of the shaft to knock the component free.
Sprocket A tooth or projection on the periphery of a wheel, shaped to engage with a chain or drivebelt. Commonly used to refer to the sprocket wheel itself.
Starter inhibitor switch On vehicles with an automatic transmission, a switch that prevents starting if the vehicle is not in Neutral or Park.
Strut See MacPherson strut.

T

Tappet A cylindrical component which transmits motion from the cam to the valve stem, either directly or via a pushrod and rocker arm. Also called a cam follower.
Thermostat A heat-controlled valve that regulates the flow of coolant between the cylinder block and the radiator, so maintaining optimum engine operating temperature. A thermostat is also used in some air cleaners in which the temperature is regulated.
Thrust bearing The bearing in the clutch assembly that is moved in to the release levers by clutch pedal action to disengage the clutch. Also referred to as a release bearing.
Timing belt A toothed belt which drives the camshaft. Serious engine damage may result if it breaks in service.
Timing chain A chain which drives the camshaft.
Toe-in The amount the front wheels are closer together at the front than at the rear. On rear wheel drive vehicles, a slight amount of toe-in is usually specified to keep the front wheels running parallel on the road by offsetting other forces that tend to spread the wheels apart.
Toe-out The amount the front wheels are closer together at the rear than at the front. On front wheel drive vehicles, a slight amount of toe-out is usually specified.
Tools For full information on choosing and using tools, refer to the *Haynes Automotive Tools Manual.*
Tracer A stripe of a second colour applied to a wire insulator to distinguish that wire from another one with the same colour insulator.
Tune-up A process of accurate and careful adjustments and parts replacement to obtain the best possible engine performance.
Turbocharger A centrifugal device, driven by exhaust gases, that pressurises the intake air. Normally used to increase the power output from a given engine displacement, but can also be used primarily to reduce exhaust emissions (as on VW's "Umwelt" Diesel engine).

U

Universal joint or U-joint A double-pivoted connection for transmitting power from a driving to a driven shaft through an angle. A U-joint consists of two Y-shaped yokes and a cross-shaped member called the spider.

V

Valve A device through which the flow of liquid, gas, vacuum, or loose material in bulk may be started, stopped, or regulated by a movable part that opens, shuts, or partially obstructs one or more ports or passageways. A valve is also the movable part of such a device.
Valve clearance The clearance between the valve tip (the end of the valve stem) and the rocker arm or tappet. The valve clearance is measured when the valve is closed.
Vernier caliper A precision measuring instrument that measures inside and outside dimensions. Not quite as accurate as a micrometer, but more convenient.
Viscosity The thickness of a liquid or its resistance to flow.
Volt A unit for expressing electrical "pressure" in a circuit. One volt that will produce a current of one ampere through a resistance of one ohm.

W

Welding Various processes used to join metal items by heating the areas to be joined to a molten state and fusing them together. For more information refer to the *Haynes Automotive Welding Manual.*
Wiring diagram A drawing portraying the components and wires in a vehicle's electrical system, using standardised symbols. For more information refer to the *Haynes Automotive Electrical and Electronic Systems Manual.*

Chapter 1 Part A
Routine maintenance and servicing – petrol models

Contents

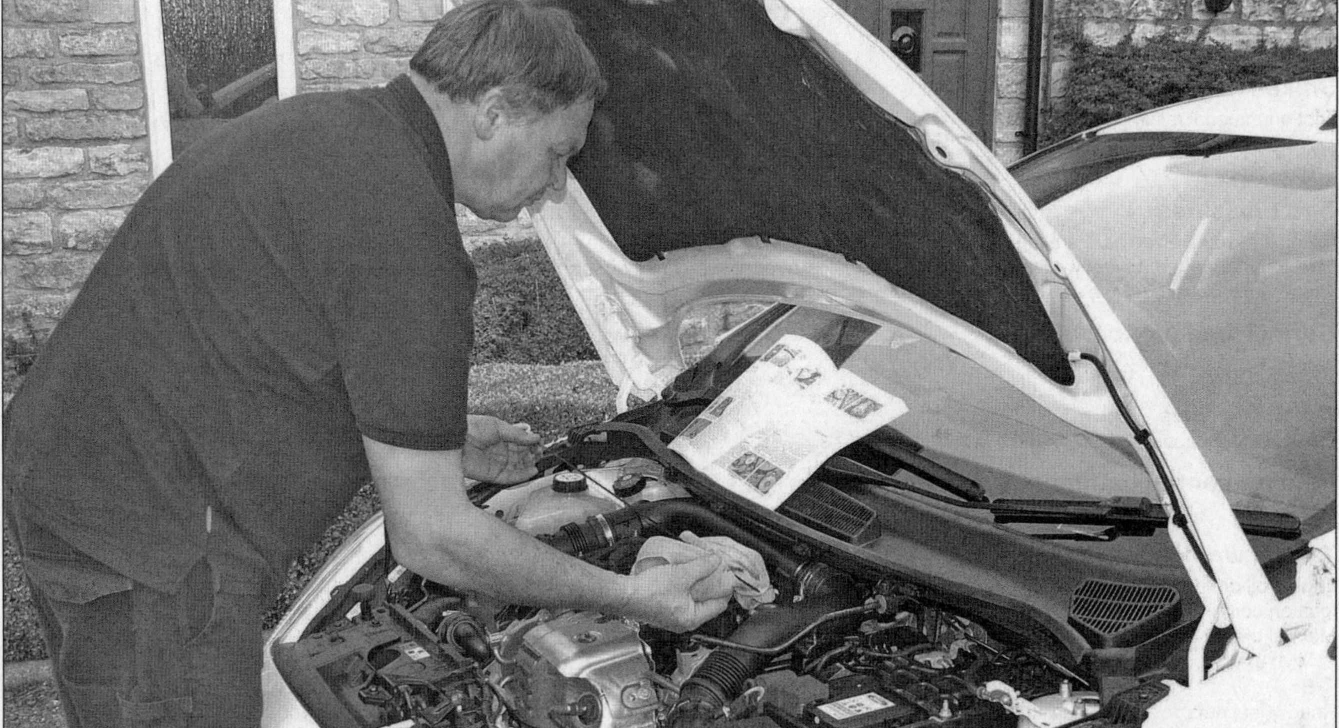

Degrees of difficulty

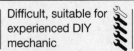

Easy, suitable for novice with little experience 	Fairly easy, suitable for beginner with some experience	Fairly difficult, suitable for competent DIY mechanic 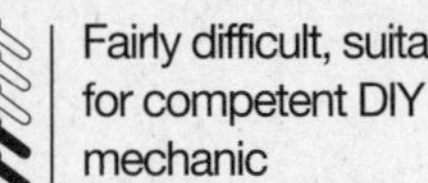	Difficult, suitable for experienced DIY mechanic	Very difficult, suitable for expert DIY or professional 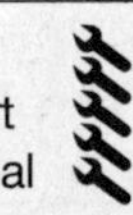

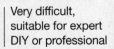

Specifications

Lubricants and fluids

Engine oil	Ford WSS-M2C950-A (For example: Ford-Castrol Magnatec Stop-Start 5W/20).
Cooling system	WSS-M97B44-D (Antifreeze Super Plus Premium / FU7J-19544-xx)
Manual transmissions (MMT6 & B6)	Ford WSS-M2C200-D2 transmission oil
Automatic transmission (6F35)	WSS-M2C938-A automatic transmission fluid
Transfer case	Ford WSL-M2C192-A SAE 75W/140
Rear differential	Ford WSP-M2C197-A SAE 80W/90
Braking system	Hydraulic fluid to DOT 4 + ESP (low viscosity)

Capacities

Engine oil (including oil filter)	4.1 litres
Cooling system (approximate)	6.2 litres
Manual transmissions:	
MMT6	1.9 litres
B6	1.6 litres
Automatic transmission (6F35)	8.5 litres
Transfer case	0.5 litres approx.
Rear differential	0.47 to 0.62 litres
Washer fluid reservoir	4.5 litres
Fuel tank	60.0 litres

Cooling system

Antifreeze mixture:	
50% antifreeze	Protection down to -37°C

Note: *Refer to the antifreeze manufacturer for latest recommendations.*

Ignition system

Type	Bosch AR 5 SII 3320 S
Spark plug gap	0.8 mm (preset)

Brakes

Friction material minimum thickness:	
Front brake pads	3.0 mm
Rear brake pads	3.0 mm

Tyre pressures

Note: *Pressures given here are a guide only, and apply to original-equipment tyres – the recommended pressures may vary if any other make or type of tyre is fitted; check with the car handbook, or the tyre manufacturer or supplier for the latest recommendations. A tyre pressure label is fitted on the driver's door pillar.*

Normal load (up to 2 people)	Front	Rear
235/55 R17 V tyres	2.4 bar (35 psi)	2.4 bar (35 psi)
235/50 R18 V tyres	2.4 bar (35 psi)	2.4 bar (35 psi)
235/45 R19 V tyres	2.4 bar (35 psi)	2.4 bar (35 psi)
Emergency (Spacesaver) 155/70 R17 M tyre	4.2 bar	4.2 bar

Remote control battery

Type	CR2032, 3V

Torque wrench settings

	Nm	lbf ft
Engine oil drain plug	35	26
Ignition coils	10	7
Manual transmission level plug:		
MMT6	35	26
B6	40	30
Roadwheel nuts	135	100
Spark plugs	13	10

1 Maintenance schedule

1 The maintenance intervals in this manual are provided with the assumption that you, not the dealer, will be carrying out the work. These are the minimum maintenance intervals based on the standard service schedule recommended by the manufacturer for vehicles driven daily. If you wish to keep your vehicle in peak condition at all times, you may wish to perform some of these procedures more often. We encourage frequent maintenance, because it enhances the efficiency, performance and resale value of your vehicle.

2 If the vehicle is driven in dusty areas, used to tow a trailer, or driven frequently at slow speeds (idling in traffic) or on short journeys, more frequent maintenance intervals are recommended.

3 When the vehicle is new, it should be serviced by a dealer service department (or other workshop recognised by the vehicle manufacturer as providing the same standard of service) in order to preserve the warranty. The vehicle manufacturer may reject warranty claims if you are unable to prove that servicing has been carried out as and when specified, using only original equipment parts or parts certified to be of equivalent quality.

Every 250 miles or weekly

- ☐ Check the engine oil level (Section 5)
- ☐ Check the coolant level (Section 6)
- ☐ Check the brake and clutch fluid level (Section 7)
- ☐ Screenwash fluid (Section 8)
- ☐ Tyre condition and pressure check (Section 9)
- ☐ Wiper blades check (Section 10)
- ☐ Battery check (Section 11)
- ☐ Check the electrical systems (Section 12)

Every 6000 miles or 6 months, whichever comes first

- ☐ Renew the engine oil and filter (Section 13)

Note: *Ford recommends that the engine oil and filter are changed every 12 500 miles or 12 months. However, oil and filter changes are good for the engine, and we recommend that the oil and filter are renewed more frequently, especially if the car is used on a lot of short journeys.*

- ☐ Reset the service indicator (Section 35)

Every 12 500 miles or 12 months, whichever comes first

In addition to the items listed above, carry out the following:

- ☐ Renew the pollen filter (Section 14)
- ☐ Check all components, pipes and hoses for fluid leaks (Section 15)
- ☐ Check the condition of the auxiliary drivebelt (Section 16)
- ☐ Check the antifreeze/inhibitor strength (Section 34)
- ☐ Check the condition and operation of the seat belts (Section 17)
- ☐ Check the front brake pads and discs for wear (Section 18)
- ☐ Check the thickness of the rear brake discs and pads (Chapter 9)
- ☐ Check the condition of the driveshaft gaiters (Section 19)
- ☐ Check the steering and suspension components for condition and security (Section 20)
- ☐ Check and if necessary adjust the handbrake (Section 21)
- ☐ Check the condition of the exhaust system components (Section 22)
- ☐ Check the roadwheel nuts are tightened to the specified torque (Section 23)
- ☐ Lubricate all door, bonnet and tailgate hinges and locks (Section 24)
- ☐ Carry out a road test (Section 25)

Every 37 500 miles or 3 years, whichever comes first

In addition to the items listed above, carry out the following:

- ☐ Renew the spark plugs (Section 26)
- ☐ Renew the air filter (Section 27)
- ☐ Check the braking system rubber hoses (Section 28)

Every 100 000 miles or 8 years, whichever comes first

- ☐ Adjust the valve clearances (Chapter 2A Section 5)
- ☐ Renew the timing belt, tensioner and idlers (Chapter 2A Section 10)

Note: *Although the normal interval for timing belt renewal is 150 000 miles or 10 years, it is strongly recommended that the interval suggested above is observed, especially on cars which are subjected to intensive use, ie, mainly short journeys or a lot of stop-start driving. The actual belt renewal interval is very much up to the individual owner, but bear in mind that severe engine damage will result if the belt breaks.*

Every 2 years, regardless of mileage

- ☐ Renew the brake fluid (Section 31)
- ☐ Check the manual transmission oil level (Section 32)
- ☐ Renew the remote control battery (Section 33)
- ☐ Renew the coolant (Section 34)

Note: *Ford states that, if the Super Plus Premium antifreeze is in the system from new, the coolant need only be changed every 10 years. If there is any doubt as to the type or quality of the antifreeze which has been used, we recommend this shorter interval be observed.*

Every 150 000 miles or 10 years, whichever comes first

- ☐ Renew the auxiliary drivebelt (Section 30)

2 General information

1 This Chapter is designed to help the home mechanic maintain his/her car for safety, economy, long life and peak performance.

2 The Chapter contains a master maintenance schedule, followed by Sections dealing specifically with each task in the schedule. Visual checks, adjustments, component renewal and other helpful items are included. Refer to the accompanying illustrations of the engine compartment and the underside of the car for the locations of the various components.

3 Servicing your car in accordance with the mileage/time maintenance schedule and the following Sections will provide a planned maintenance programme, which should result in a long and reliable service life. This is a comprehensive plan, so maintaining some items but not others at the specified service intervals, will not produce the same results.

4 As you service your car, you will discover that many of the procedures can – and should – be grouped together, because of the particular procedure being performed, or because of the proximity of two otherwise-unrelated components to one another. For example, if the car is raised for any reason, the exhaust can be inspected at the same time as the suspension and steering components.

5 The first step in this maintenance programme is to prepare yourself before the actual work begins. Read through all the Sections relevant to the work to be carried out, then make a list and gather all the parts and tools required. If a problem is encountered, seek advice from a parts specialist, or a dealer service department.

3 Component locations

Underbonnet view of a 1.5 litre EcoBoost model

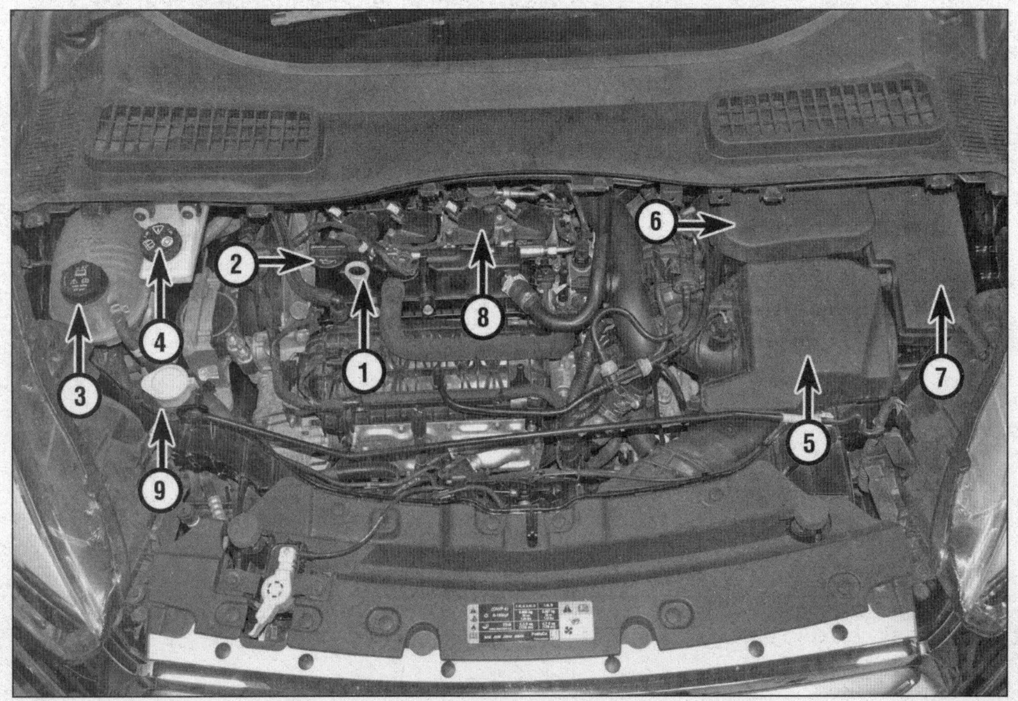

1 Engine oil level dipstick
2 Engine oil filler cap
3 Coolant reservoir (expansion tank)
4 Brake and clutch fluid reservoir
5 Air cleaner
6 Battery
7 Fuse/relay box
8 Ignition coils
9 Windscreen washer fluid filler cap

Front underbody view

1 *Brake caliper*
2 *Brake hose*
3 *Radiator bottom hose*
4 *Air conditioning compressor*
5 *Engine oil drain plug*
6 *Engine oil filter*
7 *Suspension lower arm*
8 *Driveshaft*
9 *Subframe*
10 *Track rod end*

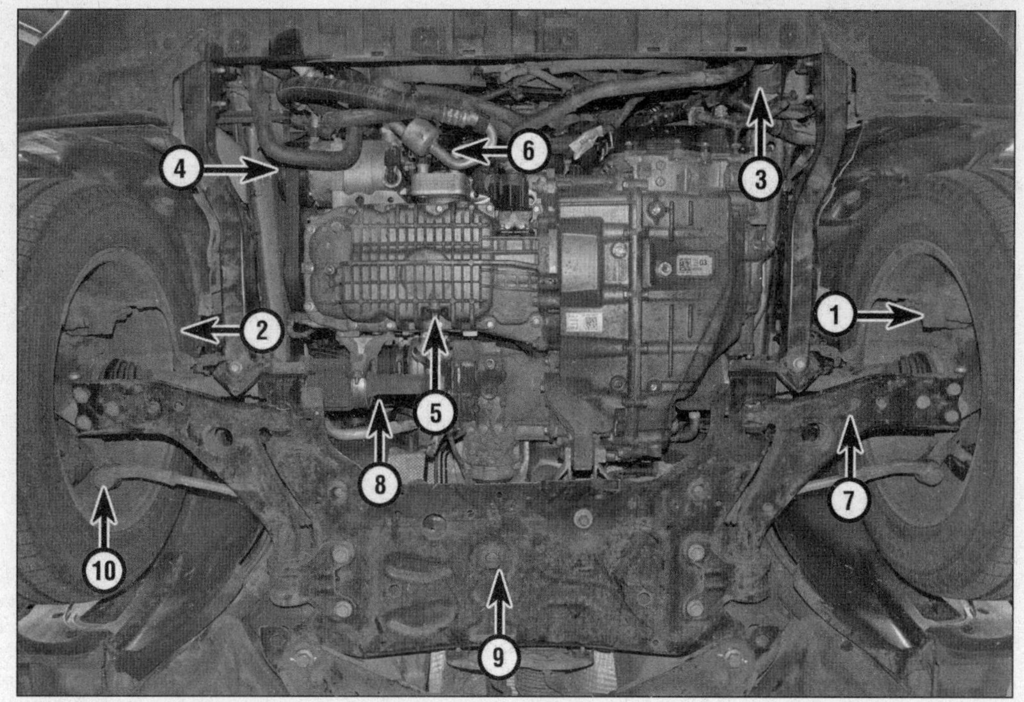

Rear underbody view

1 *Propeller shaft*
2 *Fuel filler pipe*
3 *Rear coil spring*
4 *Trailing arm*
5 *Exhaust rear silencer*
6 *Fuel tank*
7 *Handbrake cable*
8 *Driveshaft*

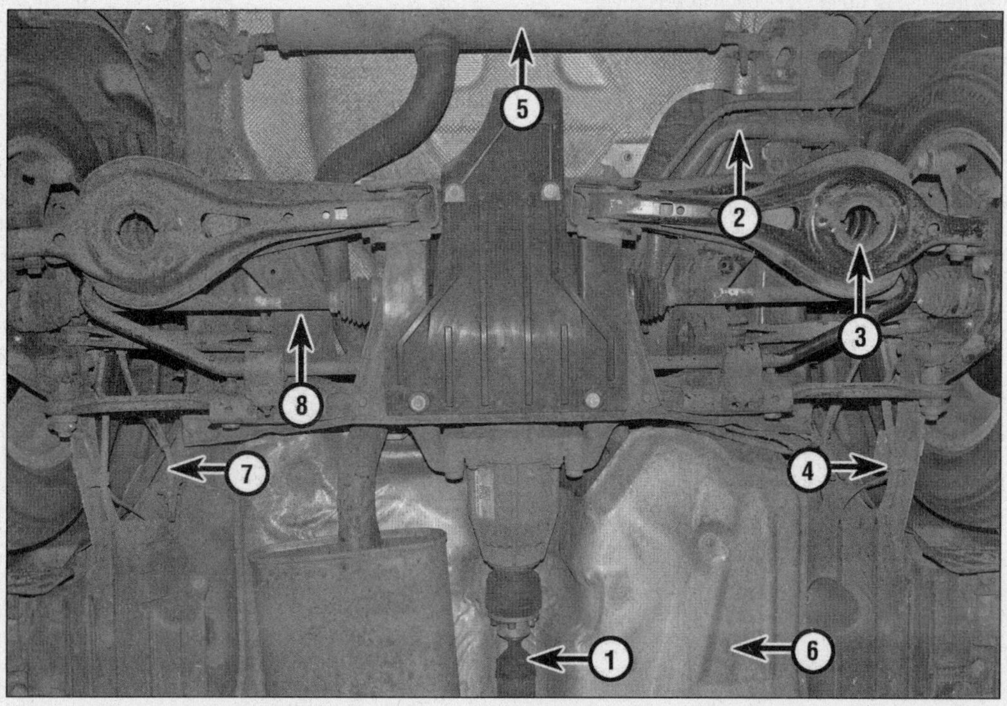

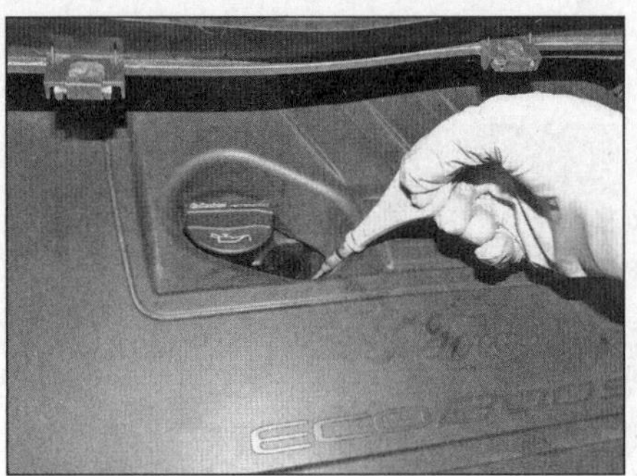

5.6 The dipstick is located next to the oil filler on the right-hand side; the dipstick is often brightly coloured and/or has a picture of an oil-can on the top for identification. Withdraw the dipstick

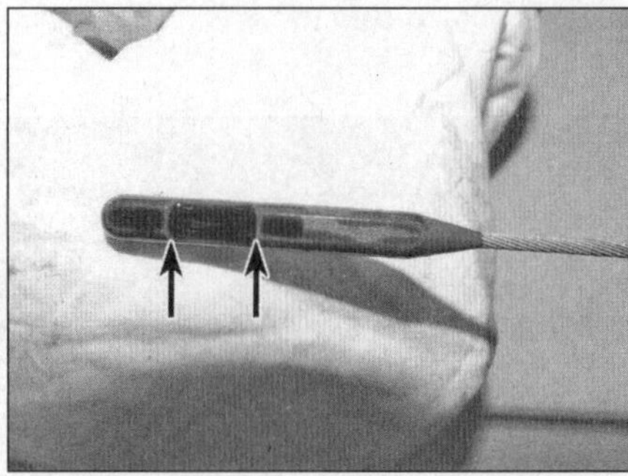

5.8 Note the oil level on the end of the dipstick, which should be between the upper (MAX) mark and lower (MIN) mark. Approximately 1.0 litre of oil will raise the level from the lower mark to the upper mark

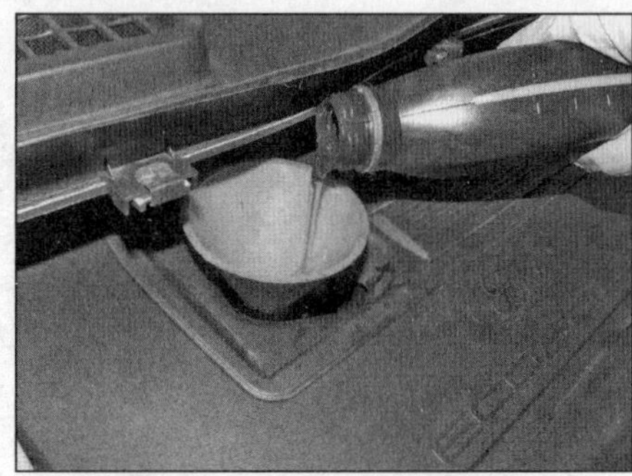

5.9 Oil is added through the filler cap aperture. Unscrew the cap and top-up the level; a funnel may help to reduce spillage. Add the oil slowly, checking the level on the dipstick often. Don't overfill

4 Regular maintenance

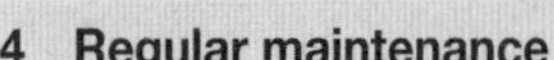

1 If, from the time the car is new, the routine maintenance schedule is followed closely, and frequent checks are made of fluid levels and high-wear items, as suggested throughout this manual, the engine will be kept in relatively good running condition, and the need for additional work will be minimised.

2 It is possible that there will be times when the engine is running poorly due to the lack of regular maintenance. This is even more likely if a used car, which has not received regular and frequent maintenance checks, is purchased. In such cases, additional work may need to be carried out, outside of the regular maintenance intervals.

3 If engine wear is suspected, a compression test (refer to Chapter 2A Section 2) will provide valuable information regarding the overall performance of the main internal components. Such a test can be used as a basis to decide on the extent of the work to be carried out. If, for example, a compression test indicates serious internal engine wear, conventional maintenance as described in this Chapter will not greatly improve the performance of the engine, and may prove a waste of time and money, unless extensive overhaul work is carried out first.

4 The following series of operations are those most often required to improve the performance of a generally poor-running engine:

Primary operations

a) Clean, inspect and test the battery (refer to Section 11)
b) Check all the engine-related fluids
c) Check the condition of all hoses, and check for fluid leaks (Section 15)
d) Check the condition of the auxiliary drivebelt (Section 16)
e) Renew the spark plugs (Section 26)
f) Check the condition of the air filter, and renew if necessary (Section 27)

5 If the above operations do not prove fully effective, carry out the following secondary operations:

Secondary operations

6 All items listed under Primary operations, plus the following:

a) Check the charging system (Chapter 5)
b) Check the ignition system (Chapter 6A)
c) Check the fuel system (Chapter 4A)
d) Check the engine control and emission systems (Chapter 6A)

5 Engine oil level check

Before you start

1 Make sure that the car is on level ground.

2 The engine must be at normal operating temperature, and switched off.

The correct oil

3 Modern engines place great demands on their oil. It is very important that the correct oil for your car is used (see *Lubricants and fluids*).

Level check

4 If you have to add oil frequently, you should check whether you have any oil leaks. Remove the engine undertray, then place some clean paper under the car overnight (ensuring it is securely weighted down), and check for stains in the morning. If there are no leaks, then the engine may be burning oil.

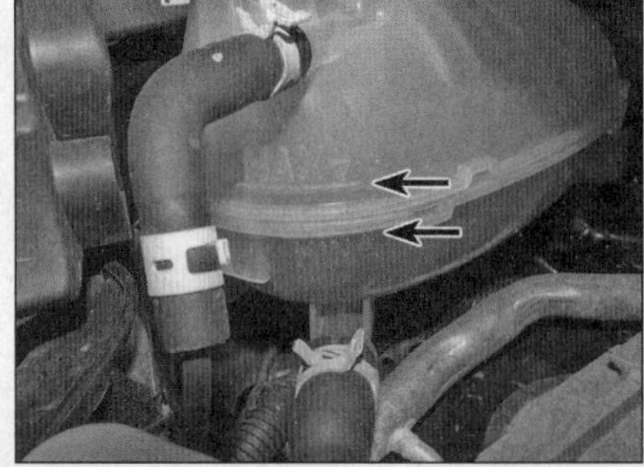

6.3 The coolant level is indicated by the minimum and maximum marks visible on the side of the expansion tank

5 Always maintain the level between the upper and lower dipstick marks. If the level is too low severe engine damage may occur. Oil seal failure may result if the engine is overfilled by adding too much oil.

6 Locate the engine oil level dipstick and pull it from place **(see illustration)**.

7 Wipe the dipstick clean, then fully insert it into the guide tube.

8 Withdraw the dipstick again and examine the oil level. It should be between the upper (MAX) and lower (MIN) marks **(see illustration)**. If it is near the lower mark, new oil needs to be added.

9 Rotate the engine oil filler cap anti-clockwise and remove it. Using a funnel, add new engine oil, a little at a time, to bring the level to the upper (MAX) mark on the dipstick **(see illustration)**. Add the oil slowly, frequently checking the level on the dipstick.

10 Securely refit the filler cap.

6 Coolant level check

Warning: Do not attempt to remove the expansion tank pressure cap when the engine is hot, as there is a very great risk of scalding. Do not leave open containers of coolant about, as it is poisonous.

1 With this type of cooling system (sealed), adding coolant should not be necessary on a regular basis. If frequent topping-up is required, it is likely there is a leak. Check the radiator, all hoses and joint faces for signs of staining or wetness, and rectify as necessary.

2 It is important that antifreeze is used in the cooling system all year round, not just during the winter months. Don't top up with water alone, as the antifreeze will become diluted. Refer to *Lubricants and fluids*.

3 With the engine completely cold, the coolant level should be between the upper and lower marks on the side of the reservoir (expansion tank) **(see illustration)**.

4 If more coolant is required, rotate the filler cap anti-clockwise and remove it **(see illustration)**.
5 Add new coolant to bring the level to the upper mark, then securely refit the cap **(see illustration)**.

7 Brake and clutch fluid level check

Warning: Brake fluid can harm your eyes and damage painted surfaces, so use extreme caution when handling and pouring it.

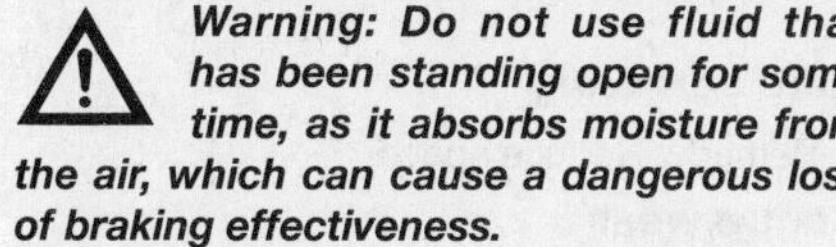

Warning: Do not use fluid that has been standing open for some time, as it absorbs moisture from the air, which can cause a dangerous loss of braking effectiveness.

1 The fluid level in the reservoir will drop slightly as the brake pads wear down, but the fluid level must never be allowed to drop below the MIN mark.

Before you start

2 Make sure that the car is on level ground.

Safety first!

3 If the reservoir requires repeated topping-up this is an indication of a fluid leak somewhere in the system, which should be investigated immediately.
4 If a leak is suspected, the car should not be driven until the braking system has been checked. Never take any risks where brakes are concerned

Level check

5 The fluid level is visible through the reservoir. The level must be kept between the MAX and MIN marks at all times **(see illustration)**.
6 If topping-up is necessary, first wipe clean the area around the filler cap to prevent dirt entering the hydraulic system, then rotate the cap anti-clockwise and remove it **(see illustration)**. If the fluid is dirty, the hydraulic system should be drained and refilled as described in Chapter 9 Section 3.
7 Add new fluid from a sealed container to bring the level to the upper mark **(see illustration)**. Use only the fluid specified in *Lubricants and fluids*; mixing different types can cause damage to the system. After topping-up to the correct level, securely refit the cap and wipe off any spilt fluid.

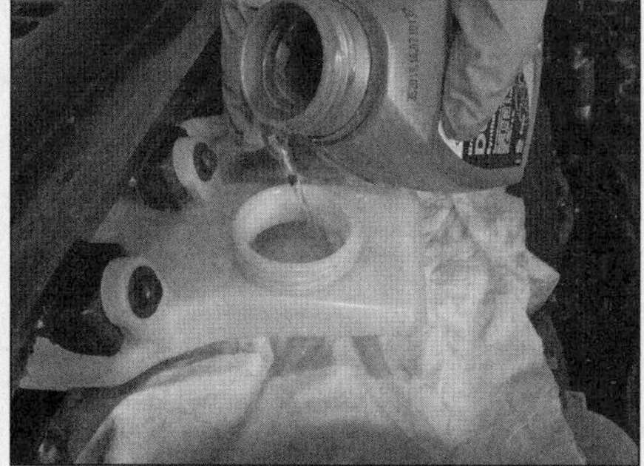

7.7 Carefully add fluid taking care not to spill it onto the surrounding components

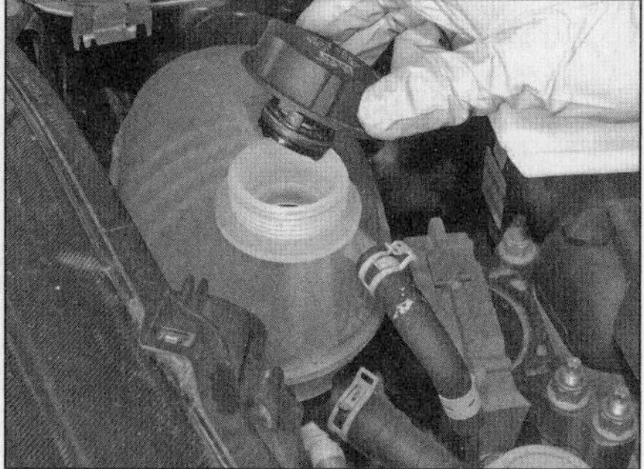

6.4 Rotate the cap anti-clockwise and remove it

7.5 The MAX and MIN marks are indicated on the side of the reservoir. The fluid level must be kept between the marks at all times

8 Screenwash fluid

1 Screenwash additives not only keep the windscreen clean during bad weather, they also prevent the washer system freezing in cold weather – which is when you are likely to need it most. Don't top-up using plain water, as the screenwash will become diluted, and will freeze in cold weather.

Warning: On no account use engine coolant antifreeze in the screen washer system – this may damage the paintwork.

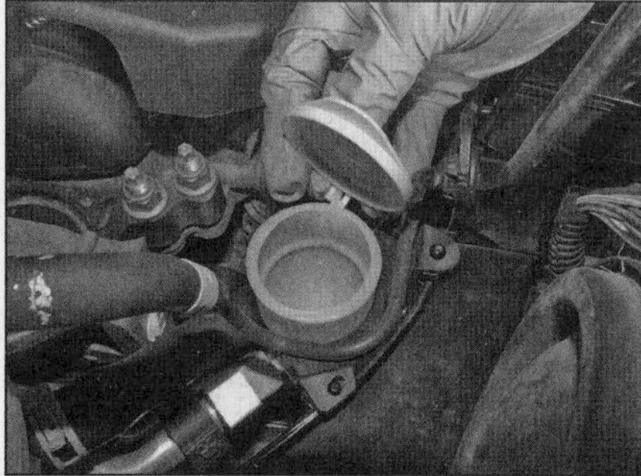

8.2 Lift the cap

6.5 Add new coolant to bring the level to the upper mark

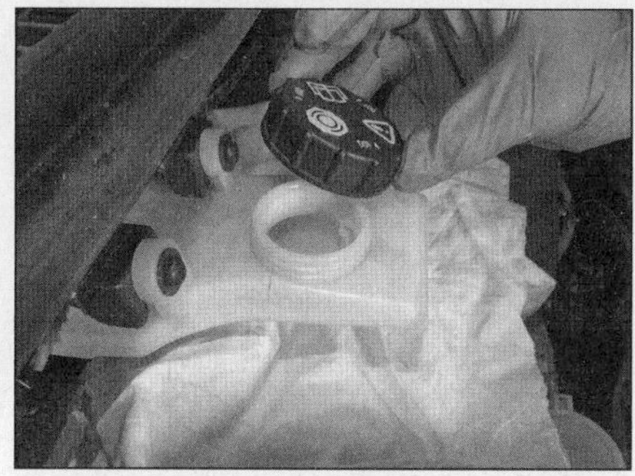

7.6 Unscrew the reservoir cap and carefully lift it out of position

2 The screen washer fluid reservoir filler cap is located on the right-hand side of the engine compartment. Carefully pull up the cap **(see illustration)**. Where fitted, the headlight washers are supplied from the same reservoir.
3 Add screenwash as per the manufacturer's instructions **(see illustration)**.

9 Tyre condition and pressure check

Tyre condition and pressure

1 It is very important that tyres are in good condition, and at the correct pressure – having a tyre failure at any speed is highly dangerous.
2 Tyre wear is influenced by driving style – harsh braking and acceleration, or fast

8.3 When topping-up, add a screenwash additive in the quantities recommended by the manufacturer

9.6 The tyres may have tread wear safety bands (B), which will appear when the tread depth reaches approximately 1.6 mm. The band positions are indicated by a mark on the tyre sidewall (A)

cornering, will all produce more rapid tyre wear. As a general rule, the front tyres wear out faster than the rears. Interchanging the tyres from front to rear ("rotating" the tyres) may result in more even wear. Non-directional tyres can be swapped diagonally front to rear, but directional tyres should be swapped on the same side only. However, if this is completely effective, you may have the expense of replacing all four tyres at once!

3 Remove any nails or stones embedded in the tread before they penetrate the tyre to cause deflation. If removal of a nail does reveal that the tyre has been punctured, refit the nail so that its point of penetration is marked. Then immediately change the wheel, and have the tyre repaired by a tyre dealer.

4 Regularly check the tyres for damage in the form of cuts or bulges, especially in the sidewalls. Periodically remove the wheels, and clean any dirt or mud from the inside and outside surfaces. Examine the wheel rims for signs of rusting, corrosion or other damage. Light alloy wheels are easily damaged by "kerbing" whilst parking; steel wheels may also become dented or buckled. A new wheel is very often the only way to overcome severe damage.

5 New tyres should be balanced when they are fitted, but it may become necessary to re-balance them as they wear, or if the balance weights fitted to the wheel rim should fall off. Unbalanced tyres will wear more quickly, as will the steering and suspension components.

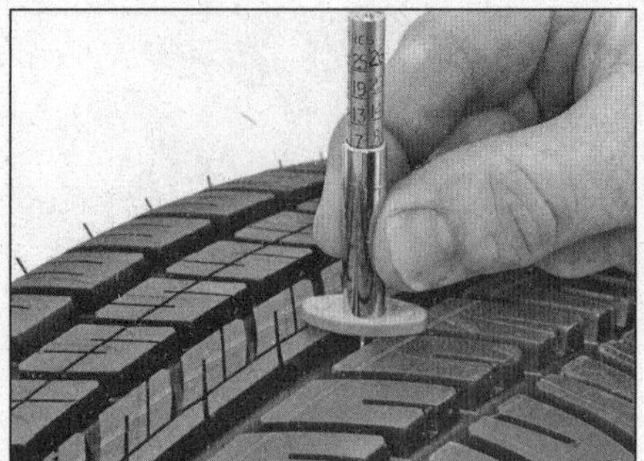

9.7 Tread wear can be monitored with a tread depth indicator gauge

Wheel imbalance is normally signified by vibration, particularly at a certain speed (typically around 50 mph). If this vibration is felt only through the steering, then it is likely that just the front wheels need balancing. If, however, the vibration is felt through the whole car, the rear wheels could be out of balance. Wheel balancing should be carried out by a tyre dealer or garage.

6 The tyres may have tread wear safety bands, which indicate when the tread depth reaches the legal limit **(see illustration)**.

7 Alternatively, monitor the tread wear with a simple, inexpensive device known as a tread depth indicator gauge **(see illustration)**.

8 Regularly check the pressures with a pressure gauge when the tyres are cold **(see illustration)**. Do not adjust the pressures immediately after the vehicle has been used, or an inaccurate setting will result.

Tyre tread wear patterns

Shoulder wear

Underinflation (wear on both sides)

Under-inflation will cause overheating of the tyre, because the tyre will flex too much, and the tread will not sit correctly on the road surface. This will cause a loss of grip and excessive wear, not to mention the danger of sudden tyre failure due to heat build-up.

Remedy: Check and adjust pressures.

Incorrect wheel camber (wear on one side)

Remedy: Repair or renew suspension parts

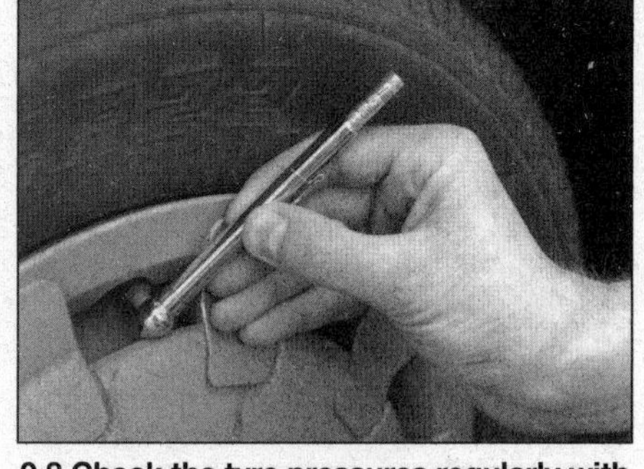

9.8 Check the tyre pressures regularly with the tyres cold

Hard cornering

Remedy: Reduce speed!

Centre wear

Overinflation

Over-inflation will cause rapid wear of the centre part of the tyre tread, coupled with reduced grip, harsher ride, and the danger of shock damage occurring in the tyre casing.

Remedy: Check and adjust pressures.

Note: *If you sometimes have to inflate your car's tyres to the higher pressures specified for maximum load or sustained high speed, don't forget to reduce the pressures to normal afterwards.*

Uneven wear

Front tyres may wear unevenly as a result of wheel misalignment. Most tyre dealers and garages can check and adjust the wheel alignment (or "tracking") for a modest charge.

Incorrect camber or castor

Remedy: Repair or renew suspension parts.

Malfunctioning suspension

Remedy: Repair or renew suspension parts.

Unbalanced wheel

Remedy: Have the wheels balanced.

Incorrect toe setting

Remedy: Adjust front wheel alignment (see Chapter 10 Section 21).

Note: *The feathered edge of the tread which typifies toe wear is best checked by feel.*

Shoulder wear

Centre wear

Uneven wear

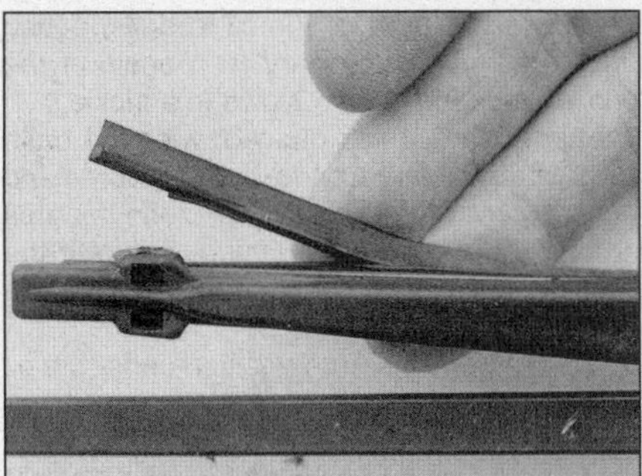

10.1 Check the condition of the wiper blades

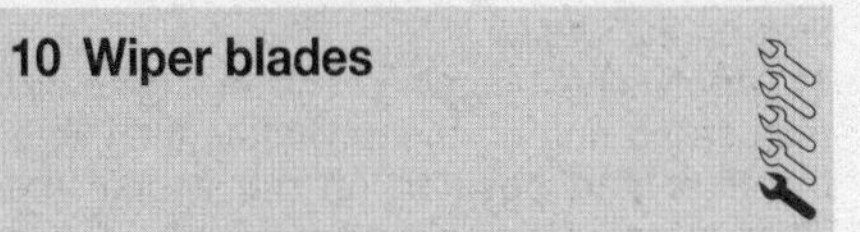

10 Wiper blades

1 Check the condition of the wiper blades; if they are cracked or show any signs of deterioration, or if the glass swept area is smeared, renew them **(see illustration)**. Wiper blades should be renewed annually.
2 To remove a front wiper blade, pull the arm away from the screen, depress the clip and slide the blade from the arm **(see illustration)**. It is prudent to lay cloth on the screen to protect it if the arm springs back.
3 To remove a rear wiper blade, pull the arm away from the screen, then prise the blade out and remove it **(see illustration)**.

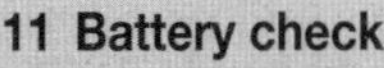

11 Battery check

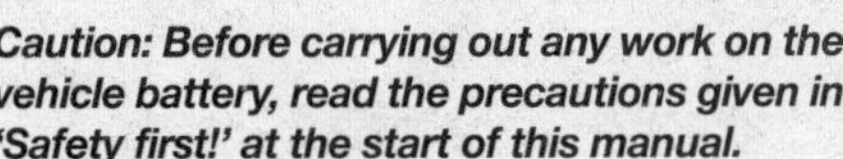

Caution: Before carrying out any work on the vehicle battery, read the precautions given in 'Safety first!' at the start of this manual.
1 Make sure that the battery tray is in good condition, and that the clamp is tight. Corrosion on the tray, retaining clamp and the battery itself can be removed with a solution of water and baking soda. Thoroughly rinse all cleaned areas with water. Any metal parts damaged by corrosion should be covered with a zinc-based primer, then painted.
2 If the battery is flat, and you need to jump start your vehicle, see *Jump starting*.

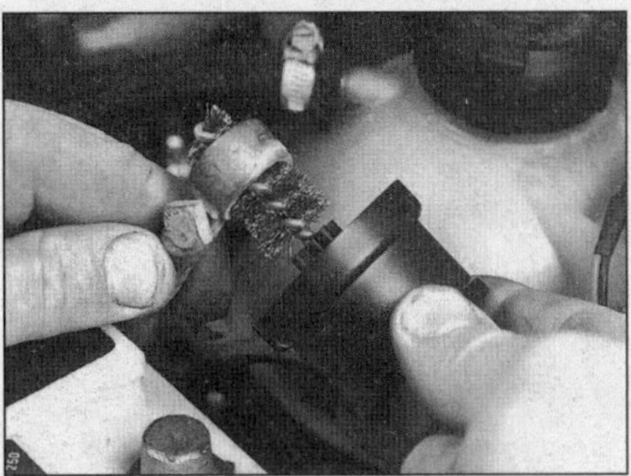

11.4 Clean the lead clamps with a small wire brush, then refit them

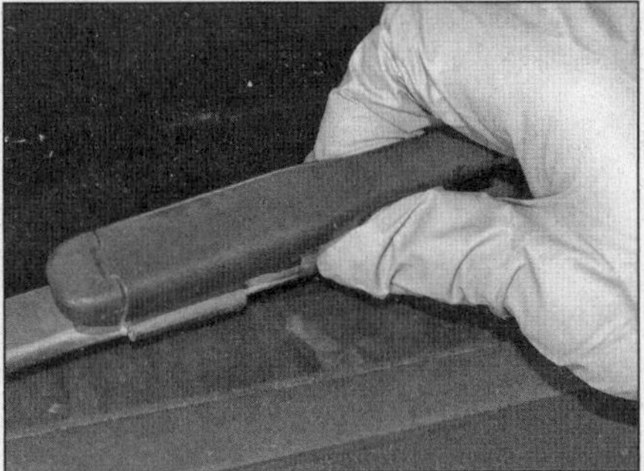

10.2 Pull the arm away from the screen, depress the clip and slide the blade down the arm

3 The battery is located under two covers on the left-hand side of the engine compartment. Lift the covers to access the battery **(see illustrations)**.
4 If corrosion (white, fluffy deposits) is evident, disconnect the leads from the battery as described in Chapter 5 Section 4, then clean the lead clamps with a small wire brush, then refit them **(see illustration)**. Automotive stores sell a tool for cleaning the battery post
5 A tool is also available for cleaning the battery posts **(see illustration)**.

Battery corrosion can be kept to a minimum by applying a layer of petroleum jelly to the clamps and terminals after they are reconnected.

11.3a Lift away the front cover...

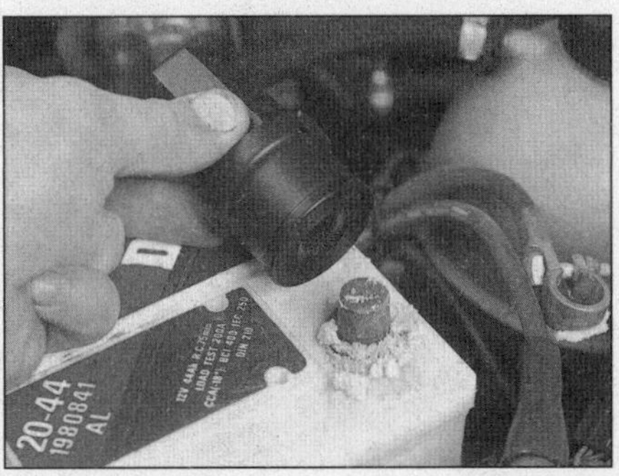

11.5 Clean the battery posts

10.3 Pull the arm away from the screen, swing the blade out, and prise it from the arm

12 Electrical systems check

1 Check all external lights and the horn. Refer to the appropriate Sections of Chapter 12 for details if any of the circuits are found to be inoperative.
2 Visually check all accessible wiring connectors, harnesses and retaining clips for security, and for signs of chafing or damage.
3 If a single indicator light, stop-light or headlight has failed, it is likely that a bulb has blown and will need to be renewed **(see illustration)**. Refer to Chapter 12 Section 7 for details. If all three stop-lights have failed, it is possible that a fuse has blown. Check the brake lamps fuse 21 (5 amp) located in the

11.3b ...and the rear cover

12.3 If a single indicator light, stop-light or headlight has failed, it is likely that a bulb has blown

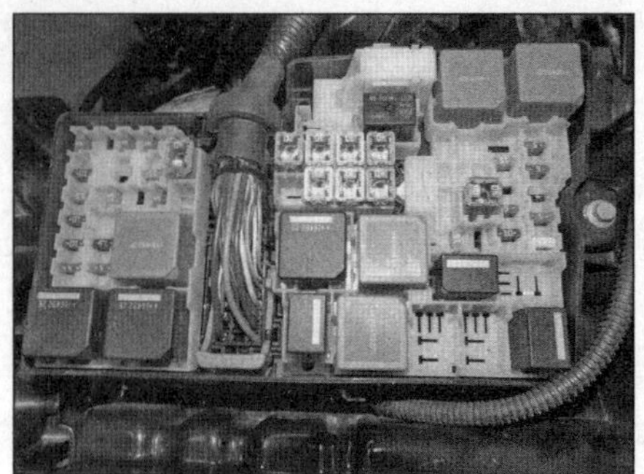

12.5 Pull out the fuse and fit a new one of the correct rating

engine bay fuse box first. If the fuse is okay, it is likely that the switch has failed (see Chapter 9 Section 17).

4 If more than one indicator light or tail light has failed, check that a fuse has not blown or that there is a fault in the circuit (see Chapter 12). High beam, rear fog, and reverse lamp fuses are located in the passenger compartment fuse box but the horn, brake lights, and lighting control fuses are located in the engine compartment fuse box. Slacken the screws, and fold down the fuseholder.

Note: *High beam, rear fog, and reverse lamp fuses are located in the passenger compartment fuse box but the horn, brake lights, and lighting control fuses are located in the engine compartment fuse box.*

5 To renew a blown fuse, simply pull it out and fit a new fuse of the correct rating (see Chapter 12) **(see illustration)**. If the fuse blows again, it is important that you find out why – a complete checking procedure is given in Chapter 12 Section 3.

13 Engine oil and filter renewal

1 Frequent oil and filter changes are the most important preventative maintenance procedures which can be undertaken by the DIY owner. As engine oil ages, it becomes diluted and contaminated, which leads to premature engine wear.

2 Before starting this procedure, gather together all the necessary tools and materials. Also make sure that you have plenty of clean rags and newspapers handy, to mop-up any spills. Ideally, the engine oil should be warm, as it will drain more easily. Take care not to touch the exhaust or any other hot parts of the engine when working under the car. To avoid any possibility of scalding, and to protect yourself from possible skin irritants and other harmful contaminants in used engine oils, it is advisable to wear gloves when carrying out this work.

3 Check the handbrake is fully on, then jack up the front of the car and support it on axle stands (see *Jacking and vehicle support*). Undo the fasteners and remove the engine undershield (where fitted) **(see illustration)**.

4 Remove the oil filler cap **(see illustration)**.

5 Using a spanner, or preferably a socket and bar, slacken the drain plug about half a turn. Position the draining container under the drain plug, then remove the plug completely **(see illustrations)**.

6 Allow some time for the oil to drain, noting that it may be necessary to reposition the container as the oil flow slows to a trickle.

7 After all the oil has drained, wipe the drain plug with a clean rag. We would recommend replacement of the drain plug. Clean the area around the drain plug opening, and refit the plug complete with the seal and tighten it to the specified torque.

8 Move a container into position under the oil filter.

9 Use an oil filter removal tool to slacken the filter initially, then unscrew it by hand the rest of the way **(see illustration)**. Empty the oil from the old filter into the container.

10 Use a clean rag to clean the filter sealing area on the engine.

11 Apply a light coating of clean engine oil to the sealing ring on the new filter, then screw the filter into position on the engine **(see illustration)**. Tighten the filter firmly by hand only – do not use any tools.

12 Remove the old oil and all tools from under the car, then lower the car to the ground.

13 Fill the engine through the filler hole, using the correct grade and type of oil (refer to Section 5 for details of topping-up). Pour in half the specified quantity of oil first, then wait a few minutes for the oil to drain into the sump. Continue to add oil, a small quantity at a time, until the level is up to the lower mark on the dipstick. Adding approximately a further 0.5 to 1.0 litre will bring the level up to the upper mark on the dipstick.

14 Start the engine and run it for a few minutes, while checking for leaks around the oil filter seal and the sump drain plug. Note that

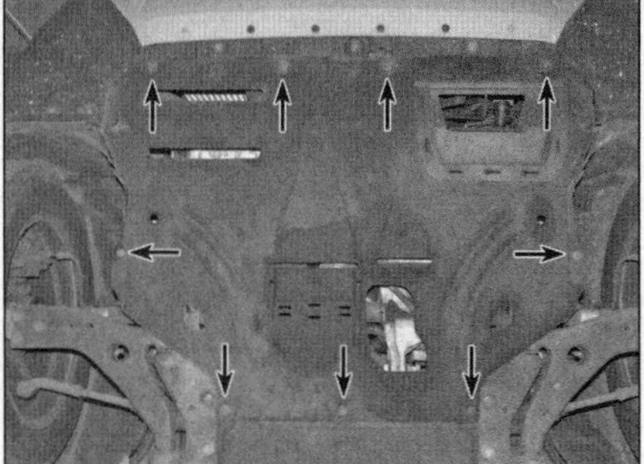

13.3 Undo the fasteners and remove the engine undershield

13.4 Rotate the oil filler cap anti-clockwise and remove it

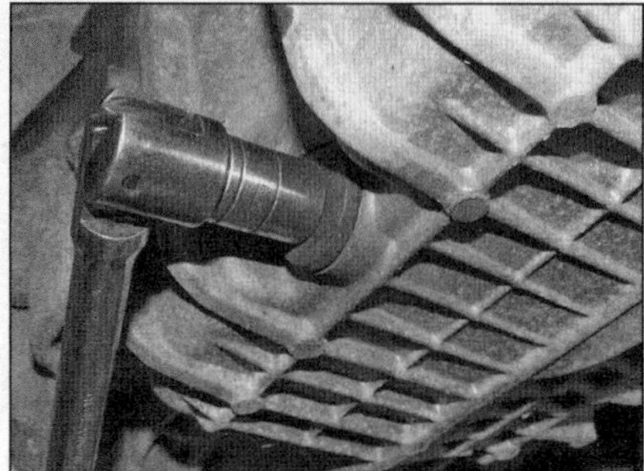

13.5a Slacken the oil drain plug on the back of the sump with a socket...

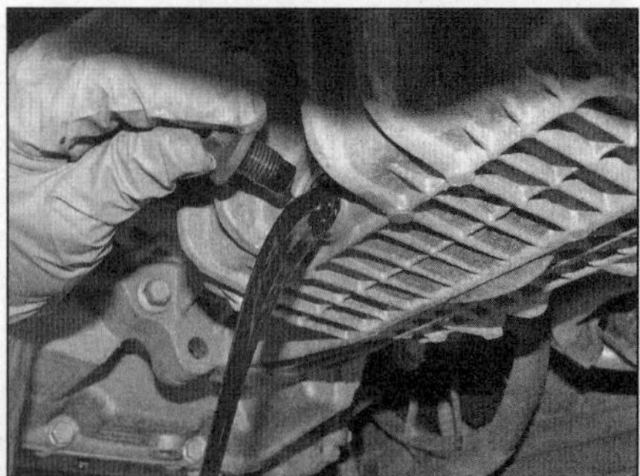

13.5b ... then unscrew it by hand, and allow the oil to drain

13.9 Use a filter removal tool to slacken the filter

13.11 Tighten the filter by hand (engine removed for clarity)

14.1 Squeeze the tangs and pull away the panel

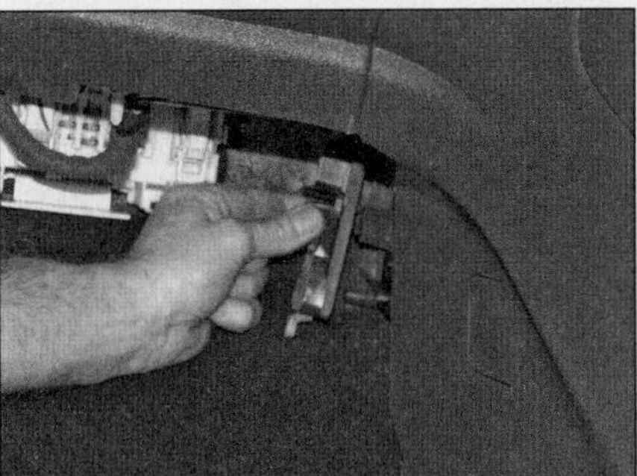

14.2 Unclip the pollen filter housing cover

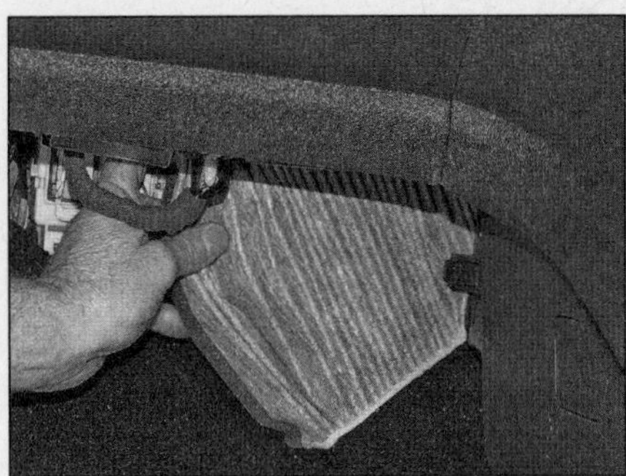

14.3 Slide out the pollen filter, into the passenger's footwell, and remove it

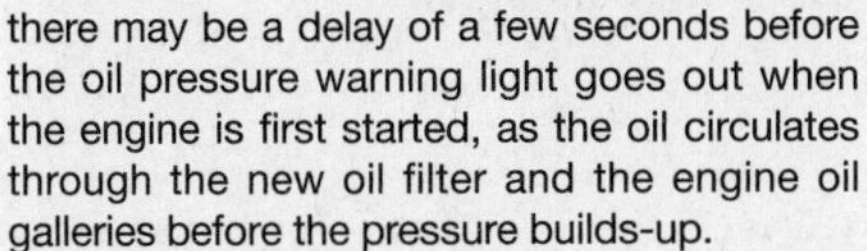

there may be a delay of a few seconds before the oil pressure warning light goes out when the engine is first started, as the oil circulates through the new oil filter and the engine oil galleries before the pressure builds-up.

15 Stop the engine, and wait a few minutes for the oil to settle in the sump once more. With the new oil circulated and the filter now completely full, recheck the level on the dipstick, and add more oil as necessary.

16 Refit the engine undertray.

17 Dispose of the used engine oil and filter safely, with reference to *General repair procedures*. Do not discard the old filter with domestic household waste. The facility for waste oil disposal provided by many local council refuse tips and/or recycling centres generally has a filter receptacle alongside.

14 Pollen filter renewal

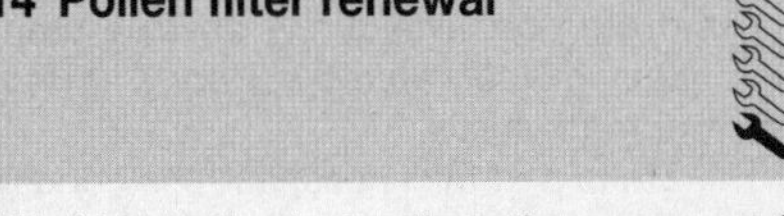

1 Working in the footwell on the passenger's side, squeeze the tangs to release the clips securing the lower trim panel to the base of the facia. Pull the panel rearward to release it from the retainer at the front and remove the trim panel **(see illustration)**.

2 Squeeze open the retaining clips and remove the pollen filter cover **(see illustration)**.

3 Slide out the pollen filter, into the passenger's footwell, and remove it **(see illustration)**.

4 When fitting the new filter, note the direction-of-airflow arrow marked on its top edge – the arrow should point into the car.

5 Slide the filter fully into position and clip the cover into place, then refit the facia lower trim panel pushing the clips onto the pins to retain panel in place.

15 Hose and fluid leak check

General

1 Visually inspect the engine joint faces, gaskets and seals for any signs of water or oil leaks. Pay particular attention to the areas around the cylinder head cover, cylinder head, oil filter and sump joint faces. Bear in mind that, over a period of time, some very slight seepage from these areas is to be expected – what you are really looking for is any indication of a serious leak. Should a leak be found, renew the offending gasket or oil seal by referring to the appropriate Chapters in this manual.

2 High temperatures in the engine compartment can cause the deterioration of the rubber and plastic hoses used for engine, accessory and emission systems operation. Periodic inspection should be made for cracks, loose clamps, material hardening and leaks.

3 When checking the hoses, ensure that all the cable-ties or clips used to retain the hoses are in place, and in good condition. Clips which are broken or missing can lead to chafing of the hoses, pipes or wiring, which could cause more serious problems in the future.

4 Carefully check the large top and bottom radiator hoses, along with the other smaller-diameter cooling system hoses and metal pipes; do not forget the heater hoses/pipes which run from the engine to the bulkhead. Inspect each hose along its entire length, renewing any that are cracked, swollen or showsigns of deterioration. Cracks may become more apparent if the hose is squeezed, and may often be apparent at the hose ends.

5 Make sure that all hose connections are tight. If the large-diameter air hoses from the air cleaner are loose, they will leak air, and upset the engine idle quality. If the spring clamps that are used to secure some of the hoses appear to be slackening, they should be updated with worm-drive clips to prevent the possibility of leaks.

6 Some other hoses are secured to their fittings with clamps. Where clamps are used, check to be sure they haven't lost their tension, allowing the hose to leak. If clamps aren't used, make sure the hose has not expanded and/or hardened where it slips over the fitting, allowing it to leak.

7 Check all fluid reservoirs, filler caps, drain plugs and fittings, etc, looking for any signs of leakage of oil, transmission and/or brake hydraulic fluid and coolant. Also check the clutch hydraulic fluid lines which lead from the fluid reservoir, master cylinder, and the slave cylinder (on the transmission).

8 Remember that some leaks will only occur with the engine running, or when the engine is hot or cold. Remove the engine undertray. With the handbrake applied, start the engine from cold, and let the engine idle while you examine the underside of the engine compartment for signs of leakage.

9 If an unusual smell is noticed inside or around the car, especially when the engine is thoroughly hot, this may point to the presence of a leak.

10 As soon as a leak is detected, its source must be traced and rectified. Where oil has been leaking for some time, it is usually necessary to clean away the accumulated dirt, so that the exact source of the leak can be identified.

Vacuum hoses

11 It's quite common for vacuum hoses, especially those in the emissions system, to be colour-coded, or to be identified by coloured stripes moulded into them. Various systems require hoses with different wall thicknesses, collapse resistance and temperature resistance. When renewing hoses, be sure the new ones are made of the same material.

12 Often the only effective way to check a hose is to remove it completely from the vehicle. If more than one hose is removed, be sure to label the hoses and fittings to ensure correct installation.

13 When checking vacuum hoses, be sure to include any plastic T-fittings in the check. Inspect the fittings for cracks, and check the hose where it fits over the fitting for distortion, which could cause leakage.

14 A small piece of vacuum hose (approximately 6 mm inside diameter) can be used as a stethoscope to detect vacuum leaks. Hold one end of the hose to your ear, and probe around vacuum hoses and fittings, listening for the 'hissing' sound characteristic of a vacuum leak.

Warning: When probing with the vacuum hose stethoscope, be very careful not to come into contact with moving engine components such as the auxiliary drivebelt, radiator electric cooling fan, etc.

18.2 With the wheel removed, the pad thickness can be seen through the front of the caliper

Fuel hoses

Warning: There are certain precautions which must be taken when inspecting or servicing fuel system components. Work in a well-ventilated area, and do not allow open flames (cigarettes, appliance pilot lights, etc) or bare light bulbs near the work area. Mop-up any spills immediately, and do not store fuel-soaked rags where they could ignite.

15 Check all fuel hoses for deterioration and chafing. Check especially for cracks in areas where the hose bends, and also just before fittings.

16 High-quality fuel line, usually identified by the word 'Fluoroelastomer' printed on the hose, should be used for fuel line renewal. Never, under any circumstances, use non-reinforced vacuum line, clear plastic tubing or water hose as a substitute for fuel lines.

17 Spring-type clamps may be used on fuel lines. These clamps often lose their tension over a period of time, and can be 'sprung' during removal. Renew all spring-type clamps with proper petrol pipe clips whenever a hose is renewed.

Metal pipes

18 Sections of metal piping are often used for fuel line between the fuel tank and the engine, and for most air conditioning applications. Check carefully to be sure the piping has not been bent or crimped, and that cracks have not started in the line; also check for signs of excessive corrosion.

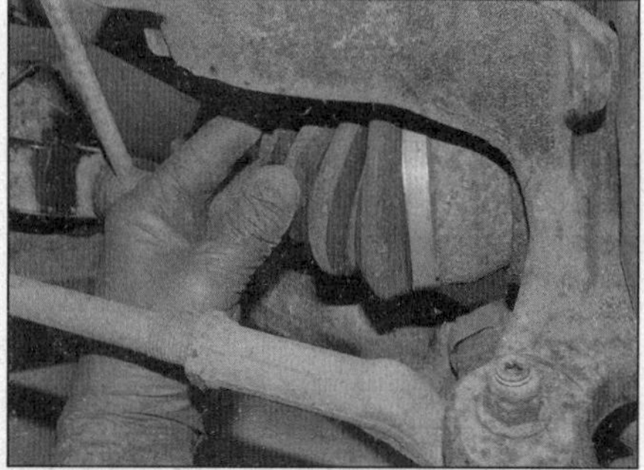

19.1 Check the outer constant velocity (CV) joint gaiters and, though less prone to wear, the inner gaiters too

19 If a section of metal fuel line must be renewed, only OE piping should be used.

20 Check the metal lines where they enter the brake master cylinder, ABS hydraulic unit or clutch master/slave cylinders (as applicable) for corrosion. Any sign of brake fluid leakage calls for an immediate and thorough inspection.

Air conditioning refrigerant

Warning: Refer to the safety information given in Safety first! and Chapter 3 Section 14, regarding the dangers of disturbing any of the air conditioning system components.

21 The air conditioning system is filled with a liquid refrigerant, which is retained under high pressure. If the air conditioning system is opened and depressurised without the aid of specialised equipment, the refrigerant will immediately turn into gas and escape into the atmosphere. If the liquid comes into contact with your skin, it can cause severe frostbite. In addition, the refrigerant contains substances which are environmentally damaging; for this reason, it should not be allowed to escape into the atmosphere.

22 Any suspected air conditioning system leaks should be immediately referred to a Ford dealer or air conditioning specialist. Leakage will be shown up as a steady drop in the level of refrigerant in the system.

23 Note that water may drip from the evaporator drain pipe, underneath the car, immediately after the air conditioning system has been in use. This is normal, and should not be cause for concern.

16 Auxiliary drivebelt check

1 A single auxiliary drivebelt is fitted at the right-hand side of the engine. The length of the drivebelt varies according to whether air conditioning is fitted.

2 Due to their function and material makeup, drivebelts are prone to failure after a long period of time, and should therefore be inspected regularly.

3 Since the drivebelt is located very close to the right-hand side of the engine compartment, it is possible to gain better access by raising the front of the car and removing the right-hand wheel and wheelarch liner.

4 With the engine stopped, inspect the full length of the drivebelt for cracks and separation of the belt plies. It will be necessary to turn the engine (using a spanner or socket and bar on the crankshaft pulley bolt) in order to move the belt from the pulleys so that the belt can be inspected thoroughly. Twist the belt between the pulleys so that both sides can be viewed. Also check for fraying, and glazing which gives the belt a shiny appearance. Check the pulleys for nicks, cracks, distortion and corrosion.

5 Small cracks in the belt ribs are not usually serious, but look closely to see whether the crack has extended into the belt plies. If the belt is in any way suspect, or is known to have seen long service, renew it as described in Section 30.

6 If the belt appears to be too slack (or has actually been slipping in service), this indicates that the 'elastic' belt is over-stretched – possibly as a result of incorrect fitting. Any slipping may also be due to external contamination of the belt (eg, by oil or water).

17 Seat belt check

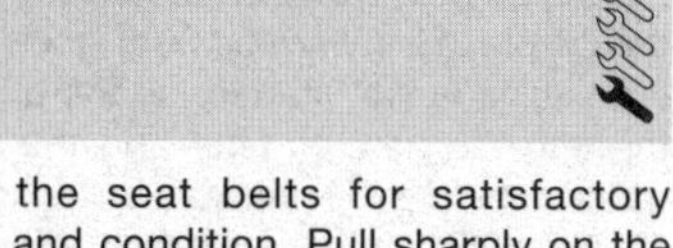

1 Check the seat belts for satisfactory operation and condition. Pull sharply on the belt to check that the locking mechanism engages correctly. Inspect the webbing for fraying and cuts. Check that they retract smoothly and without binding into their reels.

2 Check the accessible seat belt mountings, ensuring that all bolts are securely tightened.

18 Front brake pad and disc wear check

1 Apply the handbrake, slacken the front roadwheel nuts, then jack up the front of the car and support it securely on axle stands (see *Jacking and vehicle support*). Remove the front roadwheels.

2 The brake pad thickness, and the condition of the disc, can be assessed roughly with just the wheels removed **(see illustration)**. For a comprehensive check, the brake pads should be removed and cleaned. The operation of the caliper can then also be checked, and the condition of the brake disc itself can be fully examined on both sides. Refer to Chapter 9 for further information.

3 On completion, refit the roadwheels and lower the car to the ground. Tighten the roadwheel nuts to their specified torque.

19 Driveshaft gaiter check

1 With the car raised and securely supported on stands, turn the steering onto full lock, then slowly rotate the roadwheel. Inspect the condition of the outer constant velocity (CV) joint rubber gaiters while squeezing the gaiters to open out the folds. Check for signs of cracking, splits or deterioration of the rubber which may allow the grease to escape and lead to water and grit entry into the joint. Also check the security and condition of the retaining clips. Repeat these checks on the inner CV joints **(see illustration)**. If any

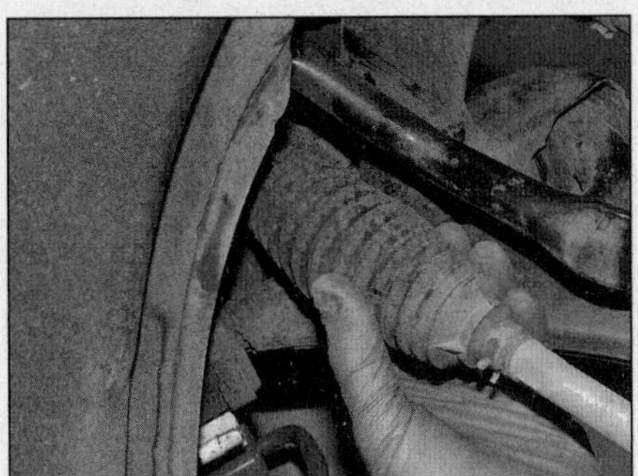

20.2 Check the steering gaiters for signs of splitting

20.3 Check for wear in the front suspension and hub bearings

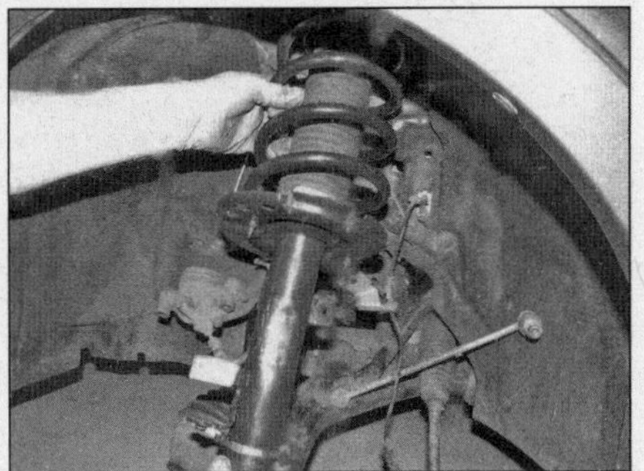

20.9 Check for signs of fluid leakage from the shock absorbers

damage or deterioration is found, the gaiters should be renewed as described in Chapter 8.

2 At the same time, check the general condition of the CV joints themselves by first holding the driveshaft and attempting to rotate the wheel. Repeat this check by holding the inner joint and attempting to rotate the driveshaft. Any appreciable movement indicates wear in the joints, wear in the driveshaft splines, or a loose driveshaft retaining nut.

20 Steering and suspension check

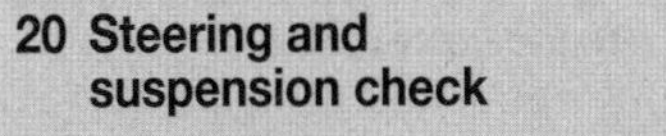

Front suspension and steering

1 Raise the front of the car, and securely support it on axle stands (see *Jacking and vehicle support*).

2 Visually inspect the balljoint dust covers and the steering rack-and-pinion gaiters for splits, chafing or deterioration **(see illustration)**. Any wear of these components will cause loss of lubricant, together with dirt and water entry, resulting in rapid deterioration of the balljoints or steering gear.

3 Grasp the roadwheel at the 12 o'clock and 6 o'clock positions, and try to rock it **(see illustration)**. Very slight free play may be felt, but if the movement is appreciable, further investigation is necessary to determine the source. Continue rocking the wheel while an assistant depresses the footbrake. If the movement is now eliminated or significantly reduced, it is likely that the hub bearings are at fault. If the free play is still evident with the footbrake depressed, then there is wear in the suspension joints or mountings.

4 Now grasp the wheel at the 9 o'clock and 3 o'clock positions, and try to rock it as before. Any movement felt now may again be caused by wear in the hub bearings or the steering track rod balljoints. If the outer balljoint is worn, the visual movement will be obvious. If the inner joint is suspect, it can be felt by placing a hand over the rack-and-pinion rubber gaiter and gripping the track rod. If the wheel is now rocked, movement will be felt at the inner joint if wear has taken place.

5 Using a large screwdriver or flat bar, check for wear in the suspension mounting bushes by levering between the relevant suspension component and its attachment point. Some movement is to be expected, as the mountings are made of rubber, but excessive wear should be obvious. Also check the condition of any visible rubber bushes, looking for splits, cracks or contamination of the rubber.

6 With the car standing on its wheels, have an assistant turn the steering wheel back-and-forth, about an eighth of a turn each way. There should be very little, if any, lost movement between the steering wheel and roadwheels. If this is not the case, closely observe the joints and mountings previously described. In addition, check the steering column universal joints for wear, and also check the rack-and-pinion steering gear itself.

Rear suspension

7 Chock the front wheels, then jack up the rear of the car and support securely on axle stands (see *Jacking and vehicle support*).

8 Working as described previously for the front suspension, check the rear hub bearings, the suspension bushes and the shock absorber mountings for wear.

Shock absorber

9 Check for any signs of fluid leakage around the shock absorber body, or from the rubber gaiter around the piston rod **(see illustration)**. Should any fluid be noticed, the shock absorber is defective internally, and should be renewed. **Note:** *Shock absorbers should always be renewed in pairs on the same axle.*

22.2 Check the condition of the exhaust rubber mountings

10 The efficiency of the shock absorber may be checked by bouncing the car at each corner. Generally speaking, the body will return to its normal position and stop after being depressed. If it rises and returns on a rebound, the shock absorber is probably suspect. Also examine the shock absorber upper and lower mountings for any signs of wear.

21 Handbrake check and adjustment

1 The handbrake should be fully applied (and capable of holding the car on a slope) after approximately 3 to 5 clicks of the ratchet. Should adjustment be necessary, refer to Chapter 9 Section 14 for the full adjustment procedure. Some models have an electrically operated parking brake, which is self-adjusting.

22 Exhaust system check

1 With the engine cold (at least three hours after the vehicle has been driven), check the complete exhaust system, from its starting point at the engine to the end of the tailpipe. Ideally, this should be done on a hoist, where unrestricted access is available; if a hoist is not available, raise and support the vehicle on axle stands (see *Jacking and vehicle support*).

2 Make sure that all brackets and rubber mountings are in good condition, and tight; if any of the mountings are to be renewed, ensure that the new ones are of the correct type – in the case of the rubber mountings, their colour is a good guide. Those nearest to the catalytic converter are more heat-resistant than the others **(see illustration)**.

3 Check the pipes and connections for evidence of leaks, severe corrosion, or damage. One of the most common points for a leak to develop is around the welded joints between the pipes and silencers. Leakage at any of the joints or in other parts of the system will usually show up as a black sooty stain in the vicinity of the leak.

Caution: Exhaust sealants should not be used on any part of the exhaust system upstream of the catalytic converter (between

26.6a The ignition coils are located above the spark plugs

the converter and engine) – even if the sealant does not contain additives harmful to the converter, pieces of it may break off and foul the element, causing local overheating.

4 At the same time, inspect the underside of the body for holes, corrosion, open seams, etc, which may allow exhaust gases to enter the passenger compartment. Seal all body openings with silicone or body putty.

5 Rattles and other noises can often be traced to the exhaust system, especially the rubber mountings. Try to move the system, silencer(s), heat shields and catalytic converter. If any components can touch the body or suspension parts, secure the exhaust system with new mountings.

23 Roadwheel nut tightness check

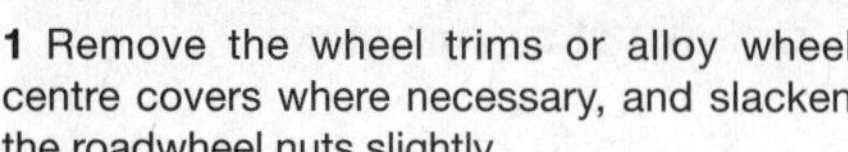

1 Remove the wheel trims or alloy wheel centre covers where necessary, and slacken the roadwheel nuts slightly.

2 Tighten the nuts evenly in a diagonal pattern to the specified torque, using a torque wrench.

24 Hinge and lock lubrication

1 Work around the car and lubricate the hinges of the bonnet, doors and tailgate with light oil.

2 Lightly lubricate the bonnet release mechanism with a smear of grease.

26.6c Undo the retaining bolts and pull each coil straight upwards

26.6b Slide out the clip and depress it to release the wiring plug

3 Check carefully the security and operation of all hinges, latches and locks, adjusting them where required. Check the operation of the central locking system.

4 Check the condition and operation of the tailgate struts, renewing them both if either is leaking or no longer able to support the tailgate securely when raised.

25 Road test

Instruments and electrical equipment

1 Check the operation of all instruments and electrical equipment.

2 Make sure that all instruments read correctly, and switch on all electrical equipment in turn, to check that it functions properly.

Steering and suspension

3 Check for any abnormalities in the steering, suspension, handling or road 'feel'.

4 Drive the car, and check that there are no unusual vibrations or noises.

5 Check that the steering feels positive, with no excessive 'sloppiness', or roughness, and check for any suspension noises when cornering and driving over bumps.

Drivetrain

6 Check the performance of the engine, clutch, transmission and driveshafts.

7 Listen for any unusual noises from the engine, clutch and transmission.

8 Make sure that the engine runs smoothly when idling, and that there is no hesitation when accelerating.

9 Check that, where applicable, the clutch action is smooth and progressive, that the drive is taken up smoothly, and that the pedal travel is not excessive. Also listen for any noises when the clutch pedal is depressed.

10 Check that all gears can be engaged smoothly without noise, and that the gear lever action is smooth and not abnormally vague or 'notchy'.

11 Listen for a metallic clicking sound from the front of the car, as the car is driven slowly in a circle with the steering on full-lock. Carry out this check in both directions. If a clicking noise is heard, this indicates wear in a driveshaft joint (see Chapter 8 Section 10).

Braking system

12 Make sure that the car does not pull to one side when braking, and that the wheels do not lock when braking hard.

13 Check that there is no vibration through the steering when braking.

14 Some models are fitted with an electrically operated parking brakem so enure that this engages and disengages correctly. Where the car is fitted with a manual parking brake, check that it operates correctly, without excessive movement of the lever, and that it holds the car stationary on a slope.

15 Test the operation of the brake servo unit as follows. Depress the footbrake 4 or 5 times to exhaust the vacuum, then start the engine. As the engine starts, there should be a noticeable 'give' in the brake pedal as vacuum builds-up. Allow the engine to run for at least 2 minutes, and then switch it off. If the brake pedal is now depressed again, it should be possible to detect a hiss from the servo as the pedal is depressed. After about 4 or 5 applications, no further hissing should be heard, and the pedal should feel considerably harder.

26 Spark plug renewal

Renewal

1 The correct functioning of the spark plugs is vital for the correct running and efficiency of the engine. It is essential that the plugs fitted are appropriate for the engine.

2 If the correct type is used and the engine is in good condition, the spark plugs should not need attention between scheduled intervals. Spark plug cleaning is rarely necessary, and should not be attempted unless specialised equipment is available, as damage can easily be caused to the firing ends.

3 Spark plug removal and refitting requires a spark plug socket, with an extension which can be turned by a ratchet handle or similar. This socket is lined with a rubber sleeve, to protect the porcelain insulator of the spark plug, and to hold the plug while you insert it into the spark plug hole. You may also need feeler blades and/or a spark plug gap checking gauge to check and adjust the spark plug electrode gap, and (ideally) a torque wrench to tighten the new plugs to the specified torque.

4 To remove the spark plugs, they are easily reached at the top of the engine.

5 Remove the engine cover by pulling it upwards from its mountings.

6 Release the clips, disconnect the wiring plugs, then undo the bolts and pull the ignition coils upwards from their locations above the spark plugs **(see illustrations)**.

7 Using a 14mm deep socket, unscrew the spark plugs, ensuring that the socket is kept in alignment with each plug – if the socket is forcibly moved to either side, the porcelain top of the plug may be broken off. Remove the plug from the engine.

8 If any undue difficulty is encountered when unscrewing any of the spark plugs, reconnect the coils and run the engine until warm, then try to remove the plugs with the engine warm.

9 As each plug is removed, examine it as follows – this will give a good indication of the condition of the engine:

a) *If the insulator nose of the spark plug is clean and white, with no deposits, this is indicative of a weak mixture.*

b) *If the tip and insulator nose are covered with hard black-looking deposits, then this is indicative that the mixture is too rich.*

c) *Should the plug be black and oily, then it is likely that the engine is fairly worn, as well as the mixture being too rich.*

d) *If the insulator nose is covered with light tan to greyish-brown deposits, then the mixture is correct, and it is likely that the engine is in good condition.*

10 If you are renewing the spark plugs, new plugs are supplied with a preset gap. Do not attempt to adjust the gap.

11 If the plugs were removed to inspect them, then the gap can be checked **(see illustration)**. The plug gap is specified in the specifications, and adjustment can be made by using a special tool to re-set the earth electrode and checking with a feeler blade or a wire-type gauge.

12 Before fitting the spark plugs, check that the threaded connector sleeves at the top of the plugs are tight (where fitted), and that the plug exterior surfaces and threads are clean. Brown staining on the porcelain, immediately above the metal body, is quite normal, and does not necessarily indicate a leak between the body and insulator.

13 On installing the spark plugs, first check that the cylinder head thread and sealing surface are as clean as possible; use a clean rag wrapped around a paintbrush to wipe clean the sealing surface. Take extra care to enter the plug threads correctly, as the cylinder head is made of aluminium alloy – it's often difficult to insert spark plugs into their holes without cross-threading them **(see Haynes Hint)**.

14 When each spark plug is started correctly on its threads, screw it down until it just seats lightly, then tighten it to the specified torque wrench setting. If a torque wrench is not available – and this is one case where the use of a torque wrench is strongly recommended. Do not exceed the specified torque setting, and NEVER overtighten spark plugs.

15 Refit the coils and tighten the retaining bolts to the specified torque.

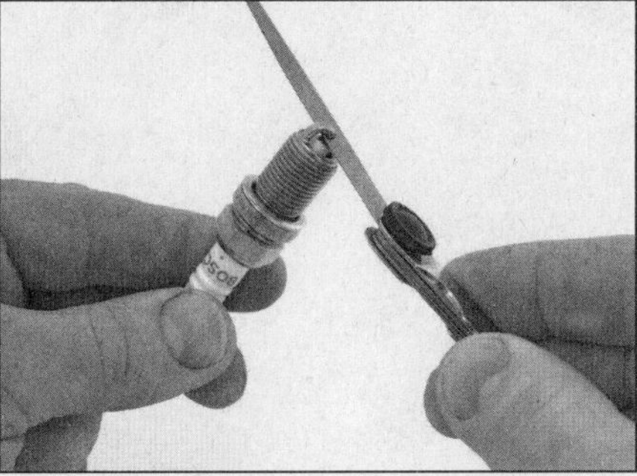

26.11 Check the electrode gap with a set of feeler gauges

27 Air filter element renewal

Caution: Never drive the vehicle with the air cleaner filter element removed. Excessive engine wear could result, and backfiring could even cause a fire under the bonnet.

1 The air filter element is located in the air cleaner assembly on the left-hand side of the engine compartment.

2 Undo the 4 bolts securing the cover to the air cleaner housing **(see illustration)**.

3 The cover can now be lifted, and the filter element removed **(see illustration)**.

4 Clean the filter housing and cover, removing any dirt or debris. A vacuum cleaner is ideal for this.

5 Position the new element in the filter housing with the locating tab downwards and refit the filter cover. Tighten the retaining bolts securely.

28 Braking system rubber hose check

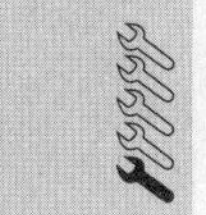

1 Position the car over an inspection pit, on car ramps, or jack it up one wheel at a time (see *Jacking and vehicle support*).

2 Inspect the braking system rubber hoses fitted to each front caliper, and on each side of the rear axle. Look for perished, swollen or hardened rubber, and any signs of cracking, especially at the metal end fittings. If there's any doubt as to the condition of any hose, renew it as described in Chapter 9 Section 4.

It's often difficult to insert spark plugs into their holes without cross-threading them. To avoid this possibility, fit a short length of rubber or plastic hose over the end of the spark plug. The flexible hose acts as a universal joint, to help align the plug with the plug hole. Should the plug begin to cross thread, the hose will slip on the spark plug,preventing thread damage to the aluminium cylinder head.

29 Timing belt renewal

1 Refer to the procedures contained in Chapter 2A Section 10.

30 Auxiliary drivebelt renewal

Renewal

1 Slacken the right-hand roadwheel nuts, firmly apply the handbrake, then jack up the front of the vehicle and support it securely on axle stands (see *Jacking and vehicle support*). Remove the right-hand front wheel.

2 Cut off the old belt with a sharp blade.

3 To fit the new belt, attach the stretchy belt

27.2 Undo the 4 bolts securing the cover to the air cleaner housing

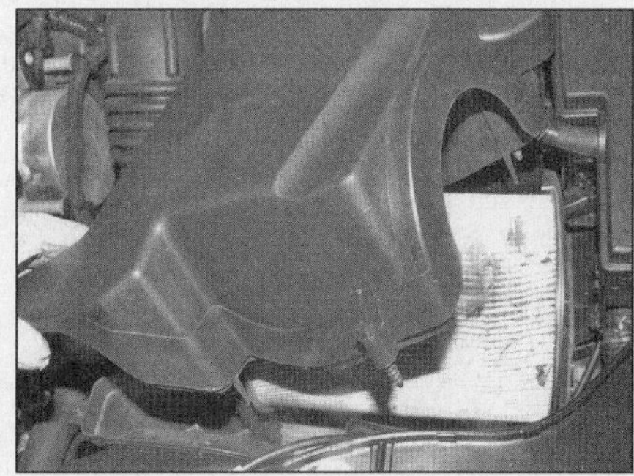

27.3 Lift the cover and remove the filter element

refitting tool to the crankshaft pulley **(see illustration)**.

4 Fit the new belt around the alternator pulley, then the air conditioning pump pulley, the coolant pump pulley, and finally, around the installation tool. Make sure the drivebelt is seated properly in the pulley grooves.

5 Turn the crankshaft pulley in the normal direction of rotation (clockwise). As the crankshaft is turned, guide the belt onto the crankshaft pulley, with the help of the plastic tool.

6 Turn the crankshaft through a full 360°, and check that the belt is sitting correctly in the pulley grooves.

7 The remainder of refitting is a reversal of removal.

31 Brake fluid renewal

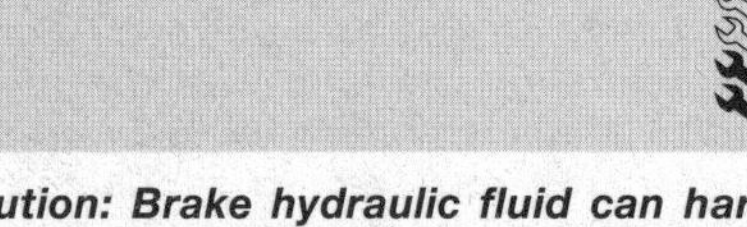

Caution: Brake hydraulic fluid can harm your eyes and damage painted surfaces, so use extreme caution when handling and pouring it. Do not use fluid that has been standing open for some time, as it absorbs moisture from the air. Excess moisture can cause a dangerous loss of braking effectiveness.

1 The procedure is similar to that for bleeding the hydraulic system as described in Chapter 9 Section 3, except that allowance should be made for the old fluid to be expelled when bleeding each section of the circuit.

2 Working as described in Chapter 9 Section 3,

30.3 Attach the tool to the crank pulley

open the first bleed screw in the sequence, and pump the brake pedal gently until the level in the reservoir is approaching the MIN mark. Top-up to the MAX level with new fluid, and continue pumping until only new fluid remains in the reservoir, and new fluid can be seen emerging from the bleed screw. Tighten the screw, and top the reservoir level up to the MAX level line.

3 Work through all the remaining bleed screws in the sequence until new fluid can be seen at all of them. Be careful to keep the master cylinder reservoir topped-up above the MIN level at all times, or air may enter the system. If this happens, further bleeding will be required, to remove the air.

4 When the operation is complete, check that all bleed screws are securely tightened, and that their dust caps are refitted. Wash off all traces of spilt fluid, and recheck the master cylinder reservoir fluid level.

5 Check that pedal travel is comparable with its pre-bled state before taking the car on the road.

32 Manual transmission oil level check

1 Position the car over an inspection pit, on car ramps, or jack it up and support it on axle stands (see *Jacking and vehicle support*), but make sure that it is level.

2 Remove all traces of dirt, then unscrew the filler/level plug from the side of the transmission **(see illustration)**.

3 The level must be just below the bottom edge of the filler/level plug hole (use a cranked tool such as an Allen key to check the level). If necessary, top-up the level with the specified grade of oil (see Section) until the oil just starts to run out. Allow any excess oil to flow out until the level stabilises **(see illustrations)**.

4 When the level is correct, clean and refit the filler/level plug, then tighten it to the specified torque.

5 Lower the car to the ground.

33 Remote control battery renewal

Note: *All the remote control units described below are fitted with a type CR 2032, 3 volt battery.*

1 Although not in the Ford maintenance schedule, we recommend that the battery is changed every 2 years, regardless of the vehicle's mileage. However, if the door locks repeatedly fail to respond to signals from the remote control at the normal distance, change the battery in the remote control before attempting to troubleshoot any of the vehicle's other systems.

Control without a folding key

2 Depress the 2 tabs on the side of the transmitter unit and carefully lift off the cover **(see illustration)**.

3 Remove the key blade from the transmitter unit **(see illustration)**.

32.2 Unscrew and remove the filler/level plug

32.3a Top-up the oil level...

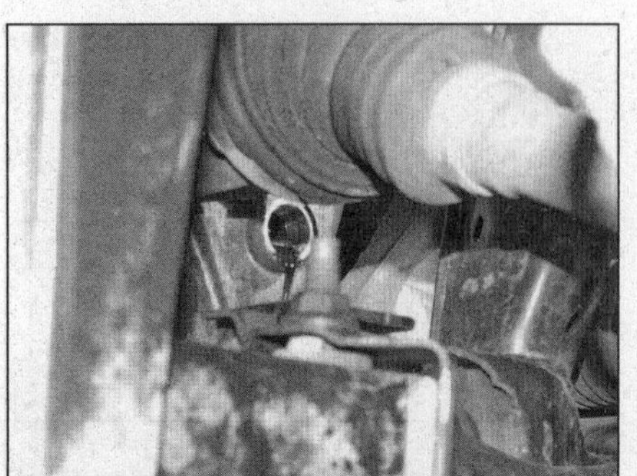

32.3b ... then allow any excess to flow out before refitting the plug

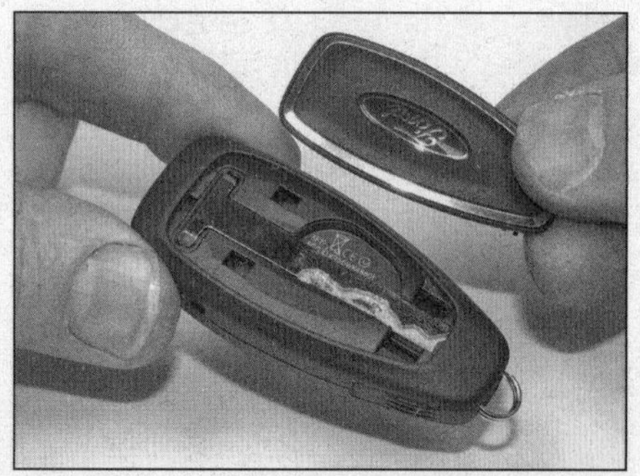

33.2 Squeeze the tabs to remove the cover

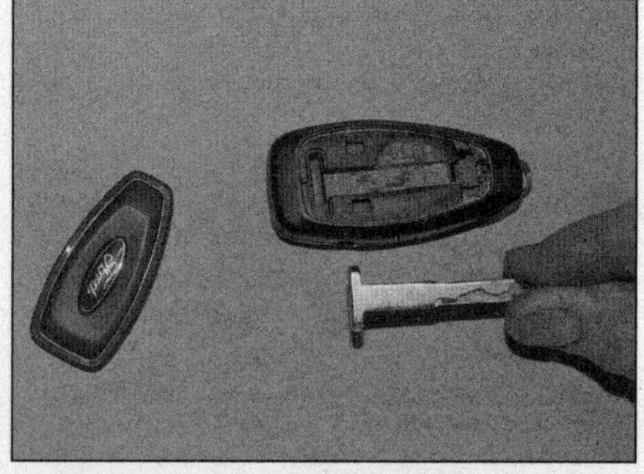

33.3 Take out the key blade from the housing

4 Use a small flat-bladed the screwdriver, to separate the 2 halves of the unit **(see illustration)**.

5 Note the fitted position of the battery (positive side down), then prise the battery from its location, and insert the new one **(see illustration)**. Avoid touching the battery or the terminals with bare fingers.

6 Snap the 2 halves of the transmitter together, place the key blade in position and refit the cover.

34 Coolant strength check and renewal

Warning: Do not allow antifreeze to come in contact with your skin or painted surfaces of the vehicle. Flush contaminated areas immediately with plenty of water. Don't store new coolant, or leave old coolant lying around, where it's accessible to children or pets – they're attracted by its sweet smell. Ingestion of even a small amount of coolant can be fatal. Wipe up garage-floor and drip-pan spills immediately. Keep antifreeze containers covered, and repair cooling system leaks as soon as they're noticed.

Warning: Never remove the expansion tank filler cap when the engine is running, or has just been switched off, as the cooling system will be hot, and the consequent escaping steam and scalding coolant could cause serious injury.

Warning: Wait until the engine is cold before starting these procedures.

Strength check

1 Use a hydrometer to check the strength of the antifreeze. Follow the instructions provided with your hydrometer. The antifreeze strength should be approximately 50%. If it is significantly less than this, drain a little coolant from the radiator (see this Section), add antifreeze to the coolant expansion tank, then run the engine for a time in order to mix the new coolant before re-testing.

Coolant draining

2 To drain the system, first remove the expansion tank filler cap.

3 Apply the handbrake, then jack up the front of the vehicle and support it securely on axle stands (see *Jacking and vehicle support*). Where applicable, release the fasteners and remove the engine undershield.

4 Place a suitable container beneath the right-hand side of the radiator.

5 Release the retaining clamp and disconnect the bottom hose from the radiator **(see illustration)**. Allow the coolant to drain into the container.

6 Once the coolant has stopped draining from the radiator, reconnect the bottom hose and secure with the retaining clamp.

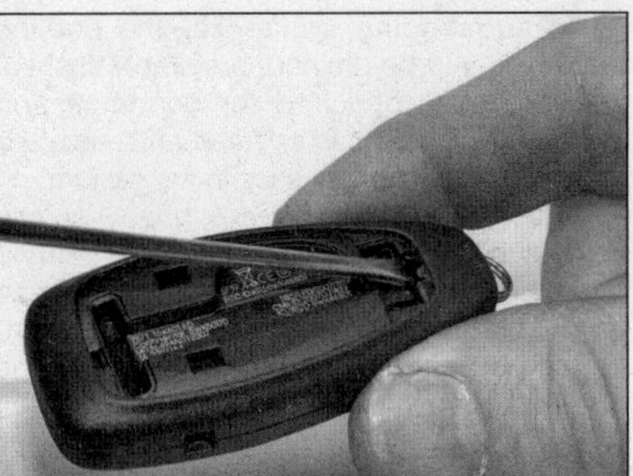

33.4 A small screwdriver can be used to prise apart the housing

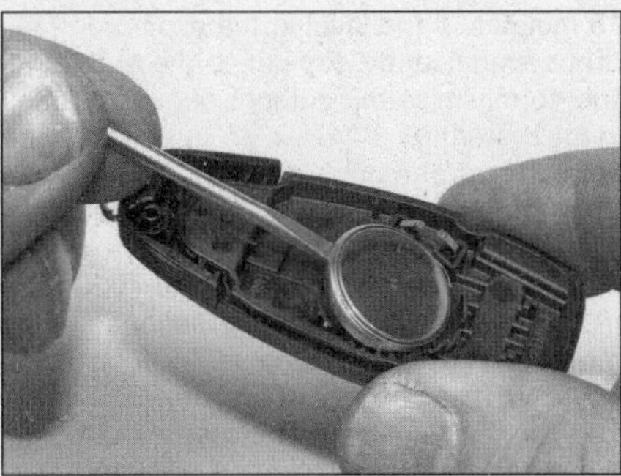

33.5 Carefully prise the battery from place

System flushing

7 With time, the cooling system may gradually lose its efficiency, as the radiator core becomes choked with rust, scale deposits from the water, and other sediment. To minimise this, as well as using only good-quality antifreeze and clean soft water, the system should be flushed as follows whenever any part of it is disturbed, and/or when the coolant is renewed.

8 With the coolant drained, refit the radiator bottom hose and refill the system with fresh water. Refit the expansion tank filler cap, start the engine and warm it up to normal operating temperature, then stop it and (after allowing it to cool down completely) drain the system again. Repeat as necessary until only clean water can be seen to emerge, then refill finally with the specified coolant mixture.

9 If only clean, soft water and good-quality antifreeze (even if not to Ford's specification) has been used, and the coolant has been renewed at the suggested intervals, the above procedure will be sufficient to keep the system clean for a considerable length of time. If, however, the system has been neglected, a more thorough operation will be required, as follows.

10 First drain the coolant, then disconnect the radiator top hose. Insert a garden hose into the radiator top hose connection, and allow water to circulate through the radiator until it runs clean from the bottom outlet.

11 To flush the engine, insert the garden hose into the radiator bottom hose, wrap a piece of rag around the garden hose to seal the connection, and allow water to circulate until it runs clear.

12 Try the effect of repeating this procedure in the top hose, although this may not be effective, since the thermostat will probably close and prevent the flow of water.

13 In severe cases of contamination, reverse-flushing of the radiator may be necessary. This may be achieved by inserting the garden hose into the bottom outlet, wrapping a piece of rag around the hose to seal the connection, then flushing the radiator until clear water emerges from the top hose outlet.

14 If the radiator is suspected of being severely choked, remove the radiator (Chapter 3 Section 6), turn it upside-down, and repeat the procedure described in paragraph 13.

15 Flushing the heater matrix can be achieved using a similar procedure to that described in paragraph 13, once the heater inlet and outlet hoses have been identified. These two hoses will be of the same diameter, and pass through the engine compartment bulkhead.

16 The use of chemical cleaners is not recommended, and should be necessary only as a last resort; the scouring action of some chemical cleaners may lead to other cooling system problems. Normally, regular renewal of the coolant will prevent excessive contamination of the system.

Coolant filling

17 With the cooling system drained and flushed, ensure that all disturbed hose unions are correctly secured. If it was raised, lower the vehicle to the ground.

18 Set the heater temperature control to maximum heat, but ensure the blower is turned off.

19 Prepare a sufficient quantity of the specified coolant mixture (see below); allow for a surplus, so as to have a reserve supply for topping-up.

20 Slowly fill the system through the expansion tank. Since the tank is the highest point in the system, all the air in the system should be displaced into the tank by the rising liquid. Slow pouring reduces the possibility of air being trapped and forming airlocks.

21 Continue filling until the coolant level reaches the expansion tank MAX level line (see Section 6), then refit the filler cap.

22 Start the engine and run it at 2500 rpm for

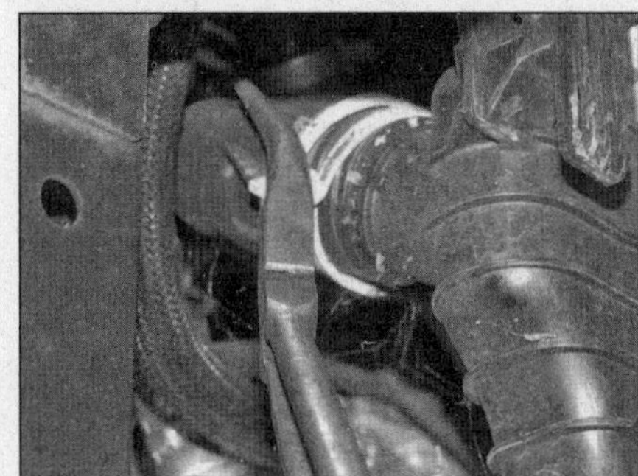

34.5 Release the clamp and disconnect the bottom hose

15 minutes. If the level in the expansion tank drops significantly, top-up to the MAX level line, to minimise the amount of air circulating in the system.

23 Increase the engine speed to 5000 rpm, then allow it to return to idle. Repeat this sequence 6 times.

24 Increase the engine speed to 4000 rpm, maintain this speed for 10 seconds, then reduce the engine speed to 2500 rpm and maintain this speed for 10 minutes.

25 Stop the engine, then leave the car to cool down completely (overnight, if possible).

26 With the system cool, open the expansion tank, and top-up the tank to the MAX level line. Refit the filler cap, tightening it securely, and clean up any spillage.

27 After refilling, always check carefully all components of the system (but especially any unions disturbed during draining and flushing) for signs of coolant leaks. Fresh antifreeze has a searching action, which will rapidly expose any weak points in the system.

Antifreeze type and mixture

Caution: Do not use engine antifreeze in the windscreen/tailgate washer system, as it will damage the vehicle's paintwork. A screenwash additive should be added to the washer system in its maker's recommended quantities.

28 If the vehicle's history (and therefore the quality of the antifreeze in it) is unknown, owners are advised to drain and thoroughly reverse-flush the system, before refilling with fresh coolant mixture.

29 If the antifreeze used is to Ford's specification, the levels of protection it affords are indicated in the coolant packaging.

30 To give the recommended standard mixture ratio for antifreeze, 50% (by volume) of antifreeze must be mixed with 50% of clean, soft water; if you are using any other type of antifreeze, follow its manufacturer's instructions to achieve the correct ratio.

31 You are unlikely to fully drain the system at any one time (unless the engine is being completely stripped), and the capacities quoted in the Specifications are therefore slightly academic for routine coolant renewal. As a guide, only two-thirds of the system's total capacity is likely to be needed for coolant renewal.

32 As the drained system will be partially filled with flushing water, in order to establish the recommended mixture ratio, measure out 50% of the system capacity in antifreeze and pour it into the hose/expansion tank as described above, then top-up with water. Any topping-up while refilling the system should be done with a suitable mixture.

33 Before adding antifreeze, the cooling system should be drained, preferably flushed, and all hoses checked for condition and security. As noted earlier, fresh antifreeze will rapidly find any weaknesses in the system.

34 After filling with antifreeze, a label should be attached to the expansion tank, stating the type and concentration of antifreeze used, and the date installed. Any subsequent topping-up should be made with the same type and concentration of antifreeze.

General cooling system checks

35 The engine should be cold for the cooling system checks, so perform the following procedure before driving the vehicle, or after it has been shut off for at least three hours.

36 Remove the expansion tank filler cap, and clean it thoroughly inside and out with a rag. Also clean the filler neck on the expansion tank. The presence of rust or corrosion in the filler neck indicates that the coolant should be changed. The coolant inside the expansion tank should be relatively clean and transparent. If it is rust-coloured, drain and flush the system, and refill with a fresh coolant mixture.

37 Carefully check the radiator hoses and heater hoses along their entire length; renew any hose which is cracked, swollen or deteriorated.

38 Inspect all other cooling system components (joint faces, etc) for leaks. A leak in the cooling system will usually show up as white- or antifreeze-coloured deposits on the area adjoining the leak. Where any problems of this nature are found on system components, renew the component or gasket with reference to Chapter 3.

Airlocks

39 If, after draining and refilling the system, symptoms of overheating are found which did not occur previously, then the fault is almost certainly due to trapped air at some point in the system, causing an airlock and restricting the flow of coolant; usually, the air is trapped because the system was refilled too quickly.

40 If an airlock is suspected, first try gently squeezing all visible coolant hoses. A coolant hose which is full of air feels quite different to one full of coolant when squeezed. After refilling the system, most airlocks will clear once the system has cooled, and been topped-up.

41 While the engine is running at operating temperature, switch on the heater and heater fan, and check for heat output. Provided there is sufficient coolant in the system, lack of heat output could be due to an airlock in the system.

42 Airlocks can have more serious effects than simply reducing heater output – a severe airlock could reduce coolant flow around the engine. Check that the radiator top hose is hot when the engine is at operating temperature – a top hose which stays cold could be the result of an airlock (or a non-opening thermostat).

43 If the problem persists, stop the engine and allow it to cool down completely, before unscrewing the expansion tank filler cap or loosening the hose clips and squeezing the hoses to bleed out the trapped air. In the worst case, the system will have to be at least partially drained (this time, the coolant can be saved for re-use) and flushed to clear the problem. If all else fails, have the system evacuated and vacuum filled by a suitably-equipped garage.

Expansion tank cap check

44 Wait until the engine is completely cold – perform this check before the engine is started for the first time in the day.

45 Place a wad of cloth over the expansion tank cap, then unscrew it slowly and remove it.

46 Examine the condition of the rubber seal on the underside of the cap. If the rubber appears to have hardened, or cracks are visible in the seal edges, a new cap should be fitted.

47 If the car is several years old, or has covered a large mileage, consider renewing the cap regardless of its apparent condition – they are not expensive. If the pressure relief valve built into the cap fails, excess pressure in the system will lead to puzzling failures of hoses and other cooling system components.

35 Reset service indicator

1 Close all doors.

2 Turn the ignition key to stage 2, or hold the start button in for 2 seconds, without touching any pedal.

3 Hold down the accelerator and brake pedals for at least 20 seconds until a "Service: Oil reset in prog." message is displayed on the instrument cluster.

4 Continue holding the accelerator and brake pedals until the display says "Service: Oil reset complete".

5 At this point the oil change reminder indicator will extinguish. This confirms that the procedure has been correctly completed.

Chapter 1 Part B
Routine maintenance and servicing – diesel models

Contents

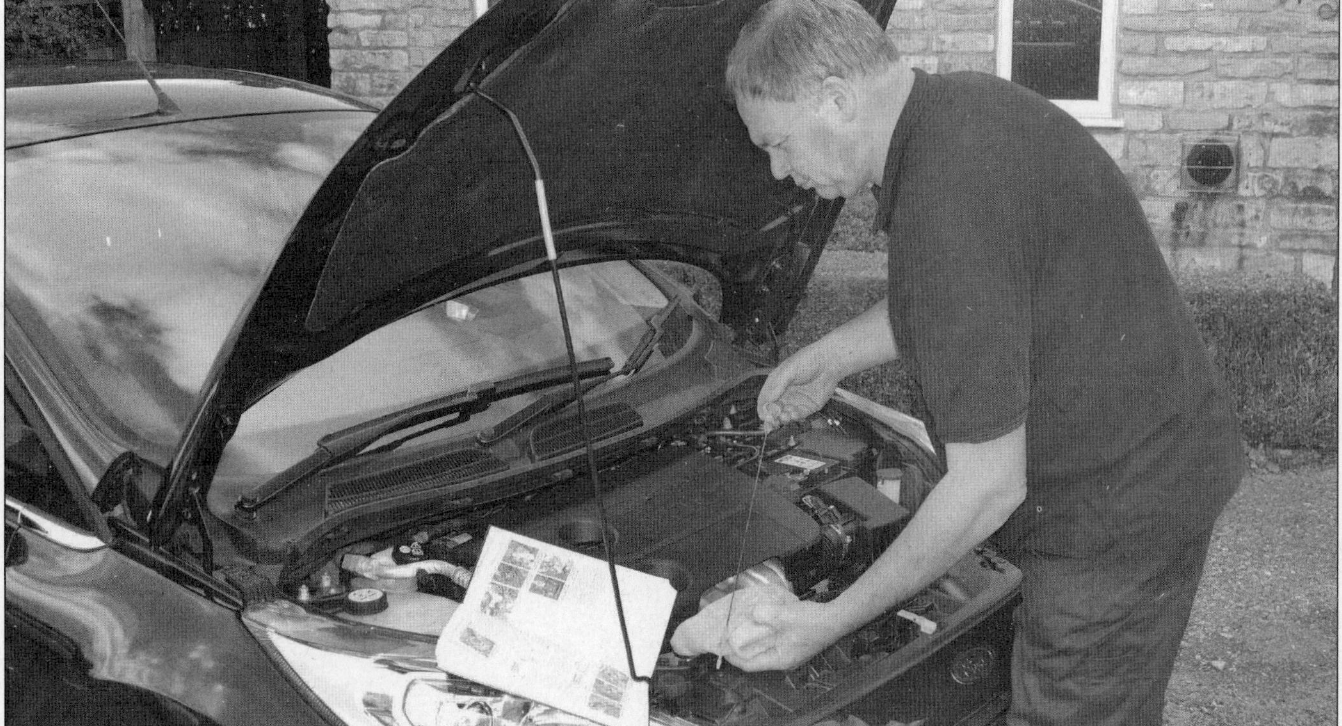

Degrees of difficulty

Easy, suitable for novice with little experience 	Fairly easy, suitable for beginner with some experience 	Fairly difficult, suitable for competent DIY mechanic 	Difficult, suitable for experienced DIY mechanic 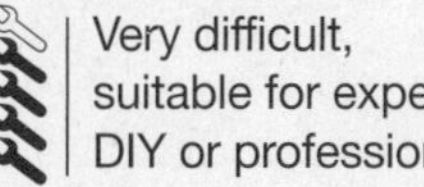	Very difficult, suitable for expert DIY or professional 

Specifications

Lubricants and fluids

Engine oil	Ford WSS-M2C950-A long-life oil or Castrol Magnatec SAE 0W-30. SAE 5W-30 (fully synthetic) to ACEA A3 may be used for topping up only.*
Cooling system	Ford WSS-M97B44-D long-life ethylene glycol based antifreeze*
Manual transmission	Ford WSS-M2C200-D2 transmission oil*
Automatic transmission	Ford WSS-M2C938-A*
Transfer case	Ford WSL-M2C192-A SAE 75W/140
Rear differential	Ford WSP-M2C197-A SAE 80W/90
Braking system	Hydraulic fluid to DOT 4 + ESP (low viscosity)

* *Check with your local dealer or specialist for the latest recommendations*

Capacities

Engine oil (including oil filter):	
1.5-litre engine	3.9 litres
2.0-litre engine	5.8 litres
Cooling system (approximate):	
1.5-litre engine	7.3 litres
2.0-litre engine	8.0 litres
Manual transmissions:	
MMT6	1.9 litres
B6	1.575 litres
Automatic transmission (6F35)	8.5 litres
Transfer case	0.5 litres approx.
Rear differential	0.47 to 0.62 litres
Washer fluid reservoir	4.5 litres
Fuel tank	60.0 litres

Cooling system

Antifreeze mixture:	
50% antifreeze	Protection down to -37°C

Note: *Refer to antifreeze manufacturer for latest recommendations.*

Brakes

Friction material minimum thickness:	
Front brake pads	3.0 mm
Rear brake pads	3.0 mm

Tyre pressures

Note: *Pressures given here are a guide only, and apply to original-equipment tyres – the recommended pressures may vary if any other make or type of tyre is fitted; check with the car handbook, or the tyre manufacturer or supplier for the latest recommendations. A tyre pressure label is fitted on the driver's door pillar.*

Normal load (up to 2 people)	Front	Rear
235/55 R17 V tyres	2.4 bar (35 psi)	2.4 bar (35 psi)
235/50 R18 V tyres	2.4 bar (35 psi)	2.4 bar (35 psi)
235/45 R19 V tyres	2.4 bar (35 psi)	2.4 bar (35 psi)
Emergency (Spacesaver) 155/70 R17 M tyre	4.2 bar	4.2 bar

Remote control battery

Type	CR2032, 3V

Torque wrench settings	Nm	lbf ft
Engine oil drain plug	35	26
Engine oil filter cap	25	18
Manual transmission level plug:		
MMT6	35	26
B6	40	30
Roadwheel nuts	135	100
Glow plugs	6	4

1 Maintenance schedule

1 The maintenance intervals in this manual are provided with the assumption that you, not the dealer, will be carrying out the work. These are the minimum maintenance intervals based on the standard service schedule recommended by the manufacturer for vehicles driven daily. If you wish to keep your vehicle in peak condition at all times, you may wish to perform some of these procedures more often. We encourage frequent maintenance, because it enhances the efficiency, performance and resale value of your vehicle.

2 If the vehicle is driven in dusty areas, used to tow a trailer, or driven frequently at slow speeds (idling in traffic) or on short journeys, more frequent maintenance intervals are recommended.

3 When the vehicle is new, it should be serviced by a dealer service department (or other workshop recognised by the vehicle manufacturer as providing the same standard of service) in order to preserve the warranty. The vehicle manufacturer may reject warranty claims if you are unable to prove that servicing has been carried out as and when specified, using only original equipment parts or parts certified to be of equivalent quality.

Every 250 miles or weekly

- ☐ Check the engine oil level (Section 5)
- ☐ Check the coolant level (Section 6)
- ☐ Check the brake and clutch fluid level (Section 7)
- ☐ Screenwash fluid (Section 8)
- ☐ Tyre condition and pressure check (Section 9)
- ☐ Wiper blades check (Section 10)
- ☐ Battery check (Section 11)
- ☐ Check the electrical systems (Section 12)

Every 6000 miles or 6 months, whichever comes first

- ☐ Renew the engine oil and filter (Section 13)

Note: *Ford recommend that the engine oil and filter are changed every 12 500 miles or 12 months. However, oil and filter changes are good for the engine, and we recommend that the oil and filter are renewed more frequently, especially if the car is used on a lot of short journeys.*

- ☐ Reset the service indicator (Section 37)

Every 12 500 miles or 12 months, whichever comes first

In addition to the items listed above, carry out the following:

- ☐ Renew the pollen filter (Section 14)
- ☐ Drain any water from the fuel filter (Section 15)
- ☐ Check all components, pipes and hoses for fluid leaks (Section 16)
- ☐ Check the condition of the auxiliary drivebelt (Section 17)
- ☐ Check the antifreeze/inhibitor strength (Section 36)
- ☐ Check the condition and operation of the seat belts (Section 18)
- ☐ Check all brake pads and discs for wear (Section 19)
- ☐ Check the condition of the driveshaft gaiters (Section 20)
- ☐ Check the steering and suspension components for condition and security (Section 21)
- ☐ Check and if necessary adjust the handbrake (Section 22)
- ☐ Check the condition of the exhaust system components (Section 23)
- ☐ Check the roadwheel nuts are tightened to the specified torque (Section 24)
- ☐ Lubricate all door, bonnet and tailgate hinges and locks (Section 25)
- ☐ Carry out a road test (Section 27)

Every 37 500 miles or 3 years, whichever comes first

In addition to the items listed above, carry out the following:

- ☐ Renew the fuel filter (Section 28)
- ☐ Renew the air filter (Section 29)
- ☐ Check the braking system rubber hoses (Section 30)

Every 112 500 miles or 10 years, whichever comes first

- ☐ Renew the auxiliary drivebelt (Section 32)
- ☐ Renew the timing belt and tensioner, as described in Chapter 2B Section 7and Chapter 2C Section 5.

Note: *Although the normal interval for timing belt renewal is 112 500 miles or 10 years, it is strongly recommended that the interval suggested above is observed, especially on cars which are subjected to intensive use, ie, mainly short journeys or a lot of stop-start driving. The actual belt renewal interval is very much up to the individual owner, but bear in mind that severe engine damage will result if the belt breaks.*

Every 2 years, regardless of mileage

- ☐ Renew the brake fluid (Section 33)
- ☐ Check the manual transmission oil level (Section 34)
- ☐ Renew the remote control battery (Section 35)

Every 6 years, regardless of mileage

- ☐ Renew the coolant (Section 36)

Note: *Ford state that, if their Super Plus antifreeze is in the system from new, the coolant need only be changed every 10 years. If there is any doubt as to the type or quality of the antifreeze which has been used, we recommend this shorter interval be observed.*

2 General information

1 This Chapter is designed to help the home mechanic maintain his/her car for safety, economy, long life and peak performance.

2 The Chapter contains a master maintenance schedule, followed by Sections dealing specifically with each task in the schedule. Visual checks, adjustments, component renewal and other helpful items are included. Refer to the accompanying illustrations of the engine compartment and the underside of the car for the locations of the various components.

3 Servicing your car in accordance with the mileage/time maintenance schedule and the following Sections will provide a planned maintenance programme, which should result in a long and reliable service life. This is a comprehensive plan, so maintaining some items but not others at the specified service intervals, will not produce the same results.

4 As you service your car, you will discover that many of the procedures can – and should – be grouped together, because of the particular procedure being performed, or because of the proximity of two otherwise-unrelated components to one another. For example, if the car is raised for any reason, the exhaust can be inspected at the same time as the suspension and steering components.

5 The first step in this maintenance programme is to prepare yourself before the actual work begins. Read through all the Sections relevant to the work to be carried out, then make a list and gather all the parts and tools required. If a problem is encountered, seek advice from a parts specialist, or a dealer service department.

3 Component location

Underbonnet view of a 2.0 litre model

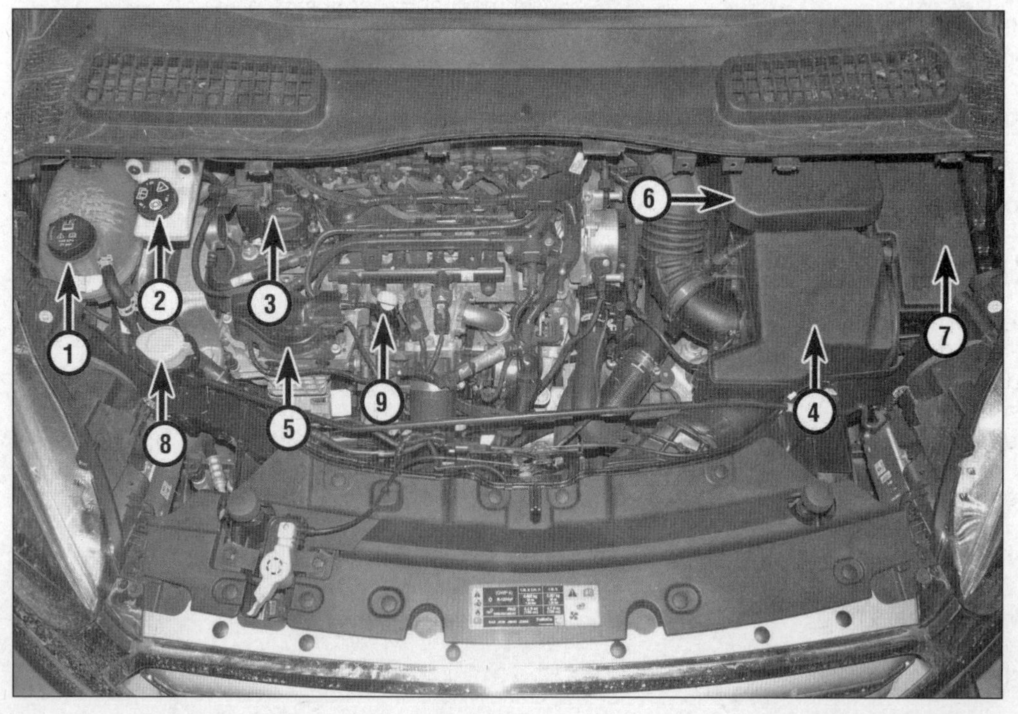

1. *Coolant reservoir (expansion tank)*
2. *Brake and clutch fluid reservoir*
3. *Engine oil filler cap*
4. *Air cleaner*
5. *Fuel filter*
6. *Battery*
7. *Fuse/relay box*
8. *Windscreen washer fluid reservoir filler*
9. *Engine oil level dipstick*

Underbonnet view of a 1.5 litre model

1. *Engine oil filler cap*
2. *Engine oil level dipstick*
3. *Coolant reservoir (expansion tank)*
4. *Brake and clutch fluid reservoir*
5. *Fuel filter*
6. *Battery*
7. *Fuse/relay box*
8. *Windscreen washer fluid reservoir filler*
9. *Air cleaner*
10. *Turbocharger*

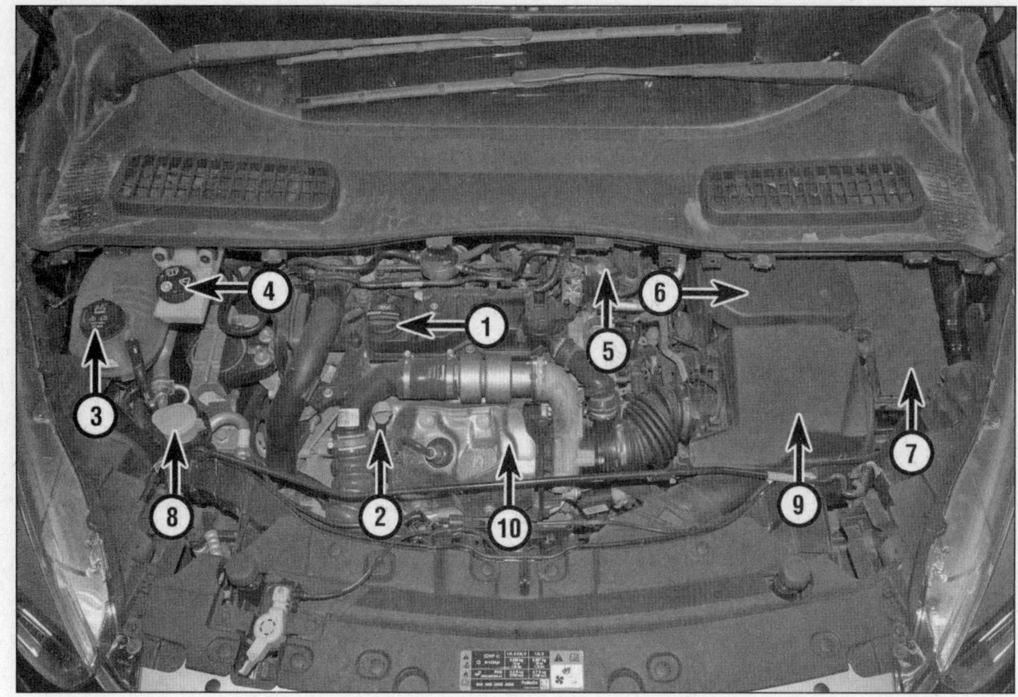

Front underbody view (2.0 litre diesel)

1. *Brake caliper*
2. *Auxiliary drivebelt*
3. *Air conditioning compressor*
4. *Engine oil drain plug*
5. *Exhaust system*
6. *Radiator bottom hose*
7. *Suspension lower arm*
8. *Driveshaft*
9. *Subframe*
10. *Track rod end*

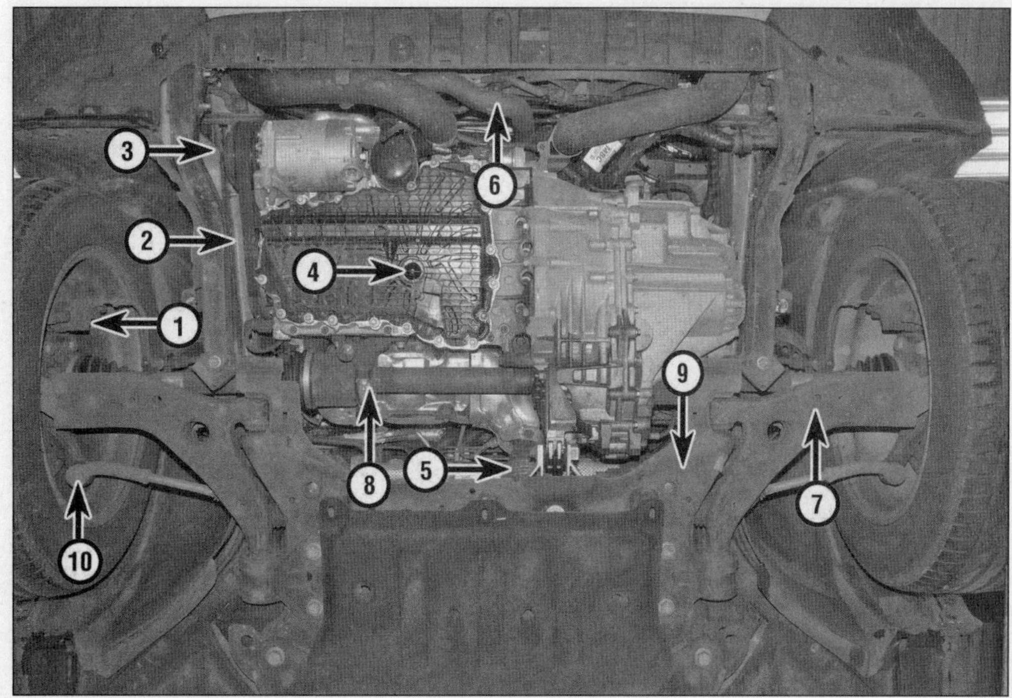

Front underbody view (1.5 litre diesel)

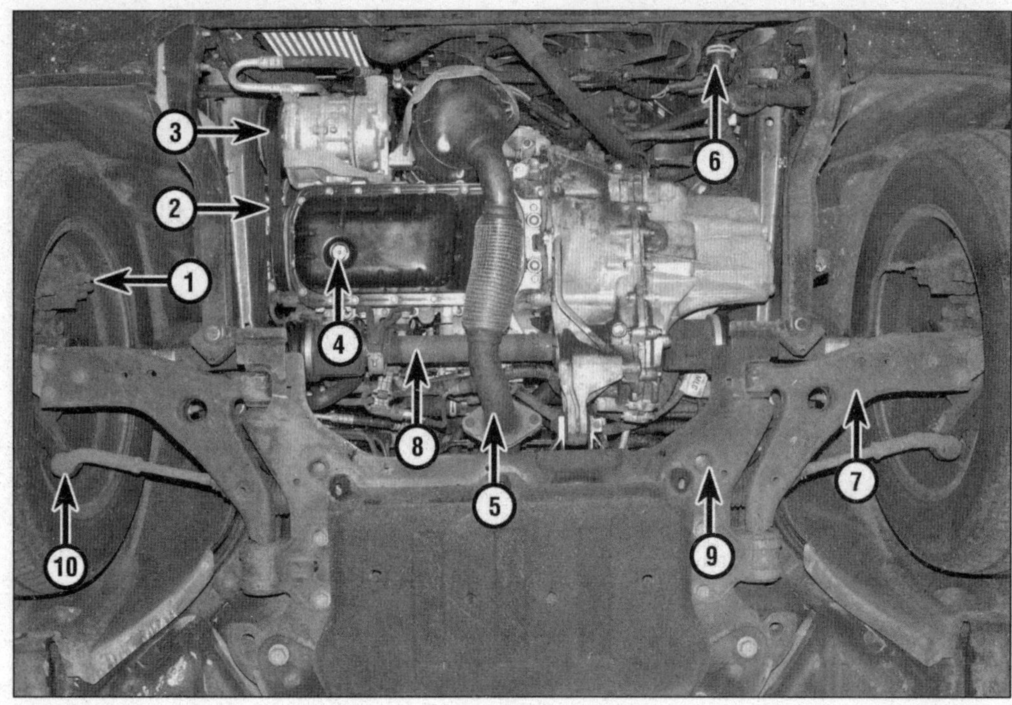

1. *Brake caliper*
2. *Auxiliary drivebelt*
3. *Air conditioning compressor*
4. *Engine oil drain plug*
5. *Exhaust*
6. *Radiator bottom hose*
7. *Suspension lower arm*
8. *Driveshaft*
9. *Subframe*
10. *Track rod end*

Rear underbody view

1. *Shock absorber*
2. *Fuel filler pipe*
3. *Rear coil spring*
4. *Trailing arm*
5. *Exhaust rear silencer*
6. *Fuel tank*
7. *Handbrake cable*

4 Regular maintenance

1 If, from the time the car is new, the routine maintenance schedule is followed closely, and frequent checks are made of fluid levels and high-wear items, as suggested throughout this manual, the engine will be kept in relatively good running condition, and the need for additional work will be minimised.

2 It is possible that there will be times when the engine is running poorly due to the lack of regular maintenance. This is even more likely if a used car, which has not received regular and frequent maintenance checks, is purchased. In such cases, additional work may need to be carried out, outside of the regular maintenance intervals.

3 If engine wear is suspected, a compression test or leakdown test (refer to Chapter 2B Section 2 or Chapter 2C Section 2) will provide valuable information regarding the overall performance of the main internal components. Such a test can be used as a basis to decide on the extent of the work to be carried out. If, for example, the test indicates serious internal engine wear, conventional maintenance as described in this Chapter will not greatly improve the performance of the engine, and may prove a waste of time and money, unless extensive overhaul work is carried out first.

4 The following series of operations are those most often required to improve the performance of a generally poor-running engine:

Primary operations

a) Clean, inspect and test the battery (Section 11)
b) Check all the engine-related fluids.
c) Check the condition of all hoses, and check for fluid leaks (Section 16)
d) Check the condition of the auxiliary drivebelt (Section 17)
e) Renew the fuel filter (Section 28)
f) Check the condition of the air filter, and renew if necessary (Section 29)

5 If the above operations do not prove fully effective, carry out the following secondary operations:

Secondary operations

6 All items listed under Primary operations, plus the following:

a) Check the charging system (Chapter 5 Section 2)
b) Check the engine control and emissions systems (Chapter 6B)
c) Check the fuel system (Chapter 4B)

5 Engine oil level check

Before you start

1 Make sure that the car is on level ground.

2 The engine must be at normal operating temperature, and switched off.

The correct oil

3 Modern engines place great demands on their oil. It is very important that the correct oil for your car is used (see *Lubricants and fluids*).

Level check

4 If you have to add oil frequently, you should check whether you have any oil leaks. Remove the engine undertray, then place some clean paper under the car overnight (ensuring it is securely weighted down), and check for stains in the morning. If there are no leaks, then the engine may be burning oil.

5 Always maintain the level between the upper and lower dipstick marks. If the level is too low severe engine damage may occur. Oil seal failure may result if the engine is overfilled by adding too much oil.

6 Locate the engine oil level dipstick and pull it from place. The dipstick is located at the front of the engine (see Section 3); the dipstick is often brightly coloured and/or has a picture of an oil-can on the top for identification. Withdraw the dipstick.

7 Wipe the dipstick clean, then fully insert it into the guide tube.

8 Withdraw the dipstick again and examine the oil level. It should be between the upper (MAX) and lower (MIN) marks **(see illustration)**. If it is near the lower mark, new engine oil needs to be added.

9 Rotate the engine oil filler cap anti-clockwise and remove it. Using a funnel, add new engine oil, a little at a time, to bring the level to the upper (MAX) mark on the dipstick. Add the oil slowly, frequently checking the level on the dipstick.

10 Securely refit the filler cap.

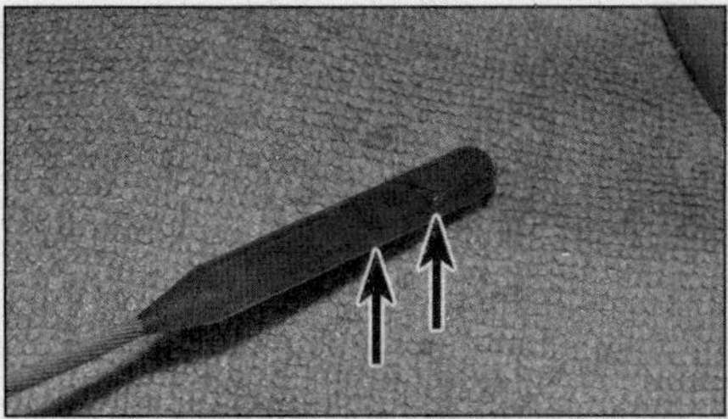

5.8 Note the oil level on the end of the dipstick, which should be between the upper (MAX) mark and lower (MIN) mark. Approximately 1.0 litre of oil will raise the level from the lower mark to the upper mark

6 Coolant level check

Warning: Do not attempt to remove the expansion tank pressure cap when the engine is hot, as there is a very great risk of scalding. Do not leave open containers of coolant about, as it is poisonous.

1 With this type of cooling system (sealed), adding coolant should not be necessary on a regular basis. If frequent topping-up is required, it is likely there is a leak. Check the radiator, all hoses and joint faces for signs of staining or wetness, and rectify as necessary.

2 It is important that antifreeze is used in the cooling system all year round, not just during the winter months. Don't top up with water alone, as the antifreeze will become diluted. Refer to Section 36.

3 With the engine completely cold, the coolant level should be between the upper and lower marks on the side of the reservoir (expansion tank) **(see illustration)**.

4 If more coolant is required, rotate the filler cap anti-clockwise and remove it **(see illustration)**.

5 Add new coolant to bring the level to the upper mark, then securely refit the cap **(see illustration)**.

6.3 The coolant level is indicated by the minimum and maximum marks visible in the filler neck.

6.4 Rotate the cap anti-clockwise and remove it

6.5 Add new coolant to bring the level to the upper mark

7.5 The MAX and MIN marks are indicated on the side of the reservoir. The fluid level must be kept between the marks at all times

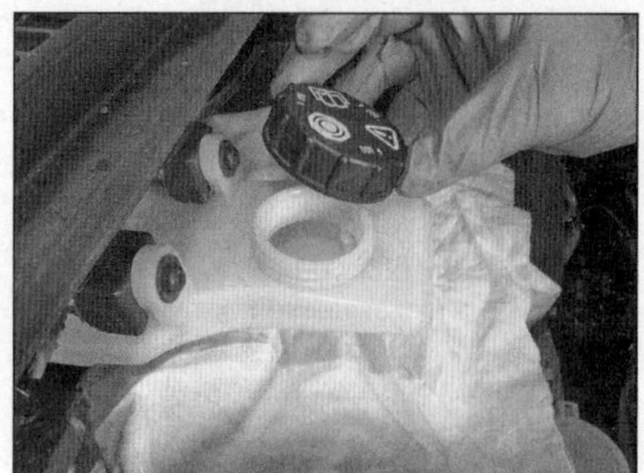

7.6 Unscrew the reservoir cap and carefully lift it out of position

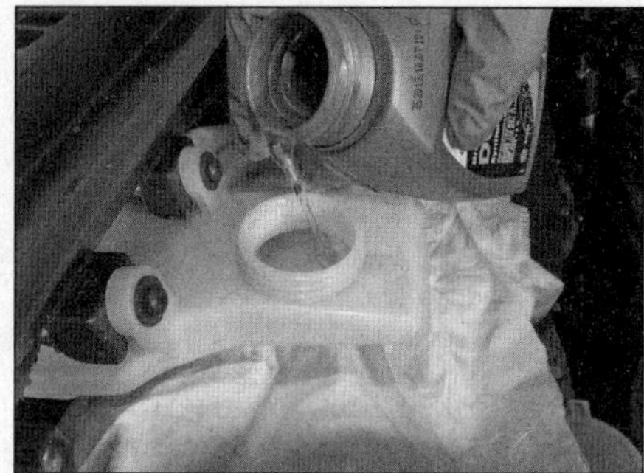

7.7 Carefully add fluid taking care not to spill it onto the surrounding components

7 Brake and clutch fluid level check

Warning: Brake fluid can harm your eyes and damage painted surfaces, so use extreme caution when handling and pouring it.

Warning: Do not use fluid that has been standing open for some time, as it absorbs moisture from the air, which can cause a dangerous loss of braking effectiveness.

1 The fluid level in the reservoir will drop slightly as the brake pads wear down, but the fluid level must never be allowed to drop below the MIN mark.

Before you start

2 Make sure that the car is on level ground.

Safety first!

3 If the reservoir requires repeated topping-up this is an indication of a fluid leak somewhere in the system, which should be investigated immediately.

4 If a leak is suspected, the car should not be driven until the braking system has been checked. Never take any risks where brakes are concerned

Level check

5 The fluid level is visible through the reservoir. The level must be kept between the MAX and MIN marks at all times **(see illustration)**.

6 If topping-up is necessary, first wipe clean the area around the filler cap to prevent dirt entering the hydraulic system, then rotate the cap anti-clockwise and remove it **(see illustration)**. If the fluid is dirty, the hydraulic system should be drained and refilled as described in Section 9 Section 3.

7 Add new fluid from a sealed container to bring the level to the upper mark **(see illustration)**. Use only the fluid specified in *Lubricants and fluids*; mixing different types can cause damage to the system. After topping-up to the correct level, securely refit the cap and wipe off any spilt fluid.

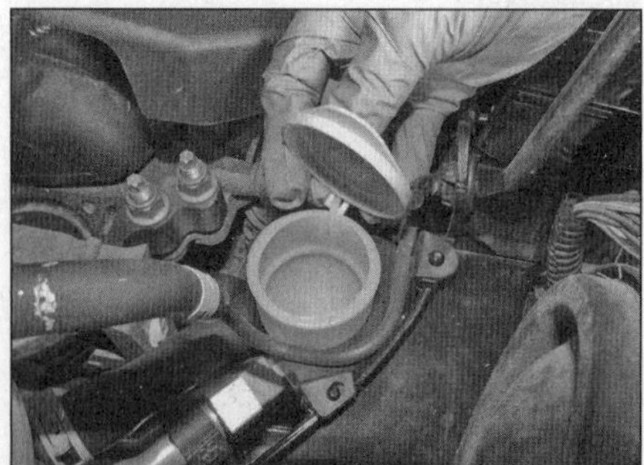

8.2 Lift the cap

8 Screenwash fluid

1 Screenwash additives not only keep the windscreen clean during bad weather, they also prevent the washer system freezing in cold weather – which is when you are likely to need it most. Don't top-up using plain water, as the screenwash will become diluted, and will freeze in cold weather.

Warning: On no account use engine coolant antifreeze in the screen washer system – this may damage the paintwork.

2 The screen washer fluid reservoir filler cap is located on the right-hand side of the engine compartment.Carefully pull up the cap **(see illustration)**. The headlight washers, where fitted, are supplied from the same reservoir.

3 Add screenwash as per the manufacturers instructions **(see illustration)**.

8.3 When topping-up, add a screenwash additive in the quantities recommended by the manufacturer

9 Tyre condition and pressure check

Tyre condition and pressure

1 It is very important that tyres are in good condition, and at the correct pressure – having a tyre failure at any speed is highly dangerous.

2 Tyre wear is influenced by driving style – harsh braking and acceleration, or fast cornering, will all produce more rapid tyre wear. As a general rule, the front tyres wear out faster than the rears. Interchanging the tyres from front to rear ("rotating" the tyres) may result in more even wear. Non-directional tyres can be swapped diagonally front to rear, but directional tyres should be swapped on the same side only. However, if this is completely effective, you may have the expense of replacing all four tyres at once!

3 Remove any nails or stones embedded in the tread before they penetrate the tyre to cause deflation. If removal of a nail does reveal that the tyre has been punctured, refit the nail so that its point of penetration is marked. Then immediately change the wheel, and have the tyre repaired by a tyre dealer.

4 Regularly check the tyres for damage in the form of cuts or bulges, especially in the sidewalls. Periodically remove the wheels, and clean any dirt or mud from the inside and outside surfaces. Examine the wheel rims for signs of rusting, corrosion or other damage. Light alloy wheels are easily damaged by "kerbing" whilst parking; steel wheels may also become dented or buckled. A new wheel is very often the only way to overcome severe damage.

5 New tyres should be balanced when they are fitted, but it may become necessary to re-balance them as they wear, or if the balance weights fitted to the wheel rim should fall off. Unbalanced tyres will wear more quickly, as will the steering and suspension components.

9.6 The tyres may have tread wear safety bands (B), which will appear when the tread depth reaches approximately 1.6 mm. The band positions are indicated by a mark on the tyre sidewall (A)

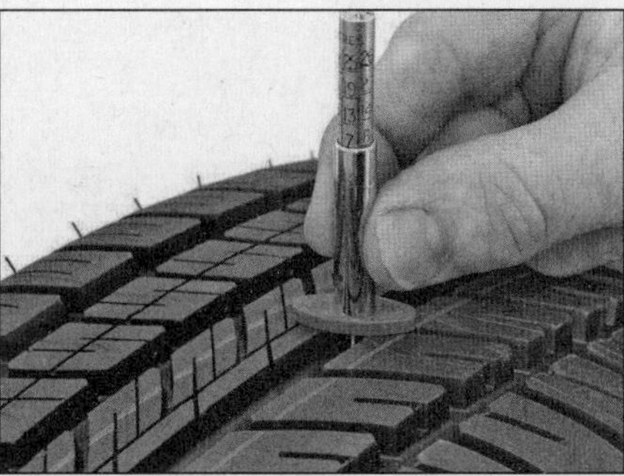

9.7 Tread wear can be monitored with a tread depth indicator gauge

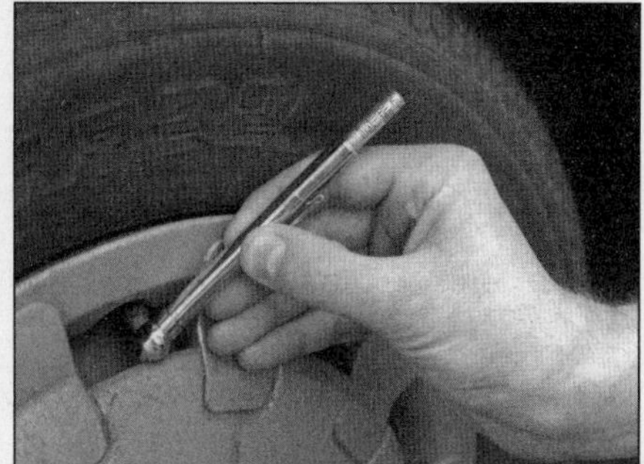

9.8 Check the tyre pressures regularly with the tyres cold

Shoulder wear

Centre wear

Uneven wear

Wheel imbalance is normally signified by vibration, particularly at a certain speed (typically around 50 mph). If this vibration is felt only through the steering, then it is likely that just the front wheels need balancing. If, however, the vibration is felt through the whole car, the rear wheels could be out of balance. Wheel balancing should be carried out by a tyre dealer or garage.

6 The tyres may have tread wear safety bands, which indicate when the tread depth reaches the legal limit **(see illustration)**.

7 Alternatively, monitor the tread wear with a simple, inexpensive device known as a tread depth indicator gauge **(see illustration)**.

8 Regularly check the pressures with a pressure gauge when the tyres are cold **(see illustration)**. Do not adjust the pressures immediately after the vehicle has been used, or an inaccurate setting will result.

Tyre tread wear patterns

Shoulder wear

Underinflation (wear on both sides)

Under-inflation will cause overheating of the tyre, because the tyre will flex too much, and the tread will not sit correctly on the road surface. This will cause a loss of grip and excessive wear, not to mention the danger of sudden tyre failure due to heat build-up.

Remedy: Check and adjust pressures.

Incorrect wheel camber (wear on one side)

Remedy: Repair or renew suspension parts

Hard cornering

Remedy: Reduce speed!

Centre wear

Overinflation

Over-inflation will cause rapid wear of the centre part of the tyre tread, coupled with reduced grip, harsher ride, and the danger of shock damage occurring in the tyre casing.

Remedy: Check and adjust pressures.

Note: *If you sometimes have to inflate your car's tyres to the higher pressures specified for maximum load or sustained high speed, don't forget to reduce the pressures to normal afterwards.*

Uneven wear

Front tyres may wear unevenly as a result of wheel misalignment. Most tyre dealers and garages can check and adjust the wheel alignment (or "tracking") for a modest charge.

Incorrect camber or castor

Remedy: Repair or renew suspension parts.

Malfunctioning suspension

Remedy: Repair or renew suspension parts.

Unbalanced wheel

Remedy: Have the wheels balanced.

Incorrect toe setting

Remedy: Adjust front wheel alignment (see Chapter 10 Section 21).

Note: *The feathered edge of the tread which typifies toe wear is best checked by feel.*

10 Wiper blades

1 Check the condition of the wiper blades; if they are cracked or show any signs of deterioration, or if the glass swept area is smeared, renew them **(see illustration)**. Wiper blades should be renewed annually.

2 To remove a front wiper blade, pull the arm

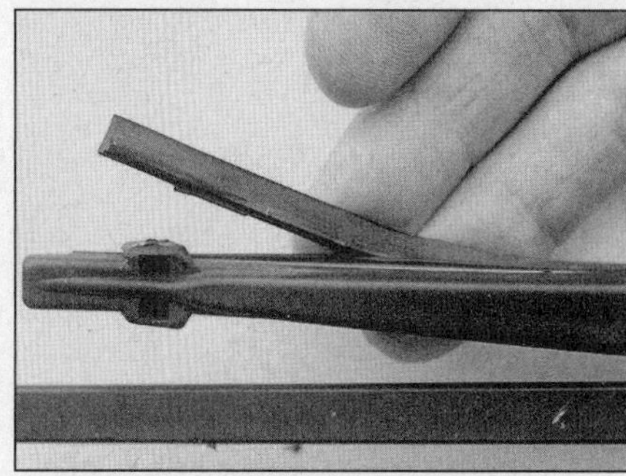

10.1 Check the condition of the wiper blades

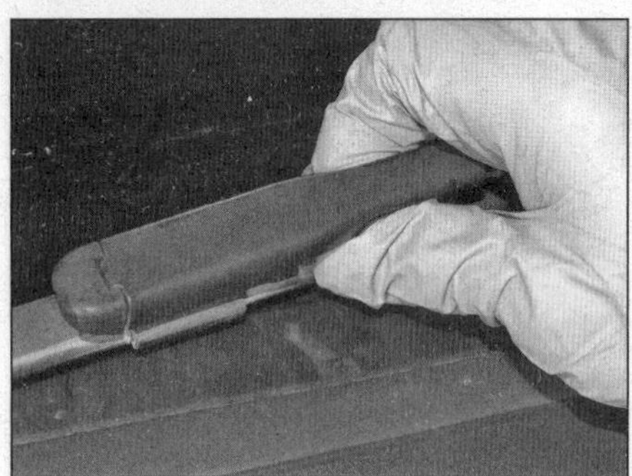

10.2 Pull the arm away from the screen, depress the clip and slide the blade down the arm

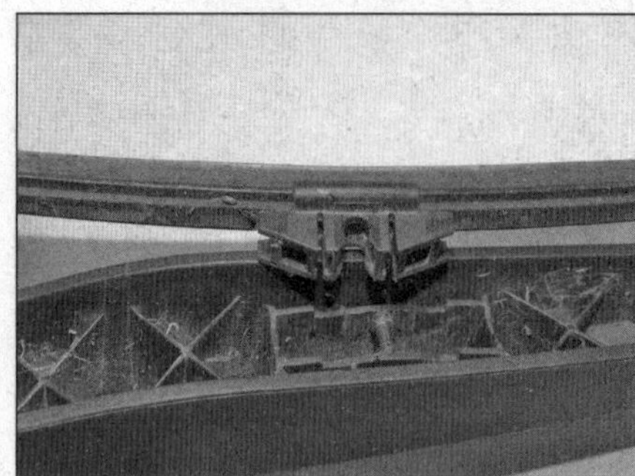

10.3 Pull the arm away from the screen, swing the blade out, and prise it from the arm

away from the screen, depress the clip and slide the blade from the arm **(see illustration)**. It is prudent to lay cloth on the screen to protect it if the arm springs back.

3 To remove a rear wiper blade, pull the arm away from the screen, then prise the blade out and remove it **(see illustration)**.

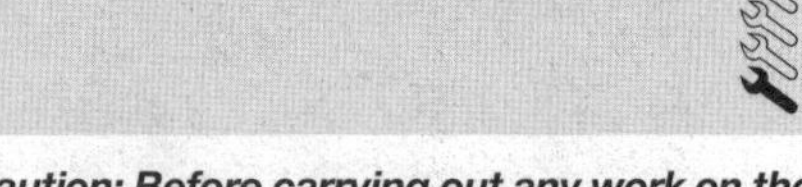

11 Battery check

Caution: Before carrying out any work on the vehicle battery, read the precautions given in 'Safety first!' at the start of this manual.

1 Make sure that the battery tray is in good condition, and that the clamp is tight. Corrosion on the tray, retaining clamp and the battery itself can be removed with a solution of water and baking soda. Thoroughly rinse all cleaned areas with water. Any metal parts damaged by corrosion should be covered with a zinc-based primer, then painted.

2 If the battery is flat, and you need to jump start your vehicle, see *Jump starting*.

3 The battery is located under two covers on the left-hand side of the engine compartment. Lift the covers to access the battery **(see illustrations)**.

4 If corrosion (white, fluffy deposits) is evident, disconnect the leads from the battery as described in Chapter 5 Section 4, then clean the lead clamps with a small wire brush, then refit them **(see illustration)**. Automotive stores sell a tool for cleaning the battery post

5 A tool is also available for cleaning the battery posts **(see illustration)**.

11.3a Lift away the front cover...

11.3b ...and the rear cover

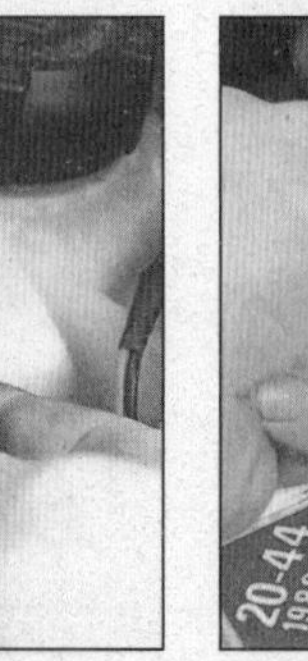

11.4 Clean the lead clamps with a small wire brush, then refit them

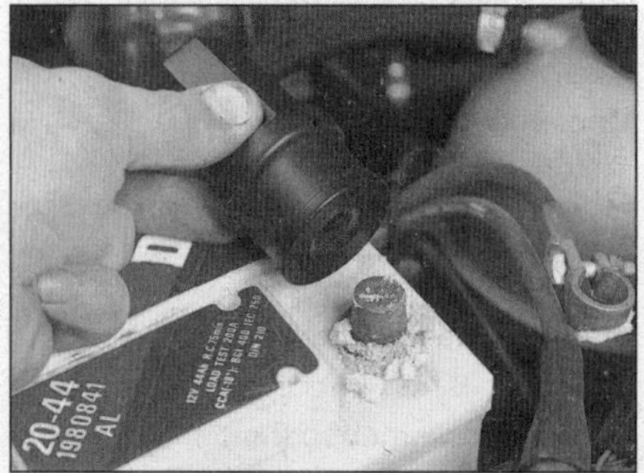

11.5 Clean the battery posts

Battery corrosion can be kept to a minimum by applying a layer of petroleum jelly to the clamps and terminals after they are reconnected.

12 Electrical systems check

1 Check all external lights and the horn. Refer to the appropriate Sections of Chapter 12 for details if any of the circuits are found to be inoperative.

2 Visually check all accessible wiring connectors, harnesses and retaining clips for security, and for signs of chafing or damage.

If you need to check your brake lights and indicators unaided, back up to a wall or garage door and operate the lights. The reflected light should show if they are working properly.

3 If a single indicator light, stop-light or headlight has failed, it is likely that a bulb has blown and will need to be renewed **(see illustration)**. Refer to Chapter 12 Section 8 for details. If all three stop-lights have failed, it is possible that a fuse has blown. Check the brake lamps fuse 21 (5 amp) located in the engine bay fuse box first. If the fuse is okay, it is likely that the switch has failed (see Chapter 12 Section 6).

4 If more than one indicator light or tail light has failed, check that a fuse has not blown or that there is a fault in the circuit (see, 12). High beam, rear fog, and reverse lamp fuses are located in the passenger compartment fuse box but the horn, brake lights, and lighting control fuses are located in the engine compartment fuse box. Slacken the screws, and fold down the fuseholder.

5 To renew a blown fuse, simply pull it out and fit a new fuse of the correct rating (see

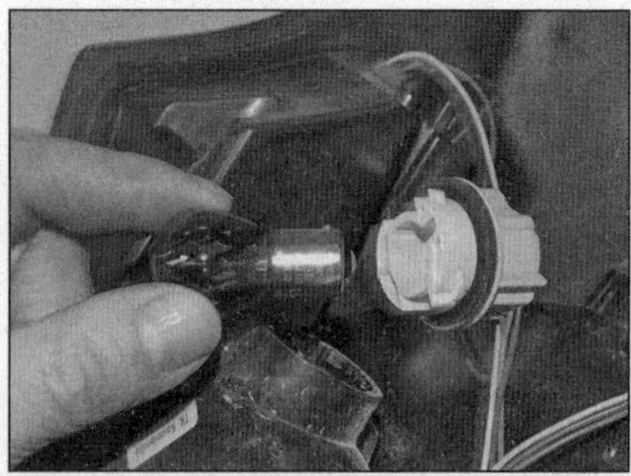

12.3 If a single indicator light, stop-light or headlight has failed, it is likely that a bulb has blown

Chapter 12 Section 3) **(see illustration)**. If the fuse blows again, it is important that you find out why – a complete checking procedure is given in Chapter 12 Section 2.

13 Engine oil and filter renewal

1 Frequent oil and filter changes are the most important preventative maintenance procedures which can be undertaken by the DIY owner. As engine oil ages, it becomes diluted and contaminated, which leads to premature engine wear.

2 Before starting this procedure, gather together all the necessary tools and materials. Also make sure that you have plenty of clean rags and newspapers handy, to mop-up any spills. Ideally, the engine oil should be warm, as it will drain better. Take care, however, not to touch the exhaust or any other hot parts of the engine when working under the vehicle. To avoid any possibility of scalding, and to protect yourself from possible skin irritants and other harmful contaminants in used engine oils, it is advisable to wear gloves when carrying out this work.

3 Check the handbrake is fully on, then jack up the front of the car and support it on axle stands (see *Jacking and vehicle support*).

4 Lift up the engine cover and remove it.

5 Undo the retaining bolts and remove the engine undertray (where fitted) **(see illustration)**.

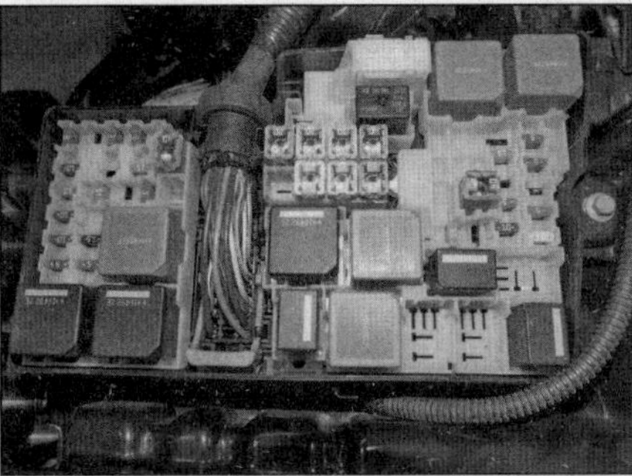

12.5 Pull out the fuse and fit a new one of the correct rating

2.0 litre engines to emissions level Stage V

6 On engines to emission level Stage V, disengage the retaining tab and lift the engine oil filler pipe from its location **(see illustration)**. Move the pipe to one side for access to the oil filter.

7 Where fitted, undo the 1 retaining nut and 2 bolts and manoeuvre the filter cover from place.

8 Using a 27 mm socket on an extension bar, undo the oil filter housing cap. Lift the cap up, with the oil filter inside it. Discard the filter and the O-ring around the circumference of the cap **(see illustrations)**.

9 Ensure the oil filter housing and cap are clean, then fit a new O-ring seal to the cap.

10 Fit the new filter element into the cap, then lubricate the O-ring seal with a little clean engine oil, and fit the cap to the housing. Tighten it securely.

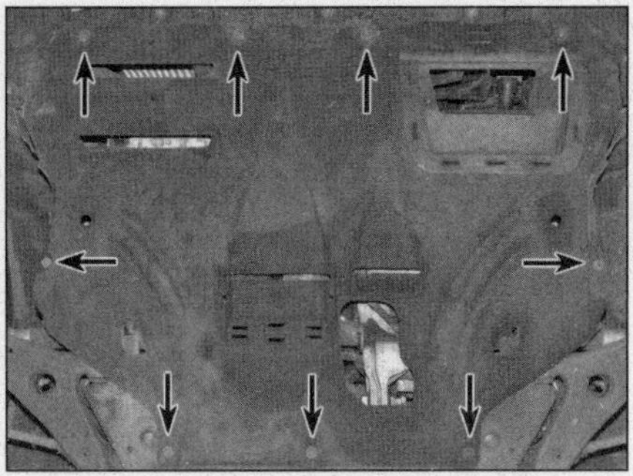

13.5 Engine undertray retaining bolts

11 Refit the oil filter cover, tightening the nut and bolts to the required torque.

12 Where applicable, refit the oil filler pipe.

13 Refit the engine cover.

14 Using a socket, slacken the drain plug about half a turn. Position the draining container under the drain plug, then remove the plug completely **(see illustration)**.

15 Allow some time for the oil to drain, noting that it may be necessary to reposition the container as the oil flow slows to a trickle.

16 After all the oil has drained, wipe the drain plug and the sealing washer (where fitted) with a clean rag. Examine the condition of the sealing washer, and renew it if it shows signs of scoring or other damage which may prevent an oil-tight seal (it is generally considered good practice to fit a new washer every time). Clean the area around the drain

13.6 Disengage the retaining tab and lift the engine oil filler pipe from its location

13.8a Undo the oil filter cap...

13.8b ... then lift up the cap with the filter element...

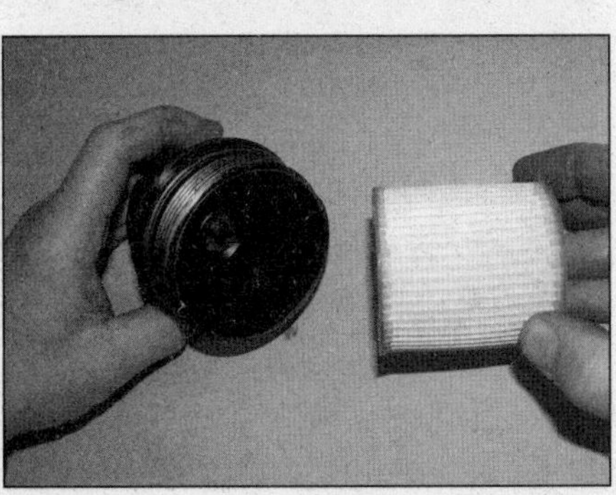

13.8c ... pull the element from the cap...

13.8d ... and discard the O-ring seal

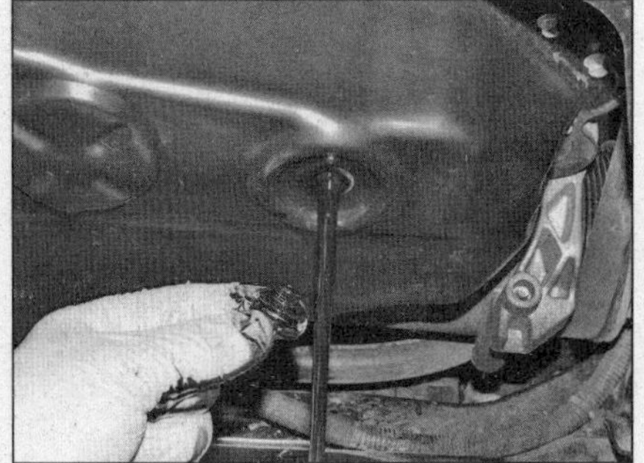

13.14 Undo the drain plug and allow the oil to drain

13.16 Renew the drain plug sealing washer

13.17 Pull out the drain plug retaining clip

13.18 Rotate the drain plug 90° anti-clockwise and pull it downwards

13.22a Loosen the filter using a tool...

13.22b ...then remove it completely

plug opening, and refit the plug complete with the washer and tighten it to the specified torque **(see illustration)**.

2.0 litre engines to emissions level Stage VI

17 Remove the draining plug retaining clip **(see illustration)**.

18 Position the draining container under the drain plug, then unscrew the plug approximately 90° anti-clockwise, pull it down and remove it **(see illustration)**. Recover the sealing ring from the drain plug.

19 Allow some time for the old oil to drain, noting that it may be necessary to reposition the container as the oil flow slows to a trickle.

20 After all the oil has drained, wipe off the drain plug with a clean rag. Clean the area around the drain plug opening, and refit the plug. Turn the plug 90° clockwise until it stops, then refit the retaining clip.

21 If the filter is also to be renewed, move the container into position under the oil filter, which is located on the front side of the cylinder block.

22 Use an oil filter removal tool to loosen the oil filter **(see illustrations)**.

23 Use a clean rag to remove all oil, dirt and sludge from the filter mating face on the engine.

24 Apply a little clean engine oil to the O-ring seal, then fit the new filter and tighten it securely.

1.5 litre engine

25 Remove the air cleaner assembly, as described in Section 4B Section 6.

26 Using a socket on an extension bar, undo the oil filter housing cap. Lift the cap up, with the filter element inside it. Discard the filter and the O-ring seal around the circumference of the cap **(see illustrations)**.

27 Using a spanner, socket or Allen key as applicable, slacken the drain plug about half a turn **(see illustration)**. Position the draining container under the drain plug, then remove the plug completely **(see Haynes Hint)**.

As the drain plug releases from the threads, move it away sharply so the stream of oil issuing from the sump runs into the container, not up your sleeve.

28 Allow some time for the oil to drain, noting that it may be necessary to reposition the container as the oil flow slows to a trickle.

29 After all the oil has drained, wipe the drain plug and the sealing washer (where fitted) with a clean rag. Examine the condition of the sealing washer, and renew it if it shows signs of scoring or other damage which may prevent an oil-tight seal (it is generally considered good practice to fit a new washer every time). Clean the area around the drain plug opening, and refit the plug complete with the washer and tighten it to the specified torque.

30 Ensure the oil filter housing and cap are clean, then fit a new O-ring seal to the cap.

31 Lubricate the cap O-ring seal with clean engine oil, insert the new filter element, then refit the cap and tighten it to the specified torque.

All engines

32 Remove the old oil and all tools from

13.26a Location of the engine oil filter

13.26b Unscrew the cap and remove it complete with filter element

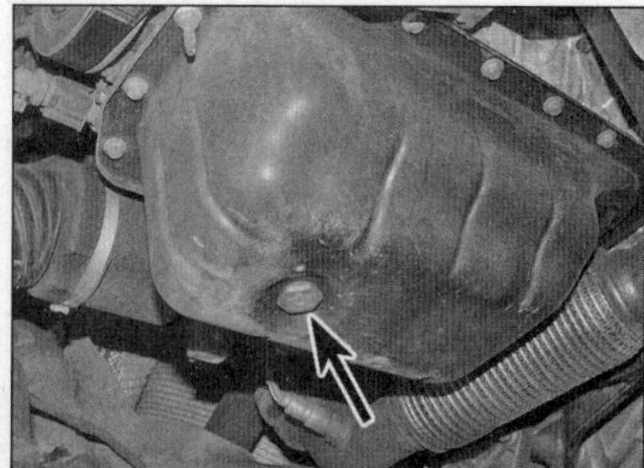

13.27 Undo the engine oil drain plug

28.4 Undo the bolts and remove the bracket

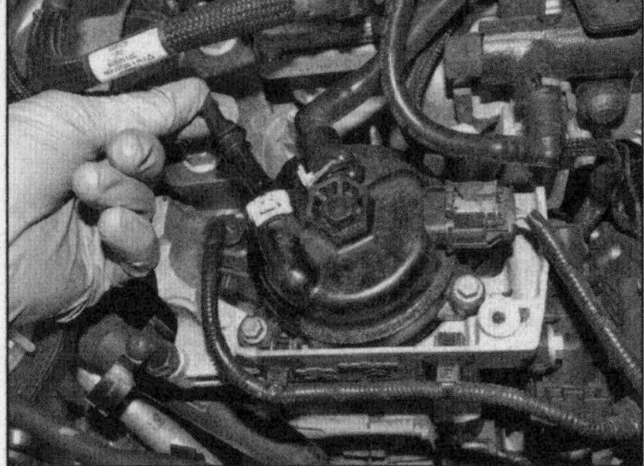
28.5 Depress the buttons and disconnect the pipes

28.6 Lift the yellow catch and disconnect the wiring plug

28.8a Unplug the connector by the filter...

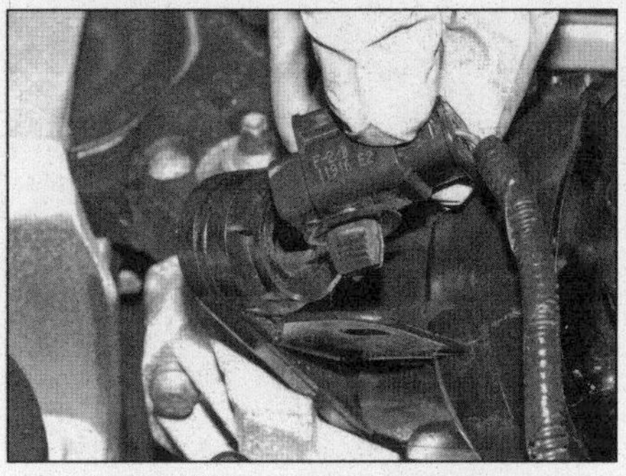
28.8b ...and detach the wiring harness from the filter housing

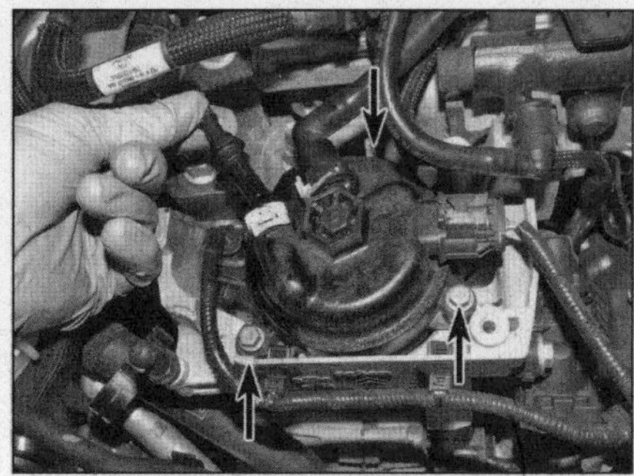
28.9 Filter retaining bolts

Braking system

12 Make sure that the car does not pull to one side when braking, and that the wheels do not lock when braking hard.

13 Check that there is no vibration through the steering when braking.

14 Some models are fitted with an electrically operated parking brakem so enure that this engages and disengages correctly. Where the car is fitted with a manual parking brake, check that it operates correctly, without excessive movement of the lever, and that it holds the car stationary on a slope.

15 Test the operation of the brake servo unit as follows. Depress the footbrake 4 or 5 times to exhaust the vacuum, then start the engine. As the engine starts, there should be a noticeable 'give' in the brake pedal as vacuum builds-up. Allow the engine to run for at least 2 minutes, and then switch it off. If the brake pedal is now depressed again, it should be possible to detect a hiss from the servo as the pedal is depressed. After about 4 or 5 applications, no further hissing should be heard, and the pedal should feel considerably harder.

28 Fuel filter renewal

Note: *Various types of fuel filters are fitted to these engines depending on model year and territory. The following procedures depict a typical example.*

Note: *After renewing the filter it will be necessary to prime and bleed the fuel system, which can occasionally prove troublesome on these engines. Refer to the procedures contained in Chapter 4B Section 5 and ensure you have the necessary equipment before proceeding.*

2.0 litre engines

1 The fuel filter is located on the top of the engine towards the front right.

2 Depressurize the fuel system as described in Chapter 4B Section 4.

3 Pull up and remove the plastic cover from the top of the engine.

4 Undo the bolts and remove the remove the bracket above the filter location **(see illustration)**.

5 Be ready to collect any spilt fuel, then depress the release buttons and disconnect the fuel pipes from the filter **(see illustration)**. Plug the openings to prevent contamination.

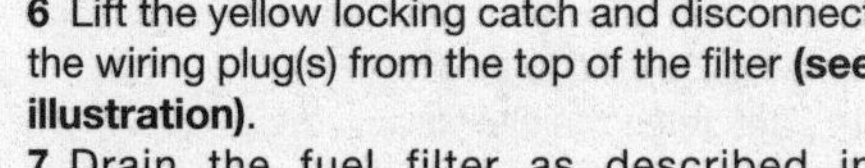

6 Lift the yellow locking catch and disconnect the wiring plug(s) from the top of the filter **(see illustration)**.

7 Drain the fuel filter as described in Section 15.

8 Disconnect the wiring plug that's down by the fuel filter, and detach the wiring harness from the front of the fuel filter housing, to allow the filter to be removed easily **(see illustrations)**.

9 Undo the 3 bolts and lift the filter assembly slightly from place, then fully detach the main fuel pipe **(see illustration)**.

10 To remove the filter from the filter housing, replace the housing in the bracket on the engine, then unscrew the top of the filter housing. Use a socket on the central moulding on top of the filter housing and undo **(see illustration)**.

11 Carefully pull the top from the filter **(see illustration)**.

12 Clean the filter top outside and inside.

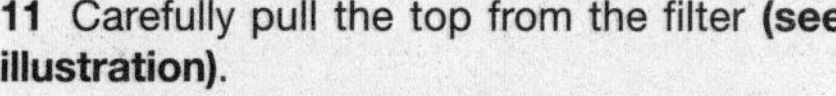

28.10 Unscrew the top of the filter housing

28.11 Pull the filter top from the element

28.13 Ensure the element is correctly located

28.20 Remove the cover locating peg

13 Locate the new filter element into the housing **(see illustration)**.

14 Retighten the filter drain screw.

15 Refit the filter top, and tighten it securely until it contacts the stop **(see illustration)**.

28.15 Tighten the top until it contact the stop

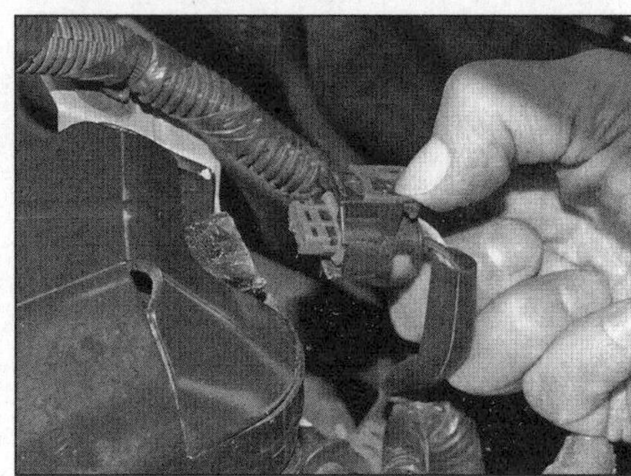
28.21 Disconnect the wiring plug

16 Slacken the filter mounting bolts to allow the fuel pipes to be reconnected to their original locations (do not fully connect the main fuel pipe at this stage), then retighten the bolts. Once the bolts are tightened, fully reconnect the main fuel pipe and reconnect the wiring plug(s).

17 Refit the bracket above the filter and tighten the retaining bolts securely.

18 The remainder of refitting is a reversal of removal, noting the following points:

a) On completion, prime and bleed the fuel system as described in Chapter 4B Section 5.

b) When the engine is running, check for any sign of leakage from the disturbed pipes.

1.5 litre diesel

19 Depressurize the fuel system as described in Chapter 4B Section 4.

20 Remove the engine cover from the top of the engine, and then slacken and remove the cover locating peg **(see illustration)**, from the top of the fuel filter bracket.

21 Release the locking clip and disconnect the wiring plug from the sensor on the top of the filter **(see illustration)**.

22 Undo the two retaining nuts and disconnect the the wiring loom mounting brackets from the top of the fuel filter housing **(see illustration)**.

23 Undo the retaining nuts/studs, and then remove the metal bracket from over the top of the fuel filter **(see illustrations)**.

24 Place a piece of cloth around the filter housing, under the fuel pipes to catch any spilt fuel **(see illustration)**.

25 Release the locking clip, then press down on the securing clip and release the fuel supply pipe from the top of the fuel filter **(see illustrations)**. Plug the opening to prevent contamination.

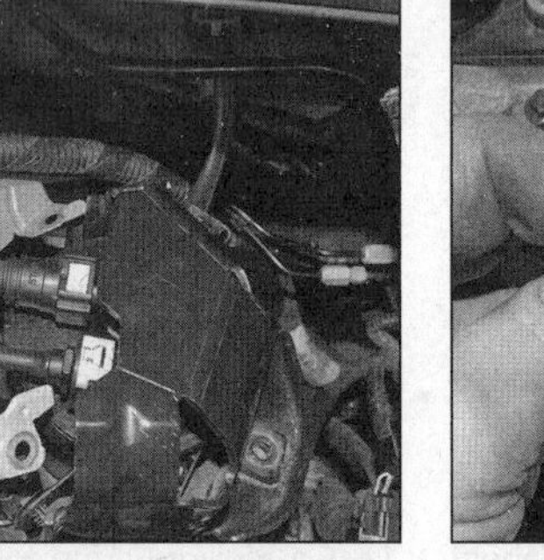
28.22 Disconnect the wiring loom brackets

28.23a Slacken and remove...

28.23b ...the retaining studs...

28.23c ...then remove the metal bracket

28.24 Place cloth around the filter housing

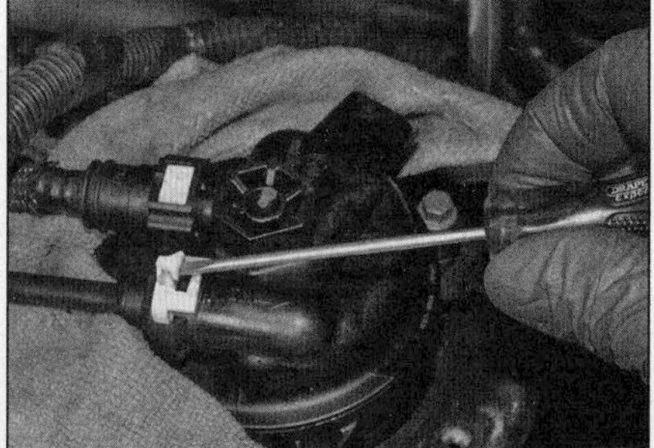
28.25a Release the locking clip...

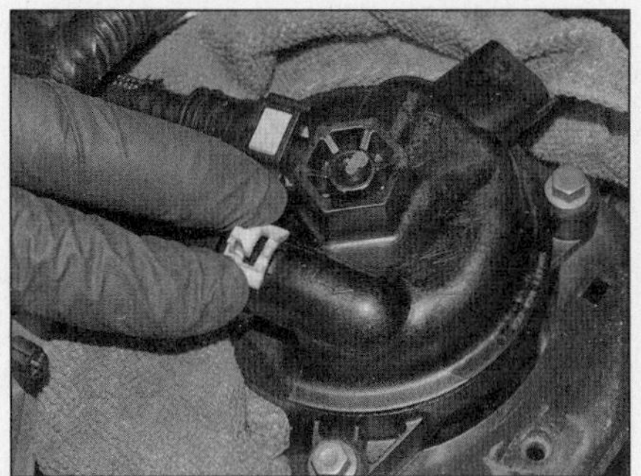

28.25b ...press down on the securing clip...

28.25c ...and disconnect the fuel supply pipe

28.25d Plug the end of the fuel pipe

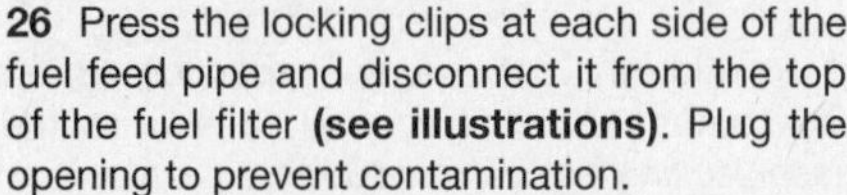

26 Press the locking clips at each side of the fuel feed pipe and disconnect it from the top of the fuel filter **(see illustrations)**. Plug the opening to prevent contamination.

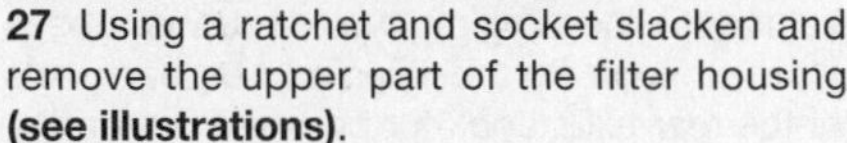

27 Using a ratchet and socket slacken and remove the upper part of the filter housing **(see illustrations)**.

28 Lift the old fuel filter element out from the lower housing **(see illustration)**.

29 If required, the fuel can be drained out from the lower housing by slackening the drain screw at the rear of the filter housing, as described in the water draining procedure. See Section 15.

30 Insert the new filter element into the lower housing, pressing it down fully into position.

31 If the lower part of the housing has been drained previously, after the new filter element is fitted, pour some clean diesel back into the lower housing, making sure it is not contaminated with dirt or water. This will aid the starting procedure, so that the system may not require bleeding.

32 Fit a new seal to the filter upper housing, making sure it is located correctly in the groove in the housing **(see illustration)**.

33 Refit the upper housing and tighten it until the stepped edge on the outer circumference of the upper housing contacts the stepped edge on the outer circumference of the lower housing **(see illustrations)**.

28.26a Release the locking clips to disconnect the fuel hose

28.26b Plug the end of the fuel pipe

28.27a Slacken the top of the fuel filter housing...

28.27b ...and unscrew it from the lower housing

28.28 Lift out the old filter element

28.32 Fit the new seal to the upper housing

28.33a Refit the upper housing...

28.33b ...until the stepped edges meet

29.2 Undo the 4 bolts securing the cover to the air cleaner housing

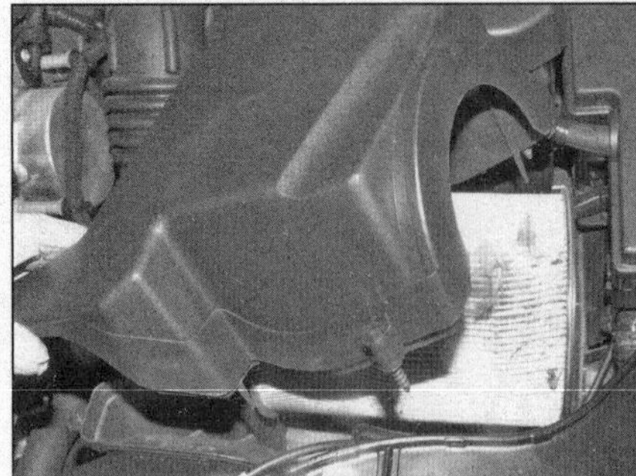
29.3 Lift the cover and remove the filter element

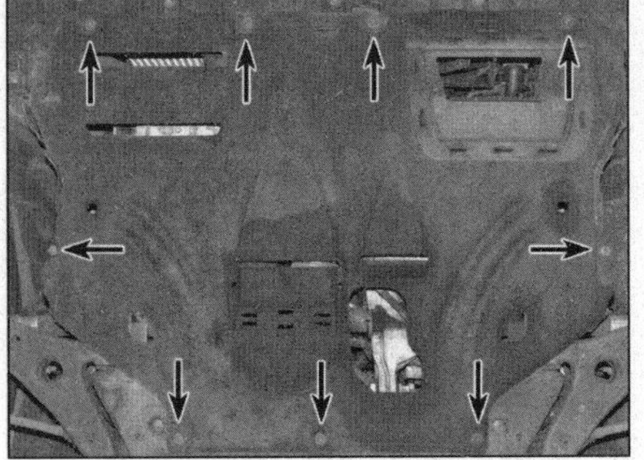
32.2 Undo the bolts and remove the undertray

32.4a Rotate the tensioner arm clockwise...

34 Refit the fuel supply and feed pipes to the top of the fuel filter housing, making sure the locking/securing clips hold the pipes in position securely.

35 Refit the upper metal bracket over the top of the fuel filter, refitting the wiring loom mounting brackets.

36 Reconnect the wiring connector to the sensor on the top of the fuel filter, making sure the locking clip is secured.

37 Refit the locating peg to the stud on the top of the filter housing and then refit the engine cover.

38 If necessary, bleed the fuel system as described in Chapter 4B Section 5.

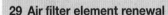

32.4b ...then insert a 4.0 mm drill bit/rod to lock it in place

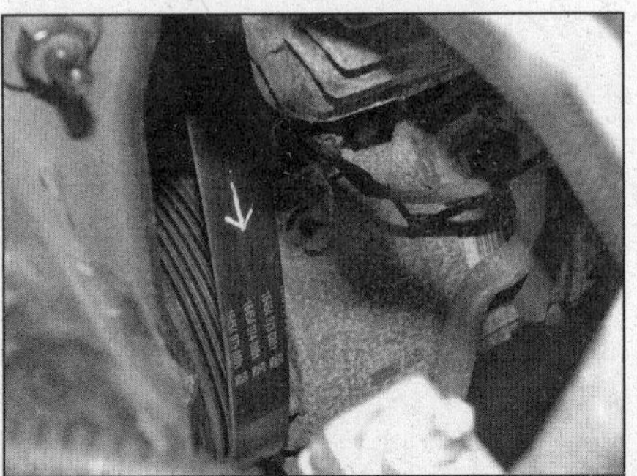
32.5 Note the belt's direction of movement

32.6 Undo the centre screw and remove the tensioner

29 Air filter element renewal

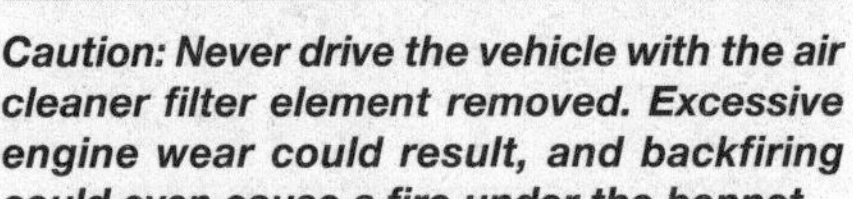

Caution: Never drive the vehicle with the air cleaner filter element removed. Excessive engine wear could result, and backfiring could even cause a fire under the bonnet.

1 The air filter element is located in the air cleaner assembly on the left-hand side of the engine compartment.

2 Undo the 4 bolts securing the cover to the air cleaner housing **(see illustration)**.

3 The cover can now be lifted, and the filter element removed **(see illustration)**.

4 Clean the filter housing and cover, removing any dirt or debris. A vacuum cleaner is ideal.

5 Position the new element in the filter housing with the locating tab downwards and refit the filter cover. Tighten the retaining bolts securely.

30 Braking system rubber hose check

1 Position the car over an inspection pit, on car ramps, or jack it up one wheel at a time (see *Jacking and vehicle support*).

2 Inspect the braking system rubber hoses fitted to each front caliper, and on each side of the rear axle. Look for perished, swollen or hardened rubber, and any signs of cracking, especially at the metal end fittings. If there's any doubt as to the condition of any hose, renew it as described in Chapter 9 Section 4.

31 Timing belt renewal

1 Refer to the procedures contained in Chapter 2B Section 7 or Chapter 2C Section 5.

32 Auxiliary drivebelt and tensioner renewal

Removal

1 Slacken the right-hand front roadwheel nuts, apply the parking brake, then jack up the front of the vehicle and support it securely on axle stands (see *Jacking and vehicle support*). Remove the right-hand roadwheel.

2 Undo the retaining bolts and remove the engine undertray **(see illustration)**.

3 Pull back the front wheelarch liner as described in Chapter 11 Section 39.

4 Engage a socket with the tensioner, then rotate the tensioner arm clockwise to release the belt tension. Insert a 4.0 mm diameter drill bit or rod through the hole in the tensioner arm, and engage with hole in tensioner body to lock arm **(see illustrations)**. It is useful to have a small mirror available to enable the alignment of the locking holes to be more easily seen in the limited space available.

5 Note how the drivebelt is routed, then remove the belt from the pulleys. Note that if the belt is to be re-used, mark the direction of rotation **(see illustration)**. The belt must be refitted the same way round.

6 To remove the tensioner, undo the retaining screw in the centre of the tensioner mount and manoeuvre from place **(see illustration)**.

Refitting

7 To refit the tensioner, engage the locating tab **(see illustration)** with the hole in the engine casting and retighten the central screw.

8 Fit the belt around the pulleys, ensuring that the ribs on the belt are correctly engaged with the grooves in the pulleys and the drivebelt is correctly routed.

9 Using a socket, hold the tensioner arm so that the locking drill bit/rod can be removed, then release the pressure so that the automatic tensioner takes up the slack in the drivebelt.

10 Refit the wheelarch liner and engine undertray. Refit the roadwheel then lower the vehicle to the ground and tighten the wheel nuts to the specified torque.

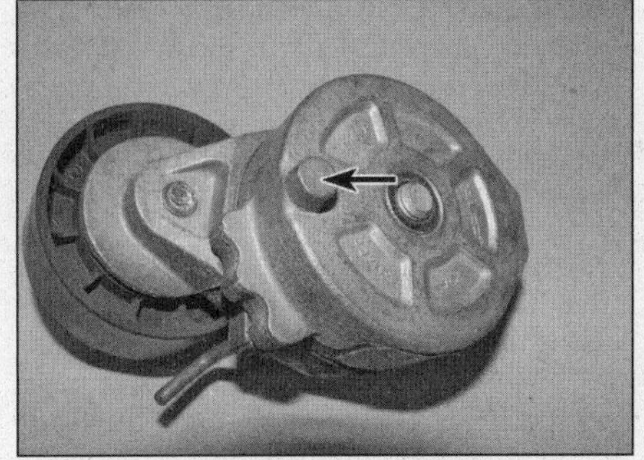

32.7 Make sure the locating tab is in the right place

34.2 Unscrew and remove the filler/level plug

33 Brake fluid renewal

Warning: Brake hydraulic fluid can harm your eyes and damage painted surfaces, so use extreme caution when handling and pouring it. Do not use fluid that has been standing open for some time, as it absorbs moisture from the air. Excess moisture can cause a dangerous loss of braking effectiveness.

1 The procedure is similar to that for bleeding the hydraulic system as described in Chapter 9 Section 3, except that allowance should be made for the old fluid to be expelled when bleeding each section of the circuit.

2 Working as described in Chapter 9 Section 3, open the first bleed screw in the sequence, and pump the brake pedal gently until the level in the reservoir is approaching the MIN mark. Top-up to the MAX level with new fluid, and continue pumping until only new fluid remains in the reservoir, and new fluid can be seen emerging from the bleed screw. Tighten the screw, and top the reservoir level up to the MAX level line.

3 Work through all the remaining bleed screws in the sequence until new fluid can be seen at all of them. Be careful to keep the master cylinder reservoir topped-up above the MIN level at all times, or air may enter the system. If this happens, further bleeding will be required, to remove the air.

4 When the operation is complete, check that all bleed screws are securely tightened, and that their dust caps are refitted. Wash off all traces of spilt fluid, and recheck the master cylinder reservoir fluid level.

5 Check that pedal travel is comparable with its pre-bled state before taking the car on the road.

34 Manual transmission oil level check

1 Position the car over an inspection pit, on car ramps, or jack it up and support it on axle stands(see *Jacking and vehicle support*), but make sure that it is level. Where fitted, undo the retaining bolts and remove the engine undertray.

2 Remove all traces of dirt, then unscrew the filler/level plug from the side of the transmission **(see illustration)**.

3 The level must be just below the bottom edge of the filler/level plug hole (use a cranked tool such as an Allen key to check the level). If necessary, top-up the level with the specified grade of oil (see *Lubricants and fluids*) until the oil just starts to run out. Allow any excess oil to flow out until the level stabilises.

4 When the level is correct, clean and refit the filler/level plug, then tighten it to the specified torque.

5 Where applicable, refit the engine undertray, then lower the car to the ground.

35.2 Squeeze the tabs to release the cover

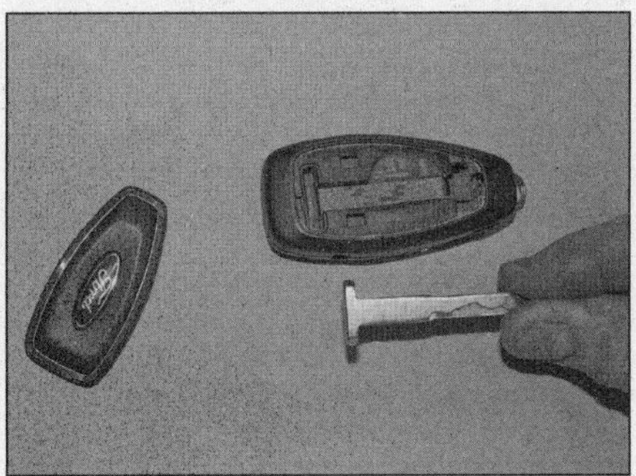

35.3 Take out the key blade from the housing

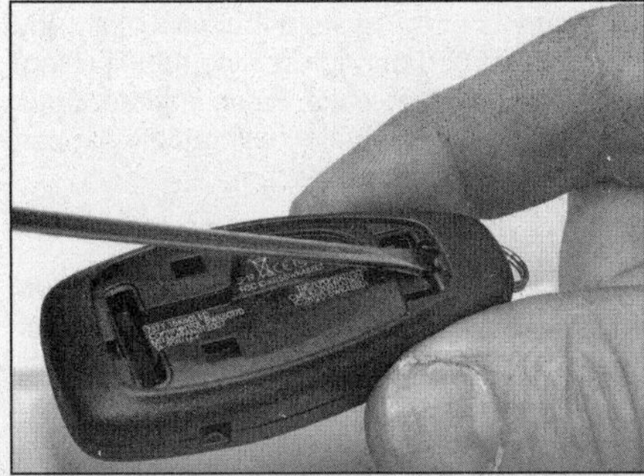

35.4 Use a screwdriver to prise open the housing

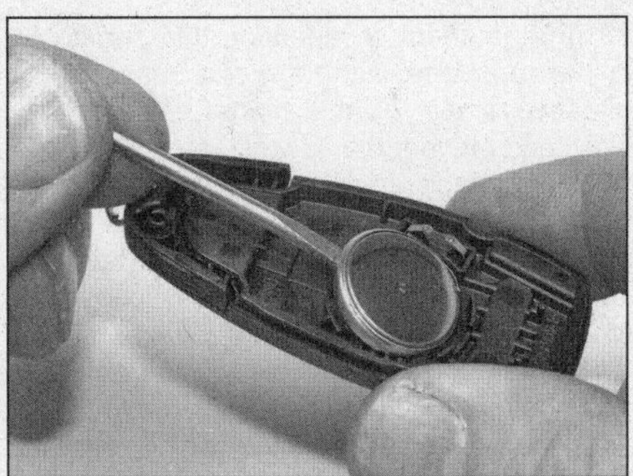

35.5 Use a screwdriver to lift out the battery

35 Remote control battery renewal

Note: *All the remote control units described below are fitted with a type CR 2032, 3 volt battery.*

1 Although not in the Ford maintenance schedule, we recommend that the battery is changed every 2 years, regardless of the vehicle's mileage. However, if the door locks repeatedly fail to respond to signals from the remote control at the normal distance, change the battery in the remote control before attempting to troubleshoot any of the vehicle's other systems.

2 Depress the two tabs on the side of the transmitter unit and carefully lift off the cover **(see illustration)**.

3 Remove the key blade from the transmitter unit **(see illustration)**.

4 Use a small flat-bladed the screwdriver to separate the 2 halves of the unit **(see illustration)**.

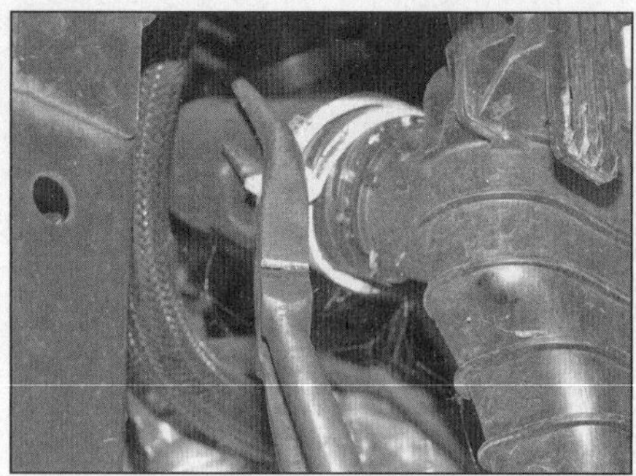
36.5 Release the clamp and disconnect the bottom hose

5 Note the fitted position of the battery (positive side down), then prise the battery from its location, and insert the new one. Avoid touching the battery or the terminals with bare fingers **(see illustration)**.

6 Snap the 2 halves of the transmitter together, place the key blade in position and refit the cover.

36 Coolant strength check and renewal

Warning: Do not allow antifreeze to come in contact with your skin or painted surfaces of the vehicle. Flush contaminated areas immediately with plenty of water. Don't store new coolant, or leave old coolant lying around, where it's accessible to children or pets – they're attracted by its sweet smell. Ingestion of even a small amount of coolant can be fatal. Wipe up garage-floor and drip-pan spills immediately. Keep antifreeze containers covered, and repair cooling system leaks as soon as they're noticed.

Warning: Never remove the expansion tank filler cap when the engine is running, or has just been switched off, as the cooling system will be hot, and the consequent escaping steam and scalding coolant could cause serious injury.

Warning: Wait until the engine is cold before starting these procedures.

Strength check

1 Use a hydrometer to check the strength of the antifreeze. Follow the instructions provided with your hydrometer. The antifreeze strength should be approximately 50%. If it is significantly less than this, drain a little coolant from the radiator (see this Section), add antifreeze to the coolant expansion tank, then run the engine for a time in order to mix the new coolant before re-testing.

Coolant draining

2 To drain the system, first remove the expansion tank filler cap.

3 Apply the handbrake, then jack up the front of the vehicle and support it securely on axle stands (see *Jacking and vehicle support*). Where applicable, release the fasteners and remove the engine undershield.

4 Place a suitable container beneath the right-hand side of the radiator.

5 Release the retaining clamp and disconnect the bottom hose from the radiator **(see illustration)**. Allow the coolant to drain into the container.

6 Once the coolant has stopped draining from the radiator, reconnect the bottom hose and secure with the retaining clamp.

System flushing

7 With time, the cooling system may gradually lose its efficiency, as the radiator core becomes choked with rust, scale deposits from the water, and other sediment. To minimise this, as well as using only good-quality antifreeze and clean soft water, the system should be flushed as follows whenever any part of it is disturbed, and/or when the coolant is renewed.

8 With the coolant drained, refit the radiator bottom hose and refill the system with fresh water. Refit the expansion tank filler cap, start the engine and warm it up to normal operating temperature, then stop it and (after allowing it to cool down completely) drain the system again. Repeat as necessary until only clean water can be seen to emerge, then refill finally with the specified coolant mixture.

9 If only clean, soft water and good-quality antifreeze (even if not to Ford's specification) has been used, and the coolant has been renewed at the suggested intervals, the above procedure will be sufficient to keep the system clean for a considerable length of time. If, however, the system has been neglected, a more thorough operation will be required, as follows.

10 First drain the coolant, then disconnect the radiator top hose. Insert a garden hose into the radiator top hose connection, and allow water to circulate through the radiator until it runs clean from the bottom outlet.

11 To flush the engine, insert the garden hose into the radiator bottom hose, wrap a piece of rag around the garden hose to seal the connection, and allow water to circulate until it runs clear.

12 Try the effect of repeating this procedure in the top hose, although this may not be effective, since the thermostat will probably close and prevent the flow of water.

13 In severe cases of contamination, reverse-flushing of the radiator may be necessary. This may be achieved by inserting the garden hose into the bottom outlet, wrapping a piece of rag around the hose to seal the connection, then flushing the radiator until clear water emerges from the top hose outlet.

14 If the radiator is suspected of being severely choked, remove the radiator (Chapter 3 Section 6), turn it upside-down, and repeat the procedure described in paragraph 13.

15 Flushing the heater matrix can be achieved using a similar procedure to that described in paragraph 13, once the heater inlet and outlet hoses have been identified. These two hoses will be of the same diameter, and pass through the engine compartment bulkhead.

16 The use of chemical cleaners is not recommended, and should be necessary only as a last resort; the scouring action of some chemical cleaners may lead to other cooling system problems. Normally, regular renewal of the coolant will prevent excessive contamination of the system.

Coolant filling

17 With the cooling system drained and flushed, ensure that all disturbed hose unions are correctly secured. If it was raised, lower the vehicle to the ground.

18 Set the heater temperature control to maximum heat, but ensure the blower is turned off.

19 Prepare a sufficient quantity of the specified coolant mixture (see below); allow for a surplus, so as to have a reserve supply for topping-up.

20 Slowly fill the system through the expansion tank. Since the tank is the highest point in the system, all the air in the system should be displaced into the tank by the rising liquid. Slow pouring reduces the possibility of air being trapped and forming airlocks.

21 Continue filling until the coolant level reaches the expansion tank MAX level line, then refit the filler cap.

22 Start the engine and run it at 2000 rpm for 3 minutes.

23 Stop the engine, check the coolant level and top-up to the MAX level line.

24 Restart the engine, run it at 2000 rpm for approximately 13 minutes until it reaches normal operating temperature.

25 Raise the engine speed to 3000 rpm for approximately 5 seconds, then lower it to 2000 rpm for a further 15 minutes.

26 Stop the engine, then leave the car to cool down completely (overnight, if possible).

27 With the system cool, open the expansion tank, and top-up the tank to the MAX level line. Refit the filler cap, tightening it securely, and clean up any spillage.

28 After refilling, always check carefully all components of the system (but especially any unions disturbed during draining and flushing) for signs of coolant leaks. Fresh antifreeze has a searching action, which will rapidly expose any weak points in the system.

Antifreeze type and mixture

Caution: Do not use engine antifreeze in the windscreen/tailgate washer system, as it will damage the vehicle's paintwork. A screenwash additive should be added to the washer system in its maker's recommended quantities.

29 If the vehicle's history (and therefore the quality of the antifreeze in it) is unknown,

owners are advised to drain and thoroughly reverse-flush the system, before refilling with fresh coolant mixture.

30 If the antifreeze used is to Ford's specification, the levels of protection it affords are indicated in the coolant packaging.

31 To give the recommended standard mixture ratio for antifreeze, 50% (by volume) of antifreeze must be mixed with 50% of clean, soft water; if you are using any other type of antifreeze, follow its manufacturer's instructions to achieve the correct ratio.

32 You are unlikely to fully drain the system at any one time (unless the engine is being completely stripped), and the capacities quoted in the Specifications are therefore slightly academic for routine coolant renewal. As a guide, only two-thirds of the system's total capacity is likely to be needed for coolant renewal.

33 As the drained system will be partially filled with flushing water, in order to establish the recommended mixture ratio, measure out 50% of the system capacity in antifreeze and pour it into the hose/expansion tank as described above, then top-up with water. Any topping-up while refilling the system should be done with a suitable mixture.

34 Before adding antifreeze, the cooling system should be drained, preferably flushed, and all hoses checked for condition and security. As noted earlier, fresh antifreeze will rapidly find any weaknesses in the system.

35 After filling with antifreeze, a label should be attached to the expansion tank, stating the type and concentration of antifreeze used, and the date installed. Any subsequent topping-up should be made with the same type and concentration of antifreeze.

General cooling system checks

36 The engine should be cold for the cooling system checks, so perform the following procedure before driving the vehicle, or after it has been shut off for at least three hours.

37 Remove the expansion tank filler cap, and clean it thoroughly inside and out with a rag. Also clean the filler neck on the expansion tank. The presence of rust or corrosion in the filler neck indicates that the coolant should be changed. The coolant inside the expansion tank should be relatively clean and transparent. If it is rust-coloured, drain and flush the system, and refill with a fresh coolant mixture.

38 Carefully check the radiator hoses and heater hoses along their entire length; renew any hose which is cracked, swollen or deteriorated.

39 Inspect all other cooling system components (joint faces, etc) for leaks. A leak in the cooling system will usually show up as white- or antifreeze-coloured deposits on the area adjoining the leak. Where any problems of this nature are found on system components, renew the component or gasket with reference to Chapter 3.

Airlocks

40 If, after draining and refilling the system, symptoms of overheating are found which did not occur previously, then the fault is almost certainly due to trapped air at some point in the system, causing an airlock and restricting the flow of coolant; usually, the air is trapped because the system was refilled too quickly.

41 If an airlock is suspected, first try gently squeezing all visible coolant hoses. A coolant hose which is full of air feels quite different to one full of coolant when squeezed. After refilling the system, most airlocks will clear once the system has cooled, and been topped-up.

42 While the engine is running at operating temperature, switch on the heater and heater fan, and check for heat output. Provided there is sufficient coolant in the system, lack of heat output could be due to an airlock in the system.

43 Airlocks can have more serious effects than simply reducing heater output – a severe airlock could reduce coolant flow around the engine. Check that the radiator top hose is hot when the engine is at operating temperature – a top hose which stays cold could be the result of an airlock (or a non-opening thermostat).

44 If the problem persists, stop the engine and allow it to cool down completely, before unscrewing the expansion tank filler cap or loosening the hose clips and squeezing the hoses to bleed out the trapped air. In the worst case, the system will have to be at least partially drained (this time, the coolant can be saved for re-use) and flushed to clear the problem. If all else fails, have the system evacuated and vacuum filled by a suitably-equipped garage.

Expansion tank cap check

45 Wait until the engine is completely cold – perform this check before the engine is started for the first time in the day.

46 Place a wad of cloth over the expansion tank cap, then unscrew it slowly and remove it.

47 Examine the condition of the rubber seal on the underside of the cap. If the rubber appears to have hardened, or cracks are visible in the seal edges, a new cap should be fitted.

48 If the car is several years old, or has covered a large mileage, consider renewing the cap regardless of its apparent condition – they are not expensive. If the pressure relief valve built into the cap fails, excess pressure in the system will lead to puzzling failures of hoses and other cooling system components.

37 Reset service indicator

1 Close all doors.

2 Turn the ignition key to stage 2, or hold the start button in for 2 seconds, without touching any pedal.

3 Hold down the accelerator and brake pedals for at least 20 seconds until a "Service: Oil reset in prog." message is displayed on the instrument cluster.

4 Continue holding the accelerator and brake pedals until the display says "Service: Oil reset complete".

5 At this point the oil change reminder indicator will extinguish. This confirms that the procedure has been correctly completed.

Chapter 2 Part A
1.5 litre petrol engine in-car repair procedures

Contents

Degrees of difficulty

Easy, suitable for novice with little experience 

Fairly easy, suitable for beginner with some experience 

Fairly difficult, suitable for competent DIY mechanic 

Difficult, suitable for experienced DIY mechanic

Very difficult, suitable for expert DIY or professional 

Specifications

Engine (general)

Capacity	1498cc
Engine codes	BNMA, M8MA, M8MB, M8MC, M9MA, M9MB, M9MC, M9MD
Bore	79.00 mm
Stroke	76.40 mm
No.1 cylinder location	Right-hand (auxiliary belt) end
Direction of crankshaft rotation	Clockwise (viewed from the right-hand side of vehicle)
Compression ratio	10.1 : 1
Compression:	
Pressure	8.0 bar approximately
Maximum difference between cylinders	3.0 bar

Camshafts

Drive	Chain

Lubrication system

Oil pump type	Gear type, chain-driven off the crankshaft
Minimum oil pressure at 80°C (with correct oil level)	0.99 bars

Lubrication system

Oil pressure (minimum temp of 80°):	
Idling (800 rpm)	1.0 bar
At 2000 rpm	2.0 bars
Oil pressure relief valve opening pressure	4 ± 0.4 bar

Torque wrench settings

	Nm	lbf ft
Air conditioning compressor mounting bolts	25	18
Alternator mounting nuts	48	35
Auxiliary drivebelt tensioner bolts	48	35
Camshaft bearing cap:		
Stage 1 (bolts 1-16)	7	5
Stage 2 (bolts1-16)	Angle-tighten a further 45°	
Stage 3 (bolts 17 and 18)	10	7
Stage 4 (bolts 17 and 18)	Angle-tighten a further 70°	
Stage 5 (bolts 19 and 20)	10	7
Stage 6 (bolts 19 and 20)	Angle-tighten a further 53°	
Camshaft position sensor	10	7
Coolant outlet to cylinder head	10	7
Coolant outlet on cylinder block	18	14
Coolant pump pulley bolts	24	17
Crankcase breather to cylinder block	10	7
Crankshaft position sensor	8	6
Crankshaft oil seal carrier	10	7
Crankshaft pulley/vibration damper: *		
Stage 1	100	74
Stage 2	Angle-tighten a further 90°	
Stage 3	Wait 20 seconds	
Stage 4	Angle-tighten a further 15°	
Cylinder head bolts: *		
Stage 1	5	3
Stage 2	15	11
Stage 3	35	26
Stage 4	Angle-tighten a further 90°	
Stage 5	Angle-tighten a further 90°	
Cylinder head cover	10	7
Driveshaft support bracket to engine block bolts	48	35
Driveshaft bearing support nuts:		
Stage 1	6	4
Stage 2	25	18
Engine mountings:		
Left-hand mounting nuts	48	35
Left-hand mounting bracket to transmission	82	60
Left-hand mounting centre bolt*	148	109
Lower-rear torque rod bolts:		
On transmission	63	46
On subframe:		
Stage 1	30	22
Stage 2	Angle-tighten a further 270°	
Right-hand mounting retaining bolts	90	66
Right-hand mounting bracket-to-engine nuts	80	59
Exhaust flexible section-to-catalytic converter nuts	48	35
Exhaust manifold nuts/bolts	21	15
Flywheel bolts: *		
Stage 1	15	11
Stage 2	25	18
Stage 3	30	22
Stage 4	Angle-tighten a further 90°	
Fuel pump bolts	13	10
Fuel pump high pressure fuel lines:		
Stage 1	21	15
Stage 2	Wait 5 minutes	
Stage 3	21	15
Fuel pump housing bolts:		
Stage 1 (bolts 1-10)	3	2
Stage 2 (bolts 1-10)	9	7
Stage 3 (bolts 1-10)	11	8
Stage 4 (bolts 1,2,5,6,7,8,9,10 only)	14	10
Fuel pump housing bolts	10	7
Fuel rail bolts	23	17
Inlet manifold:		
Lower bolts	10	7
Upper bolts	18	13
Oil baffle to cylinder block	9	7

Torque wrench settings (continued)	Nm	lbf ft
Oil drain plug	27	21
Oil filter connector (cooler)	55	41
Oil intake pipe to oil baffle	9	7
Oil pressure switch	15	11
Oil pump to cylinder block	9	7
Sump bolts:		
Sump-to-block bolts	19	14
Sump-to-transmission bolts	47	35
TDC pin hole blanking plug	20	15
Timing belt cover bolts	10	7
Timing belt tensioner bolt	25	15
Turbocharger oil pipe banjo bolts*	20	15
Vacuum pump housing	10	7

** Use new fasteners*

1 General information

Engine description

1 This Part of Chapter 2 describes those repair procedures that can reasonably be carried out on the engine while it remains in the car. If the engine has been removed from the car and is being dismantled as described in Part D, any preliminary dismantling procedures can be ignored.

2 Note that, while it may be possible physically to overhaul items such as the piston/connecting rod assemblies while the engine is in the car, such tasks are not usually carried out as separate operations. Usually, several additional procedures (not to mention the cleaning of components and oilways) have to be carried out. For this reason, all such tasks are classed as major overhaul procedures, and are described in Part D of this Chapter.

3 Part D describes the removal of the engine/transmission unit from the vehicle, and the full overhaul procedures that can then be carried out.

4 The engine is a sixteen-valve, double overhead camshaft (DOHC), four-cylinder, in-line unit. The engine is mounted transversely at the front of the car, with the transmission on its left-hand end.

5 Apart from the plastic timing belt covers, plastic cylinder head cover, plastic inlet manifold, and the cast-iron cylinder liners, the main engine components (including the sump) are manufactured entirely of aluminium alloy.

6 The crankshaft runs in five main bearings, the centre main bearing's upper half incorporating thrustwashers to control crankshaft endfloat. Due to the very fine bearing clearances and bearing shell tolerances incorporated during manufacture, it is not possible to renew the crankshaft separate to the cylinder block; in fact it is not possible to remove and refit the crankshaft accurately using conventional tooling. This means that if the crankshaft is worn excessively, it must be renewed together with the cylinder block.

Caution: Do not unbolt the main bearing cap/ladder from the cylinder block, as it is not possible to refit it accurately using conventional tooling. Additionally, the manufacturers do not supply torque settings for the main bearing cap/ladder retaining bolts.

7 The connecting rods rotate on horizontally-split bearing shells at their big-ends, however the big-ends are of unusual design in that the caps are sheared from the rods during manufacture thus making each cap individually matched to its own connecting rod. The big-end bearing shells are also unusual in that they do not have any locating tabs and must be accurately positioned during refitting. The pistons are attached to the connecting rods by gudgeon pins which are an interference fit in the connecting rod small-end eyes. The aluminium alloy pistons are fitted with three piston rings: two compression rings and an oil control ring. After manufacture, the cylinder bores and pistons are measured and classified into three grades, which must be carefully matched together, to ensure the correct piston/cylinder clearance; no oversizes are available to permit reboring.

8 The inlet and exhaust valves are each closed by coil springs; they operate in guides which are shrink-fitted into the cylinder head, as are the valve seat inserts.

9 Both camshafts are driven by the same toothed timing belt, each operating eight valves via bucket tappets. Each camshaft rotates in five bearings that are line-bored directly in the cylinder head and the (bolted-on) bearing caps; this means that the bearing caps are not available separately from the cylinder head, and must not be interchanged with caps from another engine.

10 All engines feature variable valve timing on the both the inlet and exhaust camshafts. Engine oil pressure is used to vary the positions of the camshaft sprocket in relation to the camshafts, thus varying the valves' opening and closing times. Control of the oil flow is achieved using solenoid valves, which in turn are controlled by the engine management electronic control module (ECM). Varying the valve timing is this manner results in improved driveability and output, whist reducing fuel consumption and exhaust emissions.

11 The coolant pump is bolted to the right-hand end of the cylinder block, beneath the front run of the timing belt, and is driven by the auxiliary drivebelt from the crankshaft pulley.

12 Lubrication is by means of a variable output vane type oil pump. The output of the oil pump can be altered by adjusting the outer ring of the pump, so that the output can be matched to the engines demands. Use of a variable output oil pump can reduce mechanical loss in the engine by up to 10%. The oil pump is mounted on the crankshaft right-hand end, and draws oil through a strainer located in the sump. The pump forces oil through an externally-mounted full-flow spin-on-type filter.

Operations with engine in the car

13 The following work can be carried out with the engine in the car:

a) Cylinder head cover – removal and refitting.
b) Timing belt – renewal.
c) Timing belt tensioner and sprockets – removal and refitting.
d) Camshaft oil seals – renewal.
e) Camshafts, tappets and shims – removal and refitting.
f) Cylinder head – removal and refitting.
g) Sump – removal and refitting.
h) Crankshaft oil seals – renewal.
i) Oil pump – removal and refitting.
j) Flywheel/driveplate – removal and refitting.
k) Engine/transmission mountings – removal and refitting.

2.3 Fuel pump fuse 56 – upper left-hand side fuse

2 Compression test – description and interpretation

1 When engine performance is down, or if misfiring occurs which cannot be attributed to the ignition or fuel systems, a compression test can provide diagnostic clues as to the engine's condition. If the test is performed regularly, it can give warning of trouble before any other symptoms become apparent.
2 The engine must be fully warmed-up to operating temperature, the oil level must be correct and the battery must be fully-charged. The help of an assistant will also be required.
3 Remove fuse number 56 from the passenger compartment fusebox, which is located behind the glovebox **(see illustration)**. This is the fuse for the fuel pump – further details are to be found in Section 4A Section 6. Now start the engine and allow it to run until it stalls.
4 Disable the ignition system by disconnecting the multiplugs from the individual ignition coils. Remove all ignition coils and the spark plugs with reference to Chapter 6A Section 7.
5 Remove all the spark plugs with reference to Chapter 1A Section 26.
6 Fit a compression tester to the No 1 cylinder spark plug hole – the type of tester which screws into the spark plug thread is preferable.
7 Arrange for an assistant to hold the accelerator pedal fully depressed to the floor, while at the same time cranking the engine over for several seconds on the starter motor. Observe the compression gauge reading. The compression will build-up fairly quickly in a healthy engine. Low compression on the first stroke, followed by gradually-increasing pressure on successive strokes, indicates worn piston rings. A low compression on the first stroke which does not rise on successive strokes, indicates leaking valves or a blown head gasket (a cracked cylinder head could also be the cause). Deposits on the underside of the valve heads can also cause low compression. Record the highest gauge reading obtained, then repeat the procedure for the remaining cylinders.
8 Due to the variety of testers available, and the fluctuation in starter motor speed when cranking the engine, different readings are often obtained when carrying out the compression test. For this reason, actual compression pressure figures are not quoted by Ford. However, the most important factor is that the compression pressures are uniform in all cylinders, and that is what this test is mainly concerned with.
9 Add some engine oil (about three squirts from a plunger type oil can) to each cylinder through the spark plug holes, and then repeat the test.
10 If the compression increases after the oil is added, the piston rings are probably worn. If the compression does not increase significantly, the leakage is occurring at the valves or the head gasket. Leakage past the valves may be caused by burned valve seats and/or faces, or warped, cracked or bent valves.
11 If two adjacent cylinders have equally low compressions, it is most likely that the head gasket has blown between them. The appearance of coolant in the combustion chambers or on the engine oil dipstick would verify this condition.
12 If one cylinder is about 20 percent lower than the other, and the engine has a slightly rough idle, a worn lobe on the camshaft could be the cause.
13 On completion of the checks, refit the spark plugs and reconnect the ignition coils. Refit the fuel pump relay to the fusebox.

3.13 Screw-in the timing pin

3 Top Dead Centre (TDC) for No 1 piston – locating

1 Top dead centre (TDC) is the highest point of the cylinder that each piston reaches as the crankshaft turns. Each piston reaches its TDC position at the end of its compression stroke, and then again at the end of its exhaust stroke. For the purpose of engine timing, TDC on the compression stroke for No 1 piston is used. No 1 cylinder is at the timing belt end of the engine. Proceed as follows.
2 Disconnect the battery negative (earth) lead and remove the spark plugs as described in Chapter 5 Section 4 and Chapter 1A Section 26.
3 Apply the handbrake, then jack up the front of the vehicle and support it on axle stands (see *Jacking and vehicle support*).
4 Undo the fasteners and remove the engine undershield. Remove the wheel arch liner, and auxiliary drivebelt lower cover (where fitted) for access to the crankshaft pulley and bolt.
5 Remove the engine cover.
6 Position a trolley jack under the engine. Use a block of wood on the jack head to spread the load and prevent damage to the sump. Take the weight of the engine.
7 Make alignment marks between the right-hand engine mounting bracket and the cylinder head bracket/vehicle body, then undo the nuts/bolts and remove the mounting. Discard the nuts – new ones must be fitted.
8 Slacken the 4 mounting bolts on the coolant pump pulley and then remove the auxiliary drivebelt as described in Chapter 1A Section 30.
9 Remove the coolant pump pulley and then remove the timing belt cover as described in Section 9.
10 To fit the TDC locating tool remove the right-hand drive shaft as described in Chapter 8 Section 7.
11 Remove the engine mounted section of the support bracket and then remove the blanking plug from the engine block.
12 Rotate the crankshaft pulley clockwise until the marks on the camshaft variable valve timing (VVT) units are approaching the 11 o'clock position.
13 A TDC timing pin must now be inserted and tightened into the hole **(see illustration)**. It is highly recommended that the Ford timing pin 303-748 is obtained, or alternatively, a timing pin from a reputable tool manufacturer such as Draper or AST.
14 With the timing pin in position, turn the crankshaft slowly clockwise until the specially machined surface on the crank web just touches the timing pin. No 1 piston is now at TDC on its compression stroke.
15 With the engine at TDC fit Ford special tool 303-1097 over the VVT units on the ends of the camshafts (similar tools are available from other outlets). Note that the tool is marked with a line to indicate the exhaust side, a dot to indicate the inlet side, and an arrow which must point upwards **(see illustration)**.
16 Once the work requiring the TDC setting

3.15 Fit the special tool over the VVT units

has been completed, remove the special tool from the camshaft VVT units then unscrew the timing pin and refit the blanking plug.

17 Refit the remaining components in reverse order of removal.

4 Variable valve timing control solenoids – removal and refitting

Removal

1 Pull up and remove the engine cover.

2 The valve timing solenoids are positioned at the top right-hand end of the cylinder head cover **(see illustration)**.

3 Disconnect the wiring plug for each solenoid.

4 Undo the retaining bolt for each solenoid, and manoeuvre from place **(see illustration)**.

Refitting

5 Refitting is a reversal of removal.

5 Valve clearances – checking and adjustment

1 Remove the cylinder head cover as described in Section 6.

Note: *If checking the valve clearances with the timing belt removed (eg, after refitting the camshafts), rotate the crankshaft 90° anti-clockwise back from TDC on No 1 cylinder so the pistons are halfway down the cylinder bores. Verify this by inserting a long screwdriver down the spark plug holes.*

2 Remove the spark plugs (Chapter 1A Section 26) in order to make turning the engine easier. On all vehicles (ie with manual or automatic transmissions), the engine may be turned using a spanner on the crankshaft pulley bolt. On cars with a manual transmission, you can raise the front right-hand roadwheel clear of the ground, engage top gear and turn the wheel. If the former method is used, jack up and support the front of the car (see *Jacking and vehicle support*) then unbolt the lower cover for access to the pulley bolt; if the latter method is used, apply the handbrake then jack up the front right-hand side of the car until the roadwheel is clear of the ground and support with an axle stand.

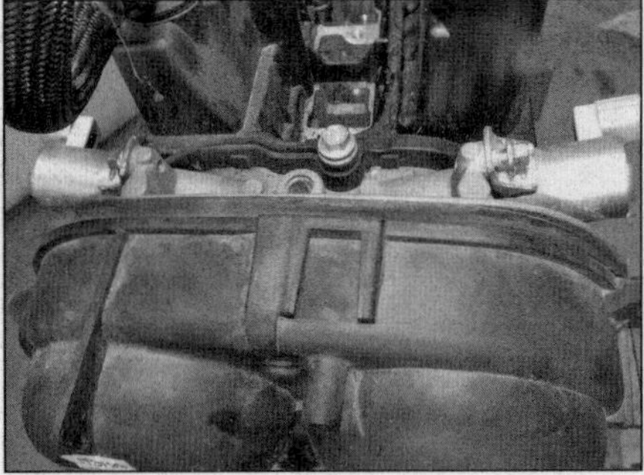

4.2 The solenoids are at the right-hand end of the engine

4.4 Remove the bolt to release each solenoid

3 Draw the valve positions on a piece of paper, numbering them 1 to 8 inlet and exhaust, from the timing belt (right-hand) end of the engine (ie, 1E, 1I, 2E, 2I and so on). As there are two inlet and two exhaust valves for each cylinder, draw the cylinders as large circles and the four valves as smaller circles. The inlet valves are at the front of the cylinder head, and the exhaust valves are at the rear. As the valve clearances are adjusted, cross them off.

4 Turn the engine in a clockwise direction until both inlet valves of No 1 cylinder are fully shut and the apex of the camshaft lobes are pointing upwards away from the valve positions.

5 Insert a feeler blade of the correct thickness (see Section) between the heel of the camshaft lobe and the tappet **(see illustration)**. It should be a firm sliding fit. If this is the case, the clearance is correct and the valve position can be crossed off. If the clearance is not correct, use feeler blades to determine the exact clearance and record this on the drawing. From this clearance it will be possible to calculate the thickness of the new tappet to be fitted. Note that no shims are fitted between the camshaft and tappet – the complete tappet must be renewed.

6 Check the clearance of the second inlet valve for No 1 cylinder, and if necessary record the existing clearance on the drawing.

7 Now turn the engine until the inlet valves of No 2 cylinder are fully shut and the camshaft lobes pointing away from the valve positions. Check the clearances as described previously, and record any that are incorrect.

8 After checking all of the inlet valve clearances, check the exhaust valve clearances in the same way, but note that the clearances are different.

9 Where adjustment is required, it is necessary to remove the camshafts as described in Section 14.

10 If the recorded clearance was too small, a thinner tappet must be fitted, and conversely if the clearance was too large, a thicker tappet must be fitted. To calculate the thickness of the new tappet, first use a micrometer to measure the thickness of the existing tappet (C) and add this to the measured clearance (B) **(see illustrations)**. Deduct the desired clearance (A) to provide the thickness (D) of the new tappet. The thickness of the tappet should be etched on the downward facing surface, however this is only the digits after the decimal point, not the total thickness of the tappet. Use a micrometer to measure the total thickness and verify the marked thickness. The formula is as follows.

11 New tappet thickness D = Existing tappet thickness C + Measured clearance B – Desired clearance A

Sample calculation

Desired clearance (A) = 0.20
Measured clearance (B) = 0.15
Existing tappet thickness (C) = 2.725
Tappet thickness required (D) = C+B-A = 2.675
All measurements in mm

12 The tappets are available in varying thicknesses in increments of 0.025 mm.

5.5 Insert a feeler gauge between the heel of the camshaft lobe and the tappet

5.10a Measure the thickness of the tappets with a micrometer

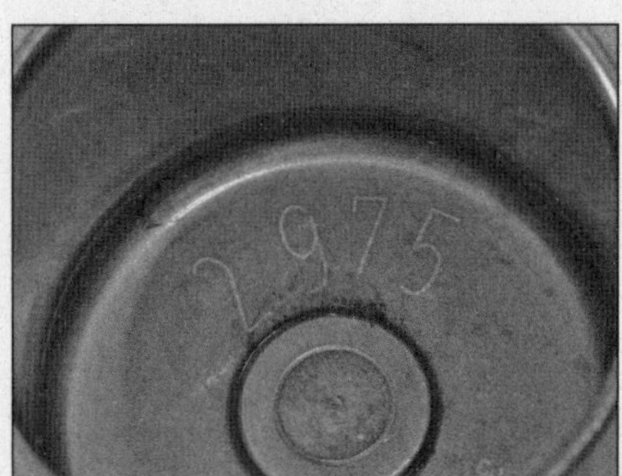

5.10b The thickness of each tappet should be etched on its underside

6.10 Undo the 11 bolts and 2 studs and lift away the cover

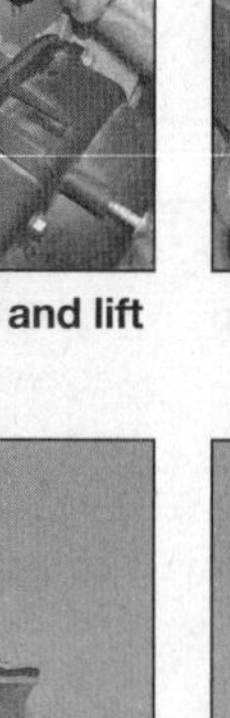

6.12b ...to the fuel pump housing...

13 It will be helpful for future adjustment if a record is kept of the thickness of tappet fitted at each position.

14 When all the clearances have been checked and adjusted, refit the lower cover (where removed), lower the car to the ground and refit the cylinder head cover.

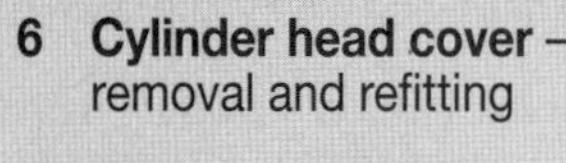

6 Cylinder head cover – removal and refitting

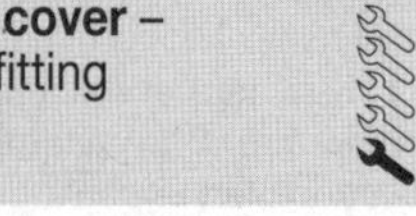

Removal

1 Depressurise the fuel system, as described in Chapter 4A Section 4.

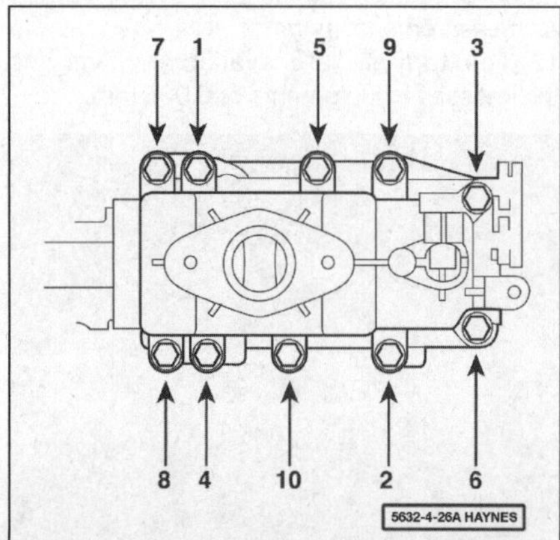

6.13 Tighten the bolts in the order shown

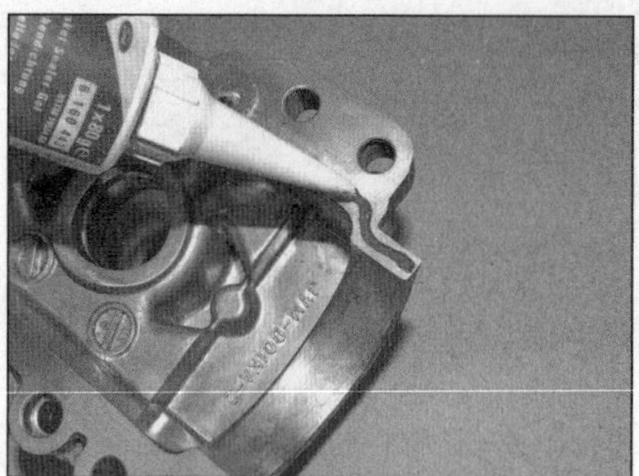

6.12a Apply a 1.5mm diameter bead of sealant...

6.12c ...and the vacuum pump housing as shown

2 Disconnect the battery negative lead as described in Chapter 5 Section 4.

3 Pull up and remove the engine cover.

4 Remove the high-pressure fuel pump and drive unit, as described in Chapter 4A Section 12.

5 Remove the vacuum pump, as described in Chapter 9 Section 20.

6 Remove the fuel rail, as described in Chapter 4A Section 9.

7 Remove the variable valve timing solenoids as described in Section 4.

8 Remove the inlet camshaft phase sensor as described in Chapter 6A Section 14.

9 Disconnect the crankcase breather pipe, release the hose clips and remove the air inlet duct from the top of the engine.

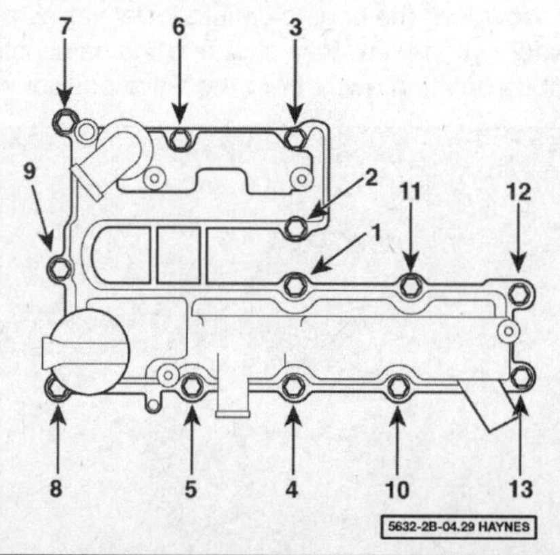

6.16 Tighten the bolts in the order shown

10 Undo the 11 retaining bolts and 2 studs and lift the cylinder head cover from place **(see illustration)**.

Refitting

11 Clean the mating surfaces of the cylinder head and the cylinder head cover. Examine the condition of the gasket – it may be reused if it is in good condition.

12 Apply sealant to the area shown (Ford WSS-M2G348-A11 or equivalent) on the vacuum pump housing and the fuel pump housing **(see illustrations)**. Ensure that the housings are fitted within 10 minutes of applying the sealant. Fit a new O-ring to the vacuum pump housing (where fitted).

13 Fit a new O-ring to the fuel pump housing and tighten the bolts in the order shown to the specified torque **(see illustration)**.

14 Lubricate the bucket tappet and refit it. Check the condition of the fuel pump O-ring. Renew it if necessary. Lubricate the O-ring with clean engine oil and refit the pump.

15 Tighten the fuel pump bolts evenly, 2 turns at a time. Fully tighten to the specified torque setting.

16 Refit the main section of the cylinder head cover (ensuring that the gasket stays in place), and tighten the bolts to the specified torque in the order shown **(see illustration)**.

17 Refit the fuel rail and then fit a new fuel pipe between the rail and the pump. Tighten to the specified torque.

18 Fit a new fuel pipe to the inlet side of the high pressure pump. Tighten to the specified torque.

19 The remainder of refitting is a reversal of removal.

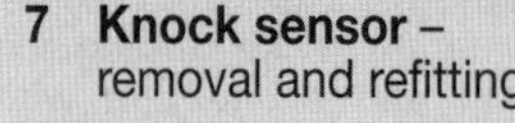

7 Knock sensor – removal and refitting

Removal

1 Remove the intake manifold, as described in Chapter 4A Section 14.

2 Unbolt the relevant knock sensor and manoeuvre from place **(see illustration)**.

Refitting

3 Refitting is a reversal of removal.

7.2 Remove the bolt to release the sensor

8 Crankshaft pulley/ vibration damper – removal and refitting

Caution: Removal of the crankshaft pulley effectively loses the valve timing setting, and it will be necessary to reset the timing.

Note: *The vibration damper/crankshaft pulley retaining bolt may only be used once. Obtain a new bolt for the refitting procedure.*

Removal

1 Remove the auxiliary drivebelt as described in Chapter 1A Section 30.

2 Set the engine to the top dead centre (TDC) position as described in Section 3.

3 Remove the starter motor as described in Chapter 5 Section 7, then use Ford tool 303-393A and 303-393-02 (or equivalent) to lock the crankshaft in position. This tool bolts across the starter motor aperture in the transmission bellhousing, and engages with the teeth of the starter ring gear on the flywheel/driveplate **(see illustrations)**.

4 With the tool installed slacken the bolt and remove the pulley. If necessary a suitable puller can be used to pull the pulley off the crankshaft.

5 Clean the end of the crankshaft and the pulley.

Refitting

6 Ensure that the crankshaft is in the Top Dead Centre (TDC) position and that the camshafts are set in the correct position.

7 If not already done so, remove the TDC sensor and install Ford special tool 303-1550 (or equivalent) **(see illustration)**.

8 Refit the pulley and rotate the pulley until the tool locates correctly in the slot in the rear of the pulley.

9 Tighten the bolt by hand and then remove the special tool. Note that the special tool is not designed to hold the pulley in position, it is designed only to locate the pulley correctly.

10 At this point, do not apply the final torque. Instead, apply just a nominal torque to hold the pulley while the engine is turned and the timing re-checked. This saves the need of a second new bolt if the timing has to be reset. Once checked and correct, the bolt can be fully tightened.

11 Remove the crankshaft locating pin, the crankshaft locking tool, the camshaft timing tool and the crankshaft pulley locating tool. Rotate the engine at least twice in the normal (clockwise) direction of rotation. Refit the TDC locating tool, the camshaft timing tool and the crankshaft pulley locating tool. If the timing and pulley position are correct, they should all fit easily, if not recheck the timing and position of the crankshaft pulley. Note that

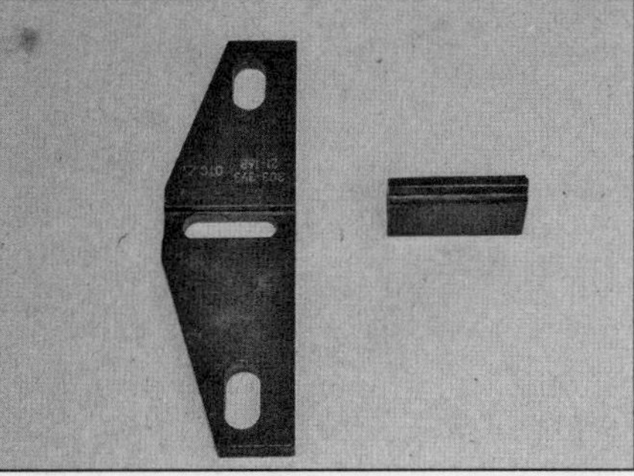

8.3a Ford tool No 303-393 and 303-393-02

8.3c ... and engages with the teeth on the flywheel ring gear

if the crankshaft pulley bolt is slackened it must be replaced again.

12 Refit the remaining components in reverse order of removal.

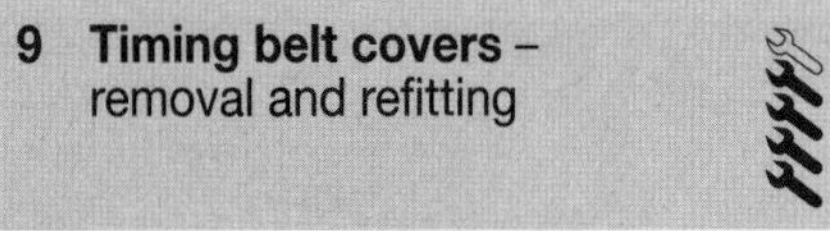

9 Timing belt covers – removal and refitting

Removal

1 This procedure is covered in the timing belt removal and refitting, as described in Section 10.

Refitting

2 Refitting is a reversal of removal. Inspect the auxiliary drivebelt and fit a new one if necessary.

10.9 Remove the driveshaft clamp bracket from place

8.3b The assembled tools bolt across the starter motor aperture...

8.7 Fit the crankshaft pulley locating tool

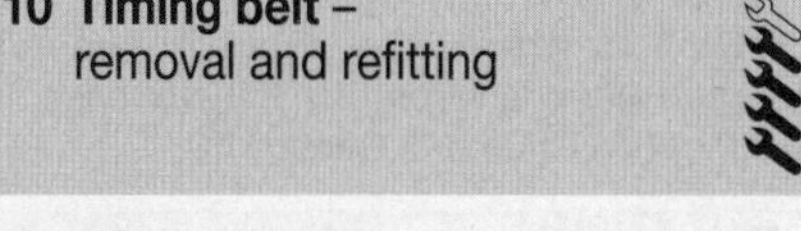

10 Timing belt – removal and refitting

Removal

1 Remove the plastic cover from the top of the engine.

2 Disconnect the battery earth lead, as described in Chapter 5 Section 4.

3 Remove the air filter assembly as described in Chapter 4A Section 3.

4 Remove the oil filter and cooler as described in Chapter 1A Section 13.

5 Lift up the cooling system expansion tank (but do not disconnect it) and rest it on top of the engine.

6 Slacken the coolant pump pulley bolts (but do not remove them at this stage), then remove the auxiliary drivebelt and tensioner as described in Chapter 1A Section 30.

7 Remove the starter motor, as described in Chapter 5 Section 7.

8 Remove the right-hand driveshaft, as described in Chapter 8 Section 7.

9 Undo the 3 mounting bolts and remove the driveshaft clamp mounting bracket **(see illustration)**.

10 Working underneath the car, undo the retaining bolts and remove the subframe cross brace **(see illustration)**.

11 Unbolt the front half of the exhaust from the rear half, and unbolt the exhaust mounts **(see illustration)**.

10.10 Remove the subframe cross brace from place

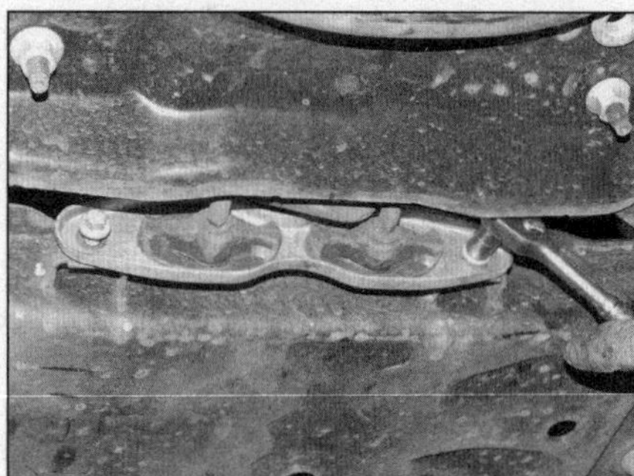
10.11 Remove the exhaust mounts from place

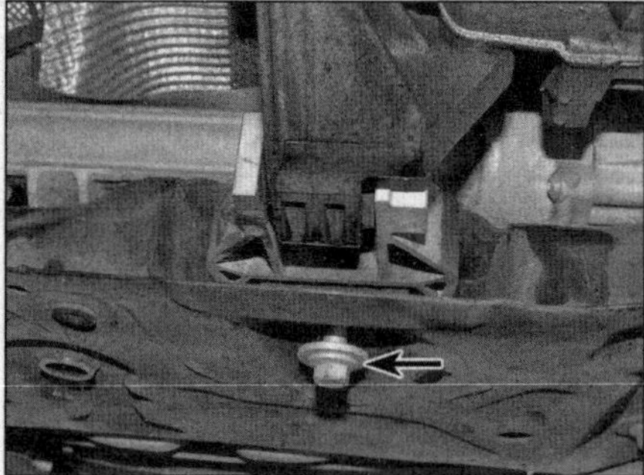
10.12 Undo the roll restrictor retaining bolt

10.17 Remove the bolt to move the pipe out of the way

10.18 Pull the strap away from the cover

10.19 Undo the bolts and remove the pulley

12 Undo the retaining bolt for the rear roll restrictor **(see illustration)**.

13 On four-wheel-drive models, separate the propeller shaft from the transfer case, as described in Chapter 8 Section 12.

14 Remove the alternator, as described in Chapter 5 Section 6.

15 Place a trolley jack beneath the engine to support it. Use a block of wood on the jack head to prevent damage.

16 Undo the retaining bolts and remove the front-right engine mounting.

17 Undo the retaining bolt and displace the turbocharger induction pipe from place **(see illustration)** to allow access to the timing belt cover rubber retaining strap.

18 Disengage the strap from the timing belt cover **(see illustration)**.

19 Fully remove the retaining bolts from the coolant pump pulley **(see illustration)** and remove the pulley from place.

20 Unscrew the retaining bolt and separate the wiring loom bracket from the top of the timing belt cover **(see illustration)**.

21 Undo the 7 retaining bolts and manoeuvre the timing belt cover from place, disengaging the rubber strap as you do so **(see illustration)**.

22 Undo the 4 retaining bolts and remove the engine mounting bracket from the engine **(see illustration)**.

23 Unscrew the TDC tool blanking plug from the rear of the engine block **(see illustration)**.

24 Use a socket on the pulley to rotate the crankshaft clockwise until the timing marks on the camshafts sprockets are in the 11 o'clock position **(see illustration)**.

25 Screw in the crankshaft locking tool to the aperture on the rear of the engine exposed by removal of the blanking bolt **(see illustration)**.

26 Rotate the engine using a socket on the crankshaft pulley until it hits a stop.

27 Install Ford special service tool 303-1097 (or equivalent) between the camshaft sprockets **(see illustration)**.

28 Insert Ford special tool 303-393A or 303-393-02 into the starter motor aperture

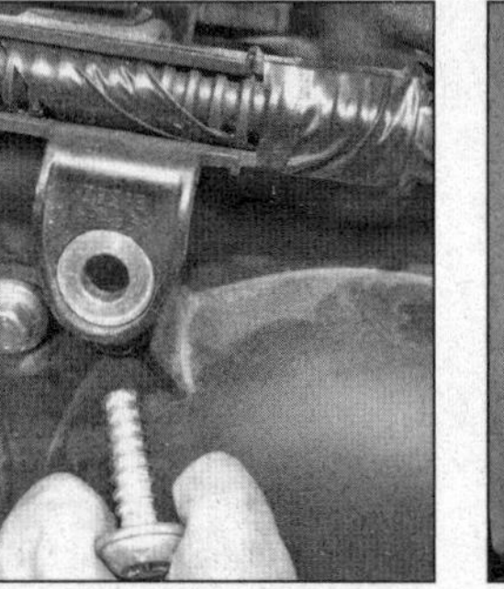
10.20 Remove the retaining bolt and displace the wiring loom

10.21 Undo the bolts and remove the timing belt cover

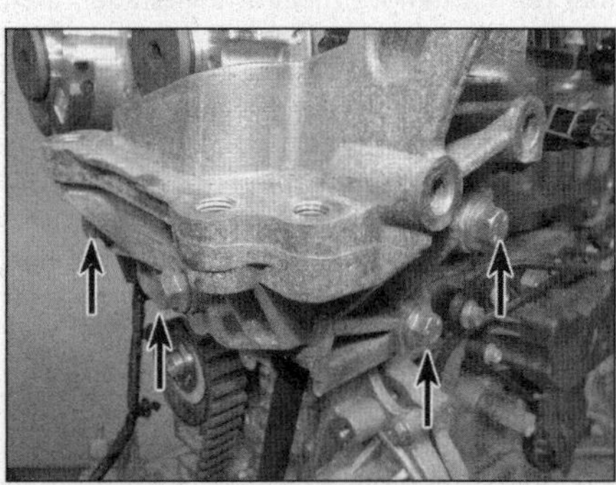
10.22 Engine mounting bracket retaining bolts

10.23 The blanking plug is located behind the bracket

10.24 Rotate the crankshaft until the camshaft sprocket marks are in the 11 o'clock position

10.25 Insert the crankshaft locking tool

10.27 Make sure the camshafts are locked in place

10.28 Insert the tool to lock the flywheel

10.29 Unbolt the crankshaft position sensor and remove

10.30 Remove the timing belt guide disc (where fitted)

and fasten securely to prevent the flywheel being rotated **(see illustration)**.

29 Disconnect the wiring plug and unbolt the crankshaft position sensor from place, to allow fitment of the crankshaft position tool (Ford part no: 303-1550) during reassembly **(see illustration)**.

30 Remove the crankshaft pulley/vibration damper as described in Section 8. Dispose of the bolt. A new one must be fitted. Where fitted remove the timing belt guide disc **(see illustration)**.

31 Turn the tensioner clockwise until the locking pin (Ford tool No 303-1054 or a suitable 4mm drill bit) can be fitted into the pulley hub to hold it in position **(see illustration)**.

32 Remove the belt and then remove the automatic tensioner.

Inspection

33 Once the belt is removed it should always be replaced. As a safety measure, the belt should be renewed irrespective of its apparent condition whenever the engine is overhauled.

34 Check the sprockets for signs of wear or damage, and replace the tensioner. This should be standard practise, as some manufacturers will not always guarantee a belt against failure if the tensioner is not replaced at the same time as the timing belt. We strongly advise replacement as an assembly including the tensioner, guide pulleys, and the coolant pump if driven from the timing belt.

35 If signs of oil or coolant contamination are found on the old belt, trace the source of the leak and rectify it, then wash down the engine timing belt area and related components to remove all traces of oil or coolant.

Refitting

36 Fit a new tensioner pulley and insert the locking pin (Ford 3030-1054, or an equivalent if using an aftermarket kit) to hold the tensioner in position.

37 Ensure the engine is still set to TDC on No 1 cylinder (Section 3), then working anti-clockwise, locate the timing belt on the crankshaft sprocket and then over the camshaft sprockets **(see illustrations)**. Finally fit the belt over the tensioner.

38 Remove the locking pin and allow the tensioner to take up the slack in the new timing belt.

39 Refit the crankshaft pulley as described in Section 8.

40 Rotate the crankshaft clockwise 2 complete revolutions and check the crankshaft and camshaft are still positioned as described in Section 3.

41 Refit the timing belt cover and tighten the bolts to the specified torque.

42 The remainder of refitting is a reversal of removal.

10.31 Insert a 4 mm drill bit or rod into the tensioner arms

10.37a Fit the belt over the crankshaft sprocket...

10.37b ...and then around the camshaft sprockets

11.5 Counterhold the camshaft with a spanner on the hexagonal section, then unscrew the blanking plug from the VCT unit

11.6a Unscrew the Torx bolt...

11.6b ... and pull the VCT unit from the camshaft

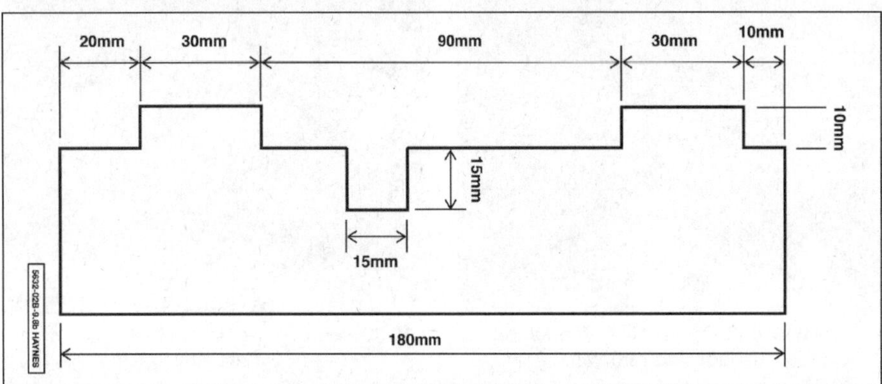

11.8a Camshaft setting tool dimensions
Drawing not to scale

11 Timing belt tensioner and sprockets – removal, inspection and refitting

Tensioner pulley

1 Removal of the tensioner pulley is described within the timing belt procedure – see Section 10.

Camshaft sprockets

2 Remove the timing belt as described in Section 10.

3 Remove the cylinder head cover as described in Section 6.

4 Remove the vacuum pump, vacuum pump housing, fuel pump and fuel pump housing (as described in Chapter 4A and Chapter 9).

5 Counterhold the camshafts using an open-ended spanner on the hexagonal sections, then unscrew the blanking plugs from the centre of the variable valve timing (VVT) units **(see illustration)**.

6 Still counterholding the camshafts, slacken and remove the VVT units centre Torx bolts **(see illustrations)**. Remove the VVT units from the ends of the camshafts. Dispose of the bolts – new ones must be fitted.

7 Examine the teeth of the sprockets for wear and damage, and renew them if necessary.

8 Insert Ford tool 303-1552 (EcoBoost models) or Ford tool 303-376B (Ti-VCT models) into the slots in the left-hand ends of the camshafts. If the Ford setting tools are notavailable, a home-made version can be fabricated out of a length of flat metal bar 5 mm thick **(see illustrations)**.

9 Locate the VVT units on the ends of the camshafts, but only finger-tighten the retaining bolts at this stage. Ensure the timing marks on the VVT units (dot on the inlet sprocket, groove on the exhaust sprocket) are at the 12 o'clock position **(see illustration)**.

10 Fit the VVT locking tool (No 303-1097) over the units. Note how the dots/holes on the VVT units align with the groove/dot on the sprockets **(see illustration)**.

11 Tighten each VVT unit retaining bolt to the specified Stage 1 torque.

12 Remove the camshaft setting bar and the VVT locking tool, then counterhold the camshafts using a spanner on the hexagonal section, and tighten each VVT unit retaining bolt to the specified Stage 2 angle setting. Do not allow the camshafts to rotate.

13 Refit the VVT locking tool, and check the marks on the sprockets align with the marks on the VVT units. If not, repeat the VVT unit refitting procedure.

14 If the timing is correct, counterhold the camshafts using a spanner on the hexagonal section, and fit the each VVT unit blanking plug. Tighten each plug to the specified torque. Renew the plug seal if necessary **(see illustrations)**.

15 Apply a 1.5 mm diameter bead of sealant

11.8b Fit the setting tool into the slots in the end of the camshafts

11.9 Ensure the groove (1) on the exhaust VVT unit and the dot (2) on the inlet unit are at the 12 o'clock position

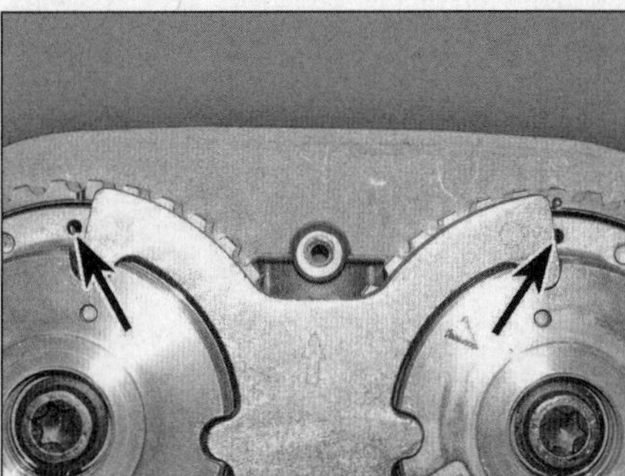
11.10 Note how the dots/holes on the VCT units align with the groove/dot on the sprockets

11.14a Renew the seal if necessary...

11.14b ... then refit the plugs to the VCT units

11.18 Slide the crankshaft sprocket from place

to the vacuum pump housing and the fuel pump housing – as described in 4A Section 11. Use Ford sealant WSS-M2G348-A11 or equivalent. Apply it to the inside of the mounting bolts holes only.

16 Fit the timing belt as described in Section 10 and the cylinder head cover as described in Section 6.

Crankshaft sprocket

17 Remove the timing belt as described in Section 10.

18 Slide the sprocket off the end of the crankshaft **(see illustration)**.

19 Examine the teeth of the sprocket for wear and damage, and renew if necessary.

20 Wipe clean the end of the crankshaft, then slide on the sprocket.

21 Refit the timing belt as described in Section 10.

12 Camshaft sprockets – removal and refitting

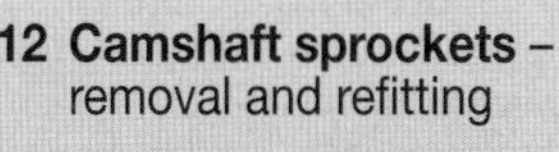

1 Removal and refitting of the camshaft sprockets is described in Section 11.

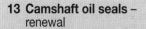

13 Camshaft oil seals – renewal

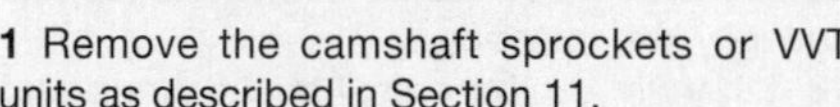

1 Remove the camshaft sprockets or VVT units as described in Section 11.

2 Note the fitted depths of the oil seals as a guide for fitting the new ones **(see illustration)**.

3 Using a screwdriver or similar tool, carefully prise the oil seals from the cylinder head/camshaft bearing caps. Take care not to damage the oil seal contact surfaces on the ends of the camshafts or the oil seal seatings **(see illustration)**.

4 Wipe clean the oil seal seatings and also the ends of the camshafts.

5 Apply a little clean engine oil to the seal lip, then locate it over the camshaft and into the cylinder head/camshaft bearing cap. Make sure that the closed end of the oil seal faces outwards **(see illustration)**.

6 Using a socket or length of metal tubing, drive the oil seals squarely into position to the previously-noted depths. Wipe away any excess oil **(see illustration)**.

7 Refit the camshaft sprockets as described in Section 11.

13.2 Measure the depth of the seals

14 Camshafts and tappets – removal, inspection and refitting

Removal

1 Disconnect the battery (see Chapter 5 Section 4) and then jack up and support the front of the vehicle (see *Jacking and vehicle support*).

2 Remove the camshaft oil seals as described in Section 13.

3 Undo the 4 retaining bolts and remove the camshaft bearing carrier **(see illustration)**.

4 Prise out the o-ring from beneath the camshaft bearing carrier and discard it **(see illustration)**. It must be replaced.

5 Lift out the camshaft seals **(see illustration)**.

6 The camshaft bearing caps may be marked

13.3 Use a screwdriver to prise out the seal

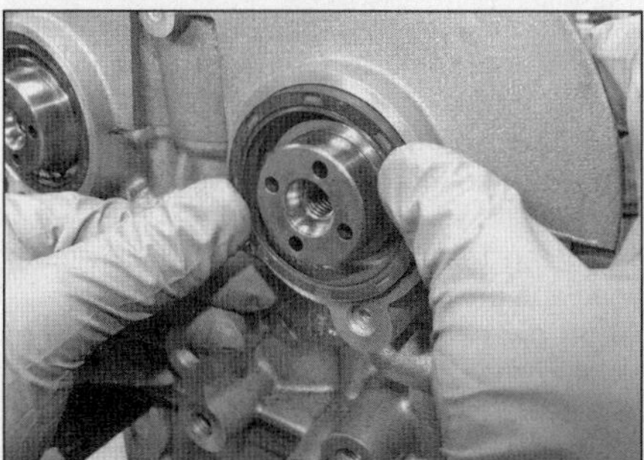

13.5 Locate the new oil seal into the cylinder/camshaft bearing cap

13.6 Drive the new seal into position with a socket

14.3 Undo the bolts and remove the bearing carrier

14.4 Hook out the o-ring beneath the bearing carrier and discard it

14.7b ...withdraw the caps

for position – the inlet caps have the numbers 1-4 (1 being the timing belt end), and should be orientated such that they can be read correctly from the exhaust side of the engine. The exhaust caps have the letters A to D, and should be orientated in the same way.

7 Progressively loosen the camshaft bearing cap retaining bolts, working in the **reverse** order shown for tightening **(see illustration 14.22)**. Work only as described to release gradually and evenly the pressure of the valve springs on the caps **(see illustrations)**. Dispose of the bolts. New ones must be fitted.

8 Withdraw the remaining caps, keeping them in order to aid refitting, then lift the camshafts from the cylinder head **(see illustration)**. The exhaust camshaft has an extra lobe for the fuel pump drive.

9 Obtain sixteen small, clean containers, and number them 1 to 8 for both the inlet and

14.18 The slots in the end of the camshafts should be just above, and approximately parallel to the cylinder head upper surface

14.5 Remove the camshaft seals from place

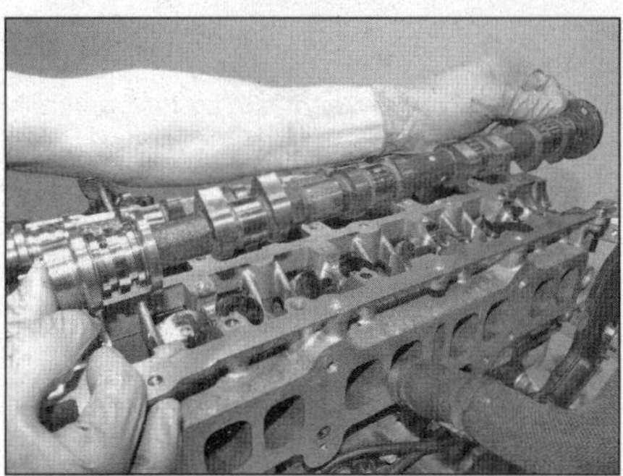

14.8 Remove the camshafts

exhaust camshafts. Lift the tappets one by one from the cylinder head.

Inspection

10 With the camshafts and tappets removed, check each for signs of obvious wear (scoring, pitting, etc) and for ovality, and renew if necessary.

11 Visually examine the camshaft lobes for score marks, pitting, and evidence of overheating (blue, discoloured areas). Look for flaking away of the hardened surface layer of each lobe. If any such signs are evident, renew the component concerned.

12 Examine the camshaft bearing journals and the cylinder head bearing surfaces for signs of obvious wear or pitting. If any such signs are evident, renew the component concerned.

13 To check camshaft endfloat, remove the tappets, clean the bearing surfaces carefully, and refit the camshafts and bearing caps.

14.20 Apply a 1.5mm diameter bead of sealant to the underside of the No 1 bearing cap as shown

14.7a Undo the camshaft bearing cap bolts...

Tighten the bearing cap bolts to the specified torque wrench setting, then measure the endfloat using a dial gauge mounted on the cylinder head so that its tip bears on the camshaft right-hand end.

14 Tap the camshaft fully towards the gauge, zero the gauge, then tap the camshaft fully away from the gauge, and note the gauge reading. If the endfloat measured is found to be more than the typical value given, fit a new camshaft and repeat the check; if the clearance is still excessive, the cylinder head must be renewed.

Refitting

15 Position the crankshaft so that No 1 piston is approximately 25 mm before TDC. This can be done by starting from the TDC position; carefully insert a large screwdriver down No 1 cylinder spark plug hole until the tip touches the top of the piston, and turn the engine anti-clockwise until the screwdriver shaft has descended 25 mm.

16 Position the camshafts so that none of the valves are at full lift (ie, fully-open, being heavily pressed down by the cam lobes). To do this, turn each camshaft using a spanner on the hexagon flats provided.

17 Lubricate the cylinder head tappet bores and the tappets with engine oil. Carefully refit the tappets to the cylinder head, ensuring each tappet is refitted to its original bore. Some care will be needed to enter the tappets squarely into their bores.

18 Liberally oil the camshaft bearings and lobes. Ensuring that each camshaft is in its original location, refit the camshafts, locating each so that the slot in its left-hand end is approximately parallel to, and just above, the cylinder head mating surface **(see illustration)**. At this stage, position the camshafts so that none of the valves are at full lift.

19 Clean the mating faces of the cylinder head and camshaft bearing caps.

20 Apply a 1.5 mm bead of sealant (Ford recommend WSS-M2G348-A11 or equivalent) to the No 1 camshaft bearing caps at the oil seal ends only **(see illustration)**. Renew the O-ring seal beneath the No 1 bearing cap.

21 Oil the bearing surfaces, then locate the camshaft bearing caps on the camshafts and

14.21 Oil the camshaft bearing surfaces

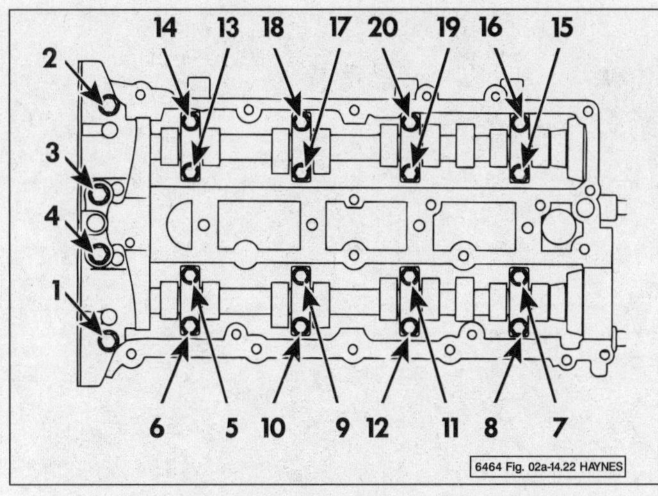

14.22 Camshaft bearing cap bolt slackening and tightening sequence

insert the retaining bolts loosely. Make sure that each cap is located in its previously-noted position **(see illustration)**.

22 Ensuring each cap is kept square to the cylinder head as it is tightened down, and working in sequence **(see illustration)**, tighten the camshaft bearing cap bolts slowly and by one turn at a time, until each cap touches the cylinder head. Next, go round again in the same sequence, tightening the bolts to the specified Stage 1 torque wrench setting specified.

23 Finally, still working in the tightening sequence, tightening the bolts further to the Stage 2 angle. It is recommended that an angle gauge is used for this, to ensure accuracy.

24 Wipe off all surplus sealant, and check the valve clearances as described in Section 4.

25 Fit new camshaft oil seals as described in Section 13.

26 The remainder of refitting is a reversal of removal.

15 Cylinder head – removal, inspection and refitting

Removal

1 Depressurise the fuel system as described in Chapter 4A Section 4.

2 Drain the cooling system as described in Chapter 1A Section 34.

3 Disconnect the battery negative lead as described Chapter 5 Section 4.

4 Remove the inlet manifold and turbocharger as described in Chapter 4A.

5 Remove the 4 turbocharger mounting studs and discard. New ones must be fitted.

6 Remove the camshafts and tappets as described in Section 14.

7 Remove the breather pipe from the front of the engine **(see illustration)**.

8 To disconnect the breathe tube from the top of the cylinder head, squeeze together the sides of the collar and pull it upwards **(see illustration)**.

9 Make a note of their fitted locations and the harness routing, then disconnect any wiring plugs attached to components on the cylinder head. Label the plugs if necessary to aid refitting.

10 Release the spring-type clip and disconnect the coolant pipe from the left-hand rear of the cylinder head.

11 Make a last check round the cylinder head, to ensure that nothing remains connected or attached which would prevent the head from being lifted off. Prepare a clean surface to lay the head down on once it has been removed.

12 Working in the **reverse** of the tightening sequence **(see illustration 15.26)**, slacken the 10 cylinder head bolts progressively and by half a turn at a time. Remove all the bolts and dispose of them. New ones will be required.

13 Lift the cylinder head away; use assistance if possible, as it is a heavy assembly. Remove the gasket, noting the two dowels. Although the gasket cannot be re-used, it is advisable to retain it for comparison with the new one, to confirm that the right part has been supplied.

Inspection

14 The mating faces of the cylinder head and cylinder block must be perfectly clean before refitting the head. Use a hard plastic or wood scraper to remove all traces of gasket and carbon; also clean the piston crowns. Take particular care during the cleaning operations, as aluminium alloy is easily damaged.

15 Make sure that the carbon is not allowed to enter the oil and coolant passages – this is particularly important for the lubrication system, as carbon could block the oil supply to the engine's components. Using adhesive tape and paper, seal the coolant, oil and bolt holes in the cylinder block. To prevent carbon entering the gap between the pistons and bores, smear a little grease in the gap. After cleaning each piston, use a small brush to remove all traces of grease and carbon from the gap, then wipe away the remainder with a clean rag. Note that there is a filter fitted into the oil supply galleries feeding the VVT system. This filter is permanently installed and cannot be removed.

16 Check the mating surfaces of the cylinder block and the cylinder head for nicks, deep scratches and other damage. If slight, they may be removed carefully with a file, but if excessive, renewal is necessary as it is not permissible to machine the surfaces.

17 If warpage of the cylinder head gasket surface is suspected, use a straight-edge to check it for distortion. Refer to Part D of this Chapter if necessary.

15.7 Undo the retaining clip and remove the breather

15.8 Squeeze together the sides of the collar to disconnect the breather tube

15.23 Locate the new cylinder head gasket over the dowels

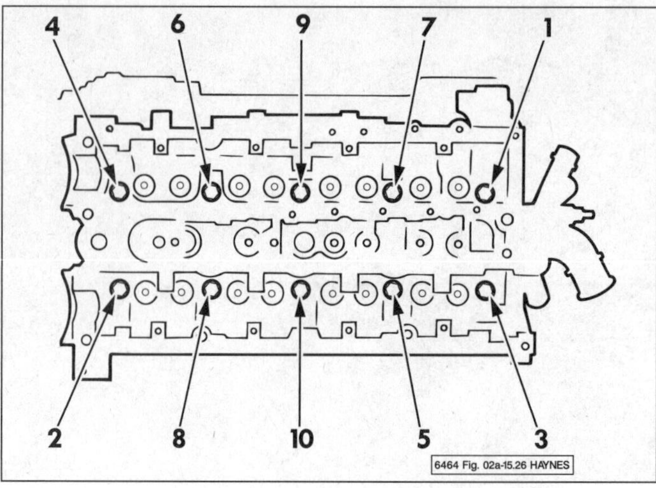

15.26 Cylinder head bolt tightening sequence

18 If possible, clean out the bolt holes in the block using compressed air, to ensure no oil or coolant is present. Screwing a bolt into an oil- or coolant filled hole can (in extreme cases) cause the block to fracture, due to the hydraulic pressure created.

19 Although not essential, if a suitable tap-and-die set is available, it's worth running the correct-size tap down the bolt threads in the cylinder block. This will clean the threads of any debris, and go some way to restoring any damaged threads. Make absolutely sure the tap is the right size and thread pitch, and lightly oil the tap before starting.

20 Ford insist that the cylinder head bolts must be renewed.

Refitting

21 Wipe clean the mating surfaces of the cylinder head and cylinder block, and check that the two locating dowels are in position in the block.

22 Turn the crankshaft anti-clockwise so that pistons 1 and 4 are approximately 25 mm before TDC, in order to avoid the risk of valve/piston contact. Turn the crankshaft using a spanner on the pulley bolt.

23 If the old gasket is still available, check that it is identical to the new one. Position the new gasket over the dowels on the cylinder block surface. It can only be fitted one way round – check carefully that the holes in the gasket align with the holes in the block surface, and that none are blocked **(see illustration)**.

24 It is useful when refitting a cylinder head to have an assistant on hand to help guide the head onto the dowels. Take care that the gasket does not get moved as the head is lowered into position. To confirm that the head is aligned correctly, once it is in place, temporarily slide in two or more of the head bolts, and check that they fit into the block holes.

25 Fit the new head bolts carefully, and screw them in by hand only until finger-tight.

26 Working progressively and in sequence, tighten the cylinder head bolts to their Stage 1 torque setting **(see illustration)**.

27 Next, go around again in the same sequence, and tighten the bolts to the Stage 2 setting. Repeat the procedure again for Stage 4.

28 The bolts should now be angle-tightened by the specified Stage 4 amount (in sequence) and again angle-tightened for the final Stage 5. This means simply that each bolt in the sequence must be turned through the stated angle. A special 'angle gauge' will be required to for Stages 4 and 5 **(see illustration)**. These are widely available.

29 The remainder of refitting is a reversal of removal, noting the following points:

a) Refit the camshafts as described in Section 14, and the timing belt as described in Section 10.

b) Tighten all fasteners to the specified torque, where given.

c) Ensure that all hoses and wiring are correctly routed, and that hose clips and wiring connectors are securely refitted.

d) Refill the cooling system as described in Chapter 1A Section 34.

e) Check all disturbed joints for signs of oil or coolant leakage once the engine has been restarted and warmed-up to normal operating temperature.

15.28 Use an angle-gauge for the final stage

16.5 Sump viewed from below, showing the engine and transmission bolts

16 Sump – removal and refitting

Removal

1 Apply the handbrake, then jack up the front of the car and support it on axle stands (see *Jacking and vehicle support*).

2 Unbolt and then remove the engine undershield.

3 Drain the engine oil, then check the drain plug sealing washer and renew if necessary. Clean and refit the engine oil drain plug together with the washer, and tighten it to the specified torque wrench setting. Although not strictly necessary, as the oil is being drained, it makes sense to fit a new oil filter at the same time (see Chapter 1A Section 13).

4 Remove the auxiliary coolant pump from place, as described in Chapter 3 Section 11. There is no need to disconnect the hoses, simply unbolt the pump from place and move it aside to allow access to the 2 obscured bellhousing bolts.

5 Unscrew the bolts securing the transmission to the sump, then progressively unscrew the sump-to-block bolts **(see illustration)**.

6 On all models, a sump gasket is not used, and sealant is used instead. Unfortunately,

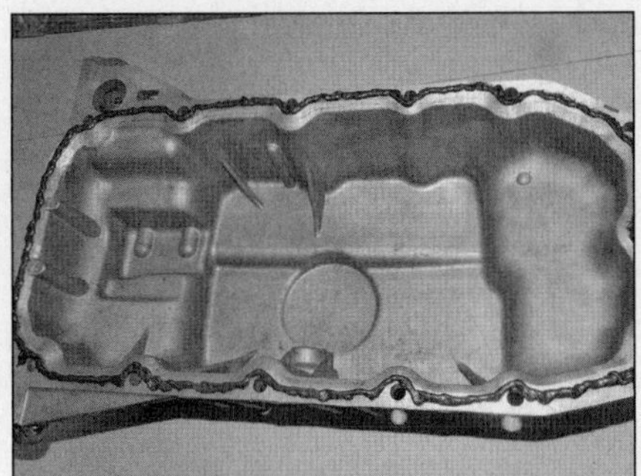
16.11 Apply a 3-4mm bead of sealant to the sump mating surface as shown

the use of sealant makes removal of the sump more difficult. If care is taken not to damage the surfaces, the sealant can be cut around using a sharp knife.

7 On no account lever between the mating faces, as this will almost certainly damage them, resulting in leaks when finished. Ford technicians have a tool comprising a metal rod which is inserted through the sump drain hole, and a handle to pull the sump downwards. Providing care is taken not to damage the threads, a large screwdriver could be used in the drain hole to prise down the sump.

8 While the sump is removed, take the opportunity to remove the oil pump pick-up/strainer pipe, and clean it with reference to Section 19.

Refitting

9 Thoroughly clean the contact surfaces of the sump and crankcase. Take care not to damage the oil pump gasket or the crankshaft oil seal, both of which are partially exposed when the sump is removed. If necessary, use a cloth rag to clean inside the sump and crankcase. If the oil pump pick-up/strainer pipe was removed, fit a new O-ring and refit the pipe with reference to Section 19.

10 To aid aligning the sump fit 2 studs (M8 X 20 mm) to engine block (at the centre and opposite each other). Cut a slot across the end of each stud, to make removal easier when the sump is in place.

11 Apply a 3 to 4 mm diameter bead of sealant (Ford recommend WSE M4G323-A4, or equivalent) to the sump pan, to the inside of the bolt holes **(see illustration)**. The sump bolts must be fitted and tightened within 10 minutes of applying the sealant.

12 Offer the sump up into position over the studs, and fully refit the remaining bolts by hand. Unscrew the studs, and refit the sump bolts in their place. The sump should be fitted flush with the block at the transmission end **(see illustration)**.

13 Insert the four sump-to-transmission bolts and tighten them to the specified torque.

14 Tighten the main sump bolts to the specified torque in the order shown **(see illustration)**.

15 Refit the auxiliary coolant pump and the engine undershield.

16 Lower the car to the ground. To be on the safe side, wait a further 30 minutes for the sealant to cure before filling the sump with fresh oil, as described in Chapter 1A Section 13.

17 The remainder of refitting is a reversal of removal.

18 Finally start the engine and check for signs of oil leaks.

16.12 Ensure the sump is perfectly aigned

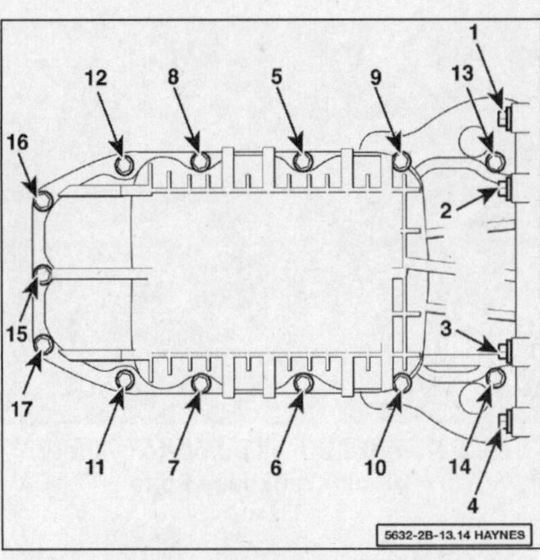

16.14 Sump bolt tightening sequence

17 Oil pick-up pipe – removal and refitting

Removal

1 Remove the sump, as described in this Section 16.

2 Undo the 3 retaining bolts and remove the pick-up pipe from place **(see illustration)**. Discard the o-ring.

Refitting

3 Refitting is a reversal of removal.

18 Oil cooler – removal and refitting

Removal

1 Raise the front of the vehicle and support it securely on axle stands (see *Jacking and vehicle support*).

2 Remove the engine undertray.

3 Drain the cooling system, as described in Chapter 1A Section 34.

4 Remove the oil filter, as described in Chapter 1A Section 13.

5 Release the clips and disconnect the pipes from the oil cooler.

6 Use a 12mm Allen key and undo the central oil cooler mounting **(see illustration)**. Renew any seals/gaskets.

Refitting

7 Refitting is a reversal of removal, ensuring that the locating tab is correctly seated in the engine casting **(see illustration)**.

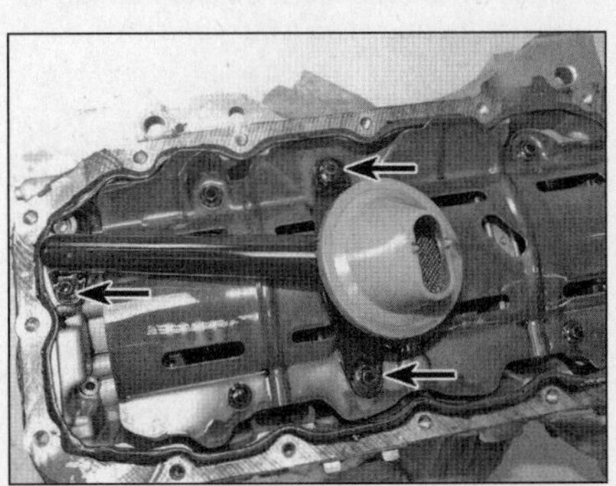
17.2 Remove the bolts to release the pick-up pipe

18.6 Use an Allen key to remove the oil cooler from place

18.7 Make sure the cooler is correctly seated

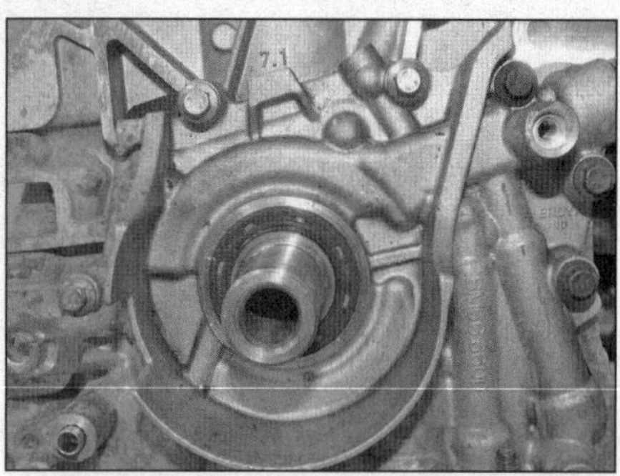
19.5 Remove the oil pump-to cylinder block/crankcase bolts

19.6 Remove the oil pump gasket

19 Oil pump – removal, inspection and refitting

Removal

1 Remove the timing belt, as described in Section 10.

2 Remove the sump as described in Section 16.

3 Unplug and remove the crankshaft position sensor.

4 Remove the oil-pick-up pipe, as described in Section 17.

5 Unscrew the bolts securing the oil pump to the cylinder block/crankcase **(see illustration)**. Note that the bolts are different lengths. Withdraw the pump over the nose of the crankshaft.

6 Recover then discard the gasket **(see illustration)**.

Inspection

7 It is not possible to obtain individual components of the oil pump, furthermore, there are no torque settings available for tightening the pump cover plate bolts. However, the following procedure is provided for owners wishing to dismantle the oil pump for examination.

8 Take out the bolts, and remove the pump cover plate; noting any identification marks on the rotors, withdraw the rotors.

9 Inspect the rotors for obvious signs of wear or damage, and renew if necessary; if either rotor, the pump body, or its cover plate are scored or damaged, the complete oil pump assembly must be renewed.

10 The oil pressure relief valve can be dismantled as follows.

11 Unscrew the threaded plug, and recover the valve spring and plunger. If the plug's sealing O-ring is worn or damaged, a new one must be obtained, to be fitted on reassembly.

12 Reassembly is the reverse of the dismantling procedure; ensure the spring and valve are refitted the correct way round, and tighten the threaded plug securely.

Refitting

13 The oil pump must be primed on installation, by pouring clean engine oil into it and rotating its inner rotor a few turns.

14 Use a little grease to stick the new gasket in place on the cylinder block/crankcase.

15 Offer the oil pump over the nose of the crankshaft, and turn the inner rotor as necessary to align its flats with the flats on the crankshaft. Insert the retaining bolts finger tight only, and then using a straight edge along the bottom of the engine block (to ensure the that the pump is flush with the block), progressively tighten the oil pump bolts. Fully tighten them to the specified torque.

16 Locate the O-ring (dipped in oil) on the pick-up/strainer pipe, then locate the pipe in the oil pump and insert the retaining bolts. Insert the bolts retaining the pipe on the baffle plate/main bearing cap. Tighten the bolts to the specified torque.

17 Where removed, refit the air conditioning compressor, tightening the bolts to the specified torque.

18 Refit the sump as described in Section 16.

19 Fit a new crankshaft oil seal as described in Section 21.

20 Refit the remaining components in the reverse order of removal.

20 Oil pressure switch – removal and refitting

1 The oil pressure switch is a vital early warning of low oil pressure. The switch operates the oil warning light on the instrument panel – the light should come on with the ignition, and go out almost immediately when the engine starts.

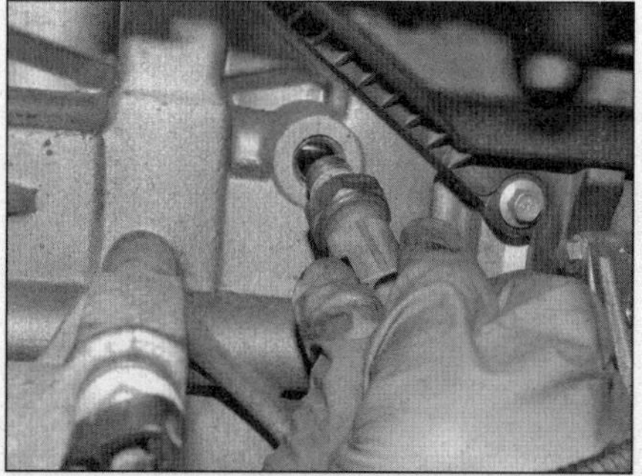
20.7 Oil pressure switch

2 If the light does not come on, there could be a fault on the instrument panel, the switch wiring, or the switch itself. If the light does not go out, low oil level, worn oil pump (or sump pick-up blocked), blocked oil filter, or worn main bearings could be to blame – or again, the switch may be faulty.

3 If the light comes on while driving, the best advice is to turn the engine off immediately, and not to drive the car until the problem has been investigated – ignoring the light could mean expensive engine damage.

Removal

4 Raise the front of the vehicle and support it securely on axle stands (see *Jacking and vehicle support*).

5 Drain the engine oil and remove the oil filter, as described in Chapter 1A Section 13.

6 Remove the oil cooler, as described in Section 18.

7 The oil pressure switch is located on the front face of the engine, above the oil filter **(see illustration)**.

8 Disconnect the wiring plug from the switch.

9 Unscrew the switch from the block, and remove it. There should only be a very slight loss of oil when this is done.

Inspection

10 Examine the switch for signs of cracking or splits. If the top part of the switch is loose, this is an early indication of impending failure.

11 Check that the wiring terminals at the switch are not loose, then trace the wire from the switch connector until it enters the main loom – any wiring defects will give rise to apparent oil pressure problems.

Refitting

12 Refitting is the reverse of the removal procedure, noting the following points:

a) *Tighten the switch securely.*
b) *Reconnect the switch connector, making sure it clicks home properly. Ensure that the wiring is routed away from any hot or moving parts.*
c) *Check the engine oil level and top-up if necessary (see Chapter 1A Section 5).*
d) *Check for signs of oil leaks once the engine has been restarted and warmed-up to normal operating temperature.*

21 Crankshaft oil seals – renewal

Right-hand oil seal

1 Remove the crankshaft sprocket as described in Section 11.

2 As a safety precaution, refit the engine right-hand mounting upper section and mounting bracket, and tighten the mounting bolts/nuts.

3 Note the fitted depth of the oil seal as a guide for fitting the new one.

21.4 Insert a screw then use pliers to remove the seal

21.15 Locate the new oil seal housing (complete with fitting sleeve) over the end of the crankshaft

21.17 With the oil seal housing bolted into position, remove the fitting ring

4 Drill a small hole into the existing oil seal. Thread a self-tapping screw into the hole and using a pair of pliers, pull on the head of the screw to extract the oil seal. Take great care to avoid drilling through into the seal housing or crankshaft sealing surface **(see illustration)**. Alternatively, prise out the seal using a suitable hooked tool.

5 Wipe clean the seating and the nose of the crankshaft.

6 Apply a little clean engine oil to the inner lip of the seal, then locate it over the crankshaft and into the oil pump housing. Make sure that the closed end of the oil seal faces outwards.

7 Using a socket or length of metal tubing, drive the oil seal squarely into position to the previously-noted depth. The Ford installation tool (303-395) is used together with an old crankshaft pulley bolt to press the oil seal into position. The same idea may be used with metal tubing and a large washer – do not use a new crankshaft pulley bolt, as it is only permissible to use the bolt once. With the oil seal in position, wipe away any excess oil.

8 With the weight of the engine once more supported, unscrew the nuts and bolts and remove the engine right-hand mounting upper section and mounting bracket.

9 Refit the crankshaft sprocket with reference to Section 11.

Left-hand oil seal

10 Remove the flywheel/driveplate as described in Section 23.

11 Unscrew the six bolts and withdraw the oil seal carrier from the end of the crankshaft. Note that the seal and carrier are made as one unit – it is not possible to obtain the seal separately.

12 Remove the sump, as described in Section 16.

13 Clean the carrier contact surface on the cylinder block, and the end of the crankshaft.

14 The new oil seal carrier is supplied complete with a fitting sleeve, which ensures that the oil seal lips are correctly located on the crankshaft. Ford state that neither the crankshaft nor the new oil seal should be lubricated before fitting.

15 Locate the oil seal carrier and fitting sleeve over the end of the crankshaft. Press the carrier into position, noting that the centre bolt holes are formed into locating dowels **(see illustration)**.

16 Insert the retaining bolts and progressively tighten them to the specified torque.

17 Remove the fitting sleeve and check that the oil seal lips are correctly located **(see illustration)**.

18 Refit the sump, as described in Section 16.

19 Refit the flywheel/driveplate as described in Section 23.

22 Crankcase vent oil separator – removal and refitting

Removal

1 Remove the intake manifold as described in Chapter 4A Section 14.

2 Remove the starter motor, as described in Chapter 5 Section 7.

3 Unclip and disconnect the hose from the crankcase vent oil separator.

4 Unclip the wiring from the separator.

5 Undo the retaining bolts and remove the oil separator from place.

Refitting

6 Refitting is a reversal of removal.

23 Flywheel/driveplate – removal, inspection and refitting

Removal

1 Remove the clutch as described in Chapter 8 Section 6.

2 Hold the flywheel/driveplate stationary using one of the following methods:

If an assistant is available, insert one of the transmission mounting bolts into the cylinder block and have the assistant engage a wide-bladed screwdriver with the starter ring gear teeth while the bolts are loosened. Alternatively, a piece of angle-iron can be engaged with the ring gear and located against the transmission mounting bolt.

A further method is to fabricate a piece of flat metal bar with a pointed end to engage the ring gear – fit the tool to the transmission bolt and use washers and packing to align it with the ring gear, then tighten the bolt to hold it in position **(see illustration)**. Fit Ford special tool 303-939A (or equivalent) and lock the flywheel in position.

3 Unscrew and remove the bolts, then lift the flywheel/driveplate off the locating dowel on the crankshaft. Dispose of the bolts. New ones must be used.

Warning: Take care – the flywheel/driveplate is heavy!

Inspection

4 Clean the flywheel/driveplate to remove grease and oil. Inspect the surface for cracks, rivet grooves, burned areas and score marks. Light scoring can be removed with emery cloth. Check for cracked and broken ring gear teeth. Lay the flywheel/driveplate on a flat surface, and use a straight-edge to check for warpage.

5 Where a dual mass flywheel is fitted check for excessive play between the stationary section and the movable section. Make paint marks on the inner and outer sections and then rotate the secondary section of the flywheel. Note the amount of rotation between the two sections **(see illustration)**. As a rule of thumb anything greater than 15mm should be considered excessive. If in doubt (and given the amount of work required to remove the flywheel) a second opinion from a Ford

23.2 Home-made flywheel locking tool

23.5 Mark the inner and outer sections (arrowed) and check for excessive play

dealer or suitably equipped garage should be sought. Note that special tools are available to accurately asses the condition of the flywheel. If the service history of the vehicle is known and the clutch is being replaced for the second time, then the dual mass flywheel should always be replaced.

6 Clean and inspect the mating surfaces of the flywheel/driveplate and the crankshaft. If the crankshaft oil seal is leaking, renew it (see Section 21) before refitting the flywheel/ driveplate. In fact, given the large amount of work needed to remove the flywheel/ driveplate, it's probably worth fitting a new seal anyway, as a precaution.

Refitting

7 Make sure that the mating faces of the flywheel/driveplate and crankshaft are clean, then locate the flywheel/driveplate on the crankshaft – it will only fit in one position.

24.8 Move the coolant expansion bottle to the side

24.14 Remove the battery support panel

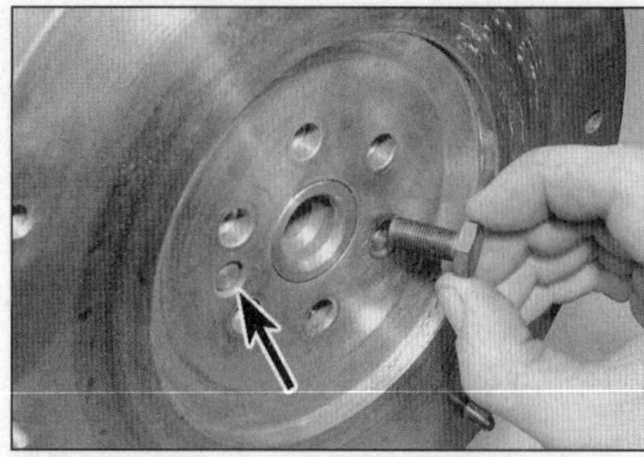

23.8 Fit the new flywheel retaining bolts. Note the dowel (arrowed) in the end of the crankshaft

8 Insert the new retaining bolts finger-tight **(see illustration)**.

9 Lock the flywheel/driveplate (see paragraph 2), then tighten the bolts in a diagonal sequence to the specified torque.

10 Refit the clutch with reference to Chapter 8 Section 6, and the transmission as described in Chapter 7A Section 6.

24 Engine/transmission mountings – inspection and renewal

General

1 The engine/transmission mountings seldom require attention, but broken or deteriorated mountings should be renewed immediately, or the added strain placed on the driveline components may cause damage or wear.

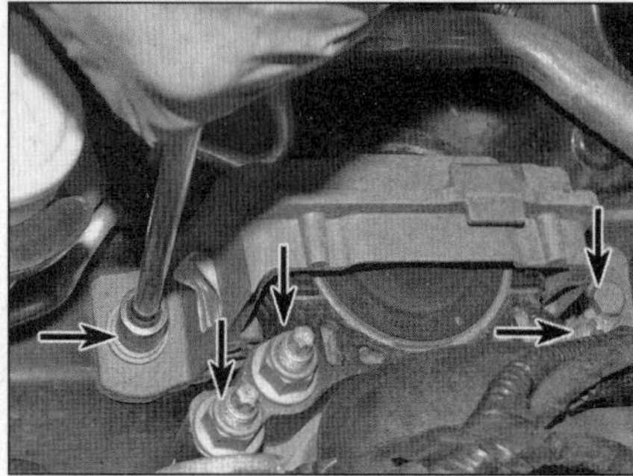

24.10 Undo the bolts and remove the mounting

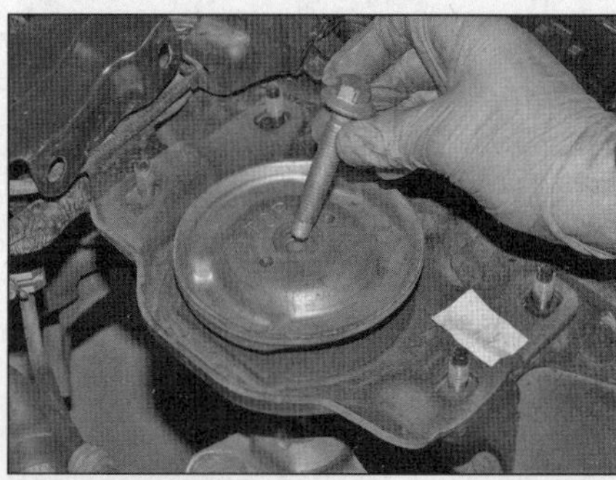

24.15 Remove the centre bolt

2 While separate mountings may be removed and refitted individually, if more than one is disturbed at a time – such as if the engine/transmission unit is removed from its mountings – they must be reassembled and their fasteners tightened in the position marked on removal.

3 On reassembly, the complete weight of the engine/transmission unit must not be taken by the mountings until all are correctly aligned with the marks made on removal. Tighten the engine/transmission mounting fasteners to their specified torque wrench settings.

Inspection

4 During the check, the engine/transmission unit must be raised slightly, to remove its weight from the mountings.

5 Raise the front of the vehicle, and support it securely on axle stands (see *Jacking and vehicle support*). Position a jack under the sump, with a large block of wood between the jack head and the sump, then carefully raise the engine/transmission just enough to take the weight off the mountings.

Warning: DO NOT place any part of your body under the engine when it is supported only by a jack.

6 Check the mountings to see if the rubber is cracked, hardened or separated from the metal components. Sometimes the rubber will split right down the centre.

7 Check for relative movement between each mounting's brackets and the engine/ transmission or body (use a large screwdriver or lever to attempt to move the mountings). If movement is noted, lower the engine and check-tighten the mounting fasteners.

Renewal

Note: *The following paragraphs assume the engine is supported beneath the sump as described earlier.*

Right-hand mounting

8 Lift up the coolant expansion tank and position it to one side **(see illustration)**. Note there is no need to disconnect the coolant pipes.

9 Mark the position of the mounting on the vehicle on the right-hand inner wing panel, and then undo the 2 bolts securing the mounting.

10 Undo the retaining bolts from the engine side of the mounting and then remove the mounting **(see illustration)**.

11 Re-align the marks made on removal. Tighten all fasteners to the torque wrench settings specified.

Left-hand mounting

12 Remove the air filter housing as described in Chapter 4A Section 3.

13 Remove the battery as described in Chapter 5 Section 4, then undo the 3 bolts and remove the battery tray. Disconnect any wiring as the tray is withdrawn.

14 Unclip the wiring loom from the battery tray support panel, remove the 4 bolts and withdraw the support panel **(see illustration)**.

15 With the transmission supported, note the position of the mounting then unscrew the centre retaining bolt to release the upper half of the mounting from the transmission **(see illustration)**.

16 Refitting is a reversal of removal. Re-align the mounting in the position noted on removal, then tighten all fasteners to the specified torque wrench settings.

Rear mounting (roll restrictor)

17 Remove the 3 mounting bolts from the transmission. Remove the single bolt from the subframe **(see illustration)**.

18 With the aid of an assistant pivot the engine (assuming the two main engine mountings are in position) and work the mounting free.

19 On refitting, ensure that the bolts are securely tightened to the specified torque wrench setting.

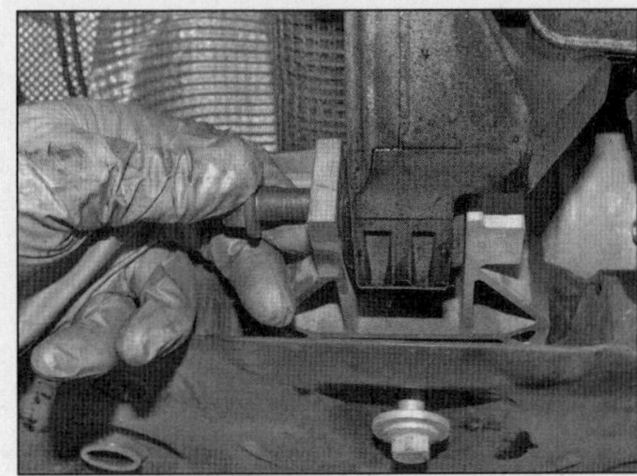

24.17 Remove the bolts

Chapter 2 Part B
1.5 litre diesel engine in-car repair procedures

Contents

Degrees of difficulty

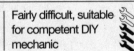

Easy, suitable for novice with little experience 	Fairly easy, suitable for beginner with some experience	Fairly difficult, suitable for competent DIY mechanic	Difficult, suitable for experienced DIY mechanic	Very difficult, suitable for expert DIY or professional

Specifications

General

Designation	Duratorq-TDCi
Engine codes*	XWMA, XWMB, XWMC
Capacity	1499 cc
Bore	73.5 mm
Stroke	88.3 mm
Direction of crankshaft rotation	Clockwise (viewed from the right-hand side of vehicle)
No 1 cylinder location	At the transmission end of block
Maximum power output:	88 kW (118 PS)
Maximum torque output:	270 Nm
Emissions level	Stage 6
Compression ratio	16: 1

** The engine code is stamped on a plate attached to the front of the cylinder block, next to the oil filter*

Compression pressures (engine hot, at cranking speed)

Normal	20 ± 5 bar
Minimum	15 bar
Maximum difference between any two cylinders	5 bar

Camshaft

Camshaft end float	0.195 – 0.3 mm

Lubrication system

Oil pump type	Gear-type, driven directly by the right-hand end of the crankshaft, by two flats machined along the crankshaft journal.
Minimum oil pressure at 80°C:	
Idle speed	1.0 to 2.0 bar
2000 rpm	2.3 to 3.7 bar

Torque wrench settings

	Nm	lbf ft
Ancillary drivebelt tensioner roller	25	18
Big-end bolts: *		
Stage 1	10	7
Stage 2	Slacken 180°	
Stage 3	10	7
Stage 4	Angle-tighten a further 130°	
Camshaft bearings:		
Stage 1	5	4
Stage 2	10	7
Camshaft bearing ladder:		
Studs	10	7
Bolts	10	7
Camshaft position sensor bolt	8	6
Camshaft sprocket bolt: *		
Stage 1	20	15
Stage 2	Angle-tighten a further 50°	
Coolant outlet housing bolts	8	6
Crankshaft position/speed sensor bolt	10	7
Crankshaft pulley/sprocket bolt: *		
Stage 1	35	26
Stage 2	Angle-tighten a further 190°	
Cylinder head bolts: *		
Stage 1	20	15
Stage 2	40	30
Stage 3	Angle-tighten a further 260°	
Cylinder head cover	10	7
EGR valve	10	7
Engine-to-transmission fixing bolts	47	35
Flywheel bolts: *		
Stage 1	30	22
Stage 2	Angle-tighten a further 90°	
Fuel pump sprocket	50	37
Left-hand engine/transmission mounting:		
Mounting-to-bracket outer nuts	48	35
Mounting bracket to transmission	80	59
Main bearing ladder outer seam bolts:		
Stage 1	5	4
Stage 2	10	7
Main bearing ladder to cylinder block:		
Stage 1	10	7
Stage 2	Slacken 180°	
Stage 3	10	7
Stage 4	30	22
Stage 5	Angle-tighten a further 140°	
Piston oil jet spray tube bolt	20	15
Oil cooler retaining bolts	10	7
Oil filter cover	25	18
Oil pick-up pipe	10	7
Oil pressure switch	30	22
Oil pump to cylinder block:		
Stage 1	5	4
Stage 2	9	7
Rear engine mounting:		
Rear through-bolt:		
Stage 1	30	22
Stage 2	Angle-tighten a further 270°	
Mounting bracket-to-transmission bolts	63	46
Right-hand engine mounting:		
Mounting to inner wing and mounting bracket (nuts/bolts)	48	35
Mounting bracket to engine block	55	41
Sump drain plug	35	26
Sump bolts/nuts	12	8
Timing belt idler pulley	37	27
Timing belt tensioner pulley	30	22
Timing cover bolts	5	4
Vacuum pump bolts	20	15

** Do not re-use*

1 General information

How to use this Chapter

1 This Part of Chapter 2 describes the repair procedures that can reasonably be carried out on the engine while it remains in the vehicle. If the engine has been removed from the vehicle and is being dismantled as described in Part D, any preliminary dismantling procedures can be ignored.

2 Note that, while it may be possible physically to overhaul items such as the piston/connecting rod assemblies while the engine is in the car, such tasks are not usually carried out as separate operations. Usually, several additional procedures are required (not to mention the cleaning of components and oilways); for this reason, all such tasks are classed as major overhaul procedures, and are described in Part D of this Chapter.

3 Part D describes the removal of the engine/transmission from the car, and the full overhaul procedures that can then be carried out.

4 The 1.5 litre Duratorq-TDCi engine is a 4-cylinder, turbocharged, single overhead cam (SOHC) 8-valve design, with direct injection. The engine is mounting transversely, with the transmission mounted on the left-hand side.

5 A toothed timing belt drives the camshaft, high-pressure fuel pump and coolant pump. The camshaft operates the inlet and exhaust valves via rocker arms which are supported at their pivot ends by hydraulic self-adjusting tappets. The camshaft Is supported by bearings machined directly in the cylinder head and camshaft bearing housing.

6 The high-pressure fuel pump supplies fuel to the fuel rail, and subsequently to the electronically-controlled injectors which inject the fuel direct into the combustion chambers. This design differs from the previous type where an injection pump supplies the fuel at high pressure to each injector. The earlier, conventional type injection pump required fine calibration and timing, and these functions are now completed by the high-pressure pump, electronic injectors and engine management ECM.

7 The crankshaft runs in five main bearings of the usual shell type. Endfloat is controlled by thrustwashers either side of No 2 main bearing.

8 The pistons are selected to be of matching weight, and incorporate fully-floating gudgeon pins retained by circlips.

Repair operations precaution

9 The engine is a complex unit with numerous accessories and ancillary components. The design of the engine compartment is such that every conceivable space has been utilised, and access to virtually all of the engine components is extremely limited. In many cases, ancillary components will have to be removed, or moved to one side, and wiring, pipes and hoses will have to be disconnected or removed from various cable clips and support brackets.

10 When working on this engine, read through the entire procedure first, look at the car and engine at the same time, and establish whether you have the necessary tools, equipment, skill and patience to proceed. Allow considerable time for any operation, and be prepared for the unexpected.

11 Because of the limited access, many of the engine photographs appearing in this Chapter were, by necessity, taken with the engine removed from the vehicle.

Warning: It is essential to observe strict precautions when working on the fuel system components of the engine, particularly the high-pressure side of the system. Before carrying out any engine operations that entail working on, or near, any part of the fuel system, refer to the special information given in Chapter 4B.

12 Operations with engine in vehicle

a) Compression pressure – testing.
b) Cylinder head cover – removal and refitting.
c) Crankshaft pulley – removal and refitting.
d) Timing belt covers – removal and refitting.
e) Timing belt – removal, refitting and adjustment.
f) Timing belt tensioner and sprockets – removal and refitting.
g) Camshaft oil seal – renewal.
h) Camshaft, rocker arms and hydraulic tappets – removal, inspection and refitting.
i) Sump – removal and refitting.
j) Oil pump – removal and refitting.
k) Crankshaft oil seals – renewal.
l) Engine/transmission mountings – inspection and renewal.
m) Flywheel – removal, inspection and refitting.

2 Compression and leakdown tests – description and interpretation

Compression test

Note: *A compression tester specifically designed for diesel engines must be used for this test.*

1 When engine performance is down, or if misfiring occurs which cannot be attributed to the fuel system, a compression test can provide diagnostic clues as to the engine's condition.

2 A compression tester specifically intended for diesel engines must be used, because of the higher pressures involved. The tester is connected to an adapter which screws into the glow plug or injector hole. On this engine, an adapter suitable for use in the glow plug holes will be required, so as not to disturb the fuel system components. It is unlikely to be worthwhile buying such a tester for occasional use, but it may be possible to borrow or hire one – if not, have the test performed by a garage.

3 Unless specific instructions to the contrary are supplied with the tester, observe the following points:

a) The battery must be in a good state of charge, the air filter must be clean, and the engine should be at normal operating temperature.
b) All the glow plugs should be removed, and the glow plug module disconnected as described in Chapter 6B Section 16 before starting the test.

4 The compression pressures measured are not so important as the balance between cylinders. Values are given in the Specifications.

5 The cause of poor compression is less easy to establish on a diesel engine than on a petrol one. The effect of introducing oil into the cylinders ('wet' testing) is not conclusive, because there is a risk that the oil will sit in the swirl chamber or in the recess on the piston crown instead of passing to the rings. However, the following can be used as a rough guide to diagnosis.

6 All cylinders should produce very similar pressures; any difference greater than that specified indicates the existence of a fault. Note that the compression should build-up quickly in a healthy engine; low compression on the first stroke, followed by gradually-increasing pressure on successive strokes, indicates worn piston rings. A low compression reading on the first stroke, which does not build-up during successive strokes, indicates leaking valves or a blown head gasket (a cracked head could also be the cause). Deposits on the undersides of the valve heads can also cause low compression.

7 A low reading from two adjacent cylinders is almost certainly due to the head gasket having blown between them; the presence of coolant in the engine oil will confirm this.

8 If the compression reading is unusually high, the cylinder head surfaces, valves and pistons are probably coated with carbon deposits. If this is the case, the cylinder head should be removed and decarbonised.

Note: *After performing this test, a fault code may be generated and stored in the PCM memory. Have the PCM self-diagnosis facility interrogated by a Ford dealer or suitably-equipped specialist, and the fault code erased. Inexpensive diagnostic code scanners are readily available.*

Leakdown test

9 A leakdown test measures the rate at which compressed air fed into the cylinder is lost. It is an alternative to a compression test, and in many ways it is better, since the escaping air provides easy identification of where pressure loss is occurring (piston rings, valves or head gasket).

10 The equipment needed for leakdown testing is unlikely to be available to the home mechanic. If poor compression is suspected, have the test performed by a suitably-equipped garage.

3.9 Insert the special tool (or a 5.0 mm drill bit/bolt) through the round hole in the sprocket flange into the hole in the oil pump housing

3.10 Insert the special tool (or an 8.0 mm bolt/rod) through the hole in the camshaft sprocket into the corresponding hole in the cylinder head

3.11 Insert a 5.0 mm rod (or similar) through the slot in the fuel pump sprocket flange

3 Engine assembly/valve timing holes – general information and usage

Note: *Disconnect the battery to eliminate the possibility of the engine being accidentally cranked on the starter motor, which is likely to cause damage with the locking pins in place. If the engine is to be left in this state for a long period of time, it is also a good idea to place suitable warning notices inside the vehicle, and in the engine compartment.*

1 Timing holes or slots are located in the crankshaft pulley flange and camshaft sprocket hub. This will ensure that the valve timing is maintained during operations that require removal and refitting of the timing belt. When the holes/slots are aligned with their corresponding holes in the cylinder block and cylinder head, suitable diameter bolts/pins can be inserted to lock the crankshaft and camshaft in position, preventing rotation.

2 Note that the fuel system used on these engines does not have a conventional diesel injection pump, but instead uses a high-pressure fuel pump. However, the fuel pump sprocket must be pegged in position in a similar fashion to the camshaft sprocket.

3 To align the engine assembly/valve timing holes, proceed as follows.

4 Apply the handbrake, then jack up the front of the vehicle and support it on axle stands (see *Jacking and vehicle support*). Remove the right-hand front roadwheel.

5 To gain access to the crankshaft pulley, to enable the engine to be turned, the wheel arch plastic liner must be removed. The liner is secured by several plastic expanding rivets/nut/bolts. To remove the rivets, push in the centre pins a little, then prise the clips from place. Remove the liner from under the front wing.

6 Remove the crankshaft pulley as described in Section 5.

7 Remove the upper and lower timing belt covers as described in Section 6.

8 Temporarily refit the crankshaft pulley bolt (without the crankshaft pulley) and then remove the crankshaft locking tool.

9 Turn the crankshaft until the timing hole in the crankshaft sprocket aligns with the hole in the oil pump casing (this is at the 12 o'clock position). Fit the special tool 303-732, or a suitable alternative (5.0 mm drill bit or rod) and lock the crankshaft in position **(see illustration)**.

10 With the crankshaft locked in position fit the camshaft locking tool (303-735 or similar). The hole in the camshaft sprocket should be at approximately the 1 o'clock position **(see illustration)**. If this is not the case remove the crankshaft locking pin and rotate the engine one revolution. Note that the crankshaft must always be turned in a clockwise direction (viewed from the right-hand side of vehicle).

11 When refitting the timing belt, rotate the fuel pump sprocket clockwise and insert a 5.0 mm bolt or drive bit through the slot in the sprocket flange and into the corresponding hole in the fuel pump mounting bracket **(see illustration)**.

12 The crankshaft and camshaft are now locked in position, preventing unnecessary rotation.

4 Cylinder head cover – removal and refitting

Removal

1 Pull up and remove the plastic cover from the top of the engine.

2 Disconnect the wiring plugs from the fuel injectors, then unclip the wiring harness from the top of the engine **(see illustration)**.

3 Disconnect the wiring plug, undo the 4 retaining bolts and remove the throttle body **(see illustration)**. The lower, left-hand bolt is accessed from the rear.

4 Undo the clamps, then undo the 3 mounting bolts and 1 nut, and remove the intercooler pipe from across the top of the engine.

5 Release the clips and disconnect the breather hose from the cylinder head cover.

6 Unclip the wiring harness, then unbolt and then remove the timing belt upper cover as described in Section 6.

7 Prise up and remove fuel return pipe assembly plastic rivet **(see illustration)**.

8 Remove the 11 bolts and then remove the

4.2 Undo the bolt and unclip the wiring harness

4.3 Throttle body retaining bolts

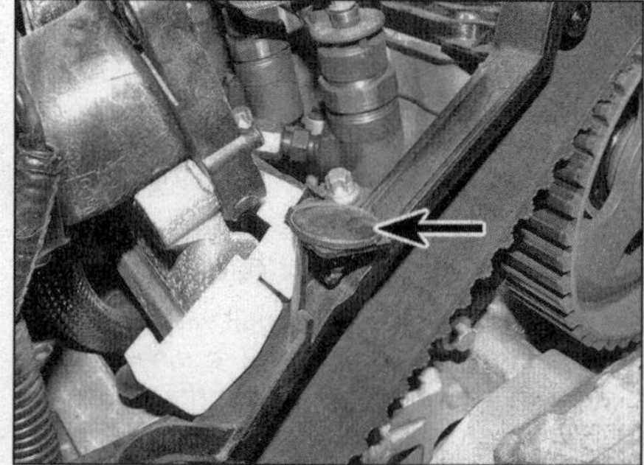

4.7 Prise up the rivet securing the fuel return pipe assembly

cover **(see illustrations)**. Recover the rubber seal. Examine the seal and renew it if there are any signs of deterioration or damage.

Refitting

9 Refitting is a reversal of removal, but ensure that the seal is correctly located **(see illustrations)**.

5 Crankshaft pulley – removal and refitting

Removal

1 Jack up and support the front of the vehicle (see *Jacking and vehicle support*) then undo the fasteners and remove the engine undershield **(see illustration)**.

2 Remove the auxiliary drivebelt as described in Chapter 1B Section 32.

3 To prevent accidental damage, undo the lower timing belt cover lower rear bolt 1.5 turns, then undo the retaining bolt and move the crankshaft position sensor to one side **(see illustrations)**.

4 To lock the crankshaft, working underneath the engine, insert Ford tool No. 303-734 or a 12 mm diameter rod into the hole in the engine block casting over the lower section of the flywheel **(see illustration)**. Note that the hole in the casting and flywheel is provided purely to lock the crankshaft while the pulley bolt is undone – it does not position the crankshaft at TDC. Rotate the crankshaft clockwise until the tool engages in the hole in the flywheel – don't rotate the crank pulley anti-clockwise.

5 Pull the central cover from the pulley **(see illustration)**.

6 Using a suitable socket and extension bar, unscrew the retaining bolt, remove the washer, then slide the pulley off the end of the crankshaft **(see illustrations)**. If the pulley is tight fit, it can be drawn off the crankshaft using a suitable puller. If a puller is being

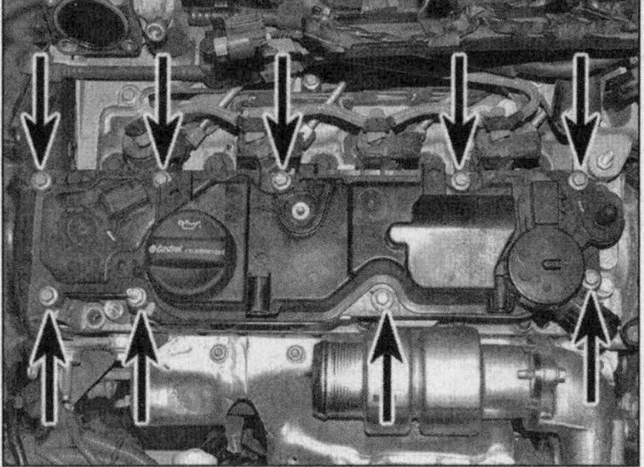

4.8a Undo the 9 bolts at the top...

4.8b ...and the 2 bolts at the right-hand end of the cover

4.9a Gently push back the clips to release the seal

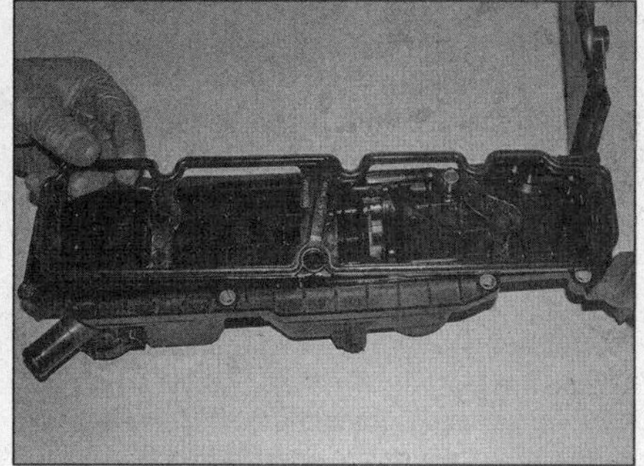

4.9b Ensure the seal is correctly seated

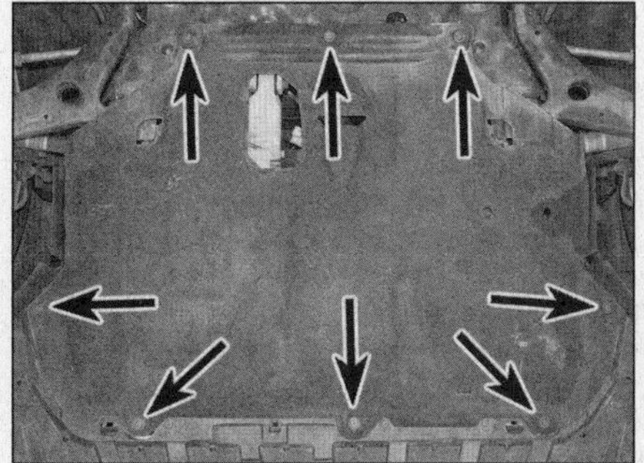

5.1 Manoeuvre the engine undershield from place

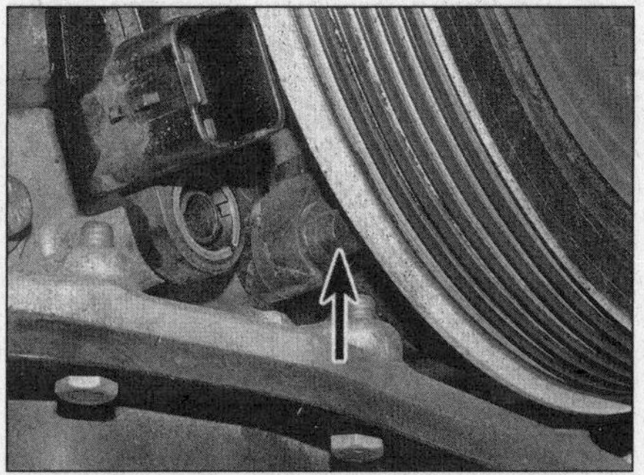

5.3a Undo the lower cover rear bolt 1.5 turns

5.3b Note the sensor locating dowel and pin

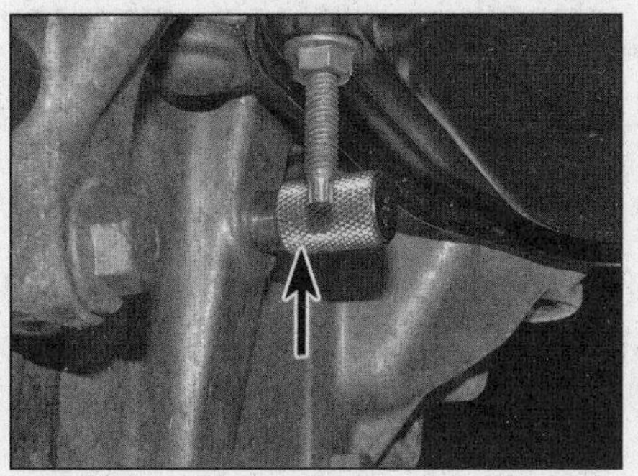

5.4 Install the flywheel locking tool

5.5 Pull the cover from the pulley

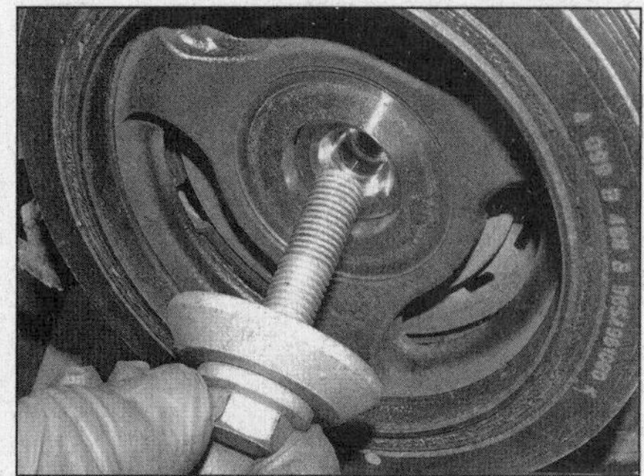

5.6a Remove the bolt and washer

5.6b The key on the crankshaft engages with the slot in the pulley

used, refit the pulley retaining bolt without the washer, to avoid damaging the crankshaft as the puller is tightened.

Caution: Do not touch the outer magnetic sensor ring of the sprocket with your fingers, or allow metallic particles to come into contact with it.

Refitting

7 Refit the pulley to the end of the crankshaft.

8 Refit the crankshaft pulley. Fit a new bolt and retaining washer. Tighten the bolt to the specified torque, then through the specified angle.

9 Refit the cover to the centre of the pulley.

10 Remove the locking tool.

11 Refit the crankshaft position sensor and tighten the retaining bolt to the specified torque.

12 Refit and tension the auxiliary drivebelt as described in Chapter 1B Section 32.

13 Refit the remaining components in reverse order of removal.

6 Timing belt covers – removal and refitting

Warning: Refer to the precautionary information contained in Section 1 before proceeding.

Removal

Upper cover

1 Pull the plastic cover on the top of the engine upwards from its' mountings.

2 Unclip the wiring loom and fuel lines from the cover.

3 Undo the 4 bolts and remove the timing belt upper cover.

Lower cover

4 Remove the crankshaft pulley as described in Section 5.

5 Position a trolley/workshop jack under the engine. Place a block of wood on the jack head (to help spread the load on the sump), then take the weight of the engine.

6 Undo the nuts/bolts, and remove the right-hand engine mounting **(see illustration)**.

7 Undo the 3 retaining bolts and move the wiring harness guide away from the engine **(see illustrations)**. The rear bolt is accessible from underneath the vehicle.

8 Undo the remaining bolt and remove the auxiliary drivebelt tensioner assembly.

9 Undo the 5 bolts and remove the lower cover **(see illustration)**.

Refitting

10 Refitting of all the covers is a reversal of the relevant removal procedure, ensuring that each cover section is correctly located, and that the cover retaining bolts are securely tightened. Ensure that all disturbed hoses are reconnected and retained by their relevant clips.

7 Timing belt – removal, inspection, refitting and tensioning

General

1 The timing belt drives the camshaft, high-pressure fuel pump, and coolant pump from a toothed sprocket on the end of the crankshaft. If the belt breaks or slips in service, the pistons are likely to hit the valve heads, resulting in expensive damage.

2 The timing belt should be renewed at the specified intervals, or earlier if it is contaminated with oil, or at all noisy in operation (a 'scraping' noise due to uneven wear).

3 If the timing belt is being removed, it is a wise precaution to renew the coolant pump at the same time. This may avoid the need to remove the timing belt again at a later stage, should the coolant pump fail. The timing belt tensioner should always be replaced when a new timing belt is fitted.

Removal

4 Disconnect the battery, as described in Chapter 5 Section 4.

5 Remove the upper and lower timing belt covers, as described in Section 6.

6 Undo the bolts and remove the mounting bracket from the right-hand end of the engine.

7 Lock the crankshaft and camshaft in the correct position as described in Section 3. If necessary, temporarily refit the crankshaft pulley bolt to enable the crankshaft to be rotated.

8 Insert a hexagon key into the belt tensioner pulley centre, slacken the pulley bolt, and allow the tensioner to rotate clockwise, relieving the belt tension **(see illustration)**. With the belt slack, temporarily tighten the pulley bolt.

9 Note its routing, then remove the timing belt from the sprockets.

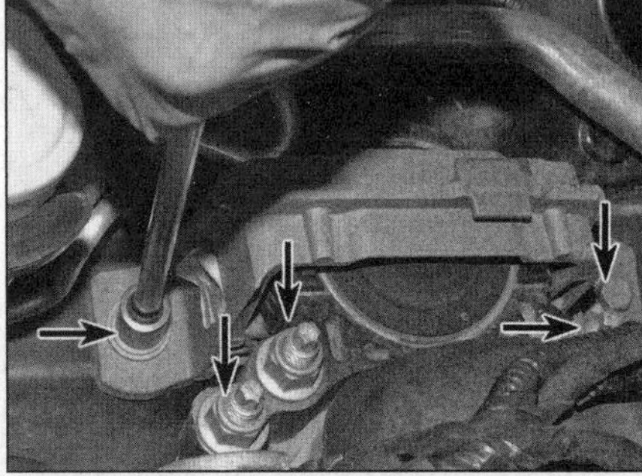

6.6 Engine mounting nuts/bolt

6.7a Undo the 2 bolts above the auxiliary drivebelt tensioner...

6.7b ... and the bolt at the rear

6.9 Lower timing belt cover bolts

7.8 Slacken the bolt and allow the tensioner to rotate, relieving the tension on the belt

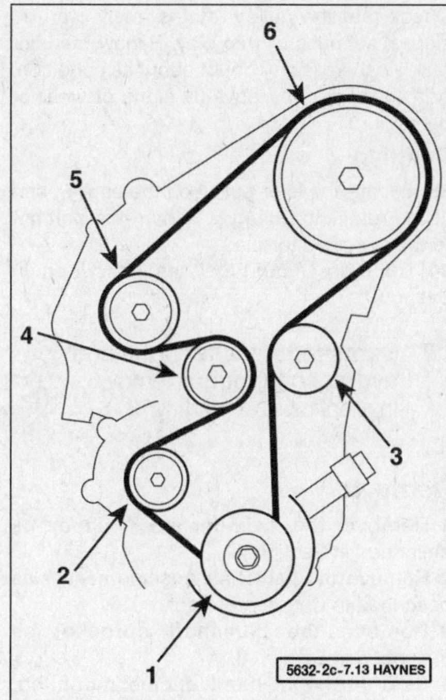

7.12 Timing belt routing

1 Crankshaft
2 Coolant pump
3 Idler
4 Tensioner
5 Fuel pump
6 Camshaft

Inspection

10 Renew the belt as a matter of course, regardless of its apparent condition. The cost of a new belt is nothing compared with the cost of repairs should the belt break in service. If signs of oil contamination are found, trace the source of the oil leak and rectify it. Wash down the engine timing belt area and all related components, to remove all traces of oil. The tensioner must always be replaced. Check that the idler pulleys rotate freely without any sign of roughness, and also check that the coolant pump pulley rotates freely. It is highly recommended that both the coolant pump and the idler pulley are replaced at the same time as the timing belt and tensioner.

TOOL TIP

A sprocket holding tool can be made from two lengths of steel strip bolted together to form a forked end. Drill holes and insert bolts in the ends of the fork to engage with the sprocket spokes.

Refitting and tensioning

11 Commence refitting by ensuring that the crankshaft, camshaft and fuel pump sprocket timing pins are in position as described in Section 3.
12 Locate the timing belt on the crankshaft sprocket, then keeping it taut, locate it around the idler pulley, camshaft sprocket, high-pressure pump sprocket, coolant pump sprocket, and the tensioner roller **(see illustration)**.
13 Slacken the tensioner pulley bolt, and using a hexagonal key, rotate the tensioner anti-clockwise, which moves the index arm clockwise, until the index arm is aligned as shown **(see illustration)**. Tighten the tensioner bolt after setting the alignment.
14 Remove the camshaft, crankshaft and fuel pump sprocket (where applicable) timing pins and, using a socket on the crankshaft pulley bolt, rotate the crankshaft clockwise 6 complete revolutions. Refit the crankshaft and camshaft locking pins.
15 Check that the tensioner index arm is still aligned **(see illustration 7.13)**. If it is not, remove and belt and begin the refitting process again, starting at Paragraph 11.
16 The remainder of refitting is a reversal of removal. Tighten all fasteners to the specified torque where given.

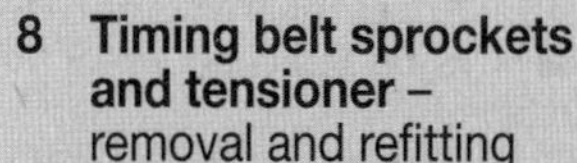

8 Timing belt sprockets and tensioner – removal and refitting

Camshaft sprocket

Removal

1 Remove the timing belt as described in Section 7.
2 Remove the locking tool from the camshaft sprocket/hub. Slacken the sprocket hub retaining bolt. To prevent the camshaft rotating as the bolt is slackened, a sprocket holding tool will be required. In the absence of the special Ford tool, an acceptable substitute can be fabricated at home **(see Tool Tip)**. Do not attempt to use the engine assembly/valve timing locking tool to prevent the sprocket from rotating whilst the bolt is slackened.
3 Remove the sprocket hub retaining bolt, and slide the sprocket and hub off the end of the camshaft.
4 Clean the camshaft sprocket thoroughly, and renew it if there are any signs of wear, damage or cracks.

Refitting

5 Refit the camshaft sprocket to the camshaft **(see illustration)**.
6 Refit the sprocket hub retaining bolt. Tighten the bolt to the specified torque, preventing the camshaft from turning as during removal.
7 Align the engine assembly/valve timing slot in the camshaft sprocket hub with the hole in the cylinder head and refit the timing pin to lock the camshaft in position.
8 Fit the timing belt around the pump sprocket and camshaft sprocket, and tension the timing belt as described in Section 7.

8.5 Ensure the lug on the sprocket hub engages with the slot on the end of the camshaft

7.13 The index arm must align with the lug

Crankshaft sprocket

Removal

9 Remove the timing belt as described in Section 7.
10 Check that the engine assembly/valve timing holes are still aligned as described in Section 3, and the camshaft sprocket and flywheel are locked in position.
11 Slide the sprocket off the end of the crankshaft and collect the Woodruff key **(see illustrations)**.

8.11a Slide the sprocket from the crankshaft...

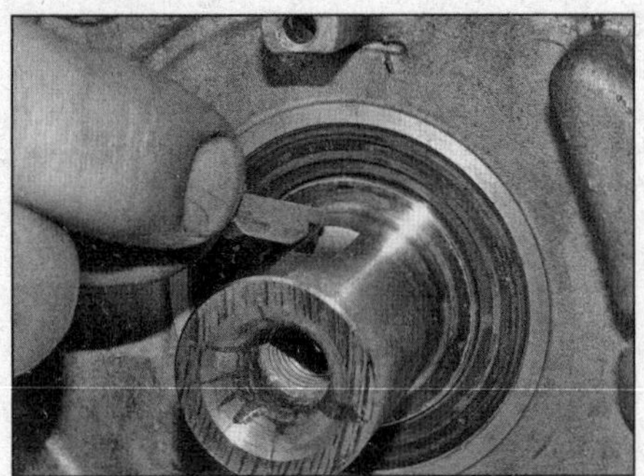

8.11b ...and recover the Woodruff key

12 Examine the crankshaft oil seal for signs of oil leakage and, if necessary, renew it as described in Section 13.

13 Clean the crankshaft sprocket thoroughly, and renew it if there are any signs of wear, damage or cracks. Recover the crankshaft locating key.

Refitting

14 Refit the key to the end of the crankshaft, then refit the crankshaft sprocket (with the flange facing the crankshaft pulley).

15 Fit the timing belt around the crankshaft sprocket, and tension the timing belt as described in Section 7.

Fuel pump sprocket

Removal

16 Remove the timing belt as described in Section 7.

17 Using a suitable socket, undo the pump sprocket retaining nut. The sprocket can be held stationary by inserting a suitably-sized locking pin, drill or rod through the slot in the sprocket flange, and into the corresponding hole in the backplate.

18 The pump sprocket is a taper fit on the pump shaft and it will be necessary to use a two-legged puller to release if from the taper.

19 Partially unscrew the sprocket retaining nut, fit the puller and release the sprocket from the taper.

20 Clean the sprocket thoroughly, and renew it if there are any signs of wear, damage or cracks.

Refitting

21 Refit the pump sprocket and retaining nut, and tighten the nut to the specified torque.

8.31 Timing belt idler pulley retaining nut

22 Refit the timing belt as described in Section 7.

Coolant pump sprocket

23 The coolant pump sprocket is integral with the pump, and cannot be removed. Coolant pump removal is described in Chapter 3 Section 10.

Tensioner pulley

Removal

24 Remove the timing belt as described in Section 7.

25 Remove the tensioner pulley retaining bolt, and then remove the tensioner.

26 Clean the tensioner pulley, but do not use any strong solvent which may enter the pulley bearings. Check that the pulley rotates freely, with no sign of stiffness or free play. The pulley should always be replaced when the timing belt is replaced.

27 Examine the pulley mounting stud for signs of damage and if necessary, renew it.

Refitting

28 Refitting is a reversal of removal.

29 Refit the timing belt as described in Section 7.

Idler pulley

Removal

30 Remove the timing belt as described in Section 7.

31 Undo the retaining bolt/nut and withdraw the idler pulley from the engine **(see illustration)**.

32 Clean the idler pulley, but do not use any strong solvent which may enter the bearings. Check that the pulley rotates freely, with no sign of stiffness or free play. Renew the idler pulley if there is any doubt about its condition, or if there are any obvious signs of wear or damage.

Refitting

33 Locate the idler pulley on the engine, and fit the retaining bolt/nut. Tighten the bolt/nut to the specified torque.

34 Refit the timing belt as described in Section 7.

9 Camshafts, rocker arms and hydraulic tappets – removal, inspection and refitting

Removal

1 Remove the cylinder head cover as described in Section 4.

2 Remove the camshaft position sensor as described in Chapter 6A Section 14.

3 Remove the camshaft sprocket as described in Section 8.

4 Refit the right-hand engine mounting, but only tighten the bolts moderately; this will keep the engine supported during the camshaft removal.

5 Undo the bolts and remove the vacuum pump as described in Chapter 9 Section 20. Recover the pump O-ring seals.

6 Unbolt the fuel filter (see Chapter 1B Section 28) and move it to one side.

7 Working in reverse order to that shown **(see illustration 9.22)** remove the retaining bolts and then remove camshaft bearing cap ladder **(see illustration)**.

8 Lift out the camshaft **(see illustration)** and dispose of the oil seal. A new one will be required.

9 Obtain 8 small, clean plastic containers, and number them 1 to 4 inlet and 1 to 4 exhaust; alternatively, divide a larger container into 8 compartments.

10 Lift out each rocker arm. Place the rocker arms in their respective positions in the box or containers **(see illustration)**.

11 A compartmentalised container filled with engine oil is now required to retain the hydraulic tappets while they are removed from the cylinder head. Withdraw each hydraulic

9.7 Remove the bearing ladder

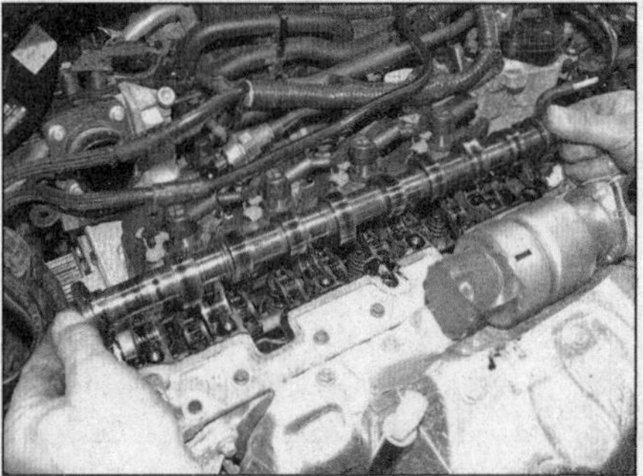

9.8 Remove the camshaft

9.10 Remove the rocker arms (cam followers)v

follower **(see illustration)** and place it in the container, keeping them each identified for correct refitting. The tappets must be totally submerged in the oil to prevent air entering them.

Inspection

12 Inspect the cam lobes and the camshaft bearing journals for scoring or other visible evidence of wear. Once the surface hardening of the cam lobes has been eroded, wear will occur at an accelerated rate.

Note: *If these symptoms are visible on the tips of the camshaft lobes, check the corresponding rocker arm, as it will probably be worn as well.*

13 Examine the condition of the bearing surfaces in the cylinder head and camshaft bearing housing. If wear is evident, the cylinder head and bearing housing will both have to be renewed, as they are a matched assembly.

14 Inspect the rocker arms and tappets for scuffing, cracking or other damage and renew any components as necessary. Also check the condition of the tappet bores in the cylinder head. As with the camshafts, any wear in this area will necessitate cylinder head renewal.

Refitting

15 Thoroughly clean the sealant from the mating surfaces of the cylinder head and camshaft bearing housing. Use a suitable liquid gasket dissolving agent (available from Ford dealers) together with a soft putty knife; do not use a metal scraper or the faces will be damaged. As there is no conventional gasket used, the cleanliness of the mating faces is of the utmost importance.

16 Clean off any oil, dirt or grease from both components and dry with a clean lint-free cloth. Ensure that all the oilways are completely clean.

17 Liberally lubricate the hydraulic tappet bores in the cylinder head with clean engine oil.

18 Insert the hydraulic tappets into their original bores in the cylinder head unless they have been renewed.

19 Lubricate the rocker arms and place them over their respective tappets and valve stems. Lubricate the bearing surfaces **(see illustration)** and then refit the camshaft.

20 Apply a thin bead of silicone sealant (Ford part No WSE-M4G323-A4) to the mating surface of the camshaft cover/bearing ladder as shown **(see illustration)**.

21 Assemble the bearing ladder within 10 minutes of applying the sealant. Ford technicians use a special tool (303-245) to align the bearing ladder, however 2 suitable bolts (with their heads and threads cut off) can be used if the tool is not available.

22 Tighten the bolts to the specified torque in sequence **(see illustration)**.

23 Fit a new camshaft oil seal as described in Section 13.

9.11 Use long nose pliers to remove the hydraulic tappets

9.20 Apply sealant to the camshaft housing

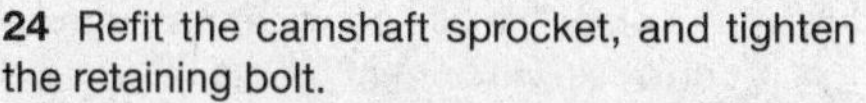

24 Refit the camshaft sprocket, and tighten the retaining bolt.

25 Refit the timing belt and temporarily refit the crankshaft pulley bolt – use the old bolt. Rotate the engine at least 20 revolutions to allow the oil pump to deliver oil to the camshaft and associated components. Refit the timing belt cover.

26 Refit the remainder of the components in the reverse order of removal.

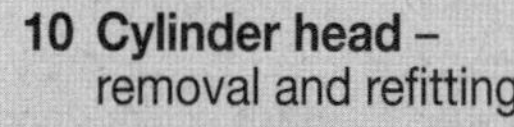

10 Cylinder head – removal and refitting

Removal

1 Apply the handbrake, then jack up the front of the vehicle and support it on axle stands (see *Jacking and vehicle support*).

10.5 Remove the air intake duct

9.19 Lubricate the bearing surfaces

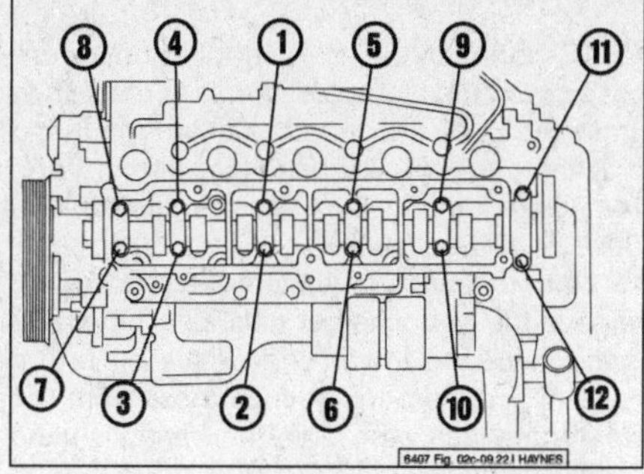

9.22 Bearing ladder bolts tightening sequence

2 Disconnect the battery negative lead as described in Chapter 5 Section 4.

3 Remove the windscreen cowl panel as described in Chapter 11 Section 12.

4 Drain the cooling system as described in Chapter 1B Section 36.

5 Release the clamps, undo the 2 bolts, remove the air intake duct between the air cleaner housing and turbocharger, and disconnect the breather hose from the cylinder head cover **(see illustration)**.

6 Remove the timing belt, camshaft, rocker arms and hydraulic tappets as described in Section 9.

7 Remove the diesel particulate filter as described in Chapter 4B Section 21.

8 Remove the EGR cooler assembly as described in Chapter 4B Section 17.

9 Disconnect the hoses and unbolt the fuel filter assembly as described in Chapter 1B Section 28.

10 Undo the upper mounting bolts, and pivot the alternator away from the engine, undo the oil dipstick guide tube bolt, then undo the bolts securing the alternator mounting bracket to the cylinder head/block.

11 Note their fitted positions, then disconnect the wiring plugs as necessary, and unbolt the wiring harness duct from above the fuel rail and injectors **(see illustration)**.

12 Undo the unions and remove the high-pressure pipes between the fuel rail and the injectors. Counterhold the pipe unions with an open-ended spanner on the injector ports to prevent them from rotating. Discard the pipes, new ones must be fitted. Plug the openings to prevent contamination.

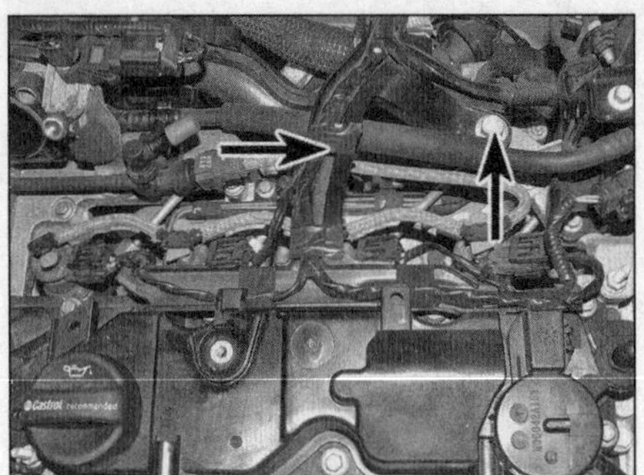

10.11 Undo the bolt, disconnect the wiring plugs, then unclip the harness duct

10.13 Depress the buttons, then disconnect the fuel supply and return hoses from the pump

10.16 Remove the coolant outlet housing

13 Disconnect the fuel supply and return hoses from the high-pressure fuel pump, then undo the bolts securing the pump mounting bracket to the cylinder head **(see illustration)**.

14 Remove the fuel injectors as described in Chapter 4B Section 14.

15 With reference to Chapter 4B Section 19, remove the turbocharger oil supply pipe, and disconnect the lower end of the oil return hose. Disconnect the vacuum hose from the wastegate actuator, and the variable vane position sensor.

16 Undo the coolant outlet housing (left-hand end of the cylinder head) retaining bolts, slacken the two bolts securing the housing support bracket to the top of the transmission bellhousing, and move the outlet housing away from the cylinder head a little **(see illustration)**. There is no need to disconnect the hoses.

17 Check that no components or electrical connectors are still fitted to the cylinder head.

18 Working in the **reverse** of the sequence shown **(see illustration 10.37)** undo the cylinder head bolts. Discard the bolts – new ones must be fitted.

19 Release the cylinder head from the cylinder block and location dowels by rocking it. The Ford tool for doing this consists simply of two metal rods with 90-degree angled ends **(see illustration)**. Do not prise between the mating faces of the cylinder head and block, as this may damage the gasket faces.

20 Lift the cylinder head from the block, and recover the gasket.

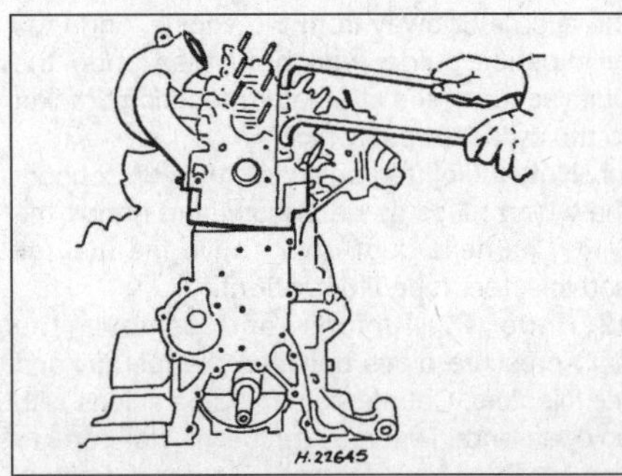

10.19 Free the cylinder head using angled rods

Preparation for refitting

21 The mating faces of the cylinder head and cylinder block must be perfectly clean before refitting the head. Ford recommend the use of a scouring agent for this purpose, but acceptable results can be achieved by using a hard plastic or wood scraper to remove all traces of gasket and carbon. The same method can be used to clean the piston crowns. Take particular care to avoid scoring or gouging the cylinder head/cylinder block mating surfaces during the cleaning operations, as aluminium alloy is easily damaged. Make sure that the carbon is not allowed to enter the oil and water passages – this is particularly important for the lubrication system, as carbon could block the oil supply to the engine's components. Using adhesive tape and paper, seal the water, oil and bolt holes in the cylinder block. To prevent carbon entering the gap between the pistons and bores, smear a little grease in the gap. After cleaning each piston, use a small brush to remove all traces of grease and carbon from the gap, then wipe away the remainder with a clean rag.

22 Check the mating surfaces of the cylinder block and the cylinder head for nicks, deep scratches and other damage. If slight, they may be removed carefully with a file, but if excessive, machining may be the only alternative to renewal. If warpage of the cylinder head gasket surface is suspected, use a straight-edge to check it for distortion. Refer to Part D of this Chapter if necessary.

23 Thoroughly clean the threads of the cylinder head bolt holes in the cylinder block. Ensure that the bolts run freely in their threads, and that all traces of oil and water are removed from each bolt hole.

Gasket selection

24 The gasket thickness is indicated by notches/holes on the front edge of the gasket. If the crankshaft or pistons/connecting rods have not been disturbed, fit a new gasket with the same number of notches/holes as the previous one. If the crankshaft/piston or connecting rods have been disturbed, it's necessary to work out the piston protrusion as follows:

25 Remove the crankshaft timing pin, then turn the crankshaft until pistons 1 and 4 are at TDC (Top Dead Centre). Position a dial test indicator (dial gauge) on the cylinder block adjacent to the rear of No 1 piston, and zero it on the block face. Transfer the probe to the crown of No 1 piston (10.0 mm in from the rear edge), then slowly turn the crankshaft back-and-forth past TDC, noting the highest reading on the indicator. Record this reading as protrusion A.

26 Repeat the check described in paragraph 25, this time 10.0 mm in from the front edge of the No 1 piston crown. Record this reading as protrusion B.

27 Add protrusion A to protrusion B, then divide the result by 2 to obtain an average reading for piston No 1.

28 Repeat the procedure described in paragraphs 25 to 27 on piston 4, then turn the crankshaft through 180° and carry out the procedure on the piston Nos 2 and 3 **(see illustration)**. Check that there is a maximum difference of 0.07 mm protrusion between any two pistons.

29 If a dial test indicator is not available, piston protrusion may be measured using a straight-edge and feeler blades or Vernier calipers. However, this is much less accurate, and cannot therefore be recommended.

30 Note the greatest piston protrusion measurement, and use this to determine the correct cylinder head gasket from the table below. The series of notches/holes on the

10.28 Measure the piston protrusion using a DTI gauge

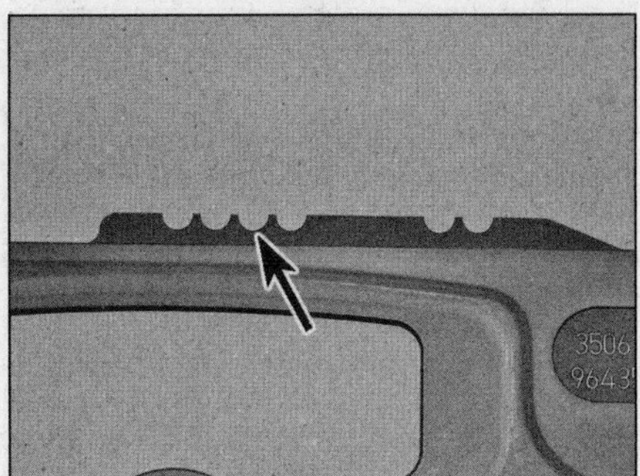

10.30 Cylinder head gasket thickness identification notches

10.33 Ensure the gasket locates over the dowels

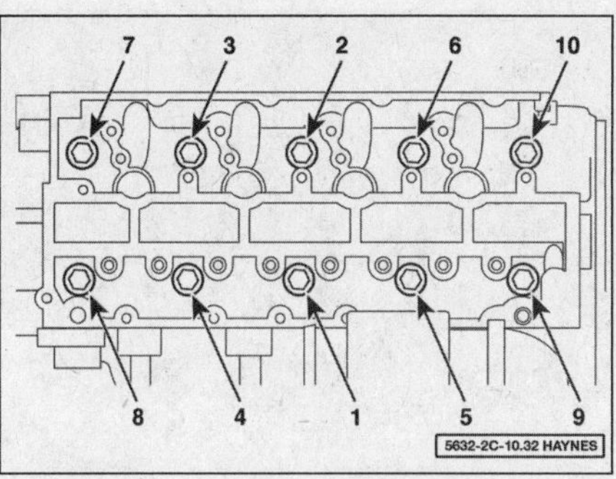

10.37 Cylinder head bolt tightening sequence

side of the gasket are used for thickness identification **(see illustration)**.

Piston protrusion (mm)	Gasket thickness (mm)	Notches
0.533 to 0.634	*1.25*	*2*
0.634 to 0.684	*1.30*	*3*
0.684 to 0.734	*1.35*	*1*
0.734 to 0.784	*1.40*	*4*
0.784 to 0.886	*1.45*	*5*

Refitting

31 Turn the crankshaft and position Nos 1 and 4 pistons at TDC, then turn the crankshaft a quarter turn (90°) anti-clockwise.

32 Thoroughly clean the surfaces of the cylinder head and block.

33 Make sure that the locating dowels are in place, then fit the correct gasket the right way round on the cylinder block **(see illustration)**.

34 Carefully lower the cylinder head onto the gasket and block, making sure that it locates correctly onto the dowels.

35 Apply a smear of grease to the threads, and to the underside of the heads of the new cylinder head bolts.

36 Carefully insert the cylinder head bolts into their holes (do not drop them in) and initially finger-tighten them.

37 Working progressively and in sequence, tighten the cylinder head bolts to their Stage 1 torque setting, using a torque wrench and suitable socket **(see illustration)**.

38 Once all the bolts have been tightened to their Stage 1 torque setting, working again in the specified sequence, tighten each bolt to the specified Stage 2 setting. Finally, angle-tighten the bolts through the specified Stage 3 angle. It is recommended that an angle-measuring gauge is used during this stage of tightening, to ensure accuracy. **Note:** *Retightening of the cylinder head bolts after running the engine is not required.*

39 Refit the hydraulic tappets, rocker arms, and camshaft housing (complete with camshafts) as described in Section 9.

40 Refit the timing belt as described in Section 7.

41 The remainder of refitting is a reversal of removal, noting the following points.

a) Use a new seal when refitting the coolant outlet housing.

b) When refitting a cylinder head, it is good practice to renew the thermostat.

c) Tighten all fasteners to the specified torque where given.

d) Refill the cooling system.

e) The engine may run erratically for the first few miles, until the engine management ECM relearns its stored values.

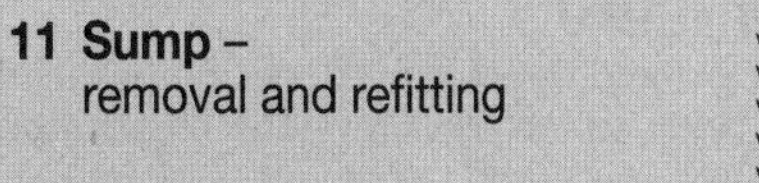

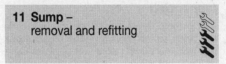

11 Sump – removal and refitting

Removal

1 Drain the engine oil, then clean and refit the engine oil drain plug, tightening it securely. If the engine is nearing its service interval when the oil and filter are due for renewal, it is recommended that the filter is also removed, and a new one fitted. After reassembly, the engine can then be refilled with fresh oil. Refer to Chapter 1B Section 13 for further information.

2 Apply the handbrake, then jack up the front of the vehicle and support it on axle stands (see *Jacking and vehicle support*). Undo the bolts and remove the engine undershield.

3 Although not strictly necessary, remove the exhaust front pipe as described in Chapter 4B Section 21.

4 Where necessary, disconnect the wiring connector from the oil temperature sender unit, which is screwed into the sump.

5 Progressively slacken and remove all the sump retaining bolts/nuts. Since the sump bolts vary in length, remove each bolt in turn, and store it in its correct fitted order by pushing it through a clearly-marked cardboard template. This will avoid the possibility of installing the bolts in the wrong locations on refitting.

11.8 Apply a bead of sealant to the sump or crankcase mating surface. Ensure the sealant is applied to the inside of the retaining bolt holes

6 Try to break the joint by striking the sump with the palm of your hand, then lower and withdraw the sump from under the car. If the sump is stuck (which is quite likely) use a putty knife or similar, carefully inserted between the sump and block. Ease the knife along the joint until the sump is released. While the sump is removed, take the opportunity to check the oil pump pick-up/strainer for signs of clogging or splitting. If necessary, remove the pump as described in Section 12, and clean or renew the strainer.

Refitting

7 Clean all traces of sealant from the mating surfaces of the cylinder block/crankcase and sump, then use a clean rag to wipe out the sump and the engine's interior.

8 Ensure that the sump mating surfaces are clean and dry, then apply a 3mm diameter bead of sealant (Ford part No WSE-M4G323-A4) to the sump mating surface **(see illustration)**. The sealant must be applied to the Inside of the bolt holes. Note that the sump must be installed within 10 minutes of applying the sealant, and the bolts tightened within a further 5 minutes.

9 Offer up the sump to the cylinder block/crankcase. Refit its retaining bolts/nuts, ensuring that each bolt is screwed into its original location. Tighten the bolts evenly and progressively to the specified torque setting **(see illustration)**.

11.9 Refit the sump and tighten the bolts

12.4 Oil pick-up tube bolts

12.5 Oil pump retaining bolts

12.6 Undo the Torx bolts and remove the pump cover

10 Reconnect the wiring connector to the oil temperature sensor (where fitted).
11 Where applicable, refit the exhaust pipe.
12 Lower the vehicle to the ground, wait at least 30 minutes (for the sealant to set), and then refill the engine with oil as described in Chapter 1B Section 13.

12 Oil pump – removal, inspection and refitting

Removal

1 Remove the sump as described in Section 11.
2 Remove the crankshaft front oil seal as described in Section 13.
3 Disconnect the wiring plug, undo the bolts and remove the crankshaft position sensor, located on the right-hand end of the cylinder block.
4 Undo the three Torx security bolts and remove the oil pump pick-up tube from the pump/block **(see illustration)**. Discard the oil seal, a new one must be fitted.
5 Undo the bolts, and remove the oil pump **(see illustration)**.

Inspection

6 Undo and remove the Torx bolts securing the cover to the oil pump **(see illustration)**. Examine the pump rotors and body for signs of wear and damage. If worn, the complete pump must be renewed.
7 Remove the circlip, and extract the cap, valve piston and spring, noting which way around they are fitted **(see illustrations)**. The condition of the relief valve spring can only be measured by comparing it with a new one; if there is any doubt about its condition, it should also be renewed.
8 Refit the relief valve piston and spring, then secure them in place with the circlip.
9 Refit the cover to the oil pump, and tighten the Torx bolts securely.

Refitting

10 Remove all traces of sealant, and thoroughly clean the mating surfaces of the oil pump and cylinder block.
11 Apply a 4 mm diameter bead of silicone sealant to the mating face of the cylinder block **(see illustration)**. Ensure that no sealant enters any of the holes in the block.
12 With a new oil seal fitted, refit the oil pump over the end of the crankshaft, aligning the flats in the pump drive gear with the flats machined in the crankshaft **(see illustrations)**. Note that new oil pumps are supplied with the oil seal already fitted, and a seal protector sleeve. The sleeve fits over the end of the crankshaft to protect the seal as the pump is fitted.

12.7a Remove the circlip...

12.7b ...cap...

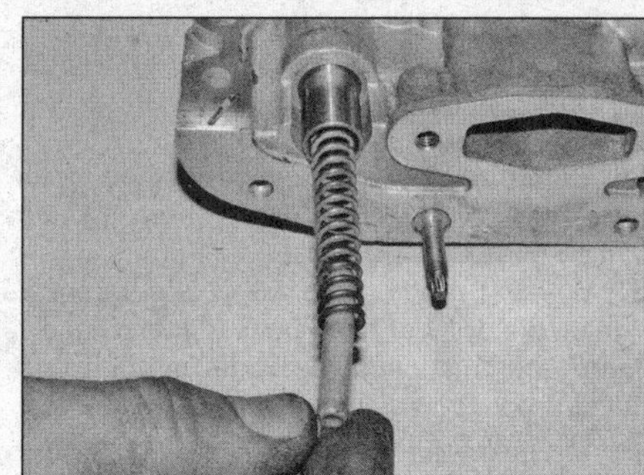
12.7c ...spring...

12.7d ...and piston

12.11 Apply a bead of sealant to the cylinder block mating surface

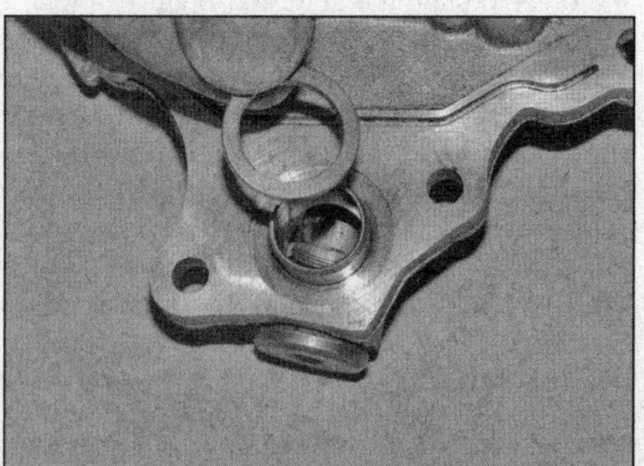
12.12a Fit a new seal...

13 Install the oil pump bolts and tighten them to the specified torque.
14 Refit the oil pick-up tube to the pump/cylinder block using a new O-ring seal. Ensure the oil dipstick guide tube is correctly refitted.
15 Refit the woodruff key to the crankshaft, and slide the crankshaft sprocket into place.
16 The remainder of refitting is a reversal of removal.

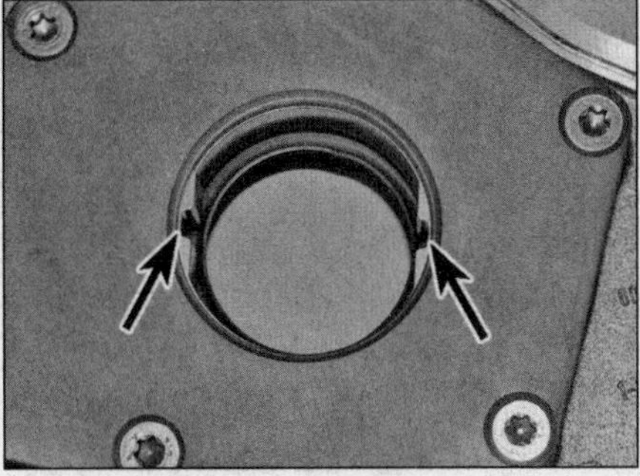

12.12b ...align the pump gear flats...

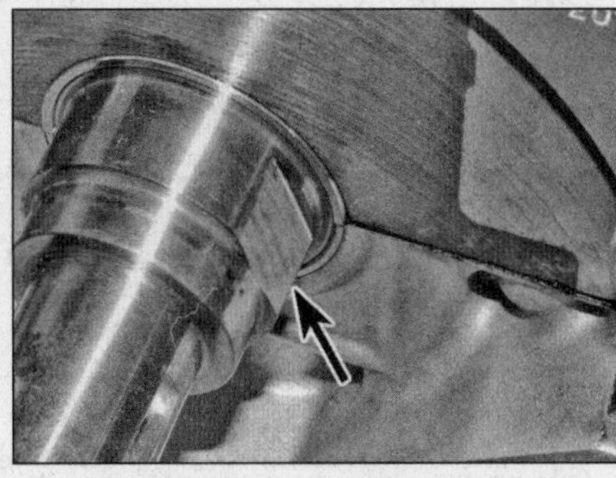

12.12c ...with those of the crankshaft

13 Oil seals – renewal

Crankshaft

Right-hand oil seal

1 Remove the crankshaft sprocket and Woodruff key as described in Section 8.
2 Measure and note the fitted depth of the oil seal.
3 Pull the oil seal from the housing using a screwdriver. Alternatively, drill a small hole in the oil seal, and use a self-tapping screw and a pair of pliers to remove it **(see illustration)**.
4 Clean the oil seal housing and the crankshaft sealing surface.
5 The new seal should be supplied with a protective sleeve, which fits over the end of the crankshaft to prevent any damage to the seal lip. With the sleeve in place, press the seal (open end first) into the pump to the previously-noted depth, using a suitable tube or socket **(see illustrations)**.
6 Where applicable, remove the plastic sleeve from the end of the crankshaft.
7 Refit the crankshaft sprocket as described in Section 8.

Left-hand oil seal

8 Remove the flywheel, as described in Section 15.
9 Measure and note the fitted depth of the oil seal.
10 Pull the oil seal from the housing using a screwdriver. Alternatively, drill a small hole in the oil seal, and use a self-tapping screw and a pair of pliers to remove it **(see illustration 13.3)**.
11 Clean the oil seal housing and the crankshaft sealing surface.
12 The new seal should be supplied with a protective sleeve, which fits over the end of the crankshaft to prevent any damage to the seal lip **(see illustration)**. With the sleeve in place, press the seal (open end first) into the housing to the previously-noted depth, using a suitable tube or socket.
13 Where applicable, remove the plastic sleeve from the end of the crankshaft.
14 Refit the flywheel, as described in Section 15.

Camshaft

15 Remove the camshaft sprocket as described in Section 8. In principle there is no need to remove the timing belt completely, but remember that if the belt has been contaminated with oil, it must be renewed.
16 Pull the oil seal from the housing using a hooked instrument. Alternatively, drill a small hole in the oil seal and use a self-tapping screw and a pair of pliers to remove it **(see illustration)**.
17 Clean the oil seal housing and the camshaft sealing surface.
18 Press the seal (open end first) into the housing to the previously-noted depth, using either the correct tool (303-684), a suitable tube or a socket which bears only of the outer edge of the seal **(see illustrations)**. If the seal was supplied with a protective sleeve, remove it.

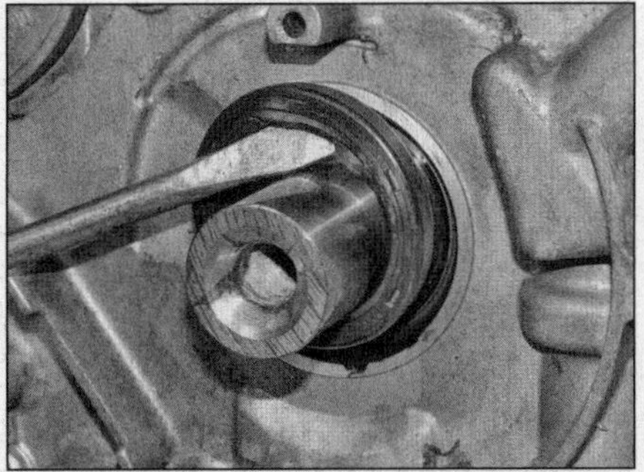

13.3 Take great care not to mark the crankshaft while levering out the oil seal

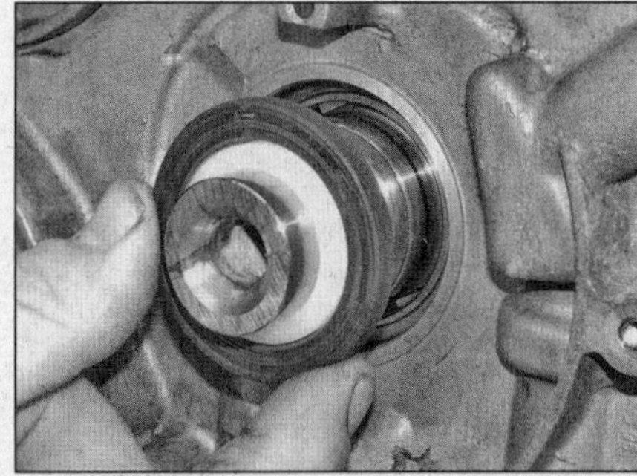

13.5a Slide the seal and protective sleeve over the end of the crankshaft...

13.5b ...and press the seal into place

13.12 Slide the seal and protective sleeve over the left-hand end of the crankshaft

13.16 Drill a hole, insert a self-tapping screw, and pull the seal from place using pliers

13.18a Use the correct tool to fit the seal...

13.18b ...or a suitable socket

19 Refit the camshaft sprocket as described in Section 8.
20 Where necessary, fit a new timing belt with reference to Section 7.

14 Oil pressure switch and level sensor – removal and refitting

Removal

Oil pressure switch

1 The oil pressure switch is located at the front of the cylinder block, adjacent to the oil dipstick guide tube. Note that on some models, access to the switch may be improved if the vehicle is jacked up and supported on axle stands, then undo the bolts and remove the engine undershield so that the switch can be reached from underneath (see *Jacking and vehicle support*).
2 Remove the protective sleeve from the wiring plug (where applicable), then disconnect the wiring from the switch.
3 Unscrew the switch from the cylinder block, and recover the sealing washer **(see illustration)**. Be prepared for oil spillage, and if the switch is to be left removed from the engine for any length of time, plug the hole in the cylinder block.

Oil level sensor

4 Where fitted, the oil level sensor is located at the rear of the cylinder block. Jack up the front of the vehicle and support it securely on axle stands (see *Jacking and vehicle support*). Undo the bolts and remove the engine undershield.
5 Reach up between the driveshaft and the cylinder block, and disconnect the sensor wiring plug **(see illustration)**.
6 Using an open-ended spanner, unscrew the sensor and withdraw it from position.

Refitting

Oil pressure switch

7 Examine the sealing washer for any signs of damage or deterioration, and if necessary renew.
8 Refit the switch, complete with washer, and tighten it to the specified torque where given.
9 Refit the engine undershield, and lower the vehicle to the ground.

Oil level sensor

10 Smear a little silicone sealant on the threads and refit the sensor to the cylinder block, tightening it securely.
11 Reconnect the sensor wiring plug.
12 Refit the engine undershield, and lower the vehicle to the ground.

15 Flywheel – removal, inspection and refitting

Removal

1 Remove the transmission as described in Chapter 7A Section 6, then remove the clutch assembly as described in Chapter 8 Section 6.
2 Prevent the flywheel from turning. Do not attempt to lock the flywheel in position using the crankshaft pulley locking tool described in Section 3. Insert a 12 mm diameter rod or drill bit through the hole in the flywheel cover casting, and into a slot in the flywheel **(see illustration)**
3 Make alignment marks between the flywheel and crankshaft to aid refitment. Slacken and remove the flywheel retaining bolts, and remove the flywheel from the end of the crankshaft. Be careful not to drop it; it is heavy. If the flywheel locating dowel (where fitted) is a loose fit in the crankshaft end, remove it and store it with the flywheel for safe-keeping. Discard the flywheel bolts; new ones must be used on refitting.

Inspection

4 Examine the flywheel for scoring of the clutch face, and for wear or chipping of the ring gear teeth. If the clutch face is scored, the flywheel may be surface-ground, but renewal is preferable. Seek the advice of a Ford dealer or engine reconditioning specialist to see if machining is possible. If the ring gear is worn or damaged, the flywheel must be renewed, as it is not possible to renew the ring gear separately.
5 All engines maybe fitted with a dual-mass flywheel. The maximum travel of the primary mass in relation to the secondary must not exceed 15 teeth (or 20 degrees). If in doubt remove the flywheel and have a suitably equipped specialist check the flywheel. Inspect the flywheel for any grease or debris from the interface between the fixed part and the movable part of the flywheel. If any doubt to the condition of the flywheel exists, despite the expense we recommend replacing it.

Refitting

6 Clean the mating surfaces of the flywheel and crankshaft. Remove any remaining locking compound from the threads of the crankshaft holes, using the correct size of tap, if available.
7 If the new flywheel retaining bolts are not supplied with their threads already pre-coated, apply a suitable thread-locking compound to the threads of each bolt.
8 Ensure that the locating dowel is in position. Offer up the flywheel, locating it on the dowel (where fitted), and fit the new retaining bolts.

14.3 The oil pressure switch is located on the front face of the cylinder block

14.5 The oil level sensor is located on the rear face of the cylinder block (arrowed)

15.2 Lock the flywheel with a 12mm diameter rod or bolt

Where no locating dowel is fitted, align the previously-made marks to ensure the flywheel is refitted in its original position.

9 Lock the flywheel using the method employed on dismantling, and tighten the retaining bolts to the specified torque **(see illustration)**.

10 Refit the clutch, then remove the flywheel locking tool, and refit the transmission.

15.9 Flywheel retaining bolts

16 Engine/transmission mountings – inspection and renewal

General

1 The engine/transmission mountings seldom require attention, but broken or deteriorated mountings should be renewed immediately, or the added strain placed on the driveline components may cause damage or wear.

2 While separate mountings may be removed and refitted individually, if more than one is disturbed at a time – such as if the engine/transmission unit is removed from its mountings – they must be reassembled and their fasteners tightened in the position marked on removal.

3 On reassembly, the complete weight of the engine/transmission unit must not be taken by the mountings until all are correctly aligned with the marks made on removal. Tighten the engine/transmission mounting fasteners to their specified torque wrench settings.

Inspection

4 During the check, the engine/transmission unit must be raised slightly, to remove its weight from the mountings.

5 Raise the front of the vehicle, and support it securely on axle stands (see *Jacking and vehicle support*). Position a jack under the sump, with a large block of wood between the jack head and the sump, then carefully raise the engine/transmission just enough to take the weight off the mountings.

Warning: DO NOT place any part of your body under the engine when it is supported only by a jack.

6 Check the mountings to see if the rubber is cracked, hardened or separated from the metal components. Sometimes the rubber will split right down the centre.

7 Check for relative movement between each mounting's brackets and the engine/transmission or body (use a large screwdriver or lever to attempt to move the mountings). If movement is noted, lower the engine and check-tighten the mounting fasteners.

Renewal

Note: *The following paragraphs assume the engine is supported beneath the sump as described earlier.*

Right-hand mounting

8 Lift up the coolant expansion tank and position it to one side **(see illustration)**. Note there is no need to disconnect the coolant pipes.

9 Mark the position of the mounting on the vehicle on the right-hand inner wing panel, and then undo the 2 bolts securing the mounting.

10 Undo the retaining bolts from the engine side of the mounting and then remove the mounting **(see illustration)**.

11 Re-align the marks made on removal. Tighten all fasteners to the torque wrench settings specified.

Left-hand mounting

12 Remove the air filter housing as described in Chapter 4A Section 3.

13 Remove the battery as described in Chapter 5 Section 4, then undo the 3 bolts and remove the battery tray. Disconnect any wiring as the tray is withdrawn.

14 Unclip the wiring loom from the battery tray support panel, remove the 4 bolts and withdraw the support panel **(see illustration)**.

15 With the transmission supported, note the position of the mounting then unscrew the centre retaining bolt to release the upper half of the mounting from the transmission **(see illustration)**.

16 Refitting is a reversal of removal. Re-align the mounting in the position noted on removal, then tighten all fasteners to the specified torque wrench settings.

Rear mounting (roll restrictor)

17 Remove the 3 mounting bolts from the transmission. Remove the single bolt from the subframe **(see illustration)**.

18 With the aid of an assistant pivot the engine (assuming the two main engine mountings are in position) and work the mounting free.

19 On refitting, ensure that the bolts are securely tightened to the specified torque wrench setting.

16.8 Move the coolant expansion bottle to the side

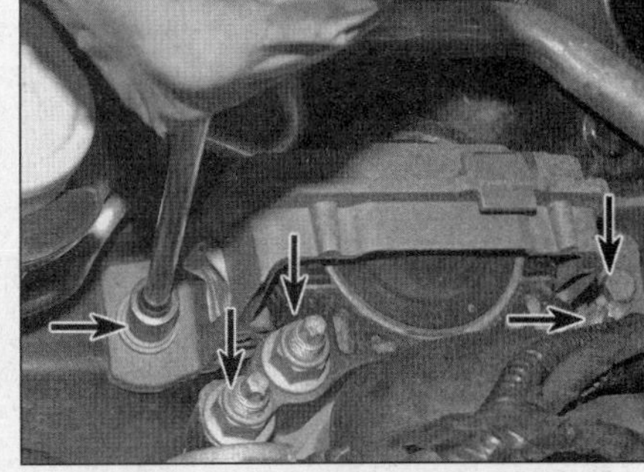

16.10 Undo the bolts and remove the mounting

16.14 Remove the battery support panel

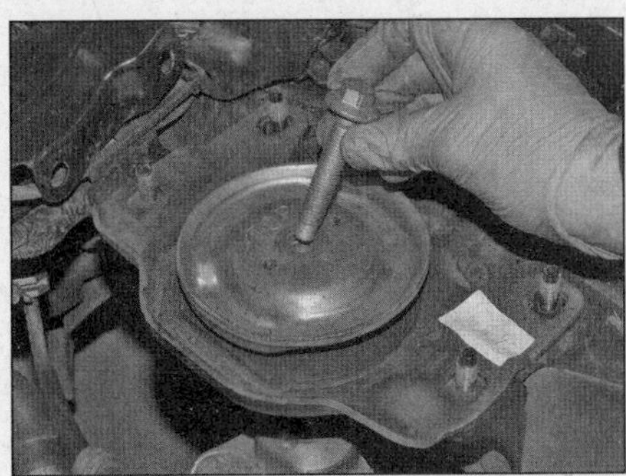

16.15 Remove the centre bolt

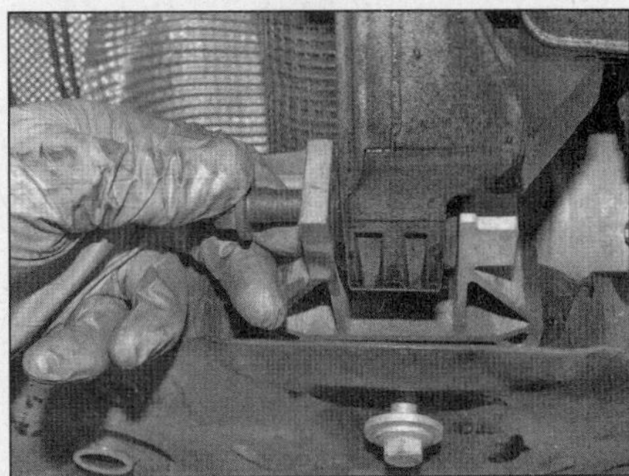

16.17 Remove the bolts

Chapter 2 Part C
2.0 litre diesel engine in-car repair procedures

Contents

Degrees of difficulty

Easy, suitable for novice with little experience	Fairly easy, suitable for beginner with some experience	Fairly difficult, suitable for competent DIY mechanic	Difficult, suitable for experienced DIY mechanic	Very difficult, suitable for expert DIY or professional

Specifications

General

Engine type	Four-cylinder, in-line, double overhead camshaft, aluminium cylinder head and cast iron engine block
Designation	Duratorq TDCi
Engine codes	TXMA, T7MA, T7MB, T8MA, T8MB, UFMA, XRMA,
Output:	
Power:	
Engine code TXMA	120 kW (161 PS) @ 4000 rpm
Engine code T7MA, T7MB	110 kW (147 PS) @ 4000 rpm
Engine code T8MA	132 kW (177 PS) @ 4000 rpm
Engine code T8MB	120 kW (163 PS) @ 4000 rpm
Engine code UFMA	103 kW (138 PS) @ 4000 rpm
Engine code XRMA	88 kW (118 PS) @ 4000 rpm
Torque	320 Nm @ 1750 rpm
Capacity	1997 cc
Bore	85.0 mm
Stroke	88.0 mm
Compression ratio	18: 1
Firing order	1-3-4-2 (No 1 cylinder at transmission end)
Direction of crankshaft rotation	Clockwise (seen from right-hand side of vehicle)

* *For details of engine code location, see 'Vehicle identification'.*

Camshaft

Camshaft bearing journal diameter	25.059 to 25.080 mm
Camshaft endfloat	0.070 to 0.168 mm

Cylinder head

Piston protrusion:	**Thickness of cylinder head gasket**
0.55 to 0.60 mm	1.21 to 1.29 mm (1 hole)
0.61 to 0.65 mm	1.26 to 1.34 mm (2 holes)
0.66 to 0.70 mm	1.31 to 1.39 mm (3 holes)
0.71 to 0.75 mm	1.36 to 1.44 mm (4 holes)
Valve clearances	Hydraulic adjusters – no adjustment necessary

Lubrication

Engine oil type/specification	See *Lubricants and fluids*
Engine oil capacity	See Chapter 1B
Oil pressure – minimum (engine at operating temperature):	
At 2000 rpm	2.0 bar
At 4000 rpm	4.0 bar

Torque wrench settings

	Nm	lbf ft
Air conditioning compressor bolts	25	18
Big-end bearing cap nuts: *		
Stage 1	20	15
Stage 2	Angle-tighten a further 70°	
Camshaft sprocket bolt:		
Stage 1	20	15
Stage 2	Angle-tighten a further 60°	
Crankshaft oil seal carrier	14	10
Crankshaft pulley bolt: *		
Stage 1	70	52
Stage 2	Angle-tighten a further 110°	
Cylinder head lower section-to-block bolts: *		
Stage 1	60	44
Stage 2	Angle-tighten a further 220°	
Cylinder head upper section-to-lower section bolts:		
Stage 1	5	4
Stage 2	10	7
Cylinder head cover/inlet manifold	8	6
Engine mountings:		
Left-hand mounting (transmission):		
Mounting-to-body bolts	48	35
Mounting-to-body nuts	80	59
Mounting-to-transmission bracket centre bolt	148	109
Rear mounting (roll restrictor) bolts	125	92
Right-hand mounting-to-engine bracket nuts	80	59
Right-hand mounting–to-body bolts	90	66
Right-hand mounting engine bracket bolts	56	41
Engine-to-transmission bolts	48	35
Flywheel bolts:*		
Stage 1	33	24
Stage 2	Angle-tighten a further 35 degrees	
Fuel accumulator rail mounting bolts	22	16
Fuel injector mounting studs	10	7
Fuel pump mounting bolts	20	15
High-pressure fuel pipe unions:		
Stage 1	17	13
Stage 2	28	21
Main bearing cap bolts:		
Stage 1	30	22
Stage 2	Angle-tighten a further 63°	
Oil pump bolts	10	7
Oil pump pick-up tube bolts	12	9
Roadwheel nuts	135	100
Subframe cross-brace retaining bolts	30	22
Subframe mounting bolts: *		
Stage 1	150	111
Stage 2	Angle-tighten a further 90°	
Sump bolts:		
Sump to cylinder block	16	12
Sump to transmission	48	35
Thermostat housing to cylinder head	10	7
Timing belt idler pulley	56	41
Timing belt tensioner	21	15
Timing chain tensioner	6	4
Vacuum pump mounting bolts	10	7

** Do not re-use*

1 General information

How to use this Chapter

1 This Part of Chapter 3 is devoted to in-car repair procedures on the 2.0 litre Duratorq TDCi diesel engines. All procedures concerning engine removal, refitting, and overhaul can be found in Chapter 2D.

2 Refer to *Vehicle identification* for details of engine code locations.

3 Most of the operations included in this Chapter are based on the assumption that the engine is still installed in the car. Therefore, if this information is being used during a complete engine overhaul, with the engine already removed, many of the steps included here will not apply.

Engine description

4 The engine is a result of a joint venture

between Ford and Peugeot. This DOHC (Double Overhead Camshaft) 16-valve engine features common rail direct injection, and a VNT (Variable Nozzle Turbine) turbocharger.

5 All major components are made from aluminium, apart from the cast-iron cylinder block – no liners are fitted, the cylinders are bored directly into the block. Engines to emission level Stage V have a lower crankcase which is bolted to the underside of the cylinder block/crankcase, with a sump bolted under that. This arrangement offers greater rigidity than the normal sump arrangement, and helps to reduce engine vibration.

6 The crankshaft runs in five main bearings, thrustwashers are fitting either side of the No 2 cylinder main bearings to control crankshaft endfloat. The connecting rods rotate on horizontally-split bearing shells at their big-ends. The pistons are attached to the connecting rods by gudgeon pins which are a floating fit in the connecting rod small-end eyes, secured by circlips. The aluminium alloy pistons are fitted with three piston rings: two compression rings and an oil control ring. After manufacture, the cylinder bores and piston skirts are measured and classified into four weight grades, which must be carefully matched together to ensure the correct piston/cylinder clearance; no oversizes are available to permit reboring.

7 The inlet and exhaust valves are each closed by coil springs; they operate in guides which are shrink-fitted into the cylinder head, as are the valve seat inserts.

8 A rubber-toothed belt, driven by the crankshaft sprocket, rotates the coolant pump and the exhaust camshaft sprocket. The inlet camshaft is driven by a short timing chain from the exhaust camshaft.

9 The camshafts operate the 16 valves via roller-rocker arms with hydraulic clearance adjusters. The camshafts rotate in five bearings that are line-bored directly into the two sections of the cylinder head.

10 The vacuum pump (used for the brake servo and other vacuum actuators) is driven from the end of the inlet camshaft, while the high-pressure fuel pump is driven from the end of the exhaust camshaft.

Lubrication system

11 The oil pump is mounted under the cylinder block, and is chain-driven from a crankshaft sprocket. The pump forces oil through an externally-mounted full-flow cartridge-type filter. From the filter, the oil is pumped into a main gallery in the cylinder block/crankcase, from where it is distributed to the crankshaft (main bearings) and cylinder head. An oil cooler is fitted next to the oil filter, at the rear of the block. The cooler is supplied with coolant from the engine cooling system.

12 While the crankshaft and camshaft bearings receive a pressurised supply, the camshaft lobes and valves are lubricated by splash, as are all other engine components. The undersides of the pistons are cooled by oil, sprayed from nozzles fitted above the upper main bearing shells. The turbocharger receives its own pressurised oil supply.

Operations with engine in car

13 The following major repair operations can be accomplished without removing the engine from the vehicle. However, owners should note that any operation involving the removal of the sump requires careful forethought, depending on the level of skill and the tools and facilities available; refer to the relevant text for details.

a) Compression pressure – testing.
b) Cylinder head cover – removal and refitting.
c) Timing belt covers – removal and refitting.
d) Timing belt/chain – renewal.
e) Timing belt tensioner and sprockets – removal and refitting.
f) Camshaft oil seal – renewal.
g) Camshafts, rocker arms and hydraulic adjusters – removal and refitting.
h) Cylinder head – removal, overhaul and refitting.
i) Cylinder head and pistons – decarbonising.
j) Sump – removal and refitting.
k) Crankshaft oil seals – renewal.
l) Oil pump – removal and refitting.
m) Piston/connecting rod assemblies – removal and refitting (but see note below).
n) Flywheel/driveplate – removal and refitting.
o) Engine/transmission mountings – removal and refitting.

Note: *It is possible to remove the pistons and connecting rods (after removing the cylinder head and sump) without removing the engine, however, this is not recommended. Work of this nature is more easily and thoroughly completed with the engine on the bench, as described in Chapter 2D.*

2 Compression and leakdown tests – description and interpretation

Compression test

Note: *A compression tester suitable for use with diesel engines will be required for this test.*

1 When engine performance is down, or if misfiring occurs which cannot be attributed to the fuel or emissions systems, a compression test can provide diagnostic clues as to the engine's condition. If the test is performed regularly, it can give warning of trouble before any other symptoms become apparent.

2 The engine must be fully warmed-up to normal operating temperature, the battery must be fully-charged and the glow plugs must be removed. The aid of an assistant will be required.

3 Note that it is necessary to disconnect the glow plug relay to allow the compression test to be performed. This will log a fault code in the engine management powertrain control module when the engine is turned over on the starter, and the fault code will have to be cleared, using Ford diagnostic equipment or a compatible alternative, on completion of the test. Unless you have access to the necessary diagnostic equipment it may be preferable to have the compression test carried out by a Ford dealer or suitably-equipped garage. Should you wish to proceed, the procedure is as follows.

2.4 Glow plug relay

4 Remove the glow plug relay from the engine compartment fuse/relay box **(see illustration)**.

5 Pull the plastic cover on the top of the engine upwards to release it from its mountings.

6 Disconnect the wiring plugs from the injectors.

7 Remove the glow plugs as described in Chapter 6B Section 16.

8 Fit a compression tester to the No 1 cylinder glow plug hole. The type of tester which screws into the plug thread is preferred.

9 Crank the engine for several seconds on the starter motor. After one or two revolutions, the compression pressure should build-up to a maximum figure and then stabilise. Record the highest reading obtained.

10 Repeat the test on the remaining cylinders, recording the pressure in each.

11 The cause of poor compression is less easy to establish on a diesel engine than on a petrol engine. The effect of introducing oil into the cylinders (wet testing) is not conclusive, because there is a risk that the oil will sit in the recess on the piston crown, instead of passing to the rings. However, the following can be used as a rough guide to diagnosis.

12 All cylinders should produce very similar pressures. Any great difference indicates the existence of a fault. Note that the compression should build-up quickly in a healthy engine. Low compression on the first stroke, followed by gradually increasing pressure on successive strokes, indicates worn piston rings. A low compression reading on the first stroke, which does not build-up during successive strokes, indicates leaking valves or a blown head gasket (a cracked head could also be the cause). Deposits on the undersides of the valve heads can also cause low compression.

3.4 Undo the retaining bolt and lift out the camshaft position sensor

3.5 Unclip the hose from the separator

3.6 Slacken the retaining bolts and lift away the cover

3.7 Fit the new rubber gasket

13 A low reading from two adjacent cylinders is almost certainly due to the head gasket having blown between them and the presence of coolant in the engine oil will confirm this.
14 If the compression reading is unusually high, the cylinder head surfaces, valves and pistons are probably coated with carbon deposits. If this is the case, the cylinder head should be removed and decarbonised (see Part D).
15 On completion, remove the compression tester, and refit the glow plugs.
16 Reconnect the injector wiring plugs and the plastic cover over the top of the engine.
17 Refit the glow plug relay, then clear the fault code from the powertrain control module.

Leakdown test

18 A leakdown test measures the rate at which compressed air fed into the cylinder is lost. It is an alternative to a compression test, and in many ways it is better, since the escaping air provides easy identification of where pressure loss is occurring (piston rings, valves or head gasket).
19 The equipment required for leakdown testing is unlikely to be available to the home mechanic. If poor compression is suspected, have the test performed by a suitably-equipped garage.

3 Oil separator – removal and refitting

Warning: Refer to the information contained in Chapter 4B Section 3, before proceeding.

Removal

1 Remove the plastic cover from the top of the engine by pulling it straight up.
2 Disconnect the battery as described in Chapter 5 Section 4.
3 Remove the windscreen cowls, as described in Chapter 11 Section 12.
4 Unplug the wiring connector for the camshaft position sensor, then undo the retaining bolt and manoeuvre from place **(see illustration)**.
5 Release the retaining clip and detach the hose from the rear of the oil separator **(see illustration)**.
6 Undo the 15 retaining bolts and manoeuvre the oil separator upwards from place **(see illustration)**.

Refitting

7 Clean the sealing surfaces of the separator and the head then fit the new rubber gasket and sealing rings **(see illustration)**.
8 Fit the cover to the cylinder head. Tighten the bolts to the specified torque.
9 The remainder of refitting is a reversal of removal.

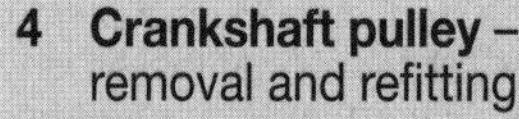

4 Crankshaft pulley – removal and refitting

Note: *Ford special tools or suitable alternatives will be required to lock the flywheel/driveplate and to retain the crankshaft and camshaft at the TDC position during this procedure.*
Note: *A new crankshaft pulley retaining bolt will be required for refitting.*

Removal

1 Disconnect the battery negative lead as described in Chapter 5 Section 4.
2 Pull the plastic cover on top of the engine straight up from its mountings.
3 Remove the auxiliary drivebelt as described in Chapter 1B Section 32.
4 Remove the starter motor as described in Chapter 5 Section 7.
5 Use pliers to remove the crankshaft pulley rubber cover **(see illustration)**.
6 Two special tools are now required to set the engine at TDC (Top Dead Centre) for No 1 cylinder (at the transmission end). Ford tool No 303-1059 locates through a hole in the rear flange of the cylinder block into a corresponding hole in the rear of the flywheel/driveplate, while tool No 303-735 locates through a hole in the exhaust camshaft sprocket into a hole in the cylinder head casting. In the absence of these tools, use an 8 mm diameter drill bit to lock the camshaft sprocket, and an 8 mm diameter rod to lock the flywheel/driveplate.
Note: *The flywheel/driveplate locking bolt must be flat (not tapered at all) at the end.*
7 Using a spanner or socket on the pulley bolt, rotate the crankshaft in a clockwise direction (viewed from the timing belt end of the engine) until the hole in the camshaft sprocket begins to align with the corresponding hole in the cylinder head.
8 Insert the crankshaft setting tool though the

4.5 Pull out the crankshaft pulley cover

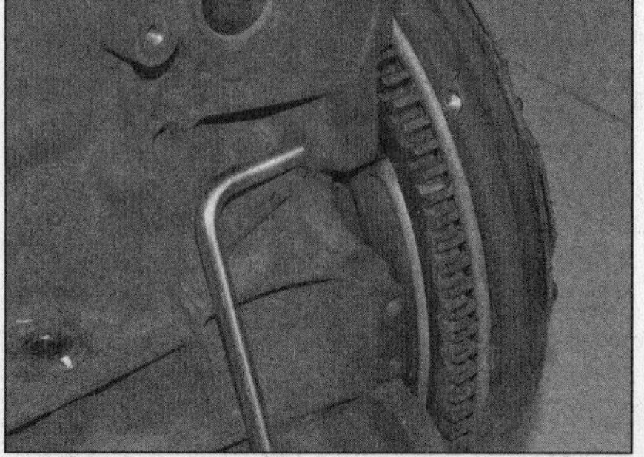
4.8a The crankshaft setting tool fits through the hole in the cylinder block flange...

4.8b ... and into a hole in the rear of the flywheel/driveplate

4.9 The camshaft locking tool fits through the hole in the camshaft sprocket, into the timing hole in the cylinder head

4.11 Crankshaft holding tool engaged with the ring gear teeth

4.12a Undo the retaining bolt...

4.12b ... remove the crankshaft pulley...

4.12c ... followed by the TDC sensor ring

hole in the cylinder block flange and press it against the back of the flywheel/driveplate. Have an assistant very slowly rotate the crankshaft clockwise, and the tool should slide into the flywheel/driveplate as the holes align **(see illustrations)**.

9 It should now be possible to insert the camshaft locking tool (303-735) or equivalent through the hole in the camshaft sprocket into the hole in the cylinder head **(see illustration)**. Note that it may be necessary to rotate the camshaft sprocket backwards or forwards very slightly to be able to insert the tool.

10 The centre bolt which secures the crankshaft pulley must now be slackened. This bolt is tightened to a very high torque, and it is first of all essential to ensure that the car is adequately supported, as considerable effort will be needed.

11 Ford technicians use a special holding tool (303-393/303-393-01) which bolts to the transmission housing and engages with the starter ring gear teeth **(see illustration)**. The use of this tool, or an equivalent, is strongly recommended. Do not rely on the crankshaft and camshaft setting/locking tools to prevent the crankshaft rotating.

12 Unscrew the bolt securing the pulley to the crankshaft, and remove the pulley. It is essential to obtain a new bolt for refitting. If required, remove the TDC sensor ring/spacer **(see illustrations)**.

Caution: Handle the sensor ring with care.

Refitting

13 Refit the TDC sensor ring/spacer and crankshaft pulley to the crankshaft, then fit the new pulley securing bolt and tighten it to the specified Stage 1 torque using a torque wrench.

14 Stage 2 involves tightening the bolt though an angle, rather than to a torque. The bolt must be rotated through the specified angle – special angle gauges are available from tool outlets.

15 The remainder of refitting is a reversal of removal.

5 Timing belt and tensioner – removal and refitting

Removal

1 Disconnect the battery, as described in Chapter 5 Section 4.

5.4 Pull away the pulley cover using pliers

2 Remove the auxiliary drivebelt as described in Chapter 1B Section 32.

3 Remove the starter motor as described in Chapter 5 Section 7.

4 Remove the rubber cover from the crankshaft pulley **(see illustration)**.

5 Use Ford special tool 303-393-01 to lock the flywheel in position **(see illustration)**.

6 Undo the crankshaft pulley bolt **(see illustration)**.

7 Remove the 6 bolts and remove the timing belt upper and lower covers **(see illustration)**.

8 Support the engine on a trolley jack.

9 Undo the 4 main mounting bolts for the right-hand engine mount, followed by the bolt attaching it to the fuel filter housing **(see illustrations)**.

10 Lock the timing belt sprocket in position using Ford special tool 303-735 **(see illustration)**.

5.5 Lock the flywheel with the special tool

5.6 Remove the pulley bolt from the crankshaft

5.7 Undo the bolts and manoeuvre the timing covers out

5.9a Remove the right-hand engine mount bolts...

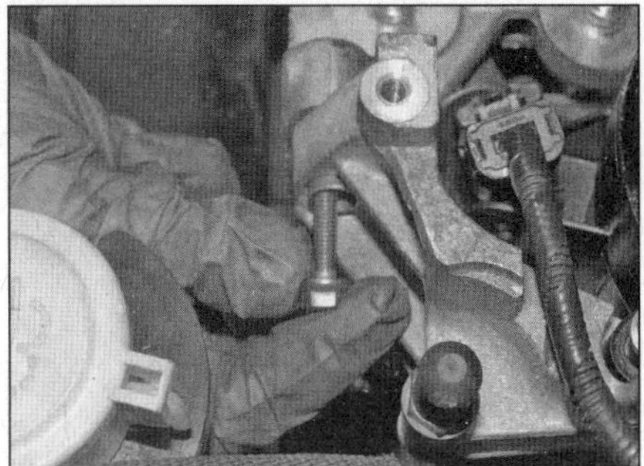

5.9b ...then the fuel filter housing bolt

5.10 Use the special tool or an 8mm drillbit to lock the timing belt sprocket in place

5.11 Slacken the tensioner pulley bolt

11 Relieve the timing belt tension by slackening the bolt/nut in the centre of the tensioner pulley **(see illustration)**.

12 Remove the crankshaft pulley from place, followed by the crankshaft position sensor ring **(see illustration)**.

13 Remove the timing belt from the sprockets. Note that the belt must not be re-used.

5.12 Remove the crankshaft pulley then the sensor ring

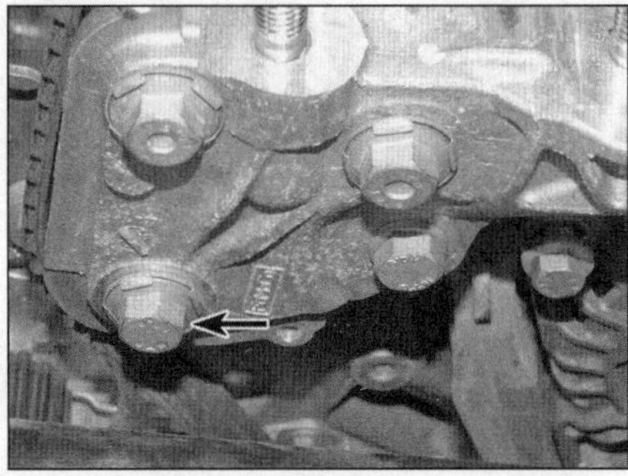

5.14a Undo the idler pulley retaining bolt...

5.14b ... and manoeuvre from place

5.19 Ensure that the slot in the tensioner backplate engages over the dowel on the cylinder block

14 Undo the engine mounting bracket lower rear retaining bolt and remove the idler pulley, together with the bolt **(see illustrations)**.

15 Undo the bolt or the nut in the centre of the tensioner and remove the tensioner. Discard both the tensioner and idler pulleys – new ones must be fitted.

Refitting

16 Ensure that the crankshaft and camshaft are still set to TDC on No 1 cylinder, with the setting/locking tools in position (see Section 4).

17 Insert the bolt into the new idler pulley, then slide the pulley and bolt into position in the engine mounting bracket. Screw in the bolt and tighten it to the specified torque.

18 Tighten all the engine mount bolts to their required torque. Note that each bolts has a different torque setting.

19 Locate the new timing belt tensioner into position, ensuring that the slot in the tensioner backplate engages over the dowel on the cylinder block **(see illustration)**. Tighten the retaining bolt/nut finger-tight only at this stage.

20 Fit the new timing belt over the various sprockets in the following order: crankshaft, idler pulley, camshaft, tensioner and coolant pump. Pay attention to any arrows on the belt indicating direction of rotation.

21 New tensioners are usually supplied with a locking pin holding the tensioner in the released position. If so, pull out the locking pin and allow the tensioner pulley to move into contact with the timing belt.

22 Using a 6 mm Allen key inserted in the

5.22a Using an Allen key in the tensioner arm hole...

5.22b ... rotate the arm anti-clockwise until the pointer is between the sides of the adjustment 'window'

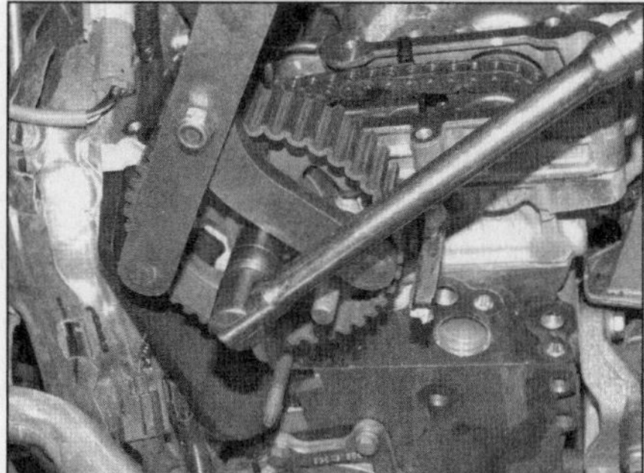
6.6 Use a tool to hold the sprocket whilst undoing retaining bolt

tensioner arm, rotate the arm anti-clockwise until the pointer is positioned between the sides of the adjustment 'window' **(see illustrations)**. Fully-tighten the tensioner retaining bolt.

23 Refit the timing belt lower cover and tighten the bolts securely.

24 Refit the sensor ring/spacer and the crankshaft pulley, then tighten the old pulley bolt to 50 Nm (37 lb ft).

25 Remove the crankshaft and camshaft setting/locking tools, then rotate the crankshaft 4 complete revolutions clockwise, until the crankshaft setting tool can be re-inserted. Check that the camshaft locking tool can also be inserted.

26 Check position of the tensioner pointer, and if necessary slacken the retaining bolt and use the Allen key to align the pointer in the centre of the adjustment 'window'. Tighten the retaining bolt securely.

27 Remove the old crankshaft pulley bolt, and fit the new one. Tighten the bolt to the specified Stage 1 torque, then through the specified Stage 2 angle using the flywheel locking tool to prevent the crankshaft from rotating. Where applicable, refit the rubber cover to the centre of the crankshaft pulley

28 Remove the crankshaft and camshaft setting/locking tools.

29 The remainder of refitting is a reversal of removal, remembering to tighten all fasteners to their specified torque where given.

6 Camshafts, rocker arms and hydraulic adjusters – removal, inspection and refitting

Note: *A new camshaft oil seal will be required for refitting.*

Removal

1 Remove the timing belt as described in Section 5.

2 Remove the vacuum pump as described in Chapter 9 Section 20.

3 Remove the cylinder head cover as described in Section 3.

4 Remove the following components as described in Chapter 4B :

a) Air cleaner assembly.
b) Fuel injectors.
c) Fuel pump.

5 Remove the fuel pump gear cassette as described in Chapter 4B Section 12.

6 Undo the retaining bolt and pull the sprocket from the exhaust camshaft. Ford technicians use a special holding tool (205-072) which locates in the holes of the sprocket and prevents it from turning as the bolt is undone. If this tool is not available, a home-made tool can easily be fabricated. **(see illustration)**

7 Gradually and evenly remove the bolts securing the upper section of the cylinder head to the lower section **(see illustration)**.

8 Remove the 4 locating dowels for the fuel injector clamps using a magnetic tool **(see illustration)**. Failure to do so risks the dowels falling into the engine.

9 Carefully tap around the edge of the cylinder head upper section and lift it from position. Note that the cover will probably be reluctant to lift due to the sealant used, and possible corrosion around the two locating dowels at the front edge.

Note: *Keep the internal and external bolts separate from each other to make refitting easier, and be aware that the four frontmost external bolts are shorter than all of the others.*

10 Undo the retaining bolts for the camchain tensioner **(see illustration)**.

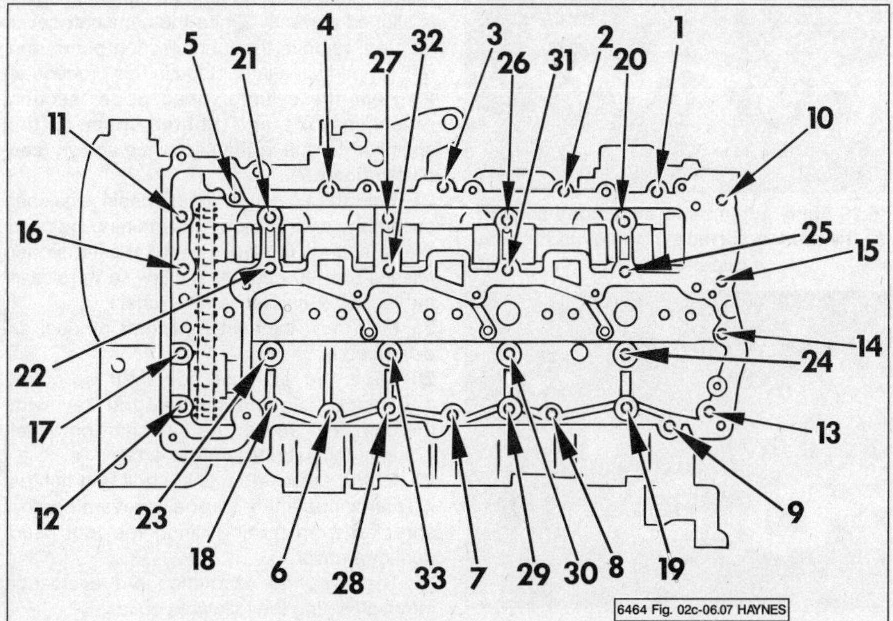

6.7 Undo the bolts in the order indicated

6.8 Lift out the dowels using a magnet

6.10 Remove the tensioner retaining bolts

6.11 Lift the camshafts from position and disengage the timing chain from the sprockets

6.13 Remove the rockers and adjusters and submerge in oil

11 Lift the camshafts from position, disengage the timing chain from the sprockets, and remove the exhaust camshaft seal **(see illustration)**.

12 Have ready a box, filled with engine oil and divided into 16 segments, or some containers or other means of storing and identifying the rockers arms and hydraulic adjusters after removal. It's essential that if they are to be refitted, they return to their original positions. Mark the segments in the box or the containers with the cylinder number for each rocker arm/adjuster, and left or right, for the particular cylinder.

13 Lift out the rockers arms and hydraulic adjusters, Keep them identified for position, and place them in their respective positions in the box or container **(see illustration)**. The hydraulic adjusters must be totally submerged in the oil to prevent air entering them.

Inspection

14 Proceed as described in paragraphs 14 to 17.

Refitting

15 Make sure that the top surfaces of the cylinder head, and in particular the camshaft bearings and the mating surfaces are completely clean.

16 Smear some clean engine oil onto the sides of the hydraulic adjusters, and offer each one into position in their original bores in the cylinder head, together with its rocker arm.

17 Locate the timing chain on the camshaft sprockets, aligning the two coloured chain links with the marks on the camshaft sprockets, then lubricate the camshaft and cylinder head bearing journals with clean engine oil, and lower the camshafts into position **(see illustrations 7.20a, 7.20b and 7.20c)**. The mark on the inlet camshaft must be in the 12 o'clock position.

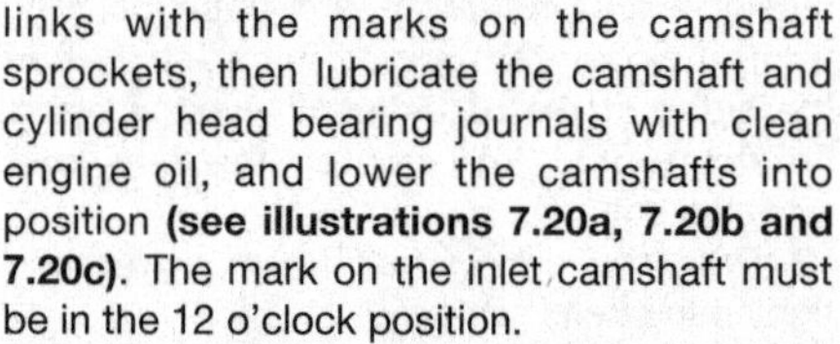

18 Place the new gasket in position between the two camshafts on the cylinder head lower section **(see illustration)**.

19 Apply a thin bead of silicone sealant (Ford part No WSE-M4G323-A4) to the mating surface of the cylinder head upper section**(see illustration)**.

20 Lower the upper section of the cylinder head into position, keeping the gasket aligned as you do so. To temporarily retain the gasket in alignment, insert two of the fuel injector clamp bolts into their locations for No 1 and No 4 injector **(see illustrations)**.

21 Remove the two injector clamp bolts used to align the gasket.

22 Refit the fuel injection pump loosely using the bottom 2 bolts, so that the camshaft cover is aligned correctly. Once the camshaft cover is fitted, remove the fuel injection pump and refit properly at a later stage in this procedure.

23 Refit the cylinder head upper section retaining bolts and tighten them to the specified torque in the sequence shown **(see illustration 6.7)**.

24 Refit the camshaft timing chain tensioner assembly, and tighten the retaining bolts to the specified torque. Rotate the tensioner release arm 90 degrees clockwise to release the tensioner and tension the chain.

25 Fit a new exhaust camshaft oil seal as described in Section 7.

26 Slide the exhaust camshaft sprocket into place, aligning the integral key with the camshaft and fit the camshaft sprocket locking tool **(see illustration 4.12)**.

27 Fit the sprocket retaining bolt and tighten it to the specified torque, preventing the sprocket from turning using the tool used during removal.

28 The remainder of refitting is a reversal of removal, noting the following points:

a) *When refitting the vacuum pump, use a new gasket and ensure the drive coupling is aligned with the slot in the camshaft.*

6.18 Place the new gasket in position on the cylinder head lower section

6.19 Apply a thin bead of silicone sealant to the mating surface of the cylinder head upper section

6.20a Lower the upper section of the cylinder head into position, keeping the gasket aligned

6.20b Insert two of the fuel injector clamp bolts to maintain the gasket alignment

b) Refit the fuel injection pump, fuel injectors and air cleaner assembly as described in Chapter 4B.
c) Fit the new timing belt, tensioner and idler pulley as described in Section 5.
d) Tighten all fasteners to their specified torque, where given.
e) Check the engine oil and coolant levels as described in Chapter 1B Section 5 and Chapter 1B Section 6.

7 Camshaft oil seal – renewal

1 Remove the camshaft sprocket as described in Section 6.
2 Carefully prise or pull the seal from position **(see Haynes Hint)**.

One of the best ways to remove an oil seal is to carefully drill or punch two holes through the seal opposite each other (taking care not to damage the surface behind the seal as this is done). Two self-tapping screws are then screwed into the holes; by pulling on the screw heads alternately with a pair of pliers, the seal can be extracted.

3 Clean out the seal housing and the sealing surface of the camshaft by wiping it with a lint-free cloth. Remove any swarf or burrs that may cause the seal to leak.
4 Apply a little oil to the new camshaft oil seal, and fit it over the end of the camshaft, lips facing inwards. To avoid damaging the seal lips, wrap a little tape over the end of the camshaft. Ford dealers have a special tool (No 303-684/1) for fitting the seal, but if this is not available, a deep socket of suitable size can be used **(see illustration)**. Drive the seal into place until it is flush with the casing surface.
Note: *Select a socket that bears only on the hard outer surface of the seal, not the inner lip which can easily be damaged. It is important that the seal is fitted square to the shaft, and is fully seated.*
5 Refit the camshaft sprocket (Section 6) and timing belt as described in Section 5.

8 Cylinder head – removal, inspection and refitting

Removal

1 Disconnect the battery negative lead as described in Chapter 5 Section 4.
2 Drain the cooling system as described in Chapter 1B Section 36.
3 Remove the thermostat as described in Section 3 Section 7.
4 Remove the camshafts, rocker arms and hydraulic adjusters as described in Section 6.
5 Remove the turbocharger/exhaust manifold as described in Chapter 4B Section 17.
6 Remove the EGR valve cooler as described in Chapter 6B Section 18.
7 Position a jack under the sump, with a large block of wood between the jack head and the sump, then carefully raise the engine just enough to take the weight off the right-hand engine/transmission mounting.
8 Unscrew the two locking nuts securing the mounting to the engine bracket, then undo the two bolts securing the mounting to the inner wing panel. Remove the mounting, then undo the three bolts and remove the engine bracket.
9 Working in the reverse order of the tightening sequence **(see illustration 8.33)**, gradually and evenly slacken and remove the cylinder head bolts. Discard the bolts, new ones must be fitted.
10 Lift the cylinder head away; use assistance if possible, as it is a very heavy assembly. Do not place the cylinder head flat on its sealing surface, as the ends of the glow plugs may be damaged – support the ends of the cylinder head on wooden blocks.
11 If the head is stuck (as is possible), be careful how you choose to free it. Striking the head with tools carries the risk of damage, and the head is located on two dowels, so its movement will be limited. Do not, under any circumstances, lever the head between the mating surfaces, as this will certainly damage the sealing surfaces for the gasket, leading to leaks.
12 Once the head has been removed, recover the gasket from the two dowels.
13 Do not discard the gasket at this stage – it will be needed for correct identification of the new gasket.

Inspection

14 If required, dismantling and inspection of the cylinder head is covered in Part D of this Chapter.

Cylinder head gasket selection

15 Examine the old cylinder head gasket for manufacturer's identification markings. These will be in the form of holes on the front edge of the gasket, which indicate the gasket's thickness.
16 Unless new components have been fitted, or the cylinder head has been machined (skimmed), the new cylinder head gasket must be of the same type as the old one. Purchase the required gasket, and proceed to paragraph 25.
17 If the head has been machined, or if new pistons have been fitted, it is likely that a head gasket of different thickness to the original will be needed.
18 Gasket selection is made on the basis of the measured piston protrusion above the cylinder head gasket surface.
19 To measure the piston protrusion, anchor

7.4 Apply a little clean oil to the oil seal inner lip before driving into place with a socket

a dial test indicator (DTI) to the top face (cylinder head gasket mating face) of the cylinder block, and zero the gauge on the gasket mating face **(see illustration)**.
20 Rest the gauge probe above No 1 piston crown, and turn the crankshaft slowly by hand until the piston reaches TDC (its maximum height). Measure and record the maximum piston projection at TDC.
21 Repeat the measurement for the remaining pistons, and record the results.
22 If the measurements differ from piston to piston, take the highest figure, and use this to determine the thickness of the head gasket required. Refer to the Specifications for details of cylinder head gasket thicknesses.

Preparation for refitting

23 The mating faces of the cylinder head and cylinder block must be perfectly clean before refitting the head. Use a hard plastic or wooden scraper to remove all traces of gasket and carbon; also clean the piston crowns.
Note: *The new head gasket has rubber-coated surfaces, which could be damaged from sharp edges or debris left by a metal scraper. Take particular care when cleaning the piston crowns, as the soft aluminium alloy is easily damaged.*
24 Make sure that the carbon is not allowed to enter the oil and water passages – this is particularly important for the lubrication system, as carbon could block the oil supply to the engine's components. Using adhesive tape and paper, seal the water, oil and bolt holes in the cylinder block.

8.19 Zero the DTI on the gasket face

8.30 Fit the new gasket over the dowels, with the thickness identification holes at the front

25 To prevent carbon entering the gap between the pistons and bores, smear a little grease in the gap.

26 After cleaning each piston, use a small brush to remove all traces of grease and carbon from the gap, then wipe away the remainder with a clean rag. Clean all the pistons in the same way.

27 Check the mating surfaces of the cylinder block and the cylinder head for nicks, deep scratches and other damage (refer to the Note in paragraph 25). If slight, they may be removed carefully with a file, but if excessive, machining may be the only alternative to renewal.

28 If warpage of the cylinder head gasket surface is suspected, use a straight-edge to check it for distortion.

29 Ensure that the cylinder head bolt holes in the crankcase are clean and free of oil. Syringe or soak up any oil left in the bolt holes. This is most important in order that the correct bolt tightening torque can be applied, and to prevent the possibility of the block being cracked by hydraulic pressure when the bolts are tightened.

Refitting

30 Ensure that the cylinder head locating dowels are in place at the corners of the cylinder block, then fit the new cylinder head gasket over the dowels, ensuring that the identification holes are at the front**(see illustration)**. Take care to avoid damaging the gasket's rubber coating.

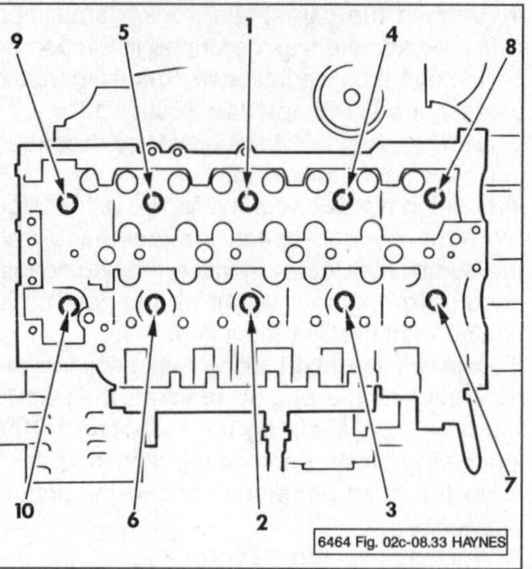

8.33 Cylinder head lower section bolt tightening sequence

31 Lower the cylinder head into position on the gasket, ensuring that it engages correctly over the dowels.

32 Fit the new cylinder head bolts and screw them in as far as possible by hand.

33 Working in sequence**(see illustration)**, tighten all the cylinder head bolts to the specified Stage 1 torque using an E14 Torx socket.

34 Stage 2 involves tightening the bolts though an angle, rather than to a torque **(see illustration)**. Each bolt in sequence must be rotated through the specified angle – special angle gauges are available from tool outlets.

35 The remainder of refitting is a reversal of the removal procedure, bearing in mind the following points:

a) *Refit the turbocharger/exhaust manifold as described in Chapter 4B Section 17.*
b) *Refit the camshafts, rocker arms and hydraulic adjusters as described in Section 6.*
c) *Refit the thermostat as described in Section 3 Section 7.*
d) *Refill the cooling system as described in Chapter 1B Section 36.*
e) *Check and if necessary top-up the engine oil level as described in Chapter 1B Section 13.*
f) *Before starting the engine, read through the section on engine restarting after overhaul in Chapter 2D Section 12.*

8.34 Use an angle gauge for the Stage 2 torque setting

9 Sump – removal and refitting

Removal

1 Firmly apply the handbrake, then jack up the front of the vehicle and support it securely on axle stands (see *Jacking and vehicle support*). Undo the fasteners and remove the engine undertray.

2 Referring to Chapter 1B Section 13 if necessary, drain the engine oil, then clean and refit the engine oil drain plug, tightening it to the specified torque wrench setting. We strongly advise renewing the oil filter element, also described in Chapter 1B Section 13.

3 Undo the retaining bolts and manouevre the sump from place **(see illustrations)**.

4 Break the joint by carefully inserting a putty knife (or similar) between the sump and cylinder block. Take care not to damage the sealing surfaces.

Refitting

5 On reassembly, thoroughly clean and degrease the mating surfaces of the cylinder block/crankcase and sump, then use a clean rag to wipe out the sump and the engine's interior.

6 Fit a new gasket to the sump **(see illustration)**.

7 Refit the sump and fit the retaining bolts, tightening them by hand only at this stage.

9.3a Undo the sump retaining bolts...

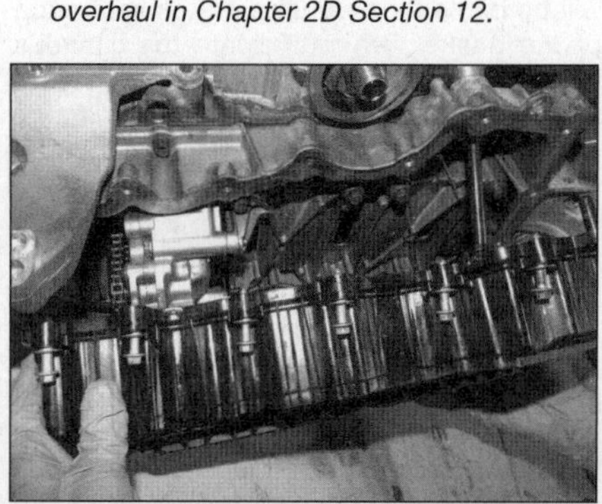

9.3b ...then lower the sump down

9.6 Ensure the gasket is correctly located in the sump grooves

8 Tighten the sump-to-cylinder block bolts gradually and evenly to the specified torque.
9 Refit the engine undertray, then lower the car to the ground. Wait at least 1 hour for the sealant to cure (or whatever time is indicated by the sealant manufacturer) before refilling the engine with oil. If removed, fit a new oil filter with reference to Chapter 1B Section 13.

10 Oil pump – removal, inspection and refitting

Removal

1 Remove the timing belt as described in Section 5, then slide off the crankshaft sprocket.
2 Remove the sump as described in Section 9.
3 Undo the bolt securing the crankshaft position sensor to the crankshaft oil seal carrier and position the sensor to one side **(see illustration)**.
4 Undo the 3 pump mounting bolts then disengage the pump from the chain and manoeuvre from place **(see illustration)**.

10.3 Remove the bolt to displace the camshaft position sensor

10.4 Undo the 3 bolts and remove the pump

Refitting

5 Before fitting the oil pump, ensure that the mating faces on the pump and the cylinder block are completely clean.
6 Engage the drive chain with the oil pump.
7 Refit the mounting bolts and tighten them to the specified torque.
8 Refit the sump, using a new gasket and tightening all the bolts to the required torque.
9 The remainder of refitting is a reversal of removal.

11 Timing chain – removal and refitting

Removal

1 Remove the oil pump as described in Section 10.
2 Disconnect the wiring plug for the air conditioning compressor **(see illustration)**.

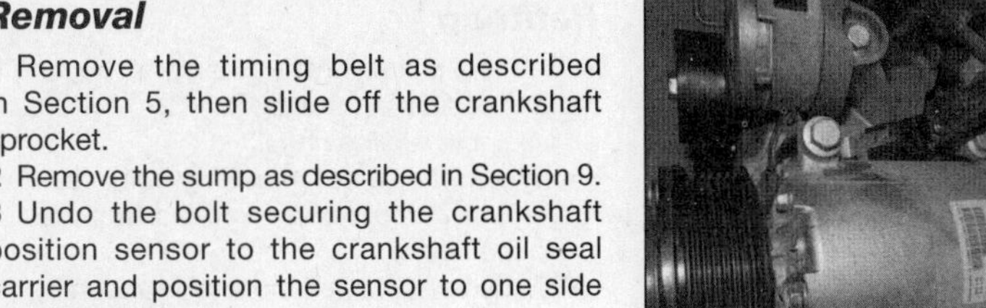
11.2 Unplug the air-con compressor

11.7 Slacken the alternator bracket mounting bolts to allow the alternator bracket to move, giving access to this bolt on the sandwich plate

3 Undo the 3 mounting bolts, and move the airconditioning compressor out of the way. **Note:** *There is no need to disconnect the air-conditiong pipes*.
4 Remove the sump as described in Section 9.
5 Undo the retaining bolts and remove the dipstick from place.
6 Remove the alternator as described in Chapter 5 Section 6.
7 Loosen the bolts for the alternator mounting bracket, to allow access to the corner bolt from the sump sandwich plate **(see illustration)**.
8 Undo the 20 retaining bolts for the sump sandwich plate **(see illustration)**. Some of the bolts are different lengths. Note their fitted positions to aid reassembly.
9 Check the deflection of the timing chain. If it is greater than 12mm the chain must be replaced.
10 Remove the retaining bolt and manoeuvre the crankshaft position sensor from place **(see illustration 10.3)**.
11 Undo the 5 bolts (they are different lengths so note their fitted positions) and remove the timing chain cover.
12 Remove the 3 retaining bolts and manoeuvre the oil pump from place **(see illustration 10.4)**.
13 To remove the timing chain sprocket, take out the key using a pair of pliers, then manouvre the sprocket from the crankshaft **(see illustrations)**.

Refitting

14 Refitting is a reversal of removal.

11.8 Remove the sandwich plate bolts

11.13a Remove the key from the crankshaft...

11.13b ...then slide the sprocket from the crankshaft

12.1 Oil pressure warning switch

12 Oil pressure warning light switch – removal and refitting

Removal

1 The switch is screwed into the oil filter housing **(see illustration)**. Access is from under the vehicle.

2 Apply the handbrake, then jack up the front of the vehicle and support it securely on axle stands (see *Jacking and vehicle support*). Undo the fasteners and remove the engine undertray.

3 To further improve access, Remove the auxiliary drivebelt as described in Chapter 1B Section 32, then undo the mounting bolts and move the air conditioning compressor to one side. Suspend the compressor from the radiator crossmember using wire or straps. There is no need to disconnect the refrigerant pipes.

4 Disconnect the switch wiring plug.

5 Unscrew the switch from the housing; be prepared for some oil loss.

Refitting

6 Refitting is the reverse of the removal procedure; fit a new pressure switch sealing washer, and tighten the switch securely.

7 Reconnect the switch wiring plug.

8 Refit all components removed for access to the switch.

9 Check the engine oil level and top-up as necessary (see Chapter 1B Section 5).

10 Check for correct warning light operation, and for signs of oil leaks, once the engine has been restarted and warmed-up to normal operating temperature.

13 Oil cooler – removal and refitting

Note: *New sealing rings will be required on refitting – check for availability prior to commencing work.*

Removal

1 The cooler is fitted to the oil filter housing on the front of the cylinder block. Access is from under the vehicle.

2 Firmly apply the handbrake, then jack up the front of the vehicle and support it securely on axle stands (see *Jacking and vehicle support*). Undo the fasteners and remove the engine undertray.

13.4a Squeeze the clip to remove the first coolant pipe from the cooler...

13.4b ...then pull out the retaining clip and detach the second pipe

13.5 Disconnect the oil switches

13.6 Oil cooler retaining bolts

3 To further improve access, remove the auxiliary drivebelt as described in Chapter 1B Section 32, then undo the mounting bolts and move the air conditioning compressor to one side. Suspend the compressor from the radiator crossmember using wire or straps. There is no need to disconnect the refrigerant pipes.

4 Working underneath the car, disconnect the 2 coolant pipes from the top of the oil cooler **(see illustrations)**.

5 Unplug the oil pressure and temperature switches **(see illustration)**.

6 Undo the 3 retaining bolts and detach the cooler from the housing **(see illustration)**. Recover the sealing rings and be prepared for oil/coolant spillage.

Refitting

7 Refitting is a reversal of removal, bearing in mind the following points:

a) *Use new sealing rings.*
b) *Tighten the cooler mounting bolts securely*
c) *Refit all components removed for access to the cooler.*
d) *On completion, refit the engine undertray, then lower the car to the ground. Check and if necessary top-up the oil and coolant levels (see Chapter 1B Section 5 and Chapter 1B Section 6), then start the engine and check for signs of oil or coolant leakage.*

14 Crankshaft oil seals – renewal

Timing belt end seal

1 Remove the timing belt as described in Section 5.

2 Slide the belt sprocket from the crankshaft, and recover the locating key from the groove on the crankshaft **(see illustrations 11.1a and 11.1b)**.

3 Note the fitted depth of the oil seal as a guide for fitting the new one.

4 Using a screwdriver or similar tool, carefully prise the oil seal from its location. Take care not to damage the oil seal contact surfaces or crankshaft. Alternatively, drill a small hole in the seal (taking care not to drill any deeper than necessary), then insert a self-tapping screw and use pliers to pull out the seal **(see illustration)**.

14.4 Drill a small hole in the seal before inserting a self-tapping screw and pulling out the seal

5 Wipe clean the oil seal contact surfaces and seating, and clean up any sharp edges or burrs which might damage the new seal as it is fitted, or which might cause the seal to leak once in place.

6 No oil should be applied to the oil seal, which is made of PTFE. Ford technicians use a special seal-fitting tool (303-255/303-395), but an adequate substitute can be achieved using a large socket or piece of tubing of sufficient size to bear on the outer edge of the new seal. Note that the new seal is supplied with a guide which fits over the end of the crankshaft.

7 Locate the new seal (with guide still fitted) over the end of the crankshaft, using the tool **(see illustration)**, socket, or tubing to press the seal squarely and fully into position, to the previously-noted depth. Remove the guide from the end of the crankshaft.

8 The remainder of reassembly is the reverse of the removal procedure, referring to the relevant text for details where required. Check for signs of oil leakage when the engine is restarted.

Flywheel/driveplate end seal

9 Remove the flywheel/driveplate as described in Section 15.

10 Using a screwdriver or similar, carefully prise the oil seal from place. Take great care not to damage the seal seating area or the crankshaft sealing surface. Alternatively, punch or drill two small holes opposite each other in the oil seal, then screw a self-tapping screw into each hole, and pull the screws with pliers to extract the seal.

11 Clean the end of the crankshaft, polishing off any burrs or raised edges, which may have caused the seal to fail in the first place. Clean also the seal mating face on the engine block, using a suitable solvent for degreasing if necessary.

12 The new oil seal is supplied fitted with a locating sleeve, which must not be removed prior to fitting (it will drop out on its own when the seal is fitted). Do not lubricate the seal.

13 Offer the new seal into position, feeding the locating sleeve over the end of the crankshaft.

14 Ford technicians use a special tool (205-307) to pull the seal into position. In the absence of the tool, use a large socket/piece of tubing which bears only on the hard outer edge of the seal, and carefully tap the seal into position.

15 If the seal locating sleeve is still in position, remove it now.

16 The remainder of the reassembly procedure is the reverse of dismantling, referring to the relevant text for details where required. Check for signs of oil leakage when the engine is restarted.

14.7 Guide the new seal over the end of the crankshaft then drive it home until it's flush with the cover

15.2 A simple home-made tool to lock the flywheel

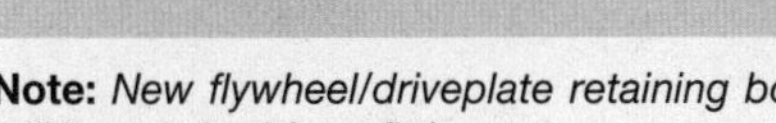

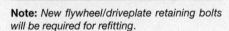

15 Flywheel/driveplate – removal, inspection and refitting

Note: *New flywheel/driveplate retaining bolts will be required for refitting.*

Removal

Manual transmission models

1 Remove the transmission as described in Chapter 7A Section 6 then remove the clutch assembly as described in Chapter 8 Section 6.

2 Prevent the flywheel from turning by locking the ring gear teeth with a similar arrangement to that shown **(see illustration)**. Alternatively, bolt a strap between the flywheel and the cylinder block/crankcase. Make alignment marks between the flywheel and crankshaft using paint or a suitable marker pen.

3 Slacken and remove the retaining bolts and remove the flywheel. Do not drop it, as it is very heavy.

Automatic transmission models

4 Remove the transmission as described in Chapter 7A Section 6 then remove the driveplate as described in paragraphs 2 and 3.

Inspection

5 On manual transmission models, examine the flywheel for scoring of the clutch face. If the clutch face is scored, the flywheel may be surface ground, but renewal is preferable.

6 On automatic transmission models closely examine the driveplate and ring gear teeth for signs of wear or damage and check the driveplate surface for any signs of cracks.

7 If there is any doubt about the condition of the flywheel/driveplate, seek the advice of a Ford dealer or engine reconditioning specialist. They will be able to advise if it is possible to recondition it or whether renewal is necessary.

Refitting

Manual transmission models

8 Clean the mating surfaces of the flywheel and crankshaft.

9 Unless they are already pre-coated, apply a drop of locking compound to each of the new retaining bolt threads then offer up the flywheel, if the original is being refitted align the marks made prior to removal. Screw in the retaining bolts.

10 Lock the flywheel by the method used on removal, and tighten the retaining bolts to the specified torque in two stages.

11 Refit the clutch as described in Section then remove the locking tool, and refit the transmission as described in Chapter 7A Section 6.

Automatic transmission models

12 Clean the mating surfaces of the driveplate and crankshaft.

13 Unless they are already pre-coated, apply a drop of locking compound to each of the new retaining bolt threads then offer up the driveplate, if the original is being refitted align the marks made prior to removal. Screw in the retaining bolts.

14 Lock the driveplate by the method used on removal, and tighten the retaining bolts to the specified torque in two stages.

15 Remove the locking tool and refit the transmission as described in Chapter 7B Section 7.

16 Engine/transmission mountings – inspection and renewal

1 Refer to Chapter 2B Section 16, but note the different torque wrench settings given in the Specifications at the beginning of this Chapter.

Chapter 2 Part D
Engine removal and overhaul procedures

Contents

Degrees of difficulty

Easy, suitable for novice with little experience 

Fairly easy, suitable for beginner with some experience 

Fairly difficult, suitable for competent DIY mechanic 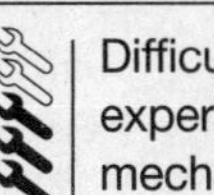

Difficult, suitable for experienced DIY mechanic

Very difficult, suitable for expert DIY or professional 

Specifications

Engine type

	Manufacturer's engine codes*
1.5 litre (1498 cc) DOHC 16-valve petrol engine	BNMA, M8MA, M8MB, M8MC, M9MA, M9MB, M9MC, M9MD
1.5 litre (1499 cc) SOHC 8-valve diesel engine	XWMA, XWMB, XWMC
2.0 litre (1998 cc) DOHC 16-valve diesel engine	TXMA, T7MA, T7MB, T8MA, T8MB, UFMA, XRMA

* *For details of engine code location, see 'Vehicle identification'.*

Petrol engines

Cylinder head

Maximum gasket face distortion .... 0.10 mm

Valves

Stem diameter:
- Inlet valves .... 5.470 to 5.485 mm
- Exhaust valves .... 5.465 to 5.480 mm

Torque wrench settings

Refer to Chapter 2A specifications

Diesel engines

Cylinder head

Maximum gasket face distortion:	
1.5 litre engines	0.025 mm
2.0 litre engines	0.03 mm

Valves

Valve stem diameter:	
1.5 litre engines	Not available
2.0 litre engines	
Inlet valves	5.978 ± 0.009 mm
Exhaust valves	5.968 ± 0.009 mm

Cylinder block

Cylinder bore diameter (nominal):	
1.5 litre engines	73.50 mm
2.0 litre engines	85.00 mm

Piston rings

End gaps:	
1.5 litre engines:	
Top compression ring	0.20 to 0.35 mm
Second compression ring	0.20 to 0.40 mm
Oil control ring	0.20 to 0.40 mm
2.0 litre engines:	
Top compression ring	0.20 to 0.35 mm
Second compression ring	0.80 to 1.00 mm
Oil control ring	0.25 to 0.50 mm

Crankshaft

Endfloat:	
1.5 litre engines	0.10 to 0.30 mm
2.0 litre engines	0.07 to 0.32 mm
Maximum bearing journal out-of-round (all engines)	0.007 mm

Torque wrench settings

Refer to Specifications in Chapter 2B or Chapter 2C.

1 General information

1 Included in this Part of Chapter 2 are details of removing the engine/transmission from the car and general overhaul procedures for the cylinder head, cylinder block/crankcase and all other engine internal components.

Note: *On all petrol engines covered by this manual, it is not possible to remove the intermediate/main bearing section or to remove the crankshaft or pistons. No separate parts are available, and replacement/exchange units are supplied with crankshaft, pistons, connecting rods, etc, already fitted. Consult a Ford dealer or parts specialist for further information.*

2 The information given ranges from advice concerning preparation for an overhaul and the purchase of parts, to detailed step-by-step procedures covering removal, inspection, renovation and refitting of engine internal components (where possible).

3 After Section 6, all instructions are based on the assumption that the engine has been removed from the car. For information concerning in-car engine repair, as well as the removal and refitting of those external components necessary for full overhaul, refer to Parts A to C of this Chapter (as applicable) and to Section 6. Ignore any preliminary dismantling operations described in Parts A to C that are no longer relevant once the engine has been removed from the car.

4 Apart from torque wrench settings, which are given at the beginning of Parts A to C (as applicable), all specifications relating to engine overhaul are at the beginning of this Part of Chapter 2.

2 Engine overhaul – general information

1 It is not always easy to determine when, or if, an engine should be completely overhauled, as a number of factors must be considered.

2 High mileage is not necessarily an indication that an overhaul is needed, while low mileage does not preclude the need for an overhaul. Frequency of servicing is probably the most important consideration. An engine which has had regular and frequent oil and filter changes, as well as other required maintenance, will most likely give many thousands of miles of reliable service. Conversely, a neglected engine may require an overhaul very early in its life.

3 Excessive oil consumption is an indication that piston rings, valve stem oil seals and/or valves and valve guides are in need of attention. Make sure that oil leaks are not responsible before deciding that the rings and/or guides are to blame. Perform a cylinder compression check to determine the likely cause of the problem.

4 Check the oil pressure with a gauge fitted in place of the oil pressure switch, and compare it with the value given in the Specifications. If it is extremely low, the main and big-end bearings and/or the oil pump are probably worn out.

5 Loss of power, rough running, knocking or metallic engine noises, excessive valve gear noise and high fuel consumption may also point to the need for an overhaul, especially if they are all present at the same time. If a complete tune-up does not remedy the situation, major mechanical work is the only solution.

6 An engine overhaul involves restoring the internal parts to the specifications of a new engine. However, at the time of writing, Ford will only sell the bottom end of an engine complete with crankshaft, shells, pistons as a complete unit. You cannot replace the parts individually.

Note: *Critical cooling system components such as the hoses, drivebelts, thermostat and coolant pump should be renewed when an engine is overhauled. The radiator should* *be checked carefully, to ensure that it is not clogged or leaking. Also, it is a good idea to renew the oil pump whenever the engine is overhauled.*

7 Before beginning the engine overhaul, read through the entire procedure to familiarise yourself with the scope and requirements of the job. Overhauling an engine is not difficult if you follow all of the instructions carefully, have the necessary tools and equipment, and pay close attention to all specifications; however, it can be time-consuming. Plan on the car being tied up for a minimum of two weeks, especially if parts must be taken to an engineering works for repair or reconditioning. Check on the availability of parts, and make sure that any necessary special tools and equipment are obtained in advance. Most work can be done with typical hand tools, although a number of precision measuring tools are required for inspecting parts to determine if they must be renewed. Often the engineering works will handle the inspection of parts, and offer advice concerning reconditioning and renewal.

8 Always wait until the engine has been completely dismantled, and all components, especially the engine block, have been inspected before deciding what service and repair operations must be performed by an engineering works. Since the condition of the block will be the major factor to consider when determining whether to overhaul the original engine or buy a reconditioned unit, do not purchase parts or have overhaul work done on other components until the block has been thoroughly inspected. As a general rule, time is the primary cost of an overhaul, so it does not pay to fit worn or substandard parts.

9 As a final note, to ensure maximum life and minimum trouble from a reconditioned engine, everything must be assembled with care, and in a spotlessly-clean environment.

3 Engine removal – methods and precautions

Warning: Always be extremely careful when removing and refitting the engine. Serious injury can result from careless actions. Plan ahead, take your time, and you will find that a job of this nature, although major, can be accomplished successfully.

1 If you have decided that an engine must be removed for overhaul or major repair work, several preliminary steps should be taken.

2 Locating a suitable place to work is extremely important. Adequate work space, along with storage space for the car, will be needed. If a garage is not available, at the very least a flat, level, clean work surface is required.

3 Cleaning the engine compartment and engine before beginning the removal procedure will help keep tools clean and organised.

4 The engine is removed complete with the transmission, by lowering it out of the car; the car's body must be raised and supported securely, sufficiently high that the engine/transmission can be unbolted as a single unit and lowered to the ground. An engine hoist will therefore be necessary. Make sure the equipment is rated in excess of the combined weight of the engine and transmission. Safety is of primary importance, considering the potential hazards involved in lifting the engine out of the car.

5 If the engine is being removed by a novice, an assistant should be available. Advice and aid from someone more experienced would also be helpful. There are many instances when one person cannot simultaneously perform all of the operations required when removing the engine from the car.

6 Plan the operation ahead of time. Arrange for, or obtain, all of the tools and equipment you will need, prior to beginning the job. Some of the equipment necessary to perform engine removal and installation safely and with relative ease are (in addition to an engine hoist) a heavy-duty trolley jack, complete sets of spanners and sockets as described at the end of this manual, wooden blocks, and plenty of rags and cleaning solvent for mopping-up spilled oil, coolant and fuel. If the hoist must be hired, make sure that you arrange for it in advance, and perform all of the operations possible without it beforehand. This will save you money and time.

7 Plan for the car to be out of use for quite a while. An engineering works will be required to perform some of the work which the do-it-yourselfer cannot accomplish without special equipment. These places often have a busy schedule, so it would be a good idea to consult them before removing the engine, in order to accurately estimate the amount of time required to rebuild or repair components that may need work.

8 During the engine/transmission removal procedure, it is advisable to make notes of the locations of all brackets, cable-ties, earthing points, etc, as well as how the wiring harnesses, hoses and electrical connections are attached and routed around the engine and engine compartment. An effective way of doing this is to take a series of photographs of the various components before they are disconnected or removed; the resulting photographs will prove invaluable when the engine/transmission is refitted.

Note: *Such is the complexity of the power unit arrangement on these vehicles, and the variations that may be encountered according to model and optional equipment fitted, that the procedures given in Sections 4 and 5 should be regarded as a guide to the work involved, rather than an accurate step-by-step procedure. Where differences are encountered, or additional component disconnection or removal is necessary, make notes of the work involved as an aid to refitting.*

4 Petrol engine – removal, separation and refitting

Note: *This procedure describes removing the engine and transmission a complete assembly downwards out the of the engine compartment. When raising the vehicle bear in mind that the front underside of the vehicle must be at least 700 mm above the ground to provide sufficient clearance.*

Removal

1 Remove the plastic cover over the top of the engine.

2 Remove the windscreen cowl panel as described in Chapter 11 Section 12.

3 Remove the radiator as described in Chapter 3 Section 6. This procedure can be completed with the radiator in place, but is much easier, and carries much less risk of damage, with the radiator removed.

4 Remove the air cleaner assembly as described in Chapter 4A Section 3.

5 Remove the battery and battery tray as described in Chapter 5 Section 4.

6 Jack up the front of the car, and support it on axle stands (see *Jacking and vehicle support*). Although not essential immediately, it would be wise at this stage to raise the car sufficiently to allow the engine and transmission to be withdrawn from underneath.

7 Undo the fasteners and remove the engine undertray.

8 Remove the auxiliary drivebelt as described in Chapter 1B Section 32.

9 Drain the cooling system as described in Chapter 1A Section 34.

10 If the engine is being dismantled, drain the engine oil with reference to Chapter 1B Section 13.

11 Undo the retaining nut and disconnect the engine positive supply lead from the battery positive terminal connector.

12 Disconnect the reversing light switch wiring connector and the earth leads at the engine/transmission left-hand mounting and at the left-hand chassis member. Release the wiring from the cable clips and ties.

13 On automatic transmission models, disconnect the wiring connector at the transmission control module, then release the wiring harness from the cable clips and ties.

14 On manual transmission models, taking precautions against fluid spillage, prise up the spring clip and disconnect the clutch slave cylinder fluid pipe from on top of the transmission. Unclip the pipe, and tie it up to the bulkhead to reduce further fluid spillage.

15 Disconnect the engine wiring harness from the engine compartment fuse/relay box. Using a small screwdriver, release the two retaining tabs and lift up the front section of the fuse/relay carrier. Release the wiring harness from the fuse/relay box so it is free to be removed with the engine.

16 Disconnect the transmission gearchange/ selector cable(s) from the transmission as described in Chapter 7A Section 3 or Chapter 7B Section 4, as applicable.
17 Disconnect the radiator top and bottom hoses, expansion tank hose, heater matrix coolant hoses and EGR cooler hoses.
18 On automatic transmission models, disconnect the two transmission fluid pipes from the fluid cooler by pressing the two tabs on the quick-release connectors and pulling the connectors off the fluid cooler pipe stubs. Be prepared for fluid spillage.
19 Disconnect the fuel supply and return pipes at the quick-release connectors on the fuel filter. Suitably cover or plug the disconnected unions, then release the fuel pipes from their retaining clips.
20 Disconnect the wiring connector at the radiator cooling fan.
21 Disconnect the brake servo vacuum hose from the vacuum pump.
22 Remove both driveshafts as described in Chapter 8 Section 7.
23 Remove the front crossmember and lock carrier assembly as described in Chapter 11 Section 10.
24 Remove the catalytic converter as described in Chapter 4A Section 17.
25 Disconnect the wiring connector from the air conditioning compressor. Undo the three bolts securing the compressor to the block, and secure the compressor to one side using cable- ties – do not disconnect any of the hoses.
26 Refer to Chapter 6A Section 6 and disconnect the three wiring connectors from the engine management powertrain control module (PCM).
27 Make a final check round the engine and transmission, to make sure nothing (apart from the left- and right-hand mountings) remains attached or in the way which will prevent it from being lowered out. Also make sure there is enough room under the front of the car for the engine/transmission to be lowered out and withdrawn.
28 Securely attach the engine/transmission unit to a suitable engine crane or hoist, and raise it so that the weight is just taken off the two remaining engine mountings. It is helpful at this stage to have an assistant available, either to work the crane or to guide the engine out.
29 With the engine securely supported, undo the nuts and bolts and remove the engine/ transmission left-hand mounting.
30 Similarly, remove the bolts from the engine right-hand mounting, on the driver's side of the engine compartment.
31 With the help of an assistant, carefully lower the assembly from the engine compartment, making sure it clears the surrounding components and bodywork. Be prepared to steady the engine when it touches down, to stop it toppling over. Withdraw the assembly from under the car, and remove it to wherever it will be worked on.

Separation

32 Remove the starter motor with reference to Chapter 5 Section 7.

Manual transmission models

33 Remove the bolts securing the transmission to the engine. Note the fitted positions of any brackets.
34 With the aid of an assistant, draw the transmission off the engine. Once it is clear of the dowels, do not allow it to hang on the input shaft.

Automatic transmission models

35 Remove the access cover over the starter motor aperture.
36 Rotate the crankshaft, using a socket on the pulley nut, until one of the torque converter-to-driveplate retaining bolts/nuts becomes accessible through the opening on the rear facing side of the engine. Working through the opening, undo the bolt. Rotate the crankshaft as necessary and remove the remaining bolts in the same way, there are six bolts in total. Note that new bolts will be required for refitting.
37 Remove the bolts securing the transmission to the engine.
38 With the aid of an assistant, draw the transmission squarely off the engine dowels making sure that the torque converter remains in position on the transmission. Use the access hole in the transmission housing to hold the converter in place.

Refitting

Manual transmission models

39 Make sure that the clutch is correctly centred and that the clutch release components are fitted to the bellhousing. Do not apply any grease to the transmission input shaft, the guide sleeve, or the release bearing itself, as these components have a friction-reducing coating which does not require lubrication.
40 Manoeuvre the transmission squarely into position, and engage it with the engine dowels. Refit the bolts securing the transmission to the engine, and tighten them to the specified torque. Refit the starter motor.

Automatic transmission models

41 Clean the contact surfaces on the torque converter and driveplate, and the transmission and engine mating faces. Lightly lubricate the torque converter guide projection and the engine/transmission locating dowels with grease.
42 Manoeuvre the transmission squarely into position, and engage it with the engine dowels. Refit the bolts securing the transmission to the engine and tighten lightly first in a diagonal sequence, then again to the specified torque.
43 Attach the torque converter to the driveplate using new bolts. Rotate the crankshaft for access to the bolts as was done for removal, then rotate the torque converter by means of the access hole in the transmission housing. Fit and tighten all the bolts hand-tight first, then tighten again to the specified torque. Refit the starter motor.

All models

44 The remainder of refitting is a reversal of removal, noting the following additional points:
a) *Make sure that all mating faces are clean, and use new gaskets where necessary.*
b) *Tighten all nuts and bolts to the specified torque setting, where given.*
c) *On manual transmission models, check and if necessary adjust the gearchange cables as described in Chapter 7A Section 3.*
d) *On automatic transmission models, reconnect and adjust the selector cable as described in Chapter 7B Section 4.*
e) *Refill the transmission with lubricant if necessary as described in the relevant parts of Chapter 7A Section 2 and Chapter 7B Section 2.*
f) *On manual transmission models, top-up and bleed the clutch hydraulic system as described in Chapter 8 Section 2.*
g) *Refill the engine with coolant and oil as described in Chapter 1A.*

5 Diesel engine – removal, separation and refitting

Warning: The diesel injection system operates at extremely high pressures when the pump is running. Wait at least one minute after stopping the engine before working on the fuel injection system components.

Note: *This procedure describes removing the engine and transmission a complete assembly downwards out the of the engine compartment. When raising the vehicle bear in mind that the front underside of the vehicle must be at least 700 mm above the ground to provide sufficient clearance.*

Removal

1 Remove the plastic cover over the top of the engine.
2 Remove the windscreen cowl panel as described in Chapter 11 Section 12.
3 Remove the radiator as described in Chapter 3 Section 6. This procedure can be completed with the radiator in place, but is much easier, and carries much less risk of damage, with the radiator removed.
4 Remove the air cleaner assembly as described in Section 4B Section 6.
5 Remove the battery and battery tray as described in Chapter 5 Section 4.
6 Jack up the front of the car, and support it on axle stands (see *Jacking and vehicle support*).
7 Undo the fasteners and remove the engine undertray.
8 Remove the auxiliary drivebelt as described in Chapter 1B Section 32.
9 Drain the cooling system as described in Section 1B Section 36.

10 If the engine is being dismantled, drain the engine oil with reference to Chapter 1B Section 13.
11 Slacken the hose clamps, undo the bracket bolt and remove the charge air pipe from the left-hand side of the engine **(see illustration)**.
12 Undo the retaining nut and disconnect the engine positive supply lead from the battery positive terminal connector.
13 Disconnect the reversing light switch wiring connector and the earth leads at the engine/transmission left-hand mounting and at the left-hand chassis member. Release the wiring from the cable clips and ties.
14 On automatic transmission models, disconnect the wiring connector at the transmission control module, then release the wiring harness from the cable clips and ties.
15 On manual transmission models, taking precautions against fluid spillage, prise up the spring clip and disconnect the clutch slave cylinder fluid pipe from on top of the transmission. Unclip the pipe, and tie it up to the bulkhead to reduce further fluid spillage.
16 Disconnect the engine wiring harness from the engine compartment fuse/relay box. Using a small screwdriver, release the two retaining tabs and lift up the front section of the fuse/relay carrier. Release the wiring harness from the fuse/relay box so it is free to be removed with the engine.
17 Disconnect the transmission gearchange/selector cable(s) from the transmission as described in Chapter 7A Section 3 or Chapter 7B Section 4, as applicable.
18 Disconnect the radiator top and bottom hoses, expansion tank hose, heater matrix coolant hoses and EGR cooler hoses.
19 On automatic transmission models, disconnect the two transmission fluid pipes from the fluid cooler by pressing the two tabs on the quick-release connectors and pulling the connectors off the fluid cooler pipe stubs. Be prepared for fluid spillage.
20 Disconnect the fuel supply and return pipes at the quick-release connectors on the fuel filter. Suitably cover or plug the disconnected unions, then release the fuel pipes from their retaining clips.
21 Disconnect the wiring connector at the radiator cooling fan.
22 Remove both driveshafts as described in Chapter 8 Section 7.
23 Remove the front crossmember and lock carrier assembly as described in Chapter 11 Section 10.
24 Remove the catalytic converter as described in Chapter 4B Section 21.
25 Disconnect the wiring connector from the air conditioning compressor. Undo the three bolts securing the compressor to the block, and secure the compressor to one side using cable ties – do not disconnect any of the hoses.
26 Refer to Chapter 6B Section 6 and disconnect the three wiring connectors from the engine management powertrain control module (PCM).
27 Make a final check round the engine and transmission, to make sure nothing (apart from the left- and right-hand mountings) remains attached or in the way which will prevent it from being lowered out. Also make sure there is enough room under the front of the car for the engine/transmission to be lowered out and withdrawn.
28 Securely attach the engine/transmission unit to a suitable engine crane or hoist, and raise it so that the weight is just taken off the two remaining engine mountings. It is helpful at this stage to have an assistant available, either to work the crane or to guide the engine out.
29 With the engine securely supported, undo the nuts and bolts and remove the engine/transmission left-hand mounting.
30 Similarly, remove the bolts from the engine right-hand mounting, on the driver's side of the engine compartment.
31 With the help of an assistant, carefully lower the assembly from the engine compartment, making sure it clears the surrounding components and bodywork. Be prepared to steady the engine when it touches down, to stop it toppling over. Withdraw the assembly from under the car, and remove it to wherever it will be worked on.

Separation

32 Remove the starter motor with reference to Chapter 5 Section 7.

Manual transmission models

33 Remove the bolts securing the transmission to the engine. Note the fitted positions of any brackets.
34 With the aid of an assistant, draw the transmission off the engine. Once it is clear of the dowels, do not allow it to hang on the input shaft.

Automatic transmission models

35 Remove the access cover over the starter motor aperture.
36 Rotate the crankshaft, using a socket on the pulley nut, until one of the torque converter-to-driveplate retaining bolts/nuts becomes accessible through the opening on the rear facing side of the engine. Working through the opening, undo the bolt. Rotate the crankshaft as necessary and remove the remaining bolts in the same way, there are six bolts in total. Note that new bolts will be required for refitting.
37 Remove the bolts securing the transmission to the engine.
38 With the aid of an assistant, draw the transmission squarely off the engine dowels making sure that the torque converter remains in position on the transmission. Use the access hole in the transmission housing to hold the converter in place.

Refitting

Manual transmission models

39 Make sure that the clutch is correctly centred and that the clutch release components are fitted to the bellhousing. Do not apply any grease to the transmission input shaft, the guide sleeve, or the release bearing itself, as

5.11 Undo the charge air pipe bracket bolt

these components have a friction-reducing coating which does not require lubrication.
40 Manoeuvre the transmission squarely into position, and engage it with the engine dowels. Refit the bolts securing the transmission to the engine, and tighten them to the specified torque. Refit the starter motor.

Automatic transmission models

41 Clean the contact surfaces on the torque converter and driveplate, and the transmission and engine mating faces. Lightly lubricate the torque converter guide projection and the engine/transmission locating dowels with grease.
42 Manoeuvre the transmission squarely into position, and engage it with the engine dowels. Refit the bolts securing the transmission to the engine and tighten lightly first in a diagonal sequence, then again to the specified torque.
43 Attach the torque converter to the driveplate using new bolts. Rotate the crankshaft for access to the bolts as was done for removal, then rotate the torque converter by means of the access hole in the transmission housing. Fit and tighten all the bolts hand-tight first, then tighten again to the specified torque. Refit the starter motor.

All models

44 The remainder of refitting is a reversal of removal, noting the following additional points:

a) *Make sure that all mating faces are clean, and use new gaskets where necessary.*
b) *Tighten all nuts and bolts to the specified torque setting, where given.*
c) *On manual transmission models, check and if necessary adjust the gearchange cables as described in Chapter 7A Section 3.*
d) *On automatic transmission models, reconnect and adjust the selector cable as described in Chapter 7B Section 4.*
e) *Refill the transmission with lubricant if necessary as described in the relevant parts of Chapter 7A Section 2 and Chapter 7B Section 2.*
f) *On manual-transmission models, top-up and bleed the clutch hydraulic system as described in Chapter 8 Section 2.*
g) *Refill the engine with coolant and oil as described in Section or Chapter 1B Section 13.*

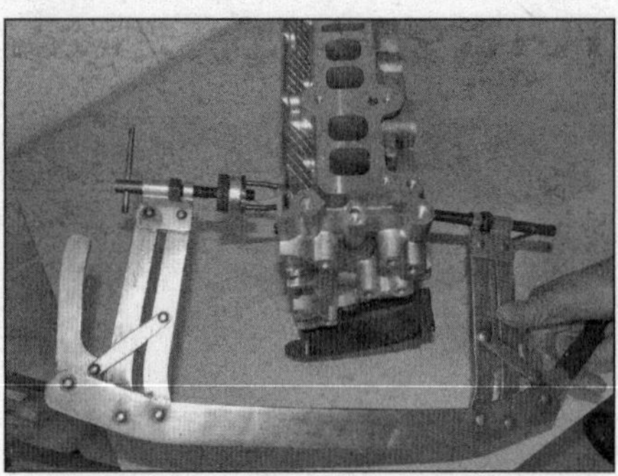

7.5 Compress the valve spring with a suitable valve spring compressor

7.6 Remove the spring retainer and the valve spring

6 Engine overhaul – dismantling sequence

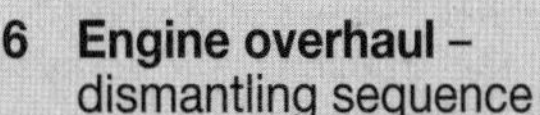

Note: *On all petrol engines covered by this manual, it is not possible to remove the intermediate/main bearing section or to remove the crankshaft or pistons. No separate parts are available, and replacement/exchange units are supplied with crankshaft, pistons, connecting rods, etc, already fitted. Consult a Ford dealer or parts specialist for further information.*

1 It is much easier to dismantle and work on the engine if it is mounted on a portable engine stand. These stands can often be hired from a tool hire shop. Before the engine is mounted on a stand, the flywheel/driveplate should be removed from the engine, so that the engine stand bolts can be tightened into the end of the cylinder block.

2 If a stand is not available, it is possible to dismantle the engine with it blocked up on a sturdy workbench or on the floor. Be extra careful not to tip or drop the engine when working without a stand.

3 If you're going to obtain a reconditioned ('recon') engine, all external components must be removed first, to be transferred to the new engine (just as they will if you are doing a complete engine overhaul yourself).

Note: *When removing the external components from the engine, pay close attention to details that may be helpful or important during refitting. Note the fitted position of gaskets, seals, spacers, pins, washers, bolts and other small items. These external components include the following:*

Petrol engines

a) Ignition system HT components including ignition coils, spark plugs and wiring as applicable.
b) All electrical switches and sensors.
c) Thermostat housing.
d) Fuel system components.
e) Inlet and exhaust manifolds.
f) Oil filter.
g) Engine mountings and lifting brackets.
h) Ancillary component mounting brackets.
i) Oil filler tube and dipstick.
j) Coolant pipes and hoses.
k) Flywheel.

Diesel engines

a) All electrical switches and sensors.
b) Fuel system components and glow plugs.
c) Thermostat housing.
d) Inlet and exhaust manifolds.
e) Oil cooler.
f) Engine lifting brackets, hose brackets and wiring brackets.
g) Ancillary component mounting brackets.
h) Wiring harnesses and brackets.
i) Coolant pipes and hoses.
j) Oil filler tube and dipstick.
k) Flywheel/driveplate.

4 If you are obtaining a 'short' motor (which consists of the engine cylinder block, crankshaft, pistons and connecting rods all assembled), then the timing belt/chain, cylinder head, sump and oil pump will have to be removed also.

7.7 Special pliers are available specifically designed to remove valve stem seals

7.8 Place each valve and its associated components in a labelled bag

5 If you are planning a complete overhaul (diesel engines only) the engine can be disassembled and the internal components removed in the following order:

a) Engine external components (including inlet and exhaust manifolds).
b) Timing belt and sprockets.
c) Cylinder head.
d) Flywheel/driveplate.
e) Sump.
f) Oil pump.
g) Pistons and connecting rods.
h) Crankshaft and main bearings.

6 Before beginning the disassembly and overhaul procedures, make sure that you have all of the correct tools necessary. Refer to the reference section at the end of this manual for further information.

7 Cylinder head – dismantling

Note: *New and reconditioned cylinder heads are available from the manufacturers and from engine overhaul specialists. Due to the fact that some specialist tools are required for the dismantling and inspection procedures, and new components may not be readily available, it may be more practical and economical for the home mechanic to purchase a reconditioned head rather than dismantle, inspect and recondition the original head.*

1 Remove the cylinder head as described in Part A, B or C of this Chapter (as applicable).

2 If not already done, remove the inlet and exhaust manifolds with reference to Chapter 4A or Chapter 4B. Also remove all external fittings, unions, pipes, sensors, brackets and elbows.

3 Proceed as follows according to engine type.

Petrol engines

4 Tap each valve stem smartly, using a light hammer and drift, to free the spring and associated items.

5 Fit a deep-reach type valve spring compressor to each valve in turn, and compress each spring until the collets are exposed **(see illustration)**. Lift out the collets; a small screwdriver, a magnet or a pair of tweezers may be useful. Carefully release the spring compressor and remove it.

6 Remove the spring retainer and the valve spring **(see illustration)**. Pull the valve out of its guide.

7 Pull off the valve stem oil seal with a pair of long-nosed pliers **(see illustration)**. It may be necessary to use a tool such as a pair of electrician's wire strippers, the 'legs' of which will engage under the seal, if the seal is tight.

8 It is essential that each valve is stored together with its collets, retainer, spring and spring seat. The valves should also be kept in their correct sequence, unless they are so badly worn or burnt that they are to be renewed. If they are going to be kept and

7.10 Remove the camshaft drive chain guide – 2.0 litre diesel engines

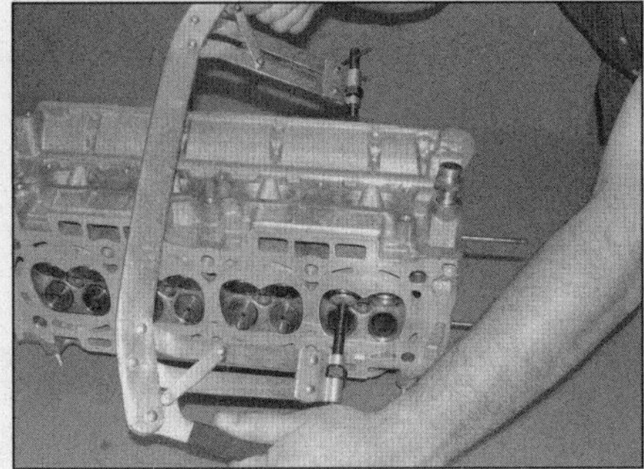
7.15a Compress the valve spring using a spring compressor...

7.15b ... then extract the collets and release the spring compressor

7.15c Remove the spring retainer...

7.15d ... followed by the valve spring...

7.15e ... and the spring seat (not all models)

used again, place each valve assembly in a labelled polythene bag or similar container **(see illustration)**. Note that No 1 valve is nearest to the timing chain end of the engine.

9 Continue removing all the remaining valves in the same way.

Diesel engines

10 Remove the camshaft drive chain guide from the cylinder head **(see illustration)**.

11 If you haven't already done so, remove the inlet and exhaust manifolds with reference to Chapter 4B Section 16 or Chapter 4B Section 17. Remove any remaining brackets or housings as required.

12 Remove the camshaft(s), tappets and rockers (as applicable) as described in Part A, B, C or D of this Chapter.

13 If you haven't already done so, remove the glow plugs as described in Chapter 6B Section 16.

14 Tap each valve stem smartly, using a light hammer and drift, to free the spring and associated items.

15 On all models, using a valve spring compressor, compress each valve spring in turn until the split collets can be removed. Release the compressor, and lift off the spring retainer, spring and, where fitted, the spring seat. Using a pair of pliers, carefully extract the valve stem oil seal from the top of the guide. On some engines, the valve stem oil seal also forms the spring seat and is deeply recessed in the cylinder head. It is also a tight fit on the valve guide making it difficult to remove with pliers or a conventional valve stem oil seal removal tool. It can be easily removed, however, using a self-locking nut of suitable diameter screwed onto the end of a bolt and locked with a second nut. Push the nut down onto the top of the seal; the locking portion of the nut will grip the seal allowing it to be withdrawn from the top of the valve guide. Access to the valves is limited, and it may be necessary to make up an adapter out of metal tube – cut out a ' window' so that the valve collets can be removed **(see illustrations)**.

16 Using a pair of pliers, carefully extract the valve stem oil seal from the top of the guide. On 2.0 litre engines, the valve stem oil seal also forms the spring seat and is deeply recessed in the cylinder head. It is also a tight fit on the valve guide making it difficult to remove with pliers or a conventional valve stem oil seal removal tool. It can be easily removed, however, using a self-locking nut of suitable diameter screwed onto the end of a bolt and locked with a second nut. Push the nut down onto the top of the seal; the locking portion of the nut will grip the seal allowing it to be withdrawn from the top of the valve guide **(see illustrations)**.

17 It is essential that each valve is stored together with its collets, retainer, spring, and spring seat. The valves should also be kept in their correct sequence, unless they are so badly worn or burnt that they are to be renewed. If they are going to be kept and used again, place each valve assembly in a labelled polythene bag or similar small container **(see illustration 7.8)**.

18 Continue removing all the remaining valves in the same way.

7.16a Remove the valve stem oil seal using a pair of pliers...

7.16b ... alternatively, secure a self-locking nut of suitable diameter to a long bolt, then use the tool to remove the valve stem seal

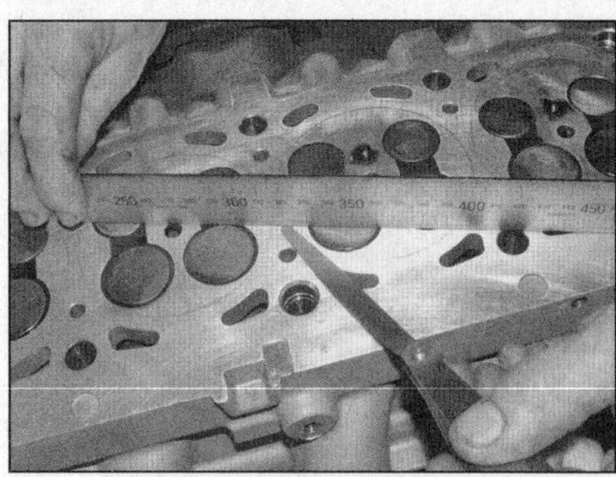
8.7 Check the cylinder head gasket surface for distortion

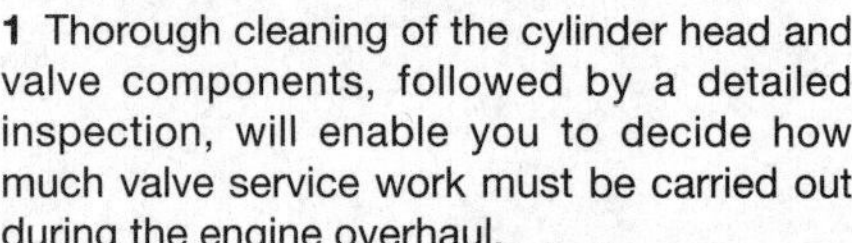

8 Cylinder head and valves – cleaning, inspection and renovation

1 Thorough cleaning of the cylinder head and valve components, followed by a detailed inspection, will enable you to decide how much valve service work must be carried out during the engine overhaul.

Cleaning

2 Scrape away all traces of old gasket material and sealing compound from the cylinder head. Take care not to damage the cylinder head surfaces.
3 Scrape away the carbon from the combustion chambers and ports, then wash the cylinder head thoroughly with paraffin or a suitable solvent.
4 Scrape off any heavy carbon deposits that may have formed on the valves, then use a power-operated wire brush to remove deposits from the valve heads and stems.
5 If the head is extremely dirty, it should be steam cleaned. On completion, make sure that all oil holes and oil galleries are cleaned.

Inspection and renovation

Note: *Be sure to perform all the following inspection procedures before concluding that the services of an engine overhaul specialist are required. Make a list of all items that require attention.*

Cylinder head

6 Inspect the head very carefully for cracks, evidence of coolant leakage and other damage. If cracks are found, a new cylinder head should be obtained.
7 Use a straight-edge and feeler blade to check that the cylinder head surface is not distorted **(see illustration)**. If the specified distortion limit is exceeded, machining of the gasket face is not recommended by the manufacturers, so the only course of action is to renew the cylinder head.
8 Examine the valve seats in each of the combustion chambers. If they are severely pitted, cracked or burned, then they will need to be renewed or recut by an engine overhaul specialist. If they are only slightly pitted, this can be removed by grinding the valve heads and seats together with coarse, then fine, grinding paste as described below.
9 If the valve guides are worn, indicated by a side-to-side motion of the valve in the guide, new guides must be fitted. If necessary, insert a new valve in the guides to determine if the wear is on the guide or valve. If new guides are to be fitted, the valves must be renewed as a matter of course. Valve guides may be renewed using a press and a suitable mandrel, and the work is best carried out by an engine overhaul specialist, since if it is not done skilfully, there is a risk of damaging the cylinder head.
10 Where applicable, check the cam follower bores in the cylinder head for wear. If excessive wear is evident, the cylinder head must be renewed.
11 Examine the camshaft bearing surfaces in the cylinder head as described in Chapter 2A Section 14, Chapter 2B Section 9 or Chapter 2C Section 6.

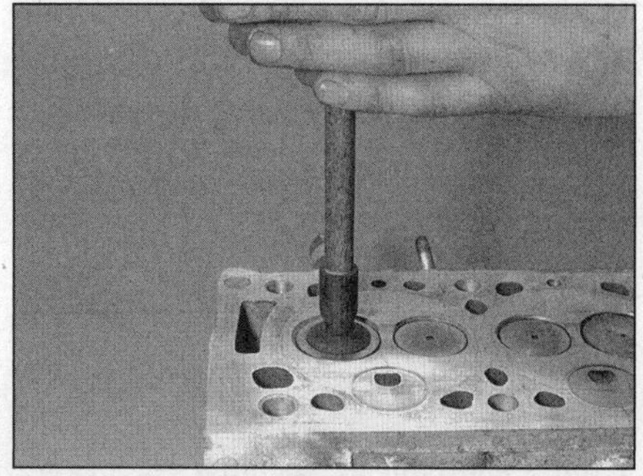
8.16 Grinding-in a valve

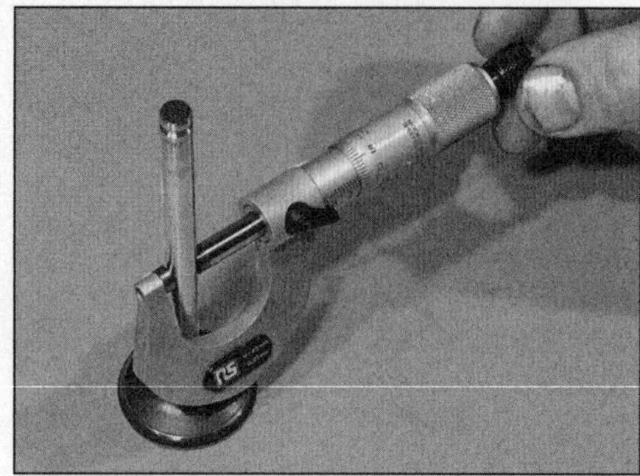
8.13 Measure the valve stem diameter with a micrometer

8.19 Valve components

Valves

12 Examine the head of each valve for pitting, burning, cracks and general wear, and check the valve stem for scoring and wear ridges. Rotate the valve, and check for any obvious indication that it is bent. Look for pits and excessive wear on the end of each valve stem.
13 If the valve appears satisfactory at this stage, measure the valve stem diameter at several points using a micrometer **(see illustration)**. Any significant difference in the readings obtained indicates wear of the valve stem. Should any of these conditions be apparent, the valve(s) must be renewed.
14 If the valves are in satisfactory condition, or if new valves are being fitted, they should be ground (lapped) into their respective seats to ensure a smooth gas-tight seal.
15 Valve grinding is carried out as follows. Place the cylinder head upside-down on a bench, with a block of wood at each end to give clearance for the valve stems. Where applicable, take care to protect the camshaft bearing surfaces.
16 Smear a trace of coarse carborundum paste on the seat face, and press a suction grinding tool onto the valve head. With a semi-rotary action, grind the valve head to its seat, lifting the valve occasionally to redistribute the grinding paste **(see illustration)**.
17 When a dull-matt even surface is produced on both the valve seat and the valve, wipe off the paste and repeat the process with fine carborundum paste. A light spring placed under the valve head will greatly ease this operation.
18 When a smooth unbroken ring of light grey matt finish is produced on both the valve and seat, the grinding operation is complete. Be sure to remove all traces of grinding paste, using paraffin or a suitable solvent, before reassembly of the cylinder head.

Valve components

19 Examine the valve springs for signs of damage and discoloration, and also measure their free length by comparing the existing spring with a new component **(see illustration)**.
20 Stand each spring on a flat surface, and check it for squareness. If any of the springs are damaged, distorted or have lost their tension, obtain a complete new set of springs. It is normal to renew the springs as a matter of course during a major overhaul.
21 Renew the valve stem oil seals regardless of their apparent condition.

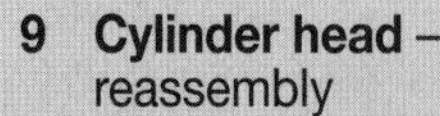

9 Cylinder head – reassembly

1 Working on the first valve assembly, refit the spring seat then dip the new valve stem

oil seal in fresh engine oil. Locate the seal on the valve guide and press the seal firmly onto the guide using a suitable socket **(see illustrations)**.

2 Lubricate the stem of the first valve, and insert it in the guide **(see illustration)**.

3 Locate the valve spring on top of its seat, then refit the spring retainer.

4 Compress the valve spring, and locate the split collets in the recess in the valve stem. Release the compressor, then repeat the procedure on the remaining valves. Ensure that each valve is inserted into its original location. If new valves are being fitted, insert them into the locations to which they have been ground.

Use a little dab of grease to hold the collets in position on the valve stem while the spring compressor is released.

5 With all the valves installed, support the cylinder head and, using a hammer and interposed block of wood, tap the end of each valve stem to settle the components.

6 The previously removed components can now be refitted with reference to Section 7.

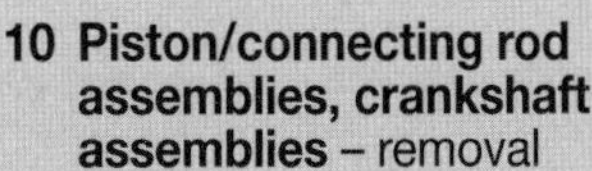

10 Piston/connecting rod assemblies, crankshaft assemblies – removal

1 The bottom half of engine is only sold by Ford as a complete unit, and so cannot be disassembled.

11 Engine overhaul – reassembly sequence

1 Before reassembly begins, ensure that all new parts have been obtained and that all necessary tools are available. Read through the entire procedure to familiarise yourself with the work involved, and to ensure that all items necessary for reassembly of the engine are at hand. In addition to all normal tools and materials, jointing and thread locking compound will be needed during engine reassembly. Do not use any kind of silicone-based sealant on any part of the fuel system or inlet manifold, and never use exhaust sealants upstream (on the engine side) of the catalytic converter.

2 In order to save time and avoid problems, engine reassembly can be carried out in the following order.

a) Crankshaft and main bearings (diesel engines)
b) Pistons/connecting rods (diesel engines).
c) Oil pump
d) Sump
e) Flywheel/driveplate
f) Cylinder head
g) Timing sprockets and belt
h) Engine external components (including inlet and exhaust manifolds)

3 Ensure that everything is clean prior to reassembly. As mentioned previously, dirt and metal particles can quickly destroy bearings and result in major engine damage. Use clean engine oil to lubricate during reassembly.

9.1a Locate the valve stem oil seal on the valve guide...

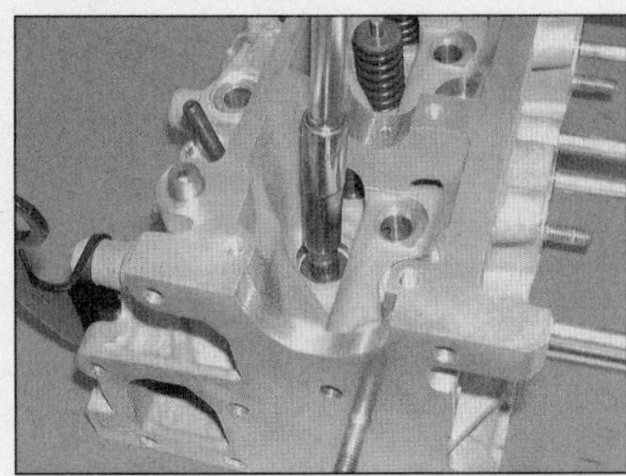

9.1b ... and press the seal firmly onto the guide using a suitable socket

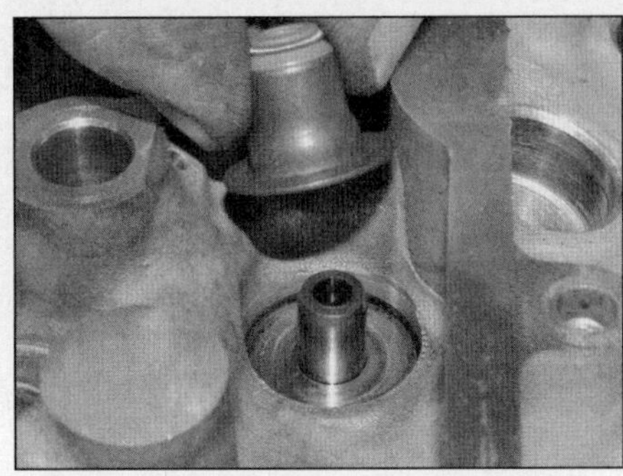

9.1c On some engines, the valve stem oil seal is integral with the spring seat

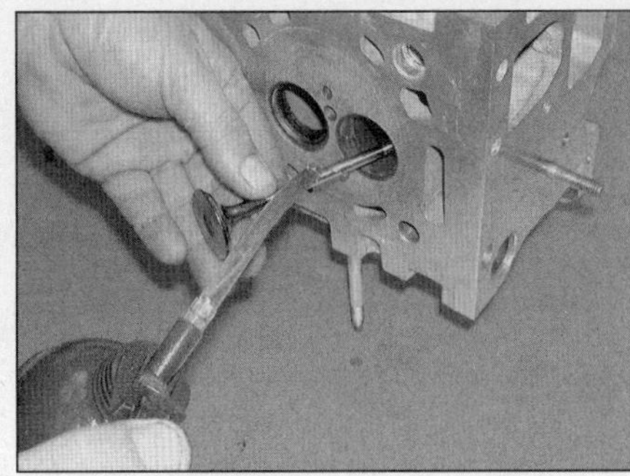

9.2 Lubricate the stem of the valve and insert it into the guide

12 Engine – initial start-up after overhaul

1 With the engine refitted in the vehicle, double-check the engine oil and coolant levels. Make a final check that everything has been reconnected, and that there are no tools or rags left in the engine compartment.

2 On diesel engines, prime and bleed the fuel system as described in Chapter 4B Section 5.

3 Start the engine, noting that this may take a little longer than usual. Make sure that the oil pressure warning light goes out.

4 While the engine is idling, check for fuel, water and oil leaks. Don't be alarmed if there are some odd smells and smoke from parts getting hot and burning off oil deposits.

5 Assuming all is well, run the engine until it reaches normal operating temperature, then switch off the engine.

6 After a few minutes, recheck the oil and coolant levels as described in Chapter 1A and Chapter 1B, and top-up as necessary.

7 Note that there is no need to retighten the cylinder head bolts once the engine has first run after reassembly.

8 If new pistons, rings or crankshaft bearings have been fitted, the engine must be treated as new, and run-in for the first 600 miles. Do not operate the engine at full-throttle, or allow it to labour at low engine speeds in any gear. It is recommended that the oil and filter be changed at the end of this period.

Notes

Chapter 3
Cooling, heating and ventilation systems

Contents

Degrees of difficulty

Easy, suitable for novice with little experience 	Fairly easy, suitable for beginner with some experience 	Fairly difficult, suitable for competent DIY mechanic 	Difficult, suitable for experienced DIY mechanic	Very difficult, suitable for expert DIY or professional 

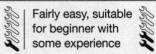

Specifications

General

Maximum system pressure	1.5 bars

Thermostat

Start of opening temperature (approximate):	
Petrol engines	N/A
Diesel engine models	N/A

Air conditioning compressor

Compressor oil:	
Quantity	135 cc

Refrigerant

	Quantity	Type
1.5 litre EcoBoost	630g	Up to Aug 2016: R134a/ After Aug 2-16: r1234yf
1.5 Duratorq	530g	Up to Aug 2016: R134a/ After Aug 2-16: r1234yf
2.0 TDCI	600g	Up to Aug 2016: R134a/ After Aug 2-16: r1234yf

Torque wrench settings

	Nm	lbf ft
Air conditioning compressor mounting bolts	25	18
Air conditioning refrigerant pipe bolts	15	11
Alternator mounting bolts	41	30
Coolant pump:		
Petrol engines	10	7
Diesel engines	15	11
Thermostat housing (diesel engines only)	10	7

1 General information and precautions

1 The cooling system is of pressurised type, comprising a pump driven by timing belt, an aluminium crossflow radiator, electric cooling fan, and a thermostat. The system functions as follows. Cold coolant from the radiator passes through the hose to the coolant pump, where it is pumped around the cylinder block and head passages. After cooling the cylinder bores, combustion surfaces and valve seats, the coolant reaches the underside of the thermostat, which is initially closed. The coolant passes through the heater, and is returned via the cylinder block to the coolant pump.

2 When the engine is cold, the thermostat is shut, and the coolant circulates only through the cylinder block, cylinder head and heater. When the coolant reaches a predetermined temperature, the thermostat opens and the coolant passes through to the radiator. As the coolant circulates through the radiator, it is cooled by the inrush of air when the car is in forward motion. Airflow is supplemented by the action of the electric cooling fan when necessary. Once the coolant has passed through the radiator, and has cooled, the cycle is repeated.

3 The temperature gauge and cooling fan are controlled by the engine coolant temperature sensor which transmits a signal to the engine management powertrain control module (PCM) to operate them.

4 An expansion tank is fitted to allow for the expansion of the coolant when hot. On models fitted with an engine oil cooler or automatic transmission fluid cooler, the coolant is also passed through the oil/fluid cooler.

5 Refer to Sections 8 and 11 for information on the heater/ventilation system and air conditioning system.

Warning: Do not attempt to remove the expansion tank filler cap, or disturb any part of the cooling system, while the engine is hot; there is a high risk of scalding. If the expansion tank filler cap must be removed before the engine and radiator have fully cooled (even though this is not recommended) the pressure in the cooling system must first be relieved. Cover the cap with a thick layer of cloth, to avoid scalding, and slowly unscrew the filler cap until a hissing sound can be heard. When the hissing has stopped, indicating that the pressure has reduced, slowly unscrew the filler cap until it can be removed; if more hissing sounds are heard, wait until they have stopped before unscrewing the cap completely. At all times, keep well away from the filler cap opening and protect your hands.

Warning: Do not allow antifreeze to come into contact with skin, or with the painted surfaces of the car. Rinse off spills immediately, with plenty of water. Never leave antifreeze lying around in an open container, or in a puddle on the driveway or garage floor. Children and pets are attracted by its sweet smell, but antifreeze can be fatal if ingested.

Warning: If the engine is hot, the electric cooling fan may start rotating even if the engine is not running; be careful to keep hands, hair and loose clothing well clear when working in the engine compartment.

Warning: Refer to Section 1 for precautions to be observed when working on models equipped with air conditioning.

2 Troubleshooting

Coolant leaks

1 A coolant leak can develop anywhere in the cooling system, but the most common causes are:

a) A loose or weak hose clamp
b) A defective hose
c) A faulty pressure cap
d) A damaged radiator
e) A defective heater core
f) A faulty coolant pump
g) A leaking gasket at any joint that carries coolant

2 Coolant leaks aren't always easy to find. Sometimes they can only be detected when the cooling system is under pressure. Which is why a coolant system pressure tester is useful. After the engine has cooled completely, the tester is attached in place of the pressure cap, then pumped up to the pressure value equal to that of the pressure cap rating. Now, leaks that only exist when the engine is fully warmed up will become apparent. The tester can be left connected to locate a persistent slow leak.

Coolant level drops, but no external leaks

3 If you find it necessary to keep adding coolant, but there are no external leaks, the probable causes include:

a) A leaking head gasket
b) A leaking intake manifold gasket (only on engines that have coolant passages in the manifold), or a cracked cylinder head or cylinder block

4 Any of the above problems will also usually result in contamination of the engine oil, which will cause it to take on a milkshake-like appearance. A leaking head gasket or cracked head or block can also result in engine oil contaminating the cooling system.

5 Combustion leak detectors (also known as block testers) are available at most auto parts stores. These work by detecting exhaust gases in the cooling system, which indicates a compression leak from a cylinder into the coolant. The tester consists of a large bulb-type syringe and bottle of test fluid. A measured amount of the fluid is added to the syringe. The syringe is placed over the cooling system filler neck and, with the engine running, the bulb is squeezed and a sample of the gases present in the cooling system are drawn up through the test fluid. If any combustion gases are present in the sample taken, the test fluid will change color.

6 If the test indicates combustion gas is present in the cooling system, you can be sure that the engine has a leaking head gasket or a crack in the cylinder head or block, and will require disassembly to repair.

Pressure cap

Warning: Wait until the engine is completely cool before beginning this check.

7 The cooling system is sealed by a spring-loaded cap, which raises the boiling point of the coolant. If the cap's seal or spring are worn out, the coolant can boil and escape past the cap. With the engine completely cool, remove the cap and check the seal; if it's cracked, hardened or deteriorated in any way, replace it with a new one.

8 Even if the seal is good, the spring might not be; this can be checked with a cooling system pressure tester. If the cap can't hold a pressure within approximately 0.13 bar of its rated pressure (which is marked on the cap), replace it with a new one.

9 The cap is also equipped with a vacuum relief spring. When the engine cools off, a vacuum is created in the cooling system. The vacuum relief spring allows air back into the system, which will equalise the pressure and prevent damage to the radiator (the radiator tanks could collapse if the vacuum is great enough). If, after turning the engine off and allowing it to cool down you notice any of the cooling system hoses collapsing, replace the pressure cap with a new one.

Thermostat

10 Before assuming the thermostat is responsible for a cooling system problem, check the coolant level (see Chapter 1A Section 6 or Chapter 1B Section 6), and temperature gauge (or light) operation.

11 If the engine takes a long time to warm up (as indicated by the temperature gauge or heater operation), the thermostat is probably stuck open. Replace the thermostat with a new one.

12 If the engine runs hot or overheats, a thorough test of the thermostat should be performed. **Note:** *The following test only applicable to vehicles with a separate thermostat. Most modern engines are now equipped with a thermostat that is integral with it's housing. In this case, no testing of the thermostat is possible, and the complete assembly may need to be replaced.*

13 Definitive testing of the thermostat can

only be made when it is removed from the vehicle. If the thermostat is stuck in the open position at room temperature, it is faulty and must be replaced.

Caution: Do not drive the vehicle without a thermostat. The engine management PCM may stay in open loop and emissions and fuel economy will suffer.

14 To test a thermostat, suspend the (closed) thermostat on a length of string or wire in a pot of cold water.

15 Heat the water while observing the thermostat. The thermostat should fully open before the water boils.

16 If the thermostat doesn't open and close as specified, or sticks in any position, replace it.

Cooling fan

17 If the engine is overheating and the cooling fan is not coming on when the engine temperature rises to an excessive level, unplug the fan motor wiring plugs(s) and connect the motor directly to the battery with fused bridging wires. If the fan motor doesn't come on, replace the motor.

18 If the radiator fan motor is okay, but it isn't coming on when the engine gets hot, the fan relay might be defective. A relay is used to control a circuit by turning it on and off in response to a control decision by the engine management Powertrain Control Module (PCM). These control circuits are fairly complex, and checking them should be left to a qualified automotive technician. Sometimes, the control system can be fixed by simply identifying and replacing a faulty relay.

19 Locate the fan relays in the engine compartment fuse/relay box.

20 Test the relay (see Chapter 12 Section 3).

21 If the relay is okay, check all wiring and connections to the fan motor. Refer to the wiring diagrams in Chapter 12. If no obvious problems are found, the problem could be the Engine Coolant Temperature (ECT) sensor or the engine management Powertrain Control Module (PCM). Have the cooling fan system and circuit diagnosed by a dealer service department or suitably equipped repairer.

Coolant pump

22 A failure in the coolant pump can cause serious engine damage due to overheating.

Auxiliary drivebelt-driven coolant pump

23 There are two ways to check the operation of the coolant pump while it's installed on the engine. If the pump is found to be defective, it should be replaced with a new or rebuilt unit.

24 Coolant pumps are normally equipped with weep (or vent) holes on the underside. If a failure occurs in the pump seal, coolant will leak from the hole.

25 If the coolant pump shaft bearings fail, there may be a howling sound at the pump while it's running. Shaft wear can be felt with the drivebelt removed if the coolant pump pulley is rocked up and down (with the engine off). Don't mistake drivebelt slippage, which causes a squealing sound, for coolant pump bearing failure.

Timing chain or timing belt-driven coolant pump

26 Coolant pumps driven by the timing chain or timing belt are located underneath the timing chain or timing belt cover.

27 Checking the coolant pump is limited because of where it is located. However, some basic checks can be made before deciding to remove the coolant pump. If the pump is found to be defective, it should be replaced with a new or rebuilt unit.

28 One sign that the coolant pump may be failing is that the heater (climate control) may not work well. Warm the engine to normal operating temperature, confirm that the coolant level is correct, then run the heater and check for hot air coming from the ducts.

29 Check for noises coming from the coolant pump area. If the coolant pump impeller shaft or bearings are failing, there may be a howling sound at the pump while the engine is running.

Note: *Be careful not to mistake drivebelt noise (squealing) for coolant pump bearing or shaft failure.*

30 It you suspect coolant pump failure due to noise, wear can be confirmed by feeling for play at the pump shaft. This can be done by rocking the drive sprocket on the pump shaft up and down. To do this you will need to remove the tension on the timing chain or belt as well as access the coolant pump.

All coolant pumps

31 Finding coolant in the engine oil could indicate other serious issues besides a failed coolant pump, such as a leaking head gasket or a cracked cylinder head or block.

32 Even a pump that exhibits no outward signs of a problem, such as noise or leakage, can still be due for replacement. Removal for close examination is the only sure way to tell. Sometimes the fins on the back of the impeller can corrode to the point that cooling efficiency is diminished significantly.

Heater system

33 If the fan motor will run at all speeds, the electrical part of the system is okay. The three basic heater problems fall into the following general categories:

a) *Not enough heat*
b) *Heat all the time*
c) *No heat*

34 If there's not enough heat, the control valve or flap is stuck in a partially open position, the coolant coming from the engine isn't hot enough, or the heater matrix is restricted. If the coolant isn't hot enough, the thermostat in the engine cooling system is stuck open, allowing coolant to pass through the engine so rapidly that it doesn't heat up quickly enough. If the vehicle is equipped with a temperature gauge instead of a warning light, watch to see if the engine temperature rises to the normal operating range after driving for a reasonable distance.

35 If there's heat all the time, the control valve or the flap is stuck wide open.

36 If there's no heat, coolant is probably not reaching the heater matrix, or the heater matrix core is blocked. The likely cause is a collapsed or blocked hose, matrix, or a seized heater control valve. If the heater is the type that flows coolant all the time, the cause is a stuck flap or a broken or kinked control cable.

Air conditioning system

37 If the cool air output is inadequate:

a) *Inspect the condenser coils and fins to make sure they're clear*
b) *Check the compressor clutch for slippage*
c) *Check the blower motor for proper operation*
d) *Inspect the blower discharge passage for obstructions*
e) *Check the system air intake filter for clogging*

38 If the system provides intermittent cooling air:

a) *Check the fuse, blower switch and blower motor for a malfunction*
b) *Make sure the compressor clutch isn't slipping*
c) *Inspect the plenum flap to make sure it's operating properly*
d) *Inspect the evaporator to make sure it isn't blocked*
e) *If the unit is icing up, it may be caused by excessive moisture in the system, defective evaporator temperature sensor, control unit*

39 If the system provides no cooling air:

a) *Inspect the compressor drivebelt; make sure it isn't loose or broken*
b) *Make sure the compressor clutch engages; if it doesn't, check for a blown fuse*
c) *Inspect the wire harness for broken or disconnected wires*
d) *If the compressor clutch doesn't engage, bridge the terminals of the AC pressure switch(es) with a jumper wire; if the clutch now engages, and the system is properly charged, the pressure switch is bad*
e) *Make sure the blower motor is not disconnected or burned out*
f) *Make sure the compressor isn't partially or completely seized*
g) *Inspect the refrigerant pipes for leaks*
h) *Check the components for leaks*
i) *Inspect the receiver-drier/accumulator or expansion valve/tube for blocked screens*

40 If the system is noisy:

a) *Look for loose panels in the passenger compartment*
b) *Inspect the compressor drivebelt; it may be loose or worn*
c) *Check the security of the compressor mounting bolts*
d) *Listen carefully to the compressor; it may be worn out*
e) *Listen to the idler pulley and bearing, and the clutch; either may be defective*
f) *The winding in the compressor clutch coil or solenoid may be defective*
g) *The compressor oil level may be low*

3.5 To release the spring-type clips, squeeze together the clip 'ears' with pliers

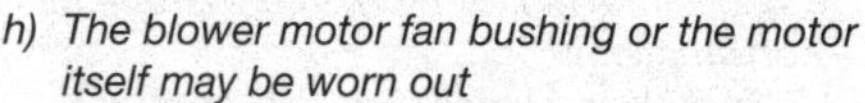

3.12 Where click-fit connectors are used, prise out the wire clip then disconnect the hose

3.13 Ensure the sealing ring and clip are correctly fitted to the hose union before reconnecting

h) The blower motor fan bushing or the motor itself may be worn out

i) If there is an excessive charge in the system, you'll hear a rumbling noise in the high pressure pipe, or a thumping noise in the compressor

j) If there is a low charge in the system, you might hear hissing in the evaporator case at the expansion valve

3 Cooling system hoses – disconnection and renewal

Note: *Refer to the warnings given in Section 1 of this Chapter before proceeding. Hoses should only be disconnected once the engine has cooled sufficiently to avoid scalding.*

1 If the checks described in Chapter 1A Section 15 or Chapter 1B Section 16 reveal a faulty hose, it must be renewed as follows.

2 First drain the cooling system (see Chapter 1A Section 34 or Chapter 1B Section 36). If the coolant is not due for renewal, it may be re-used, providing it is collected in a clean container.

3 To disconnect a hose, proceed as follows, according to the type of hose connection.

Conventional connections

4 On conventional connections, the clips used to secure the hoses in position may be standard worm-drive (Jubilee) clips, spring clips or disposable crimped types. The crimped type of clip is not designed to be re-used and should be renewed with a worm-drive type on reassembly.

5 To disconnect a hose, release the retaining clips and move them along the hose, clear of the relevant inlet/outlet. Carefully work the hose free. The hoses can be removed with relative ease when new – on an older car; they may have stuck **(see illustration)**.

6 If a hose proves to be difficult to remove, try to release it by rotating its ends before attempting to free it. Gently prise the end of the hose with a blunt instrument (such as a flat-bladed screwdriver), but do not apply too much force, and take care not to damage the pipe stubs or hoses. Note in particular that the radiator inlet stub is fragile; do not use excessive force when attempting to remove the hose. If all else fails, cut the hose with a sharp knife, then slit it so that it can be peeled off in two pieces. Although this may prove expensive if the hose is otherwise undamaged, it is preferable to buying a new radiator. Check first, however, that a new hose is readily available.

7 When fitting a hose, first slide the clips onto the hose, then work the hose into position. If crimped-type clips were originally fitted, use standard worm-drive clips when refitting the hose.

8 Work the hose into position, checking that it is correctly routed, and then slide each clip back along the hose until it passes over the flared end of the relevant inlet/outlet, before tightening the clip securely.

9 Refill the cooling system (see Chapter 1A Section 34 or Chapter 1B Section 36).

10 Check thoroughly for leaks as soon as possible after disturbing any part of the cooling system.

Click-fit connections

Note: *New sealing ring should be used when reconnecting the hose.*

11 On certain models, some cooling system hoses are secured in position with click-fit connectors where the hose is retained by a large circlip.

12 To disconnect this type of hose fitting, carefully prise the wire clip out of position then disconnect the hose connection **(see illustration)**. Once the hose has been disconnected, refit the wire clip to the hose union. Inspect the hose unit sealing ring for signs of damage or deterioration and renew if necessary.

13 On refitting, ensure that the sealing ring is in position and the wire clip is correctly located in the groove in the union **(see illustration)**. Lubricate the sealing ring with a smear of soapy water, to ease installation, and then push the hose into its union until it is heard to click into position.

14 Ensure the hose is securely retained by the wire clip then refill the cooling system as described in Chapter 1A Section 34 or Chapter 1B Section 36.

15 Check thoroughly for leaks as soon as possible after disturbing any part of the cooling system.

4 Coolant expansion tank – removal and refitting

Removal

1 Referring to Chapter 1A Section 34 or Chapter 1B Section 36, drain the cooling system sufficiently to empty the Specifications of the expansion tank. Do not drain any more coolant than is necessary.

2 Release the clip and detach the coolant hose from the expansion tank **(see illustration)**.

3 Slide the expansion tank upwards off its mountings to manoeuvre from place, releasing the clips as you do so **(see illustration)**.

4.2 Unclip the coolant hose

4.3 Slide the expansion tank upwards off its hoses

5.3 Unplug the temperature sensor connector

5.5a Remove the left lower mounting screw...

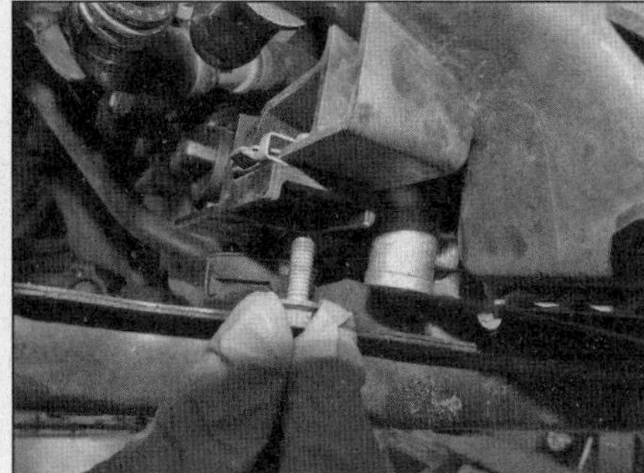

5.5b ...then the right screw

5.6a Remove the grommet from the front left of the radiator...

5.6b ...then the front right

5.7 Lower the radiator from the vehicle

Refitting

4 Refitting is the reverse of removal, ensuring the hoses are securely reconnected. On completion, top-up the coolant level as described in Chapter 1A or Chapter 1B.

5 Auxiliary radiator – removal and refitting

Removal

1 Remove the front bumper assembly, as described in Chapter 11 Section 5.
2 Drain the cooling system, as described in Chapter 1A Section 34.
3 Disconnect the temperature sensor wiring plug **(see illustration)**.
4 Disconnect the radiator hoses from the left-hand end of the auxiliary radiator.
5 Undo the lower mounting screw from the each end of the radiator **(see illustrations)**.
6 Prise out the grommet from each end of the radiator **(see illustrations)**.
7 Disengage the radiator from its mountings and lower from the vehicle **(see illustration)**.

Refitting

8 Refitting is a reversal of removal.

6 Radiator – removal, inspection and refitting

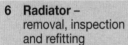

Removal

2.0-litre diesel

1 Have the refrigerant circuit evacuated by a suitably equipped repairer.
2 Raise the front of the vehicle and support it securely on axle stands (see *Jacking and vehicle support*). Undo the fasteners and remove the engine undershield.
3 Drain the cooling system (see Chapter 1B Section 36).
4 Remove the front bumper assembly, as described in Chapter 11 Section 5.
5 Remove the intercooler, as described in Chapter 4B Section 20.
6 Slacken the jubilee clip on the inner end of the right-hand intercooler pipe and remove the pipe **(see illustration)**, to ease access to the bottom radiator hose.
7 Release the clips and disconnect the coolant hoses from the radiator **(see illustrations)**.
8 Insert a retaining pin in both of the radiator top mounts, to prevent the radiator falling out once all the bolts are undone **(see illustration)**.

6.6 Remove the right-hand intercooler pipe

6.7a Detach the expansion tank hose...

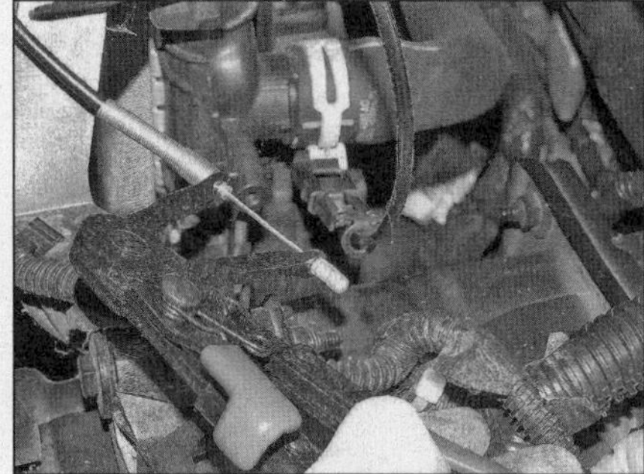

6.7b ...then the radiator top hose...

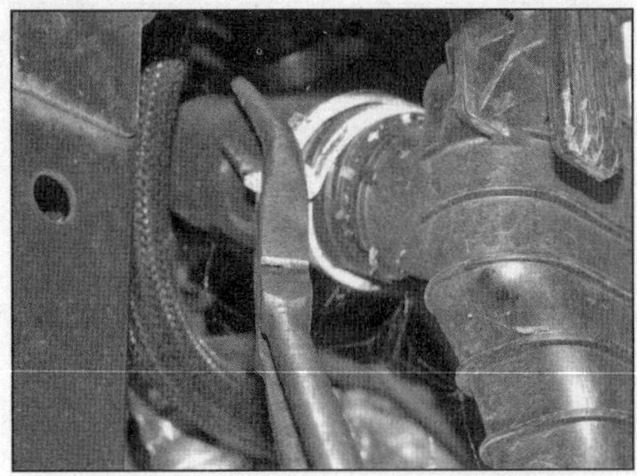
6.7c ...and finally the bottom hose

6.8 Insert a pin to support the radiator

6.9 Loosen the rearmost subframe mounting bolts

6.10 Remove the rear bolts on the triangular panel

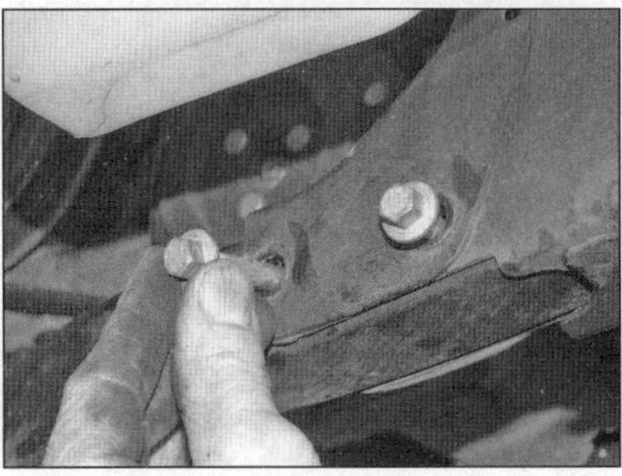
6.11 Undo the 2 bolts holding the subframe to the radiator support

6.12 Support the radiator assembly on a trolley jack

9 Slacken the mounting bolt at the rear of the each subframe leg **(see illustration)**.

10 Undo the 2 retaining bolts on the triangular panel at the rear of each subframe leg **(see illustration)**.

11 Remove the 2 retaining bolts holding the subframe leg to the radiator support **(see illustration)**.

12 Support the radiator and subframe on a transmission jack or 2 trolley jacks **(see illustration)**.

13 Use a long socket extension bar to reach up through the front corner of the subframe to reach the upper mounting bolts **(see illustration)**.

14 Prise open the clip to separate the bottom radiator hose from the radiator **(see illustration)**.

15 Lower the radiator and cooling fan assembly from the vehicle **(see illustration)**.

6.13 Reach up to slacken the upper mounting bolts

6.14 Prise open the bottom hose clip behind the radiator

6.15 The radiator and cooling must be lowered from the vehicle

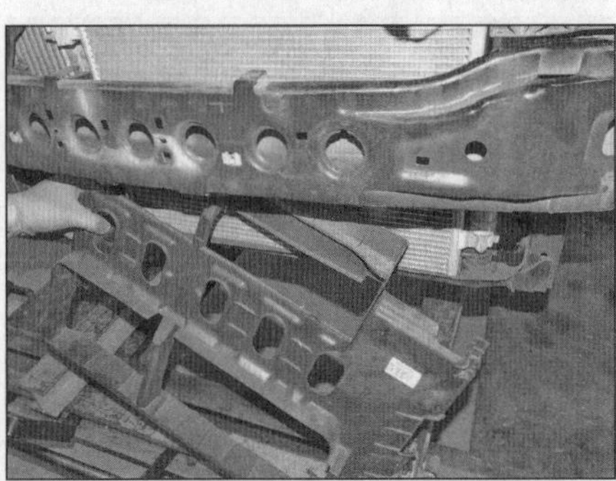
6.20 Undo the clips and lower the intercooler shroud

1.5-litre diesel

16 Raise the front of the vehicle and support it securely on axle stands (see *Jacking and vehicle support*). Undo the fasteners and remove the engine undershield.

17 Drain the cooling system, as described in Chapter 1B Section 36.

18 Disconnect the battery, as described in Chapter 5 Section 4.

19 Remove the active shutter grille, as described in Chapter 11 Section 6.

20 Release the 3 clips and remove the intercooler front shroud downwards from place **(see illustration)**.

21 Undo the jubilee clips and disengage the pipes from the top and bottom of the intercooler **(see illustrations)**.

22 Unclip the bleed valve from the left-hand end of the radiator **(see illustration)**.

23 Release the clip and remove the radiator hose, then unplug the wiring plug **(see illustrations)**.

6.21a Undo the clip to remove the top pipe...

6.21b ...then the bottom one

6.22 Depress the tabs to release the bleed valve

6.23a Remove the radiator hose...

6.23b ...then unplug the wiring plug

6.24 Unplug the wiring connector

24 Disconnect the wiring plug from the radiator mounting member **(see illustration)**.

25 Detach the radiator hose from the right-hand side of the radiator.

26 Undo the 3 mounting bolts from each frame rail and remove from place **(see illustration)**.

27 Support the radiator mounting crossmember using a trolley jack.

28 Reach up through the crossmember and undo the mounting bolts at each end **(see illustration)**.

29 Use cable ties or split pins to hang the intercooler and radiator from the upper radiator crossmember.

30 Lower the bottom crossmember from place, disengaging it from the rubber feet as you do so **(see illustration)**.

31 Undo the bolt to separate the right-hand end of the condenser from the radiator **(see illustration)**.

32 Disengage the left-hand end of the condenser from the retaining clip **(see illustration)**.

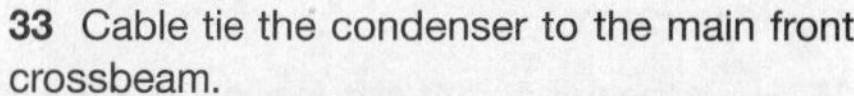

33 Cable tie the condenser to the main front crossbeam.

34 Cut the cable ties for the radiator and lower from place **(see illustration)**.

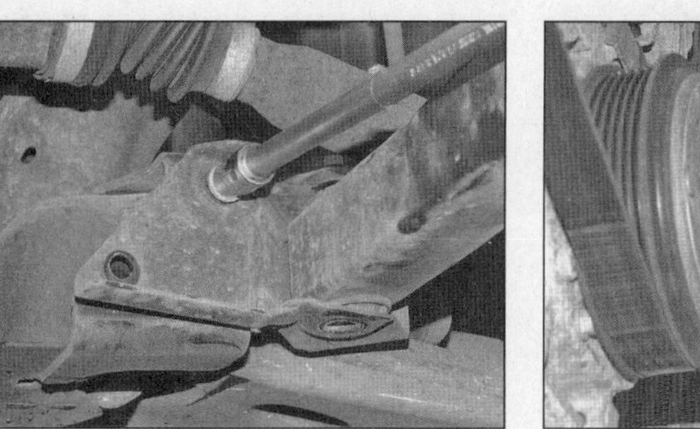

6.26 Undo the bolts and remove the rails

6.28 Undo the bolts at each end of the crossmember

6.30 Lower the crossmember

6.31 Undo the bolt to release the condenser

6.32 Disengage the condenser from the clip

6.34 Cut the cable ties and lower the radiator from the vehicle

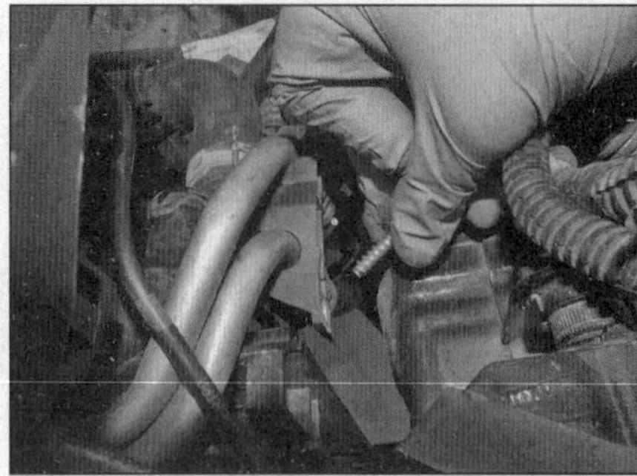

6.41 Unscrew the transmission fluid cooler pipe bracket

6.42a Undo the fluid cooler pipe clamp bolts...

6.42b ...be prepared for fluid loss

6.43 Replace the fluid cooler pipe seals

6.44 Ensure the fluid cooler pipes are sealed to prevent contamination

1.5-litre petrol

35 Have the refrigerant circuit evacuated by a suitably equipped repairer.

36 Raise the front of the vehicle and support it securely on axle stands (see *Jacking and vehicle support*). Undo the fasteners and remove the engine undershield.

37 Drain the cooling system (see Chapter 1A Section 34).

38 Remove the front bumper assembly, as described in Chapter 11 Section 5.

39 Remove the auxiliary radiator as described in Section 5.

40 Remove the active shutter grille, as described in Chapter 11 Section 6.

41 Remove the retaining bolts from the mounting bracket for the transmission fluid cooler pipes **(see illustration)**.

42 Unscrew the retaining bolts for the transmission fluid cooler pipe clamp bolts **(see illustrations)**. Be prepare for fluid loss.

43 Remove the seals from the transmission fluid cooler pipes. These must be replaced **(see illustration)**.

44 Plug the ends of the fluid cooler pipes, to prevent any dirt ingress **(see illustration)**.

45 Release the clips and disconnect the coolant hoses from the radiator **(see illustrations)**.

46 Slacken the jubilee clip on the inner end of the right-hand intercooler pipe and remove the pipe **(see illustration)**, to ease access to the bottom radiator hose.

47 Insert a retaining pin in both of the radiator top mounts, to prevent the radiator falling out once all the bolts are undone **(see illustration)**.

48 Slacken the mounting bolt at the rear of the each subframe leg **(see illustration)**.

49 Undo the 2 retaining bolts on the triangular panel at the rear of each subframe leg **(see illustration)**.

50 Remove the 2 retaining bolts holding the

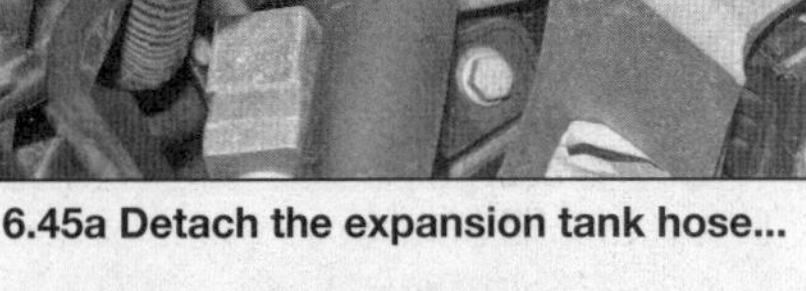

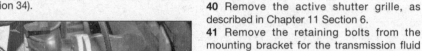

6.45a Detach the expansion tank hose...

6.45b ...then the radiator top hose...

6.45c ...and finally the bottom hose

6.46 Remove the right-hand intercooler pipe

6.47 Insert a pin to support the radiator

6.48 Loosen the rearmost subframe mounting bolts

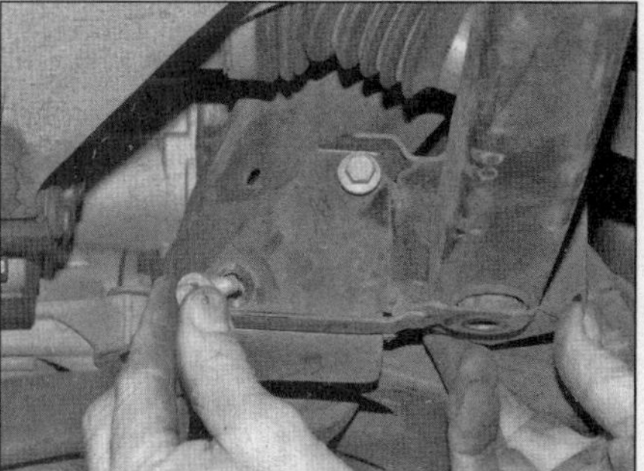
6.49 Remove the rear bolts on the triangular panel

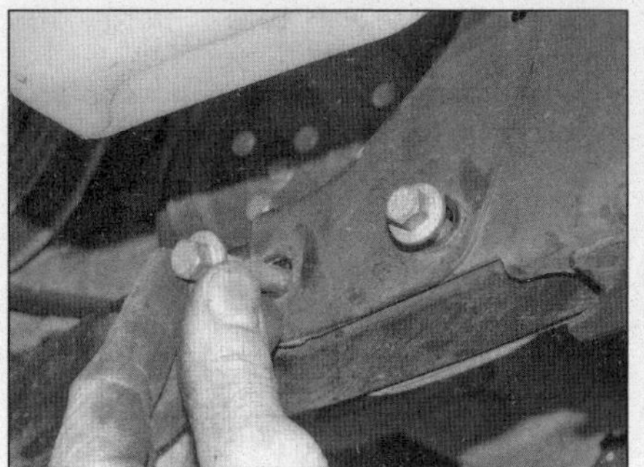
6.50 Undo the 2 bolts holding the subframe to the radiator support

6.51 Support the radiator assembly on a trolley jack

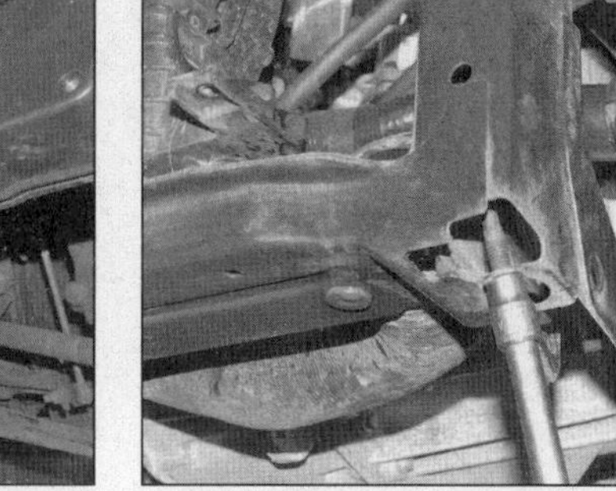
6.52 Reach up to slacken the upper mounting bolts

subframe leg to the radiator support **(see illustration)**.

51 Support the radiator and subframe on a transmission jack or 2 trolley jacks **(see illustration)**.

52 Use a long socket extension bar to reach up through the front corner of the subframe to reach the upper mounting bolts **(see illustration)**.

53 Prise open the clip to separate the bottom radiator hose from the radiator **(see illustration)**.

54 Lower the radiator and cooling fan assembly from the vehicle **(see illustration)**.

Inspection

55 Insert a garden hose into the radiator top inlet. Direct a flow of clean water through the radiator, and continue flushing until clean water emerges from the radiator bottom outlet.

56 If after a reasonable period, the water still does not run clear, the radiator can be flushed with a good proprietary cleaning agent. It is important that their manufacturer's instructions are followed carefully. If the contamination is particularly bad, insert the hose in the radiator bottom outlet, and reverse-flush the radiator.

57 Clean dirt and debris from the radiator fins, using an airline (in which case, wear eye protection) or a soft brush. Be careful, as the fins are sharp, and easily damaged.

58 If necessary, a radiator specialist can perform a 'flow test' on the radiator, to establish whether an internal blockage exists.

59 A leaking radiator must be referred to a specialist for permanent repair. Do not attempt to weld or solder a leaking radiator, as damage to the plastic components may result.

60 Inspect the condition of the radiator mounting rubbers, and renew them if necessary.

Refitting

61 Refitting is a reversal of removal, bearing in mind the following points:

a) Ensure that the lower lugs on the radiator are correctly engaged.

b) Reconnect the hoses with reference to Section 3.

c) On completion, refill the cooling system as described in Chapter 1A Section 34 or Chapter 1B Section 36.

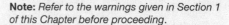

7 Thermostat – removal and refitting

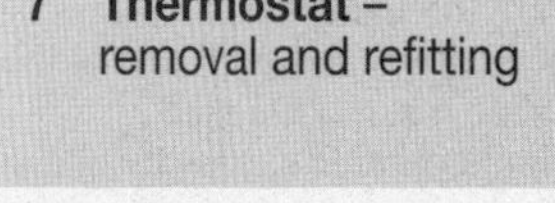

Note: *Refer to the warnings given in Section 1 of this Chapter before proceeding.*

Removal

1 Disconnect the battery negative lead as described in Chapter 5 Section 4.

2 Drain the cooling system (see Chapter 1A Section 34 or Chapter 1B Section 36). If the coolant is relatively new or in good condition, drain it into a clean container and re-use it.

1.5 litre petrol engine

3 Remove the plastic cover from the top of the engine.

4 Remove the alternator, as described in Chapter 5 Section 6.

6.53 Prise open the bottom hose clip behind the radiator

6.54 The radiator and cooling must be lowered from the vehicle

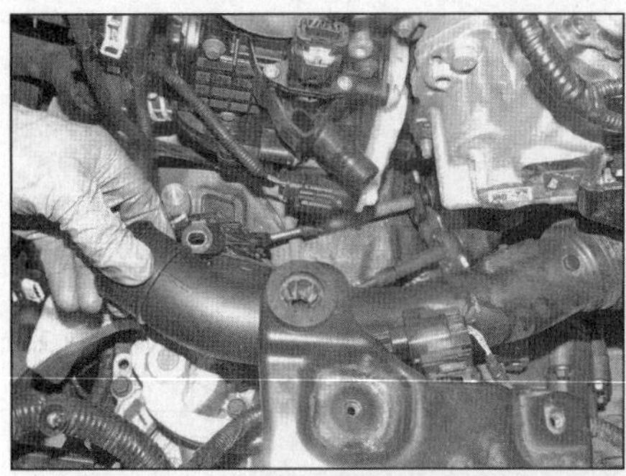
7.12 Disconnect and displace the pipe

7.13 Unplug the thermostat sensor

7.14 Unplug the wiring connector

7.16 Remove the rearmost bolt

7.17 Thermostat housing retaining bolts

5 Release the clips and disconnect the coolant hoses from the thermostat.

6 Slacken and remove the bolt from the thermostat and slide it along the stud.

7 Use pliers or mole grips to grasp the shank of the stud, and unscrew it from place.

8 Remove the thermostat.

9 Check the condition of the cover rubber seal and renew it if necessary.

2.0 litre diesel engines

10 Remove the plastic cover from the top of the engine. The thermostat housing is located at the left-hand end of the cylinder head.

11 Remove the air cleaner assembly as described in Chapter 4B Section 6.

12 Disconnect the intercooler pipe by the thermostat, then undo the 2 mounting bolts and move it to one side **(see illustration)**.

13 Remove the wiring plug from the thermostat sensor **(see illustration)**.

14 Disconnect the wiring plug from the thermostat housing **(see illustration)**.

15 Release the clamps and disconnect the hoses from the thermostat housing.

16 Undo the retaining bolt at the rear of the thermostat housing **(see illustration)**.

17 Undo the 4 retaining bolts and remove the housing. Renew the seals regardless of their apparent condition **(see illustration)**. Note that the thermostat is integral with the housing – if faulty the complete assembly must be renewed.

Refitting

18 Refitting is the reverse of the removal procedure, noting the following points:

a) *Clean the mating surfaces carefully and, renew the thermostat's sealing rings.*

b) *Fit the thermostat in the same position as noted on removal. Lubricate the sealing rings with clean anti-freeze or rubber lubrication paste.*

c) *Tighten the thermostat cover/housing bolts/nuts to the specified torque wrench setting*

d) *Remake all the coolant hose connections, then refill the cooling system as described in Chapter 1A Section 34 or Chapter 1B Section 36.*

e) *Start the engine and allow it to reach normal operating temperature, then check for leaks and proper thermostat operation.*

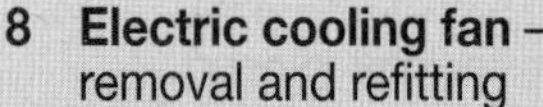

8 Electric cooling fan – removal and refitting

Removal

1 Raise the front of the car and support it on axle stands as described in *Jacking and vehicle support*.

2 Remove the radiator and cooling fan assembly, as described in Section 6.

3 Release the four tabs (one at each corner of the radiator assembly) to separate the cooling fans and housing from the radiator **(see illustration)**.

4 Gently prise away the foam along the top of the radiator and cooling fan assembly, then manoeuvre the fan assembly from place **(see illustration)**.

5 To separate each fan motor from the housing, first disconnect the wiring plug **(see illustration)**.

8.3 Release the tabs to release the fan housing

8.4 Prise away the foam to release the fan assembly

8.5 Disconnect the motor wiring plug

8.6 Remove the 3 screws to detach the fan motor

6 Undo the 3 retaining screws for each fan and manoeuvre from place **(see illustration)**.

Refitting

7 Refitting is a reversal of removal.

9 Coolant temperature sensor – removal and refitting

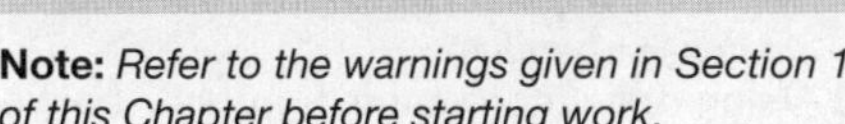

Note: *Refer to the warnings given in Section 1 of this Chapter before starting work.*

Warning: Ensure the coolant is cold before attempting this procedure.

Petrol engines

1 The sensor is located at the coolant outlet housing at the left-hand end of the cylinder head.

2 Remove the plastic cover from the top of the engine.

3 Disconnect the wiring plug from the sensor **(see illustration)**.

4 Two different types of sensor may be fitted. The first type is screwed into the coolant outlet housing, and the second type is clipped into place. Unscrew the sensor from the housing, or pull out the clip as applicable. Be prepared for coolant spillage and have rag or a rubber plug handy to force into the sensor aperture. This way only a little coolant will be lost.

5 Refitting is the reverse of the removal procedure, noting the following points:

a) Renew the sensor seal if necessary.

b) Screw the sensor into position and tighten it to the specified torque, or refit the sensor and insert the clip, as applicable.

c) Top-up or refill the cooling system as described in Chapter 1A Section 6 or Chapter 1B Section 6.

Diesel engines

6 The sensor is located in the thermostat housing at the left-hand end of the cylinder head.

7 Remove the plastic cover from the top of the engine.

8 Remove the air cleaner assembly and intake duct as described in Chapter 4A Section 3 or Chapter 4B Section 6.

9 Prise out the retaining clip, and disconnect the coolant hose from the heater to the thermostat housing.

9.3 Unplug the sensor wiring plug

10 Disconnect the sensor wiring plug, and undo the engine coolant temperature sensor retaining screws **(see illustration)**. Be prepared for coolant spillage and have rag or a rubber plug handy to force into the sensor aperture to minimise coolant loss.

11 Refitting is the reverse of the removal procedure, noting the following points:

a) Renew the sensor seal if necessary.

b) Top-up or refill the cooling system as described in Chapter 1A Section 6 or Chapter 1B Section 6

10 Coolant pump – checking, removal and refitting

Note: *Refer to the warnings given in Section 1 of this Chapter before starting work.*

Checking

1 A failure in the coolant pump can cause serious engine damage due to overheating.

2 There are three ways to check the operation of the coolant pump while it's installed on the engine. If the pump is defective, fit a new or rebuilt unit.

3 With the engine running at normal operating temperature, squeeze the radiator top hose. If the coolant pump is working properly, a pressure surge should be felt as the hose is released.

4 Coolant pumps are equipped with weep or vent holes. If a failure occurs in the pump seal, coolant will leak from the hole. In most cases you'll need an electric torch to find the hole on the coolant pump from underneath to check for leaks. It will also be necessary to remove the timing belt upper cover on 2.0 litre diesel engines (Chapter 2C Section 5).

10.9 Slacken the bolts and remove the pump

9.10 Undo the sensor retaining screws

5 If the coolant pump shaft bearings fail, there may be a howling sound at the drivebelt end of the engine while it's running. Shaft wear can be felt if the coolant pump pulley or sprocket is rocked up and down.

6 Don't mistake drivebelt slippage, which causes a squealing sound, for coolant pump bearing failure.

Removal

7 Drain the cooling system (see Chapter 1A Section 34 or Chapter 1B Section 36).

1.5 litre petrol engine

Note: *Ford says the coolant pump can be replaced without removing the timing belt, but the procedure is so complex and lengthy that we strongly suggest the timing belt is replaced at the same time. The timing belt MUST be replaced if it is contaminated with water or oil.*

8 Remove the timing belt, as described in Chapter 2A Section 10.

9 Undo the 6 retaining bolts and remove the coolant pump from place **(see illustration)**. Be prepared for some fluid spillage.

Diesel engines

10 Remove the timing belt as described in Chapter 2C Section 5.

11 Undo the retaining bolts and remove the coolant pump. Recover the gasket **(see illustration)**.

10.11 Unbolt and remove the coolant pump

10.12 Renew the coolant pump gasket

Refitting

12 Clean the pump mating surfaces carefully; the gasket/O-ring must be renewed whenever it is disturbed**(see illustration)**. Refit the pump and tighten the bolts to the specified torque wrench setting.

13 The remainder of the refitting procedure is the reverse of dismantling, noting the following points:

a) *Tighten all fixings to the specified torque wrench settings (where given).*

b) *Where applicable, check the timing belt for contamination and renew if required, as described in Chapter 2C Section 5.*

c) *On completion, refill the cooling system as described in Chapter 1A Section 34 or Chapter 1B Section 36.*

11 Auxiliary coolant pump – removal and refitting

Removal

1 Jack up the vehicle and support it on axle stands, as described in *Jacking and vehicle support*.

2 Undo the fixings and remove the engine undertray.

3 Drain the cooling system, as described in Chapter 1A Section 34.

4 Disconnect the wiring plug from the auxiliary pump **(see illustration)**.

5 Squeeze the clips and disconnect the coolant hoses from the auxiliary pump.

6 Undo the 2 retaining bolts and manoauvre the pump from place **(see illustration)**. Be prepared for some fluid spillage.

Refitting

7 Refitting is a reversal of removal, ensuring that the locating tab on the top of the pump is inserted into the corresponding aperture on the engine **(see illustration)**.

12 Heating and ventilation system – general information

Note: *Refer to Section 14 for information on the air conditioning side of the system.*

Manually controlled system

1 The heating/ventilation system consists of a variable speed blower motor (housed behind the facia), face level vents in the centre and at each end of the facia, and air ducts to the front footwells.

2 The control unit is located in the facia, and the controls operate flap valves to deflect and mix the air flowing through the various parts of the heating/ventilation system. The flap valves are contained in the air distribution housing, which acts as a central distribution unit, passing air to the various ducts and vents.

3 Cold air enters the system through the grille in the scuttle. If required, the airflow is boosted by the blower, and then flows through the various ducts, according to the settings of the controls. Stale air is expelled through ducts at the rear of the vehicle. If warm air is required, the cold air is passed over the heater matrix, which is heated by the engine coolant.

4 A recirculation lever enables the outside air supply to be closed off, while the air inside the vehicle is recirculated. This can be useful to prevent unpleasant odours entering from outside the vehicle, but should only be used briefly, as the recirculated air inside the vehicle will soon become stale.

5 On some engine models an electric heater is fitted into the heater housing. When the coolant temperature is cold, the heater warms the air before it enters the heater matrix. This quickly increases the temperature of the heater matrix on cold starts, resulting in warm air being available to heat the vehicle interior soon after start-up.

Automatic climate control

6 A fully-automatic electronic climate control system was offered as an option on some models. The main components of the system are exactly the same as those described for the manual system, the only major difference being that the temperature and distribution flaps in the heating/ventilation housing are operated by electric motors rather than cables.

7 The operation of the system is controlled by the electronic control module (which is incorporated in the blower motor assembly) along with the following sensors.

a) *The passenger compartment sensor – informs the control module of the temperature of the air inside the passenger compartment.*

b) *Evaporator temperature sensor – informs the control module of the evaporator temperature.*

c) *Heater matrix temperature sensor – informs the control module of the heater matrix temperature.*

8 Using the information from the above sensors, the control module determines the appropriate settings for the heating/ventilation system housing flaps to maintain the passenger compartment at the desired setting on the control panel.

9 If the system develops a fault, the vehicle should be taken to a Ford dealer. A complete test of the system can then be carried out, using a special electronic diagnostic test unit, which is simply plugged into the system's diagnostic connector.

13 Heater/ventilation components – removal and refitting

Caution: Prior to working on any electrical component, we recommend that the battery is disconnected as described in Chapter 5 Section 4.

Control panel

1 Using a trim removal tool, prise up the leather gearlever surround.

11.4 Disconnect the auxiliary pump wiring plug

11.6 Remove the bolts to release the pump

11.7 Unsure the pump tab engages with the locating recess

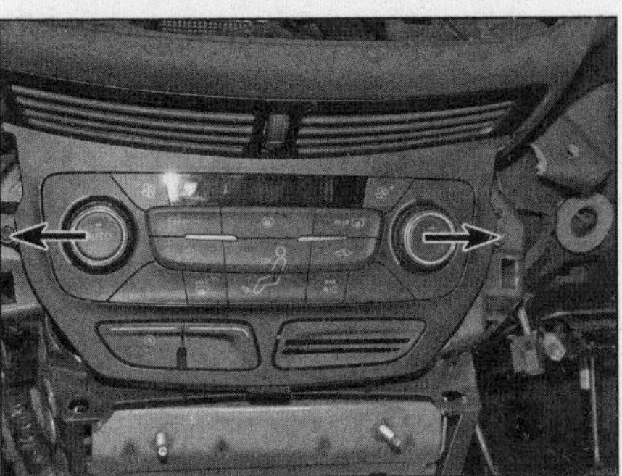
13.3 Undo the heater panel retaining screws

13.4 Disconnect the heater control panel wiring plugs

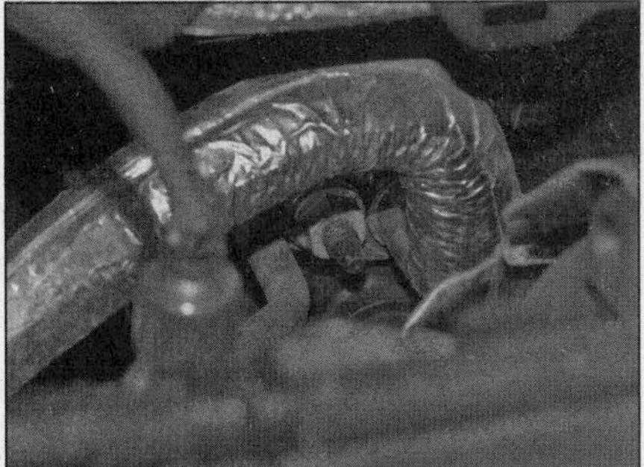
13.7 Undo the retaining nut for the pipe bracket

13.8 Prise off the rubber drain pipe

13.10 Undo the retaining rings to disconnect the pipes

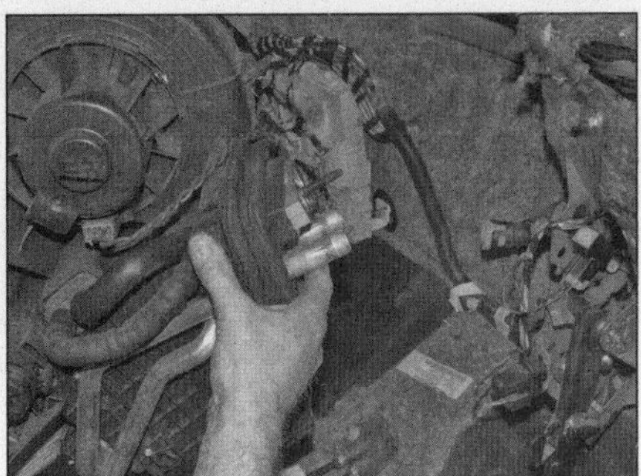
13.11 Remove the heater box from the vehicle

2 Remove the gearlever surround panel as described in Chapter 11 Section 38.

3 Remove the 2 retaining screws to release the heater control panel **(see illustration)** and manoeuvre the panel rearward from place.

4 Disconnect the 3 wiring plugs from the heater control panel **(see illustration)**.

5 Refitting is a reversal of removal.

Heater matrix removal

6 The heater matrix can only be removed once the heater box has been removed. Drain the cooling system as described in Chapter 1A Section 34 or Chapter 1B Section 36, have the air conditioning refrigerant circuit evacuated, then remove the facia crossmember, as described in Chapter 11 Section 38.

7 Working in the engine bay, undo the retaining nut for the heater pipe bracket **(see illustration)**.

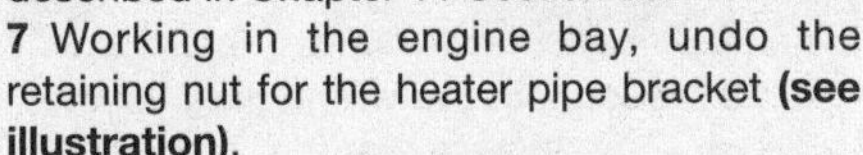

8 Disconnect all wiring plugs from the heater box and the air conditioning drain pipe **(see illustration)**.

9 Pull the heater box assembly towards the rear of the cabin to allow access to the 2 heater pipes.

10 Rotate the retaining rings for each pipe anti-clockwise and pull the hoses from the rear of the heater box **(see illustration)**.

Note: *Have a small container handy to catch any coolant fluid when the pipes are removed.*

11 Manoeuvre the entire heater assembly from place **(see illustration)** taking care not to tilt it and spill any more coolant.

12 Remove the screw that locks the inlet and outlet pipes in position and then remove the foam insulation **(see illustration)**.

13 Undo the 4 retaining screws holding on the heater box side panel **(see illustration)**.

14 Turn the heater box over and remove the 5 screws from the lower section. Separate the lower section and lift out the heater matrix **(see illustrations)**.

15 Refitting is the reverse of the removal procedure. Refill the cooling system with

13.12 Remove the foam insulation

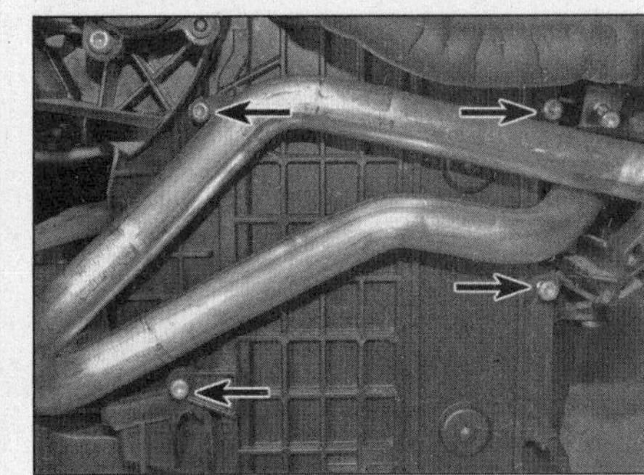
13.13 Remove the 4 side panel screws

13.14a Remove the screws and...

13.14b ...lift off the cover...

13.14c ...and remove the matrix

13.17 Press the plug through the casing

13.18 Lift the side cover away

the recommended coolant (see Chapter 1A Section 34 or Chapter 1B Section 36). Start the engine and allow it to reach normal operating temperature, indicated by the radiator top hose becoming hot. Recheck the coolant level and add more if required, then check for leaks. Check the operation of the heater.

Evaporator

16 Remove the heater matrix as described earlier in this Section.

17 Gently push the retaining pug for the heat sensor through the heater box casing **(see illustration)**.

18 Pull away the side cover from the evaporator **(see illustration)**.

19 Gently remove the evaporator from place **(see illustration)**.

Heater blower motor

20 Access is extremely limited. Remove the facia and crossmember, as described in Chapter 11 Section 38.

21 Disconnect all the wiring plugs and remove the fusebox as described in Chapter 12 Section 4.

22 Undo the 3 retaining screws and remove the cover from the left-hand side of the fan assembly **(see illustration)**.

23 Working on the right-hand side of the heater housing, disconnect the wiring plug from the blower motor **(see illustration)**.

24 Release the locking tab using a screwdriver, then rotate the blower motor anti-clockwise to disengage **(see illustrations)**.

25 Working on the left-hand side of the heater box, pull the fan assembly and motor through to remove.

26 Refitting is a reversal of removal.

Heater blower motor controller

27 Remove the facia end panel as described in Chapter 11 Section 38.

28 Remove the glovebox as described in Chapter 11 Section 37.

29 Remove the passenger-side lower facia panel as described in Chapter Section.

30 Remove the passenger-side centre console kick panel as described in Chapter 11 Section 38.

31 Disconnect the wiring plugs, undo the retaining screw and withdraw the controller from beside the blower motor **(see illustration)**.

32 Refitting is a reversal of removal.

Heater housing assembly

33 On models with air conditioning, have

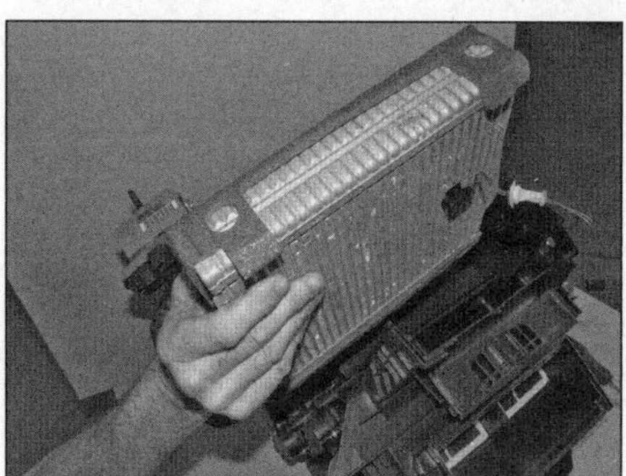
13.19 Pull the evaporator from the heater box

13.22 Undo the screws and remove the cover

13.23 Disconnect the wiring plug for the blower motor

13.24a Release the tab...

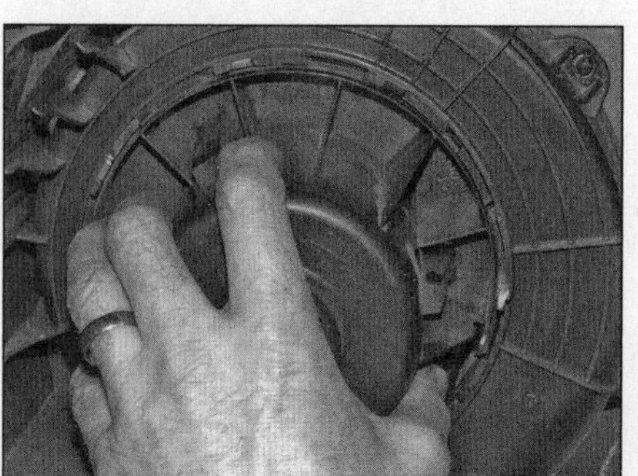
13.24b ...then rotate the motor to release

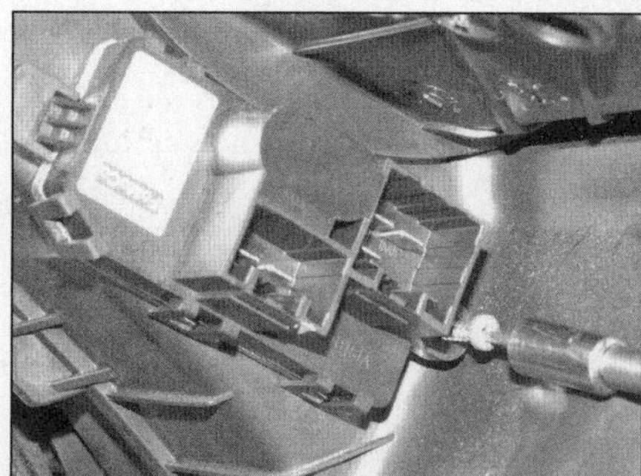
13.31 Slacken the screw to remove the blower controller

13.39 Disconnect the recirculation flap motor wiring plug

13.42a Disconnect the wiring plug...

13.42b ...then undo the screws and remove the motor

the refrigerant circuit evacuated by an air conditioning specialist and obtain some plugs to seal the air conditioning pipe unions whilst the system is disconnected.

Warning: Failure to seal the refrigerant pipe unions will result in the dehydrator reservoir become saturated, necessitating its renewal.

34 Drain the cooling system (see Chapter 1A Section 34 or Chapter 1B Section 36). Alternatively, working in the engine compartment, clamp the heater matrix coolant hoses to minimise coolant loss.

35 Remove the heater housing as described earlier in this Section.

36 Refitting is the reverse of removal ensuring the seals are in position on the pipes and housing mounting. On completion, refill the cooling system (see Chapter 1A Section 34 or Chapter 1B Section 36).

Air recirculation/temperature blend/distribution motors

Air recirculation flap motor

37 Remove the driver's-side lower facia panel as described in Chapter 11 Section 38.

38 Undo the retaining screw and remove the footwell air duct.

39 Undo the screws, disconnect the wiring plug and remove the air recirculation flap motor **(see illustration)**.

40 Refitting is a reversal of removal.

Passenger-side footwell flap motor

41 Remove the passenger side glovebox as described in Chapter 11 Section 37.

42 Disconnect the wiring plug, undo the screws and remove the footwell flap motor **(see illustrations)**.

43 Refitting is a reversal of removal.

Defroster flap motor

44 Remove the passengers side glovebox as described in Chapter 11 Section 37.

45 Unclip and remove the passengers footwell air duct.

46 Disconnect the motor wiring plug, undo the screw, and remove the motor.

47 Refitting is a reversal of removal.

Centre console vent

48 Remove the centre console as described in Chapter 11 Section 36.

49 Undo the retaining screw in the small aperture at the rear of the vent **(see illustration)**.

Footwell vents

50 Remove the centre console side panels as described in Chapter 11 Section 36.

51 Remove the lower facia panels on both sides of the dashboard, as described in Chapter 11 Section 38.

52 Undo the retaining screw and pull the vent from place **(see illustration)**.

53 Refitting is a reversal of removal.

Facia vent temperature sensor

54 Remove the infotainment screen as described in Section 12 Section 20.

55 Disconnect the wiring plug for each sensor, then rotate the sensor anti-clockwise and remove it **(see illustration)**.

56 Refitting is a reversal of removal.

Driver's side climate control air temperature sensor

57 Remove the driver's side lower facia panel as described in Chapter 11 Section 38.

58 Remove the driver's side centre console side panel, as described in Chapter 11 Section 36.

59 Reach behind the facia and disconnect the wiring plug from the rear of the temperature sensor **(see illustration)**.

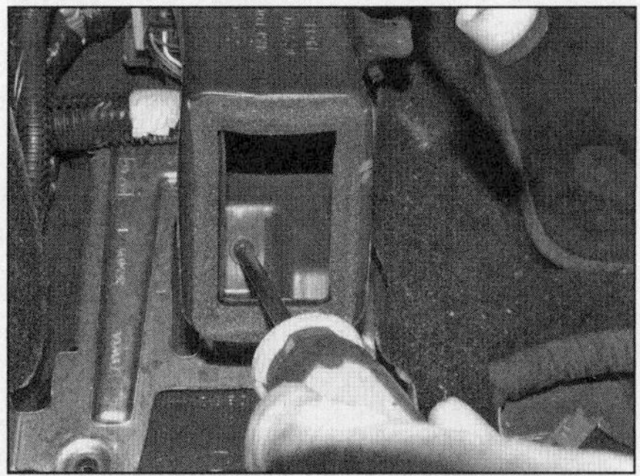
13.49 Remove the retaining screw and pull away the vent tube

13.52 Remove the retaining screw to detach the vent

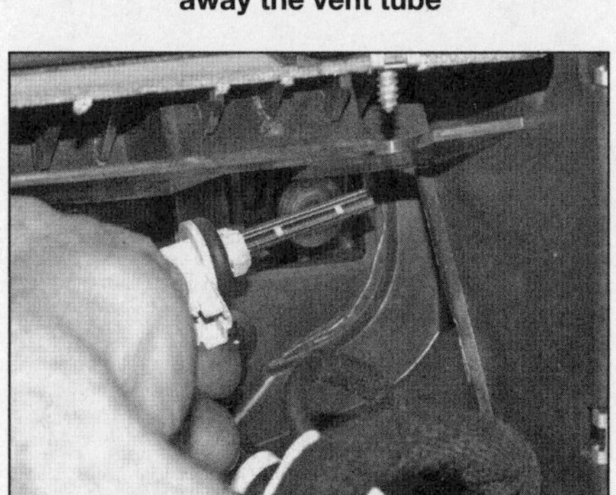
13.55 Disconnect the wiring plug, then rotate the sensor anti-clockwise

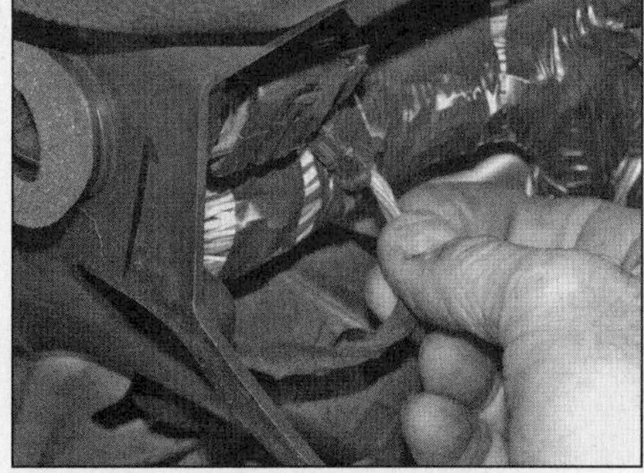
13.59 Disconnect the sensor wiring plug

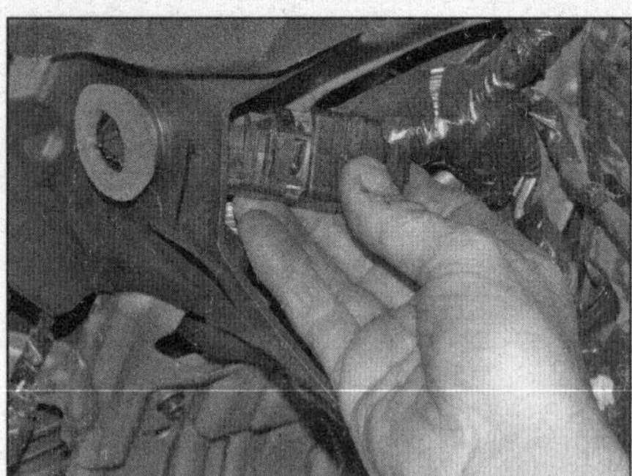

13.60 Rotate the sensor anti-clockwise

60 Rotate the sensor anti-clockwise to remove from behind the facia **(see illustration)**.

61 Refitting is a reversal of removal.

14 Air conditioning system – general information and precautions

General information

1 An air conditioning system is available on certain models. It enables the temperature of incoming air to be lowered, and also dehumidifies the air, which makes for rapid demisting and increased comfort.

2 The cooling side of the system works in the same way as a domestic refrigerator. Refrigerant gas is drawn into a belt-driven compressor, and passes into a condenser mounted on the front of the radiator, where it loses heat and becomes liquid. The liquid passes through an expansion valve to an evaporator, where it changes from liquid under high pressure to gas under low pressure. This change is accompanied by a drop in temperature, which then cools the evaporator. The refrigerant returns to the compressor, and the cycle begins again.

3 Air blown through the evaporator passes to the heating/ventilation housing, where it is mixed with hot air blown through the heater matrix to achieve the desired temperature in the passenger compartment.

4 The heating side of the system works in the same way as on models without air conditioning (see Section 12).

5 Any problems with the system should be referred to a Ford dealer, or suitably-equipped specialist.

6 The air conditioning refrigerant circuit service ports are located in the engine compartment. One is by the right-hand headlight and the other is lower down, in front of the fuel filter bracket.

Precautions

7 When an air conditioning system is fitted, it is necessary to observe special precautions whenever dealing with any part of the system, or its associated components. The refrigerant is potentially dangerous, and should only be handled by qualified persons. Uncontrolled discharging of the refrigerant is dangerous and damaging to the environment for the following reasons.

a) If it is splashed onto the skin, it can cause frostbite.

b) The refrigerant is heavier then air and so displaces oxygen. In a confined space, which is not adequately ventilated, this could lead to a risk of suffocation. The gas is odourless and colourless so there is no warning of its presence in the atmosphere.

c) Although not poisonous, in the presence of a naked flame (including a cigarette) it forms a noxious gas that causes headaches, nausea, etc.

Warning: Never attempt to open any air conditioning system refrigerant pipe/hose union without first having the system fully discharged by an air conditioning specialist. On completion of work, have the system recharged with the correct type and amount of fresh refrigerant.

Note: *Always seal disconnected refrigerant pipe/hose unions as soon as they are disconnected. Failure to form an airtight seal on any union will result in the dehydrator reservoir become saturated, necessitating its renewal. Also renew all sealing rings disturbed.*

Caution: Do not operate the air conditioning system if it is known to be short of refrigerant as this could damage the compressor.

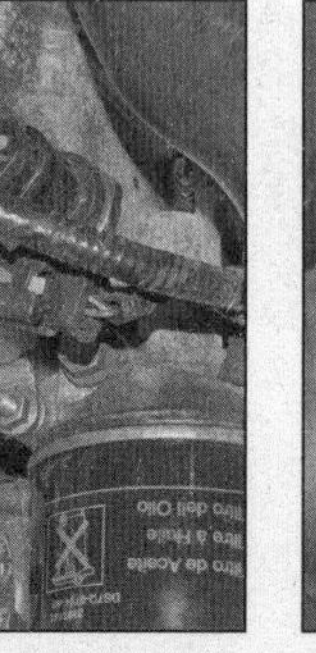

15.6 Detach the pipes from the compressor

15.7 Undo the bolts and remove the compressor

15 Air conditioning system components – removal and refitting

Warning: Refer to the precautions given in Section 14 and have the system discharged by an air conditioning specialist before carrying out any work on the air conditioning system.

1 Have the air conditioning refrigerant circuit evacuated by a Ford dealer or suitably equipped specialist.

Compressor

Removal

2 Remove the auxiliary drivebelt as described in Chapter 1A Section 30 or Chapter 1B Section 32.

3 Disconnect the battery negative lead as described in Chapter 5 Section 4.

4 Remove the electric cooling fan and shroud assembly as described in Section 8. There is no need to do this step on 1.5-litre diesel models.

5 Disconnect the compressor wiring plug.

6 Unscrew the bolts securing the refrigerant pipes retaining plates to the compressor **(see illustration)**. Separate the pipes from the compressor and quickly seal the pipe and compressor unions to prevent the entry of moisture into the refrigerant circuit. Discard the sealing rings, new ones must be used on refitting. Release the pipes from any retaining clips as necessary.

Warning: Failure to seal the refrigerant pipe unions will result in the dehydrator reservoir become saturated, necessitating its renewal.

7 Unscrew the compressor mounting bolts, then free the compressor from its mounting bracket and remove it from the engine **(see illustration)**.

8 If the compressor is to be renewed, drain the refrigerant oil from the old compressor. The specialist who recharges the refrigerant system will need to add this amount of oil to the system.

Refitting

9 If a new compressor is being fitted, drain the refrigerant oil.

10 Manoeuvre the compressor into position and fit the mounting bolts. Tighten the compressor mounting bolts to the specified torque.

11 Lubricate the new refrigerant pipe sealing rings with compressor oil. Remove the plugs and install the sealing rings then quickly fit the refrigerant pipes to the compressor. Ensure the refrigerant pipes are correctly joined then refit the retaining bolts, tightening them to the specified torque.

12 The remainder of refitting is a reversal of removal.

13 Have the air conditioning system recharged with the correct type and amount

15.18a Disconnect the refrigerant pipes...

15.18b ..and plug the openings

15.19 Remove the right-hand retaining bolt

of refrigerant by a specialist before using the system. Remember to inform the specialist which components have been renewed, so they can add the correct amount of oil.

Condenser

Removal

14 Have the air-conditioning system evacuated by a suitably equipped repairer.

15 Remove the front bumper as described in Chapter 11 Section 5.

16 Remove the active shutter grille as described in Chapter 11 Section 6.

17 To improve access, remove the right-hand headlight, as described in Chapter 12 Section 9.

18 Disconnect the refrigerant pipes, and seal them with plugs to prevent the ingress of dirt **(see illustrations)**.

19 Undo the retaining bolt at the right-hand end of the condenser **(see illustration)**.

20 Depress the retaing tab in the locator at the top left of the condenser.

21 Carefully lift the condenser to disengage it from all locating tabs **(see illustration)**.

22 Remove the condenser downwards from the vehicle **(see illustration)**.

Refitting

23 Refitting is a reversal of removal. Noting the following points:

a) *Ensure the mountings are secure when the condenser is in position in the front panel.*

b) *Lubricate the sealing rings with compressor oil. Remove the plugs and install the sealing rings then quickly fit the refrigerant pipes to the condenser. Securely tighten the dehydrator pipe union nut and ensure the compressor pipe is correctly joined.*

c) *Have the air conditioning system recharged with the correct type and amount of refrigerant by a specialist before using the system.*

Receiver/drier

24 The receiver/drier is located on the side of the condenser. It would appear that the receiver/drier is not available separately from the condenser. Check with your dealer or parts specialist.

15.21 Raise the condenser to disengage it from the fixing tabs

Evaporator

Removal

25 Remove the heating/ventilation housing and matrix as described in Section 13.

26 Unclip the rear air duct from the housing.

27 Note the fitted positions of the various wiring plugs, then disconnect them and unclip the wiring harness from the housing.

28 Undo the screws and remove the fresh air/air recirculation housing.

29 Prise open the clips and remove the pollen filter.

30 Undo the retaining screws and manoeuvre the evaporator housing from place.

31 Remove the evaporator itself from place, taking care to plug the ends of the pipes to prevent contamination.

Refitting

32 Refitting is a reversal of removal but have the air conditioning system recharged with the correct type and amount of refrigerant by a specialist prior to using the system.

16.2 Disconnect the sensor wiring plug

15.22 Take the condenser out downwards from behind the crossmember

16 Outside temperature sensor – removal and refitting

Removal

1 Remove the engine undertray as described in Section 11 Section 5.

2 Reach up from below, disconnect the temperature sensor wiring plug **(see illustration)**.

3 Gently prise the sensor upwards to release the 2 mounting plugs **(see illustration)**.

Refitting

4 Refitting is a reversal of removal.

16.3 Lift the sensor from its mounting place

Chapter 4 Part A
Fuel and exhaust systems – petrol models

Contents

Degrees of difficulty

Easy, suitable for novice with little experience 

Fairly easy, suitable for beginner with some experience 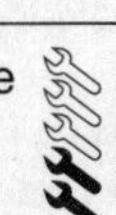

Fairly difficult, suitable for competent DIY mechanic 

Difficult, suitable for experienced DIY mechanic 

Very difficult, suitable for expert DIY or professional 

Specifications

General

Engine codes*	BNMA, M8MA, M8MB, M8MC, M9MA, M9MB, M9MC, M9MD

** For details of engine code location, see 'Vehicle identification'.*

System type

Sequential, multipoint fuel direct injection	MED17 with CAN-Bus and individual cylinder knock control. FGEC Software

Fuel system data

Fuel pump type	Electric, immersed in tank, and engine driven high-pressure pump
Specified idle speed	Not adjustable – controlled by ECU
Idle mixture CO content	Not adjustable – controlled by ECU

Recommended fuel

Minimum octane rating	95 RON unleaded (UK unleaded premium). Leaded/lead replacement fuel (LRP) must not be used

Torque wrench settings

	Nm	lbf ft
Accelerator pedal assembly nuts	8	6
Camshaft position sensor	8	6
Crankshaft position sensor	8	6
Exhaust heat shield bolts	10	7
Manifold to exhaust flexible section	48	35
Fuel rail high pressure pipe:		
Stage 1	21	16
Stage 2	Wait 5 minutes	
Stage 3	21	16
Fuel rail mounting bolts	24	17
Fuel rail pressure sensor	35	26
Fuel tank strap retaining bolts	25	18
Inlet manifold nuts/bolts:		
Upper bolts	18	13
Lower bolts	10	7
Oxygen sensors	48	35
Throttle body retaining bolts	12	8
Turbocharger oil drain pipe bolts	10	7
Turbocharger oil supply pipe bolt	26	19
Turbocharger to cylinder head nuts: *		
Stage 1	19	14
Stage 2	24	17
Stage 3	Wait 30 seconds	
Stage 4	24	17
Variable camshaft timing oil control solenoid	10	7

** Do not re-use*

1 General information and precautions

1 The fuel supply system consists of a fuel tank, which is mounted under the rear of the car, with an electric fuel pump immersed in it, a fuel filter (depending on model), fuel feed and return pipes. All petrol models are equipped with a direct injection system, where the tank-immersed electric pump supplies fuel to an engine-driven high-pressure pump. This pump supplies fuel to a common fuel rail, where it is distributed under high-pressure to the injectors. Fuel is then injected directly into the combustion chambers, resulting in lower emissions, higher engine output, for reduced consumption.

2 Refer to Chapter 6A for further information on the operation of the engine management system, and to Section 17 for information on the exhaust system.

Warning: Many of the procedures in this Chapter require the removal of fuel pipes and connections, which may result in some fuel spillage. Before carrying out any operation on the fuel system, refer to the precautions given in 'Safety first!' at the beginning of this manual, and follow them implicitly. Petrol is a highly dangerous and volatile liquid, and the precautions necessary when handling it cannot be overstressed.

Note: *Residual pressure may remain in the fuel pipes long after the vehicle was last used. When disconnecting any fuel line, first depressurise the fuel system as described in Section 4.*

2 Troubleshooting

Low pressure fuel pump

1 The lower pressure fuel pump is located inside the fuel tank. Sit inside the vehicle with the windows closed, turn the ignition key to ON (not START) and listen for the sound of the fuel pump as it's briefly activated. You will only hear the sound for a second or two, but that sound indicates that the pump is working. Alternatively, have an assistant listen at the fuel filler cap.

2 If the pump does not come on, check the relevant fuses and relays as described in Chapter 12 Section 3.

3 If the fuses and relays are okay, check the wiring back to the fuel pump. If the wiring is okay, the fuel pump control module may be defective. If the pump runs continuously with the ignition key in the ON position, engine management ECU may be defective. Have the circuit checked by a dealer or suitably equipped repairer.

2.10 An automotive stethoscope is used to listen to the fuel injectors in operation

Fuel injection system

Note: *The following procedure is based on the assumption that the fuel pump is working and the fuel pressure is adequate.*

4 Check all electrical connectors that are related to the system. Check the earth wire connections for tightness (see Chapter 12 Section 2).

5 Verify that the battery is fully charged (see Chapter 5 Section 3).

6 Inspect the air filter element (see Chapter 1A Section 27).

7 Check all fuses related to the fuel system (see Chapter 12 Section 3).

8 Check the air intake system between the throttle body and the intake manifold for leaks. Also inspect the condition of all vacuum hoses connected to the intake manifold and to the throttle body.

9 Remove the air intake duct from the throttle body and look for dirt, carbon, varnish, or other residue in the throttle body, particularly around the throttle plate. If it's dirty, clean it with carburettor cleaner, a toothbrush and a clean rag.

10 With the engine running, place an automotive stethoscope against each injector, one at a time, and listen for a clicking sound that indicates operation **(see illustration)**.

Warning: Stay clear of the drivebelt and any rotating or hot components.

11 If you can hear the injectors operating, but the engine is misfiring, the electrical circuits are functioning correctly, but the injectors might be dirty or blocked. Try a commercial injector cleaning product (available at auto parts suppliers). If cleaning the injectors doesn't help, the injectors may need to be replaced.

12 If an injector is not operating (it makes no sound), disconnect the injector electrical plug and measure the resistance across the injector terminals with an ohmmeter. Compare this measurement to the other injectors. If the resistance of the non-operational injector is quite different from the other injectors, replace it.

13 If the injector is not operating, but the resistance reading is within the range of resistance of the other injectors, the ECU or the circuit between the ECU and the injector might be faulty.

3 Air cleaner assembly – removal and refitting

Removal

1 Remove the air filter as described in Chapter 1A Section 27.

2 Release the strap and remove the air intake duct **(see illustration)**.

3 Release the clamp securing the air outlet duct to the air cleaner housing **(see illustration)**.

4 Disconnect the air mass meter wiring plug **(see illustration)**.

5 Pull the air cleaner housing upwards from place **(see illustrations)**.

Refitting

6 Refitting is a reversal of the removal procedure, ensuring that all hoses and ducts are properly reconnected and correctly seated and, where necessary, securely held by their retaining clips. Do not use any grease or lubricant when refitting the air hoses/ducts.

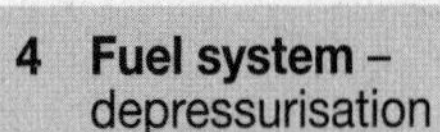

4 Fuel system – depressurisation

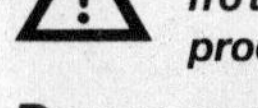

Warning: Refer to the warning note in Section 1 before proceeding.

Depressurisation

Warning: The following procedure will merely relieve the pressure in the fuel system – remember that fuel will still be present in the system components and take precautions accordingly before disconnecting any of them.

1 The fuel system referred to in this Section is defined as the tank-mounted fuel pump, the fuel filter (where fitted), the fuel injectors, high-pressure pump (where applicable), the fuel rail and the pipes of the fuel pipes between these components. All these contain fuel, which will be under pressure while the engine is running, and/or while the ignition is switched on. The pressure will remain for some time after the ignition has been switched off, and must be relieved in a controlled fashion when any of these components are disturbed for servicing work.

2 To relieve the system pressure, start the engine and allow it to idle. In the engine bay, remove the fuel pump fuse and allow the engine to stall. Crank the engine for 5 seconds to fully depressurise the system.

5 Fuel pipes and fittings – general information and disconnection

1 Disconnect the battery negative lead as described in Chapter 5 Section 4.

2 The fuel supply pipe connects the fuel pump in the fuel tank to the fuel rail on the engine.

3 Whenever you're working under the vehicle, be sure to inspect all fuel and evaporative emission pipes for leaks, kinks, dents and other damage. Always replace a damaged fuel pipe immediately.

4 If you find signs of dirt in the pipes during disassembly, disconnect all pipes and blow them out with compressed air. Inspect the fuel strainer on the fuel pump pick-up unit for damage and deterioration.

Steel tubing

5 It is critical that the fuel pipes be replaced with pipes of equivalent type and specification.

6 Some steel fuel pipes have threaded fittings. When loosening these fittings, hold the stationary fitting with a spanner while turning the union nut.

Plastic tubing

Warning: When removing or installing plastic fuel tubing, be careful not to bend or twist it too much, which can damage it. Also, plastic fuel tubing is NOT heat resistant, so keep it away from excessive heat.

7 When replacing fuel system plastic tubing, use only original equipment replacement plastic tubing.

Flexible hoses

8 When replacing fuel system flexible hoses,

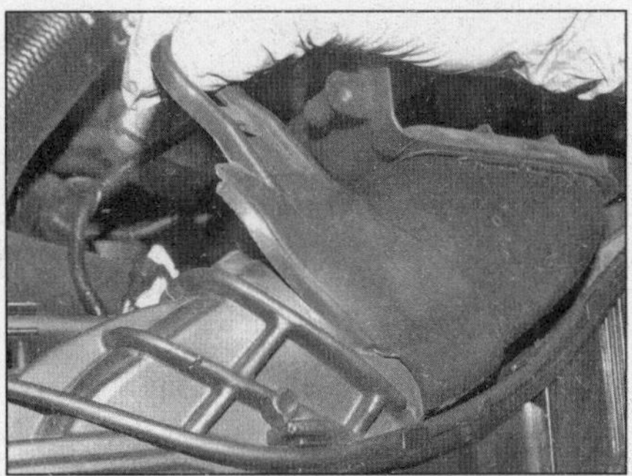

3.2 Undo the strap to release the intake duct

3.3 Slacken the clip to free the outlet duct

3.4 Disconnect the air mass meter wiring plug

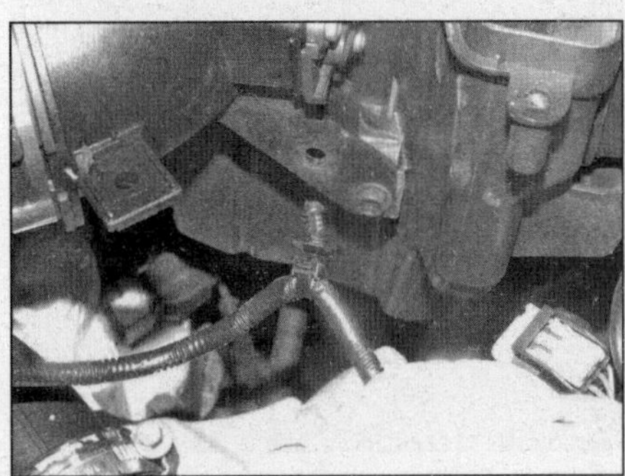

3.5a Unclip the wiring from the side of the air cleaner housing...

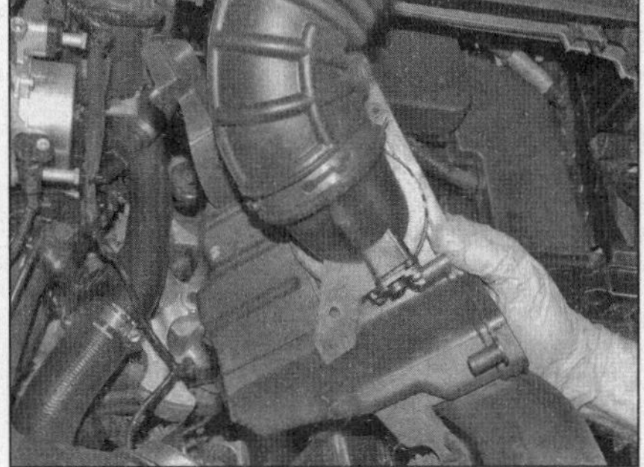

3.5b ...then lift away the housing itself

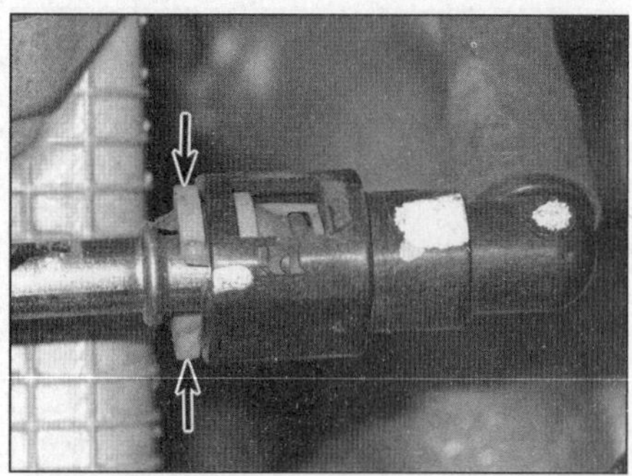
5.10a Two-tab type fitting; depress both tabs with your fingers, then pull the fuel pipe and the fitting apart

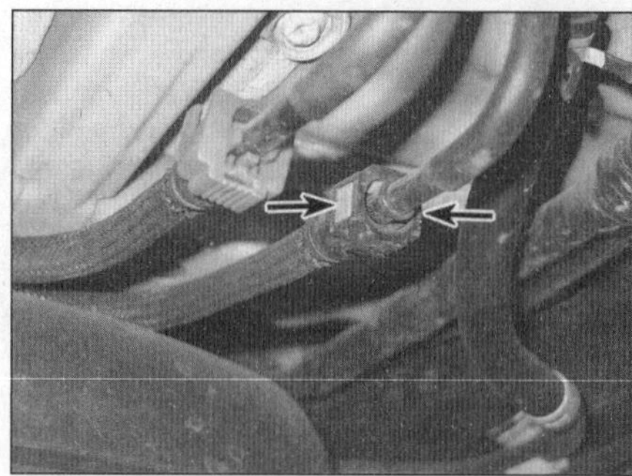
5.10b On this type of fitting, depress the two buttons on opposite sides of the fitting, then pull it off the fuel pipe

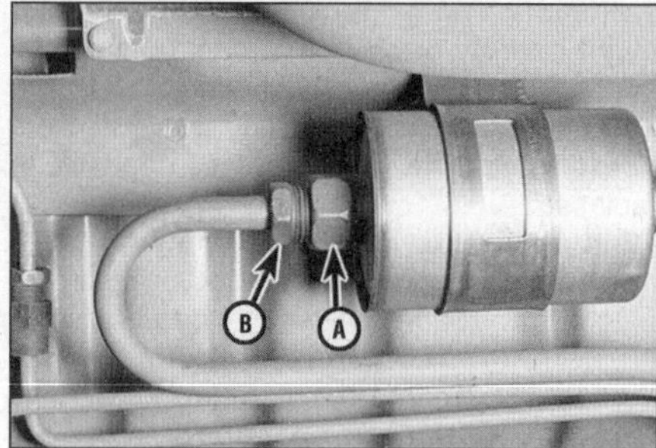

5.10c Threaded fuel pipe fitting; hold the stationary portion of the pipe or component (A) while loosening the union nut (B) with a flare-nut spanner

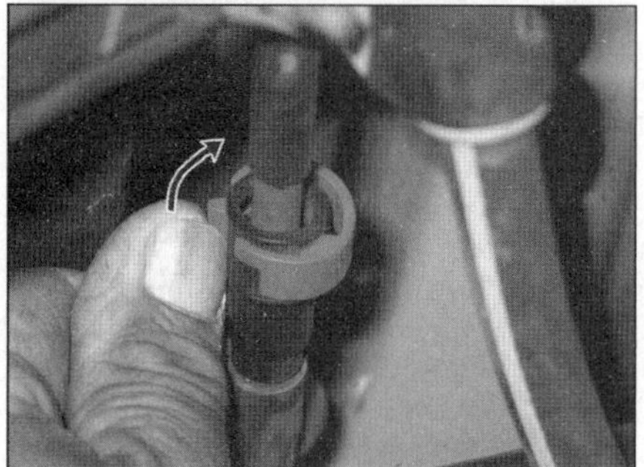
5.10d Plastic collar-type fitting; rotate the outer part of the fitting

5.10e Metal collar quick-connect fitting; pull the end of the retainer off the fuel pipe and disengage the other end from the female side of the fitting...

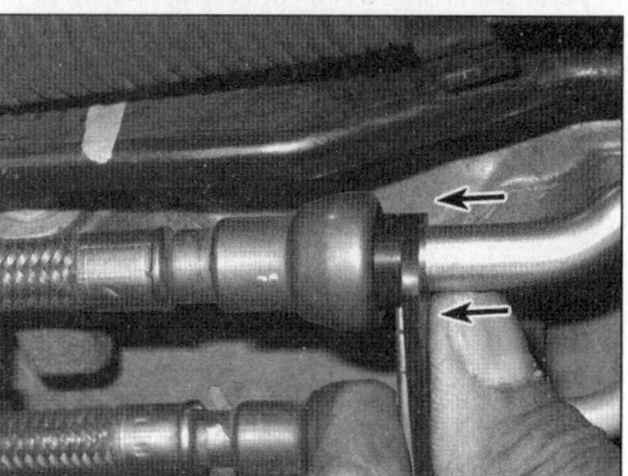
5.10f ... insert a fuel pipe separator tool into the female side of the fitting, push it into the fitting and pull the fuel pipe off the pipe

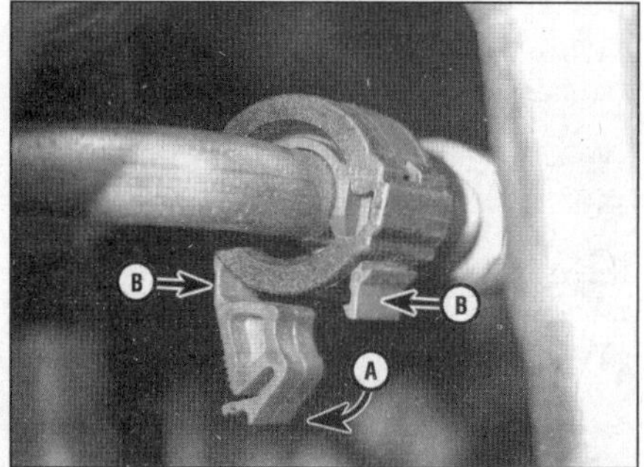

5.10g Some fittings are secured by lock tabs. Release the lock tab (A) and rotate it to the fully-opened position, squeeze the two smaller lock tabs (B)...

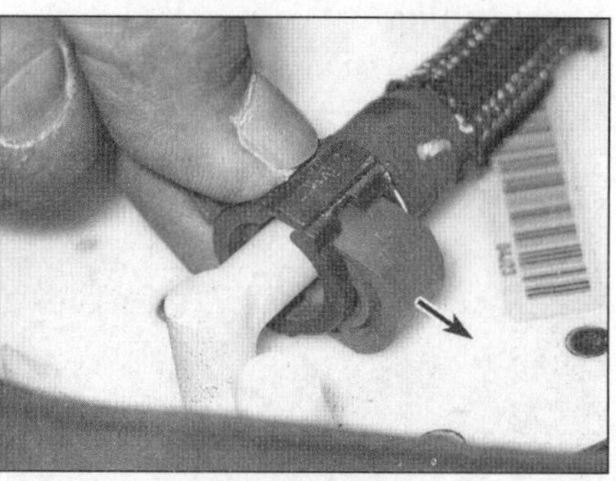
5.10h ... then push the retainer out and pull the fuel pipe off the pipe

use original equipment replacements, or hose to the same specification.

9 Don't route fuel hoses (or metal pipes) within 100 mm of the exhaust system or within 280 mm of the catalytic converter. Make sure that no rubber hoses are installed directly against the vehicle, particularly in places where there is any vibration. If allowed to touch some vibrating part of the vehicle, a hose can easily become chafed and it might start leaking. A good rule of thumb is to maintain a minimum of 8.0 mm clearance around a hose (or metal pipe) to prevent contact with the vehicle underbody.

Disconnecting Fuel pipe Fittings

10 Typical fuel pipe fittings:

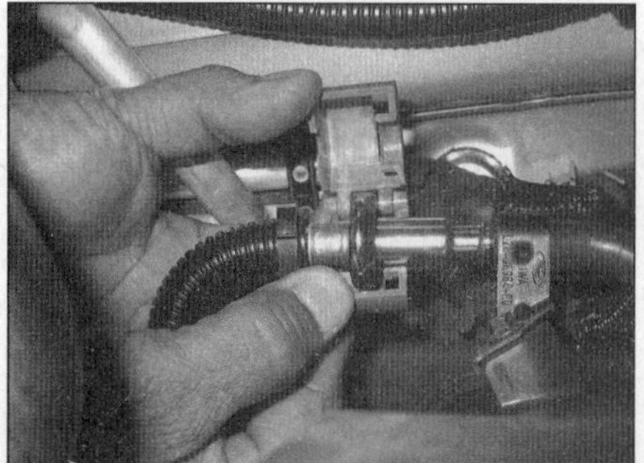
5.10i Spring-lock coupling; remove the safety cover, install a coupling release tool and close the tool around the coupling...

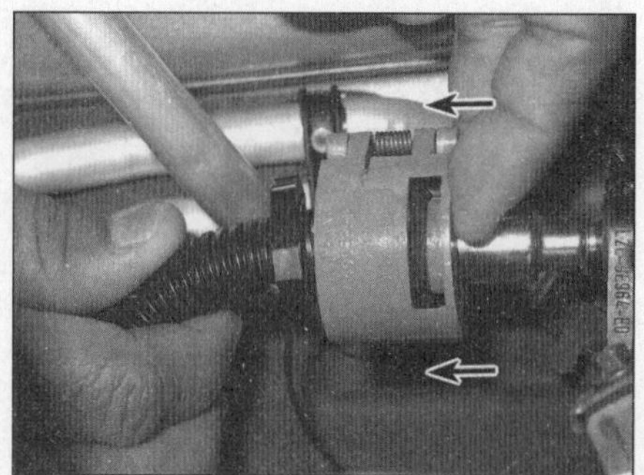
5.10j ... push the tool into the fitting, then pull the two pipes apart

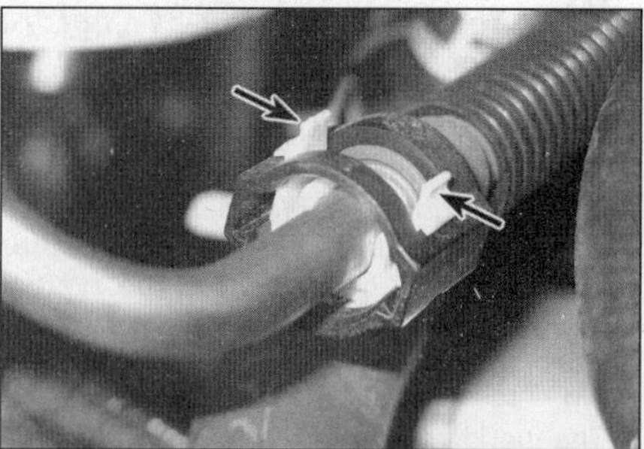
5.10k Hairpin clip type fitting: push the legs of the retainer clip together, then push the clip down all the way until it stops and pull the fuel pipe off the pipe

6 Fuel pump/level sensor – removal and refitting

Removal

1 Remove the fuel tank, as described in Section 7.

2 Unscrew the fuel pump/level sensor unit locking ring and remove it from the tank. Although a Ford tool (310-169) is available for this task, suitable alternative tools are available from good tool suppliers. Turn the ring anti-clockwise until it can be unscrewed by hand **(see illustration)**.

3 Carefully manoeuvre the pump assembly from the tank, taking care not to damage the level sensor arm **(see illustrations)**. Renew the sealing ring.

Level sensor replacement

4 Disconnect the level sensor wiring plug.

5 Release the clips and slide the sensor upwards from place.

6 The function of the level sender can be checked using a digital multimeter. Connect the multimeter across the sender terminals, and measure the resistance with the float in the empty position (zero deflection) and full position (maximum deflection) **(see illustration)**. If the resistances vary significantly from those specified, the sender may be defective.

Full tank:
Maximum float deflection) 510 ohms
Empty tank:
Minimum float deflection) 464 ohms

Pump replacement

7 The in-tank pump cannot be renewed separately. If faulty, the complete assembly must be renewed.

Refitting

8 Refitting is a reversal of removal, noting the following points:

a) Use a new sensor sealing ring.
b) To allow the unit to pass through the opening in the fuel tank, insert the float arm first.

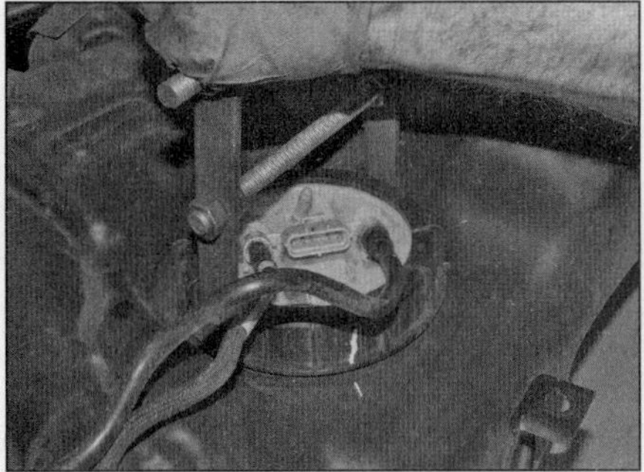

6.2 Unscrew the locking ring

6.3a Take care not to damage the sensor arm

6.3b Renew the sealing ring

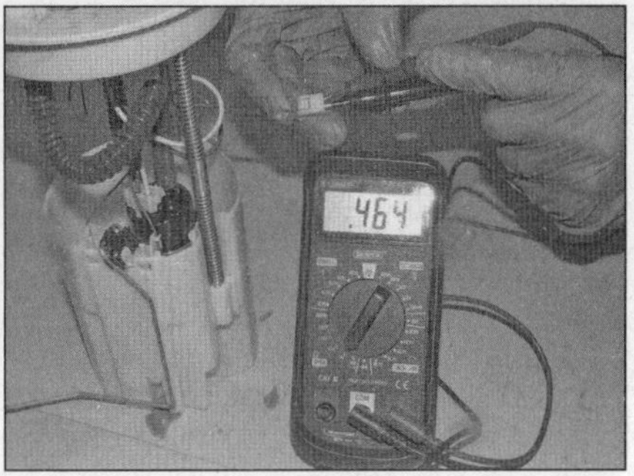

6.6 Check the sender using a multimeter

7 Fuel tank – removal and refitting

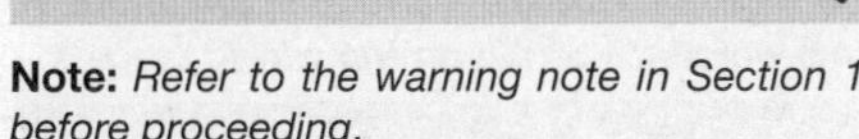

Note: *Refer to the warning note in Section 1 before proceeding.*

Removal

1 Disconnect the battery negative lead as described in Chapter 5 Section 4.

2 Before removing the fuel tank, all fuel should be drained from the tank. Since a fuel tank drain plug is not provided, it is preferable to carry out the removal operation when the tank is nearly empty.

Warning: If it's necessary to siphon the fuel out, use a siphoning kit, available at most automotive parts stores. Never start the siphoning action by mouth.

3 Slacken the right-hand rear roadwheel bolts, raise the rear of the vehicle and support it securely on axle stands (see *Jacking and vehicle support*). Remove the roadwheel.

4 On undo the plastic nuts/screw, release the plastic expansion rivets and remove the underbody panelling **(see illustration)**.

5 Remove the rear section of the exhaust system, and any heat shields that would interfere with removal of the fuel tank. **Note:** *Undo the right rear subframe bolts a few turns (but do not remove all the way) to allow you to manoeuvre out the exhaust rear section*.

6 Release the fasteners and remove the right-hand wheelarch liner **(see illustration)**.

7 Slacken the clamp and disconnect the fuel filler hose from the tank.

8 Disconnect and unclip the fuel vent hose from the filler neck **(see illustration)**.

9 Support the fuel tank using a floor jack and a wooden plank.

7.4 Undo the fasteners and remove the underbody panelling each side

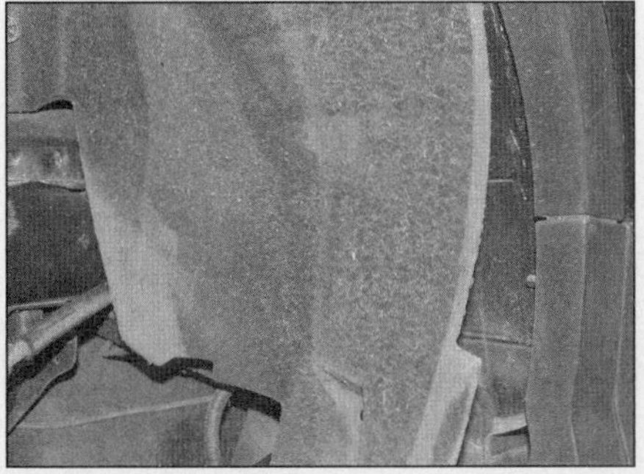

7.6 Take out the front-right wheelarch liner

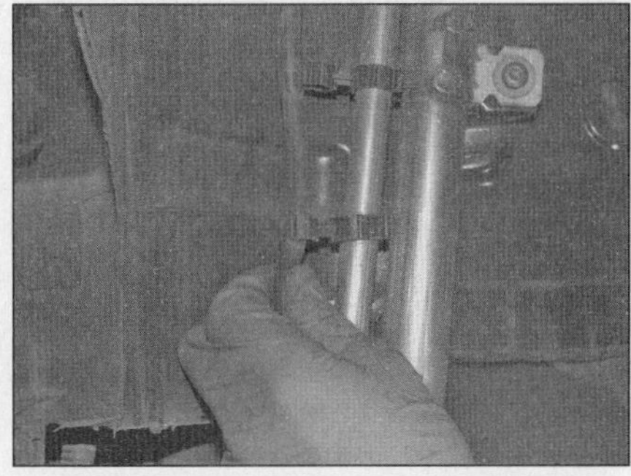

7.8 Unclip the vent hose from the filler neck

7.10 Unclip the fuel lines to separate from tank

7.12 Lower the tank and disconnect the wiring plug

8.3 Slacken the clamp to remove the intake pipe

8.4 Unplug the throttle body wiring connector

10 Release the retaining clips and separate the fuel lines from the fuel tank **(see illustration)**. Have a container ready to catch any fuel.

11 Remove the 4 retaining bolts securing the tank retaining straps.

12 Lower the tank by 10 cm, which will allow you access to disconnect the wiring plug on top of the tank **(see illustration)**.

Caution: Do not lower the tank any more or this will place strain on the wiring plug.

8.5a Undo the mounting bolts, remove the throttle body...

8.5b ...and replace the sealing ring

9.7a Disconnect the fuel injector wiring plugs...

9.7b ...then unclip the harness from the fuel rail

13 With the aid of an assistant, lower the tank from the vehicle.

Refitting

14 Refitting is a reversal of removal.

8 Throttle body – removal and refitting

Removal

1 Remove the engine cover.

2 Remove the air cleaner assembly as described in Section 3.

3 Slacken the clamp and remove the air intake pipe **(see illustration)**.

4 Disconnect the throttle body wiring plug **(see illustration)**.

5 Undo the 4 retaining bolts and remove the throttle body **(see illustrations)**. Renew the sealing ring.

Refitting

6 Position the throttle body with a new sealing ring, then tighten the retaining bolts to the specified torque.

7 The remainder of refitting is a reversal of removal.

9 Fuel rail and injectors – removal and refitting

Removal

Caution: Refer to the warning note in Section 1 before proceeding.

Note: *If a faulty injector is suspected, before condemning the injector, it is worth trying the effect of one of the proprietary injector cleaning treatments, which are available from car accessory shops.*

1 Depressurise the fuel system as described in Section 4.

2 Disconnect the battery as described in Chapter 5 Section 4.

3 Remove the windscreen cowl panel as described in Chapter 11 Section 12.

4 Pull up and remove the cover from the top of the engine.

5 Remove the ignition coils as described in Chapter 6A Section 7.

6 Disconnect the wiring plug from the fuel pressure sensor, and detach the wiring loom from the fuel rail.

7 Disconnect the fuel injectors' wiring plugs, and unclip the wiring harness from the fuel rail **(see illustrations)**.

8 Undo the union nuts, and remove the high-pressure fuel supply pipe **(see illustration)**. Discard it, because it must be replaced.

9 Undo the 4 retaining bolts on top of the fuel rail **(see illustration)**.

10 Gently prise up and lift the fuel rail from place (the fuel injectors will be removed along with the fuel rail) **(see illustration)**.

9.8 Undo the pipe union nuts

9.9 Remove the fuel rail retaining bolts

9.10 Lift the fuel rail and injectors together

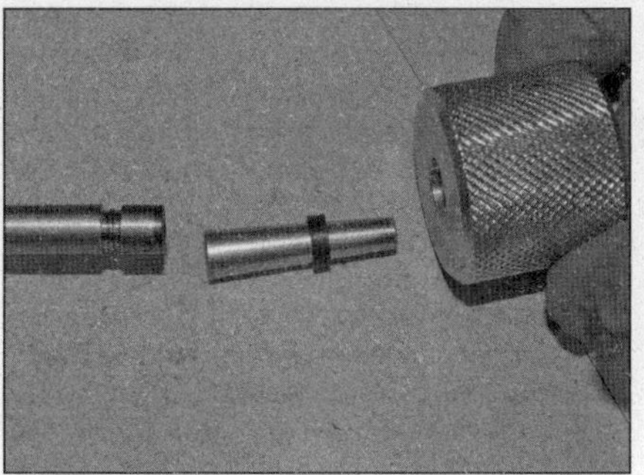
9.12a Place the seal onto the special tool...

9.12b ...then use the tool to slide it onto the injector

9.13 Disengage the clip to separate the injector from the fuel rail

Refitting

11 Before installing the new Teflon seal on each injector, thoroughly clean the groove for the seal and the injector shaft. Remove all combustion residue and varnish with a clean rag.

Caution: Do not clean the injector tip.

12 The manufacturer insists that you use the tools included in the special injector tool set (No. 310-128) to install the Teflon lower seals on the injectors: Install the special seal assembly cone on the injector, install the special sleeve on the injector and use the sleeve to push on the assembly cone, which pushes the Teflon seal into place on its groove **(see illustrations)**. Do NOT use any lubricants to do so.

13 To separate an injector from the fuel rail, prise open the retaining clip **(see illustration)**. Discard the clip, which must be replaced.

14 Remove the blue rubber seal and green plastic collar from the injector and discard **(see illustration)**.

15 Check the condition of the metal seat round the injector. If it is fine, just leave it. If it need to be replaced, first prise off the circlip **(see illustrations)** then slide the seat off the injector.

16 Check that the injector are free to rotate, then align their electrical sockets parallel to the fuel rail, pointing towards the pressure sensor end.

17 Manoeuvre the fuel rail and injectors into position, then use hand pressure alone, press them down into place.

18 As soon as resistance can be felt, insert and finger-tighten the fuel rail retaining bolts. Now tighten them gradually and evenly until the fuel rail is flush with the cylinder head, and the bolts have reached the required torque.

19 Fit a new high-pressure fuel pump-to-rail pipe, hand tighten each union nut, then tighten them to the specified torque.

20 The remainder of refitting is a reversal of removal.

10 Fuel pressure sensor – removal and refitting

Removal

1 Pull up and remove the acoustic cover from the top of the engine.

2 Depressurise the fuel system as described earlier in this Section 4.

3 Disconnect the wiring plug for the fuel pressure sensor **(see illustration)**.

4 Unscrew the sensor. Be prepared for

9.14 Prise off the rubber seal (blue) and plastic collar (green)

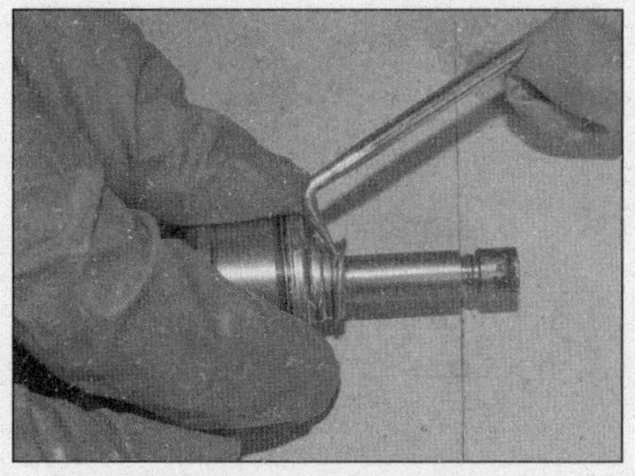
9.15a Remove the circlip...

9.15b ...the slide off the seat

10.3 Disconnect the pressure sensor wiring plug

11.4 Unplug the pump wiring connector

11.6 Separate the fuel supply pipe from the pump

11.7 Undo the retaining bolts and remove the pump

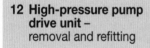

fluid spillage. Plug the openings to prevent contamination.

Refitting

5 Fit the sensor to the fuel rail, and tighten it to the specified torque.

6 The remainder of refitting is a reversal of removal.

11 High-pressure pump – removal and refitting

Removal

1 Disconnect the battery negative lead as described in Chapter 5 Section 4.

2 Pull up and remove the acoustic cover from the top of the engine.

11.9 Renew the O-ring seal

3 Depressurise the fuel system, as decscribed in Section 4.

4 Unlock and disconnect the wiring plug from the high-pressure pump **(see illustration)**.

5 Undo the unions and remove the fuel pipe between the pump and the fuel rail. Be prepared for fuel spillage.

6 Release the clips and disconnect the fuel supply pipe from the pump **(see illustration)**.

7 Gradually and evenly, slacken and remove the pump retaining bolts **(see illustration)**. Be prepare for oil spillage.

8 Discard the O-ring between the pump and cylinder head cover.

Refitting

9 Clean the mating surfaces of the pump and cylinder head cover. Install a new O-ring on the pump **(see illustration)**.

10 Prior to installing the pump, the cam lobe driving the pump must be turned to BDC (bottom dead centre). This is best achieved using a vernier caliper (or similar) inserted through the pump mounting hole, resting against the drive roller tappet. Rotate the crankshaft clockwise until the caliper/depth gauge shows the drive roller tappet is at its lowest point (BDC).

11 Manoeuvre the pump into position, then gradually, squarely and evenly, tighten the retaining bolts to their specified torque.

12 Reconnect the fuel supply pipe to the pump, and tighten the union to the specified torque.

13 Refit the fuel rail-to-pump pipe, and finger-tighten the union nuts.

14 Starting at the fuel rail, tighten the pipe union nuts to their specified torque.

15 Reconnect the high-pressure pump wiring plug.

16 The remainder of refitting is the reverse of removal.

12 High-pressure pump drive unit – removal and refitting

Removal

1 Remove the cylinder head valve cover, as described in Chapter 2A Section 6.

2 Remove the high-pressure fuel pump, as described in Section 11.

3 Undo the 10 retaining bolts and gently prise up the fuel pump drive unit from place **(see illustrations)**.

4 Remove the O-ring seal **(see illustration)**.

12.3a Remove the 10 retaining bolts...

12.3b ...and gently prise up the drive unit

12.4 Prise up the seal

13.6 Make sure the flexible exhaust pipe is braced

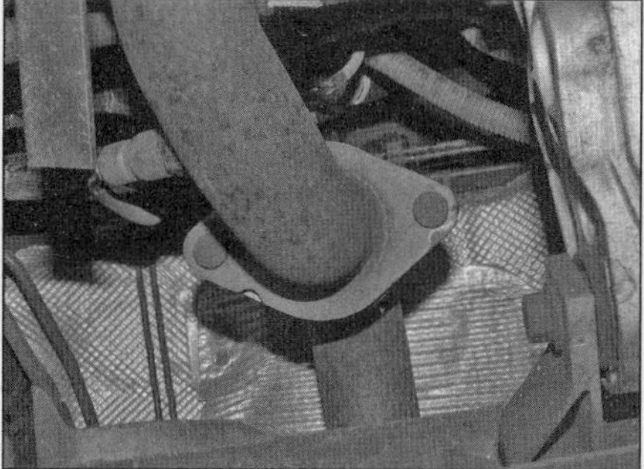
13.7 Separate the two halfs of the exhaust

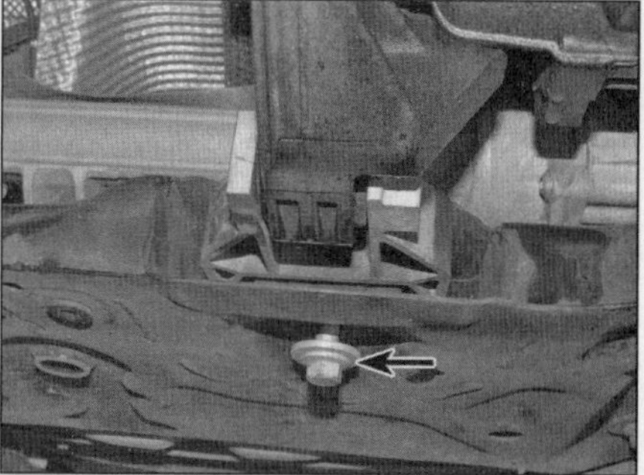
13.8 Remove the rear roll restrictor bolt

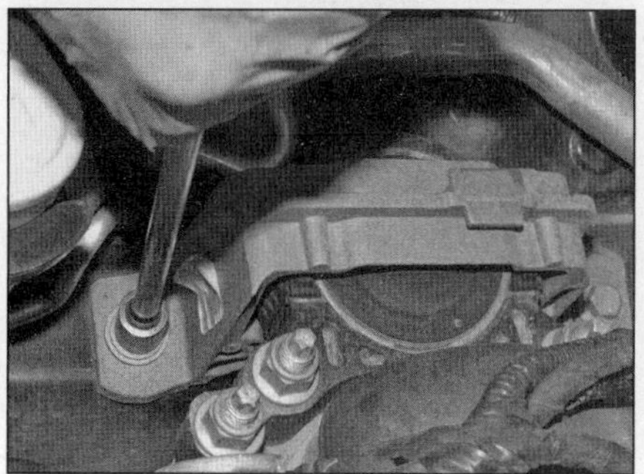
13.13 Unbolt the engine mounting

13.15 Undo the charge air cooler bolts

13.17 Manoeuvre the charge air cooler from place

Refitting

5 Clean up the drive unit mating faces.

6 Insert a new O-ring seal.

7 Apply Ford sealant WSS-M2G348-A11, then refit the fuel pump drive unit within 5 minutes. Retighten the bolts to the required torque.

8 The remainder of refitting is a reversal of removal.

13 Charge air cooler – removal and refitting

Removal

1 Have the air-conditioning refrigerant circuit evacuated by a suitably equipped repairer.

2 Lift up and remove the engine cover.

3 Disconnect the battery as described in Chapter 5 Section 3.

4 Drain the cooling system as described in Chapter 1A Section 34.

5 Undo the retaining bolts and remove the engine undertray.

6 Brace the exhaust flexible pipe using bracing bars and cable ties **(see illustration)**.

7 Unbolt the front section of the exhaust from the rear, and undo the two exhaust mounts **(see illustration)**.

8 Undo the bolt and remove the rear roll restrictor **(see illustration)**.

9 Unbolt the front of the propeller shaft, as described in Chapter 8 Section 12.

10 Unbolt and remove the air-conditioning pipe.

11 Disengage the 2 cooling pipes from the front of the charge air cooler.

12 Prise out the wiring holder from the edge of the charge air cooler.

13 Remove the 2 engine mounting-to-body retaining bolts **(see illustration)**.

14 Place a trolley jack underneath the engine and raise it by 50mm.

15 Undo the retaining bolts around the front of the charge air cooler **(see illustration)**.

16 Push the engine backwards by 70mm, and secure it.

17 Slide the charge air cooler forward from place **(see illustration)**.

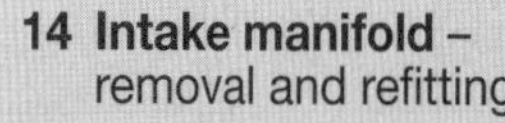

14 Intake manifold – removal and refitting

Note: *Refer to the warning note in Section 1 before proceeding.*

Intake manifold

Removal

1 Remove the charge air cooler, as described earlier in this Section 13.

2 Remove the alternator, as described in Chapter 5 Section 6.

3 Unplug the wiring connectors for the knock sensors at each end of the intake manifold, and the boost pressure sensor on top of it **(see illustrations)**.

14.3a Unplug the knock sensors...

14.3b ...and the boost pressure sensor

14.5 Remove the throttle body bracket

14.8 Remove the bolts to release the intake manifold

4 Unclip the female ends of the knock sensor plugs from each end of the intake manifold and set aside.

5 Undo the retaining bolts for the throttle body bracing bracket **(see illustration).**

16.7 Unplug the oxygen sensors

16.9 Disconnect the cooling pipe hoses

14.7 Squeeze together the sides of the collar and disconnect the breather pipe

14.9 Renew the manifold seals

6 Unclip the wiring looms from the intake manifold and move out of the way.

7 Squeeze together the sides of the collar, and pull the breather pipe from the top of the intake manifold **(see illustration).**

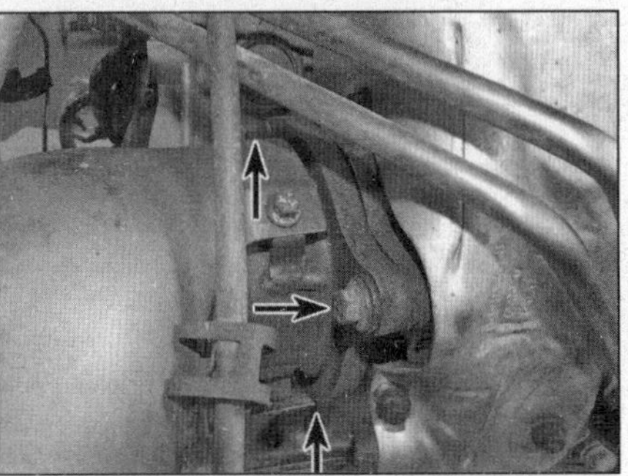
16.8 Slacken 2 bolts and remove the third, then remove the catalytic converter

16.10 Remove the bracket for the cooling pipes

8 Undo the retaining bolts (the bolts are all captive, so cannot be removed from the manifold) and manoeuvre the intake manifold from place **(see illustration).**

Refitting

9 Ensure the mating faces of the cylinder head and manifold are clean, then renew the manifold seals **(see illustration).**

10 Manoeuvre the manifold into position, then working from the centre outwards, tighten the retaining bolts to the specified torque.

11 The remainder of refitting is a reversal of removal.

15 Exhaust manifold – removal and refitting

1 The exhaust manifold is integral with the turbocharger. Refer to Section 16.

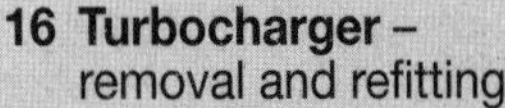

16 Turbocharger – removal and refitting

Removal

1 Slacken the right-hand front roadwheel bolts, raise the front of the vehicle and support it securely on axle stands (see *Jacking and vehicle support*). Remove the roadwheel.

2 Remove the windscreen scuttle panel, as described in Chapter 11 Section 12.

3 Drain the coolant as described in Chapter 1A Section 34.

4 Release the fasteners and remove the engine undershield.

5 Pull up and remove the acoustic cover from the top of the engine.

6 Remove the air filter assembly as described in Section 3.

7 Disconnect the wiring plugs from the exhaust oxygen sensors **(see illustration).**

8 Slacken the rearmost and bottom retaining bolts and remove the top one nearest the engine block, and manoeuvre the cataclytic converter from place **(see illustration).**

9 Release the clips and disconnect the hoses from the ends of the turbo cooling pipes **(see illustration).**

10 Undo the retaining bolt and manoeuvre the forwardmost cooling pipe bracket from place **(see illustration).**

11 Undo the retaining bolt and remove the middle mounting bracket for the cooling pipes **(see illustration).**

12 Undo the retaining bolt at each end and remove the cooling pipe from the turbocharger **(see illustration).** Discard the pipes, which must be replaced.

13 Undo the 2 retaining bolts, slacken the pipe clamp and manoeuvre the induction pipe from place **(see illustrations).**

14 Slacken the clamp and separate the turbo charge pipe from the turbo **(see illustration).**

15 Undo the 2 mounting bolts and disconnect

16.11 Remove the middle cooling pipe bracket

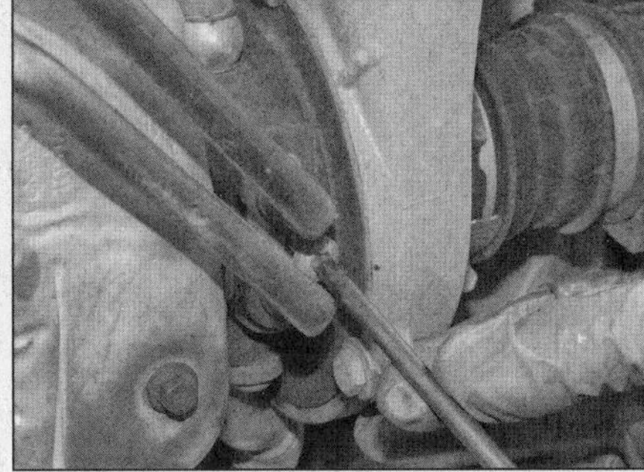

16.12 Undo the bolt and remove the pipes from the turbocharger

16.13a Undo the first retaining bolt...

16.13b ...then the second...

16.13c ...and finally the pipe clamp

16.14 Disconnect the turbo charge pipe

the 2 wiring plugs from the turbo charge pipe **(see illustrations)**.

16 Disconnect the breather pipe from the top of the oil separator and move out of the way **(see illustration)**.

17 Slacken the clamps and disconnect the charge pipe from the throttle body **(see illustration)**.

18 Release the clip and disconnect the turbo vacuum pipe **(see illustration)**.

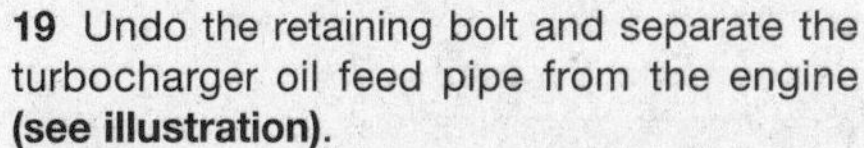

19 Undo the retaining bolt and separate the turbocharger oil feed pipe from the engine **(see illustration)**.

20 Remove the transfer case, as described in Chapter 8 Section 11.

16.15a Unplug the turbo pressure bypass valve...

16.15b ...then the MAP sensor...

16.15c ...and then the air temparature sensor

16.16 Disconnect the turbo breather pipe from the oil separator

16.17 Pull the pipe from the throttle body

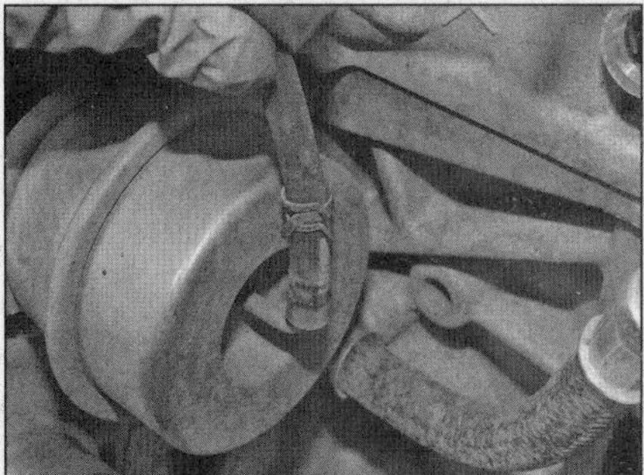

16.18 Release the clip and disconnect the vacuum pipe

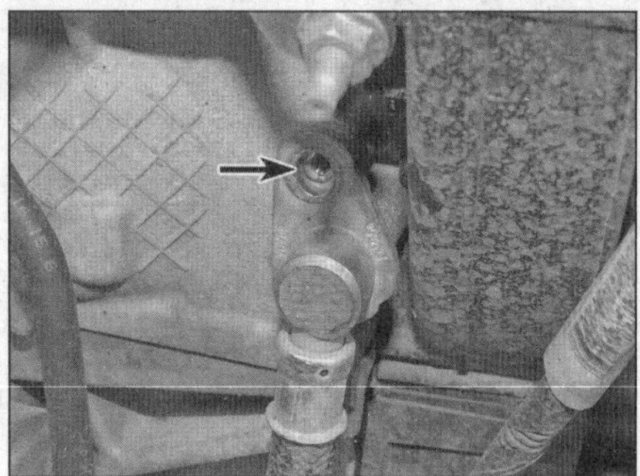
16.19 Turbocharger oil feed pipe bolt

16.21 Support the flexible pipe with a brace and cable ties

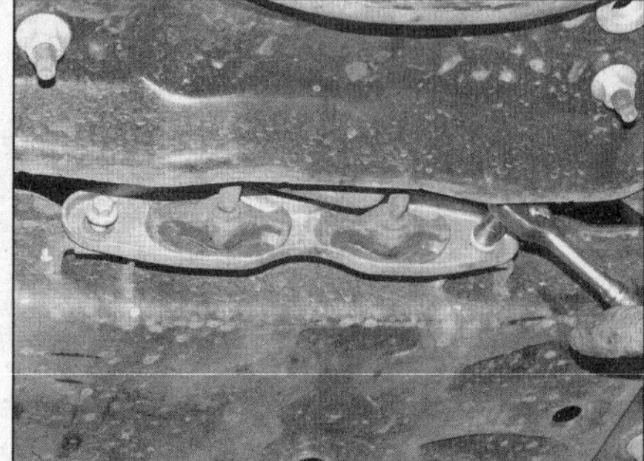
16.22 Unbolt and remove the exhaust mounts

16.23 Remove the bolts and disconnect the oil return pipe

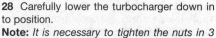

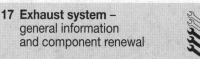

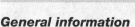

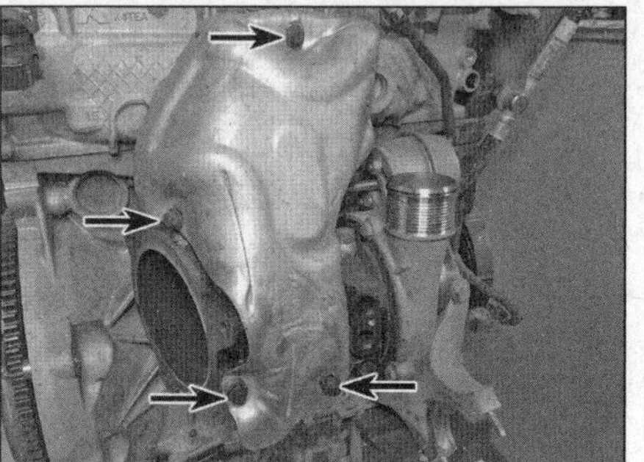
16.24 Remove the turbocharger heat shield

21 Brace the exhaust flexible pipe, to prevent damage **(see illustration)**.

22 Undo the retaining bolts and remove the exhaust mounts from beneath the car **(see illustration)**.

23 Undo the 3 retaining bolts and remove the turbo oil return pipe from place **(see illustration)**.

24 Undo the 4 retaining bolts and remove the turbo heat shield **(see illustration)**.

25 Undo the 4 retaining nuts and manoeuvre the turbocharger assembly from place **(see illustration)**. Discard the nuts and gasket, which must be replaced.

Refitting

26 Ensure the mating faces of the manifold and cylinder head are clean.

27 Position the new gasket over the locating studs on the cylinder head. Ensure the side of the gasket with a part number is against the cylinder head **(see illustration)**.

28 Carefully lower the turbocharger down in to position.

Note: *It is necessary to tighten the nuts in 3 stages to the specified torque. This process allows for the gasket to compress at each stage.*

29 The remainder of refitting is a reversal of removal.

17 Exhaust system – general information and component renewal

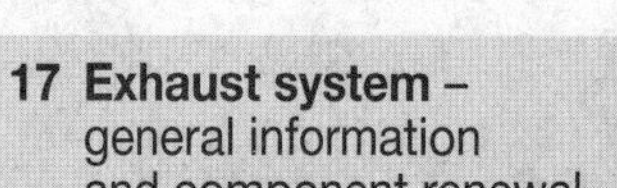

General information

Note: *Allow exhaust system components to cool before inspection or repair. Also, when working under the vehicle, make sure it is securely supported on axle stands (see Jacking and vehicle support).*

1 The exhaust system consists of the exhaust manifolds, catalytic converter, muffler, tailpipe and all connecting pipes, flanges and clamps. The exhaust system is isolated from the vehicle body and from chassis components by a series of rubber hangers. Periodically inspect these hangers for cracks or other signs of deterioration, replacing them as necessary.

2 Conduct regular inspections of the exhaust system to keep it safe and quiet. Look for any damaged or bent parts, open seams, holes, loose connections, excessive corrosion or other defects which could allow exhaust fumes to enter the vehicle. Do not repair deteriorated exhaust system components; replace them with new parts.

3 If the exhaust system components are extremely corroded, or rusted together, a cutting torch is the most convenient tool for removal. Consult a properly-equipped repairer. If a cutting torch is not available, you can use a hacksaw, or if you have compressed air, there are special pneumatic cutting chisels that can also be used. Wear safety goggles to protect your eyes from metal chips and wear work gloves to protect your hands.

4 Here are some simple guidelines to follow when repairing the exhaust system:

a) *Work from the back to the front when removing exhaust system components.*
b) *Apply penetrating oil to the exhaust system component fasteners to make them easier to remove.*
c) *Use new gaskets, hangers and clamps.*
d) *Apply anti-seize compound to the threads of all exhaust system fasteners during reassembly.*
e) *Be sure to allow sufficient clearance between newly installed parts and all points on the underbody to avoid overheating the floor pan and possibly damaging the interior carpet and insulation. Pay particularly close attention to the catalytic converter and heat shield.*

Catalytic converter renewal

5 Renewal of the catalytic converter is described in Chapter 6A Section 18.

16.25 Undo the nuts and remove the turbocharger

16.27 Make sure the gasket is the right way round, with the part number against the cylinder head

Chapter 4 Part B
Fuel and exhaust systems – diesel models

Contents

Degrees of difficulty

Easy, suitable for novice with little experience	Fairly easy, suitable for beginner with some experience	Fairly difficult, suitable for competent DIY mechanic	Difficult, suitable for experienced DIY mechanic	Very difficult, suitable for expert DIY or professional

Specifications

General

Engine codes: *	
1.5 litre	XWMA, XWMB
2.0-litre	XRMA, T7MA, T8MA

** For details of engine code location, see 'Vehicle identification'.*

System type	High-pressure direct injection with full electronic control, intercooler and turbocharger
Fuel system operating pressure	200 to 2500 bars (according to engine speed)
Idle speed	750 ± 20 rpm (controlled by ECU)
Engine cut-off speed	5500 rpm (controlled by ECU)
Injectors type	Piezo

Torque wrench settings

	Nm	lbf ft
Accumulator rail mounting bolts	22	16
Accumulator rail-to-fuel injector fuel pipe unions:		
Stage 1	17	13
Stage 2	28	21
Exhaust manifold nuts*	20	15
Fuel injector clamp bolt:		
Stage 1	8	6
Stage 2	Angle-tighten a further 120°	
Fuel injector clamp stud:		
Stage 1	10	7
Stage 2	Angle-tighten a further 70°	
Fuel pump-to-accumulator rail fuel pipe unions:		
Stage 1	17	13
Stage 2	28	21
High-pressure fuel pump mounting bolts	20	15
High-pressure fuel pump gear cassette:		
Stage 1	2	1
Stage 2	10	7
Inlet manifold bolts	10	7
Intercooler bolts	5	4
Throttle body bolts	10	7
Turbocharger-to-cylinder block bracket	22	16
Turbocharger-to-manifold clamp*	25	18
Turbocharger-to-particulate filter clamp*	15	10
Turbocharger oil feed pipe banjo bolt	40	30
Turbocharger oil return pipe	8	6

** Do not re-use*

1 General information and system operation

1 The fuel system consists of a rear-mounted fuel tank and fuel lift pump, a fuel filter, and an electronically-controlled high-pressure direct injection system, together with a turbocharger and intercooler.

2 The exhaust system is conventional, but to meet the latest emission levels a catalytic converter/particulate filter and an exhaust gas recirculation system are fitted to all models.

3 The injection system (generally known as a 'common rail' system) derives its name from the fact that a common rail (referred to as an accumulator rail), or fuel reservoir, is used to supply fuel to all the fuel injectors. Instead of an in-line or distributor type injection pump, which distributes the fuel directly to each injector, a high-pressure pump is used, which generates a very high fuel pressure (2000+ bars at high engine speed) in the accumulator rail. The accumulator rail stores fuel, and maintains a constant fuel pressure, with the aid of a pressure control valve. Each injector is supplied with high-pressure fuel from the accumulator rail, and the injectors are individually controlled via signals from the system electronic control unit (ECU). The injectors are electronically operated.

4 In addition to the various sensors used on models with a conventional fuel injection pump; common rail systems also have a fuel pressure sensor. The fuel pressure sensor allows the ECU to maintain the required fuel pressure, via the pressure control valve.

System operation

5 For the purposes of describing the operation of a common rail injection system, the components can be divided into three sub-systems; the low-pressure fuel system, the high-pressure fuel system and the electronic control system.

6 Details of the engine and emissions control systems are given in Chapter 6B.

Low-pressure fuel system

7 The low-pressure fuel system consists of the following components:

a) Fuel tank.
b) Fuel lift pump.
c) Fuel filter.
d) Low-pressure fuel lines.

8 The low-pressure system (fuel supply system) is responsible for supplying clean fuel to the high-pressure fuel system.

High-pressure fuel system

9 The high-pressure fuel system consists of the following components:

a) High-pressure fuel pump with pressure control valve.
b) High-pressure fuel accumulator rail.
c) Fuel injectors.
d) High-pressure fuel lines.

10 After passing through the fuel filter, the fuel reaches the high-pressure pump, which forces it into the accumulator rail. As diesel fuel has certain elasticity, the pressure in the accumulator rail remains constant, even though fuel leaves the rail each time one of the injectors operates. Additionally, a pressure control valve mounted on the high-pressure pump ensures that the fuel pressure is maintained within preset limits.

11 The pressure control valve is operated by the PCM (Powertrain Control Module). When the valve is opened, fuel is returned from the high-pressure pump to the tank, via the fuel return lines, and the pressure in the accumulator rail falls. To enable the PCM to trigger the pressure control valve correctly, a fuel pressure sensor measures the pressure in the accumulator rail.

12 The electronically-controlled fuel injectors are operated individually, via signals from the PCM, and each injector injects fuel directly into the relevant combustion chamber. The fact that high fuel pressure is always available allows very precise and highly flexible injection in comparison to a conventional injection pump: for example, combustion during the main injection process can be improved considerably by the pre-injection of a very small quantity of fuel.

System components

Fuel lift pump

13 The fuel lift pump and integral fuel gauge sender unit/level sensor is electrically operated, and is mounted in the fuel tank.

High-pressure pump

14 The high-pressure pump is mounted on the engine in the position normally occupied by the conventional distributor fuel injection pump. The pump is driven by the timing chain at the left-hand end of the engine, and is lubricated by the fuel, which it pumps.

15 The fuel lift pump forces the fuel into the high-pressure pump chamber, via a safety valve.

16 The high-pressure pump consists of three radially-mounted pistons and cylinders. The pistons are operated by an eccentric cam mounted on the pump drive spindle. As a piston moves down, fuel enters the cylinder through an inlet valve. When the piston reaches bottom dead centre (BDC), the inlet valve closes, and as the piston moves back up the cylinder, the fuel is compressed. When the pressure in the cylinder reaches the pressure in the accumulator rail, an outlet valve opens, and fuel is forced into the accumulator rail. When the piston reaches top dead centre (TDC), the outlet valve closes, due to the pressure drop, and the pumping cycle is repeated. The use of multiple cylinders provides a steady flow of fuel, minimising pulses and pressure fluctuations.

17 As the pump needs to be able to supply sufficient fuel under full-load conditions, it will supply excess fuel during idle and part-load conditions. This excess fuel is returned from the high-pressure circuit to the low-pressure circuit (to the tank) via the pressure control valve.

18 The pump incorporates a facility to effectively switch off one of the cylinders to improve efficiency and reduce fuel consumption when maximum pumping capacity is not required. When this facility is operated, a solenoid-operated needle holds the inlet valve in the relevant cylinder open during the delivery stroke, preventing the fuel from being compressed.

Accumulator rail

19 As its name suggests, the accumulator rail (also known as common rail) acts as an accumulator, storing fuel and preventing pressure fluctuations. Fuel enters the rail from the high-pressure pump, and each injector has its own connection to the rail. The fuel pressure sensor is mounted in the rail, and the rail also has a connection to the fuel pressure control valve on the pump.

Pressure control valve

20 The pressure control valve is operated by the PCM, and controls the system pressure. The valve is integral with the high-pressure pump and cannot be separated.

21 If the fuel pressure is excessive, the valve opens, and fuel flows back to the tank. If the pressure is too low, the valve closes, enabling the high-pressure pump to increase the pressure.

22 The valve is an electronically-operated ball valve. The ball is forced against its seat, against the fuel pressure, by a powerful spring, and also by the force provided by the electromagnet. The force generated by the electromagnet is directly proportional to the current applied to it by the PCM. The desired pressure can therefore be set by varying the current applied to the electromagnet. Any pressure fluctuations are damped by the spring.

Fuel pressure sensor

23 The fuel pressure sensor is mounted in the accumulator rail, and provides very precise information on the fuel pressure to the PCM.

Fuel injector

24 The injectors are mounted on the engine in a similar manner to conventional diesel fuel injectors. The injectors are Piezo crystal type, electronically-operated via signals from the PCM, and fuel is injected at the pressure existing in the accumulator rail. The injectors are high-precision instruments and are manufactured to very high tolerances.

PCM (Powertrain Control Module) and sensors

25 The PCM and sensors are described earlier in Chapter 6B.

Air inlet sensor and turbocharger

26 An airflow sensor is fitted downstream of the air filter to monitor the quantity of air supplied to the turbocharger. The air from the high-pressure side of the turbocharger is channelled through the intercooler. The turbochargers are of the variable nozzle geometry type.

2 Troubleshooting

Fuel pump

1 The fuel pump is located inside the fuel tank. Sit inside the vehicle with the windows closed, turn the ignition key to ON (not START) and listen for the sound of the fuel pump as it's briefly activated. You will only hear the sound for a second or two, but that sound indicates that the pump is working. Alternatively, have an assistant listen at the fuel filler cap.

2 If the pump does not operate, check all of the fuses and relays (see Chapter 12 Section 3).

3 If the fuses are okay, check the wiring back to the fuel pump. If the wiring is okay, the fuel pump control module may be defective. If the pump runs continuously with the ignition key in the ON position, the PCM may be defective. Have the circuit checked by a dealer or suitably equipped repairer.

Fuel injection system

Note: *The following procedure is based on the assumption that the fuel pump is working and the fuel pressure is adequate.*

4 Check all electrical wiring plugs that are related to the system. Check the earth wire connections for tightness (see Chapter 12 Section 2).

5 Verify that the battery is fully charged (see Chapter 5 Section 3).

6 Inspect the air filter element (see Chapter 4A Section 3).

7 Check all fuses and relays related to the fuel system (see Chapter 12 Section 3).

8 Check the air intake system between the throttle body and the intake manifold for air leaks. Also inspect the condition of all vacuum hoses connected to the intake manifold and to the throttle body.

9 Remove the air intake duct from the throttle body and look for dirt, carbon, varnish, or other residue in the throttle body, particularly around the throttle plate. If it's dirty, clean it with carburettor cleaner, a toothbrush and a clean rag.

10 With the engine running, place an automotive stethoscope against each injector, one at a time, and listen for a clicking sound that indicates operation **(see illustration)**.

Warning: Stay clear of the drivebelt and any rotating or hot components.

11 If you can hear the injectors operating, but the engine is misfiring, the electrical circuits are functioning correctly, but the injectors might be dirty or blocked. Try a commercial injector cleaning product (available at auto parts suppliers). If cleaning the injectors doesn't help, they may need replacing.

12 If the injector is not operating, the circuit between the PCM and the injector might be faulty.

3 High-pressure diesel injection system – special information

Warnings and precautions

1 It is essential to observe strict precautions when working on the fuel system components, particularly the high-pressure side of the system. Before carrying out any operations on the fuel system, refer to the precautions given in *Safety first!* at the beginning of this manual, and to the following additional information.

a) Do not carry out any repair work on the high-pressure fuel system unless you are competent to do so, have all the necessary tools and equipment required, and are aware of the safety implications involved.

b) Before starting any repair work on the fuel system, wait at least 30 seconds after switching off the engine to allow the fuel circuit pressure to reduce.

c) Never work on the high-pressure fuel system with the engine running.

d) Keep well clear of any possible source of fuel leakage, particularly when starting the engine after carrying out repair work. A leak in the system could cause an extremely high pressure jet of fuel to escape, which could result in severe personal injury.

e) Never place your hands or any part of your body near to a leak in the high-pressure fuel system.

f) Do not use steam cleaning equipment or compressed air to clean the engine or any of the fuel system components.

Procedures and information

2 Strict cleanliness must be observed at all times when working on any part of the fuel system. This applies to the working area in general, the person doing the work, and the components being worked on.

3 Before working on the fuel system components, they must be thoroughly cleaned with a suitable degreasing fluid. Specific cleaning products may be obtained from Ford dealers. Alternatively, a suitable brake cleaning fluid may be used. Cleanliness is particularly important when working on the fuel system connections at the following components:

a) Fuel filter.

b) High-pressure fuel pump.

2.10 An automotive stethoscope is used to listen to the fuel injectors in operation

c) Accumulator rail.

d) Fuel injectors.

e) High-pressure fuel pipes.

4 After disconnecting any fuel pipes or components, the open union or orifice must be immediately sealed to prevent the entry of dirt or foreign material. Plastic plugs and caps in various sizes are available in packs from motor factors and accessory outlets, and are particularly suitable for this application **(see illustration)**. Fingers cut from disposable rubber gloves should be used to protect components such as fuel pipes, fuel injectors and wiring connectors, and can be secured in place using elastic bands. Suitable gloves of this type are available at no cost from most petrol station forecourts.

5 Whenever any of the high-pressure fuel pipes are disconnected or removed, new pipes must be obtained for refitting.

6 On the completion of any repair on the high-pressure fuel system, Ford recommend the use of a leak-detecting compound. This is a powder which is applied to the fuel pipe unions and connections, and turns white when dry. Any leak in the system will cause the product to darken indicating the source of the leak.

7 The torque wrench settings given in the Specifications must be strictly observed when tightening component mountings and connections. This is particularly important when tightening the high-pressure fuel pipe unions. To enable a torque wrench to be used on the fuel pipe unions, two crow-foot adapters are required. Suitable alternatives are available from motor factors and accessory outlets **(see illustration)**.

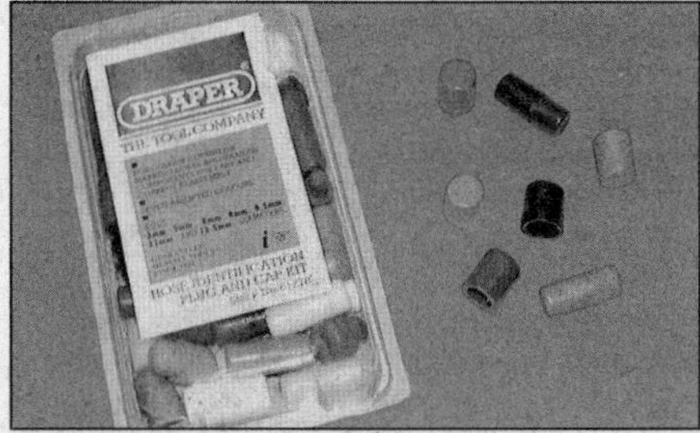

3.4 Typical plastic plug and cap set for sealing disconnected fuel pipes and components

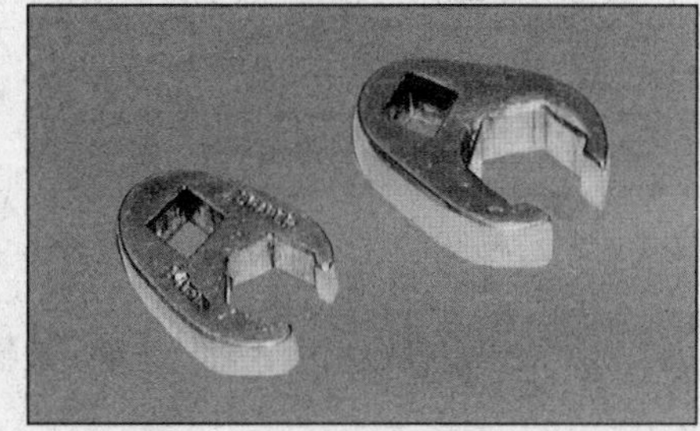

3.7 Two crow-foot adapters will be necessary for tightening the fuel pipe unions

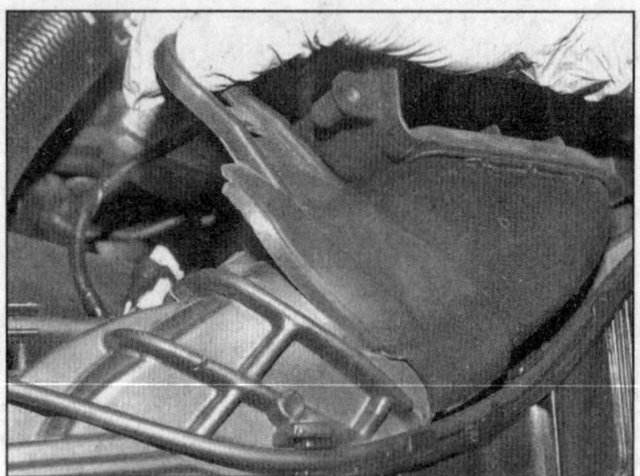

6.2 Undo the strap to release the intake duct

6.3 Slacken clamp to free the outlet duct

4 Fuel system – depressurisation

Warning: Refer to the warning note in Section 1 before proceeding.

Depressurisation

Warning: The following procedure will merely relieve the pressure in the fuel system – remember that fuel will still be present in the system components and take precautions accordingly before disconnecting any of them.

1 The fuel system referred to in this Section is defined as the tank-mounted fuel pump, the fuel filter (where fitted), the fuel injectors, high-pressure pump (where applicable), the fuel rail and the pipes of the fuel pipes between these components. All these contain fuel, which will be under pressure while the engine is running, and/or while the ignition is switched on. The pressure will remain for some time after the ignition has been switched off, and must be relieved in a controlled fashion when any of these components are disturbed for servicing work.

2 To relieve the system pressure, start the engine and allow it to idle. In the engine bay, remove the fuel pump fuse and allow the engine to stall. Crank the engine for 5 seconds to fully depressurise the system.

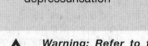

6.4 Disconnect the air mass meter wiring plug

6.5a Unclip the wiring from the side of the air cleaner housing...

5 Fuel system – priming and bleeding

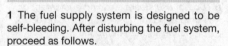

1 The fuel supply system is designed to be self-bleeding. After disturbing the fuel system, proceed as follows.

2 Switch on the ignition, and leave it for approximately 1 minute. Do not attempt to start the engine. During this time the electric fuel pump is activated and the system vented.

3 Depress the accelerator pedal to the floor then start the engine as normal (this may take longer than usual, especially if the fuel system has been allowed to run dry – operate the starter in ten second bursts with 5 seconds rest in between each operation). Run the engine at a fast idle speed for a minute or so to purge any remaining trapped air from the fuel lines. After this time the engine should idle smoothly at a constant speed.

4 If the engine idles roughly, then there is still some air trapped in the fuel system. Increase the engine speed again for another minute or so then recheck the idle speed. Repeat this procedure as necessary until the engine is idling smoothly.

5 If the engine still fails to start, the system must be primed using Ford diagnostic equipment. Entrust this task to a Ford dealer or suitably equipped repairer.

6.5b ...then lift away the housing itself

6 Air cleaner assembly – removal and refitting

Removal

1 If desired, remove the air filter as described in Chapter 1B Section 29.

2 Unstrap the clip and remove the air intake duct **(see illustration)**.

3 Release the clamp securing the air outlet duct to the air cleaner housing **(see illustration)**.

4 Disconnect the air mass meter wiring plug **(see illustration)**.

5 Pull the air cleaner housing upwards from place **(see illustrations)**.

Refitting

6 Refitting is a reversal of the removal procedure, ensuring that all hoses and ducts are properly reconnected and correctly seated and, where necessary, securely held by their retaining clips. Do not use any grease or lubricant when refitting the air hoses/ducts.

7 Fuel pipes and fittings – general information and disconnection

1 Disconnect the battery negative lead as described in Chapter 5 Section 4.

2 The fuel supply pipe connects the fuel pump in the fuel tank to the fuel rail on the engine.

3 Whenever you're working under the vehicle, be sure to inspect all fuel and evaporative emission pipes for leaks, kinks, dents and other damage. Always replace a damaged fuel pipe immediately.

4 If you find signs of dirt in the pipes during disassembly, disconnect all pipes and blow them out with compressed air. Inspect the fuel strainer on the fuel pump pick-up unit for damage and deterioration.

Steel tubing

5 It is critical that the fuel pipes be replaced with pipes of equivalent type and specification.

6 Some steel fuel pipes have threaded fittings. When loosening these fittings, hold the stationary fitting with a spanner while turning the union nut.

Plastic tubing

Warning: When removing or installing plastic fuel tubing, be careful not to bend or twist it too

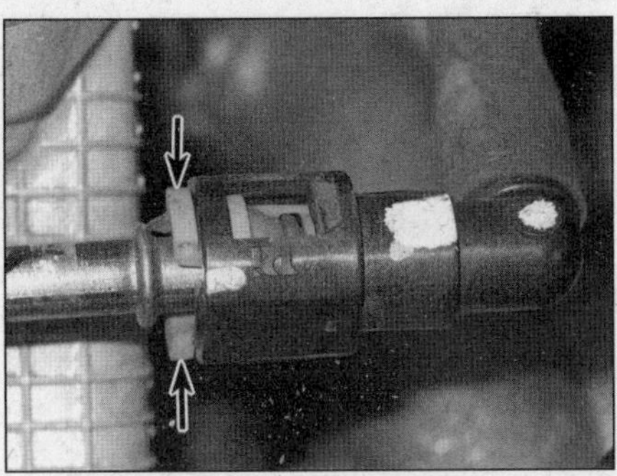

7.10a Two-tab type fitting; depress both tabs with your fingers, then pull the fuel pipe and the fitting apart

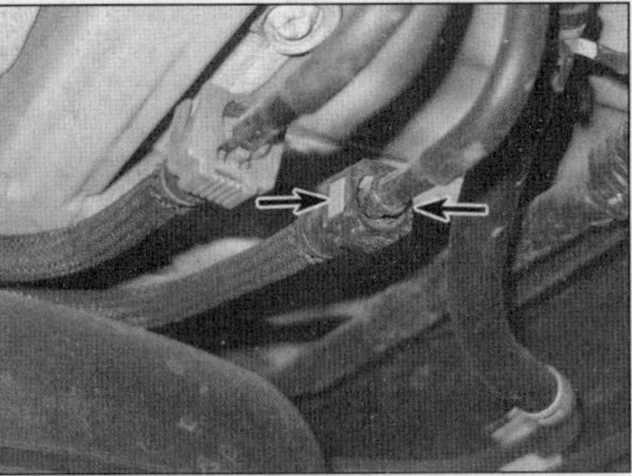

7.10b On this type of fitting, depress the two buttons on opposite sides of the fitting, then pull it off the fuel pipe

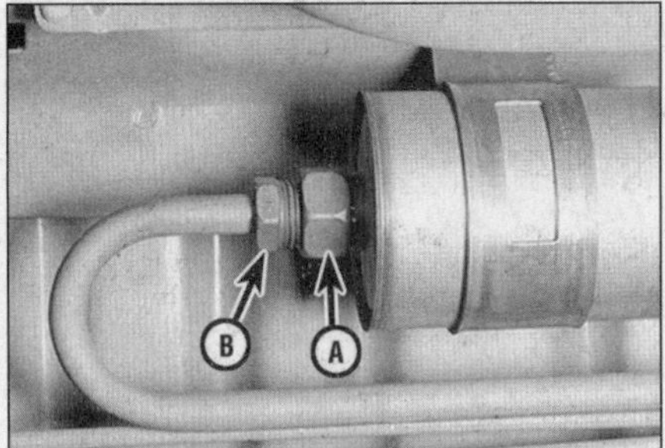

7.10c Threaded fuel pipe fitting; hold the stationary portion of the pipe or component (A) while loosening the union nut (B) with a flare-nut spanner

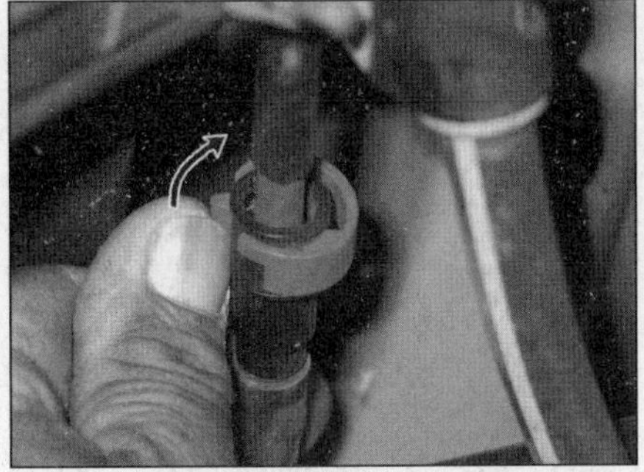

7.10d Plastic collar-type fitting; rotate the outer part of the fitting

7.10e Metal collar quick-connect fitting; pull the end of the retainer off the fuel pipe and disengage the other end from the female side of the fitting...

7.10f ... insert a fuel pipe separator tool into the female side of the fitting, push it into the fitting and pull the fuel pipe off the pipe

much, which can damage it. Also, plastic fuel tubing is NOT heat resistant, so keep it away from excessive heat.

7 When replacing fuel system plastic tubing, use only original equipment replacement plastic tubing.

Flexible hoses

8 When replacing fuel system flexible hoses, use original equipment replacements, or hose to the same specification.

9 Don't route fuel hoses (or metal pipes) within 100 mm of the exhaust system or within 280 mm of the catalytic converter/particulate filter. Make sure that no rubber hoses are installed directly against the vehicle, particularly in places where there is any vibration. If allowed to touch some vibrating part of the vehicle, a hose can easily become chafed and it might start leaking. A good rule of thumb is to maintain a minimum of 8.0 mm clearance around a hose (or metal pipe) to prevent contact with the vehicle underbody.

Disconnecting Fuel pipe Fittings

10 Typical fuel pipe fittings:

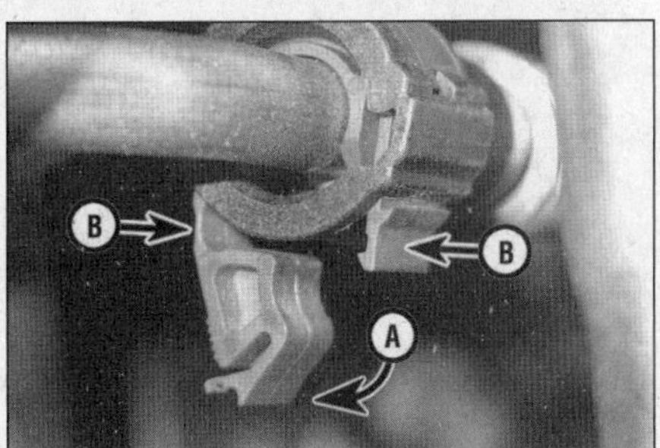
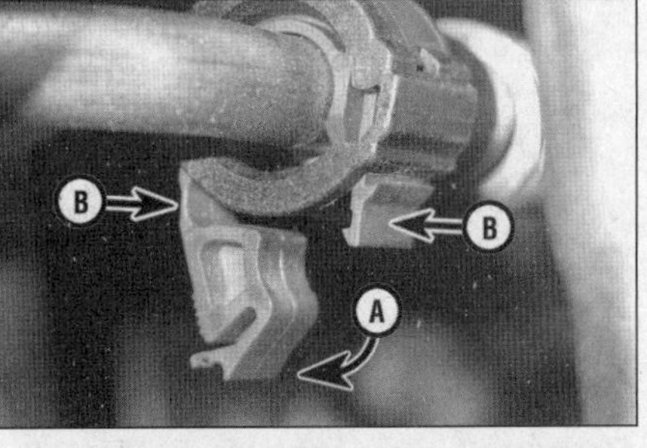

7.10g Some fittings are secured by lock tabs. Release the lock tab (A) and rotate it to the fully-opened position, squeeze the two smaller lock tabs (B)...

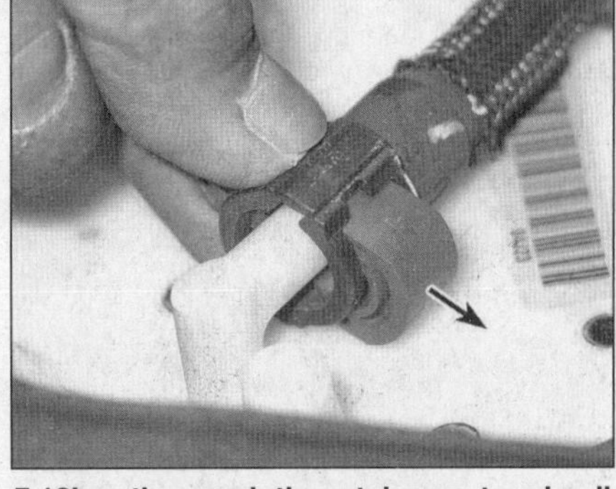

7.10h ... then push the retainer out and pull the fuel pipe off the pipe

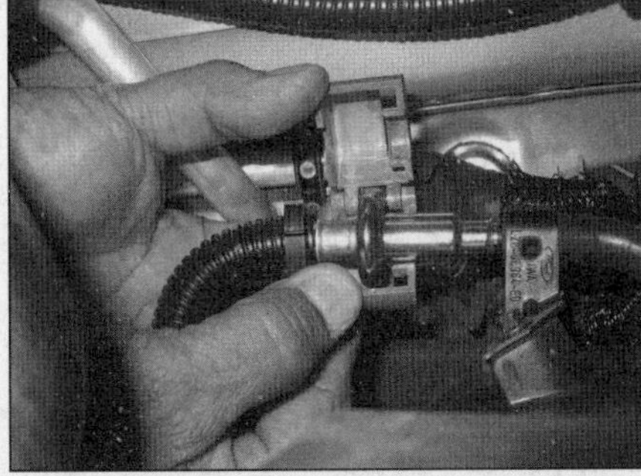

7.10i Spring-lock coupling; remove the safety cover, install a coupling release tool and close the tool around the coupling...

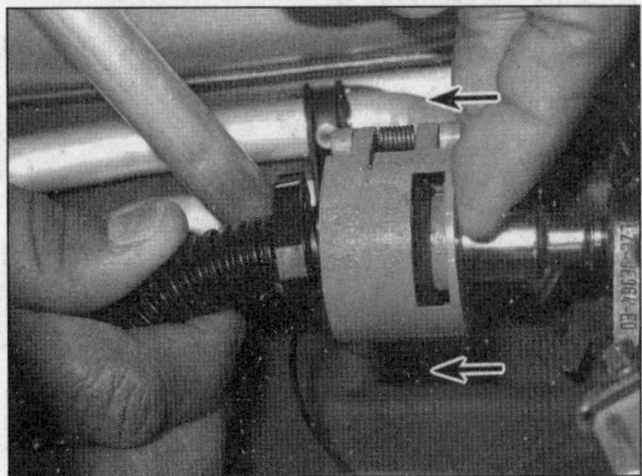

7.10j ... push the tool into the fitting, then pull the two pipes apart

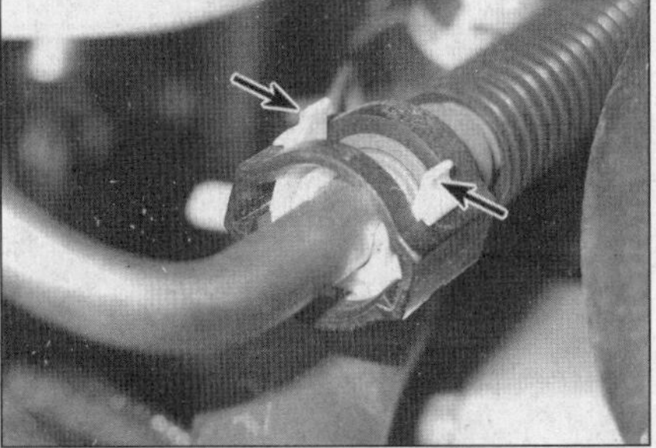

7.10k Hairpin clip type fitting: push the legs of the retainer clip together, then push the clip down all the way until it stops and pull the fuel pipe off the pipe

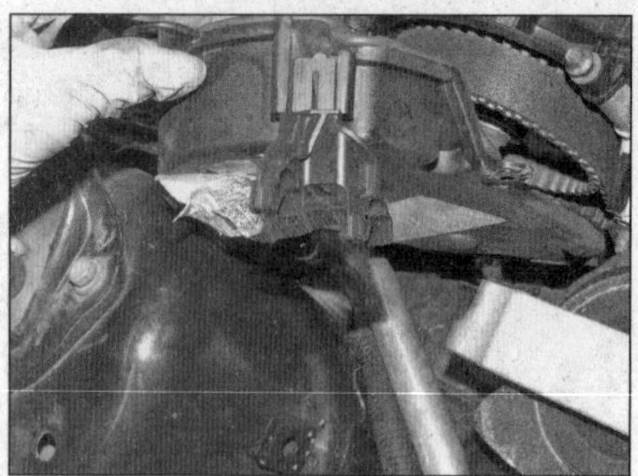
11.6 Move the timing belt cover aside

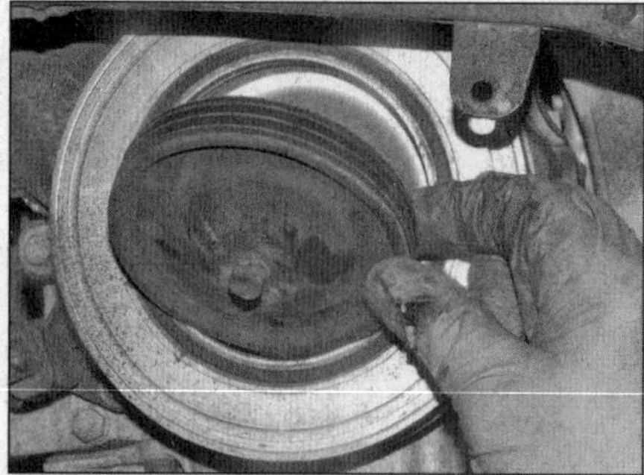
11.7 Pull away the crankshaft pulley cover

11.9a Disconnect the wiring plug...

11.9b ...and unbolt the air intake pipe

11.10 Remove the rubber cover from the fuel pump

11.11 Move the intercooler pipe out of the way

8 Fuel lift pump – removal and refitting

The diesel fuel lift pump is located in the same position as the conventional fuel pump on petrol models, and the removal and refitting procedures are virtually identical. Refer to Chapter 4A Section 6.

9 Fuel level sensor – removal and refitting

The fuel level sensor is located in the same position as the unit fitted to petrol models, and the removal and refitting procedures are virtually identical. Refer to Chapter 4A Section 6.

10 Fuel tank – removal and refitting

Refer to Chapter 4A Section 7.

11 High-pressure fuel pump – removal and refitting

Warning: Refer to the information contained in Section 3 before proceeding.

Removal

2.0-litre engine

1 Drain the cooling system as described in Chapter 1B Section 36.

2 Remove the air cleaner assembly as described in Section 6.

3 Remove the auxiliary drivebelt as decribed in Chapter 1B Section 32.

4 Unclip and move the fuel pipes at the right-hand end of the engine to one side.

5 Unclip the wiring harness from the rear edge of the upper timing belt cover.

6 Undo the upper 2 bolts and move the top part of the timing belt cover to one side **(see illustration)**.

7 Remove the rubber cover from the crankshaft pulley **(see illustration)**.

8 Use a socket and turn the crankshaft (clockwise only), then use Ford special tool 303-1667 or an 8 mm drill bit to lock the camshaft in place as described in Chapter 2C Section 5.

9 Disconnect the wiring plug, then undo the 3 retaining bolts (1 at the front and 2 at the rear) and remove the air intake pipe from place **(see illustrations)**.

10 Pull away the rubber fuel pump cover **(see illustration)**.

11 Unbolt the left-hand intercooler pipe and move downwards out of the way below the battery carrier **(see illustration)**.

12 Undo the 4 retaining bolts from the fuel pump bracket (access behind is extremely limited) and remove. Unplug the wiring connector that is routed through the bracket as it becomes available **(see illustrations)**.

13 Place a rag below the fuel pipes to soak up any spilled fuel **(see illustration)**.

14 Prise out the clips and detach the fuel pipes from the pump **(see illustration)**.

15 Undo the union nut and disconnect the

11.12a Remove the retaining bolts and detach the bracket

11.12b Disconnect the wiring plug

11.13 Put a rag below the fuel pipes

11.14 Disconnect the fuel pipes from the pump

11.15 Disconnect the high-pressure pipe

11.16 Undo the bolts and remove the pump

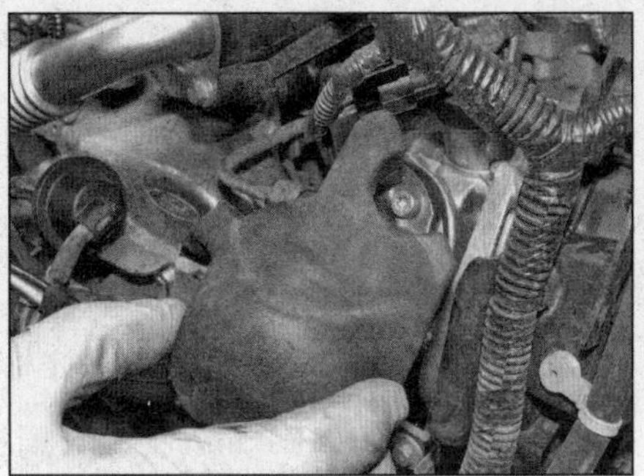
11.23 Remove the rubber pump guard

11.24 Disconnect the wiring plugs and fuel pipes

high-pressure fuel pipe from the pump **(see illustration)**.

16 Undo the 3 mounting bolts and manoeuvre the pump from place **(see illustration)**.

1.5-litre engine

17 Drain the coolant as described in Chapter 1B Section 36.

18 Remove the windscreen cowl as described in Chapter 11 Section 12.

19 Remove the timing belt as described in Chapter 2B Section 7.

20 Undo the retaining bolt and move the EGR bypass valve solenoid to one side.

21 Undo the 2 retaining bolts and move the cylinder block coolant drain out of the way.

22 Use a suitable drill bit or pin to stop the oil pump pulley rotating, then undo the central bolt and manoeuvre the pulley from place.

23 Working at the rear of the engine, remove the rubber guard from around the high-pressure pump **(see illustration)**.

24 Disconnect any wiring plugs from the pump, then disconnect the fuel supply hose and the metal high-pressure fuel pipe **(see illustration)**. Discard the pipe – a new one must be fitted upon reassembly.

25 Undo the 3 retaining bolts and manoeuvre the pump from place.

Refitting

26 Ensure the pump and cylinder block mating surfaces are clean, then align the keyway on the pump shaft with the key in the tapered bore in the pump drive sprocket.

27 Fit a new O-ring seal, then offer the pump into position.

28 Engage the shaft with the drive sprocket. Ensure the key and keyway engage correctly.

29 Tighten the bolts securing the pump to the required torque.

30 Thereafter, refitting is a reversal of removal, noting the following:

a) Tighten all fasteners to their specified torque where given.
b) Reconnect the battery negative lead as described in Chapter 5 Section 4.
c) Refill the cooling system as described in Chapter 1B Section 36.

12 High-pressure fuel pump gear cassette – removal and refitting

Removal

1 Remove the the high-pressure fuel pump as described in this Section 11.

2 Undo the 4 mounting bolts and manoeuvre the gear cassette from place **(see illustration)**. Discard the bolts because they must be replaced.

3 Use a magnet to remove the drive from the cylinder head **(see illustration)**.

Refitting

4 Refitting is a reversal of removal, ensuring that you fit a new gasket.

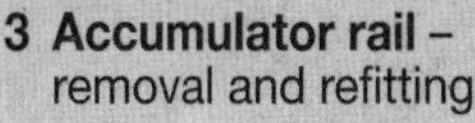

13 Accumulator rail – removal and refitting

Warning: Refer to the information contained in Section 3 before proceeding.

Removal

Note: *A complete new set of high-pressure fuel pipes will be required for refitting.*

12.2 Remove the bolts to detach the cassette

12.3 The drive can be removed using a magnet

13.4 Disconnect the sensor wiring plug

13.5 Slacken the high-pressure pipe unions

2.0-litre engine

1 Disconnect the battery negative lead as described in Chapter 5 Section 4.

2 Pull up and remove the plastic cover from the top of the engine.

3 Displace all the pipes and wiring on top of the engine, as described in Section 14.

4 Disconnect the wiring plug for the fuel pressure sensor **(see illustration)**.

5 Use a spanner to slacken unions, and remove the high-pressure fuel pipes between the accumulator and the injectors. Discard the pipes, because they must be replaced **(see illustration)**.

6 Undo the 2 mounting bolts and remove the fuel (accumulator) rail from place.

1.5-litre engine

7 Remove the starter motor as described in Chapter 5 Section 7.

8 Disconnect the battery negative lead as described in Chapter 5 Section 4.

9 Remove the windscreen grille cowl as described in Chapter 11 Section 12.

10 Remove the air cleaner as described in Section 6.

11 Slacken the clamps, undo the retaining bolts/nuts and remove the air intake ducting assembly from the top of the engine.

12 Remove the fuel filter as described in Chapter 1B Section 28 then undo the retaining bolts and remove the fuel filter mounting bracket.

13 Remove the EGR valve assembly as described in Chapter 6B Section 18.

14 Undo the bolts/nut and remove the throttle body/duct assembly from the intake manifold.

15 Undo the unions and remove the high pressure pipes from the accumulator (fuel) rail.

16 Undo the retaining bolts and remove the fuel rail.

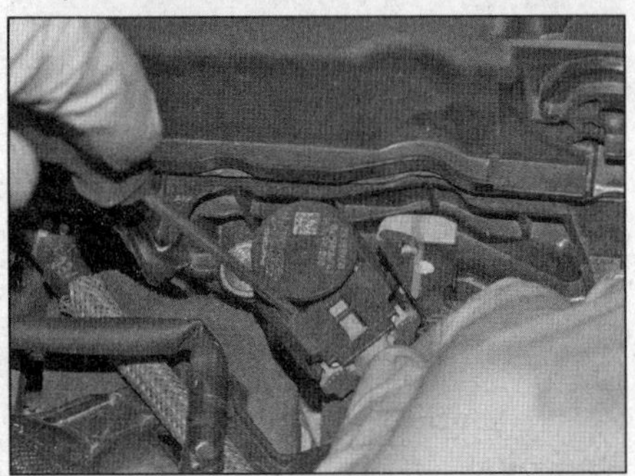
14.2 Disconnect the injector wiring plugs

14.3 Unclip the loom and move out of the way

14.4 Undo the 3 bolts and remove the fuel filter protection bracket

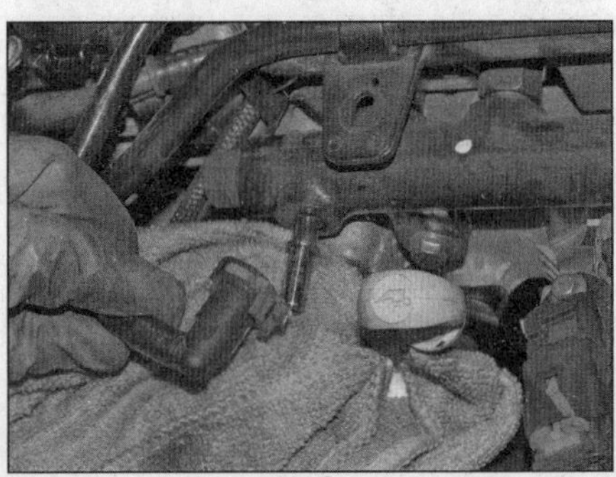
14.5 Detach the fuel pipes from the filter and fuel rail

All engines

17 Plug the openings in the accumulator rail and fuel pump to prevent dirt ingress.

Note: *The fuel pressure sensor on the accumulator rail must not be removed.*

Refitting

18 Locate the accumulator rail in position, refit and tighten the mounting bolts to the specified torque.

19 Fit the high-pressure pipes to the injectors, accumulator and pump. Only finger-tighten the unions at this stage. Refit the rubber mountings where applicable.

20 Tighten the high-pressure pipe unions to the specified torque in the following order:

a) Accumulator
b) Pump
c) Injectors

21 The remainder of refitting is a reversal of removal, noting the following points:

a) Ensure all wiring connectors and harnesses are correctly refitting and secured.
b) Reconnect the battery as described in Chapter 5 Section 4.
c) Observing the precautions listed in Section 3, start the engine and allow it to idle. Check for leaks at the high-pressure fuel pipe unions with the engine idling. If satisfactory, increase the engine speed to 3000 rpm and check again for leaks. Take the car for a short road test and check for leaks once again on return. If any leaks are detected, obtain and fit additional new high-pressure fuel pipes as required.
d) Do not attempt to cure even the slightest leak by further tightening of the pipe unions.

14 Fuel injectors – removal and refitting

Warning: Refer to the information contained in Section 3 before proceeding.

Removal

1 Pull up the plastic cover from the top of the engine, then undo the screws and remove the sound insulation material above the injectors.

2 Prise up the locking catches, then disconnect the wiring plugs for the injectors **(see illustration)**.

3 Disconnect all wiring plugs and unclip all mounting clips holding the wiring loom across the top of the engine **(see illustration)**, and move to one side.

4 Undo the retaining bollts and remove the protection bracket from the top of the fuel filter **(see illustration)**.

5 Disconnect the pipes from the fuel filter and fuel rail **(see illustration)**.

Note: *Have a rag handy to catch any excess fuel.*

6 Raise the locking tabs and disconnect the fuel return pipes from the injectors **(see illustration)**.

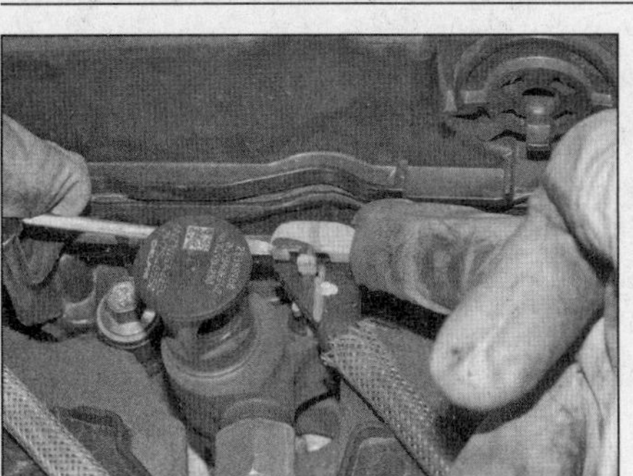
14.6 Raise the tabs to detach the pipes

14.7 Move the fuel pipes out of the way

14.8 Displace the turbocharger actuator vacuum pipe

14.9 Undo the bolts and remove the shroud

14.10 Undo the fuel pipe using a 17 mm spanner

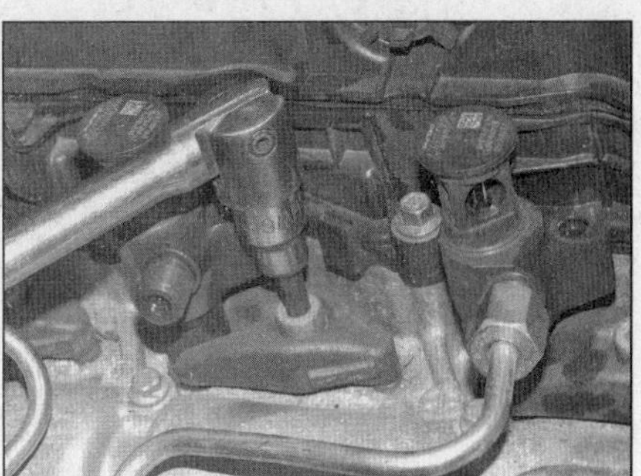
14.11 Undo the injector retaining bolt

7 Displace the fuel pipes from the top of the engine **(see illustration)**.

8 Detach the turbocharger actuator vacuum pipe and move out of the way **(see illustration)**.

9 Undo the 5 mounting bolts and lift the fuel pipe shroud out of the way **(see illustration)**.

10 Using a 17 mm spanner, undo the fuel pipe from the injector **(see illustration)**. Discard the pipe – new ones will be required upon reassembly.

11 Use an Allen key to undo the fuel injector mounting bolt **(see illustration)**.

12 Remove the injector from place, then discard the sealing washer **(see illustrations)**.

Refitting

13 Ensure the injectors and seats in the cylinder head are clean and dry.

14 Fit new sealing washers to the injectors, apply a little high-temperature anti-seize grease to the injector stems and refit them.

15 Fit the new injector pipes, and tighten the unions finger tight, then to the specified torque.

16 The remainder of refitting is a reversal of removal, noting the following points:

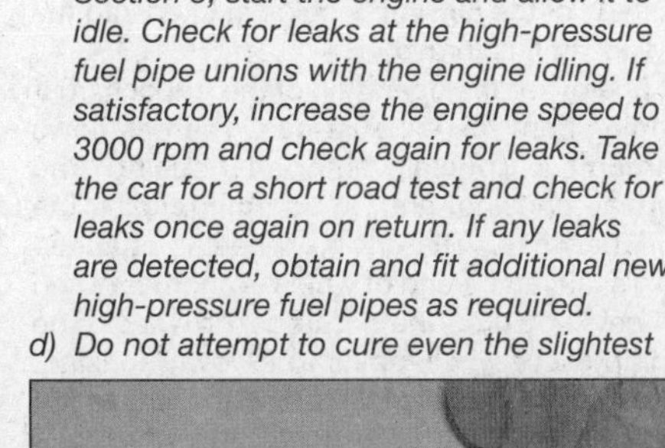

a) *Ensure all wiring connectors and harnesses are correctly refitting and secured.*
b) *Reconnect the battery as described in Chapter 5 Section 4.*
c) *Observing the precautions listed in Section 3, start the engine and allow it to idle. Check for leaks at the high-pressure fuel pipe unions with the engine idling. If satisfactory, increase the engine speed to 3000 rpm and check again for leaks. Take the car for a short road test and check for leaks once again on return. If any leaks are detected, obtain and fit additional new high-pressure fuel pipes as required.*
d) *Do not attempt to cure even the slightest leak by further tightening of the pipe unions.*

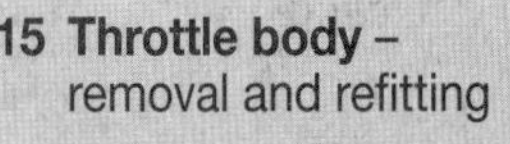

15 Throttle body – removal and refitting

Removal

2.0-litre engine

1 Remove the plastic cover from the top of the engine.

2 Disconnect the battery as described in Chapter 5 Section 4.

3 Note their fitted positions, then disconnect any wiring plugs from the throttle body.

4 Undo the 4 retaining screws and detach the throttle body from the intake elbow **(see illustration)**. Discard the seal.

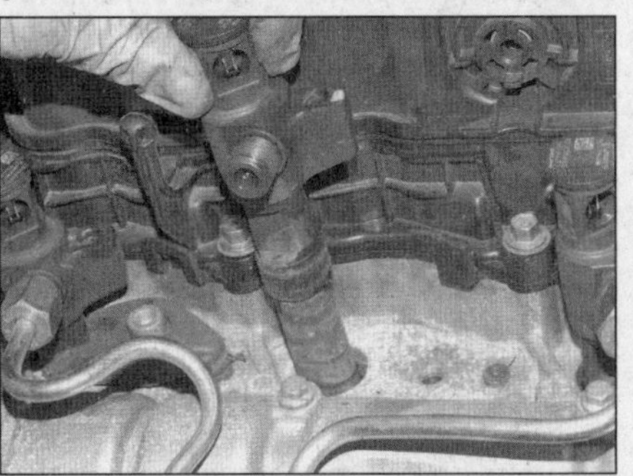
14.12a Take out the fuel injector...

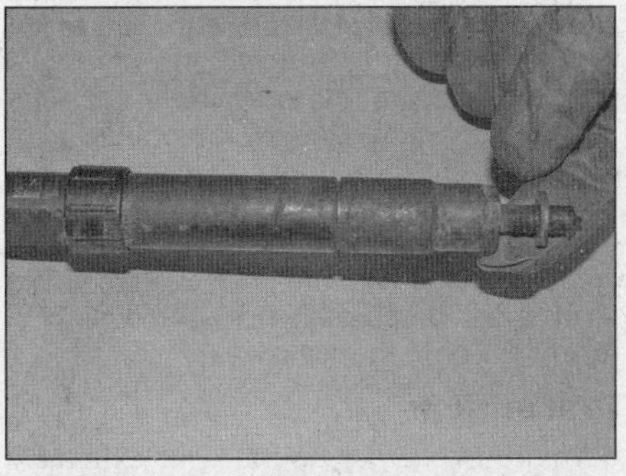
14.12b ...and discard the sealing washer

15.4 Remove the retaining screws and sepaarte the throttle body from the elbow

15.5 Disconnect the lower wiring plug

5 Disconnect the bottom wiring plug as it becomes available **(see illustration)**.

1.5-litre engine

6 Slacken the clamp and disconnect the intercooler pipe from the throttle body.
7 Disconnect the wiring plug, undo the 4 retaining bolts and remove the throttle body **(see illustration)**. The lower, left-hand bolt is accessed from the rear.

Refitting

8 Renew the seal, then refit the throttle body to the manifold. Tighten the retaining bolts to the specified torque.
9 The remainder of refitting is a reversal of removal.

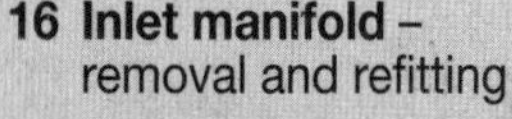

16 Inlet manifold – removal and refitting

Removal

1 Disconnect the battery negative lead as described in Chapter 5 Section 4.
2 Pull the plastic cover on the top of the engine upwards from its mountings.
3 Remove the electric cooling fan and shroud as described in Chapter 3 Section 8.
4 Raise the front of the vehicle and support it securely on axle stands (see *Jacking and vehicle support*). Release the fasteners and remove the engine undershield.
5 Note their fitted positions/routing, then disconnect the following from around the intake manifold:

15.7 Throttle body retaining bolts

a) *Vacuum hose from the EGR valve.*
b) *Wiring harness from the left-hand end of the manifold.*
c) *Battery positive cable from the alternator, then unclip the cable from the holder.*
d) *Fuel supply and return pipes retaining clip screw*
e) *Pre-heating control unit wiring plug.*
f) *Coolant temperature sensor wiring plug.*

6 Release the clips and move the wiring harness tray on the top of the engine to one side **(see illustration 14.3)**.
7 Undo the bolts securing the manifold and EGR cooler.
8 Pull the EGR pipe from place. Renew the O-ring seal.
9 Manoeuvre the inlet manifold upwards from place.

Refitting

10 Refitting is a reversal of removal, remembering to renew the manifold seals. Tighten the retaining bolts to the specified torque, working from the centre outwards.

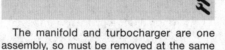

17 Exhaust manifold – removal and refitting

The manifold and turbocharger are one assembly, so must be removed at the same time, as described in Section 19.

18 Turbocharger – description and precautions

Description

1 A turbocharger is fitted to increase engine efficiency by raising the pressure in the inlet manifold above atmospheric pressure. Instead of the air simply being sucked into the cylinders, it is forced in.
2 Energy for the operation of the turbocharger comes from the exhaust gas. The gas flows through a specially shaped housing (the turbine housing) and, in so doing, spins the turbine wheel. The turbine wheel is attached to a shaft, at the end of which is another vaned wheel known as the compressor wheel. The compressor wheel spins in its own housing, and compresses the inlet air on the way to the inlet manifold.
3 Boost pressure (the pressure in the inlet manifold) is controlled by a variable inlet nozzle to improve boost pressure at low engine speeds.
4 The turbo shaft is pressure-lubricated by an oil feed pipe from the main oil gallery. The shaft 'floats' on a cushion of oil. A drain pipe returns the oil to the sump.

Precautions

5 The turbocharger operates at extremely high speeds and temperatures. Certain precautions must be observed, to avoid premature failure of the turbo, or injury to the operator.
6 Do not operate the turbo with any of its parts exposed, or with any of its hoses removed. Foreign objects falling onto the rotating vanes could cause excessive damage, and (if ejected) personal injury.
7 Do not race the engine immediately after start-up, especially if it is cold. Give the oil a few seconds to circulate.
8 Always allow the engine to return to idle speed before switching it off – do not blip the throttle and switch off, as this will leave the turbo spinning without lubrication.
9 Allow the engine to idle for several minutes before switching off after a high-speed run.
10 Observe the recommended intervals for oil and filter changing, and use a reputable oil of the specified quality. Neglect of oil changing, or use of inferior oil, can cause carbon formation on the turbo shaft, leading to subsequent failure.

19 Turbocharger – removal, inspection and refitting

Removal

1 Apply the handbrake, then jack up the front of the vehicle and support it on axle stands (see *Jacking and vehicle support*). Undo the screws and remove the engine undershield.
2 Disconnect the battery negative lead as described in Chapter 5 Section 4.
Note: *Although it is possible to remove the turbocharger with the engine in situ, access is extremely limited. If greater access is required, remove the engine and transmission unit as described in Chapter 2D Section 5.*
3 Pull the plastic acoustic cover from the top of the engine.
4 Remove the windscreen scuttle panel as described in Chapter 11 Section 11.
5 Remove the air cleaner assembly as described in Section 6.
6 Disconnect the breather pipe, undo the retaining bolt, release the clamp and remove the air intake pipe at the rear of the cylinder head.
7 Following the procedure description in Section 6B Section 18, move the particulate filter to one side. Note that a new turbocharger-to-particulate filter clamp and gasket will be required.
8 Undo the 4 mounting bolts and remove the DPF heat shield **(see illustration)**.
9 Release the clamp and remove the air intake pipe from the turbocharger **(see illustration)**.
10 Using an Allen key and socket, undo the retaining bolts and remove the oil feed and return pipes from the turbocharger **(see illustration)**.
11 Undo the turbocharger oil supply pipe banjo bolt **(see illustration)**. Discard the sealing rings. Be prepared for oil

19.8 Undo the bolts to remove the heat shield

19.9 Disconnect the air intake from the turbocharger

19.10 Remove the bolts and detach the oil pipes

19.11 Unbolt the turbocharger oil supply pipe

19.14 Remove the bolts from the lifting eye

19.15 Remove the turbocharger retaining bolts

spillage. Plug/seal the openings to prevent contamination.

12 Undo the bolts and remove the heatshields at the front of the turbocharger.

13 Disconnect all wiring plugs from the turbocharger.

14 Undo the bolts securing the turbocharger to the engine lifting eye **(see illustration)**.

15 Undo the bolts securing the turbocharger to the cylinder block **(see illustration)**.

16 Manoeuvre the turbocharger, complete with oil return pipe, upwards from place.

Inspection

17 With the turbocharger removed, inspect the housing for cracks or other visible damage.

18 Spin the turbine or the compressor wheel, to verify that the shaft is intact and to feel for excessive shake or roughness. Some play is normal, since in use, the shaft is 'floating' on a film of oil. Check that the wheel vanes are undamaged.

19 If oil contamination of the exhaust or induction passages is apparent, it is likely that turbo shaft oil seals have failed.

20 No DIY repair of the turbo is possible and none of the internal or external parts are available separately. If the turbocharger is suspect in any way a complete new unit must be obtained. Do not attempt to dismantle the turbocharger control assemblies.

21 If the turbocharger has failed, it is essential that all debris/dirt is removed from the air/intercooler hoses, and the oil lines.

Refitting

22 Refitting is a reverse of the removal procedure, bearing in mind the following points:

a) Renew the manifold gasket.
b) If a new turbocharger is being fitted, change the engine oil and filter.
c) Prime the turbocharger by injecting clean engine oil through the oil feed pipe union before reconnecting the union.
d) Renew the oil return pipe O-ring seal, and feed pipe sealing washers.
e) If a new turbocharger is being fitted, remove all traces of oil or grease from all air pipes/ducts. Any such residue could cause premature failure of the turbocharger.
f) Tighten all fasteners to their specified torque where given.

20.4a Slacken the clamps...

20 Intercooler – removal and refitting

Removal

2.0-litre diesel

1 Raise the front of the vehicle and support it securely on axle stands (see *Jacking and vehicle support*). Undo the fasteners and remove the engine undershield.

2 Remove the front bumper cover as described in Chapter 11 Section 5.

3 Release the lower side clips for the active shutter grille to allow the bottom edge to be pulled forward when required.

4 Slacken the clamps on the pipes at each end of the intercooler and disengage the pipes **(see illustrations)**.

20.4b ...then disengage the left- and right-hand pipes

20.5a Remove the 2 bottom mounting bolts...

20.5b ...then manoeuvre the intercooler forward to remove

20.9a Release the retaining clips...

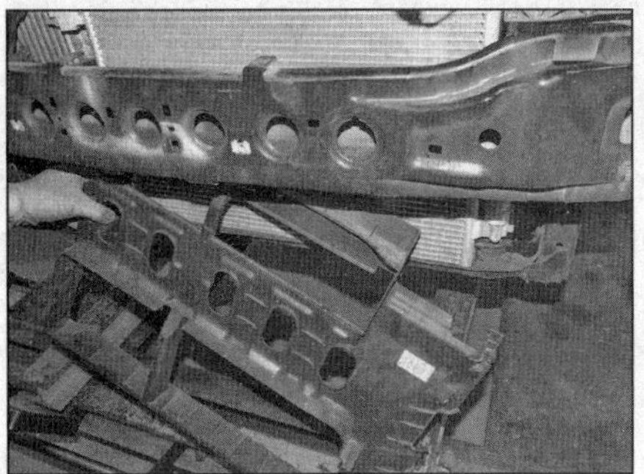

20.9b ...and lower the front shroud

20.10 Undo the clips and lower the intercooler shroud

5 Undo the 2 bottom retaining bolts and hinge the intercooler forward on the upper 2 mounting **(see illustrations)**.

1.5-litre diesel

6 Drain the cooling system, as described in Chapter 1B Section 36.

7 Disconnect the battery, as described in Chapter 5 Section 4.

8 Remove the active shutter grille, as described in Chapter 11 Section 6.

9 Release the clips and remove the plastic radiator front shroud downwards from place **(see illustrations)**.

10 Release the 3 clips and remove the intercooler front shroud downwards from place **(see illustration)**.

11 Slacken the clamps and disengage the pipes from the top and bottom of the intercooler **(see illustrations)**.

12 Unclip the air-conditioning pipe from the intercooler, then lower the intercooler from place **(see illustration)**.

Refitting

13 Refitting is a reversal of removal. The charge air pipes must be free from oil, grease and debris. They must be refitted without using oil or grease as a lubricant. Any such residue could cause premature failure of the turbocharger.

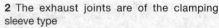

21 Exhaust system – general information and component renewal

General information

1 The exhaust system fitted during production consists of a catalytic converter/particulate filter, and rear exhaust section incorporating the silencer box.

2 The exhaust joints are of the clamping sleeve type

3 The system is suspended throughout its entire length by rubber mountings.

4 To remove the system or part of the system, first jack up the front or rear of the car and support it on axle stands (see *Jacking and vehicle support*). Alternatively, position the car over an inspection pit or on car ramps. Undo the screws and remove the engine undershield.

5 If the rear silencer section of the exhaust needs renewing, it is available as a two-part system, check with your local exhaust dealer. The original exhaust will need to be cut, just in front of the rear axle. Before making any cuts, it is advisable to get the new part of the exhaust system; this can then be measured to fit the original.

6 Each section is refitted by reversing the removal sequence, noting the following points:

a) Inspect the rubber mountings for signs of damage or deterioration, and renew as necessary.

b) Apply a smear of exhaust system jointing paste to the pipes and clamping sleeves.

c) Prior to tightening the exhaust system fasteners, ensure that all rubber mountings are correctly located, and that there is adequate clearance between the exhaust system and vehicle underbody.

Catalytic converter/ particulate filter renewal

7 Renewal of the catalytic converter/ particulate filter is described in Chapter 6B Section 18.

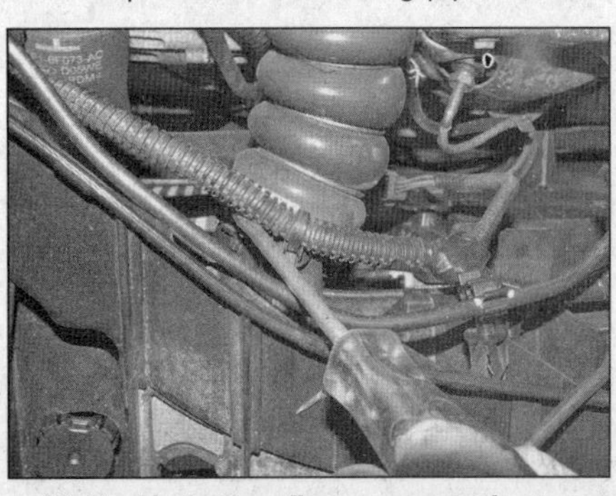

20.11a Undo the clip to remove the top pipe...

20.11b ...then the bottom one

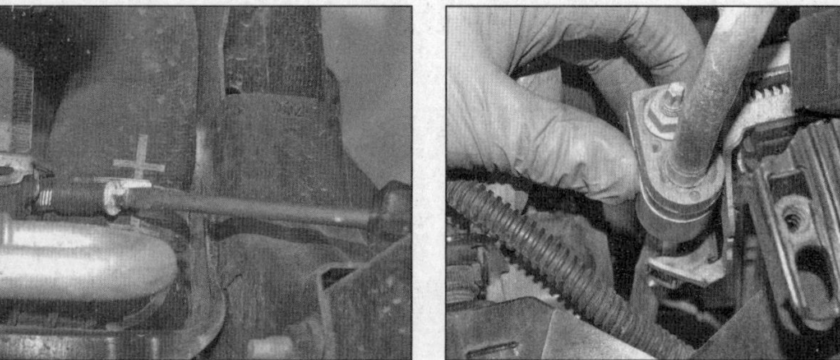

20.12 Unclip the aircon pipe, then lower the intercooler from place

Chapter 5
Starting and charging systems

Contents

Degrees of difficulty

Easy, suitable for novice with little experience 

Fairly easy, suitable for beginner with some experience 

Fairly difficult, suitable for competent DIY mechanic 

Difficult, suitable for experienced DIY mechanic

Very difficult, suitable for expert DIY or professional 

Specifications

System type .... 12 volt, negative earth

Battery

Type	EFB (Enhanced Flooded Battery), or AGM (Absorbent Glass Mat) 'maintenance-free' sealed for life

Alternator

Type	Denso
Rating	180 amp

Starter motor

Type	N/A

Torque wrench settings	**Nm**	**lbf ft**
Alternator mounting bolts	41	30
1.5-litre:		
Right-hand bolts	45	33
Left-hand bolts	39	29
2.0-litre	41	30
Battery terminals	12	9
Starter motor:		
1.5-litre	25	18
2.0-litre	35	26

1 General information and precautions

General information

1 The engine electrical system consists mainly of the charging and starting systems. Because of their engine-related functions, these components are covered separately from the body electrical devices such as the lights, instruments, etc (which are covered in Chapter 12). On petrol engine models refer to Chapter 6A for information on the ignition system, and on diesel models refer to Chapter 6B for information on the preheating system.

2 The electrical system is of the 12 volt negative earth type.

3 The battery is of the low maintenance or 'maintenance-free' (sealed for life) type and is charged by the alternator, which is belt-driven from the crankshaft pulley.

4 The starter motor is of the pre-engaged type incorporating an integral solenoid. On starting, the solenoid moves the drive pinion into engagement with the flywheel ring gear before the starter motor is energised. Once the engine has started, a one-way clutch prevents the motor armature being driven by the engine.

Precautions

5 While some repair procedures are given, the usual course of action is to renew the component concerned.

6 It is necessary to take extra care when working on the electrical system to avoid damage to semi-conductor devices (diodes and transistors), and to avoid the risk of personal injury. In addition to the precautions given in *Safety first*! at the beginning of this manual, observe the following when working on the system:

a) *Always remove rings, watches, etc, before working on the electrical system. Even with the battery disconnected, capacitive discharge could occur if a component's live terminal is earthed through a metal object. This could cause a shock or nasty burn.*

b) *Do not reverse the battery connections. Components such as the alternator, electronic control units, or any other components having semi-conductor circuitry could be irreparably damaged.*

c) *If the engine is being started using jump leads and a slave battery, make use of the built-in jump lead connections points (see 'Jump starting'). This also applies when connecting a battery charger.*

d) *Never disconnect the battery terminals, the*

alternator, any electrical wiring or any test instruments when the engine is running.

e) Never 'test' for alternator output by 'flashing' the output lead to earth.

f) Never use an ohmmeter of the type incorporating a hand-cranked generator for circuit or continuity testing.

g) Always ensure that the battery is disconnected when working on the electrical system.

h) Before using electric-arc welding equipment on the car, disconnect the battery, alternator and components such as the fuel injection/ ignition electronic control unit to protect them from the risk of damage.

2 Troubleshooting

Battery

Note: *The following is intended as a guide only. Always refer to the manufacturer's recommendations (often printed on a label attached to the battery) before charging a battery.*

1 General electrical fault finding is described in Chapter 12 Section 2.

2 All models are fitted with a maintenance-free battery in production, which should require no maintenance under normal operating conditions.

3 In all cases, a 'sealed for life' maintenance-free battery is fitted, and topping-up and testing of the electrolyte in each cell is not possible. The condition of the battery can therefore only be tested using a battery condition indicator or a voltmeter.

4 Generally speaking, if the voltage reading is less than 12.2 volts, then the battery is discharged, whilst a reading of 12.2 to 12.4 volts indicates a partially discharged condition.

Charging system

Note: *Refer to the warnings given in 'Safety first!' and in Section 1 of this Chapter before starting work.*

5 If the ignition warning light fails to illuminate when the ignition is switched on, first check the alternator wiring connections for security. If satisfactory, check that the warning light bulb (where applicable) has not blown, and that the bulbholder is secure in its location in the instrument panel. If the light still fails to illuminate, check the continuity of the warning light feed wire from the alternator to the bulbholder. On most vehicles, the warning light is an LED integral with the instrument cluster, and no repair is possible. Any malfunction of the instrument panel should generate an error code. The systems self-diagnosis facility can be interrogated using suitable diagnostic equipment connected via the vehicles 16-pin diagnostic plug located under the drivers side of the facia. If all is satisfactory, the alternator may be at fault and should be renewed or taken to an auto-electrician for testing and repair.

6 If the ignition warning light illuminates when the engine is running, stop the engine and check that the drivebelt is correctly fitted and tensioned (see Chapter 1A Section 30 or Chapter 1B Section 32) and that the alternator connections are secure. If all is so far satisfactory, have the alternator checked by an auto-electrician for testing and repair.

7 If the alternator output is suspect even though the warning light functions correctly, the regulated voltage may be checked as follows.

8 Connect a voltmeter across the battery terminals and start the engine.

9 Increase the engine speed until the voltmeter reading remains steady; the reading should be approximately 12 to 13 volts, and no more than 15 volts.

10 Switch on as many electrical accessories (eg, the headlights, heated rear window and heater blower) as possible, and check that the alternator maintains the regulated voltage of around 13 to 14 volts.

11 If the regulated voltage is not as stated, the fault may be due to worn brushes, weak brush springs, a faulty voltage regulator, a faulty diode, a severed phase winding or worn or damaged slip-rings. The alternator should be renewed or taken to an auto-electrician for testing and repair.

Starting system

The starter motor rotates, but the engine doesn't

12 Remove the starter motor (see Section 7). Have the starter motor checked by a automotive electrician or suitably equipped repairer.

13 Check the flywheel/driveplate ring gear for missing teeth and other damage. With the ignition turned off, rotate the flywheel/ driveplate so you can check the entire ring gear.

The starter motor is noisy

14 If the solenoid is making a chattering noise, first check the battery as described previously in this Section. If the battery is okay, check the cables and connections.

15 If you hear a grinding, crashing metallic sound when you turn the key to Start, check for loose starter mounting bolts. If they're tight, remove the starter and inspect the teeth on the starter pinion gear and flywheel ring gear. Look for missing or damaged teeth.

16 If the starter sounds fine when you first turn the key to Start, but then stops rotating the engine and emits a zinging sound, the problem may be a defective starter motor drive pinion. Remove the starter motor (see Section), check the pinion gear teeth and the flywheel/driveplate ring gear teeth. Replace as necessary.

The starter motor rotates slowly

17 Check the battery as previously described in this Section.

18 If the battery is okay, verify all connections (at the battery, the starter solenoid and motor) are clean, corrosion-free and secure. Make sure the cables aren't frayed or damaged.

19 Check that the starter mounting bolts are secure so it earths properly. Also check the pinion gear and flywheel/driveplate ring gear for evidence of mechanical damage (galling, deformed gear teeth or other damage).

The starter motor does not rotate at all

20 Check the battery as previously described in this Section.

21 If the battery is okay, verify all connections (at the battery, the starter solenoid and motor) are clean, corrosion-free and secure. Make sure the cables aren't frayed or damaged.

22 Check all of the fuses in the fuse/relay box.

23 Check that the starter mounting bolts are secure so it earths properly.

24 Check for voltage at the starter solenoid "S" terminal when the ignition key is turned to the start position. If voltage is present, replace the starter/solenoid assembly. If no voltage is present, the problem could be the starter relay, the ignition/starter switch, the inhibitor/gear position switch (automatic transmission models), or with an electrical connector somewhere in the circuit (see the wiring diagrams – Chapter 12). Also, on many modern vehicles, the engine management PCM and/or Body Control Module (BCM) control the voltage signal to the starter solenoid; on such vehicles a special scan tool is required for diagnosis.

3 Battery – testing and charging

Note: *The following is intended as a guide only. Always refer to the manufacturer's recommendations (often printed on a label attached to the battery) before charging a battery.*

1 All models are fitted with a maintenance-free battery in production, which should require no maintenance under normal operating conditions.

2 In all cases, a 'sealed for life' maintenance-free battery is fitted, and topping-up and testing of the electrolyte in each cell is not possible. The condition of the battery can therefore only be tested using a battery condition indicator or a voltmeter.

3 Generally speaking, if the voltage reading is less than 12.2 volts, then the battery is discharged, whilst a reading of 12.2 to 12.4 volts indicates a partially discharged condition.

4 Battery and tray – disconnection, removal and refitting

Note: *Prior to disconnecting the battery, wait 15 minutes after switching off the ignition to allow the vehicle's ECU's to store all learnt values in their memories.*

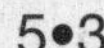

4.6 Undo the nut and disconnect the battery negative lead

4.7 Disconnect the positive lead clamp

4.8 Unclip the fusebox wiring

Removal

1 Prior to disconnecting the battery, close all windows and the sunroof, and ensure that the vehicle alarm system is deactivated (see Owner's Handbook).

Warning: Make sure the keys are not left in the car, in case of the vehicle locking system activating and locking all the doors.

2 The battery is located on the left-hand side of the engine compartment.

3 Remove the upper and lower windscreen cowl panels, as described in Chapter 11 Section 12.

4 Remove the air filter assembly as described in Chapter 4A Section 3 or Chapter 4B Section 6.

5 Unclip and remove the two battery covers.

6 Disconnect the battery negative (earth) lead **(see illustration)**.

7 Slacken the battery positive lead clamp nut and using a twisting motion, pull the clamp upwards from the battery terminal **(see illustration)**.

8 Unclip the wiring for the fuse box from the front of the battery box **(see illustration)**.

9 Pull up the and unclip the wiring junction box and place to one side **(see illustration)**.

10 Undo the 2 retaining nuts and remove the battery retainer **(see illustration)**.

11 Pull the battery forwards, disconnect the negative lead clamp and unplug any wiring plugs **(see illustrations)**.

Refitting and reconnection

12 Refitting is a reversal of removal. Always reconnect the positive lead first, and the negative lead last.

4.9 Move the wiring unit to one side

13 After reconnecting the battery, several of the vehicle's ECMs will require time to relearn certain values. This will normally be complete within a normal driving pattern of 15 miles (approximately). In addition, several systems may require re-initialisation as follows: **Note:** *If a new battery has been fitted, the vehicles body control module (BCM) may need to be configured with the new batteries' details. This is easily accomplished using a readily-available after-market configuration tool. Alternatively, entrust this task to a Ford dealer or suitably equipped repairer.*

Sunroof

a) *With the battery reconnected, and the ignition on, press the sunroof operating switch into the 'closed' position and hold it there.*
b) *The sunroof will move a few centimetres – continue to hold the switch in the 'closed' position for approximately 75 seconds. During this time the roof will open completely, then close completely. Now release the switch.*

4.10 Undo the nuts and remove the battery retainer

Electric windows

a) *Operate the button to fully open the window, then press the switch into the 'open, one-touch operation' (second switch position) and hold it there for 20 seconds.*
b) *Release the switch, then press the switch into the 'close, one-touch operation (second switch position) and hold it there until the window closes completely.*

Battery tray

14 Remove the battery as described previously in this Section.

15 Undo the 3 bolts securing the battery tray **(see illustration)**.

16 Manoeuvre the battery tray from place.

17 Refitting is a reversal of removal.

4.11a Pull the battery forward to access the negative lead clamp...

4.11b ...then disconnect it and unplug the wiring connectors

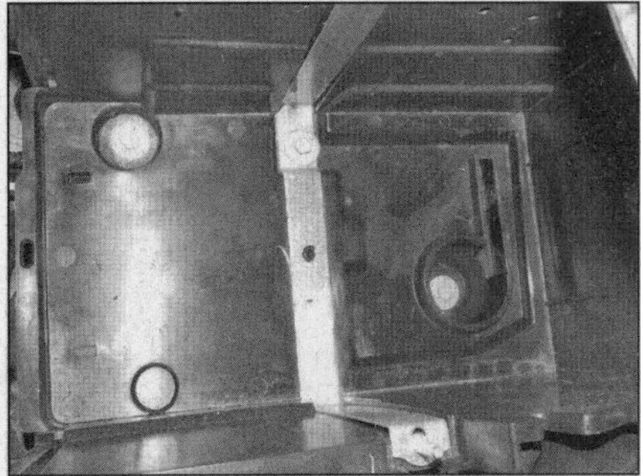

4.15 Undo the battery tray bolts

6.9a Remove the upper bolt...

6.9b ...and swivel the solenoid unit to one side

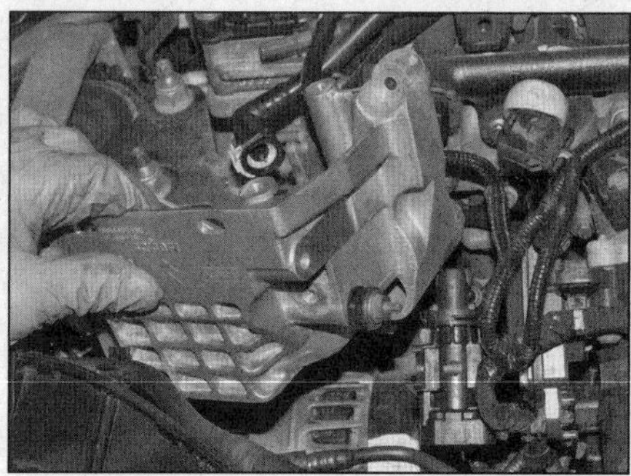
6.10 Unbolt and remove the fuel filter bracket

5 Alternator drivebelt – removal, refitting and tensioning

1 Refer to the procedure given for the auxiliary drivebelt in Chapter 1A Section 30 or Chapter 1B Section 32 as applicable.

6 Alternator – removal and refitting

Removal

2.0-litre diesel

1 Disconnect the battery negative lead as described in Section 4.

2 Pull up and remove the cover from the engine.

3 Remove the metal bracket from above the fuel filter, then unclip the wiring harness, and place it to one side.

4 Disconnect any wiring plugs from the filter housng.

5 Undo the 3 captive fuel filter housing-to-bracket bolts.

6 Unclip the fuel supply and return hoses. There's no need to disconnect them.

7 Lift the filter assembly from the bracket. Rotate the filter anti-clockwise and position to the rear.

8 Remove the auxiliary drivebelt as described in Chapter 1B Section 32.

9 Undo the upper bolt from the solenoid unit on the side of the fuel filter bracket and swivel out of the way **(see illustrations)**.

10 Undo the fasteners from the fuel filter bracket and manoeuvre the bracket from place **(see illustration)**.

11 Remove the cover, undo the nut from the battery positive lead connection on the alternator, disconnect the wiring plug **(see illustrations)**.

12 Reaching down from the top, slacken the upper alternator mounting bolt **(see illustration)**.

13 Working through the right front wheelarch, hold the auxiliary belt tensioner in position, remove the locking pin, then allow the tensioner to rotate to its stop.

14 Remove the lower alternator bolt **(see illustration)**.

15 Manoeuvre the alternator upwards from place.

1.5-litre diesel

16 Disconnect the battery as described in Section 4.

17 Pull up and remove the engine cover from the top of the engine.

18 Remove the auxiliary drivebelt, as described in Chapter 1B Section 32.

19 Disconnect and unbolt the air intake pipe, ensuring that the wiring bracket at the rear of the pipe is released **(see illustration)**.

20 Unbolt and remove the top intercooler pipe **(see illustration)**.

21 Undo the retaining bolts and manoeuvre the auxiliary drivebelt tensioner downwards from place.

22 Disconnect the wiring plug, then unbolt the other connections from the alternator **(see illustration)**.

23 Using a spanner, slacken (but do not remove) the alternator rear mounting bolts **(see illustration)**.

6.11a Prise off the rubber cover...

6.11b ...then disconnect the wiring

6.12 Slacken the upper the alternator mounting bolt

6.14 Undo the lower mounting bolt for the alternator

6.19 Unbolt and remove the intake pipe

6.20 Disconnect and remove the top intercooler pipe

6.22 Disconnect the electrical connections

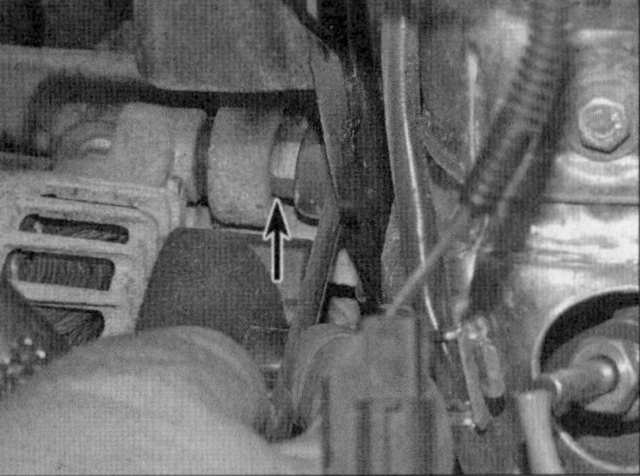

6.23 Loosen the alternator rear bolts

24 Undo the 2 front mounting bolts and manoeuvre the alternator upwards from place **(see illustration)**.

1.5-litre petrol

25 Pull up and remove the engine cover.

26 Remove the auxiliary drivebelt as described in Chapter 1A Section 30.

27 Unbolt the brake fluid reservoir and move out of the way **(see illustration)**.

28 Prise up the coolant header tank and move it to one side **(see illustration)**.

29 Working underneath the car, remove the engine undertray.

30 Undo the 2 bolts and separate the 2 parts of the exhaust **(see illustration)**.

31 Remove the 2 engine mounting-to-body bolts at the right-hand end of the engine **(see illustration)**.

32 Place a trolley jack beneath the engine and raise it by 60mm **(see illustration)**.

6.24 Undo the bolts and lift out the alternator

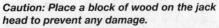

6.27 Unbolt the brake fluid reservoir and move aside

Caution: Place a block of wood on the jack head to prevent any damage.

33 Unclip the neck of the windscreen washer fluid reservoir and remove **(see illustration)**.

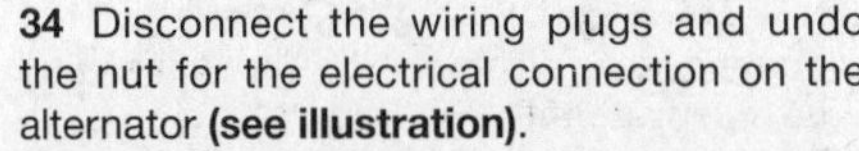

34 Disconnect the wiring plugs and undo the nut for the electrical connection on the alternator **(see illustration)**.

35 Undo the lower alternator mounting bolt **(see illustration)**.

6.28 Move the coolant header tank to one side

6.30 Undo the bolts and separate the exhaust parts

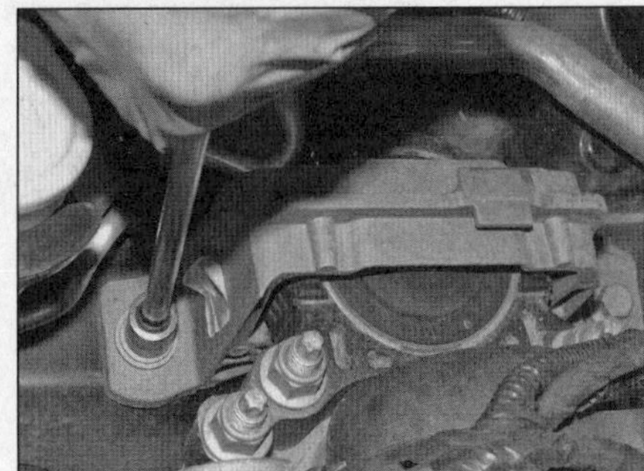

6.31 Undo the bolts on the right-hand engine mounting

6.32 Use a trolley jack to raise the engine by 60mm

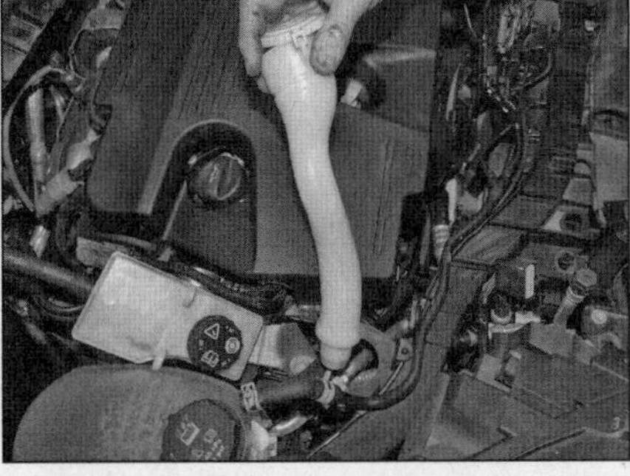

6.33 Unclip and remove the washer fluid reservoir neck

6.34 Disconnect all the wiring plugs and connections

6.35 Undo the lower bolt for the alternator

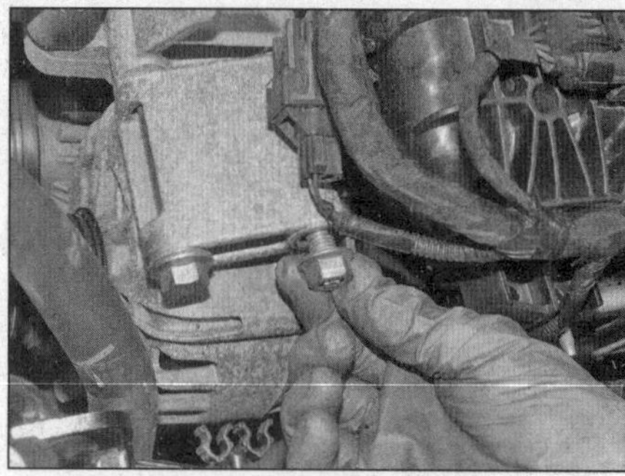
6.36a Undo the nut...

6.36b ...then unscrew the stud

6.37 Remove the upper mounting bolt

6.38 Remove the alternator through the opening

36 Remove the nut from the upper alternator mounting, then unscrew the mounting stud **(see illustrations)**.

37 Undo the upper mounting bolt **(see illustration)**.

38 Manoeuvre the alternator upwards from place **(see illustration)**. If the alternator won't come out of the gap raise the engine slightly.

Refitting

39 Refitting is a reversal of removal, noting the following points:

a) *Tighten all fasteners to their specified torque where given.*
b) *Refit the auxiliary drivebelt as described in Chapter 1A Section 30 or Chapter 1B Section 32 as applicable.*

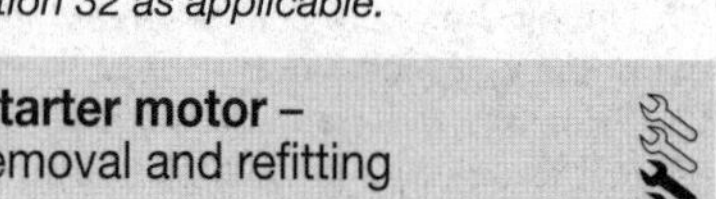

7 Starter motor – removal and refitting

2.0-litre diesel

Removal

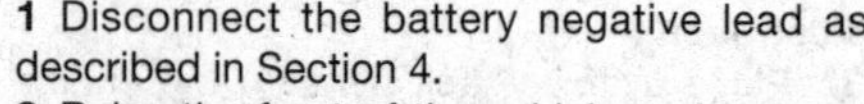

1 Disconnect the battery negative lead as described in Section 4.

2 Raise the front of the vehicle and support it securely on axle stands (see *Jacking and vehicle support*). Release the fasteners and remove the engine undershield **(see illustration)**.

3 Disconnect the wiring from the starter motor solenoid and the stop/start solenoid **(see illustration)**.

4 Working underneath the car, undo the 2 nuts for the pipe brackets from the ends of the mounting bolts **(see illustration)**.

5 Still working underneath the car, undo 2 of the 3 starter motor retaining bolts **(see illustration)**.

6 Working from above, undo the retaining clip and remove the intercooler pipe to one side **(see illustration)**.

7.2 Undo the fasteners and remove the undertray

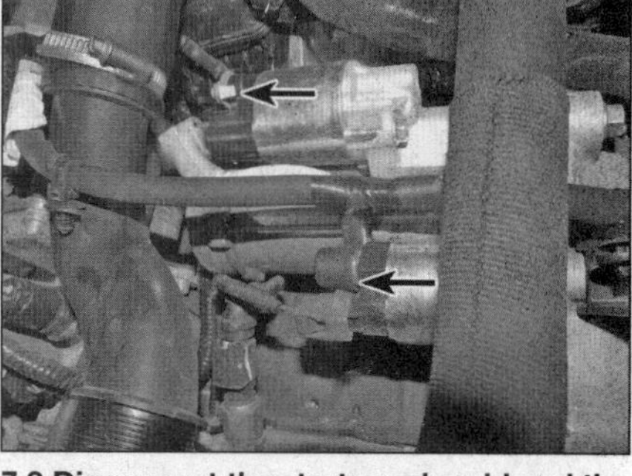
7.3 Disconnect the starter solenoid and the stop/start solenoid

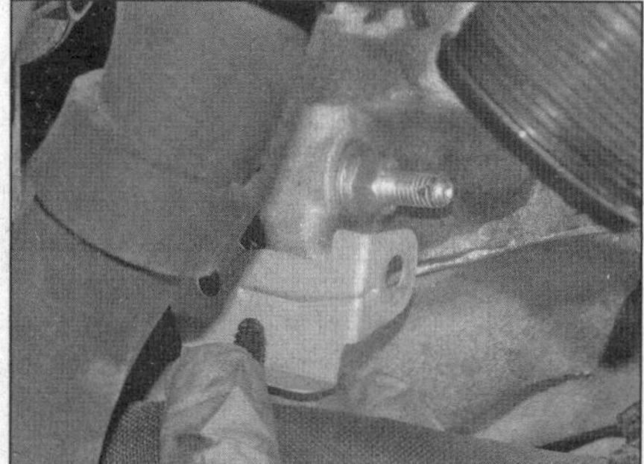
7.4 Undo the nuts holding the pipe brackets

7.5 Remove 2 of the starter motor retaining bolts

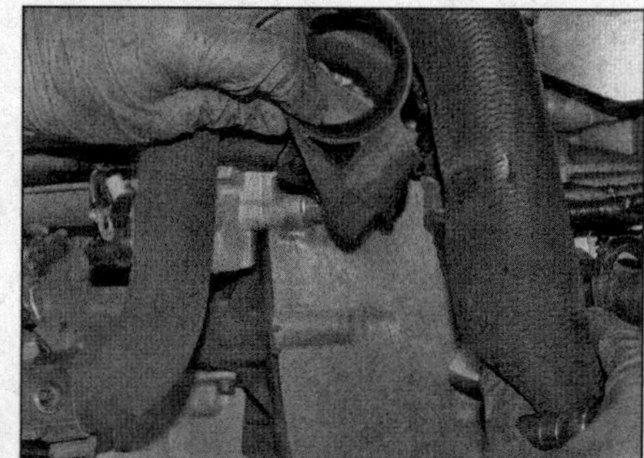
7.6 Unclip and move the intercooler pipe

7 Use a spanner to undo and remove the top starter motor mounting bolt **(see illustration)**.

8 Manoeuvre the starter downwards from place

Refitting

9 Refitting is a reversal of removal, ensuring that all fasteners are tightened to the specified torque where given.

1.5-litre diesel

Removal

10 The starter motor is located on the rear of the cylinder block **(see illustration)**.

11 Remove the battery and tray, as described in Section 4.

12 Undo the starter motor lower mounting bolt from underneath, noting the wiring loom mounting bracket located on the bolt **(see illustration)**.

13 Note their fitted positions, then undo the two securing nuts and disconnect the wiring connections from the starter motor **(see illustration)**.

14 Unclip the wiring loom retaining clip from one of the upper mounting bolts, then undo the upper mounting bolts, and remove the starter motor. The starter motor will need to be lowered down and out from under the vehicle. As the upper bolts are removed, an assistant will be required to support the starter from underneath. To make removal easier, disconnect the wiring connector from the oxygen sensor to make more room for the starter to be lowered and removed.

Refitting

15 Refitting is a reversal of removal.

1.5-litre petrol

Removal

16 Disconnect the battery negative lead as described in Section 4.

17 Raise the front of the vehicle and support it securely on axle stands (see *Jacking and vehicle support*). Release the fasteners and remove the engine undershield **(see illustration)**.

18 Remove the air filter assembly as described in Chapter 4A Section 3.

19 Disconnect the selector cable from the transmission **(see illustration)**.

20 Use a suitable lever to manoeuvre the coolant hose out of the way, allowing access to the top starter motor retaining bolt **(see illustration)**.

21 Use as extension and flexible joint to undo the top retaining bolt **(see illustration)**.

22 Remove the oil filter as described in Chapter 1A Section 13.

23 Displace the oil cooler, as described in Chapter 2A Section 18. However, there is no need to fully disconnect the cooling pipes from the oil cooler for this procedure.

24 Disconnect the wiring from the starter motor **(see illustration)**.

7.7 Remove the final starter bolt

7.10 Location of starter motor

7.12 Note location of wiring loom bracket

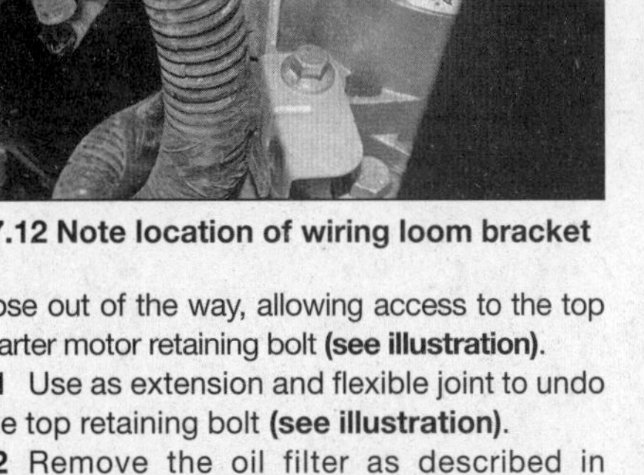

7.13 Undo the two wiring securing nuts

7.17 Undo the fastenings and remove the undertray

7.19 Prise the selector cable from the transmission

7.20 Lever the hose out of the way

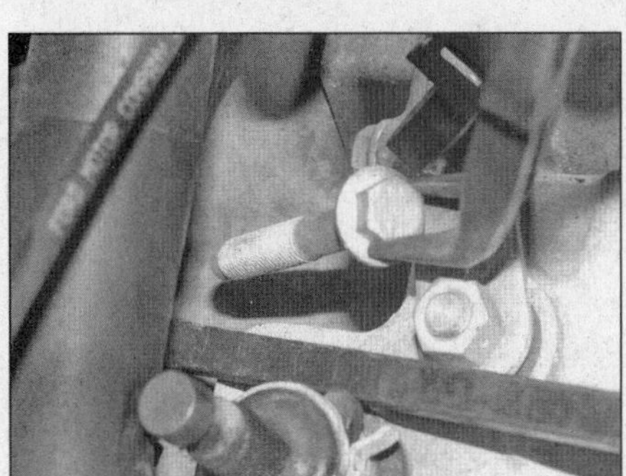

7.21 Remove the top starter motor bolt

7.24 Disconnect the starter wiring

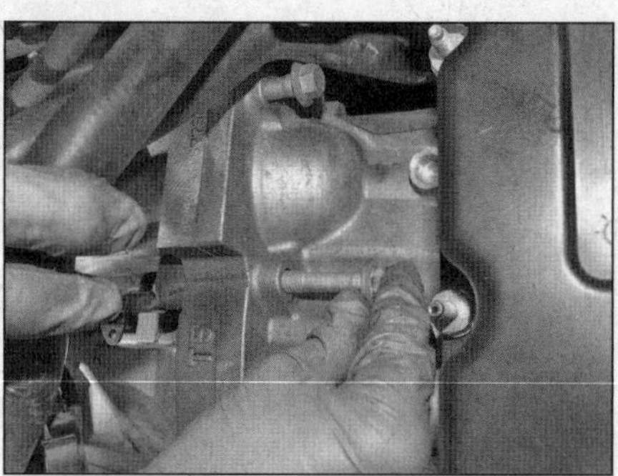

7.25 Undo the remaining starter mounting bolts

7.26 Remove the starter downwards

25 Working underneath the car, undo the 2 remaining mounting bolts **(see illustration)**.

26 Manoeuvre the starter downwards from place (radiator removed for clarity) **(see illustration)**.

Refitting

27 Refitting is a reversal of removal.

Chapter 6 Part A
Engine and emission control systems – petrol models

Contents

Degrees of difficulty

Easy, suitable for novice with little experience		Fairly easy, suitable for beginner with some experience		Fairly difficult, suitable for competent DIY mechanic		Difficult, suitable for experienced DIY mechanic		Very difficult, suitable for expert DIY or professional	

Specifications

Ignition system

Type	Distributorless ignition system controlled by engine management PCM, 1 coil per spark plug
Spark plugs	See Chapter 1A Specifications
Ignition timing	Controlled by engine management PCM (Powertrain Control Module)

Engine management system

Petrol engines	MED17 with CAN-Bus and individual cylinder knock control. FGEC Software

Torque wrench settings

Torque wrench settings	Nm	lbf ft
Camshaft position sensors	9	7
Catalytic converter:		
To-turbocharger clamp	13	10
Mounting bracket nuts	20	15
Common fuel rail pressure sensor	35	26
Crankshaft position sensor	10	7
Ignition coil retaining bolt	10	7
Knock sensor retaining bolt	18	13
Oxygen sensors	48	36

1 Engine management system

Electronic control system

1 On all engines, the fuel injection and ignition functions are combined into a single engine management system. The system incorporates a closed-loop catalytic converter and an evaporative emission control system, and complies with the latest emission control standards. The fuel side of the system operates as follows.

2 The fuel pump, which is situated in the fuel tank, supplies fuel from the tank to the high-pressure fuel pump. The pump motor is permanently immersed in fuel, to keep it cool. The fuel rail is mounted directly above the fuel injectors and acts as a fuel reservoir.

3 Fuel rail supply pressure is controlled by the pressure regulator, also located in the fuel tank. The regulator contains a spring-loaded valve, which lifts to allow excess fuel to recirculate within the tank when the optimum operating pressure of the fuel system is exceeded (eg, during low speed, light load cruising).

4 The fuel injectors are electromagnetic valves, which spray atomised fuel into the combustion chambers under the control of the engine management system control unit. Ford call this unit a PCM (Powertrain Control Module). There is one injector per cylinder, mounted in the cylinder head. The fuel is injected directly in the top of the combustion chambers. The PCM controls the volume of fuel injected by varying the length of time for which each injector is held open. The fuel injection systems are of the sequential type, whereby each injector operates individually in cylinder sequence.

5 The electrical control system consists of the PCM, along with the following sensors:

b) Coolant temperature sensor – informs the PCM of engine temperature.

c) Inlet air temperature sensor – informs the PCM of the temperature of the air passing through the throttle housing.

d) Oxygen sensors – inform the PCM of the oxygen content of the exhaust gases.

e) Charge/Manifold pressure sensor – informs the PCM of the charge pressure in the intake manifold.

f) Charge pressure sensor (upstream of the throttle valve) – informs the PCM of the charge pressure from the turbocharger.

g) Crankshaft position sensor – informs the PCM of engine speed and crankshaft angular position.

h) Knock sensor – informs the PCM of pre-ignition (detonation) within the cylinders.

i) Camshaft sensors – informs the PCM on the camshaft positions.

j) Accelerator pedal position sensor – informs the PCM of the pedal position and rate of change.

k) Clutch and brake pedal position sensor – informs the PCM of the pedal positions (not all models).

6 Signals from each of the sensors are compared by the PCM and, based on this information, the ECU selects the response appropriate to those values, and controls the fuel injectors (varying the pulse width – the length of time the injectors are held open – to provide a richer or weaker air/fuel mixture, as appropriate). The air/fuel mixture is constantly varied by the PCM, to provide the best settings for cranking, starting (with either a hot or cold engine) and engine warm-up, idle, cruising and acceleration.

7 The PCM also has full control over the engine idle speed, via the motorised throttle body. A sensor informs the PCM of the position, and rate of change, of the accelerator pedal. The PCM then controls the throttle body – no accelerator cable is fitted. The PCM also carries out 'fine tuning' of the idle speed by varying the ignition timing to increase or reduce the torque of the engine as it is idling. This helps to stabilise the idle speed when electrical or mechanical loads (such as headlights, air conditioning, etc) are switched on and off.

8 If there is any abnormality in any of the readings obtained from the coolant temperature sensor, the inlet air temperature sensor or the oxygen sensor, the PCM enters its 'back-up' mode. If this happens, the erroneous sensor signal is overridden, and the PCM assumes a pre-programmed 'back-up' value, which will allow the engine to continue running, albeit at reduced efficiency. If the PCM enters this mode, the warning lamp on the instrument panel will be illuminated, and the relevant fault code will be stored in the PCM memory.

9 If the warning light illuminates, the vehicle should be taken to a Ford dealer or specialist at the earliest opportunity. Once there, a complete test of the engine management system can be carried out, using a special electronic diagnostic test unit, which is plugged into the system's diagnostic connector, located behind the trim panel under the driver's side of the facia.

Ignition system

10 The ignition system is integrated with the fuel injection system to form a combined engine management system under the control of one PCM. The ignition side of the system is of the static (distributorless) type, consisting of the ignition coils and spark plugs. Each ignition coil is mounted directly above the spark plugs. The coils are integral with the spark plug caps and are pushed directly onto the spark plugs, one for each plug. This removes the need for any HT leads connecting the coils to the plugs.

11 The PCM uses its inputs from the various sensors to calculate the required ignition advance setting and coil charging time, depending on engine temperature, load and speed. At idle speeds, the PCM varies the ignition timing to alter the torque characteristic of the engine, enabling the idle speed to be controlled.

12 A knock sensor is also incorporated into the ignition system. Mounted onto the cylinder block, the sensor detects the high-frequency vibrations caused when the engine starts to pre-ignite, or 'pink'. Under these conditions, the knock sensor sends an electrical signal to the PCM, which in turn retards the ignition advance setting in small steps until the 'pinking' ceases.

2 Emissions systems – general information

1 All petrol engines use unleaded petrol and also have various other features built into the fuel system to help minimise harmful emissions. In addition, all engines are equipped with the crankcase emission control system described below. All engines are also equipped with a catalytic converter and an evaporative emission control system.

2 The emission control systems function as follows.

Crankcase emission control

3 To reduce the emission of unburned hydrocarbons from the crankcase into the atmosphere, the engine is sealed and the blow-by gases and oil vapour are drawn from inside the crankcase, through a wire mesh oil separator, into the inlet tract to be burned by the engine during normal combustion.

4 Under all conditions the gases are forced out of the crankcase by the (relatively) higher crankcase pressure; if the engine is worn, the raised crankcase pressure (due to increased blow-by) will cause some of the flow to return under all manifold conditions.

Exhaust emission control

5 To minimise the amount of pollutants which escape into the atmosphere, a catalytic converter is fitted in the exhaust system. On all models where a catalytic converter is fitted, the system is of the closed-loop type, in which oxygen (lambda) sensors in the exhaust system provides the fuel injection/ ignition system PCM with constant feedback, enabling the PCM to adjust the mixture to provide the best possible conditions for the converter to operate.

6 The oxygen sensors have a heating element built-in that is controlled by the PCM through the oxygen sensor relay to quickly bring the sensor's tip to an efficient operating temperature. The sensor's tip is sensitive to oxygen and sends the PCM a varying voltage depending on the amount of oxygen in the exhaust gases; if the inlet air/fuel mixture is too rich, the exhaust gases are low in oxygen so the sensor sends a low-voltage signal, the voltage rising as the mixture weakens and the amount of oxygen rises in the exhaust gases. Peak conversion efficiency of all major pollutants occurs if the inlet air/fuel mixture is maintained at the chemically correct ratio for the complete combustion of petrol of 14.7 parts (by weight) of air to 1 part of fuel (the 'stoichiometric' ratio). The sensor output voltage alters in a large step at this point, the PCM using the signal change as a reference point and correcting the inlet air/fuel mixture accordingly by altering the fuel injector pulse width.

Evaporative emission control

7 To minimise the escape into the atmosphere of unburned hydrocarbons, an evaporative emission control system is fitted to all models. The fuel tank filler cap is sealed and a charcoal canister is mounted underneath the fuel tank to collect the petrol vapours generated in the tank when the car is parked. It stores them until they can be cleared from the canister (under the control of the fuel injection/ignition system PCM) via the purge valve into the inlet tract to be burned by the engine during normal combustion.

8 To ensure that the engine runs correctly when it is cold and/or idling and to protect the catalytic converter from the effects of an over-rich mixture, the purge control valve is not opened by the PCM until the engine has warmed-up, and the engine is under load; the valve solenoid is then modulated on and off to allow the stored vapour to pass into the inlet tract.

3 European On Board Diagnosis (EOBD) system

General description

1 All models are equipped with the European On-Board Diagnosis (EOBD) system. This system consists of an on-board computer known as the ECU (Electronic Control Unit), Electronic Control Module (ECM) or Powertrain Control Module (PCM), and information sensors, which monitor various functions of the engine and send data to the ECU/ECM/PCM. This system incorporates a series of diagnostic monitors that detect and identify fuel injection and emissions control system faults and store the information in the computer memory. This system also tests sensors and output actuators, diagnoses drive cycles, freezes data and clears codes.

2 The ECU/ECM/PCM is the brain of the electronically controlled fuel and emissions system. It receives data from a number of sensors and other electronic components (switches, relays, etc.). Based on the information it receives, the ECU/ECM/PCM generates output signals to control various relays, solenoids (fuel injectors) and other actuators. The ECU/ECM/PCM is specifically calibrated to optimise the emissions, fuel economy and driveability of the vehicle.

3.4a Simple code readers are an economical way to extract trouble codes when the CHECK ENGINE light comes on

3.4b Hand-held scan tools like these can extract computer codes and also perform diagnostics

3 Whilst the vehicle is within the manufactures warranty, have any faults diagnosed and rectified by the dealer service department.

Scan tool information

4 As extracting the Diagnostic Trouble Codes (DTCs) from an engine management system is now the first step in troubleshooting many computer-controlled systems and components, a code reader, at the very least, will be required. More powerful scan tools can also perform many of the diagnostics once associated with expensive factory scan tools **(see illustrations)**. If you're planning to obtain a generic scan tool for your vehicle, make sure that it's compatible with EOBD systems. If you don't plan to purchase a code reader or scan tool and don't have access to one, you can have the codes extracted by a dealer service department or a suitably equipped repairer.

4 Obtaining and clearing Diagnostic Trouble Codes (DTCs)

1 All models covered by this manual are equipped with on-board diagnostics. When the ECU/ECM/PCM recognises a malfunction in a monitored emission or engine control system, component or circuit, it turns on the Malfunction Indicator Light (MIL) on the dash. The ECU/ECM/PCM will continue to display the MIL until the problem is fixed and the Diagnostic Trouble Code (DTC) is cleared from the ECU/ECM/PCM's memory. You'll need a scan tool to access any DTCs stored in the ECU/ECM/PCM.

2 Before outputting any DTCs stored in the ECU/ECM/PCM, thoroughly inspect ALL electrical connectors and hoses. Make sure that all electrical connections are secure, clean and free of corrosion. And make sure that all hoses are correctly connected, fit securely and are in good condition.

Accessing the DTCs

3 The Diagnostic Trouble Codes (DTCs) can only be accessed with a code reader or scan tool. Professional scan tools are expensive, but relatively inexpensive generic code readers or scan tools **(see illustrations 3.4a and 3.4b)** are available at most auto parts stores. Simply plug the connector of the scan tool into the diagnostic connector **(see illustration)**. Then follow the instructions included with the scan tool to extract the DTCs.

4 Once you have outputted all of the stored DTCs, look them up on the accompanying DTC chart.

5 After troubleshooting the source of each DTC, make any necessary repairs or replace the defective component(s).

Clearing the DTCs

6 Clear the DTCs with the code reader or scan tool in accordance with the instructions provided by the tool's manufacturer.

Diagnostic Trouble Codes

7 The accompanying tables are a sample list of the Diagnostic Trouble Codes (DTCs) that can be accessed by a do-it-yourselfer working at home (there are many, many more DTCs available to professional mechanics with proprietary scan tools and software, but those codes cannot be accessed by a generic scan tool). If, after you have checked and repaired the connectors, wire harness and vacuum hoses (if applicable) for an emission-related system, component or circuit, the problem persists, have the vehicle checked by a dealer service department or suitably equipped repairer.

4.3 The 16-pin Data Link Connector (DLC) is located under the right-hand side of the facia

EOBD trouble codes

Code	Probable cause
P000A	Camshaft 1 position, (bank no.1), slow response
P000B	Camshaft 2 position, (bank no.1), slow response
P0010	Camshaft 1 position, (bank no.1), actuator circuit open
P0013	Camshaft 2 position, (bank no.1), actuator circuit open
P0016	Crankshaft/camshaft timing (bank no.1. sensor no.1) misalignment
P0017	Crankshaft/camshaft timing (bank no.1. sensor no.2) misalignment
P0031	Upstream oxygen sensor (cylinder bank no. 1), heater circuit low voltage
P0032	Upstream oxygen sensor heater (cylinder bank no. 1), heater circuit high voltage
P0037	Downstream oxygen sensor (cylinder bank no. 1), heater circuit low voltage
P0038	Downstream oxygen sensor (cylinder bank no. 1), heater circuit high voltage
P0068	Manifold pressure/throttle position correlation – high-flow/ vacuum leak
P0070	Ambient temperature sensor stuck
P0071	Ambient temperature sensor performance
P0072	Ambient temperature sensor, low voltage
P0073	Ambient temperature sensor, high voltage
P0107	Manifold Absolute Pressure (MAP) sensor, low voltage
P0108	Manifold Absolute Pressure (MAP) sensor, high voltage
P0110	Intake Air Temperature (IAT) sensor, stuck
P0111	Intake Air Temperature (IAT) sensor performance
P0112	Intake Air Temperature (IAT) sensor, low voltage
P0113	Intake Air Temperature (IAT) sensor, high voltage
P0116	Engine Coolant Temperature (ECT) sensor performance
P0117	Engine Coolant Temperature (ECT) sensor, low voltage
P0118	Engine Coolant Temperature (ECT) sensor, high voltage
P0121	Throttle Position (TP) sensor performance
P0122	Throttle Position (TP) sensor, low voltage
P0123	Throttle Position (TP) sensor, high voltage
P0125	Insufficient coolant temperature for closed-loop control; closed-loop temperature not reached
P0128	Thermostat rationality
P0129	Barometric pressure out-of-range (low)
P0131	Upstream oxygen sensor (cylinder bank no. 1), low voltage or shorted to ground
P0132	Upstream oxygen sensor (cylinder bank no. 1), high voltage or shorted to voltage
P0133	Upstream oxygen sensor (cylinder bank no. 1), slow response
P0134	Upstream oxygen sensor (cylinder bank no. 1), sensor remains at center (not switching)
P0135	Upstream oxygen sensor (cylinder bank no. 1), heater failure
P0137	Downstream oxygen sensor (cylinder bank no. 1), low voltage or shorted to ground
P0138	Downstream oxygen sensor (cylinder bank no. 1), high voltage or shorted to voltage
P0139	Downstream oxygen sensor (cylinder bank no. 1), slow response
P0140	Downstream oxygen sensor (cylinder bank no. 1), sensor remains at center (not switching)
P0141	Downstream oxygen sensor (cylinder bank no. 1), heater failure
P0171	Fuel control system too lean (cylinder bank no. 1)
P0172	Fuel control system too rich (cylinder bank no. 1)
P0201	Injector circuit malfunction – cylinder no. 1
P0202	Injector circuit malfunction – cylinder no. 2
P0203	Injector circuit malfunction – cylinder no. 3
P0204	Injector circuit malfunction – cylinder no. 4

Code	Probable cause
P0300	Multiple cylinder misfire detected
P0301	Cylinder no. 1 misfire detected
P0302	Cylinder no. 2 misfire detected
P0303	Cylinder no. 3 misfire detected
P0304	Cylinder no. 4 misfire detected
P0315	No crank sensor learned
P0320	No crankshaft reference signal at Powertrain Control Module (PCM)
P0325	Knock sensor circuit malfunction
P0335	Crankshaft Position (CKP) sensor circuit
P0339	Crankshaft Position (CKP) sensor intermittent
P0340	Camshaft Position (CMP) sensor circuit
P0344	Camshaft Position (CMP) sensor intermittent
P0351	Ignition coil no. 1, primary circuit
P0352	Ignition coil no. 2, primary circuit
P0353	Ignition coil no. 3, primary circuit
P0354	Ignition coil no. 4, primary circuit
P0365	Camshaft Position (CMP) sensor circuit (bank no.1. sensor no.2)
P0369	Camshaft Position (CMP) sensor intermittent (bank no.1. sensor no.2)
P0440	General Evaporative Emission Control (EVAP) system failure
P0441	Evaporative Emission Control (EVAP) system, incorrect purge flow
P0442	Evaporative Emission Control (EVAP) system, medium leak (0.040-inch) detected
P0443	Evaporative Emission Control (EVAP) system, purge solenoid circuit malfunction
P0452	Natural Vacuum Leak Detector (NVLD) pressure sensor circuit, low voltage
P0453	Natural Vacuum Leak Detector (NVLD) pressure sensor circuit, high input
P0455	Evaporative Emission Control (EVAP) system, large leak detected
P0456	Evaporative Emission Control (EVAP) system, small leak (0.020-inch) detected
P0460	Fuel level sending unit, no change as vehicle is operated
P0461	Fuel level sensor circuit, range or performance problem
P0462	Fuel level sending unit or sensor circuit, low voltage
P0463	Fuel level sending unit or sensor circuit, high voltage
P0480	Low-speed fan control relay circuit malfunction
P0498	Natural Vacuum Leak Detector (NVLD) canister vent valve solenoid circuit, low voltage
P0499	Natural Vacuum Leak Detector (NVLD) canister vent valve solenoid circuit, high voltage
P0500	No vehicle speed signal (four-speed automatic transaxles)
P0501	Vehicle speed sensor, range or performance problem
P0503	Vehicle speed sensor 1, erratic
P0506	Idle speed control system, rpm lower than expected
P0507	Idle speed control system, rpm higher than expected
P0508	Idle Air Control (IAC) valve circuit, low voltage
P0509	Idle Air Control (IAC) valve circuit, high voltage
P0513	Invalid SKIM key (engine immobilizer problem)
P0516	Battery temperature sensor, low voltage
P0517	Battery temperature sensor, high voltage
P0519	Idle speed performance
P0522	Engine oil pressure sensor/switch circuit, low voltage
P0532	Air conditioning refrigerant pressure sensor, low voltage
P0533	Air conditioning refrigerant pressure sensor, high voltage
P0551	Power Steering Pressure (PSP) switch circuit, range or performance problem
P0562	Battery voltage low
P0563	Battery voltage high
P0579	Speed control switch circuit, range or performance problem
P0580	Speed control switch circuit, low voltage

Code	Probable cause	Code	Probable cause
P0581	Speed control switch circuit, high voltage	P0632	Odometer not programmed in Powertrain Control Module (PCM)
P0582	Speed control vacuum solenoid circuit	P0633	SKIM key not programmed in Powertrain Control Module (PCM)
P0858	Speed control switch 1/2 correlation	P0642	Sensor reference voltage 2 circuit, low voltage
P0586	Speed control vent solenoid circuit	P0643	Sensor reference voltage 2 circuit, high voltage
P0591	Speed control switch 2 circuit, performance problem	P0645	Air conditioning clutch relay circuit
P0592	Speed control switch 2 circuit, low voltage	P0685	Automatic Shutdown (ASD) relay control circuit
P0593	Speed control switch circuit 2, high voltage	P0688	Automatic Shutdown (ASD) relay sense circuit, low voltage
P0594	Speed control servo power circuit	P0700	Electronic Automatic Transaxle (EATX) control system malfunction or DTC present
P0600	Serial communication link malfunction	P0703	Brake switch circuit malfunction
P0601	Powertrain Control Module (PCM), internal controller failure	P0833	Clutch released switch circuit
P0622	Alternator field control circuit malfunction or field not switching correctly	P0850	Park/Neutral switch malfunction
P0627	Fuel pump relay circuit	P0856	Traction control torque request circuit
P0630	Vehicle Identification Number (VIN) not programmed in Powertrain Control Module (PCM)		

5 Accelerator pedal – removal and refitting

Removal

1 Remove the driver's side facia lower panel, as described in Chapter 11 Section 38.

2 Disconnect the battery negative lead as described in Chapter 5 Section 4.

3 Disconnect the wiring plug from the throttle position sensor, then unscrew the 2 mounting nuts and remove the pedal/sensor assembly from the bulkhead studs **(see illustration)**. Note that the sensor is not available separately from the pedal assembly.

Note: *Ford insist that the sensor wiring plug can only be disconnected 10 times before is becomes irreversibly damaged. Use a marker pen to record each disconnection on the side of the connector. Only disconnect the plug if it is absolutely necessary.*

Refitting

4 Refit in the reverse order of removal. On completion, check the action of the pedal to ensure that the throttle has full unrestricted movement, and fully returns when released.

5 Reconnect the battery as described in Chapter 5 Section 4.

6 Powertrain Control Module (PCM) – removal and refitting

Removal

Note: *Disconnecting the battery will erase any fault codes stored in the PCM. It is strongly recommended that the fault code memory of the unit is interrogated using a code reader or scanner prior to battery disconnection.*

1 Disconnect the battery as described in Chapter 5 Section 4.

2 Pull back the left-hand front wheelarch liner, as described in Chapter 11 Section 39.

3 The PCM cover is held on by rivets. To remove these, first drill 2 small holes in the surface of the rivet **(see illustration)**.

4 Insert the tip of circlip pliers into the holes drilled in the rivet surface, and turn **(see illustration)**.

Note: *The use of penetrating fluid will help to ease out the bolts. If they are stuck, you will need to remove the front foglight as described in Chapter 12 Section 9, and spray the rear of the bolts.*

5 Remove the cover from the PCM **(see illustration)**.

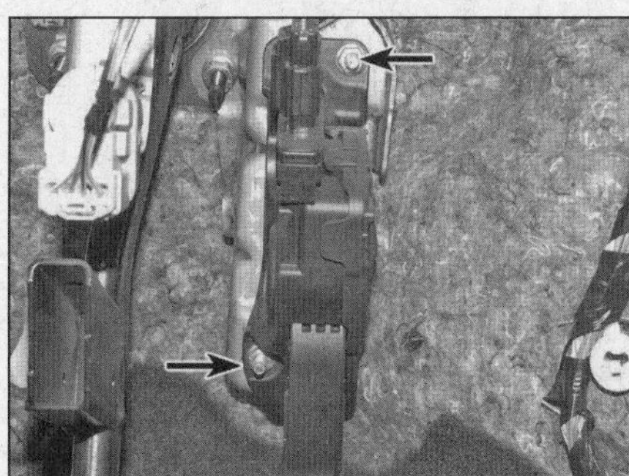

5.3 Accelerator pedal/sensor assembly mounting nuts

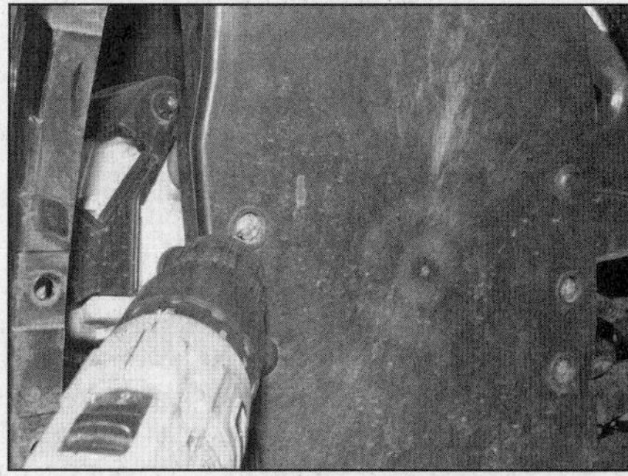

6.3 Drill 2 small holes in each rivet

6.4 Use circlip pliers to turn each rivet

6.5 Once the rivets are removed, pull away the PCM cover

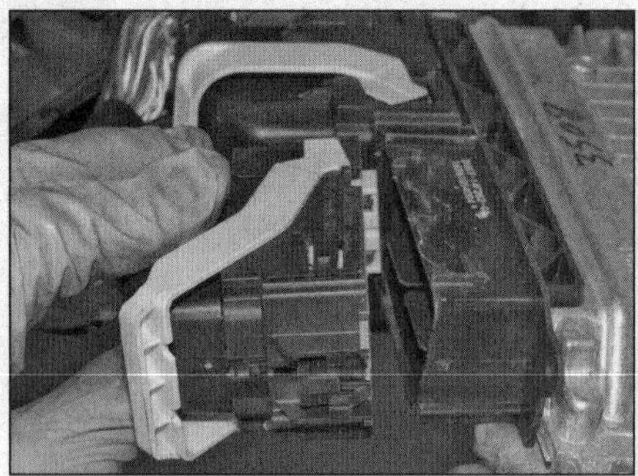

6.6a Lift the locking bar to disconnect the first plug...

6.6b ...then do the same for the second plug

6.7 The PCM can be pulled off its locating pins

6.9a Slacken the 2 bolts in the wheelarch area...

6.9b ...and the one through the foglight aperture

6 Prise up the locking bars and disconnect the wiring plugs from the PCM **(see illustrations)**.

7 Pull the PCM from its rubber locating pins **(see illustration)**.

8 If not already done, remove the front foglight assembly from place, as described in Chapter 12 Section 9.

9 Undo the 2 retaining bolts in the wheelarch area, and the one bolt accessed through the foglight aperture and manoeuvre the PCM housing from place **(see illustrations)**.

Refitting

10 Refitting is a reversal of removal. After reconnection, the vehicle must be driven for several miles so that the PCM can re-learn its basic settings. If the engine still runs erratically, the basic setting may be reinstated by a Ford dealer or suitably equipped repairer. **Note:** *If a new PCM has been fitted, it will need to be coded using Ford diagnostic equipment. Entrust this task to a Ford dealer or suitably equipped repairer.*

7 Ignition coils – removal and refitting

Removal

1 Pull up and remove the plastic cover from the top of the engine.

2 Slide out the locking catch and disconnect the wiring plug from the top of the ignition coil **(see illustration)**.

3 Undo the retaining bolt, and gently pull the coil upwards, from the spark plug **(see illustration)**.

Caution: Pull the coil units upwards smoothly and slowly. The silicone tube that

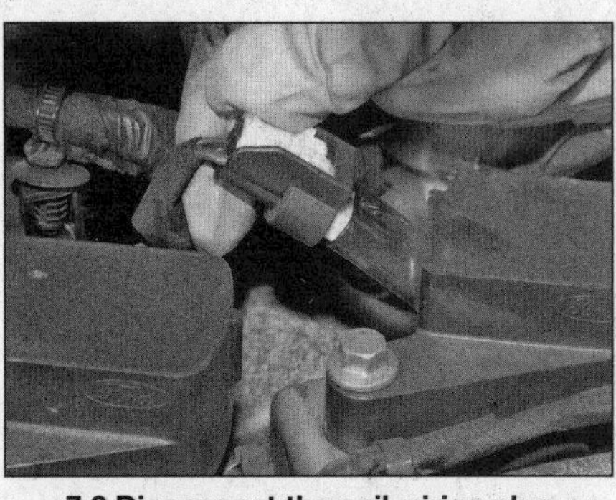

7.2 Disconnect the coil wiring plug

7.3 Remove the bolt and lift up the coil

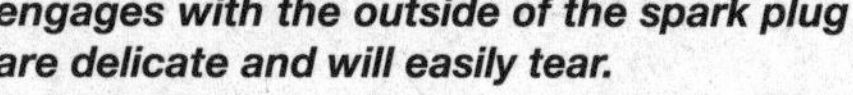

engages with the outside of the spark plug are delicate and will easily tear.

4 Repeat this procedure on the remaining ignition coils.

Testing

5 The circuitry arrangement of the ignition coil unit on these engines is such that testing of an individual coil in isolation from the remainder of the engine management system is unlikely to prove effective in diagnosing a particular fault. Should there be any reason to suspect a faulty individual coil, the engine management system self-diagnosis system should be interrogated as described in Section 4.

Refitting

6 Refitting is a reversal of the relevant removal procedure ensuring the wiring plugs are securely reconnected, and the coil retaining bolts are tightened to their specified torque.

Note: *The silicone tubes that engage with the spark plugs are pre-coated to aid fitting and removal. Under no circumstances should they be lubricated with oil or grease.*

8 Ignition timing – checking and adjustment

1 There are no timing marks on the flywheel or crankshaft pulley. The timing is constantly being monitored and adjusted by the engine management ECU, and nominal values cannot be given. Therefore, it is not possible for the home mechanic to check the ignition timing.

2 The only way in which the ignition timing can be checked is using special electronic test equipment, connected to the engine management system diagnostic connector; see Section 4 for further information.

9 Knock sensor – removal and refitting

Removal

1 The knock sensor(s) is screwed into the cylinder block below the intake manifold.

Remove the intake manifold as described in Chapter 4A Section 14.

2 Disconnect the wiring plug, undo the retaining bolt and remove the sensor **(see illustration)**.

Refitting

3 Ensure the mating surfaces of the cylinder block and knock sensor are clean.

4 Position the sensor on the cylinder block, insert the retaining bolt and tighten it to the specified torque.

Note: *It's essential for the correct functioning of the knock sensor that the retaining bolt is tightened to the specified torque.*

5 Refitting is a reversal of the removal procedure.

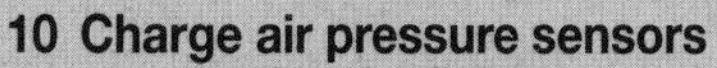

10 Charge air pressure sensors – removal and refitting

Manifold pressure sensor

Removal

1 Unlock and disconnect the sensor wiring plug.

2 Remove the sensor **(see illustration)**.

Refitting

3 Check the condition of the sensor O-ring seal and renew if necessary.

4 Apply a thin smear of grease to the O-ring seal, then refit the sensor.

5 Reconnect the wiring plug.

11 Engine coolant temperature sensor – removal and refitting

Removal

1 Partially drain the cooling system to just below the level of the sensor (as described in Chapter 1A Section 34). Alternatively, have ready a suitable bung to plug the sensor aperture whilst the sensor is removed. If this method is used, take great care not to damage the switch aperture or use anything which will allow foreign matter to enter the cooling system.

11.3 Disconnect then unscrew the coolant temperature sensor

9.2 Unbolt and remove the sensor

2 Remove the air intake pipe as described in Chapter 4A Section 3.

3 Prise out the clip, disconnect the wiring plug, then unscrew the sensor from the cylinder block **(see illustration)**. If the system has not been drained, plug the sensor aperture to prevent further coolant loss.

Refitting

4 Where the sensor was screwed into place, check the condition of the O-ring seal, and fit the sensor, tightening it securely.

5 Reconnect the wiring plug.

6 The remainder of refitting is a reversal of removal. Top-up the cooling system as described in Chapter 1A Section 34.

12 Crankshaft position sensor – removal and refitting

Removal

1 Remove the right-hand front wheelarch liner, as described in Chapter 11 Section 39.

2 The sensor is located at the back of the cylinder block, behind the crankshaft pulley. Unlock and disconnect the sensor wiring plug **(see illustration)**.

3 Undo the retaining bolt and remove the sensor.

Refitting

4 Refitting is reverse of the removal procedure. Tighten the sensor retaining bolt to the specified torque.

12.2 Disconnect the crankshaft sensor wiring plug

10.2 Unclip and remove the sensor

13 Vehicle speed sensor

1 The engine management PCM receives vehicle speed data from the wheel speed sensors, via the ABS ECU.

14 Camshaft position sensors – removal and refitting

Removal

1 Pull up and remove the acoustic cover from the top of the engine.

2 There are two camshaft position sensors located on the left-hand end of the cylinder head **(see illustration)**.

3 Disconnect the wiring plug, then undo the bolt and remove the relevant sensor from the cylinder head cover.

Refitting

4 Refitting is the reverse of removal ensuring the sensor seal is in good condition. Tighten the retaining bolt to the specified torque.

15 Accelerator pedal position sensor

1 The sensor is integral with the accelerator pedal assembly – see Section 5.

14.2 Camshaft position sensors are on the left-hand end of the cylinder head cover

16 Air mass/hot film air mass sensor – removal and refitting

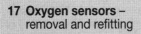

Removal

1 The sensor is fitted to the air outlet duct from the air cleaner housing. Unlock and disconnect the sensor wiring plug **(see illustration)**.

2 Undo the 2 retaining screws and detach the sensor from the air cleaner.

Refitting

3 Refitting is the reverse of removal. If a new meter has been fitted, the adaption values stored in the engine management PCM may need to be reset using diagnostic equipment. Entrust this task to a Ford dealer or suitably equipped repairer.

17 Oxygen sensors – removal and refitting

Removal

Warning: Ensure the exhaust system/turbocharger is completely cool before proceeding.

1 Pull up and remove the acoustic cover from the top of the engine.

2 Release the clamps securing the air duct to the air cleaner housing and intake pipe.

3 Undo the bolts and move the wiring harness of the top of the engine to one side.

16.1 Disconnect the sensor wiring plug

4 Remove the insulation material from around the wiring harness on the cylinder head.

5 Disconnect the breather pipe, release the clamp undo the retaining bolt and manoeuvre the air intake pipe from the rear of the engine **(see illustration)**. Disconnect any wiring plugs as the pipe is withdrawn.

6 Trace the wiring back from the oxygen sensor(s), which are located before and after the catalytic converter. Disconnect both wiring connectors and free the wiring from any relevant retaining clips or ties.

7 Unscrew the sensor from the exhaust system front pipe/manifold and remove it **(see illustration)**.

Caution: The oxygen sensors are delicate and will not work if they are dropped or knocked, if their power supply is disrupted, or if any cleaning materials are used on them.

Refitting

8 Refitting is a reverse of the removal procedure. Prior to installing the sensor apply a smear of high temperature grease to the sensor threads. Ensure that the sensor is tightened to the specified torque, and that the wiring is correctly routed and in no danger of contacting either the exhaust system or engine.

17.5 Unbolt and remove the air intake pipe

17.7 Unscrew the sensor from the manifold

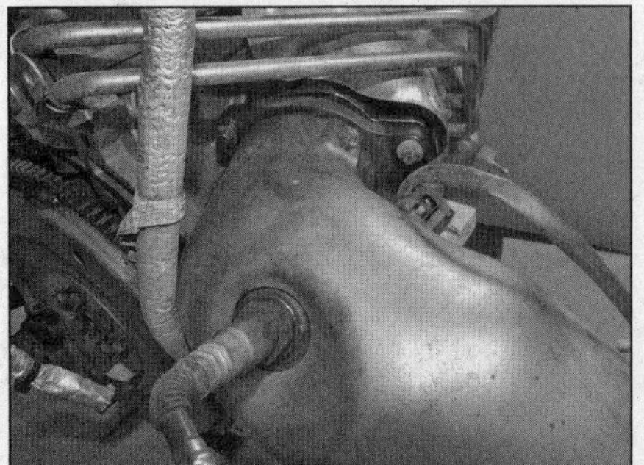

18.10 Undo the catalytic converter bolts

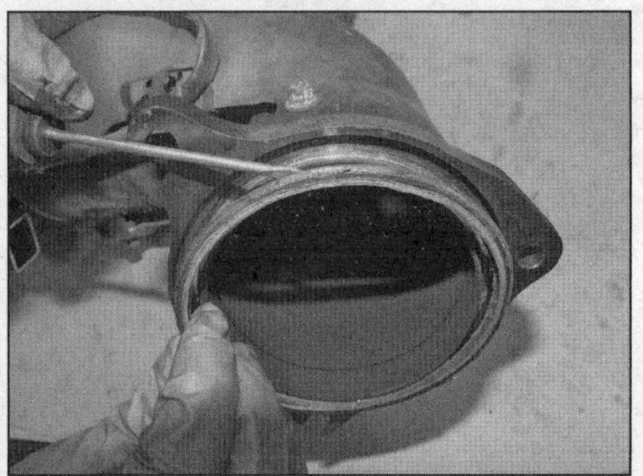

18.11 Refit the catalytic converter with a new gasket

18 Emission control systems – testing and component renewal

Crankcase emission control

1 The components of this system require no attention other than to check that the hose(s) are clear and undamaged at regular intervals.

Evaporative emission control

2 If the system is thought to be faulty, disconnect the hoses from the charcoal canister and purge control valve and check that they are clear by blowing through them. If the purge control valve or charcoal canister is thought to be faulty, they must be renewed.

Exhaust emission control

3 The performance of the catalytic converter can be checked only by measuring the exhaust gases using a good-quality, carefully-calibrated exhaust gas analyser.

4 If the CO level at the tailpipe is too high, the vehicle should be taken to a Ford dealer or specialist so that the complete fuel injection and ignition systems, including the oxygen sensor, can be thoroughly checked using the special diagnostic equipment.

Oxygen sensor renewal

5 Refer to Section 17.

Catalytic converter renewal

6 Raise the front of the vehicle and support it securely on axle stands (see *Jacking and vehicle support*). Release the fasteners and remove the engine undershield.

7 Remove both oxygen sensors as described in Section 17.

8 Unbolt the front pipe from the rest of the exhaust system.

9 Unclip the rubber exhaust mountings from the rear of the catalytic converter.

10 Undo the 3 boltssecuring the catalytic converter to the turbocharger **(see illustration)**. Note that a new clamp and seal will be required for refitting.

11 Prior to refitting, locate a new clamp on the turbocharger output flange, and position the new gasket **(see illustration)**.

12 Manoeuvre the catalytic converter upwards into position against the turbocharger flange (ensure the new gasket and clamp remain in place), then refit and finger-tighten the mounting bracket nuts.

13 Tighten the turbocharger-to-catalytic converter clamp to the specified torque.

14 Tighten the catalytic converter mounting bracket nuts to the specified torque.

15 The remainder of refitting is a reversal of removal.

Chapter 6 Part B
Engine and emission control systems – diesel models

Contents

Degrees of difficulty

Easy, suitable for novice with little experience 	Fairly easy, suitable for beginner with some experience	Fairly difficult, suitable for competent DIY mechanic	Difficult, suitable for experienced DIY mechanic	Very difficult, suitable for expert DIY or professional 

Specifications

Engine management system

Diesel engines	DDE High-pressure direct injection with full electronic control, intercooler and turbocharger

Torque wrench settings

Torque wrench settings	Nm	lbf ft
Camshaft position sensor	6	4
Common fuel rail pressure sensor	70	52
Crankshaft position sensor	8	6
Exhaust gas/particulate filter temperature sensor	15	10
Glow plugs	6	4
Oxygen sensors	15	10
Particulate filter-to-turbocharger clamp*	15	10

** Do not re-use*

1 Engine management system

Electronic control system

1 The electronic control system consists of the following components:

a) Powertrain Control Module (PCM).
b) Crankshaft speed/position sensor – informs the PCM of the engine speed and crankshaft angular position.
c) Camshaft position sensor – informs the PCM of the camshafts' positions.
d) Accelerator pedal position sensor – informs the PCM of the pedal position and rate of change.
e) Coolant temperature sensor – informs the PCM of the engine coolant temperature.
f) Fuel temperature sensor – informs the PCM of the fuel temperature.
g) Air mass meter – informs the PCM of the intake air quantity.
h) Fuel pressure sensor – informs the PCM of the fuel pressure within the accumulator (common) rail.
i) Fuel injectors.
j) Fuel pressure control valve – allows the PCM to control the pressure of the fuel in the accumulator (common) rail.
k) Preheating control unit – controls the voltage and duty-cycle of the glow plugs.
l) EGR solenoid valve – allows the PCM to control the flow of exhaust gasses recirculated in to the intake system.
m) Charge air temperature/pressure sensor – informs the PCM of the pressure and temperature of the intake air.
n) Charge pressure sensor – informs the PCM of the air pressure in the intake manifold.
o) Exhaust gas temperature sensor – informs the PCM of the temperature of the exhaust gasses.
p) Particulate filter pressure differential sensor – informs the PCM of the difference in pressure between gasses entering and leaving the particulate filter.

2 The information from the various sensors is passed to the PCM, which evaluates the signals. The PCM contains electronic 'maps' which enable it to calculate the optimum quantity of fuel to inject, the appropriate start of injection, and even pre- and post-injection fuel quantities, for each individual engine cylinder under any given condition of engine operation.

3 Additionally, the PCM carries out monitoring and self-diagnostic functions. Any faults in the system are stored in the PCM memory, which enables quick and accurate fault diagnosis using appropriate diagnostic equipment (such as a suitable fault code reader/scan tool).

Pre/post-heating system

4 To assist cold starting, diesel engines are fitted with a preheating system, which consists of three glow plugs (one per cylinder), a glow plug relay unit, a facia-mounted warning lamp, the engine management PCM, and the associated electrical wiring.

5 The glow plugs are miniature electric heating elements, encapsulated in a ceramic case with a probe at one end and electrical connection at the other. Each combustion chamber has one glow plug threaded into it, with the tip of the glow plug probe positioned directly in line with incoming spray of fuel from the injectors. When the glow plug is energised, it heats up rapidly, causing the fuel passing over the glow plug probe to be heated to its optimum temperature, ready for combustion. In addition, some of the fuel passing over the glow plugs is ignited and this helps to trigger the combustion process.

6 The preheating system begins to operate as soon as the ignition key is switched to the second position. A facia-mounted warning lamp informs the driver that preheating is taking place. The lamp extinguishes when sufficient preheating has taken place to allow the engine to be started, but power will still be supplied to the glow plugs for a further period until the engine is started. If no attempt is made to start the engine, the power supply to the glow plugs is switched off after 10 seconds to prevent battery drain and glow plug burnout.

7 With the electronically-controlled diesel injection systems fitted to models in this manual, the glow plug relay unit is controlled by the engine management system PCM, which determines the necessary preheating time based on inputs from the various system sensors. The system monitors the temperature of the inlet air, and then alters the preheating time (the length for which the glow plugs are supplied with current) to suit the conditions.

8 Post-heating takes place after the ignition key has been released from the 'start' position. The glow plugs continue to operate for a maximum of 60 seconds, helping to improve fuel combustion whilst the engine is warming-up, resulting in quieter, smoother running and reduced exhaust emissions.

9 The glow plug for cylinder No.2 incorporates a pressure sensor to monitor the combustion chamber pressure. This steel cased glow plug element incorporates a strain gauge. The deformation of the strain gauge is converted into a voltage signal, and is used by the engine management PCM to determine fuel quality, and engine condition.

Testing

10 The glow plugs are not supplied with battery voltage in order to operate. They are provided with a voltage of between 5 and 7 volts, but the pulse-width of the voltage is modulate. This makes it impossible to test the plugs using traditional methods. If a fault is suspected, have the engine management self-diagnosis system interrogated using diagnostic equipment connected to the 16-pin diagnostic plug located under the driver's side of the facia.

2 Emissions systems – general information

1 All petrol engines use unleaded petrol and also have various other features built into the fuel system to help minimise harmful emissions. In addition, all engines are equipped with the crankcase emission control system described below. All engines are also equipped with a catalytic converter and an evaporative emission control system.

2 All diesel engines are also designed to meet the strict emission requirements and are equipped with a crankcase emission control system and a catalytic converter/particulate filter. To further reduce exhaust emissions, all diesel engines are also fitted with an exhaust gas recirculation (EGR) system. The particulate uses porous silicon carbide substrate to trap particulates of carbon as the exhaust gases pass through.

3 The emission control systems function as follows.

Crankcase emission control

4 Refer to the description for petrol engines.

Exhaust emission control

5 To minimise the level of exhaust pollutants released into the atmosphere, a catalytic converter/particulate filter is fitted in the exhaust system of all models.

6 The catalytic converter consists of a canister containing a fine mesh impregnated with a catalyst material, over which the hot exhaust gases pass. The catalyst speeds up the oxidation of harmful carbon monoxide, un-burnt hydrocarbons and soot, effectively reducing the quantity of harmful products released into the atmosphere via the exhaust gases.

Exhaust gas recirculation system

7 This system is designed to recirculate small quantities of exhaust gas into the inlet tract, and therefore into the combustion process. This process reduces the level of oxides of nitrogen present in the final exhaust gas, which is released into the atmosphere.

8 The volume of exhaust gas recirculated is controlled by the system electronic control unit.

9 A vacuum-operated valve is fitted to the manifold, to regulate the quantity of exhaust gas recirculated. The valve is operated by the vacuum supplied by the solenoid valve, or electrically powered solenoid.

Particulate filter system

10 The particulate filter is combined with the catalytic converter in the exhaust system, and its purpose it to trap particulates of carbon (soot) as the exhaust gases pass through, in order to comply with latest emission regulations.

3.4a Simple code readers are an economical way to extract trouble codes when the CHECK ENGINE light comes on

3.4b Hand-held scan tools like these can extract computer codes and also perform diagnostics

4.3 The 16-pin Data Link Connector (DLC) is located under the right-hand side of the facia

11 The filter can be automatically regenerated (cleaned) by the system's PCM on-board the vehicle. The engine's high-pressure injection system is utilised to inject fuel into the exhaust gases during the post-injection period; this causes the filter temperature to increase sufficiently to oxidise the particulates, leaving an ash residue. The regeneration period is automatically controlled by the on-board PCM.

3 European On Board Diagnosis (EOBD) system

General description

1 All models are equipped with the European On-Board Diagnosis (EOBD) system. This system consists of an on-board computer known as the ECU (Electronic Control Unit), Electronic Control Module (ECM) or Powertrain Control Module (PCM), and information sensors, which monitor various functions of the engine and send data to the ECU/ECM/PCM. This system incorporates a series of diagnostic monitors that detect and identify fuel injection and emissions control system faults and store the information in the computer memory. This system also tests sensors and output actuators, diagnoses drive cycles, freezes data and clears codes.

2 The ECU/ECM/PCM is the brain of the electronically controlled fuel and emissions system. It receives data from a number of sensors and other electronic components (switches, relays, etc.). Based on the information it receives, the ECU/ECM/PCM generates output signals to control various relays, solenoids (fuel injectors) and other actuators. The ECU/ECM/PCM is specifically calibrated to optimise the emissions, fuel economy and driveability of the vehicle.

3 Whilst the vehicle is within the manufactures warranty, have any faults diagnosed and rectified by the dealer service department.

Scan tool information

4 As extracting the Diagnostic Trouble Codes (DTCs) from an engine management system is now the first step in troubleshooting many computer-controlled systems and components, a code reader, at the very least, will be required. More powerful scan tools can also perform many of the diagnostics once associated with expensive factory scan tools **(see illustrations)**. If you're planning to obtain a generic scan tool for your vehicle, make sure that it's compatible with EOBD systems. If you don't plan to purchase a code reader or scan tool and don't have access to one, you can have the codes extracted by a dealer service department or a suitably equipped repairer.

4 Obtaining and clearing Diagnostic Trouble Codes (DTCs)

1 All models covered by this manual are equipped with on-board diagnostics. When the ECU/ECM/PCM recognises a malfunction in a monitored emission or engine control system, component or circuit, it turns on the Malfunction Indicator Light (MIL) on the dash. The ECU/ECM/PCM will continue to display the MIL until the problem is fixed and the Diagnostic Trouble Code (DTC) is cleared from the ECU/ECM/PCM's memory. You'll need a scan tool to access any DTCs stored in the ECU/ECM/PCM.

2 Before outputting any DTCs stored in the ECU/ECM/PCM, thoroughly inspect ALL electrical connectors and hoses. Make sure that all electrical connections are secure, clean and free of corrosion. And make sure that all hoses are correctly connected, fit securely and are in good condition.

Accessing the DTCs

3 The Diagnostic Trouble Codes (DTCs) can only be accessed with a code reader or scan tool. Professional scan tools are expensive, but relatively inexpensive generic code readers or scan tools **(see illustrations 3.4a and 3.4b)** are available at most auto parts stores. Simply plug the connector of the scan tool into the diagnostic connector **(see illustration)**. Then follow the instructions included with the scan tool to extract the DTCs.

4 Once you have outputted all of the stored DTCs, look them up on the accompanying DTC chart.

5 After troubleshooting the source of each DTC, make any necessary repairs or replace the defective component(s).

Clearing the DTCs

6 Clear the DTCs with the code reader or scan tool in accordance with the instructions provided by the tool's manufacturer.

Diagnostic Trouble Codes

7 The accompanying tables are a sample list of the Diagnostic Trouble Codes (DTCs) that can be accessed by a do-it-yourselfer working at home (there are many, many more DTCs available to professional mechanics with proprietary scan tools and software, but those codes cannot be accessed by a generic scan tool). If, after you have checked and repaired the connectors, wire harness and vacuum hoses (if applicable) for an emission-related system, component or circuit, the problem persists, have the vehicle checked by a dealer service department or suitably equipped repairer.

EOBD trouble codes

Code	Probable cause
P000A	Camshaft 1 position, (bank no.1), slow response
P000B	Camshaft 2 position, (bank no.1), slow response
P0010	Camshaft 1 position, (bank no.1), actuator circuit open
P0013	Camshaft 2 position, (bank no.1), actuator circuit open
P0016	Crankshaft/camshaft timing (bank no.1. sensor no.1) misalignment
P0017	Crankshaft/camshaft timing (bank no.1. sensor no.2) misalignment
P0031	Upstream oxygen sensor (cylinder bank no. 1), heater circuit low voltage

Code	Probable cause
P0032	Upstream oxygen sensor heater (cylinder bank no. 1), heater circuit high voltage
P0037	Downstream oxygen sensor (cylinder bank no. 1), heater circuit low voltage
P0038	Downstream oxygen sensor (cylinder bank no. 1), heater circuit high voltage
P0068	Manifold pressure/throttle position correlation – high-flow/ vacuum leak
P0070	Ambient temperature sensor stuck
P0071	Ambient temperature sensor performance
P0072	Ambient temperature sensor, low voltage
P0073	Ambient temperature sensor, high voltage
P0107	Manifold Absolute Pressure (MAP) sensor, low voltage
P0108	Manifold Absolute Pressure (MAP) sensor, high voltage
P0110	Intake Air Temperature (IAT) sensor, stuck
P0111	Intake Air Temperature (IAT) sensor performance
P0112	Intake Air Temperature (IAT) sensor, low voltage
P0113	Intake Air Temperature (IAT) sensor, high voltage
P0116	Engine Coolant Temperature (ECT) sensor performance
P0117	Engine Coolant Temperature (ECT) sensor, low voltage
P0118	Engine Coolant Temperature (ECT) sensor, high voltage
P0121	Throttle Position (TP) sensor performance
P0122	Throttle Position (TP) sensor, low voltage
P0123	Throttle Position (TP) sensor, high voltage
P0125	Insufficient coolant temperature for closed-loop control; closed-loop temperature not reached
P0128	Thermostat rationality
P0129	Barometric pressure out-of-range (low)
P0131	Upstream oxygen sensor (cylinder bank no. 1), low voltage or shorted to ground
P0132	Upstream oxygen sensor (cylinder bank no. 1), high voltage or shorted to voltage
P0133	Upstream oxygen sensor (cylinder bank no. 1), slow response
P0134	Upstream oxygen sensor (cylinder bank no. 1), sensor remains at center (not switching)
P0135	Upstream oxygen sensor (cylinder bank no. 1), heater failure
P0137	Downstream oxygen sensor (cylinder bank no. 1), low voltage or shorted to ground
P0138	Downstream oxygen sensor (cylinder bank no. 1), high voltage or shorted to voltage
P0139	Downstream oxygen sensor (cylinder bank no. 1), slow response
P0140	Downstream oxygen sensor (cylinder bank no. 1), sensor remains at center (not switching)
P0141	Downstream oxygen sensor (cylinder bank no. 1), heater failure
P0171	Fuel control system too lean (cylinder bank no. 1)
P0172	Fuel control system too rich (cylinder bank no. 1)
P0201	Injector circuit malfunction – cylinder no. 1
P0202	Injector circuit malfunction – cylinder no. 2
P0203	Injector circuit malfunction – cylinder no. 3
P0204	Injector circuit malfunction – cylinder no. 4
P0300	Multiple cylinder misfire detected
P0301	Cylinder no. 1 misfire detected
P0302	Cylinder no. 2 misfire detected
P0303	Cylinder no. 3 misfire detected
P0304	Cylinder no. 4 misfire detected
P0315	No crank sensor learned
P0320	No crankshaft reference signal at Powertrain Control Module (PCM)
P0325	Knock sensor circuit malfunction
P0335	Crankshaft Position (CKP) sensor circuit
P0339	Crankshaft Position (CKP) sensor intermittent
P0340	Camshaft Position (CMP) sensor circuit
P0344	Camshaft Position (CMP) sensor intermittent
P0351	Ignition coil no. 1, primary circuit
P0352	Ignition coil no. 2, primary circuit
P0353	Ignition coil no. 3, primary circuit
P0354	Ignition coil no. 4, primary circuit
P0365	Camshaft Position (CMP) sensor circuit (bank no.1. sensor no.2)
P0369	Camshaft Position (CMP) sensor intermittent (bank no.1. sensor no.2)
P0440	General Evaporative Emission Control (EVAP) system failure
P0441	Evaporative Emission Control (EVAP) system, incorrect purge flow
P0442	Evaporative Emission Control (EVAP) system, medium leak (0.040-inch) detected
P0443	Evaporative Emission Control (EVAP) system, purge solenoid circuit malfunction
P0452	Natural Vacuum Leak Detector (NVLD) pressure sensor circuit, low voltage
P0453	Natural Vacuum Leak Detector (NVLD) pressure sensor circuit, high input
P0455	Evaporative Emission Control (EVAP) system, large leak detected
P0456	Evaporative Emission Control (EVAP) system, small leak (0.020-inch) detected
P0460	Fuel level sending unit, no change as vehicle is operated
P0461	Fuel level sensor circuit, range or performance problem
P0462	Fuel level sending unit or sensor circuit, low voltage
P0463	Fuel level sending unit or sensor circuit, high voltage
P0480	Low-speed fan control relay circuit malfunction
P0498	Natural Vacuum Leak Detector (NVLD) canister vent valve solenoid circuit, low voltage
P0499	Natural Vacuum Leak Detector (NVLD) canister vent valve solenoid circuit, high voltage
P0500	No vehicle speed signal (four-speed automatic transaxles)
P0501	Vehicle speed sensor, range or performance problem
P0503	Vehicle speed sensor 1, erratic
P0506	Idle speed control system, rpm lower than expected
P0507	Idle speed control system, rpm higher than expected
P0508	Idle Air Control (IAC) valve circuit, low voltage
P0509	Idle Air Control (IAC) valve circuit, high voltage
P0513	Invalid SKIM key (engine immobilizer problem)
P0516	Battery temperature sensor, low voltage
P0517	Battery temperature sensor, high voltage
P0519	Idle speed performance
P0522	Engine oil pressure sensor/switch circuit, low voltage
P0532	Air conditioning refrigerant pressure sensor, low voltage
P0533	Air conditioning refrigerant pressure sensor, high voltage
P0551	Power Steering Pressure (PSP) switch circuit, range or performance problem
P0562	Battery voltage low
P0563	Battery voltage high
P0579	Speed control switch circuit, range or performance problem
P0580	Speed control switch circuit, low voltage
P0581	Speed control switch circuit, high voltage
P0582	Speed control vacuum solenoid circuit
P0858	Speed control switch 1/2 correlation
P0586	Speed control vent solenoid circuit
P0591	Speed control switch 2 circuit, performance problem
P0592	Speed control switch 2 circuit, low voltage
P0593	Speed control switch circuit 2, high voltage
P0594	Speed control servo power circuit
P0600	Serial communication link malfunction
P0601	Powertrain Control Module (PCM), internal controller failure
P0622	Alternator field control circuit malfunction or field not switching correctly

Code	Probable cause
P0627	Fuel pump relay circuit
P0630	Vehicle Identification Number (VIN) not programmed in Powertrain Control Module (PCM)
P0632	Odometer not programmed in Powertrain Control Module (PCM)
P0633	SKIM key not programmed in Powertrain Control Module (PCM)
P0642	Sensor reference voltage 2 circuit, low voltage
P0643	Sensor reference voltage 2 circuit, high voltage
P0645	Air conditioning clutch relay circuit
P0685	Automatic Shutdown (ASD) relay control circuit
P0688	Automatic Shutdown (ASD) relay sense circuit, low voltage
P0700	Electronic Automatic Transaxle (EATX) control system malfunction or DTC present
P0703	Brake switch circuit malfunction
P0833	Clutch released switch circuit
P0850	Park/Neutral switch malfunction
P0856	Traction control torque request circuit

5 Accelerator pedal – removal and refitting

1 This procedure is covered in Chapter 6A Section 5.

6 Powertrain Control Module (PCM) – removal and refitting

Removal

1 Disconnect the battery negative lead as described in Chapter 5 Section 4.

Note: *Disconnecting the battery will erase any fault codes stored in the PCM. It is strongly recommended that the fault code memory of the unit is interrogated using a code reader or scanner prior to battery disconnection.*

2 If not already done, remove the front foglight assembly from place, as described in Chapter 12 Section 9.

3 Undo the 2 retaining bolts in the wheelarch area, and the one bolt accessed through the foglight aperture and manoeuvre the PCM housing from place **(see illustrations)**.

4 Turn around the PCM housing to access the glow plug relay wiring plug, raise the locking bar and disconnect **(see illustration)**.

Refitting

5 Refitting is a reversal of removal. After reconnection, the vehicle must be driven for several miles so that the PCM can re-learn its basic settings. If the engine still runs erratically, the basic setting may be reinstated by a Ford dealer or suitably equipped repairer.

Note: *If a new PCM has been fitted, it will need to be coded using Ford diagnostic equipment. Entrust this task to a Ford dealer or suitably equipped repairer.*

7 Charge air pressure sensors – removal and refitting

Manifold pressure sensor

Removal

1 Unlock and disconnect the sensor wiring plug.

2 Remove the sensor **(see illustration)**.

Refitting

3 Check the condition of the sensor O-ring seal and renew if necessary.

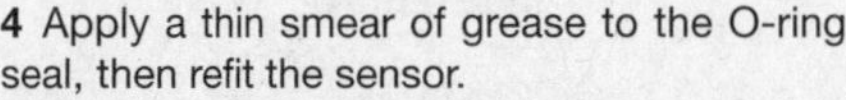

4 Apply a thin smear of grease to the O-ring seal, then refit the sensor.

5 Reconnect the wiring plug.

8 Charge air temperature sensor – removal and refitting

Removal

1 Remove the air cleaner assembly as described in Chapter 4B Section 6.

2 The sensor is located on the side of the throttle body **(see illustration)**. Disconnect the sensor wiring plug.

3 Rotate the sensor 45° anti-clockwise and remove it from the throttle body. Check the condition of the sealing ring, and renew if necessary.

Refitting

4 Refitting is a reversal of removal.

6.3a Slacken the 2 bolts in the wheelarch area...

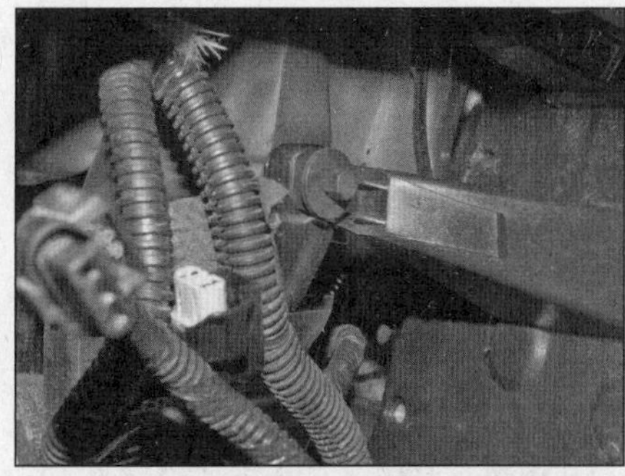

6.3b ..and the one through the foglight aperture

6.4 Lift the locking bar and unplug the glow plug relay

7.2 The sensor is retained by a single bolt

8.2 The charge air temperature sensor is located on the underside of the throttle body

10.2 Unplug the sensor then undo the bolt and remove

12.2 Disconnect and unbolt the camshaft position sensor

14.1 Disconnect the sensor wiring plug

9 Engine coolant temperature sensor – removal and refitting

Removal

1 Partially drain the cooling system to just below the level of the sensor (as described in Chapter 1B Section 36). Alternatively, have ready a suitable bung to plug the sensor aperture whilst the sensor is removed. If this method is used, take great care not to damage the switch aperture or use anything which will allow foreign matter to enter the cooling system.
2 Pull up and remove the acoustic cover from the top of the engine.
3 Remove the air cleaner assembly, as described in Section 4B Section 6.
4 Release the clips to disconnect the hoses, then unplug the wiring connectors, then unscrew the coolant temperature sensor from the right-hand end of the cylinder head. If the system has not been drained, plug the sensor aperture to prevent further coolant loss.

Refitting

5 Reconnect the wiring plug and cooling system hoses.
6 The remainder of refitting is a reversal of removal. Top-up the cooling system as described in Chapter 1B Section 36.

10 Crankshaft position sensor – removal and refitting

Removal

1 Remove the right-hand front wheelarch liner, as described in Chapter 11 Section 39.
2 The sensor is located adjacent to the crankshaft pulley. Unlock and disconnect the sensor wiring plug **(see illustration)**.
3 Undo the retaining bolt and remove the sensor.

Refitting

4 Refitting is reverse of the removal procedure. Tighten the sensor retaining bolt to the specified torque.

11 Vehicle speed sensor

General information

1 The engine management PCM receives vehicle speed data from the wheel speed sensors, via the ABS ECU.

12 Camshaft position sensor(s) – removal and refitting

Removal

1 The camshaft position sensor is located at the right-hand end of the cylinder head. Pull the plastic cover on the top of the engine upwards from its mountings.
2 Disconnect the sensor wiring plug **(see illustration)**.
3 Undo the retaining bolt and remove the sensor.

Refitting

4 Unclip the wiring from the timing belt upper cover, then unbolt the cover and remove it.
5 Insert the sensor back into the cylinder head, and tighten its retaining bolt finger-tight at this stage.
6 Use a feeler gauge to position the sensor correctly (0.9mm ± 0.3mm) from the rear face of the camshaft sprocket/signal wheel.
7 Tighten the retaining bolt to the required torque.

15.5 Use a split socket to remove the sensors

8 Reinstall the timing belt upper cover, and reconnect the sensor's wiring plug.
9 Refit the engine cover.

13 Accelerator pedal position sensor

1 The sensor is integral with the accelerator pedal assembly – see Section 5.

14 Air mass/Hot film air mass sensor – removal and refitting

Removal

1 The sensor is fitted to the air outlet duct from the air cleaner housing. Unlock and disconnect the sensor wiring plug **(see illustration)**.
2 Undo the 2 retaining screws and detach the sensor from the air cleaner.

Refitting

3 Refitting is the reverse of removal. If a new meter has been fitted, the adaption values stored in the engine management PCM may need to be reset using diagnostic equipment. Entrust this task to a Ford dealer or suitably equipped repairer.

15 Oxygen sensors – removal and refitting

Removal

1 Pull the plastic cover on the top of the engine upwards from its mountings.
2 Jack up the front of the vehicle, as described in *Jacking and Vehicle Support*, then remove the engine undertray.
3 Disconnect the breather hose, undo the retaining screw, release the clamps and remove the air intake pipe behind the cylinder head.
4 Trace the sensor wiring back to the wiring plugs and disconnect them.
5 Using a split-type socket unscrew and remove the sensors **(see illustration)**.

16.4 Remove the bolts then the EGR pipe

16.5 Undo the bolts and remove the manifold

16.7 Remove the dispstick mounting bolt and move aside

Refitting

6 Refitting is a reversal of removal. New sensors have their threads pre-coated with anti-seize compound (Never-Seez – available from Ford dealers). If a sensor is being refitted, apply a little anti-seize compound to the threads. Tighten it to the specified torque.

16 Glow plugs – removal and refitting

Warning: If the preheating system has just been energised, or if the engine has been running, the glow plugs will be very hot.

Removal

1 Ensure the ignition is turned off, and cold.

2 Pull up the plastic cover from its mountings at the top of the engine.

3 Remove the throttle body as described in Chapter 4B Section 15.

4 Undo the 4 bolts and manoeuvre the EGR pipe from place **(see illustration)**.

5 Remove the 3 retaining bolts then remove the throttle-body-to-cylinder-head manifold **(see illustration)**.

6 Remove the fuel filter and mount as described in Chapter 1B Section 28.

7 Remove the mounting bolt for the dipstick, to allow you to move the distick aside for ease of access to the second glow plug **(see illustration)**.

8 Squeeze together the sides, and pull each connector from the glow plugs **(see illustration)**.

9 Using a deep socket, unscrew the glow plugs from the cylinder head **(see illustration)**. ***Caution: Handle the glow plugs with care. They are extremely fragile.***

Refitting

10 Refit by reversing the removal operations. Apply a smear of copper-based anti-seize compound to the plug threads and tighten the glow plugs to the specified torque. Do not overtighten, as this can damage the glow plug element.

11 Refit any components removed for access.

16.8 Detach the wiring connector from the glow plug

16.9 Remove the glow plugs from place

17 Pre/post-heating system relay unit – removal and refitting

Removal

1 Disconnect the battery negative lead as described in Chapter 5 Section 4.

2 Remove the front left-hand foglight as described in Chapter 12 Section 9.

3 Lift the locking brace and remove the wiring plug from place (PCM housing removed for clarity) **(see illustration)**.

4 Undo the glow plug relay retaining screw (PCM housing removed for clarity) **(see illustration)**.

5 Use a thin screwdriver to get behind the relay and release the 2 locking tabs **(see illustration)**.

6 Manoeuvre the glow plug relay from place.

Refitting

7 Refitting is a reversal of removal, ensuring that the wiring connectors are correctly connected.

17.3 Disconnect the glow plug relay

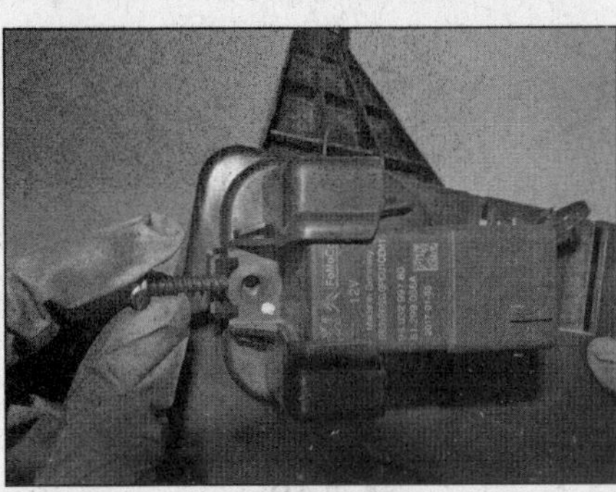
17.4 Remove the bolt that retains the glow plug relay

17.5 Insert a screwdriver to release the locking tabs

18.12a Disconnect the EGR bypass valve

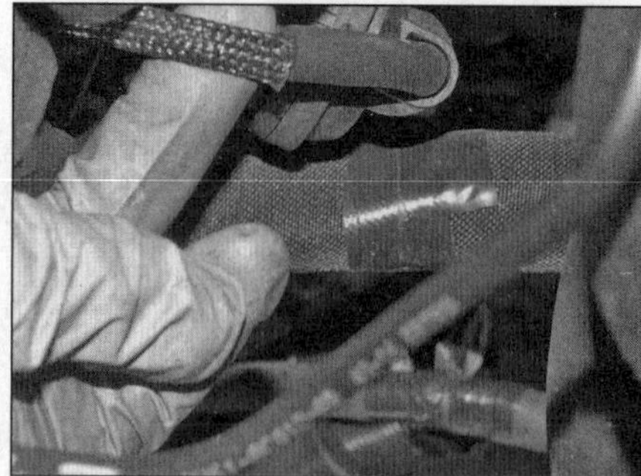

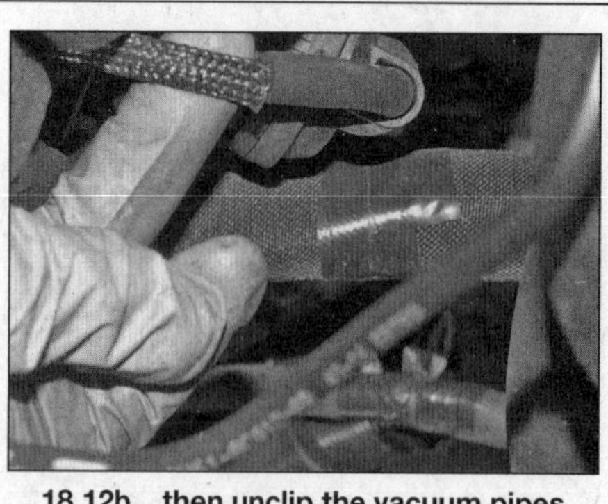

18.12b ...then unclip the vacuum pipes

18 Emission control systems – testing and component renewal

Crankcase emission control

1 The components of this system require no attention other than to check that the hose(s) are clear and undamaged at regular intervals.

Exhaust emission control

2 The performance of the catalytic converter and particulate filter can be checked only by measuring the exhaust gases using a good-quality, carefully-calibrated exhaust gas analyser.

3 If the catalytic converter or particulate filter is thought to be faulty, it is worth checking the problem is not due to a faulty injector. Refer to your Ford dealer for further information.

Exhaust gas recirculation system

4 Testing of the system should ideally be entrusted to a Ford dealer or suitably equipped repairer.

EGR valve renewal

5 The EGR valve and cooler are one unit. See Section 18 for the renewal procedure.

EGR cooler renewal

6 Drain the cooling system as described in Chapter 1B Section 36.

7 Remove the windscreen cowl panel as described in Chapter 11 Section 12.

8 Pull up the plastic cover from the top of the engine, then undo the screws and remove the sound insulation material from the cylinder head cover.

9 Remove the air filter housing and the battery and battery box (Chapter 5 Section 4).

10 Remove the fuel filter as described in Chapter 1B Section 28.

11 Undo the 4 retaining bolts and displace the fuel filter housing from place.

12 Disconnect the vacuum pipe from the EGR cooler bypass valve, and unclip the vacuum pipes from place **(see illustrations)**.

13 Disconnect the coolant hose at the left-hand side of the engine, then unbolt the coolant hose junction from the EGR cooler and move out of the way. The bolt is captive.

14 Disconnect the wiring plug from the EGR control valve **(see illustration)**.

15 Reach over the engine and undo the 2 retaining bolts securing the EGR pipe to the throttle body manifold **(see illustration)**.

16 Undo the retaining bolts and manoeuvre the EGR cooler/valve assembly from place **(see illustration)**.

17 Upon refitting, renew all gaskets and seals, regardless of their apparent condition.

18 The remainder of refitting is a reversal of removal.

Catalytic converter/ particulate filter renewal

19 Raise the vehicle and support it securely on axle stands (see *Jacking and vehicle support*).

20 Remove the windscreen scuttle panel as described in Chapter 11 Section 11. There is no need to do this step on 1.5-litre diesel models.

21 Remove the engine from the vehicle as described in Chapter 2D Section 5.

22 Remove the following:

a) *Oxygen sensors (Section 15).*
b) *Exhaust gas temperature sensors.*
c) *Differential pressure sensor.*

23 On 1.5-litre diesel models, undo the 4 retaining bolts and remove the upper heat shield.

24 Release the clamp securing the catalytic converter/particulate filter to the turbocharger **(see illustration)**. Note that a new clamp and gasket will be required.

25 On 1.5-litre diesels, brace the exhaust flexible pipe, to avoid damage.

26 On 1.5-litre diesels, working under the vehicle, unbolt the front of the exhaust system from the rear.

27 Undo the mounting nut then disconnect all wiring plugs and unclip all cables from the DPF.

28 On 1.5-litre diesels, undo the mounting bolts and manoeuvre downwards from place.

29 On 2.0-litre diesels, undo the 4 mounting bolts and remove the lower DPF mounting bracket.

30 Undo the upper 2 mounting bolts and manoeuvre the DPF assembly from place.

31 Refitting is a reversal of removal, noting the following:

a) *Prior to refitting, ensure the exhaust pipe flexible section is protected from excessive bending, as described above.*
b) *Tighten all fasteners to their specified torque where given.*
c) *Ford insist that the pressure differential sensor rubber hoses must be renewed.*

18.14 Unplug the EGR control unit

18.15 Undo the EGR pipe bolts

18.16 Manoeuvre the EGR assembly from the engine

18.24 Release the turbocharger securing clamp

Chapter 7 Part A
Manual transmission

Contents

Degrees of difficulty

Easy, suitable for novice with little experience 	Fairly easy, suitable for beginner with some experience 	Fairly difficult, suitable for competent DIY mechanic 	Difficult, suitable for experienced DIY mechanic	Very difficult, suitable for expert DIY or professional 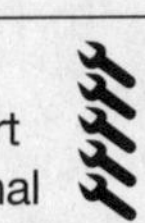

Specifications

General

Type	Manual, six forward speeds and reverse. Synchromesh on all forward speeds
Designation:	
1.5 litre engines	B6
2.0 litre engines	MMT6
Capacity:	
MMT6	1.9 litres
B6	1.58 litres
Recommended oil type	See *Lubricants and fluids* in Chapter 1A or Chapter 1B

Torque wrench settings	**Nm**	**lbf ft**
Engine-to-transmission fixing bolts	48	35
Gear position sensor	6	4
Oil drain plug	35	26
Oil filler/level plug:		
MMT6	35	26
B6	40	30

1 General information

1 The transmission is contained in a cast-aluminium alloy casing bolted to the engine's left-hand end, and consists of the gearbox and final drive differential – often called a transaxle.

2 Drive is transmitted from the crankshaft via the clutch to the input shaft, which has a splined extension to accept the clutch friction plate, and rotates in sealed ball-bearings. From the input shaft, drive is transmitted to the output shaft, which rotates in a roller bearing at its right-hand end, and a sealed ball-bearing at its left-hand end. From the output shaft, the drive is transmitted to the differential crownwheel, which rotates with the differential case and planetary gears, thus driving the sun gears and driveshafts. The rotation of the planetary gears on their shaft allows the inner roadwheel to rotate at a slower speed than the outer roadwheel when the car is cornering.

3 The input and output shafts are arranged side by side, parallel to the crankshaft and driveshafts, so that their gear pinion teeth are in constant mesh. In the neutral position, the output shaft gear pinions rotate freely, so that drive cannot be transmitted to the crownwheel.

4 Gear selection is via a floor-mounted lever and cable mechanism. The selector/gearchange cables causes the appropriate selector fork to move its respective synchro-sleeve along the shaft, to lock the gear pinion to the synchro-hub. Since the synchro-hubs are splined to the output shaft, this locks the pinion to the shaft, so that drive can be transmitted. To ensure that gear-changing can be made quickly and quietly, a synchromesh system is fitted to all forward gears, consisting of baulk rings and spring-loaded fingers, as well as the gear pinions and synchro-hubs. The synchromesh cones are formed on the mating faces of the baulk rings and gear pinions.

2 Manual transmission fluid – draining and refilling

Note: *There are two manual gearboxes: MMT6 fitted to the 2.0 diesel and B6 fitted to the 1.5 diesel – the petrol engines can be fitted with either gearbox. The level/drain plugs are situated in different locations, and the plug torque values and capacities are different.*

1 This operation is much quicker and

2.3a Transmission oil filler/level plug (MMT6 gearbox shown)...

2.3b ...and drain plug

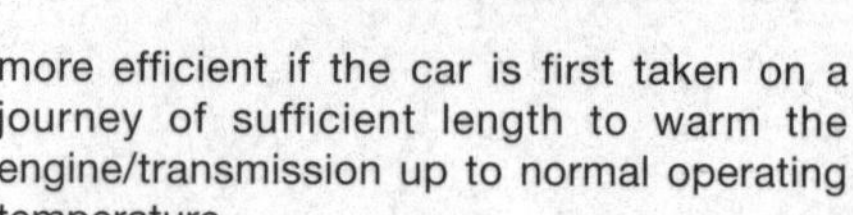

more efficient if the car is first taken on a journey of sufficient length to warm the engine/transmission up to normal operating temperature.

2 Park the car on level ground, switch off the ignition and apply the handbrake. For improved access, jack up the front of the car and support it securely on axle stands (see *Jacking and vehicle support*). Note that the car must be level to ensure accuracy when refilling and checking the oil level. Undo the fasteners and remove the engine undershield.

3 Wipe clean the area around the filler/level plug, which is situated adjacent to the left-hand driveshaft on the MMT6 transmission and and at the front on the B6 transmission. The drain plugs are in the same location for both manual transmissions. Unscrew the filler/level plug from the transmission **(see illustrations)**.

4 Position a container under the drain plug and unscrew the plug.

5 Allow the oil to drain completely into the container. If the oil is hot, take precautions against scalding.

6 When the oil has finished draining, clean the drain plug threads and those of the transmission casing, and refit the drain plug, tightening it to the specified torque wrench setting.

7 Refill the transmission carefully until oil begins to run out of the filler plug hole, then refit the filler/level plug and tighten it to the specified torque. Take the car on a short journey so that the new oil is distributed fully around the transmission components, then check the level again on your return.

8 Refit the engine undershield, and lower the vehicle to the ground.

3 Gearchange lever and cables – removal and refitting

Removal

Gearshift lever

1 Firmly apply the handbrake, then jack up the front of the vehicle and support it on axle stands (see *Jacking and vehicle support*).

2 Remove the air cleaner assembly as described in Chapter 4A Section 3 or Chapter 4B Section 6.

3 Remove the battery tray as described in Chapter 5 Section 4.

4 Remove the centre console as described in Chapter 11 Section 36.

5 Use a pair of thin-nosed plier to prise away the cables from the gearlever assembly **(see illustration)**.

6 Undo the 2 lower mounting bolts and 2 upper retaining nuts and manoeuvre the gearlever assembly from place **(see illustration)**.

7 Push the outer cable collar downwards to release it from the lever assembly **(see illustration)**.

8 Use a pair of thin-nosed pliers to prise the cable ball joints from the levers on the transmission **(see illustration)**.

9 Release the retaining clips and prise the outer cables upwards from the bracket.

10 Working underneath the vehicle, release the gearchange cables from the grommets/brackets along their length.

Gearshift cables

11 Remove the gearlever assembly as described earlier in this Section.

12 Disconnect and remove the left-hand intercooler pipe, as described in Chapter 4A Section 13 or Chapter 4B Section 20.

13 Disengage the cables from the mounting brackets on the gearbox **(see illustration)**.

Note: *Tie a piece of string to the gearbox end of the gearshift cables, to make the new cables easier to pull through.*

14 Working under the centre console, undo the 2 retaining bolts and pull the cables through.

3.5 Prise away the cables from the gearlever assembly

3.6 Undo the fixing to remove the gearlever assembly

3.7 Push the cable collar downwards to release it

3.8 Prise away the cables from the levers using thin pliers

3.13 Disengage the mounting clips for the gearshift cables

Gearlever gaiter

15 Unscrew and remove the gearknob, and withdraw the spring for the reversing collar **(see illustration)**.

16 Pull up the gaiter, and detach the gearshift actuation collar **(see illustration)**.

Refitting

17 Refitting is a reversal of the removal procedure, noting the following points:

a) Apply grease to the ball joints before refitting.

b) No adjustment of the gear change cables is possible.

4 Oil seals – renewal

Driveshaft oil seals

1 Remove the appropriate driveshaft as described in Chapter 8 Section 7.

2 Carefully prise the oil seal out of the transmission, using a large flat-bladed screwdriver or similar **(see illustration)**.

3 Remove all traces of dirt from the area around the oil seal aperture. Fit the new seal into its aperture, and drive it squarely into position using a suitable tubular drift (such as a socket) which bears only on the hard outer edge of the seal, until it abuts its locating shoulder **(see illustration)**.

4 Lubricate the seal lips with clean transmission oil, then refit the driveshaft as described in Chapter 8 Section 7.

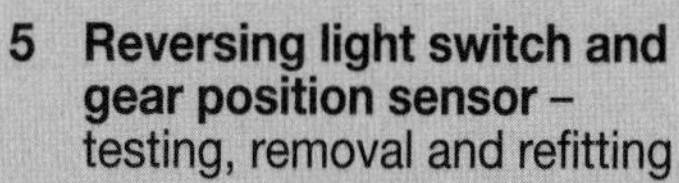

5 Reversing light switch and gear position sensor – testing, removal and refitting

B6 transmission only

1 The switch is located on top of the transmission in the gear selector housing. Remove the air cleaner as described in Chapter 4A Section 3 or Chapter 4B Section 6.

2 Select 4th gear before removing the reversing light switch from the gear selector housing.

3 Disconnect the switch wiring plug **(see illustration)**.

4 Unscrew the switch from the gear selector housing.

5 Refitting is a reversal of the removal procedure. Before refitting, make sure the switch is clean, including the mating faces. Tighten the switch to the specified torque.

6 Manual transmission – removal and refitting

Removal

1 Remove the battery and tray as described in Chapter 5 Section 4.

2 Remove the air cleaner assembly as described in Chapter 4A Section 3 or Chapter 4B Section 6.

3 Remove the front subframe as described in Chapter 10 Section 8.

4 Remove both driveshafts as described in Chapter 8 Section 7.

5 Remove the starter motor as described in Chapter 5 Section 7.

6 Install an engine support fixture to the engine, with the chain connected to the engine on the transmission end. Tighten the support fixture chain screw/nut to remove all slack in the chain.

7 Disconnect the gearchange cables from the transmission as described in Section 3.

8 Undo the bolt and disconnect the earth strap from the transmission casing **(see illustration)**.

9 Disconnect the gear position sensor wiring plug.

10 Leaving the fluid pipe connected, unbolt the clutch slave cylinder from the transmission casing, with reference to Chapter 8 Section 4 if necessary.

11 Undo the 3 bolts securing the left-hand mounting to the transmission.

12 Support the transmission with a jack – preferably one made for this purpose.

Note: *Transmission jack head adapters are available that replace the round head on a floor jack.*

13 Noting their installed locations, remove the bolts securing the transmission to the engine.

14 Using the jack, and with the help of an assistant, slide the transmission from the engine.

Note: *It may be necessary to lower the engine, using the support fixture, to facilitate transmission removal.*

Warning: Take care because the transmission is heavy!

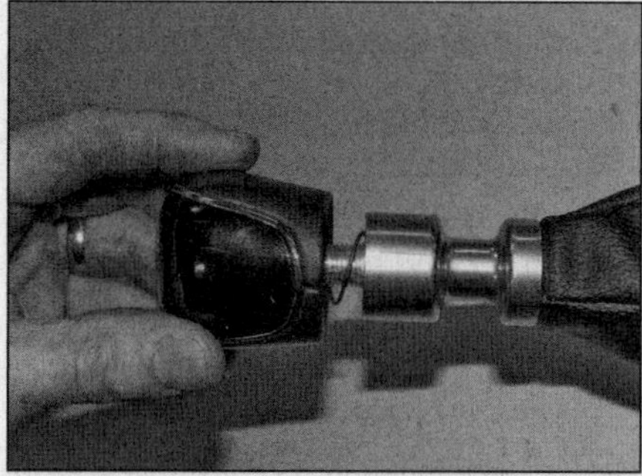

3.15 Unscrew the gearknob and collect the spring

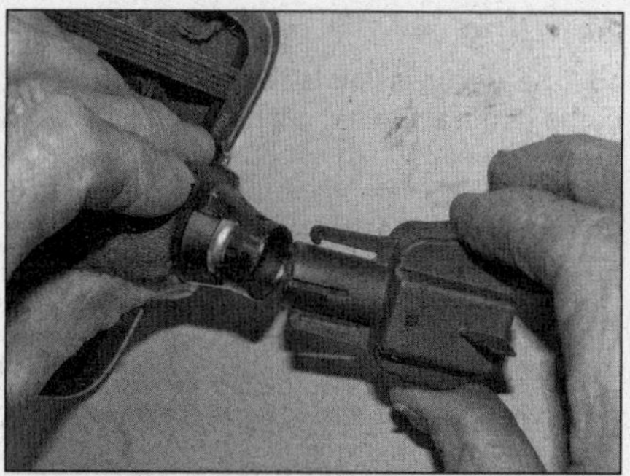

3.16 Prise open the tabs to separate the gaiter from the gearshift actuator

4.2 Carefully prise the seal from the transmission

4.3 Drive the new seal into place using a seal driver or large socket

5.3 Disconnect the switch wiring plug

6.8 Unbolt the earth strap from the gearbox

Refitting

15 The transmission is refitted by a reversal of the removal procedure, bearing in mind the following points:

a) Prior to refitting, check the clutch assembly and release mechanism components (see Chapter 8 Section 6). Do not lubricate the input shaft splines with oil or grease.

b) Ensure that the locating dowels are correctly positioned prior to installation.

c) Tighten all nuts and bolts to the specified torque (where given).

d) Renew the driveshaft oil seals, then refit the driveshafts (see Chapter 8 Section 7).

e) Refit the clutch slave cylinder (see Chapter 8 Section 4).

f) Refit the front subframe as described in Chapter 10 Section 8.

g) On completion, refill the transmission with the specified type and quantity of lubricant, as described in Section 2.

7 Manual transmission overhaul – general information

1 Overhauling a manual transmission is a difficult and involved job for the DIY home mechanic. In addition to dismantling and reassembling many small parts, clearances must be precisely measured and, if necessary, changed by selecting shims and spacers. Internal transmission components are also often difficult to obtain, and in many instances, extremely expensive. Because of this, if the transmission develops a fault or becomes noisy, the best course of action is to have the unit overhauled by a specialist repairer, or to obtain an exchange reconditioned unit.

2 Nevertheless, it is not impossible for the more experienced mechanic to overhaul the transmission, provided the special tools are available, and the job is done in a deliberate step-by-step manner, so that nothing is overlooked.

3 The tools necessary for an overhaul include internal and external circlip pliers, bearing pullers, a slide hammer, a set of pin punches, a dial test indicator, and possibly a hydraulic press. In addition, a large, sturdy workbench and a vice will be required.

4 During dismantling of the transmission, make careful notes of how each component is fitted, to make reassembly easier and more accurate.

5 Before dismantling the transmission, it will help if you have some idea what area is malfunctioning. Certain problems can be closely related to specific areas in the transmission, which can make component examination and replacement easier.

Chapter 7 Part B
Automatic transmission

Contents

Degrees of difficulty

Easy, suitable for novice with little experience 

Fairly easy, suitable for beginner with some experience 

Fairly difficult, suitable for competent DIY mechanic 

Difficult, suitable for experienced DIY mechanic 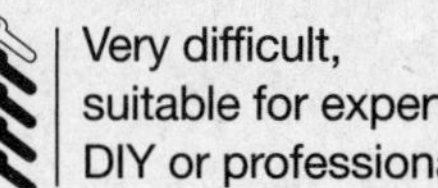

Very difficult, suitable for expert DIY or professional 

Specifications

General

Type	6-forward speeds, one reverse, with electronic control.
Designation	6F35

Lubrication

Capacity:	
Refilling after draining	4.0 litres
From dry	8.5 litres
Recommended fluid	See *Lubricants and fluids* in Chapter 1A or Chapter 1B

Torque wrench settings

	Nm	lbf ft
Engine-to-transmission fixing bolts	48	35
Fluid cooler bolts	24	18
Fluid drain plug	12	9
Fluid level plug	35	26
Torque converter-to-driveplate nuts*	48	35

* *Do not re-use*

1 General information

1 Certain models were offered with the option of a 6-speed electronically-controlled automatic transmission, consisting of a torque converter, an epicyclic geartrain, and hydraulically-operated clutches and brakes. The unit is controlled by the electronic control unit (ECU) via the electrically operated solenoid valves in the hydraulic block within the transmission unit. The gearchanges can be left completely automatic, or changed using the selector lever or steering wheel controls in Steptronic mode.

2 The torque converter provides a fluid coupling between the engine and transmission, which acts as an automatic clutch, and also provides a degree of torque multiplication when accelerating.

3 The epicyclic geartrain provides either of the six forward or one reverse gear ratios, according to which of its component parts are held stationary or allowed to turn. The components of the geartrain are held or released by brakes and clutches, which are controlled by the ECU via the electrically-operated solenoid valves in the hydraulic unit. A fluid pump within the transmission provides the necessary hydraulic pressure to operate the brakes and clutches.

4 Driver control of the transmission is by a floor mounted selector lever. The 'drive' position D provides automatic changing throughout the range of all six gear ratios, and is the one to select for normal driving. An automatic kickdown facility shifts the transmission down a gear if the accelerator pedal is fully depressed.

5 On some models, the selector lever is equipped with a shift-lock function. This prevents the selector lever being moved from the P position unless the brake pedal is depressed.

6 When the selector lever is moved to the M/S position, each of the six ratios can be selected sequentially, by moving the lever forwards/backwards.

7 Due to the complexity of the automatic transmission, any repair or overhaul work must be left to Ford dealer or specialist with the necessary special equipment for fault diagnosis and repair. The Specifications of the following Sections are therefore confined to supplying general information, and any service information and instructions that can be used by the owner. **Note:** *The automatic transmission unit is of the 'auto-adaptive' type. This means that it takes into account your driving style and modifies the transmission shift points to provide optimum performance and economy to suit. When the battery is disconnected, the transmission will lose its memory and will resort to one of its many base shift programs. The transmission will then relearn the optimum shift points when the vehicle is driven a few miles. During these first few miles of driving, there maybe a noticeable difference in performance whilst the transmission adapts to your individual style.*

3.3 Slacken the clamping bolt on the transmission casing

4.5 Remove the cable retaining bolt

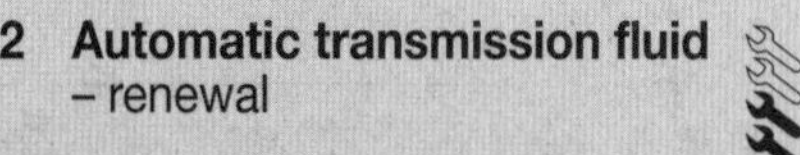

2 Automatic transmission fluid – renewal

Note: *The following fluid replacement procedures do not include replacing the fluid that remains in the torque converter. For a complete fluid change, inquire at a dealer service department or other properly equipped repair shop for a transaxle fluid flush/replacement.*

Renewal

1 Ensure the selector lever is in position 'P', then raise the vehicle and support it securely on axle stands (see *Jacking and vehicle support*). **Note:** *The front AND rear of the vehicle must be raised an equal amount.*

2 Remove the engine undershield, then place a drain pan underneath the transmission.

3 Unscrew the fluid drain plug.

Note: *Be prepared for fluid spillage.*

4 Wait until the fluid stops flowing, then refit the drain plug, tightening it to the specified torque.

5 Measure the amount of transmission fluid has been collected.

6 Remove the air cleaner assembly as described in Chapter 4A Section 3 or Chapter 4B Section 6 (it is possible to carry out this procedure with the assembly in place, but is significantly easier with it removed).

7 Undo the transmission fluid fill plug from the top of the transmission.

8 Top up the fluid with the required level of automatic transmission fluid and refit the plug.

9 Start the engine, and holding the vehicle with the footbrake, select Park for 5 seconds, followed by Reverse, Neutral, Drive and Sport, each for 5 seconds.

10 Return the gear selector to Park and allow the gearbox to warm up fully.

11 Working underneath the vehicle, remove the transmission level plug and allow the fluid to dribble out until it stops. If no fluid dribbles out, top up the fluid through the refilling hole until it does.

12 Refit the filler plug and refit the level bung, tightening to the required torque.

13 Refit the engine undertray, and lower the vehicle to the ground.

3 Selector cable – adjustment

1 To gain access to the transmission end of the selector cable, remove the air cleaner assembly and intake ducts above the transmission (see Chapter 4A Section 3 or Chapter 4B Section 6).

2 Position the selector lever firmly against its detent in the P (park) position.

3 Slacken the clamping bolt securing the end of the selector cable at the transmission lever end **(see illustration)**.

4 Move the lever on the transmission fully rearwards, then tighten the clamping bolt.

5 Check the operation of the selector lever before refitting the air cleaner and ducting.

4 Selector lever and cable – removal and refitting

Removal

1 Shift the transmission selector lever into position 'P', then raise the vehicle and support it securely on axle stands (see *Jacking and vehicle support*). Release the fasteners and remove the engine undershield.

2 Disconnect the battery negative lead as described in Chapter 5 Section 4.

3 Remove the centre console as described in Chapter 11 Section 36.

4 Remove the air cleaner and intake ducts above the transmission as described in Chapter 4A Section 3 or Chapter 4B Section 6.

5 Undo the retaining bolt for the cable mounting **(see illustration)**.

6 Slide the cable from the selector housing.

7 Undo the 4 upper mounting bolts and manoeuvre the selector lever from place **(see illustration)**.

8 Undo the fasteners and remove the heat shield below the selector lever housing.

9 Unclip the selector cable from any grommets/bracket on the vehicle underside.

10 Working at the transmission end, carefully prise the end fitting balljoint from the lever on the transmission **(see illustration)**.

11 Undo the retaining bolt and slide the cable outer fitting from the transmission bracket **(see illustration)**.

12 Undo the nuts securing the selector lever housing/selector cable to the vehicle floor **(see illustration)**.

4.7 Remove the 4 selector mounting bolts

4.10 Prise the balljoint from the gearbox

4.11 Remove the retaining bolt to release the cable mount

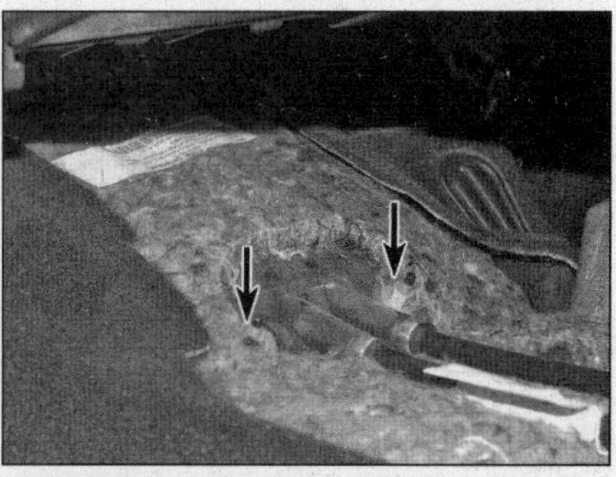
4.12 Undo the 2 nuts to remove the floor cable bracket

13 Disconnect the wiring plug, then manoeuvre the selector lever housing and cable assembly from under the vehicle. Note that the cable is integral with the housing, and cannot be renewed separately.

Refitting

14 Refitting is the reverse of removal, adjust the cable as described in Section 3.

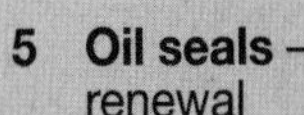

5 Oil seals – renewal

Driveshaft oil seals

1 Remove the appropriate driveshaft as described in Chapter 8 Section 7.
2 Note its fitted depth, then carefully punch two small holes opposite each other into the seal. Screw a self-tapping screw into each hole and pull on the screws to extract the seal.
3 Remove all traces of dirt from the area around the oil seal aperture, then apply a smear of clean transmission fluid to the sealing lip of the new oil seal. Drive the seal squarely into position using a suitable tubular drift (such as a socket), which bears only on the hard outer edge of the seal.
4 Refit the driveshaft as described in Chapter 8 Section 7.

Torque converter oil seal

5 Remove the transmission unit as described in Section 7.
6 Carefully slide the torque converter off the transmission shaft whilst being prepared for fluid spillage.
7 Note the correct fitted position of the seal in the housing then carefully lever it out of position, taking care not to mark the housing or shaft.
8 Remove all traces of dirt from the area around the oil seal aperture. Apply a little clean transmission fluid to the sealing lips, then ease the new seal into its aperture, ensuring its sealing lip is facing inwards, then press it squarely into position.
9 Engage the torque converter with the transmission shaft splines and slide it into position, taking care not to damage the oil seal.
10 Refit the transmission unit as described in Section 2.

6 Fluid cooler – removal and refitting

Caution: Be careful not to allow dirt into the transmission unit during this procedure.

1 Remove the radiator, as described in Chapter 3 Section 6.
2 Prise up the foam that lies along the top of the transmission fluid cooler, to expose the retaining clips **(see illustration)**.
3 Disengage the retaining clips and remove the fluid cooler **(see illustration)**.
4 Refitting is a reversal of removal.

6.2 Lift up the foam to reveal the clips

6.3 Release the clips and remove the fluid cooler

7 Automatic transmission – removal and refitting

Removal

1 Drain the transmission as described earlier in this Section 2.
2 Remove the battery and battery tray, as described in Chapter 5 Section 4.
3 Remove the left-hand front wheelarch liner, as described in Chapter 11 Section 39.
4 Undo the 4 retaining nuts and remove the battery tray support bracket from place **(see illustration)**.
5 Disconnect the selector cable from the transmission as described in Section 4.
6 Drain the transmission cooler fluid, as described in Section 6.
7 Undo the clamp bolt and separate the fluid pipe from the top of the transmission **(see illustration)**.
8 Working through the wheelarch, undo the oil cooler fluid pipe clamp bolt and separate the pipe from the transmission **(see illustration)**.
9 Undo the earth strap retaining bolt on the front of the transmission **(see illustration)**.
10 Remove all wiring plugs from the transmission **(see illustration)**.
11 Undo the retaining bolts and remove the two brackets holding on the wiring loom and cooling pipes.
12 Prise open the retaining clip for the cooling pipe by the engine, to allow access to the transmission retaining bolts **(see illustration)**.
13 Undo the two nuts that hold the cooling pipe bracket to the side of the engine **(see illustration)**.

7.4 Battery tray support bracket bolts

7.7 Undo the clamp bolt and separate the fluid pipe from the transmission

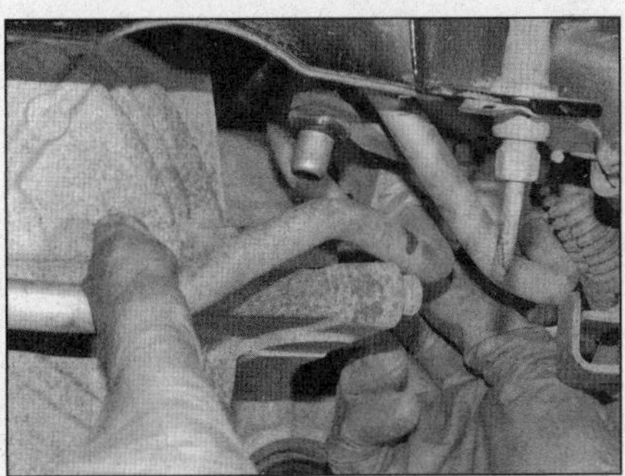

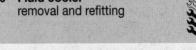

7.8 Disconnect the fluid cooler pipe

7.9 Remove the earth strap from the transmission

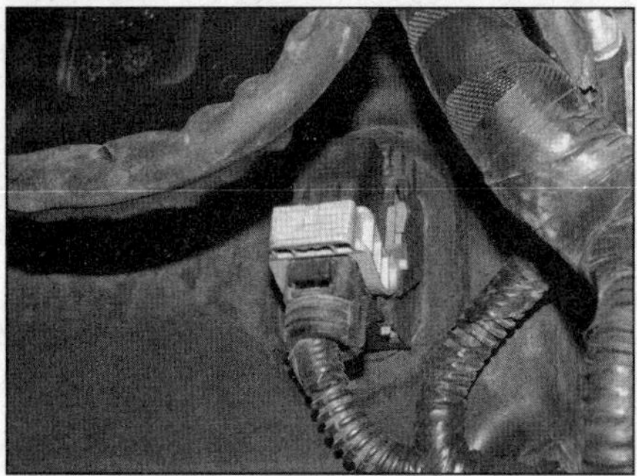
7.10 Unplug all the transmission wiring plugs

7.12 Open the clip to move the pipe out of the way

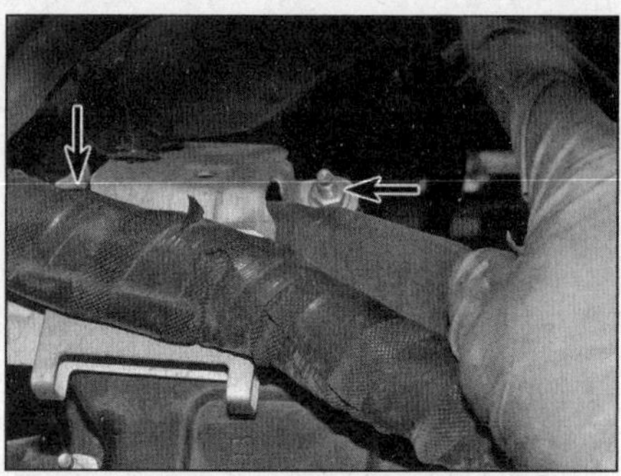
7.13 Coolant pipe bracket retaining nuts

14 Undo the transmission-to-engine upper bolts **(see illustration)**.

15 Remove the rubber grommet from the starter aperture **(see illustration)**.

16 Working through the starter aperture, undo the 4 torque converter nuts one at a time **(see illustration)**. Have and assistant rotate the crankshaft clockwise, using a spanner/ socket on the crankshaft pulley bolt, until each nut becomes accessible.

Note: *Do not allow the bolt to fall into the bell housing. Place some grease on the inside of the socket to retain the bolt.*

17 Undo the retaining bolts and remove the left-hand side front subframe leg.

18 Undo the 2 retaining bolts and manoeuvre the auxiliary coolant pump out of the way **(see illustration)**. There's no need to disconnect the hoses.

19 Support the engine and transmission using a brace and trolley jack.

20 Slacken the central mounting bolt and remove the top of the transmission mounting **(see illustration)**.

21 Undo the 4 retaining bolts and remove the transmission mounting **(see illustration)**.

22 Use a jack to support the transmission, then undo the 6 remaining mounting bolts and carefully slide the transmission from the engine, and lower it from place. Enlist the help of an assistant.

Warning: Take care as the transmission is extremely heavy!

Refitting

23 Refitting is a reversal of removal, ensuring all fastening are tightened to the correct torque and all fluids are replenished.

24 When fitting the torque converter to driveplate nuts, Ford recommend use of a magnetic socket, to lessen the possibility of a nut dropping into the transmission. If you do not have such a socket, a blob of grease on the nut will prevent it from falling out of your socket.

8 Automatic transmission overhaul – general information

1 In the event of a fault occurring with the transmission, it is first necessary to determine whether it is of an electrical, mechanical or hydraulic nature and, to do this, special test equipment is required. It is therefore essential to have the work carried out by a Ford dealer or specialist if a transmission fault is suspected.

2 Do not remove the transmission from the car for possible repair before professional fault diagnosis has been carried out, since most tests require the transmission to be in the vehicle.

7.14 Undo the 2 transmission retaining bolts

7.15 Take out the starter grommet

7.16 Undo the torque converter nuts one at a time

7.18 Unbolt the auxiliary coolant pump

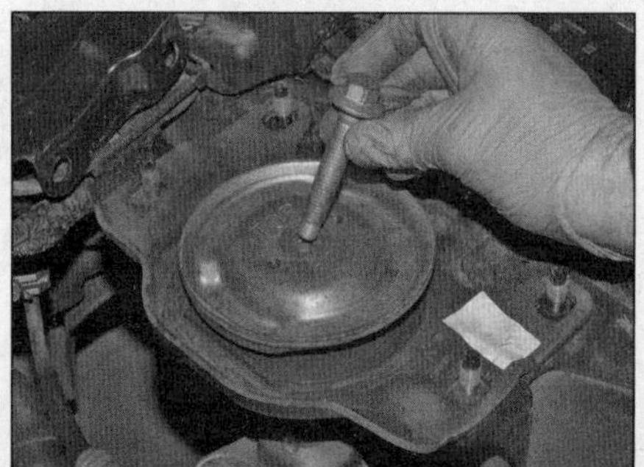
7.20 Remove the central bolt from the transmission mounting

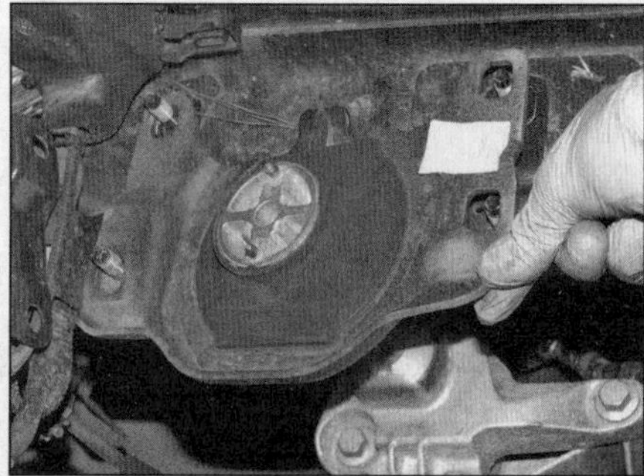
7.21 Undo the bolts and remove the mounting assembly

Chapter 8
Clutch, transfer case and driveshafts

Contents

Degrees of difficulty

Easy, suitable for novice with little experience 	Fairly easy, suitable for beginner with some experience 	Fairly difficult, suitable for competent DIY mechanic	Difficult, suitable for experienced DIY mechanic	Very difficult, suitable for expert DIY or professional 

Specifications

General

Clutch type	Single dry plate, diaphragm spring, hydraulically-operated release mechanism

Driven plate

Driven plate minimum thickness:	
Petrol engines	6.0 mm
1.5 litre diesel engines	5.7 mm
2.0 litre diesel engines	5.7 mm

Torque wrench settings

	Nm	lbf ft
Clutch master cylinder nuts	23	17
Driveshaft nut: *		
Stage 1	80	59
Stage 2	Angle-tighten a further 90°	
Pedal assembly retaining nuts*	23	17
Pressure plate retaining bolts: *		
Stage 1	10	7
Stage 2	20	5
Stage 3	29	21
Rear driveshaft hub nut*	133	98
Right-hand intermediate shaft bearing holder cap nuts: *		
Stage 1	5	4
Stage 2	25	18
Roadwheel nuts	135	100
Slave cylinder	11	8

** Do not re-use*

1 General information

Clutch

1 All models are fitted with a single dry plate clutch, which consists of five main components; friction disc, pressure plate, diaphragm spring, cover and release bearing.

2 The friction disc is free to slide along the splines of the gearbox input shaft, and is held in position between the flywheel and the pressure plate by the pressure exerted on the pressure plate by the diaphragm spring. Friction lining material is riveted to both sides of the friction disc. All models are fitted with a Self-Adjusting Clutch (SAC), which compensates for friction disc wear by altering the attitude of the diaphragm spring fingers by means of a sprung mechanism within the pressure plate cover. This ensures a consistent clutch pedal 'feel' over the life of the clutch.

3 The diaphragm spring is mounted on pins, and is held in place in the cover by annular fulcrum rings.

4 The release bearing is located on a guide sleeve at the front of the gearbox, and the bearing is free to slide on the sleeve, under the action of the slave cylinder bellhousing.

5 The release mechanism is operated by the clutch pedal, using hydraulic pressure. The pedal acts on the hydraulic master cylinder pushrod, and a slave cylinder, mounted in the gearbox bellhousing.

6 When the clutch pedal is depressed, the slave cylinder pushes the release bearing forwards, to bear against the centre of the diaphragm spring, thus pushing the centre of the diaphragm spring inwards. The diaphragm spring acts against the fulcrum rings in the cover, and so, as the centre of the spring is pushed in, the outside of the spring is pushed out, allowing the pressure plate to move backwards away from the friction disc.

7 When the clutch pedal is released, the diaphragm spring forces the pressure plate into contact with the friction linings on the friction disc, and simultaneously pushes the friction disc forwards on its splines, forcing it against the flywheel. The friction disc is now firmly sandwiched between the pressure plate and the flywheel, and drive is taken up.

Driveshafts

8 Drive is transmitted from the transmission differential to the front wheels by means of two driveshafts. The right-hand driveshaft is in two sections, and incorporates a support bearing.

9 Each driveshaft consists of three main components: the sliding (tripod type) inner joint, the driveshaft itself, and the outer CV (constant velocity) joint. The inner end of the left-hand tripod joint is secured in the differential side gear by the engagement of a circlip. The inner tripod of the right-hand driveshaft is located in the intermediate shaft tripod housing. The intermediate shaft is held in the transmission by the support bearing, which in turn is supported by a bracket bolted to the rear of the cylinder block. The outer CV joint on both driveshafts is of ball-bearing type, and is secured in the front hub by the driveshaft bolt.

2 Clutch hydraulic system – bleeding

Warning: Hydraulic fluid is poisonous; wash off immediately and thoroughly in the case of skin contact, and seek immediate medical advice if any fluid is swallowed or gets into the eyes. Certain types of hydraulic fluid are inflammable, and may ignite when allowed into contact with hot components; when servicing any hydraulic system, it is safest to assume that the fluid IS inflammable, and to take precautions against the risk of fire as though it is petrol that is being handled. Hydraulic fluid is also an effective paint stripper, and will attack plastics; if any is spilt, it should be washed off immediately, using copious quantities of clean water. When topping-up or renewing the fluid, always use the recommended type, and ensure that it comes from a freshly-opened sealed container.

2.4 Pull off the bleed nipple dust cap

1 Obtain a clean jar, a suitable length of rubber or clear plastic tubing, which is a tight fit over the bleed screw on the clutch slave cylinder, and a tin of the specified hydraulic fluid. The help of an assistant will also be required. (If a one-man do-it-yourself bleeding kit for bleeding the brake hydraulic system is available, this can be used quite satisfactorily for the clutch also. Full information on the use of these kits may be found in Chapter 9 Section 3.)

2 Raise the front of the vehicle and support it securely on axle stands (see *Jacking and vehicle support*). Release the fasteners and remove the engine undershield.

3 Remove the filler cap from the brake master cylinder reservoir, and if necessary top-up the fluid. Keep the reservoir topped-up during subsequent operations.

4 Remove the dust cap from the slave cylinder bleed nipple, located on the top of the transmission **(see illustration)**.

5 Connect one end of the bleed tube to the bleed screw, and insert the other end of the tube in the jar containing sufficient clean hydraulic fluid to keep the end of the tube submerged.

6 Open the bleed screw half a turn and have your assistant depress the clutch pedal and then slowly release it. Continue this procedure until clean hydraulic fluid, free from air bubbles, emerges from the tube. Now tighten the bleed screw at the end of a downstroke. Make sure that the brake master cylinder reservoir is checked frequently to ensure that the level does not drop too far, allowing air into the system.

7 Check the operation of the clutch pedal. After a few strokes it should feel normal. Any sponginess would indicate air still present in the system.

8 On completion remove the bleed tube and refit the dust cover. Top-up the master cylinder reservoir if necessary and refit the cap. Fluid expelled from the hydraulic system should now be discarded, as it will be contaminated with moisture, air and dirt, making it unsuitable for further use.

3 Clutch master cylinder – removal and refitting

Note: *Before starting work, refer to the warning at the beginning of Section 2 concerning the dangers of hydraulic fluid.*

Removal

Note: *Access is extremely limited.*

1 Siphon out fluid from the brake fuid reservoir, until it reaches the minimum mark.

2 Disconnect the wiring plug from the side of the master cylinder.

3 Using for special tool 308-651 or equivalent, remove the sensor from the side of the master cylinder.

4 Disconnect the hydraulic hoses from the master cylinder.

Caution: Be prepared for fluid spillage.

5 Remove the driver's knee airbag, as described in Chapter 12 Section 24.

6 Disconnect the wiring plug(s) from the clutch pedal position switch(es). Depending on model, there may be two sensors fitted to the clutch pedal bracket. The lower is the clutch pedal switch and the upper one, the starter inhibitor switch.

7 Undo the retaining nuts and manoeuvre the clutch pedal complete with the bracket and master cylinder from place.

Refitting

8 Refitting the master cylinder is the reverse sequence to removal, bearing in mind the following points.

a) Ensure all fasteners are tightened to their specified torque where given.

b) On completion, bleed the clutch hydraulic system as described in Section 2.

4 Clutch slave cylinder – removal and refitting

Note: *Before starting work, refer to the warning at the beginning of Section 2 concerning the dangers of hydraulic fluid.*

Removal

1 Raise the front of the vehicle and support it securely on axle stands (see *Jacking and vehicle support*). Release the fasteners and remove the engine undershield.

2 Separate the transmission from the engine, as described in Chapter 7A Section 6.

3 Place absorbent rags under the clutch slave cylinder. Be prepared for hydraulic fluid loss.

4 Undo the 3 retaining bolts and remove the cylinder from the transmission housing. Do not pull the pushrod from the slave cylinder. Note that any movement of the pushrod may lead to a slight leakage of fluid. This is normal and doesn't necessarily indicate the cylinder is damaged.

5 Suitably plug or cap the pipe end to prevent further fluid loss and dirt entry.

Refitting

6 Refitting the slave cylinder is the reverse sequence to removal, bearing in mind the following points.

a) Apply a little grease to the end of the slave cylinder pushrod.

b) Tighten the slave cylinder retaining bolts to the specified torque.

c) On completion, bleed the clutch hydraulic system as described in Section 4.

5 Clutch pedal – removal and refitting

1 Removal and refitting of the clutch pedal is included in the master cylinder removal and refitting procedure described in Section 3.

6 Clutch components – removal, inspection and refitting

Warning: Dust created by clutch wear and deposited on the clutch components may contain asbestos, which is a health hazard. DO NOT blow it out with compressed air, and do not inhale any of it. DO NOT use petrol or petroleum-based solvents to clean off the dust. Brake system cleaner or methylated spirit should be used to flush the dust into a suitable receptacle. After the clutch components are wiped clean with rags, dispose of the contaminated rags and cleaner in a sealed, marked container.

Removal

1 Access to the clutch may be gained in one of two ways. The engine/transmission unit can be removed, as described in Chapter 2D, and the transmission separated from the engine on the bench. Alternatively, the engine may be left in the vehicle and the transmission removed independently, as described in Chapter 7A.

2 Having separated the transmission from the engine, check if there are any marks identifying the relation of the clutch pressure plate to the flywheel. If not, make your own marks using a dab of paint or a scriber. These marks will be used if the original pressure plate is refitted, and will help to maintain the balance of the unit. A new pressure plate may be fitted in any position allowed by the locating dowels.

3 Unscrew the six clutch pressure plate retaining bolts, working in a diagonal sequence, and slackening the bolts only a turn at a time. If necessary, the flywheel may be held stationary using a wide-bladed screwdriver, inserted in the teeth of the starter ring gear and resting against part of the cylinder block. Ford state that new pressure plate bolts must be used when refitting.

4 Ease the clutch pressure plate off its locating dowels. Be prepared to catch the clutch driven plate, which will drop out as the pressure plate is removed. Note which way round the driven plate is fitted.

Inspection

Note: *On models equipped with a self-adjusting clutch, Ford insist that if a new driven plate is fitted, the pressure plate must also be renewed.*

5 The most common problem which occurs in the clutch is wear of the clutch driven plate (friction disc). However, all the clutch components should be inspected at this time, particularly if the engine has covered a high mileage. Unless the clutch components are known to be virtually new, it is worth renewing them all as a set (driven plate, pressure plate and release bearing). Renewing a worn driven plate by itself is not always satisfactory, especially if the old one was slipping and causing the pressure plate to overheat.

6 Examine the linings of the driven plate for wear and loose rivets, and the plate hub and rim for distortion, cracks, broken torsion springs, and worn splines (where applicable). The surface of the friction linings may be highly glazed, but as long as the friction material pattern can be clearly seen, and the rivet heads are at least 1 mm below the lining surface, this is satisfactory. The plate must be renewed if the lining thickness has worn down to the minimum thickness given in the Specifications.

7 If there is any sign of oil contamination, indicated by shiny black discoloration, the driven plate must be renewed, and the source of the contamination traced and rectified. This will be a leaking crankshaft oil seal or transmission input shaft oil seal. The renewal procedure for the former is given in the relevant Part of Chapter 2. The renewal procedure for the transmission input shaft oil seal is contained in Chapter 7B Section 5.

8 Check the machined faces of the flywheel and pressure plate. If either is grooved, or heavily scored, renewal is necessary. The pressure plate must also be renewed if any cracks are apparent, or if the diaphragm spring is damaged or its pressure suspect. Pay particular attention to the tips of the spring fingers, where the release bearing acts upon them.

9 With the transmission removed, it is also advisable to check the condition of the release bearing, although having got this far, it is almost certainly worth renewing it. Note that the release bearing is integral with the slave cylinder – the two must be renewed together; however, given that access to the slave cylinder is only possible with the transmission removed, not to renew it at this time is probably a false economy.

Refitting

10 It is important that no oil or grease is allowed to come into contact with the friction material of the driven plate or the pressure plate and flywheel faces. To ensure this, it is advisable to refit the clutch assembly with clean hands, and to wipe down the pressure plate and flywheel faces with a clean dry rag before assembly begins.

11 Ford technicians use a special tool for centralising the driven plate at this stage. The tool holds the driven plate centrally on the pressure plate, and locates in the middle of the diaphragm spring fingers. If the tool is not available, it will be necessary to centralise the driven plate after assembling the pressure plate loosely on the flywheel, as described in the following paragraphs.

12 Place the driven plate against the flywheel, ensuring that it is the right way round **(see illustrations)**. It may be marked FLYWHEEL SIDE, but if not, position it so that the raised hub with the cushion springs is facing away from the flywheel.

13 Place the clutch pressure plate over the dowels. Fit the new retaining bolts, and tighten them finger-tight so that the driven plate is gripped lightly, but can still be moved.

14 The driven plate must now be centralised so that, when the engine and transmission are mated, the splines of the transmission input shaft will pass through the splines in the centre of the driven plate hub.

15 Centralisation can be carried out by inserting a round bar through the hole in the centre of the driven plate, so that the end of the bar rests in the hole in the rear end of the crankshaft. Move the bar sideways or up-and-down, to move the driven plate in whichever direction is necessary to achieve centralisation. Centralisation can then be checked by removing the bar and viewing the driven plate hub in relation to the diaphragm spring fingers, or by viewing through the side apertures of the pressure plate, and checking that the disc is central in relation to the outer edge of the pressure plate.

16 An alternative and more accurate method of centralisation is to use a commercially-available clutch-aligning tool, obtainable from most accessory shops **(see illustration 6.12b)**.

6.12a The clutch driven plate should be marked to indicate which side faces the transmission or flywheel

6.12b Position the driven plate using a clutch aligning tool

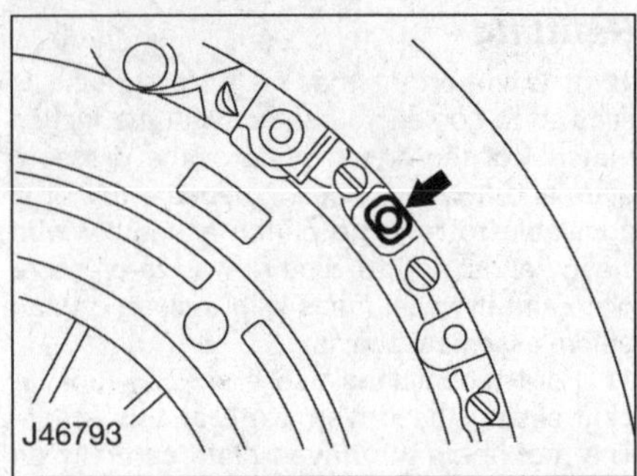

6.17 Check the 'stop-pin' is moveable as the bolts are tightened

17 Once the clutch is centralised, progressively tighten the pressure plate bolts in a diagonal sequence to the torque setting given in the Specifications. On models with a self-adjusting clutch, Check that the 'stop-pin' is moveable during the tightening of the bolts **(see illustration)**.

18 Ensure that the input shaft splines and driven plate splines are clean. Apply a thin smear of high melting-point grease to the input shaft splines – do not apply excessively, however, or it may end up on the driven plate, causing the new clutch to slip.

19 Refit the transmission to the engine.

7 Driveshafts – removal and refitting

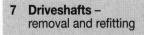

Removal

1 Prise out the centre cap, then have an assistant depress the brake pedal to prevent the hub from rotating, and slacken the driveshaft nut **(see illustration)**. Alternatively, a forked tool can be used to counterhold the hub once the wheel has been removed. Discard the nut – a new one must be fitted.

2 Slacken the relevant front roadwheel nuts, then jack the front of the vehicle up and support it securely on axle stands (see *Jacking and vehicle support*). Remove the relevant roadwheel.

3 Undo the retaining bolts and remove the engine undertray.

4 To avoid spillage when the driveshafts are separated from the transmission, drain the transmission fluid, as described in Chapter 7A Section 2 or Chapter 7B Section 2, or use a suitable container to catch the oil/fluid when the driveshaft has been removed.

5 Remove the bolt securing the brake hose to the strut to avoid straining the hose.

6 Remove the nut and bolt securing the bottom ball joint.

7 Use a lever/chain to lever down the lower arm and separate from the hub carrier. Use a wedge or chisel to slightly prise apart the balljoint clamp.

8 Separate the outer CV joint from the hub by tapping the end of the shaft with a hammer and a block of wood. It is very likely that a puller will be needed as the CV joint splines can often be reluctant to slide out of the hub.

Left-hand driveshaft

9 With the steering on full left-hand lock, pull the driveshaft outer joint back through the hub.

10 Use a tyre lever or large flat-bladed screwdriver to prise the inner joint from the transmission **(see illustration)**. Take care not to damage the casing. The circlip at the inner end of the driveshaft must be replaced.

Right-hand driveshaft

11 With the steering on full right-hand lock, pull the driveshaft outer joint back through the hub.

12 Undo the 2 nuts securing the driveshaft intermediate bearing holder cap to the mounting bracket **(see illustration)**. Discard the cap and nuts – new ones must be fitted upon reassembly.

13 Carefully pull the right-hand inner driveshaft from the transmission, and manoeuvre it from place.

14 Check the intermediate bearing. At the time of writing, it would appear that the bearing is not available separately from the driveshaft – check with your Ford dealer or parts specialist.

Refitting

15 Before refitting, clean the splines, threads and seal mating surfaces. Examine the gaiters and clips for damage/wear.

16 Fit a new circlip to the groove on the inner end of the left-hand driveshaft – the 20 mm diameter round circlip is for manual transmission models, and the 25 x 16 mm oval circlip is for automatics.

17 Fit the driveshaft(s) into the transmission. Turn the driveshaft until it engages the splines on the differential gears. Make sure the circlip is fully engaged.

18 If refitting the right-hand driveshaft, fit the new bearing holder cap, then tighten the nuts to the specified torque. Where applicable, refit the heat shield and tighten the retaining bolts securely.

19 On either driveshaft, slide the hub carrier/hub assembly over the end of the driveshaft, ensuring the hub splines engage correctly with the splines of the driveshaft.

Note: *It may be necessary to draw the driveshaft through the hub using the old hub nut. Remove the nut when in place.*

20 Reconnect the lower ball joint to the hub carrier using a chain or lever.

21 Fit and tighten the ball joint nut and bolt to the specified torque.

22 Fit the bolt securing the brake hose to the strut.

23 Fit the new driveshaft/hub nut, and tighten to the specified torque, whilst an assistant depresses the brake pedal to prevent the hub from rotating.

24 Fill the transmission with oil, and check the level as described in Chapter 7A Section 2 or Chapter 7B Section 2.

25 Refit the wheel, and lower the vehicle to the ground. Tighten the wheel retaining nuts to the specified torque.

8 Driveshaft inner tripod joint gaiter – renewal

1 Remove the driveshaft as described in Section 7, then cut off the gaiter clamps and slide the inner joint housing from place.

2 Remove the circlip from the end of the shaft, then remove the tripod from the shaft, noting how it's oriented (the flat side faces the end of the shaft).

Note: *If the tripod is stuck on the shaft, use a three-legged puller or hammer and drift to remove it.*

3 Remove the gaiter from the shaft and clean the components.

7.1 Slacken the driveshaft nut through the centre cap hole

7.10 Gently prise the driveshaft from the transmission

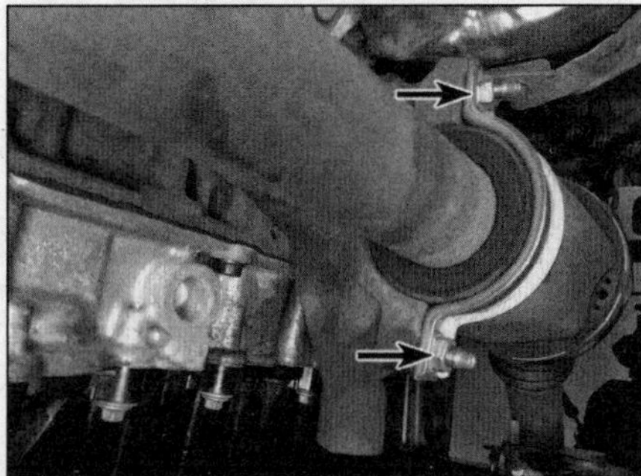

7.12 Remove the two bearing holder cap nuts

4 Slide the new small clamp and gaiter onto the shaft, then refit the tripod with the flat side of the spider (centre portion) facing the end of the shaft. Secure the tripod with a new circlip.

5 Fill the housing with the grease supplied in the kit, then install it onto the tripod. Make sure the gaiter sealing area on the housing is clean, then install the gaiter over the housing, making sure it seats properly. Install the new large gaiter clamp.

6 Position the joint mid-way through its travel. Ensure that the gaiter is not twisted or distorted, then insert a small screwdriver under the small end of the gaiter. This will allow trapped air to escape.

7 Install the new retaining clamps and tighten them securely **(see illustrations)**.

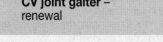

9 Driveshaft outer CV joint gaiter – renewal

1 Remove the inner CV joint (see Section 8).

2 Cut the clamps from the outer gaiter, and slide the gaiter off the inner end of the driveshaft. Do not disassemble the outer CV joint.

3 Clean the inner and outer joints. The outer joint will be more difficult to clean since it can't be removed, but with an ample supply of solvent or brake system cleaner, and flexing the joint through its range of motion, you should be able to get all of the old grease out. Allow the joint to dry thoroughly (used compressed air, if possible).

4 Slide the new outer gaiter and clamps onto the driveshaft. Fill the gaiter with the grease supplied in the kit. Make sure the outer joint housing is clean where the gaiter fits, then pull the gaiter onto the housing.

5 Make sure the small-diameter end of the gaiter is seated properly in its groove, then insert a small screwdriver under the lip of the gaiter at the housing end to allow any trapped air to escape.

6 Remove the screwdriver, install the retaining clamps in their previously noted positions, and tighten them **(see illustration)**.

7 Refit the inner CV joint as described in Section 8.

10 Driveshafts – inspection and joint renewal

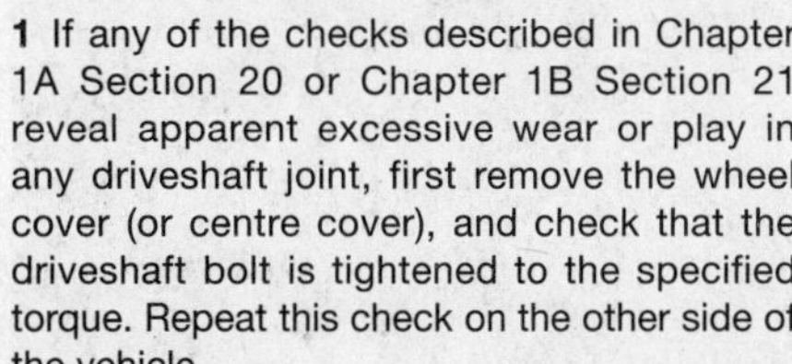

1 If any of the checks described in Chapter 1A Section 20 or Chapter 1B Section 21 reveal apparent excessive wear or play in any driveshaft joint, first remove the wheel cover (or centre cover), and check that the driveshaft bolt is tightened to the specified torque. Repeat this check on the other side of the vehicle.

2 Road test the vehicle, and listen for a metallic clicking from the front as the vehicle is driven slowly in a circle on full-lock. If a clicking noise is heard, this indicates wear in the outer constant velocity joint, which means that the joint must be renewed; reconditioning is not possible.

3 Note that the outer CV joint cannot be renewed. If faulty, the complete driveshaft must be replaced.

4 If vibration, consistent with road speed, is felt through the car when accelerating, there is a possibility of wear in the inner tripod joints.

5 To renew an inner tripod joint, remove the driveshaft as described in Section 7, then separate the joint from the driveshaft with reference to Section 8.

6 Continual noise from the right-hand driveshaft, increasing with road speed, may indicate wear in the support bearing. To renew this bearing, the driveshaft must be removed and then the bearing unbolted from the engine.

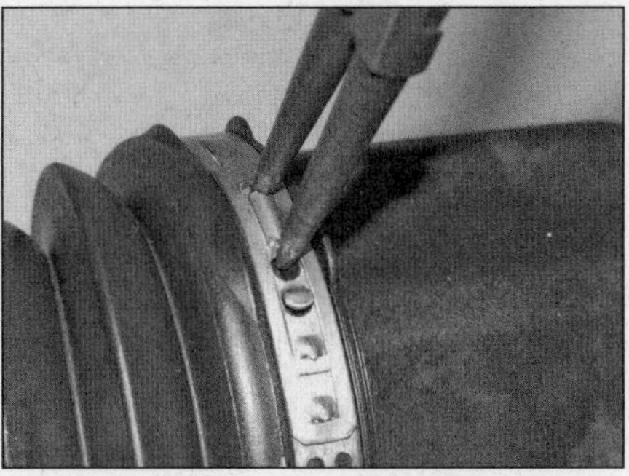

8.7a Tighten the large clamp with thin-nosed pliers...

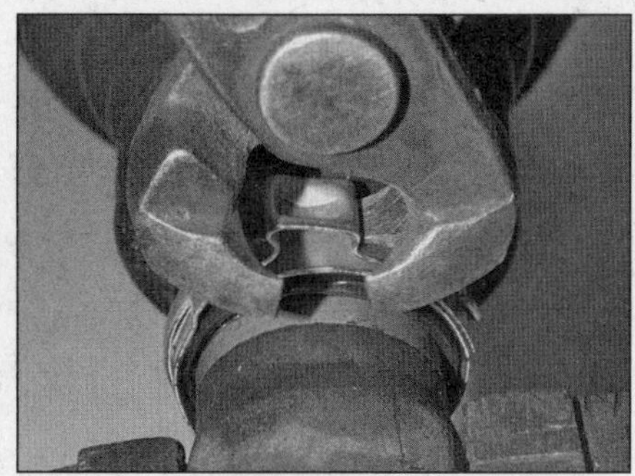

8.7b ...and the small clamp with gaiter clamp crimping pliers

9.6 Install the clamps and tighten with gaiter clamp crimping pliers

11.3 Disconnect the wiring plug from the transfer case

11 Transfer case – removal and refitting

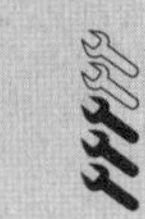

Removal

1 Remove the front right-hand driveshaft as described in Section 7.

2 Remove the 3 bolts holding the heat shield on top of the transfer case **(see illustration)**.

3 Disconnect the wiring plug from the side of the transfer case **(see illustration)**.

4 Undo the 4 retaining bolts and remove the engine rear roll restrictor **(see illustration)**.

5 Mark and disconnect the front of the propeller shaft, as described in Section 12.

6 Undo the 3 bolts holding the retaining

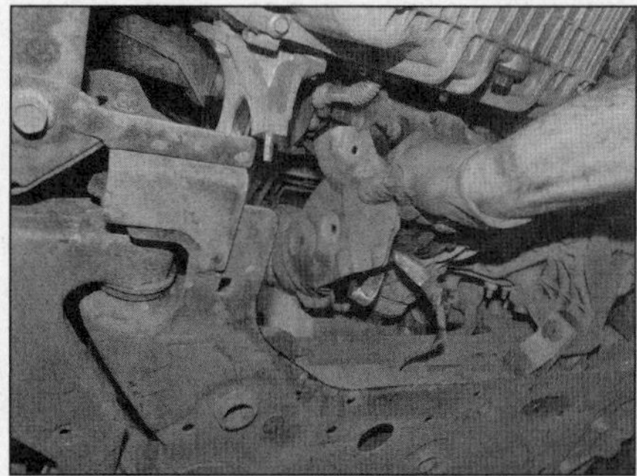

11.2 Undo the 3 bolts holding the transfer case heat shield

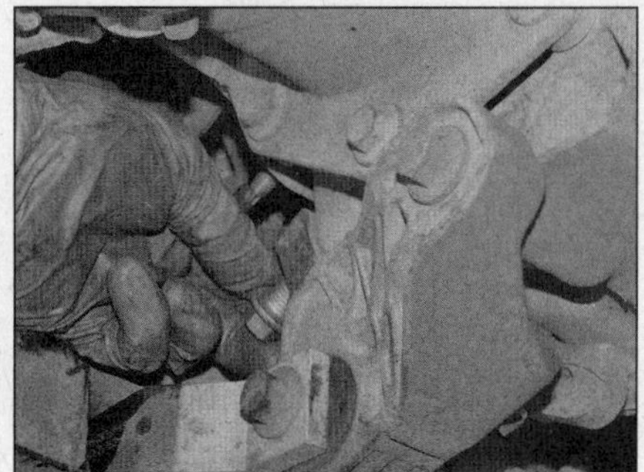

11.4 Remove the engine roll restrictor

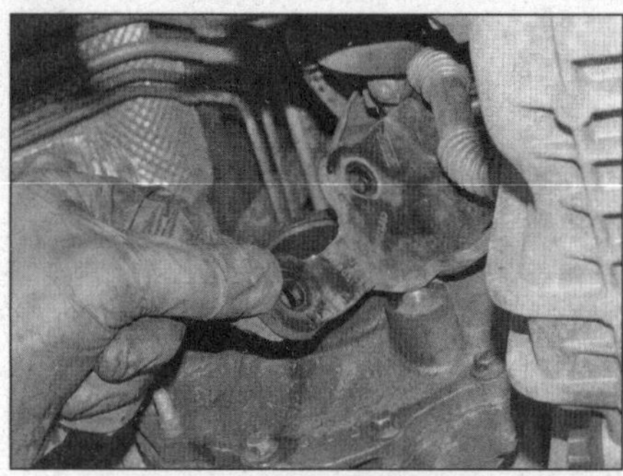
11.6 Remove the transfer case retaining bracket

11.8b ...and disconnect the vent hose

bracket to the side of the transfer case **(see illustration)**.

7 Remove the 3 lower and 2 upper bolts holding the transfer case to the side of the transmission.

8 Manoeuvre the transfer case downwards

11.8a Remove the transfer case downwards...

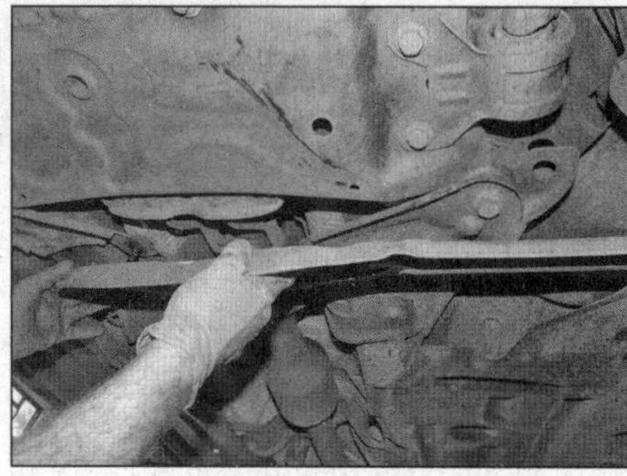
12.4 Remove the bolts and the bracing bar

from place, disconnecting the vent hose as it becomes available **(see illustrations)**.

Refitting

9 Refitting is a reversal of removal.

12 Propeller shaft – removal and refitting

Removal

1 Place your vehicle's transmission in the Neutral position.

2 Apply the handbrake, then jack up the vehicle and support it on axle stands (see *Jacking and vehicle support*).

3 Prise out the clips and move the underbody plastic shielding to one side.

4 Undo the 8 retaining bolts and remove the subframe bracing bar **(see illustration)**.

5 Make alignment marks at each end of the propeller shaft to aid refitting **(see illustration)**.

6 Slacken the 6 bolts at the rear end of the propeller shaft, but do not remove them at this stage **(see illustration)**.

7 Remove the 6 bolts at the front of the propeller shaft **(see illustration)**.

8 Undo the bolt for the engine roll restrictor and pull the bottom of the engine forward to disengage it from the propeller shaft **(see illustration)**.

9 Undo the 2 retaining bolts for the propeller shaft centre bearing **(see illustration)**.

10 Fully remove the rear propeller shaft bolts and manoeuvre the shaft rearwards from place **(see illustration)**.

Refitting

11 Refitting is a reversal of removal, ensuring that the previously made alignment marks line up and all fastenings are tightened securely.

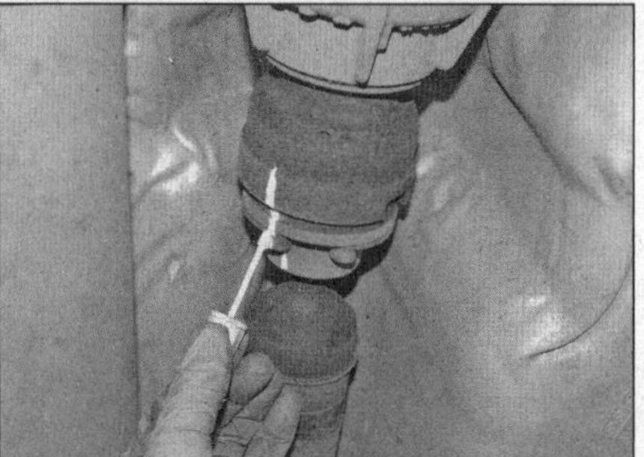
12.5 Mark each end of the propeller shaft

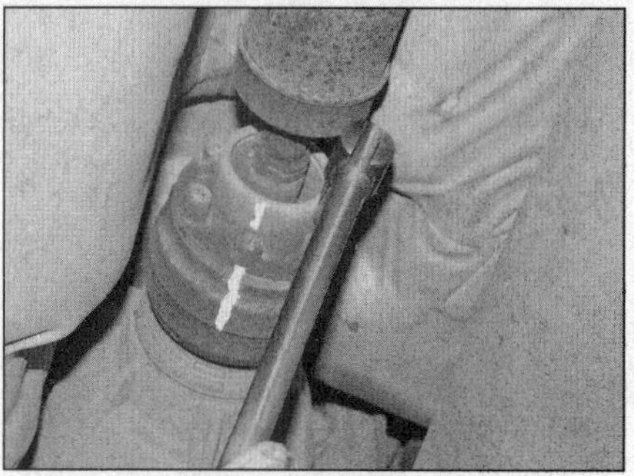
12.6 Loosen but do not remove the rear propshaft bolts

12.7 Remove the bolts from the front of the propeller shaft

12.8 Remove the roll restrictor bolt and pull the engine forward

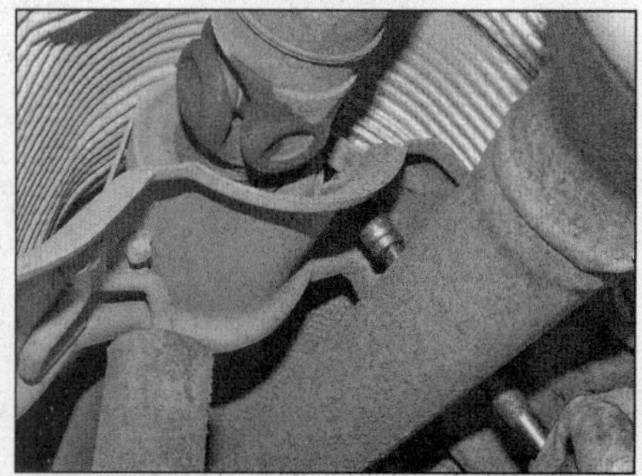
12.9 Remove the propeller shaft centre bearing bolts

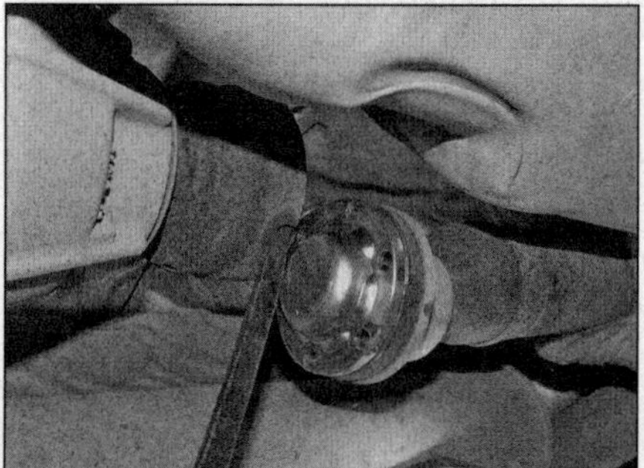
12.10 Remove the propeller shaft rearwards

13.2 Use a forked tool to brace the disc and remove the hub nut

13.3 Remove the rear wheel sensor

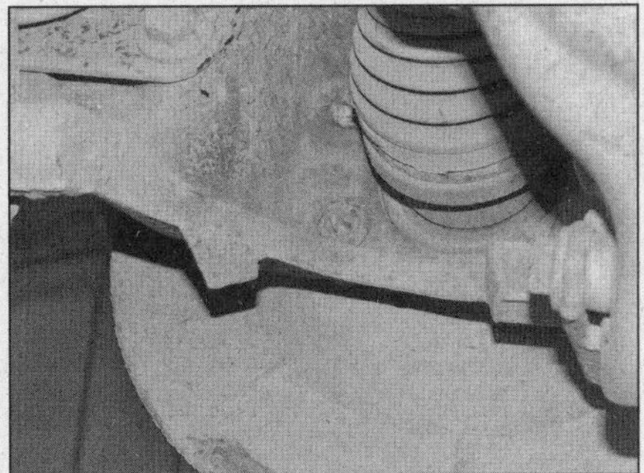

13.4 Remove the 4 bolts from the inside of the hub assembly

13.6 Drive the disc assembly off the shaft

13.7 Drive the shaft out of the differential with a drift

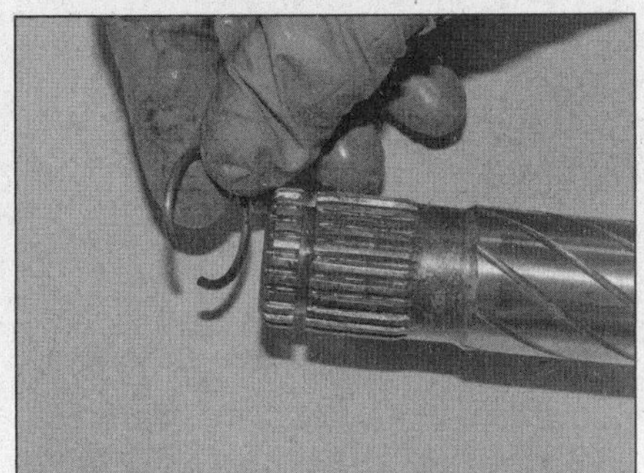

13.8 Remove the circlip

13 Rear axle halfshaft – removal and refitting

Removal

1 Raise the front of the vehicle and support it securely on axle stands (see *Jacking and vehicle support*). Remove the relevant rear roadwheel.

2 Fabricate a forked tool to prevent the brake disc from turning, and undo the central hub nut **(see illustration)**.

3 Disconnect the wiring plug, then unbolt and remove the sensor **(see illustration)**.

4 Undo 4 mounting bolts from the inside of the hub assembly **(see illustration)**.

5 Remove the brake caliper and caliper mounting bracket as described in Chapter 9 Section 10.

6 If necessary, use a hammer and drift to drive the brake disc assembly from the end of the halfshaft **(see illustration)**.

7 In order to pull the halfshaft from the differential, secure a u-shaped clamp around the end of the shaft nearest the differential, then drive it out using a hammer and drift **(see illustration)**.

8 Remove the circlip around the inner end of the halfshaft **(see illustration)**. Discard the circlip – a new one must fitted upon reassembly.

Refitting

9 Refitting is a reversal of removal, ensuring that all necessary bolts are replaced and are all tightened to the required torque.

Chapter 9
Braking system

Contents

Degrees of difficulty

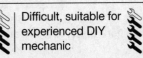

Easy, suitable for novice with little experience	Fairly easy, suitable for beginner with some experience	Fairly difficult, suitable for competent DIY mechanic	Difficult, suitable for experienced DIY mechanic	Very difficult, suitable for expert DIY or professional

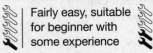

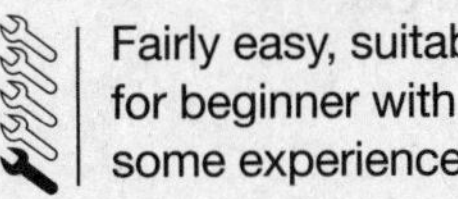
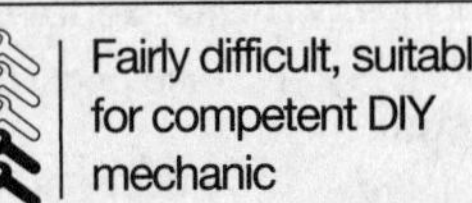
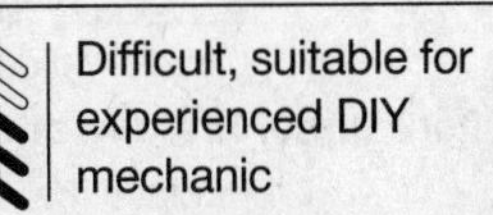

Specifications

Front brakes

Type	Ventilated disc, with single-piston sliding caliper
Disc diameter	300 or 320 mm
Disc minimum thickness	23 mm
Maximum disc run-out	0.05 mm
Brake pad friction material minimum	3 mm

Rear brakes

Disc diameter	280 mm
Disc minimum thickness:	
Manual parking brake	9 mm
Electric parking brake	9.5 mm
Brake pad friction material minimum thickness	3 mm

Torque wrench settings

	Nm	lbf ft
DSC yaw rate sensor	8	6
Front brake caliper:		
Guide pins	28	21
Mounting bracket bolts*	175	129
Hydraulic hose/pipe union nuts	15	11
Master cylinder retaining nuts*	23	17
Rear brake caliper:		
Guide pins	28	21
Mounting bracket bolts*	63	47
Roadwheel nuts	135	100
Vacuum servo unit mounting nuts*	25	18
Wheel speed sensor bolts:		
Front sensor	5	4
Rear sensor	5	4

** Do not re-use*

1 General information

1 The braking system is of the servo-assisted, dual-circuit hydraulic type. The arrangement of the hydraulic system is such that each circuit operates one front and one rear brake from a tandem master cylinder. Under normal circumstances, both circuits operate in unison. However, in the event of hydraulic failure in one circuit, full braking force will still be available at two wheels.

2 All models are equipped with disc brakes on all wheels. ABS is fitted as standard (refer to Section 18 for further information on ABS operation).

3 The disc brakes are actuated by single-piston sliding type calipers, which ensure that equal pressure is applied to each disc pad.

4 On all models, the handbrake provides an independent mechanical means of rear brake application. All models are fitted with rear brake calipers with an integral handbrake function. The handbrake cable operates a lever on the caliper which forces the piston to press the pad against the disc surface. A self-adjust mechanism is incorporated, to automatically compensate for brake pad wear.

Note: *When servicing any of the system, work carefully and methodically; also observe scrupulous cleanliness when overhauling any of the hydraulic system. Always renew components (in axle sets, where applicable) if in doubt about their condition, and use only genuine Ford replacement parts, or at least those of known good quality. Note the warnings given in 'Safety first!' and at relevant points in this Chapter concerning the dangers of asbestos dust and hydraulic fluid.*

2 Troubleshooting

PROBABLE CAUSE	CORRECTIVE ACTION
No brakes – pedal travels to floor	
1 Low fluid level	1 and 2 Low fluid level and air in the system are symptoms of another problem – a leak somewhere in the hydraulic system. Locate and repair the leak
2 Air in system	
3 Defective seals in master cylinder	3 Replace master cylinder
4 Fluid overheated and vaporised due to heavy braking	4 Bleed hydraulic system (temporary fix). Replace brake fluid (proper fix)
Brake pedal slowly travels to floor under braking or at a stop	
1 Defective seals in master cylinder	1 Replace master cylinder
2 Leak in a hose, line, caliper or wheel cylinder	2 Locate and repair leak
3 Air in hydraulic system	3 Bleed the system, inspect system for a leak
Brake pedal feels spongy when depressed	
1 Air in hydraulic system	1 Bleed the system, inspect system for a leak
2 Master cylinder or power booster loose	2 Tighten fasteners
3 Brake fluid overheated (beginning to boil)	3 Bleed the system (temporary fix). Replace the brake fluid (proper fix)
4 Deteriorated brake hoses (ballooning under pressure)	4 Inspect hoses, replace as necessary (it's a good idea to replace all of them if one hose shows signs of deterioration)
Brake pedal feels hard when depressed and/or excessive effort required to stop vehicle	
1 Servo unit faulty	1 Replace servo unit
2 Engine not producing sufficient vacuum, or hose to servo clogged, collapsed or cracked	2 Check vacuum to servo with a vacuum gauge. Replace hose if cracked or clogged, repair engine if vacuum is extremely low
3 Brake linings contaminated by grease or brake fluid	3 Locate and repair source of contamination, replace brake pads or shoes
4 Brake linings glazed	4 Replace brake pads or shoes, check discs and drums for glazing, service as necessary
5 Caliper piston(s) or wheel cylinder(s) binding or seized	5 Replace calipers or wheel cylinders
6 Brakes wet	6 Apply pedal to boil-off water (this should only be a momentary problem)
7 Kinked, clogged or internally split brake hose or line	7 Inspect lines and hoses, replace as necessary
Excessive brake pedal travel (but will pump up)	
1 Drum brakes out of adjustment	1 Adjust brakes
2 Air in hydraulic system	2 Bleed system, inspect system for a leak

PROBABLE CAUSE	CORRECTIVE ACTION
Excessive brake pedal travel (but will not pump up)	
1 Master cylinder pushrod misadjusted	1 Adjust pushrod
2 Master cylinder seals defective	2 Replace master cylinder
3 Brake linings worn out	3 Inspect brakes, replace pads and/or shoes
4 Hydraulic system leak	4 Locate and repair leak
Brake pedal doesn't return	
1 Brake pedal binding	1 Inspect pivot bushing and pushrod, repair or lubricate
2 Defective master cylinder	2 Replace master cylinder
Brake pedal pulsates during brake application	
1 Brake drums out-of-round	1 Have drums machined by an automotive machine shop
2 Excessive brake disc runout or disc surfaces out-of-parallel	2 Have discs machined by an automotive machine shop
3 Loose or worn wheel bearings	3 Adjust or replace wheel bearings
4 Loose wheel nuts	4 Tighten wheel nuts
Brakes slow to release	
1 Malfunctioning servo unit	1 Replace servo unit
2 Pedal linkage binding	2 Inspect pedal pivot bushing and pushrod, repair/lubricate
3 Malfunctioning proportioning valve	3 Replace proportioning valve
4 Sticking caliper or wheel cylinder	4 Repair or replace calipers or wheel cylinders
5 Kinked or internally split brake hose	5 Locate and replace faulty brake hose
Brakes grab (one or more wheels)	
1 Grease or brake fluid on brake lining	1 Locate and repair cause of contamination, replace lining
2 Brake lining glazed	2 Replace lining, deglaze disc or drum
Vehicle pulls to one side during braking	
1 Grease or brake fluid on brake lining	1 Locate and repair cause of contamination, replace lining
2 Brake lining glazed	2 Deglaze or replace lining, deglaze disc or drum
3 Restricted brake line or hose	3 Repair line or replace hose
4 Tyre pressures incorrect	4 Adjust tyre pressures
5 Caliper or wheel cylinder sticking	5 Repair or replace calipers or wheel cylinders
6 Wheels out of alignment	6 Have wheels aligned
7 Weak suspension spring	7 Replace springs
8 Weak or broken shock absorber	8 Replace shock absorbers

Brakes drag (indicated by sluggish engine performance or wheels being very hot after driving)

PROBABLE CAUSE	CORRECTIVE ACTION
1 Brake pedal pushrod incorrectly adjusted	1 Adjust pushrod
2 Master cylinder pushrod (between servo and master cylinder)	2 Adjust pushrod incorrectly adjusted
3 Obstructed compensating port in master cylinderr	3 Replace master cylinde
4 Master cylinder piston seized in bore	4 Replace master cylinder
5 Contaminated fluid causing swollen seals throughout system	5 Flush system, replace all hydraulic components
6 Clogged brake lines or internally split brake hose(s)	6 Flush hydraulic system, replace defective hose(s)
7 Sticking caliper(s) or wheel cylinder(s)	7 Replace calipers or wheel cylinders
8 Parking brake not releasing	8 Inspect parking brake linkage and parking brake mechanism, repair as required
9 Improper shoe-to-drum clearance	9 Adjust brake shoes
10 Faulty proportioning valve	10 Replace proportioning valve

Brakes fade (due to excessive heat)

PROBABLE CAUSE	CORRECTIVE ACTION
1 Brake linings excessively worn or glazed	1 Deglaze or replace brake pads and/or shoes
2 Excessive use of brakes	2 Downshift into a lower gear, maintain a constant slower speed (going down hills)
3 Vehicle overloaded	3 Reduce load
4 Brake drums or discs worn too thin	4 Measure drum diameter and disc thickness, replace drums or discs as required
5 Contaminated brake fluid	5 Flush system, replace fluid
6 Brakes drag	6 Repair cause of dragging brakes
7 Driver resting left foot on brake pedal	7 Don't ride the brakes

Brakes noisy (high-pitched squeal)

PROBABLE CAUSE	CORRECTIVE ACTION
1 Glazed lining	1 Deglaze or replace lining
2 Contaminated lining (brake fluid, grease, etc.)	2 Repair source of contamination, replace linings
3 Weak or broken brake shoe hold-down or return spring	3 Replace springs
4 Rivets securing lining to shoe or backing plate loose	4 Replace shoes or pads
5 Excessive dust buildup on brake linings	5 Wash brakes off with brake system cleaner
6 Brake drums worn too thin	6 Measure diameter of drums, replace if necessary
7 Wear indicator on disc brake pads contacting disc	7 Replace brake pads
8 Anti-squeal shims missing or installed improperly	8 Install shims correctly

Brakes noisy (scraping sound)

PROBABLE CAUSE	CORRECTIVE ACTION
1 Brake pads or shoes worn out; rivets, backing plate or brake shoe metal contacting disc or drum	1 Replace linings, have discs and/or drums machined (or replace)

Brakes chatter

PROBABLE CAUSE	CORRECTIVE ACTION
1 Worn brake lining	1 Inspect brakes, replace shoes or pads as necessary
2 Glazed or scored discs or drums	2 Deglaze discs or drums with sandpaper (if glazing is severe, machining will be required)
3 Drums or discs heat checked	3 Check discs and/or drums for hard spots, heat checking, etc. Have discs/drums machined or replace them
4 Disc runout or drum out-of-round excessive	4 Measure disc runout and/or drum out-of-round, have discs or drums machined or replace them
5 Loose or worn wheel bearings	5 Adjust or replace wheel bearings
6 Loose or bent brake backing plate (drum brakes)	6 Tighten or replace backing plate
7 Grooves worn in discs or drums	7 Have discs or drums machined, if within limits (if not, replace them)
8 Brake linings contaminated (brake fluid, grease, etc.)	8 Locate and repair source of contamination, replace pads or shoes
9 Excessive dust buildup on linings	9 Wash brakes with brake system cleaner
10 Surface finish on discs or drums too rough after machining	10 Have discs or drums properly machined (especially on vehicles with sliding calipers)
11 Brake pads or shoes glazed	11 Deglaze or replace brake pads or shoes

Brake pads or shoes click

PROBABLE CAUSE	CORRECTIVE ACTION
1 Shoe support pads on brake backing plate grooved or	1 Replace brake backing plate excessively worn
2 Brake pads loose in caliper	2 Loose pad retainers or anti-rattle clips
3 Also see items listed under Brakes chatter	

Brakes make groaning noise at end of stop

PROBABLE CAUSE	CORRECTIVE ACTION
1 Brake pads and/or shoes worn out	1 Replace pads and/or shoes
2 Brake linings contaminated (brake fluid, grease, etc.)	2 Locate and repair cause of contamination, replace brake pads or shoes
3 Brake linings glazed	3 Deglaze or replace brake pads or shoes
4 Excessive dust buildup on linings	4 Wash brakes with brake systemcleaner
5 Scored or heat-checked discs or drums	5 Inspect discs/drums, have machined if within limits (if not, replace discs or drums)
6 Broken or missing brake shoe attaching hardware	6 Inspect drum brakes, replace missing hardware

Rear brakes lock up under light brake application

PROBABLE CAUSE	CORRECTIVE ACTION
1 Tyre pressures too high	1 Adjust tyre pressures
2 Tyres excessively worn	2 Replace tyres
3 Defective proportioning valve	3 Replace proportioning valve

Brake warning light on instrument panel comes on (or stays on)

PROBABLE CAUSE	CORRECTIVE ACTION
1 Low fluid level in master cylinder reservoir (reservoirs with fluid level sensor)	1 Add fluid, inspect system for leak, check the thickness of the brake pads and shoes
2 Failure in one half of the hydraulic system	2 Inspect hydraulic system for a leak
3 Piston in pressure differential warning valve not centered	3 Center piston by bleeding one circuit or the other (close bleeder valve as soon as the light goes out)
4 Defective pressure differential valve or warning switch	4 Replace valve or switch
5 Air in the hydraulic system	5 Bleed the system, check for leaks
6 Brake pads worn out (vehicles with electric wear sensors – small)	6 Replace brake pads (and sensors) probes that fit into the brake pads and ground out on the disc when the pads get thin)

Brakes do not self adjust

PROBABLE CAUSE	CORRECTIVE ACTION
1 Defective caliper piston seals	1 Replace calipers. Also, possible contaminated fluid causing soft or swollen seals (flush system and fill with new fluid if in doubt)
2 Corroded caliper piston(s)	2 Same as above
3 Adjuster screw frozen	3 Remove adjuster, disassemble, clean and lubricate with high-temperature grease
4 Adjuster lever does not contact star wheel or is binding	4 Inspect drum brakes, assemble correctly or clean or replace parts as required
5 Adjusters mixed up (installed on wrong wheels after brake job)	5 Reassemble correctly
6 Adjuster cable broken or installed incorrectly (cable-type adjusters)	6 Install new cable or assemble correctly

Rapid brake lining wear

PROBABLE CAUSE	CORRECTIVE ACTION
1 Driver resting left foot on brake pedal	1 Don't ride the brakes
2 Surface finish on discs or drums too rough	2 Have discs or drums properly machined
3 Also see Brakes drag	

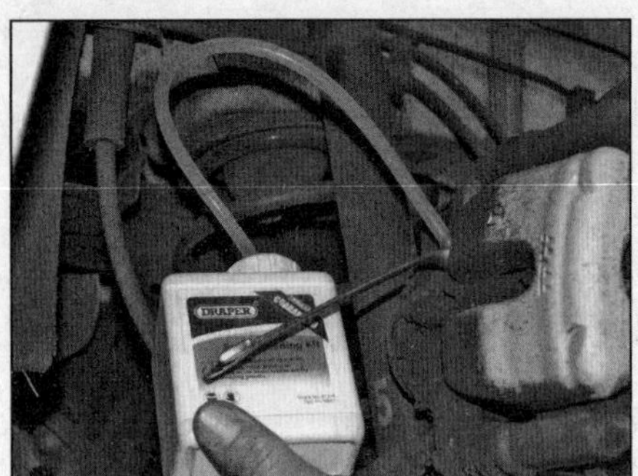

3.22 Connect the kit to the bleed screw

3 Hydraulic system – bleeding

Warning: Hydraulic fluid is poisonous; wash off immediately and thoroughly in the case of skin contact, and seek immediate medical advice if any fluid is swallowed or gets into the eyes. Certain types of hydraulic fluid are inflammable, and may ignite when allowed into contact with hot components; when servicing any hydraulic system, it is safest to assume that the fluid is inflammable, and to take precautions against the risk of fire as though it is petrol that is being handled. Hydraulic fluid is also an effective paint stripper, and will attack plastics; if any is spilt, it should be washed off immediately, using copious quantities of fresh water. Finally, it is hygroscopic (it absorbs moisture from the air) – old fluid may be contaminated and unfit for further use. When topping-up or renewing the fluid, always use the recommended type, and ensure that it comes from a freshly-opened sealed container.

Note: *If difficulty is experienced in bleeding the braking circuit on models with ABS, this maybe due to air being trapped in the ABS regulator unit. If this is the case then the vehicle should be taken to a Ford dealer or suitably equipped specialist, so that the system can be bled using special electronic test equipment.*

Note: *A hydraulic clutch shares its fluid reservoir with the braking system, and may also need to be bled (see Chapter 8 Section 2).*

Caution: Ensure the ignition is switched off before starting the bleeding procedure, to avoid any possibility of voltage being applied to the hydraulic modulator before the bleeding procedure is complete. Ideally, the battery should be disconnected. If voltage is applied to the modulator before the bleeding procedure is complete, this will effectively drain the hydraulic fluid in the modulator, rendering the unit unserviceable. Do not, therefore, attempt to 'run' the modulator in order to bleed the brakes.

General

1 The correct operation of any hydraulic system is only possible after removing all air from the components and circuit; this is achieved by bleeding the system.

2 During the bleeding procedure, add only clean, unused hydraulic fluid of the recommended type; never re-use fluid that has already been bled from the system. Ensure that sufficient fluid is available before starting work.

3 If there is any possibility of incorrect fluid being already in the system, the brake components and circuit must be flushed completely with uncontaminated, correct fluid, and new seals should be fitted to the various components.

4 If hydraulic fluid has been lost from the system, or air has entered because of a leak, ensure that the fault is cured before proceeding further.

5 Park the vehicle on level ground, switch off the engine and select first or reverse gear, then chock the wheels and release the handbrake.

6 Check that all pipes and hoses are secure, unions tight and bleed screws closed. Clean any dirt from around the bleed screws.

7 Unscrew the master cylinder reservoir cap, and top the master cylinder reservoir up to the MAX level line; refit the cap loosely, and remember to maintain the fluid level at least above the MIN level line throughout the procedure, or there is a risk of further air entering the system.

8 There are a number of one-man, do-it-yourself brake bleeding kits currently available from motor accessory shops. It is recommended that one of these kits is used whenever possible, as they greatly simplify the bleeding operation, and also reduce the risk of expelled air and fluid being drawn back into the system. If such a kit is not available, the basic (two-man) method must be used, which is described in detail below.

9 If a kit is to be used, prepare the vehicle as described previously, and follow the kit manufacturer's instructions, as the procedure may vary slightly according to the type being used; generally, they are as outlined below in the relevant sub-section.

10 Whichever method is used, the same sequence must be followed (paragraphs 11 and 12) to ensure that the removal of all air from the system.

Bleeding

Sequence

11 If the system has been only partially disconnected, and suitable precautions were taken to minimise fluid loss, it should be necessary only to bleed that of the system (ie, the primary or secondary circuit).

12 If the complete system is to be bled, then it should be done working in the following sequence:

a) Right-hand rear brake.
b) Left-hand rear brake.
c) Right-hand front brake.
d) Left-hand front brake.

Basic (two-man) method

13 Collect a clean glass jar, a suitable length of plastic or rubber tubing which is a tight fit over the bleed screw, and a ring spanner to fit the screw. The help of an assistant will also be required.

14 Remove the dust cap from the first screw in the sequence. Fit the spanner and tube to the screw, place the other end of the tube in the jar, and pour in sufficient fluid to cover the end of the tube.

15 Ensure that the master cylinder reservoir fluid level is maintained at least above the MIN level line throughout the procedure.

16 Have the assistant fully depress the brake pedal several times to build-up pressure, then maintain it on the final downstroke.

17 While pedal pressure is maintained, unscrew the bleed screw (approximately one turn) and allow the compressed fluid and air to flow into the jar. The assistant should maintain pedal pressure, following it down to the floor if necessary, and should not release it until instructed to do so. When the flow stops, tighten the bleed screw again, have the assistant release the pedal slowly, and recheck the reservoir fluid level.

18 Repeat the steps given in paragraphs 16 and 17 until the fluid emerging from the bleed screw is free from air bubbles. If the master cylinder has been drained and refilled, and air is being bled from the first screw in the sequence, allow approximately five seconds between cycles for the master cylinder passages to refill.

19 When no more air bubbles appear, tighten the bleed screw securely, remove the tube and spanner, and refit the dust cap. Do not overtighten the bleed screw.

20 Repeat the procedure on the remaining screws in the sequence, until all air is removed from the system and the brake pedal feels firm again.

Using a one-way valve kit

21 As their name implies, these kits consist of a length of tubing with a one-way valve fitted, to prevent expelled air and fluid being drawn back into the system; some kits include a translucent container, which can be positioned so that the air bubbles can be more easily seen flowing from the end of the tube.

22 The kit is connected to the bleed screw, which is then opened **(see illustration)**. The user returns to the driver's seat, depresses the brake pedal with a smooth, steady stroke, and slowly releases it; this is repeated until the expelled fluid is clear of air bubbles.

23 Note that these kits simplify work so much that it is easy to forget the master cylinder reservoir fluid level; ensure that this is maintained at least above the MIN/DANGER level line at all times.

Using a pressure-bleeding kit

24 These kits are usually operated by the reservoir of pressurised air contained in the spare tyre. However, note that it will probably be necessary to reduce the pressure to a lower level than normal; refer to the instructions supplied with the kit.

25 By connecting a pressurised, fluid-filled container to the master cylinder reservoir, bleeding can be carried out simply by opening each screw in turn (in the specified sequence), and allowing the fluid to flow out until no more air bubbles can be seen in the expelled fluid.

26 This method has the advantage that the large reservoir of fluid provides an additional safeguard against air being drawn into the system during bleeding.

27 Pressure-bleeding is particularly effective when bleeding 'difficult' systems, or when bleeding the complete system at the time of routine fluid renewal.

All methods

28 When bleeding is complete, and firm pedal feel is restored, wash off any spilt fluid, tighten the bleed screws securely, and refit their dust caps.

29 Check the hydraulic fluid level in the master cylinder reservoir, and top-up if necessary (see Chapter 1A Section 7 or Chapter 1B Section 7).

30 Discard any hydraulic fluid that has been bled from the system; it will not be fit for re-use.

31 Check the feel of the brake pedal. If it feels at all spongy, air must still be present in the system, and further bleeding is required. Failure to bleed satisfactorily after a reasonable repetition of the bleeding procedure may be due to worn master cylinder seals.

4 Hydraulic pipes and hoses – renewal

Note: *Before starting work, refer to the warning at the beginning of Section 3 concerning the dangers of hydraulic fluid.*

1 If any pipe or hose is to be renewed, minimise fluid loss by first removing the master cylinder reservoir cap, then tightening it down onto a piece of polythene to obtain an airtight seal. Alternatively, flexible hoses can be sealed, if required, using a proprietary brake hose clamp; metal brake pipe unions can be plugged (if care is taken not to allow dirt into the system) or capped immediately they are disconnected. Place a wad of rag under any union that is to be disconnected, to catch any spilt fluid.

2 To unscrew the union nuts, it is preferable to obtain a brake pipe spanner of the correct size; these are available from most large motor accessory shops. Failing this, a close-fitting open-ended spanner will be required, though if the nuts are tight or corroded, their flats may be rounded-off if the spanner slips. In such a case, a self-locking wrench is often the only way to unscrew a stubborn union, but it follows that the pipe and the damaged nuts must be renewed on reassembly. Always clean a union and surrounding area before disconnecting it. If disconnecting a component with more than one union, make a careful note of the connections before disturbing any of them.

3 If a brake pipe is to be renewed, it can be obtained, cut to length and with the union nuts and end flares in place, from Ford dealers. All that is then necessary is to bend it to shape, following the line of the original, before fitting it to the car. Alternatively, most motor accessory shops can make up brake pipes from kits, but this requires very careful measurement of the original, to ensure that the replacement is of the correct length. The safest answer is usually to take the original to the shop as a pattern.

4 On refitting, do not overtighten the union nuts. It is not necessary to exercise brute force to obtain a sound joint.

5 Ensure that the pipes and hoses are correctly routed, with no kinks, and that they are secured in the clips or brackets provided. After fitting, remove the polythene from the reservoir, and bleed the hydraulic system as described in Section 3. Wash off any spilt fluid, and check carefully for fluid leaks.

5 Front brake pads – renewal

Warning: Renew both sets of front brake pads at the same time – never renew the pads on only one wheel, as uneven braking may result. Note that the dust created by wear of the pads may contain asbestos, which is a health hazard. Never blow it out with compressed air, and don't inhale any of it. An approved filtering mask should be worn when working on the brakes. DO NOT use petrol or petroleum-based solvents to clean brake parts; use brake cleaner or methylated spirit only.

1 Apply the handbrake, then slacken the front roadwheel nuts. Jack up the front of the vehicle and support it on axle stands (see *Jacking and vehicle support*). Remove both front roadwheels.

2 Follow the accompanying photos **(see illustrations 5.2a to 5.2r)** for the actual pad replacement procedure. Be sure to stay in order and read the caption under each illustration, and note the following points:

Thoroughly clean the caliper guide surfaces, and apply a little brake assembly grease.

When pushing the caliper piston back to accommodate new pads, keep a close eye on the fluid level in the reservoir. Brake fluid is corrosive, and it could be pushed out of the reservoir, causing damage in the engine bay.

3 Depress the brake pedal repeatedly, until the pads are pressed into firm contact with the brake disc, and normal (non-assisted) pedal pressure is restored.

4 Repeat the above procedure on the remaining front brake caliper.

5 Before refitting the roadwheels, use a wire brush or mildly abrasive cloth (Scotchbrite, etc.) to clean the mating surfaces of the hub and wheel. Apply a little anti-seize grease (Copperslip) to the hub and wheel surface prior to refitting.

6 Refit the roadwheels, then lower the vehicle to the ground and tighten the roadwheel nuts to the specified torque.

7 Check the hydraulic fluid level as described in Chapter Section or Chapter Section.

Caution: New pads will not give full braking efficiency until they have bedded-in. Be prepared for this, and avoid hard braking as far as possible for the first hundred miles or so after pad renewal.

5.2a Use a screwdriver to remove the caliper retaining spring...

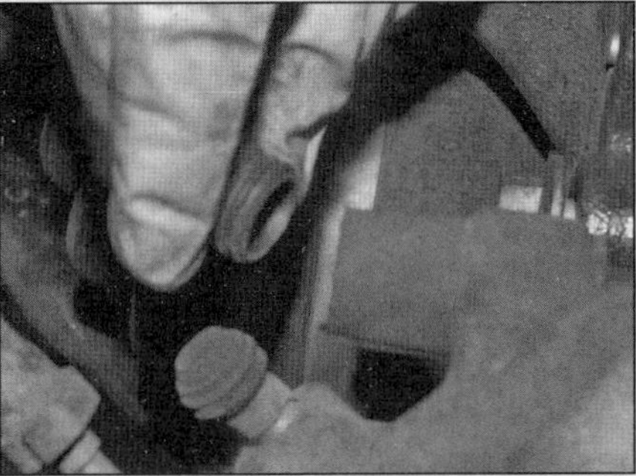

5.2b Prise the rubber caps from the upper, and lower guide pins

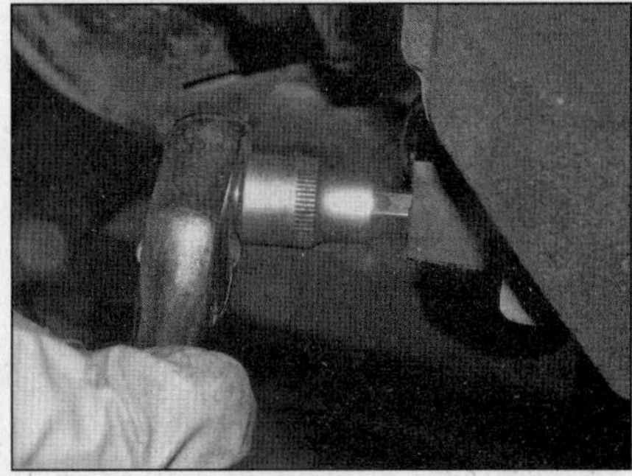

5.2c Use an Allen bit/key to unscrew both guide pins

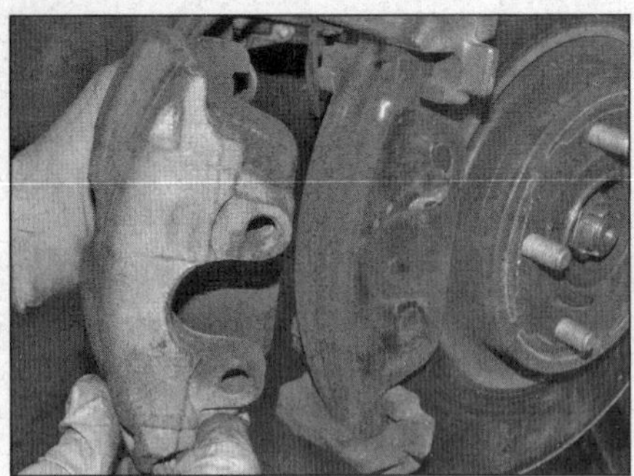
5.2d Slide the caliper from place...

5.2e ...and pull the inner brake pad from the caliper piston

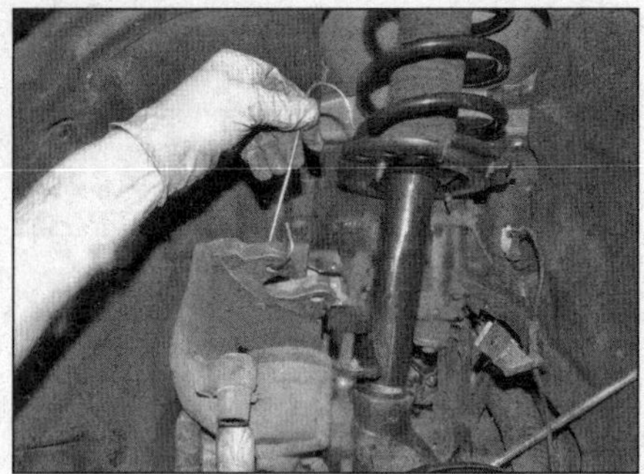
5.2f Suspend the caliper from the strut. Take care not to strain the brake hose

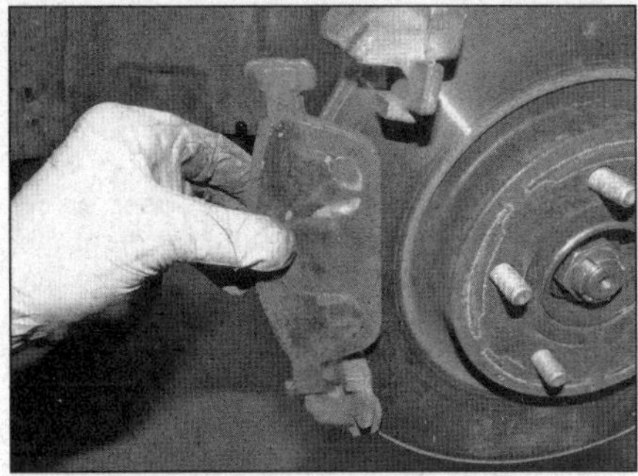
5.2g Remove the outer brake pad from the caliper mounting bracket

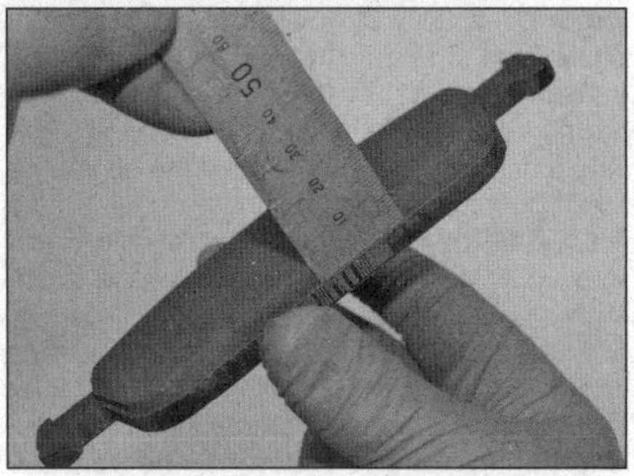
5.2h Measure the thickness of the pads friction material – if any pad is worn down to 3.0 mm or less, renew all 4 pads

5.2i Use brake cleaner and a brush to remove any brake dust or debris from the caliper and mounting bracket

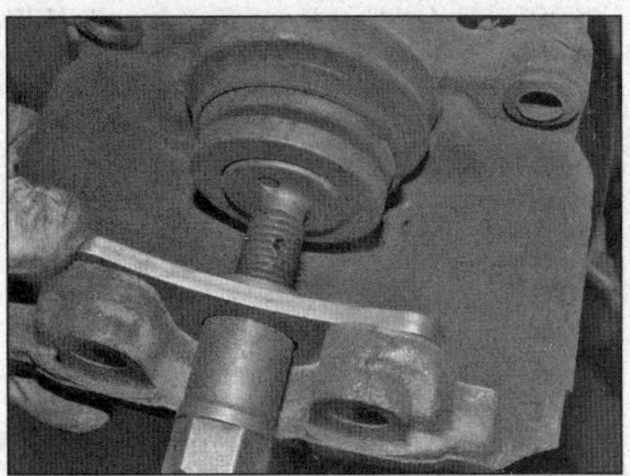
5.2j If new pads are to be fitted, use a retraction tool to push the piston back into the caliper. Keep an eye on the fluid level in the master cylinder reservoir – if the fluid level rises to the top of the reservoir, then remove excess fluid using a syringe or pipette

5.2k Apply a little high-temperature anti-seize grease to the pad contact surfaces of the caliper mounting bracket

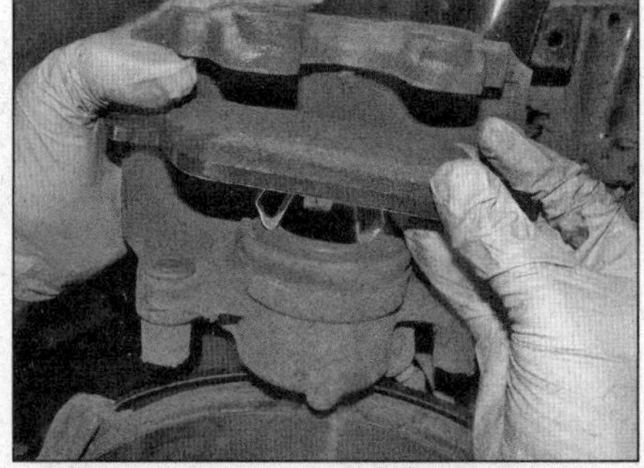
5.2l Press the inner pad into the caliper piston...

5.2m ...and the outer pad to the mounting bracket. Remove the backing sheet where applicable

5.2n Slide the caliper back into place over the pads

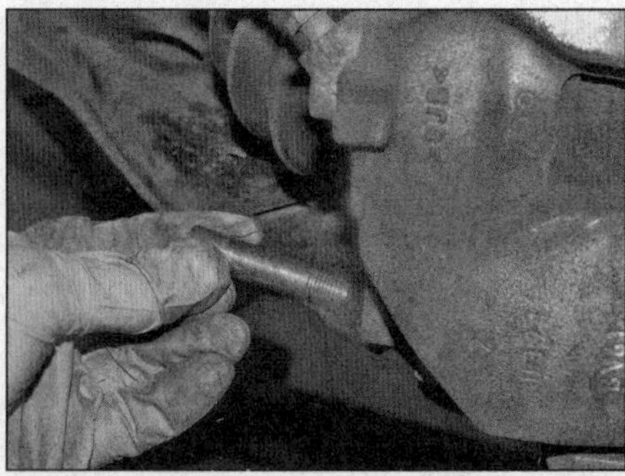
5.2o Insert both guide pin bolts...

5.2p ...and tighten them to the specified torque

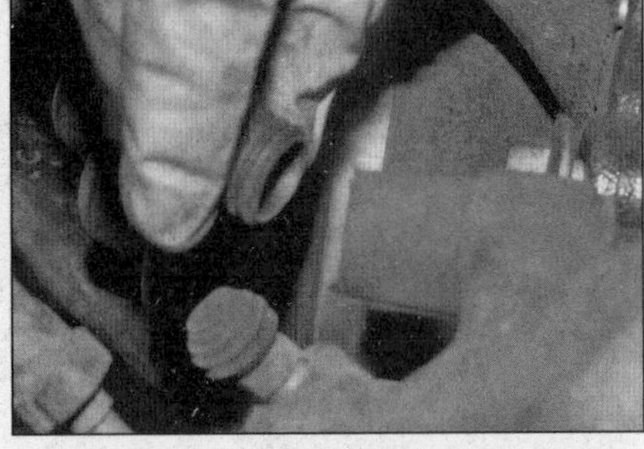
5.2q Refit the rubber caps over the ends of the guide pins

5.2r Don't forget to refit the caliper retaining spring

6 Rear brake pads – renewal

Warning: Renew BOTH sets of rear brake pads at the same time – NEVER renew the pads on only one wheel, as uneven braking may result. Note that the dust created by wear of the pads may contain asbestos, which is a health hazard. Never blow it out with compressed air, and don't inhale any of it. An approved filtering mask should be worn when working on the brakes. DO NOT use petroleum-based solvents to clean brake parts – use brake cleaner or methylated spirit only.

1 Chock the front wheels, slacken the rear roadwheel nuts, then release the parking brake. Jack up the rear of the vehicle and support it securely on axle stands (see *Jacking and vehicle support*). Remove both rear roadwheels.

2 On vehicles with an electric parking brake, you must place the parking brake in service mode before starting work. Otherwise, there is a greater risk of injury.

a) Set the ignition to ON.

b) Press the accelerator all the way down, and press down the Electric Parking Brake switch. Continue to hold both the pedal and switch in this position.

c) Switch the ignition to OFF, then switch the ignition back on again withing 5 seconds. Service mode will now be activated.

3 Follow the accompanying photos **(see illustrations 6.3a to 6.3q)** for the actual pad replacement procedure. Be sure to stay in order and read the caption under each illustration, and note the following points:

a) New pads may have an adhesive foil on the backplates. Remove this foil prior to installation.

b) Thoroughly clean the caliper guide surfaces, and apply a little brake assembly grease.

c) When pushing the caliper piston back to accommodate new pads, keep a close eye on the fluid level in the reservoir.

d) It is recommended that the pad mounting shims are renewed at the same time as the pads.

4 Depress the brake pedal repeatedly, until the pads are pressed into firm contact with the brake disc, and normal (non-assisted) pedal pressure is restored.

5 Repeat the above procedure on the remaining rear brake caliper.

6 At this stage, you must deactivate the service mode on the Electric Parking Brake (if fitted).

a) Set the ignition to ON.

b) Press the accelerator all the way down, and pull up the Electric Parking Brake switch. Continue to hold both the pedal and switch in this position.

c) Switch the ignition to OFF, then switch it back ON within 5 seconds. The parking brake will activate, and service mode is now deactivated.

7 Refit the roadwheels, then lower the vehicle to the ground and tighten the roadwheel nuts to the specified torque.

8 Check the hydraulic fluid level as described in Chapter 1A Section 7 or Chapter 1B Section 7.

Caution: New pads will not give full braking efficiency until they have bedded-in. Be prepared for this, and avoid hard braking as far as possible for the first hundred miles or so after pad renewal.

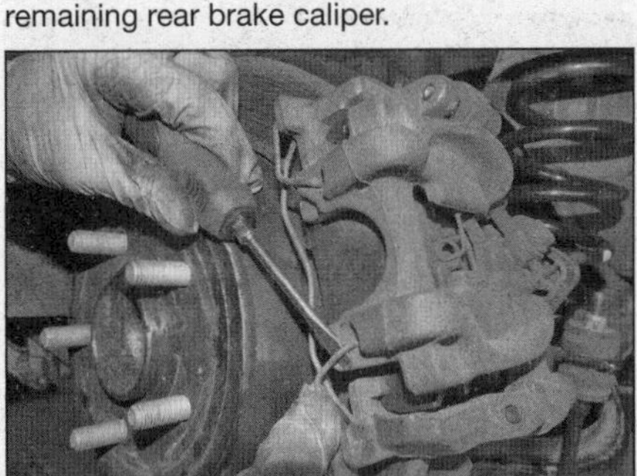
6.3a Carefully detach the brake caliper retaining spring using a large screwdriver

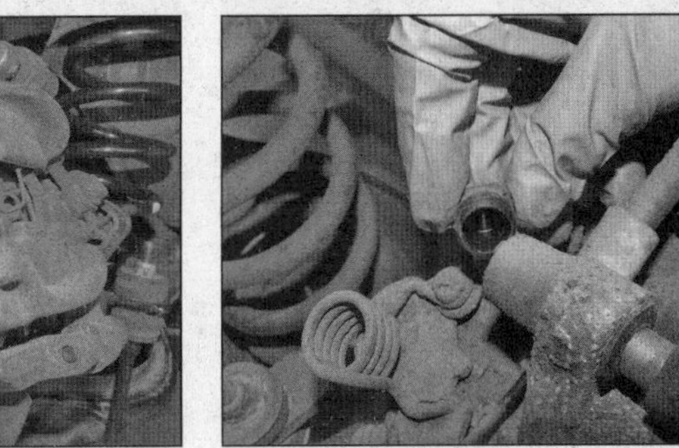
6.3b Prise out the rubber caps...

6.3c ...then unscrew the upper and lower guide pins using a hex key/bit

6.3d Unclip the wiring harness, lift the caliper from place, and suspend it from the coil spring. Take care not to strain the hose or cable

6.3e Remove the outer pad...

6.3f ...and inner pad

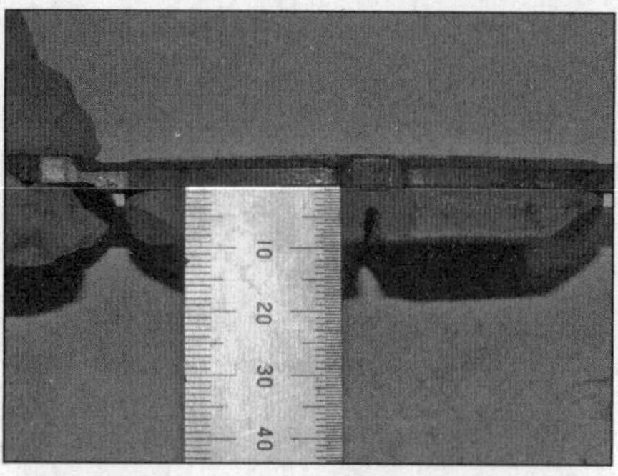

6.3g Measure the thickness of the pad's friction material. If any pad is worn down to the minimum thickness – all four pads must be renewed

6.3h Remove any dirt and debris from the caliper and mounting bracket, using an aerosol brake cleaner and brush

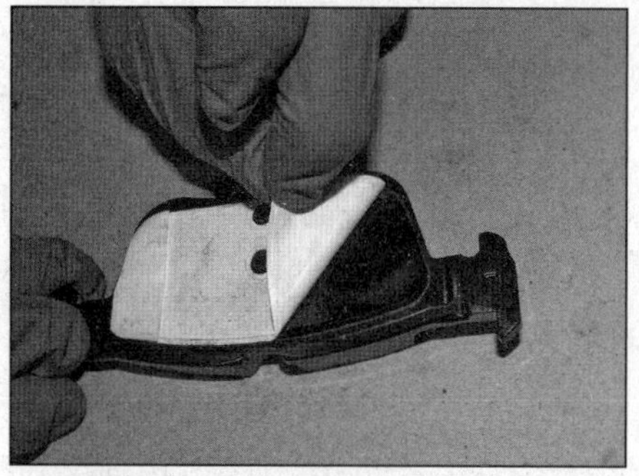

6.3i Remove the adhesive backing from the rear of the pads...

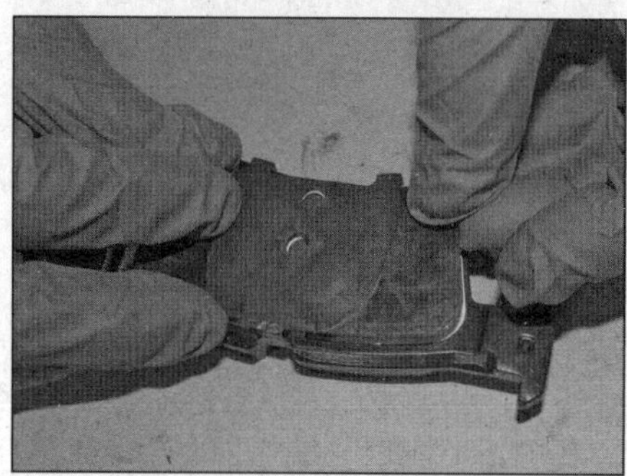

6.3j ...then position the anti-rattle shims

6.3k If new pads are fitted, the caliper piston must be pushed back and rotated clockwise into the housing at the same time – use a piston retraction tool. Keep an eye on the fluid level in the master cylinder reservoir

6.3l Apply a little high-temperature anti-seize grease to the pad contact points on the caliper mounting bracket

6.3m Fit the outer pad followed by the inner pad, which has the spring fitted. Ensure the friction material is against the disc!

6.3n Slide the caliper back into place without disturbing the pads

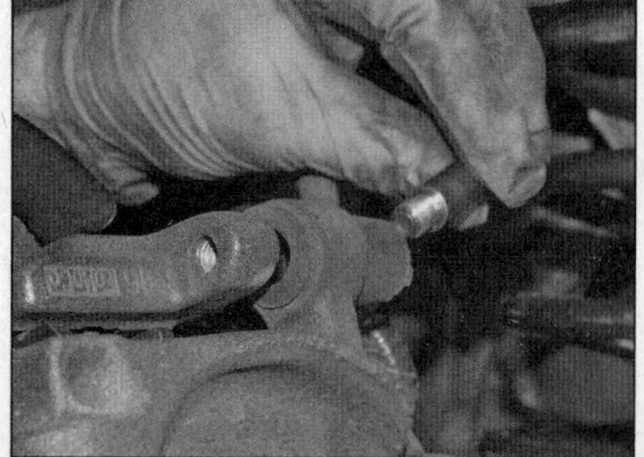

6.3o Insert the upper and lower guide pins, then tighten them to the specified torque

6.3p Press the rubber caps into place over the ends of the guide pins

6.3q Refit the caliper retaining spring

7.3 Measure the disc thickness using a micrometer

7 Front brake disc – inspection, removal and refitting

Note: *Before starting work, refer to the note at the beginning of Section 5 concerning the dangers of asbestos dust.*

Inspection

Note: *If either disc requires renewal, BOTH should be renewed at the same time, to ensure even and consistent braking. New brake pads should also be fitted.*

1 Apply the handbrake, slacken the front roadwheel nuts, then jack up the front of the car and support it on axle stands (see *Jacking and vehicle support*). Remove the appropriate front roadwheel.

2 Slowly rotate the brake disc so that the full area of both sides can be checked; remove the brake pads if better access is required to the inboard surface. Light scoring is normal in the area swept by the brake pads, but if heavy scoring or cracks are found, the disc must be renewed.

3 It is normal to find a lip of rust and brake dust around the disc's perimeter; this can be scraped off if required. If, however, a lip has formed due to excessive wear of the brake pad swept area, then the disc's thickness must be measured using a micrometer. Take measurements at several places around the disc, at the inside and outside of the pad swept area; if the disc has worn at any point to the specified minimum thickness or less, the disc must be renewed **(see illustration)**.

4 If the disc is thought to be warped, it can be checked for run-out. Either use a dial gauge mounted on any convenient fixed point, while the disc is slowly rotated, or use feeler blades to measure (at several points all around the disc) the clearance between the disc and a fixed point, such as the caliper mounting bracket. If the measurements obtained are at the specified maximum or beyond, the disc is excessively warped, and must be renewed; however, it is worth checking first that the hub bearing is in good condition. Also try the effect of removing the disc and turning it through 180°, to reposition it on the hub; if the run-out is still excessive, the disc must be renewed.

5 Check the disc for cracks, especially around the wheel bolt holes, and any other wear or damage, and renew if necessary.

7.7 Undo the 2 caliper mounting bracket bolts

Removal

6 Remove the brake pads as described in Section 5, then undo the remaining guide pin bolt, and remove the caliper. Suspend the caliper from the suspension strut coil spring to prevent straining the fluid hose. Note that new guide pin bolts will be required.

7 Slacken and remove the two bolts securing the brake caliper mounting bracket to the hub carrier **(see illustration)**. Slide the assembly off the disc and tie it to the coil spring, using a piece of wire or string, to avoid placing any strain on the hydraulic brake hose.

8 Pull the brake disc from the hub **(see illustration)**. If it is tight, lightly tap its rear face with a hide or plastic mallet.

Refitting

9 Refitting is the reverse of the removal procedure, noting the following points:

a) Ensure that the mating surfaces of the disc and hub are clean and flat.

b) Tighten the disc retaining screw and the new caliper mounting bracket bolts to the specified torque setting.

c) If a new disc has been fitted, use a suitable solvent to wipe any preservative coating from the disc, before refitting the caliper.

d) Refit the roadwheel then lower the vehicle to the ground and tighten the wheel nuts to the specified torque. Apply the foot brake several times to force the pads back into contact with the disc before driving the vehicle.

8.4 Rear brake caliper mounting bracket bolts

7.8 The disc can be pulled away from the hub

8 Rear brake disc – inspection, removal and refitting

Note: *Before starting work, refer to the note at the beginning of Section 6 concerning the dangers of asbestos dust.*

Inspection

Note: *If either disc requires renewal, BOTH should be renewed at the same time, to ensure even and consistent braking. New brake pads should also be fitted.*

1 Firmly chock the front wheels, slacken the appropriate rear roadwheel nuts, then jack up the rear of the car and support it on axle stands (see *Jacking and vehicle support*). Remove the relevant rear roadwheel.

2 Inspect the disc as described in Section 7.

Removal

3 Remove the brake pads (see Section 6.

4 Undo the two bolts securing the caliper mounting bracket to the stub axle **(see illustration)**. Discard the bolts – new ones must be fitted.

5 Use chalk or paint to mark the relationship of the disc to the hub, then if necessary, gently tap the disc from behind and release it from the hub **(see illustration)**.

Refitting

6 Refitting is the reverse of the removal procedure, noting the following points:

a) Ensure that the mating surfaces of the disc and hub are clean and flat.

8.5 Gently manoeuvre the disc away from the hub

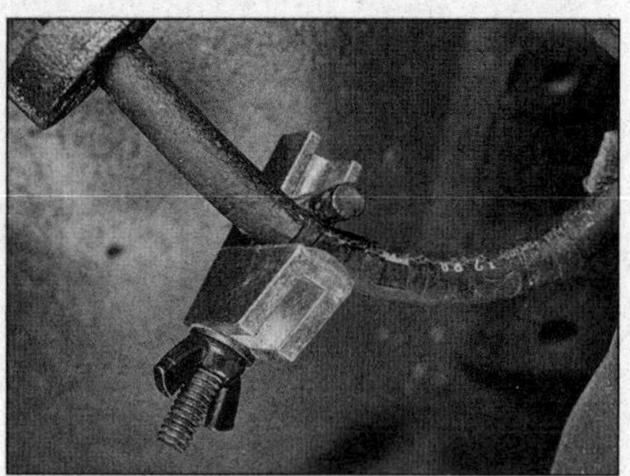

9.2 To minimise fluid loss, fit a brake hose clamp to the flexible hose

b) *Align (if applicable) the marks made on removal, and tighten the disc retaining screw and the new caliper mounting bracket bolts to the specified torque.*
c) *If a new disc has been fitted, use a suitable solvent to wipe any preservative coating from the disc, before refitting the caliper.*
d) *Refit the roadwheel, then lower the vehicle to the ground and tighten the roadwheel nuts to the specified torque. Depress the brake pedal several times to force the pads back into contact with the disc.*

9 Front brake caliper – removal, overhaul and refitting

Caution: Ensure the ignition is switched off before disconnecting any braking system hydraulic union and do not switch it on until after the hydraulic system has been bled. Failure to do this could lead to air entering the regulator unit requiring the unit to be bled using special Ford test equipment (see Section 3).

Note: *Before starting work, refer to the note at the beginning of Section 3 concerning the dangers of hydraulic fluid, and to the warning at the beginning of Section 5 concerning the dangers of asbestos dust.*

Removal

1 Apply the handbrake, slacken the relevant front roadwheel nuts, then jack up the front of the vehicle and support it on axle stands (see *Jacking and vehicle support*). Remove the appropriate roadwheel.

2 Minimise fluid loss by first removing the master cylinder reservoir cap, and then tightening it down onto a piece of polythene, to obtain an airtight seal. Alternatively, use a brake hose clamp, a G-clamp or a similar tool to clamp the flexible hose **(see illustration)**.

3 Clean the area around the caliper hose union, then loosen the union.

4 Slacken and remove the upper and lower caliper guide pins **(see illustration 5.2c)**. Lift the caliper away from the brake disc, then unscrew the caliper from the end of the brake hose.

5 If required, the caliper mounting bracket can be unbolted from the hub carrier. Note that new bolts will be required.

Overhaul

Note: *Check the availability of repair kits for the caliper before dismantling.*

6 With the caliper on the bench, wipe away all traces of dust and dirt, but avoid inhaling the dust, as it is a health hazard.

7 Withdraw the partially ejected piston from the caliper body, and remove the dust seal.

HAYNES HiNT ***If the piston cannot be withdrawn by hand, it can be pushed out by applying compressed air to the brake hose union hole. Only low pressure should be required, such as is generated by a foot pump. As the piston is expelled, take great care not to trap your fingers between the piston and caliper.***

8 Using a small screwdriver, extract the piston hydraulic seal, taking great care not to damage the caliper bore.

9 Thoroughly clean all components, using only methylated spirit, isopropyl alcohol or clean hydraulic fluid as a cleaning medium. Never use mineral-based solvents such as petrol or paraffin, as they will attack the hydraulic system's rubber components. Dry the components immediately, using compressed air or a clean, lint-free cloth. Use compressed air to blow clear the fluid passages.

10 Check all components, and renew any that are worn or damaged. Check particularly the cylinder bore and piston; these should be renewed (note that this means the renewal of the complete body assembly) if they are scratched, worn or corroded in any way. Similarly check the condition of the guide pins and their gaiters; both pins should be undamaged and (when cleaned) a reasonably tight sliding fit in the caliper bracket. If there is any doubt about the condition of any component, renew it.

11 If the assembly is fit for further use, obtain the appropriate repair kit; the components should be available from Ford dealers in various combinations. All rubber seals should be renewed as a matter of course; these should never be re-used.

12 On reassembly, ensure that all components are clean and dry.

13 Soak the piston and the new piston (fluid) seal in clean brake fluid. Smear clean fluid on the cylinder bore surface.

14 Fit the new piston (fluid) seal, using only your fingers (no tools) to manipulate it into the cylinder bore groove.

15 Fit the new dust seal to the rear of the piston and seat the outer lip of the seal in the caliper body groove. Carefully ease the piston squarely into the cylinder bore using a twisting motion. Press the piston fully into position, and seat the inner lip of the dust seal in the piston groove.

16 If the guide pins are being renewed, lubricate the pin shafts with the special grease supplied in the repair kit. Insert the pins into the caliper bracket.

Refitting

17 If previously removed, refit the caliper mounting bracket to the hub carrier, and tighten the new bolts to the specified torque.

18 Screw the caliper body fully onto the flexible hose union.

19 Slide the caliper into position over the brake pads.

20 Fit the guide pins, and tighten them to the specified torque. Refit the plastic caps.

21 Tighten the brake hose union nut securely, then remove the brake hose clamp or polythene (where fitted).

22 Bleed the hydraulic system as described in Section 3. Note that, providing the precautions described were taken to minimise brake fluid loss, it should only be necessary to bleed the relevant front brake.

23 Refit the roadwheel, then lower the vehicle to the ground and tighten the roadwheel nuts to the specified torque.

10 Rear brake caliper – removal, overhaul and refitting

Caution: Ensure the ignition is switched off before disconnecting any braking system hydraulic union and do not switch it back on until after the hydraulic system has been bled. Failure to do this could lead to air entering the regulator unit.

Note: *Before starting work, refer to the note at the beginning of Section 3 concerning the dangers of hydraulic fluid, and to the warning at the beginning of Section 5 concerning the dangers of asbestos dust.*

Removal

1 Chock the front wheels, slacken the relevant rear roadwheel nuts, then jack up the rear of the vehicle and support on axle stands (see *Jacking and vehicle support*). Remove the relevant rear wheel.

2 Remove the brake pads as described in Section 6.

3 Minimise fluid loss by first removing the master cylinder reservoir cap, and then tightening it down onto a piece of polythene, to obtain an airtight seal. Alternatively, use a brake hose clamp, a G-clamp or a similar tool to clamp the flexible hose at the nearest convenient point to the brake caliper **(see illustration 8.2)**.

4 Wipe away all traces of dirt around the brake hose union on the caliper, then slacken the hose union.

5 Remove the caliper from the vehicle and unscrew it from the hose. If required, the caliper mounting bracket can be unbolted from the hub carrier – note that new bolts will be required. Plug the pipe and caliper unions to minimise fluid loss and prevent dirt entry.

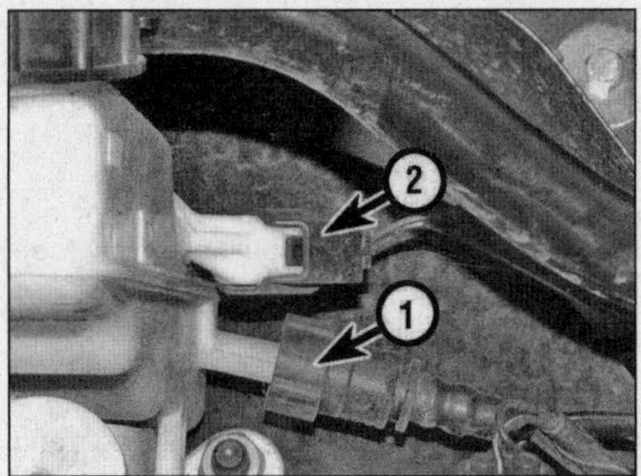

11.3 Disconnect the clutch master cylinder fluid supply hose (1) and the level sensor wiring plug (2) along with the metal brake pipes

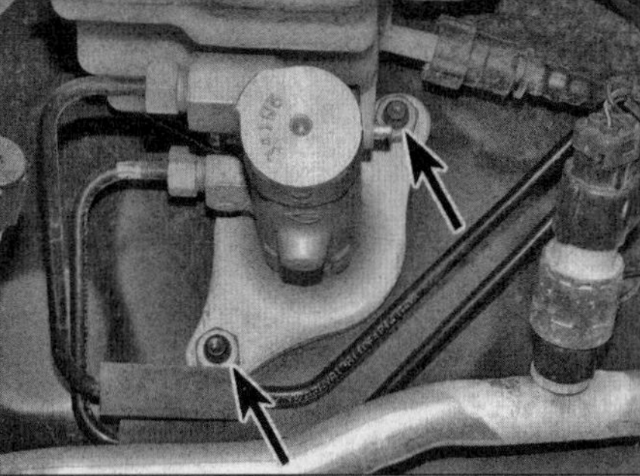
11.4 Undo the nuts and remove the master cylinder

11.5 Unscrew the reservoir retaining pin

Overhaul

6 At the time of writing, no parts were available to recondition the rear caliper assembly, with the excepting of the guide pins. Check the condition of the guide pins; both pins should be undamaged and (when cleaned) a reasonably tight sliding fit in the caliper bracket. If there is any doubt about the condition of any component, renew it.

Refitting

7 If previously removed, refit the caliper mounting bracket to the hub carrier, and tighten the new bolts to the specified torque.

8 Reconnect the brake pipe to the caliper, and tighten the brake hose union nut securely. Remove the brake hose clamp or polythene (where fitted).

9 Refit the brake pads as described in Section 6.

10 Bleed the hydraulic system as described in Section 3. Note that, providing the precautions described were taken to minimise brake fluid loss, it should only be necessary to bleed the relevant front brake.

11 Refit the roadwheel, then lower the vehicle to the ground and tighten the roadwheel nuts to the specified torque.

11 Master cylinder – removal, overhaul and refitting

Caution: Ensure the ignition is switched off before disconnecting any braking system hydraulic union and do not switch it back on until after the hydraulic system has been bled. Failure to do this could lead to air entering the regulator unit requiring the unit to be bled using special Ford test equipment (see Section 3).

Note: *Before starting work, refer to the warning at the beginning of Section 3 concerning the dangers of hydraulic fluid.*

Removal

1 Remove the windscreen cowl panel, as described in Chapter 11 Section 12.

2 Remove the master cylinder reservoir cap, and siphon the hydraulic fluid from the reservoir. Alternatively, open any convenient bleed screw in the system, and gently pump the brake pedal to expel the fluid through a plastic tube connected to the screw until the reservoir is emptied (see Section 3).

Warning: Do not siphon the fluid by mouth, as it is poisonous; use a syringe or an antifreeze tester

3 Disconnect the wiring plug from the side of the fluid reservoir, then disconnect all hydraulic connections – be prepared for fluid spillage **(see illustration)**.

4 Undo the 2 retaining nuts and remove the master cylinder from the servo unit **(see illustration)**.

5 Unscrew the retaining pin and separate the reservoir from the master cylinder **(see illustration)**. Examine the condition of the reservoir seals, and renew if necessary.

6 Wipe clean the area around the brake pipe unions on the side of the master cylinder, and place absorbent rags beneath the pipe unions to catch any surplus fluid. Make a note of the correct fitted positions of the unions, then unscrew the union nuts and carefully withdraw the pipes. Plug or tape over the pipe ends and master cylinder orifices, to minimise the loss of brake fluid, and to prevent the entry of dirt into the system. Wash off any spilt fluid immediately with cold water.

7 Slacken and remove the two nuts securing the master cylinder to the vacuum servo unit, then withdraw the unit from the engine compartment. If the sealing ring fitted to the rear of the master cylinder shows signs of damage or deterioration, it must be renewed. Discard the retaining nuts, new ones must be fitted.

Overhaul

8 At the time of writing, no parts were available to overhaul the master cylinder. Check with your Ford dealer, or specialist.

Refitting

9 Remove all traces of dirt from the master cylinder and servo unit mating surfaces and ensure that the sealing ring is correctly fitted to the rear of the master cylinder.

10 Fit the master cylinder to the servo unit. Fit the new master cylinder mounting nuts, and tighten them to the specified torque.

11 Wipe clean the brake pipe unions and refit them to the master cylinder ports, tightening them to the specified torque.

12 Press the mounting seals fully into the master cylinder ports then carefully ease the fluid reservoir into position. Slide the reservoir retaining pin into position and tighten it securely.

13 Reconnect the clutch master cylinder supply pipe, level sensor wiring plug, and pressure sensor (where fitted).

14 Refit any components removed to improve access then refill the master cylinder reservoir with new fluid. Bleed the complete hydraulic system as described in Section 3.

Note: *A hydraulic clutch shares its fluid reservoir with the braking system, and may also need to be bled (see Chapter 8 Section 2).*

12 Brake pedal – removal and refitting

Removal

1 Working inside the driver's footwell, remove the trim panel from above the pedals, as described in Chapter 11 Section 38.

2 Disconnect the wiring plug from the brake switch **(see illustration)**.

3 Carefully release the securing clip and disconnect the master cylinder pushrod from the brake pedal **(see illustration)**.

12.2 Disconnect the brake light switch wiring plug

12.3 Lift the edge and slide off the retaining clip

4 Undo the retaining nuts/bolt and manoeuvre the pedal assembly downwards, and out from the vehicle **(see illustration)**. Discard the nuts – new ones must be fitted.

Refitting

5 Refitting is a reversal of removal. Bleed the clutch hydraulic system as described Section 3.

13 Vacuum servo unit – testing, removal and refitting

Testing

1 To test the operation of the servo unit, depress the footbrake several times to exhaust the vacuum, then start the engine whilst keeping the pedal firmly depressed. As the engine starts, there should be a noticeable 'give' in the brake pedal as the vacuum builds-up. Allow the engine to run for at least two minutes, then switch it off. If the brake pedal is now depressed it should feel normal, but further applications should result in the pedal feeling firmer, with the pedal stroke decreasing with each application.

2 If the servo does not operate as described, first inspect the servo unit check valve.

3 If the servo unit still fails to operate satisfactorily, the fault lies within the unit itself. Repairs to the unit are not possible – if faulty, the servo unit must be renewed.

Removal

4 Remove the master cylinder as described in Section 11.

12.4 Pedal bracket retaining bolt/nuts locations

5 Carefully prise the vacuum check valve from the servo body.

6 Undo the 3 screws, pull the down the rear edge of the facia panel above the pedals, and disengage it from the retaining clips.

7 Remove the clip and slide out the clevis pin securing the servo pushrod to the brake pedal.

8 Slacken and remove the two nuts securing the servo to the bulkhead.

9 Manoeuvre the servo unit out of position, along with its gasket (where fitted). Renew the gasket if it shows signs of damage.

Refitting

10 Refitting is the reverse of removal, noting the following points.

a) *Renew the servo mounting nuts and tighten them to the specified torque.*
b) *Refit the master cylinder as described in Section 11 and bleed the complete hydraulic system as described in Section 3.*

14 Handbrake – adjustment

1 To check the handbrake adjustment, applying normal moderate pressure, pull the handbrake lever to the fully-applied position, counting the number of clicks emitted from the handbrake ratchet mechanism. If adjustment is correct, there should be 2 clicks before the brakes begins to apply, and no more than 6 before the handbrake is fully applied. If this is not the case, adjust as follows.

2 Remove the top of the centre console, as described in Chapter 11 Section 36.

3 Chock the front wheels, then jack up the rear of the vehicle and support it on axle stands (see *Jacking and vehicle support*).

4 Completely slacken the adjuster nut on the rod from the equaliser plate **(see illustration)**.

5 Tighten the adjuster nut on the rod until the gap between the lever on the caliper and the stop is 0.7 mm.

6 Fully apply the handbrake lever 3 times, and press the brake pedal down 3 times. Recheck the gap as described in paragraph 5.

7 Release the lever and check by hand that the rear wheels rotate freely, then check that no more than six clicks are emitted before the handbrake is fully applied.

8 Refit the gaiter, then lower the vehicle to the floor.

15 Handbrake lever – removal and refitting

Removal

1 Remove the centre console as described in Chapter 11 Section 36.

Note: *If your vehicle has an automatic transmission, you will need to move the selector lever to the Neutral position to lift the surround over the lever itself. Then return the lever to the Park position.*

2 Chock the road wheels to prevent the vehicle moving once the handbrake lever is released.

3 Referring to Section 14, release the hand-brake lever and remove the adjuster nut to release the cable.

4 Disconnect the wiring plug for the handbrake switch **(see illustration)**.

5 Undo the fasteners and manoeuvre the handbrake assembly from place **(see illustration)**.

Refitting

6 Refitting is a reversal of removal. Tighten the lever retaining nuts to the specified torque, and adjust the handbrake (see Section 14).

14.4 Slacken the handbrake adjustment nut

15.4 Disconnect the handbrake warning switch wiring plug

15.5 Undo the nuts and bolt and remove the handbrake lever from place

16 Handbrake cables – removal and refitting

Removal

1 The handbrake cable consists of a left-hand section and a right-hand section connecting the rear brakes to the adjuster mechanism on the handbrake lever rod. The cables can be removed separately.

2 Firmly chock the front wheels, slacken the relevant rear roadwheel bolts, then jack up the rear of the vehicle and support it on axle stands (see *Jacking and vehicle support*). Remove the relevant rear roadwheel.

3 Undo the screws and remove the floor covering beneath the fuel tank each side.

4 Release the fasteners and remove the heat shield beneath the handbrake cables.

5 Completely slacken the handbrake cable adjuster nut.

6 Slacken the handbrake adjuster nut sufficiently to be able to disengage the relevant cable end fitting from the equaliser plate **(see illustration)**.

7 Release the cable end fitting from the lever on the brake caliper.

8 Working inside the vehicle, slide a short length of 12 mm diameter tube over the end of the cable and depress the clips securing the cable outer end fitting to the vehicle body.

9 Working underneath the vehicle, note its fitted location, then free the cable from the various retaining clips/brackets along its route, detach the bracket from the subframe and pull the front end of the cable from the opening in the floor. Withdraw the cable from underneath the vehicle

Refitting

10 Refitting is a reversal of the removal procedure, adjusting the handbrake as described in Section 14.

17 Stop-light switch – removal, refitting and adjustment

Removal

1 Remove the driver's side lower facia panel as described in Chapter 11 Section 38.

2 Disconnect the wiring plug, then pull the switch from the pedal bracket holder **(see illustrations)**.

Refitting and adjustment

3 Depress the brake pedal, then refit the switch to the bracket, inserting it as far as possible.

4 Slowly pull the pedal back to its stop. The switch is now correctly adjusted.

5 Reconnect the wiring plug and refit the trim panel.

18 Anti-lock braking system (ABS) – general information

1 ABS is fitted to all models as standard, the system comprises a hydraulic regulator unit and the four roadwheel sensors. The regulator unit contains the electronic control unit (ECU), the hydraulic solenoid valves and the electrically-driven return pump. The purpose of the system is to prevent the wheel(s) locking during heavy braking. This is achieved by automatic release of the brake on the relevant wheel, followed by re-application of the brake.

2 The solenoid valves are controlled by the ECU, which itself receives signals from the four wheel sensors (front sensors are fitted to the hubs, and the rear sensors are fitted to the caliper mounting brackets), which monitor the speed of rotation of each wheel. By comparing these signals, the ECU can determine the speed at which the vehicle is travelling. It can then use this speed to determine when a wheel is decelerating at an abnormal rate, compared to the speed of the vehicle, and therefore predicts when a wheel is about to lock. During normal operation, the system functions in the same way as a non-ABS braking system.

3 If the ECU senses that a wheel is about to lock, it closes the relevant outlet solenoid valves in the hydraulic unit, which then isolates the relevant brake(s) on the wheel(s) which is/are about to lock from the master cylinder, effectively sealing-in the hydraulic pressure.

4 If the speed of rotation of the wheel continues to decrease at an abnormal rate, the ECU opens the inlet solenoid valves on the relevant brake(s), and operates the electrically-driven return pump which pumps the hydraulic fluid back into the master cylinder, releasing the brake. Once the speed of rotation of the wheel returns to an acceptable rate, the pump stops; the solenoid valves switch again, allowing the hydraulic master cylinder pressure to return to the caliper, which then re-applies the brake. This cycle can be carried out many times a second.

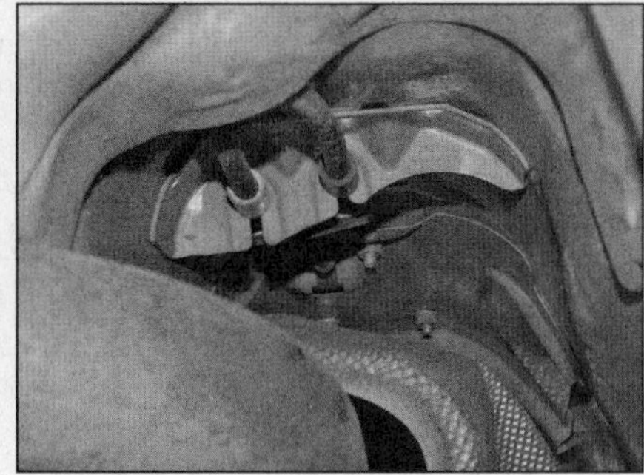

16.6 Slacken the adjuster nut and disengage the cables from the equaliser plate

5 The action of the solenoid valves and return pump creates pulses in the hydraulic circuit. When the ABS system is functioning, these pulses can be felt through the brake pedal.

6 The operation of the ABS system is entirely dependent on electrical signals. To prevent the system responding to any inaccurate signals, a built-in safety circuit monitors all signals received by the ECU. If an inaccurate signal or low battery voltage is detected, the ABS system is automatically shut-down, and the warning light on the instrument panel is illuminated, to inform the driver that the ABS system is not operational. Normal braking should still be available, however.

7 The Ford Kuga is also equipped with additional safety features built around the ABS system. These systems include EBFD (Electronic Brake Force Distribution), which automatically apportions braking effort between the front and rear wheels, and DSC (Dynamic Stability Control) which monitors the vehicles cornering forces and steering wheel angle, then applies the braking force to the appropriate roadwheel to enhance the stability of the vehicle. The DSC motion sensor is fitted beneath the rear centre console, and incorporates both the Yaw rate sensor and the lateral acceleration sensor. The DSC steering angle sensor is fitted to the upper steering column.

8 If a fault does develop in the any of these systems, the vehicle must be taken to a Ford dealer or suitably equipped specialist for fault diagnosis and repair.

17.2a Disconnect the stop light switch wiring plug...

17.2b ...then pull the switch from the holder

19.6 Undo the retaining bolt and pull out the front wheel speed sensor

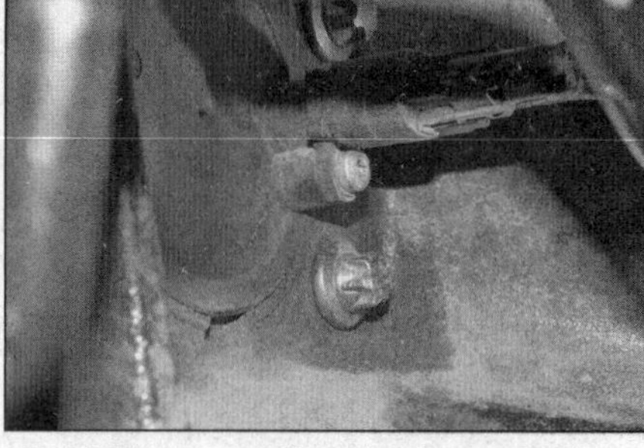

19.14 Disconnect the wheel speed sensor wiring plug

19.15 Rear wheel speed sensor retaining screw

19 Anti-lock braking system (ABS) components – removal and refitting

Regulator assembly

Removal

1 Renewal of the regulator assembly requires access to specialist diagnostic and testing equipment in order to purge air from the system, initialise and code the ECM. Consequently, we recommend this task is entrusted to a Ford dealer or suitably equipped specialist.

Electronic control unit (ECU)

2 The ECU is integral with the regulator assembly, and may not available separately. Check with a Ford dealer or parts specialist. Note that if a new ECU is fitted, it must be programmed using Ford diagnostic equipment. Entrust this task to a Ford dealer or suitably equipped repairer.

Front wheel sensor

Removal

3 Ensure the ignition is turned off.

4 Apply the handbrake, slacken the appropriate front roadwheel bolts, then jack up the front of the vehicle and support securely on axle stands (see *Jacking and vehicle support*). Remove the appropriate front roadwheel.

5 Trace the wiring back from the sensor, releasing it from all the relevant clips and ties whilst noting its correct routing, and disconnect the wiring plug.

6 Slacken and remove the retaining screw and withdraw the sensor from the hub carrier **(see illustration).**

Refitting

7 Ensure that the mating faces of the sensor and the hub carrier are clean, and apply a little anti-seize grease to the hub carrier hub bore before refitting.

8 Make sure the sensor tip is clean and ease it into position in the hub carrier.

9 Clean the threads of the sensor bolt and apply a few drops of thread-locking compound. Refit the retaining bolt and tighten it to the specified torque.

10 Work along the sensor wiring, making sure it is correctly routed, securing it in position with all the relevant clips and ties. Reconnect the wiring plug.

11 Refit the wheelarch liner, refit the wheel, then lower the vehicle and tighten the wheel bolts to the specified torque.

Rear wheel sensor

Removal

12 Ensure the ignition is turned off.

13 Chock the front wheels, slacken the appropriate rear roadwheel bolts, then jack up the rear of the vehicle and support it on axle stands (see *Jacking and vehicle support*). Remove the appropriate roadwheel.

14 Disconnect the wiring plug **(see illustration).**

15 Slacken and remove the retaining screw and withdraw the sensor **(see illustration).**

Refitting

16 Ensure that the mating faces of the sensor and the hub are clean, and apply a little anti-seize grease to the hub bore before refitting.

17 Make sure the sensor tip is clean and ease it into position in the swivel hub.

18 Clean the threads of the sensor bolt and apply a few drops of thread-locking compound. Refit the retaining bolt and tighten it to the specified torque.

19 Work along the sensor wiring, making sure it is correctly routed, securing it in position with all the relevant clips and ties. Reconnect the wiring connector, then refit the wheelarch liner.

20 Refit the wheel, then then lower the vehicle and tighten the wheel bolts to the specified torque.

20.4 Disconnect the wiring plug, undo the bolts and remove the sensor

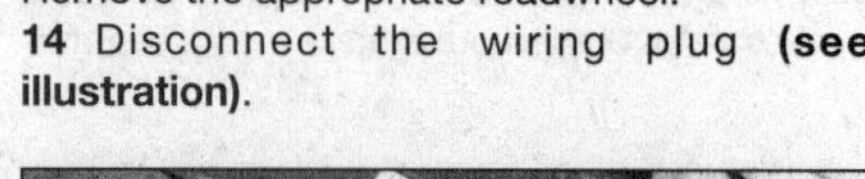

20.5a Disconnect the vacuum hose...

20 Vacuum pump – removal and refitting

1 The pump primarily supplies vacuum for the brake servo, but it can also supplies vacuum to the various engine controls (depending on model), that are vacuum operated, e.g. the turbocharger wastegate.

Removal

2 Pull up and remove the engine cover.

Diesel engines

3 To improve access remove the air filter housing and associated pipe work – as described in Chapter 4B Section 6.

4 The vacuum pump will not manoeuvre past the thermostat sensor, so you must drain the cooling system (Chapter 1B Section 36) and remove the sensor **(see illustration).**

Note: *The sensor is secured using tamperproof Torx screws – use hollow a hollow Torx bit to remove them.*

5 Pull the vacuum hose from the top of vacuum pump, then release the securing clip and disconnect the main vacuum hose to the brake servo unit **(see illustrations).**

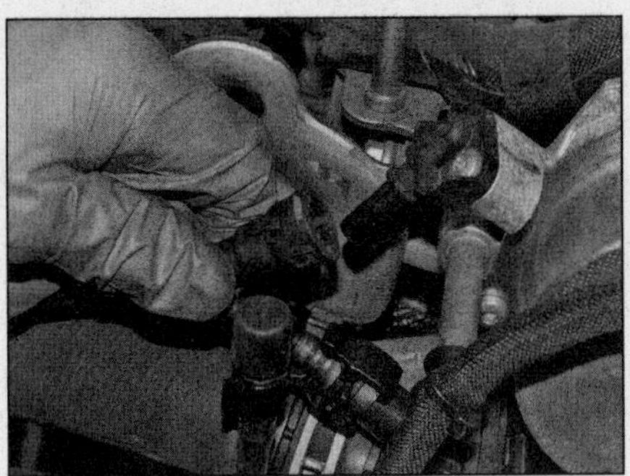

20.5b ...and release the brake servo hose

20.6 Detach the wiring harness from the bolts

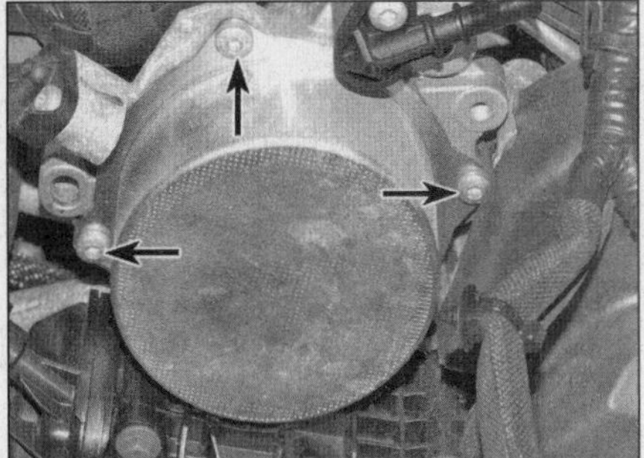

20.7 Remove the 3 securing nuts

20.11 Disconnect the turbocharger boost valve wiring plug

20.12 Disengage the wiring loom from the bracket then unbolt the bracket itself

20.13 Undo the bolts, disconnect the pipe to move the valve out of the way

6 Unclip the wiring harness and place it to one side **(see illustration)**.

7 Undo the 3 retaining bolts and remove the vacuum pump **(see illustration)**. Discard the gasket/seal, new ones must be fitted.

1.5-litre petrol engine

8 Remove the engine cover.

9 Remove the air cleaner assembly, as described in Chapter 4A Section 3.

10 Remove the air intake pipe, and unplug any wiring connectors as they become available.

11 Disconnect the turbocharger boost control valve wiring plug **(see illustration)**.

12 Disengage the wiring loom from the end of the bracket mounting studs, and unbolt the brackets **(see illustration)**.

13 Undo the 2 mounting bolts, and disconnect the turbocharger solenoid vacuum pipe, then manoeuvre the valve from place **(see illustration)**.

14 Undo the 3 retaining bolts for the vacuum pump and remove the pump from place **(see illustration)**. Replace the gasket.

Refitting

15 Refitting is a reversal of removal, noting the following points:

a) Ensure the pump and cylinder head mating surfaces are clean and dry. Fit a new gasket/seal.

b) Ensure the drive coupling is aligned with the slot in the camshaft.

c) Start the engine and check for correct operation of the pump (check brakes have servo action).

d) Make sure all the hose connections are secure, and check for leaks.

20.14 Undo the 3 bolts and lift away the vacuum pump

Chapter 10
Suspension and steering

Contents

Degrees of difficulty

Easy, suitable for novice with little experience 

Fairly easy, suitable for beginner with some experience

Fairly difficult, suitable for competent DIY mechanic 

Difficult, suitable for experienced DIY mechanic

Very difficult, suitable for expert DIY or professional 

Specifications

Front wheel alignment

Toe setting	0°20' ± 20' toe-in
Camber	–0.74° ± 1.25°
Caster (max difference between left/right)	1.00°

Rear wheel alignment

Toe setting	0°11' ± 0°05' toe-in
Camber	–2°47' to 0°17'

Chassis alignment

Normal position	68 kg on each front seat, 14 kg in the luggage compartment, and a full fuel tank

Tyre pressures

See sticker in driver's door aperture

Torque wrench settings

	Nm	lbf ft
Front suspension		
Anti-roll bar clamp bolts: *		
Stage 1	115	85
Stage 2	Angle-tighten a further 90°	
Anti-roll bar link nuts: *		
Lower nut	62	46
Upper nut	48	35
Driveshaft nut: *		
Stage 1	80	59
Stage 2	Angle-tighten a further 90°	
Front subframe bolts: *		
Rear bolts M14:		
Stage 1	140	103
Stage 2	Angle-tighten a further 180°	
Front bolts M12	115	85
Lower arm rear mounting bolts:		
Inner bolts (M12)	18	13
Outer bolts (M10)*	115	85
Lower arm outer balljoint-to-hub carrier bolt/nut*	83	61
Lower arm front pivot bolt: *		
Stage 1	115	85
Stage 2	Angle-tighten a further 90°	
Roadwheel nuts	135	100
Suspension strut thrust bearing retaining nut*	55	41
Suspension strut-to-hub carrier pinch-bolt/nut: *		
Stage 1	80	59
Stage 2	Angle-tighten a further 180°	
Suspension strut upper mounting bolts*	35	26
** Do not re-use*		
Rear suspension		
Anti-roll bar clamp bolts	60	44
Anti-roll bar link nuts	10	7
Control arms-to-trailing arm nuts*	115	85
Control arms-to-subframe nuts*	18	13
Rear hub-to-trailing arm bolts*	115	85
Roadwheel nuts	135	100
Shock absorber upper mounting bolts*	28	21
Shock absorber lower mounting bolt*	115	85
Subframe mounting bolts	115	85
Trailing arm bush/bracket-to-vehicle body*	115	85
** Do not re-use*		
Steering		
Roadwheel nuts	135	100
Steering column mounting nuts	28	21
Steering column lower universal joints pinch bolts*	28	21
Steering rack-to-subframe bolts: *		
Stage 1	115	85
Stage 2	Angle-tighten a further 90°	
Steering wheel	48	35
Track rod end clamp bolt	90	66
Track rod end balljoint-to-hub carrier*	48	35
** Do not re-use*		

1 General information

1 The independent front suspension is of MacPherson strut type, incorporating coil springs, integral telescopic shock absorbers, and an anti-roll bar. The struts are attached to hub carriers at their lower ends, and the hub carriers are in turn attached to the lower suspension arm by balljoints. The anti-roll bar is bolted to the rear of the subframe, and is connected to the front suspension struts by links **(see illustration)**.

2 The multi-link rear suspension is fully independent with trailing arms attached to the vehicle body, and control arms mounted between the body-mounted subframe and the trailing arms. Gas-pressurised shock absorbers are fitted with separate coil springs, and are mounted between the vehicle body and the trailing arms. A rear anti-roll bar is fitted to all models **(see illustration)**.

3 Both front and rear wheel bearings are integral with the hubs, and no adjustment is possible.

4 A power steering type rack-and-pinion steering gear is fitted, together with a conventional column and telescopic coupling. Unlike conventional power steering, assistance is provided by an electric motor attached to the steering rack pinion housing (EPS). This is an energy efficient design as assistance is only provided to the steering rack when required.

5 When working on the suspension or steering, you may come across nuts or bolts which seem impossible to loosen. These nuts and bolts on the underside of the vehicle are continually subjected to water, road grime, mud, etc,

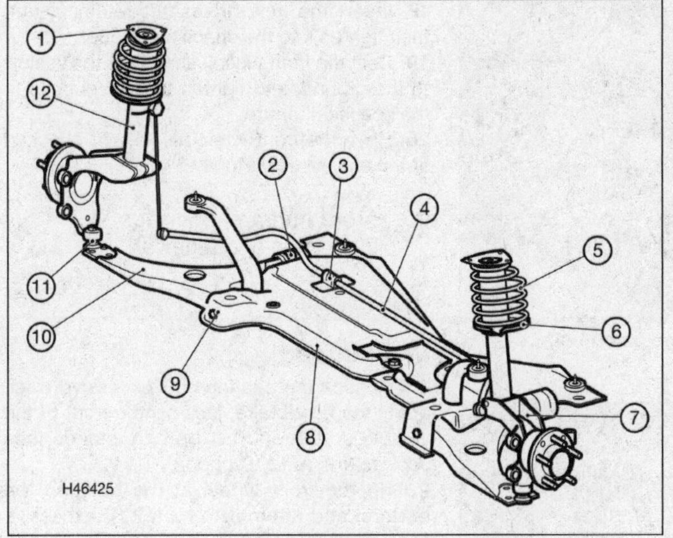

1.1 Front axle

1 *Upper bearing, mounting and spring seat*
2 *Rear bush*
3 *Clamp*
4 *Anti-roll bar*
5 *Spring*
6 *Lower spring seat*
7 *Hub carrier*
8 *Front subframe*
9 *Front bush*
10 *Control arm*
11 *Balljoint*
12 *MacPherson strut*

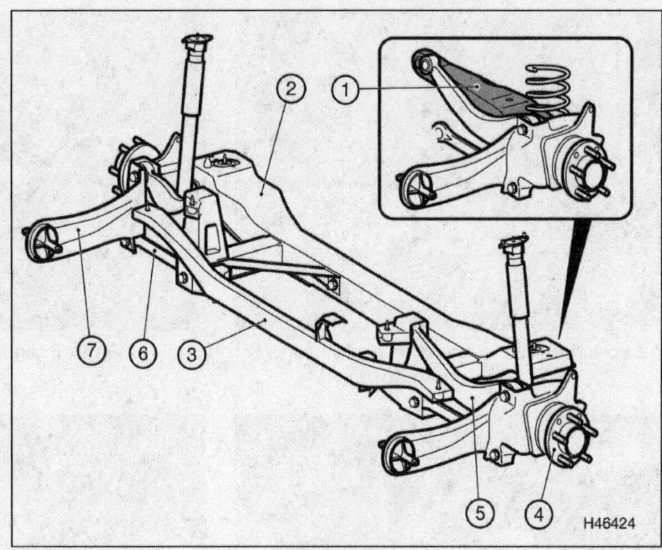

1.2 Rear axle

1 *Lower control arm*
2 *Subframe*
3 *Anti-roll bar*
4 *Rear hub*
5 *Upper control arm*
6 *Tie rod*
7 *Trailing arm/hub carrier*

and can become rusted or seized, making them extremely difficult to remove. In order to unscrew these stubborn nuts and bolts without damaging them (or other components), use lots of penetrating oil, and allow it to soak in for a while. Using a wire brush to clean exposed threads will also ease removal of the nut or bolt, and will help to prevent damage to the threads. Sometimes, a sharp blow with a hammer and punch will break the bond between a nut and bolt, but care must be taken to prevent the punch from slipping off and ruining the threads. Using a longer bar or spanner will increase leverage, but never use an extension bar/pipe on a ratchet, as the internal mechanism could be damaged. Actually tightening the nut or bolt slightly first, may help to break it loose. Nuts or bolts which have required drastic measures to remove them should always be renewed. As a general rule, all self-locking nuts (with nylon inserts) should be renewed.

6 Since most of the procedures dealt with in this Chapter involve jacking up the vehicle and working underneath it, a good pair of axle stands will be needed. A hydraulic trolley jack is the preferred type of jack to lift the vehicle, and it can also be used to support certain components during removal and refitting operations.

Warning: Never, under any circumstances, rely on a jack to support the vehicle while working beneath it. It is not recommended, when jacking up the rear of the vehicle, to lift beneath the rear crossmember.

2 Front hub carrier – removal and refitting

Removal

1 Slacken the relevant front roadwheel bolts, then jack up the front of the vehicle and support it securely on axle stands (see *Jacking and vehicle support*). Remove the roadwheel.

2 Undo the retaining bolts and remove the engine undertray.

3 Have an assistant press the brake pedal, and then slacken and remove the driveshaft nut (see Chapter 8 Section 7). Discard the nut, a new one must be fitted.

4 Remove the front brake disc as described in Chapter 9 Section 7.

5 Undo the bolts and remove the brake disc shield **(see illustration)**.

6 Unscrew and detach the track rod end from the hub carrier using a ball joint separating tool **(see illustration)**. Take care not to damage the ball joint gaiter.

7 Disconnect the wiring plug from the wheel speed sensor.

8 Unscrew and remove the pinch-bolt securing the hub carrier assembly to the front suspension strut **(see illustrations)**. Prise open the clamp a little using a wedge-shaped tool or a chisel, and release the hub carrier from the strut. If necessary, tap the hub carrier downwards with a soft-headed mallet to separate the two components. Slide the hub and carrier over the end of the driveshaft. Note that a new bolt will be required.

2.5 Remove the 3 brake shield bolts

2.6 Separate the ball joint

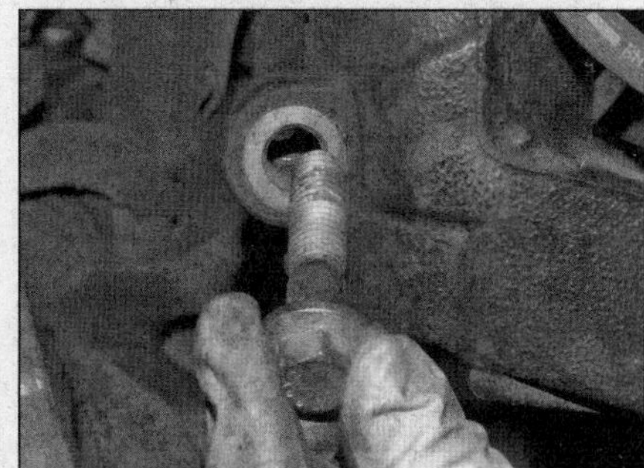
2.8a Undo the hub carrier pinch bolt...

2.8b ...then use a chisel to wedge slightly open the gap

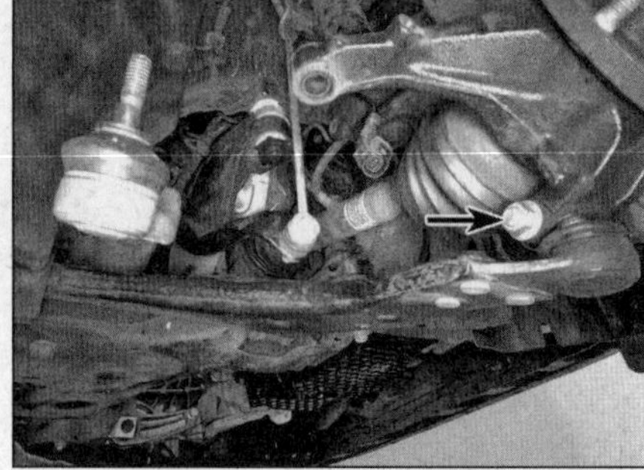
2.9a Remove the pinch bolt...

2.9b ...then separate from the hub carrier using a bar and chain

2.12 If necessary, use an old nut to pull the hub onto the driveshaft

9 Remove the pinch bolt and pull down the lower arm using a bar and chain to separate the balljoint from the hub carrier **(see illustrations)**.

10 Withdraw the driveshaft outer joint from the hub by tapping the end of the shaft using a block of woodand a hammer, if this method fails it is likely that a puller will be needed as the splines can be very tight.

Refitting

11 Locate the assembly on the strut. Ensure alignment of the lug on the strut with the opening in the hub carrier and that the carrier is pushed onto the strut until it reaches the stop. Use a jack to support the hub carrier while the clamp bolt is being installed. Tighten the new nut to the specified torque. Refit the wiring harness support bracket where applicable.

12 Pull the hub carrier assembly outwards, and insert the driveshaft into the hub. Ensure the splines of the driveshaft and hub engage correctly **(see illustration)**. It may be necessary to pull the driveshaft into the hub using the old driveshaft nut. Remove the nut when the driveshaft is in place.

13 Refit the lower arm balljoint into the lower arm, then fit the new bolt and nut, and tighten it to the specified torque. Note that the bolt must be inserted from the front.

14 Refit the brake disc shield and tighten the retaining bolts securely.

15 Refit the brake disc as described in Chapter 9 Section 7.

16 Reconnect the wheel speed sensor wiring plug.

17 Reconnect the track rod end balljoint to the hub carrier, and tighten the new nut to the specified torque.

18 Insert the new driveshaft retaining nut, then tighten it to the specified torque.

19 Refit the front wheel, and lower the vehicle to the ground, and tighten the wheel bolts to the specified torque.

20 Have the front wheel alignment checked at the earliest opportunity.

3 Front hub and bearings – inspection and renewal

Inspection

1 To check the bearings for excessive wear, apply the handbrake, jack up the front of the vehicle and support it on axle stands (see *Jacking and vehicle support*).

2 Grip the front wheel at the top and the bottom, and attempt to rock it. If excessive movement is noted, it may be that the hub bearings are worn. Do not confuse wear in the driveshaft outer joint or front suspension lower arm balljoint with wear in the bearings. Hub bearing wear will show up as roughness or vibration when the wheel is spun; it will also be noticeable as a rumbling or growling noise when driving. No adjustment of the wheel bearings is possible.

Renewal

3 Slacken the relevant front roadwheel nuts, then raise the front of the vehicle and support it securely on axle stands (see *Jacking and vehicle support*). Remove the roadwheel.

4 Undo the driveshaft nut as described in Chapter 8 Section 7.

5 Remove the relevant front brake disc as described in Chapter 9 Section 7.

6 Remove the bolts holding the brake disc backing plate to the hub assembly **(see illustration 2.5)**.

7 Undo the bolt holding the hub carrier to the front strut assembly **(see illustration 2.6)**.

8 Remove the bolt from the tapered stub and pull down using a bar and chain to separate **(see illustration 2.9b)**.

9 Manoeuvre the hub carrier and hub from place.

10 Refitting is a reversal of removal.

Bearing – removal and refitting

11 Removal and refitting of the wheel bearing requires the use of a hydraulic press. If you do not have access to one, entrust this procedure to a suitably equipped repairer.

12 Remove the hub carrier as described in this Section.

13 Use a hydraulic press to separate the hub from the hub carrier **(see illustration)**.

14 Turn over the hub carrier and remove the circlip **(see illustration)**.

15 Use a chisel to dislodge the wheel bearing race from the hub flange, then use a puller to remove it **(see illustrations)**.

16 Clean up any burrs on the hub flange using a file **(see illustration)**.

3.13 Drive out the flange from the hub carrier

3.14 Remove the circlip

3.15a Start to move the bearing race with a chisel...

3.15b ...then remove it completely using a puller

3.16 Use a file to smooth the back of the hub flange

3.17 Drive out the old bearing from the hub carrier

3.18 Offer up the new bearing, ensuring it is the right way up

3.19 Drive the new bearing into place

17 Use the press to push the old bearing from place **(see illustration)**.

18 Inspect the inside fo the hub for wear, then offer up the new bearing to the back of the hub carrier with the black magnetic strip facing towards the ABS sensor mounting **(see illustration)**.

19 Use the press and the old bearing to drive the new bearing into place **(see illustration)**. Do not press the bearing too far or the old bearing could become stuck!

20 When the bearing is almost in its correct position, insert the new circlip, then continue to drive the bearing down until you hear the circlip click into its slot **(see illustration)**.

21 Finally, use the press to drive the hub flange back into the outside surface of the hub carrier **(see illustration)**. Ensure that you press on the inner bearing race to do this, or the outer magnetic race could become damaged.

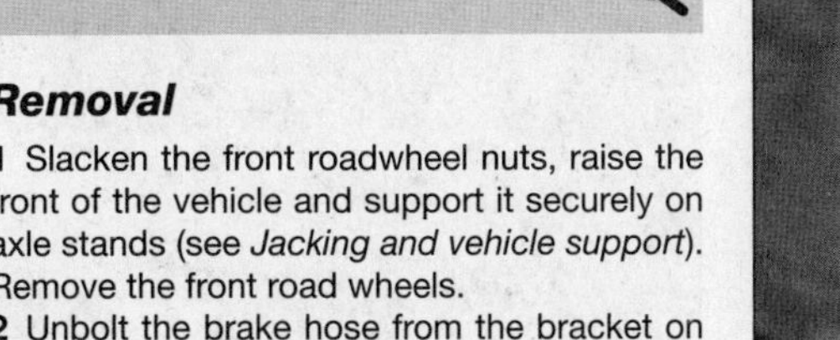

4 Front suspension strut assembly – removal and refitting

Removal

1 Slacken the front roadwheel nuts, raise the front of the vehicle and support it securely on axle stands (see *Jacking and vehicle support*). Remove the front road wheels.

2 Unbolt the brake hose from the bracket on the strut **(see illustration)**.

3 Remove the nut and disconnect the anti-roll bar link rod from the strut **(see illustration)**. Note that the ABS sensor bracket is also held by this nut.

4 Remove the front hub carrier and hub as described in Section 3.

5 Remove the windscreen cowl panels as described in Chapter 11 Section 12 and Chapter 11 Section 11.

6 Support the strut/spring assembly under

3.20 Click the new circlip into place

3.21 Press the wheel flange back into place

4.2 Undo the bolt and detach the hose from the strut

4.3 Counterhold the anti-roll bar link rod shank whilst undoing the nut

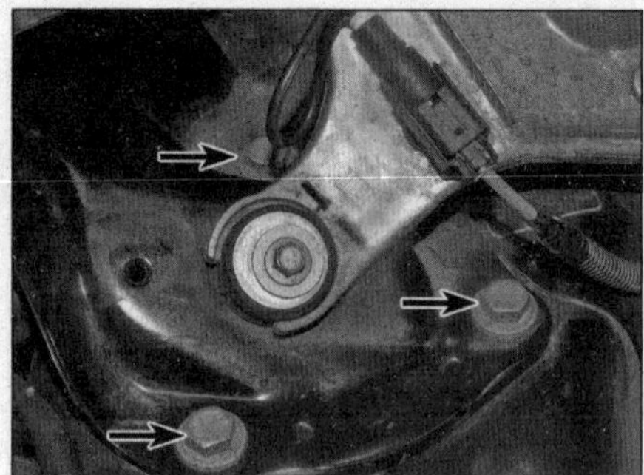

4.6 Undo the upper mounting bolts from the strut

the wheelarch, then remove the upper mounting bolts **(see illustration)**.

7 Lower the suspension strut from under the wheelarch, withdrawing it from the vehicle.

Refitting

8 Ensure the mating faces of the strut and wing are clean, then manoeuvre the strut into position, fit the new upper mounting bolts, and tighten them to the specified torque.

9 The remainder of refitting is a reversal of removal.

5 Front suspension strut – overhaul

Warning: Before attempting to dismantle the front suspension strut, a tool to hold the coil spring in compression must be obtained. Do not attempt to use makeshift methods. Uncontrolled release of the spring could cause damage and personal injury. Use a high-quality spring compressor, and carefully follow the tool manufacturer's instructions provided with it. After removing the coil spring with the compressor still fitted, place it in a safe, isolated area.

1 If the front suspension struts exhibit signs of wear (leaking fluid, loss of damping capability, sagging or cracked coil springs) then they should be dismantled and overhauled as necessary. The struts themselves cannot be serviced, and should be renewed if faulty; the springs and related components can be renewed individually. To maintain balanced characteristics on both sides of the vehicle, the components on both sides should be renewed at the same time.

2 With the strut removed from the vehicle (see Section 4), clean away all external dirt and mark each piece to ensure correct alignment on refitting.

3 Fit the coil spring compressor tools (ensuring that they are fully engaged), and compress the spring until all tension is relieved from the upper mounting.

4 Hold the strut piston rod with an Allen key, and unscrew the thrust bearing retaining nut with a ring spanner or spark plug type socket with the hexagon section on the outside (or similar) **(see illustration)**. Discard the nut, a new one must be fitted.

5 Withdraw the top mounting/thrust bearing, gaiter, bump stop and spring from the shock absorber **(see illustrations)**.

5.4 Undo the thrust bearing nut

5.5a Remove the top mounting/thrust bearing...

5.5b ...plus the gaiter and spring

6 If a new spring is to be fitted, the original spring must now be carefully released from the compressor. If it is to be re-used, the spring can be left in compression.

7 With the strut assembly now completely dismantled, examine all the components for wear and damage, and check the bearing for smoothness of operation. Renew components as necessary.

8 Examine the strut for signs of fluid leakage. Check the strut piston rod for signs of pitting along its entire length, and check the strut body for signs of damage. Test the operation of the strut, while holding it in an upright position, by attempting to move the piston. It should only be possible to move the piston a very small amount. If it's easy to move or shows little/uneven resistance, or if there is any visible sign of wear or damage to the strut, renewal is necessary.

9 Reassembly is a reversal of dismantling, noting the following points:

*a) Make sure that the coil spring ends are correctly located in the upper and lower seats before releasing the compressor **(see illustration)**.*

b) Check that the bearing is correctly fitted to the piston rod seat.

c) Tighten the new thrust bearing retaining nut to the specified torque.

d) The smaller diameter coil must be fitted against the upper spring seat.

5.9 Ensure the ends of the spring are correctly located in the seats

6 Front anti-roll bar and links – removal and refitting

Removal

Anti-roll bar

1 Remove the front subframe as described in Section 8.

2 Undo the retaining bolts and remove the heatshield over the steering rack and anti-roll bar **(see illustration)**.

3 Slacken and remove the four bolts securing the anti-roll bar clamps to the subframe, then manoeuvre the anti-roll bar from position **(see illustration)**. Discard the bolts – new ones must be fitted.

4 It would appear that at the time of writing,

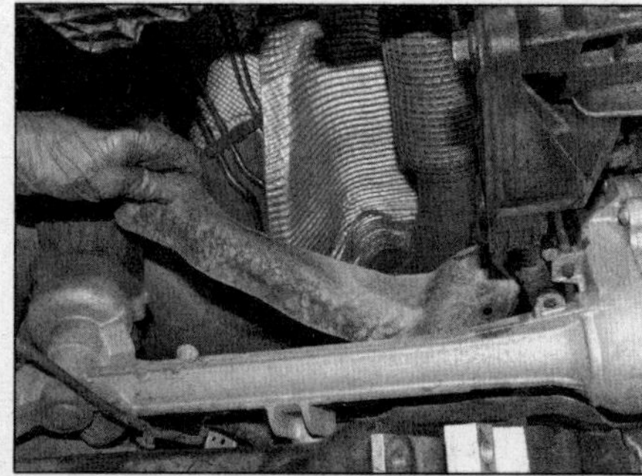

6.2 Remove the steering rack heat shield

the rubber bushes are integral with the anti-roll bar. Check with a Ford dealer or parts specialist.

Anti-roll bar links

5 Slacken the relevant front roadwheel nuts, then jack up the front of the vehicle and support it securely on axle stands (see *Jacking and vehicle support*). Remove the roadwheel.

6 Undo the nuts securing the links to the anti-roll bar and suspension strut.

Refitting

Anti-roll bar

7 Manoeuvre the anti-roll bar into position, and finger-tighten the new clamp bolts.

8 Refit the heatshield over the steering rack and anti-roll bar.

9 Refit the front subframe as described in Section 8.

10 Tighten the anti-roll bar clamp bolts to the specified torque.

11 Reconnect the anti-roll bar links and tighten the new nuts to the specified torque.

Anti-roll bar links

12 Reconnect the links to the anti-roll bar and suspension strut, then tighten the new nuts to the specified torque.

13 Refit the roadwheel and lower the vehicle to the ground. Tighten the roadwheel bolts to the specified torque.

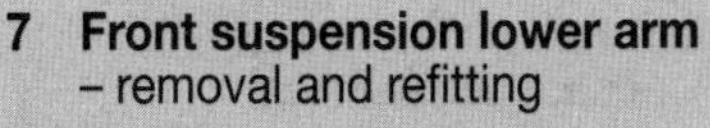

7 Front suspension lower arm – removal and refitting

Removal

1 Slacken the front roadwheel nuts, raise the front of the vehicle and support it securely on axle stands (see *Jacking and vehicle support*). Remove the front road wheel.

2 Where fitted, release the fasteners and remove the engine undertray.

3 If removing the right-hand side lower arm, undo the retaining screw and remove the ride height sensor arm bracket (where fitted) from the lower arm.

4 Release the fasteners and pull back the front section of the wheelarch liner.

5 Undo the lower arm rear mounting bracket retaining bolts **(see illustration)**. Discard the bolts – new ones must be fitted.

6 Undo the nut and remove the outer balljoint pinch bolt, noting how it is fitted (from the rear) **(see illustration 1.9a)**. Discard the nut and bolt – new ones must be fitted.

7 Use a wedge to slightly spread the hub carrier clamp, then press the lower arm downwards to release the outer balljoint from the clamp **(see illustration 1.9b)**.

8 Undo the 2 rear retaining bolts for the lower support arm **(see illustration)**.

9 Remove the front pivot bolt and manoeuvre the lower arm from place **(see illustration)**. Discard the bolt – a new one must be fitted.

10 The lower arm rear bush and mounting

6.3 Undo the anti-roll bar clamp bolts each side

assembly must be pressed from the arm. If a press is available, note the fitted depth and position of the bush prior to removing the arm/bush to enable refitting. If a press is not available, entrust this task to a Ford dealer or suitably equipped specialist.

11 The outer balljoint is integral with the lower arm.

Refitting

12 Manoeuvre the lower arm into position, insert and finger-tighten the new front pivot bolt.

13 Insert the rear mounting bolts and tighten them to the specified torque.

14 Align the outer balljoint shank with the hole in the base of the hub carrier, and press it into place. Insert the new pinch bolt (from the rear), fit the new nut, and tighten the bolt to the specified torque.

15 Tighten the lower arm front pivot bolt to the specified torque.

16 The remainder of removal is a reversal of removal, noting the following points:

a) Replace all self-locking nuts removed.

b) Tighten all fasteners to their specified torque where given.

c) Have the front wheel alignment checked as described in Section 21.

8 Front subframe – removal and refitting

Removal

1 Slacken the front wheel bolts, raise the front of the vehicle and support it securely on axle stands (see *Jacking and vehicle support*). Remove the front wheels.

2 Release the fasteners and remove the engine undershield.

3 Release the fasteners and remove both front wheelarch liners as described in Chapter 11 Section 39.

4 Disconnect the battery negative lead as described in Chapter 5 Section 4.

5 Ensure the wheels are in the 'straight-ahead' position, engage the steering lock, then remove the pinch bolt securing the universal joint to the steering rack pinion. Move the joint to the side, disengaging it from the pinion **(see illustration)**. Discard the bolt – a new one must be fitted upon reassemby.

Caution: The steering wheel/column must not be turned when disconnected from the steering rack pinion.

7.5 Remove the bracket retaining bolts

7.8 Remove the 2 rear bolts from the support arm

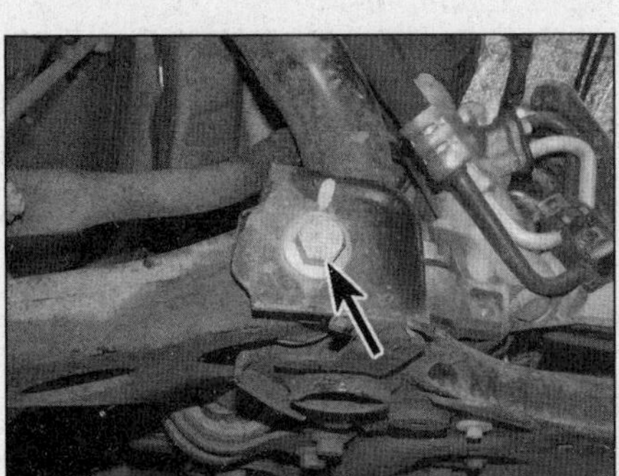

7.9 Undo the front pivot bolt to remove the arm

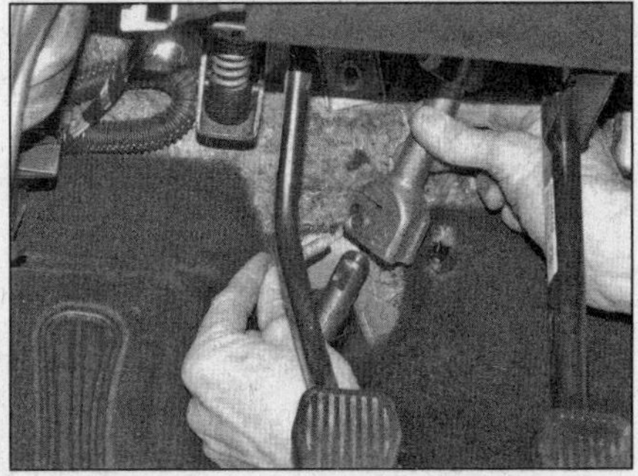

8.5 Undo the steering column pinch bolt and separate the column

8.6 Use pins to secure the radiator

8.7 Remove the underbody shielding by the subframe

8.14 Unbolt the rear roll restrictor link

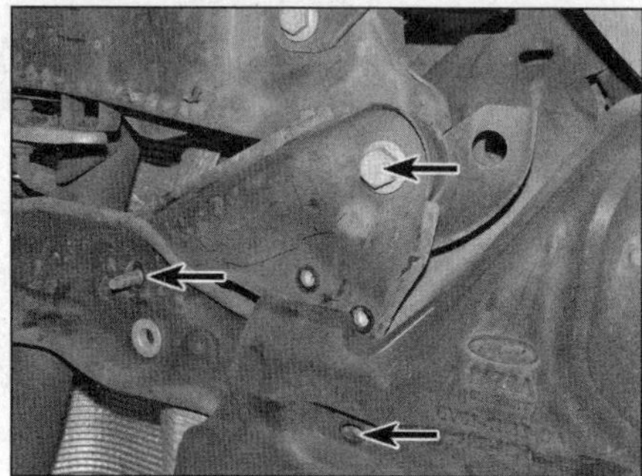
8.18 Remove the triangular panels at each end of the subframe

6 Using suitable pins/rods secure the radiator to the bonnet slam panel **(see illustration)**.

7 Where applicable, release the fasteners and remove the rear underbody protection at the rear of the subframe **(see illustration)**.

8 If the subframe is being removed as a precursor to removing the engine, remove the driveshafts, as described in Chapter 8 Section 7. If you are only removing the subframe, there is no need to do this.

9 Disconnect the lower ends of the anti-roll bar links as described in Section 6.

10 Release the exhaust system from the front rubber mountings at the rear of the subframe.

11 Disconnect any wiring plugs, and release any wiring harnesses from the front subframe and steering rack. Note the routing of the harnesses to aid reassembly.

12 On both sides, undo the 3 bolts securing the deformation elements to the subframe.

13 Slide down the locking catches and remove the intercooler lower holder each side. Refer to Chatper 4A Section 13 or Chapter 4B Section 20 if necessary.

14 Remove the bolt securing the rear engine roll restrictor link rod to the subframe **(see illustration)**.

15 Detach both lower arms from the subframe as described in Section 7.

16 Detach both trackrod ends from the hub carriers as described in Section 2.

17 Position a workshop jack under the vehicle, and using a combination of wooden planks/blocks support the front subframe.

18 Undo the retaining bolts and remove the triangular subframe elements at each end of the rear of the subframe **(see illustration)**.

19 To aid refitment, make alignment marks between the subframe mounting bolts, subframe and vehicle body.

20 Undo the subrame mounting bolts, and with the help of an assistant, carefully lower it from position. Take care not to strain any hoses or wiring. Discard the bolts – new ones must be fitted.

21 Undo the 4 retaining bolts and remove the the steering column heat shield as it becomes available **(see illustration 6.2)**.

22 Unplug any wiring connectors as they become available.

Caution: Ensure the steering rack pinion does not contact the bulkhead as the subframe is lowered. The pinion is easily damaged.

Refitting

23 Raise the subframe into position, aligning the previously made marks. Take care to ensure the steering rack pinion enters aperture in the bulkhead without contact.

24 Insert the new subframe retaining bolts and tighten them to the specified torque.

25 The remainder of refitting is a reversal of removal, noting the following points:

a) Renew all fasteners where specified.
b) Tighten all fasteners to their specified torque where given.
c) Ensure all wiring plugs are securely reconnected, and the wiring harnesses routed as noted during removal.
d) Reconnect the battery negative lead as described in Chapter 5 Section 4.
e) Have the front wheel alignment checked at the earliest opportunity.

9 Rear hub and bearings – inspection and renewal

Inspection

1 The rear hub bearings are non-adjustable.

2 To check the bearings for excessive wear, chock the front wheels, then jack up the rear of the vehicle and support it on axle stands (see *Jacking and vehicle support*). Fully release the handbrake.

3 Grip the rear wheel at the top and bottom, and attempt to rock it. If excessive movement is noted, or if there is any roughness or vibration felt when the wheel is spun, it is indicative that the hub bearings are worn.

Renewal

4 Remove the rear brake disc (see Chapter 9 Section 8).

5 Disconnect the wiring plug for the ABS sensor **(see illustration)**.

6 Undo the four mounting bolts and remove the hub and bearing assembly from the hub trailing arm **(see illustration)**. Discard the bolts – new ones must be fitted.

Note: *If the hub proves difficult to remove, it is worth reinserting the bolts for a couple of turns, then use an aluminium drift and hammer to dislodge the hub. Use an aluminium drift to avoid damaging the bolt heads, which could make them difficult to remove thereafter.*

7 Clean the hub seating face on the trailing arm.

9.5 Disconnect the ABS sensor wiring plug

9.6 Undo the bolts and remove the hub

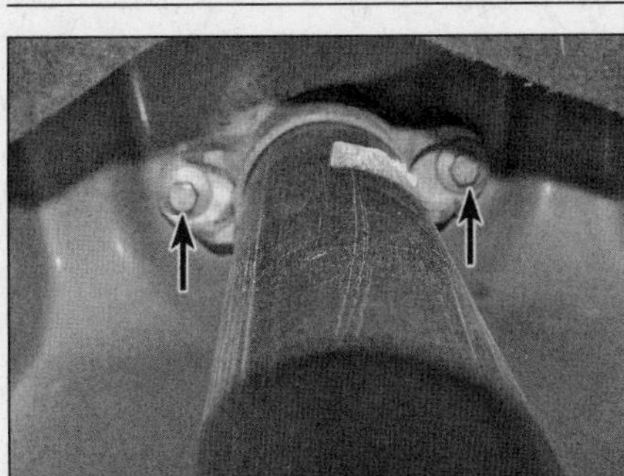
10.2 Undo the 2 top mounting bolts for the shock absorber

10.3 Then undo the lower mounting bolt

10.4 Undo the retaining nut to remove the bump stop

8 Position the new hub/bearing assembly against the trailing arm, fit the new bolts and tighten them to the specified torque.
9 Refit the rear brake disc as described in Chapter 9 Section 8.

10 Rear shock absorber – removal and refitting

Removal

1 Slacken the rear roadwheel nuts, chock the front wheels, then jack up the rear of the vehicle and support it on axle stands (see *Jacking and vehicle support*). Remove the wheels.
2 Unscrew and remove the shock absorber upper mounting bolts **(see illustration)**.
3 Undo the lower mounting bolt, and manoeuvre the shock absorber from place **(see illustration)**.
4 If required, undo the nut and remove the upper mounting from the shock absorber, followed by the bump stop and protective sleeve **(see illustration)**.

Refitting

5 Refitting is a reversal of the removal procedure, noting the following points:
a) *Where fitted, the gasket between the upper mounting and vehicle body must be discarded. It is not required post-production.*
b) *Tighten all fasteners to their specified torque where given.*
c) *The final tightening of the lower mounting bolt must be carried out with the vehicle weight on the road wheels.*

11 Rear coil spring – removal and refitting

Removal

1 Slacken the relevant rear roadwheel bolts, chock the front wheels, then jack up the rear of the vehicle and support it on axle stands (see *Jacking and vehicle support*). Remove the wheel.
2 Undo the bolt and detach the lower end of the anti-roll bar link as described in Section 12.
3 Place a trolley jack under the trailing arm and slightly compress the rear suspension.
4 Remove the bolt that attaches the lower arm to the hub carrier **(see illustration)**.
5 Carefully lower the trailing arm until the coil spring can be manoeuvred from position. It may be necessary to use a pry bar to pull the arm down a little to remove the spring **(see illustrations)**.
6 If required, remove the upper and lower spring pads.

Refitting

7 If removed, refit the upper and lower spring pads to the coil spring **(see illustration)**.
8 Manoeuvre the spring into position, ensuring the lower end locates correctly against the lower pad as described previously.
9 The remainder of refitting is a reversal of removal.

12 Rear anti-roll bar, bushes and links – removal and refitting

Removal

1 Slacken the rear roadwheel nuts, then jack up the rear of the vehicle, and support it securely on axle stands (see *Jacking and vehicle support*). Remove both rear roadwheels.

Anti-roll bar

2 Undo the fasteners and remove the central underbody panelling.

11.4 Remove the lower arm bolt

11.5a Use a pry bar to release the lower arm...

11.5b ...and remove the spring from place

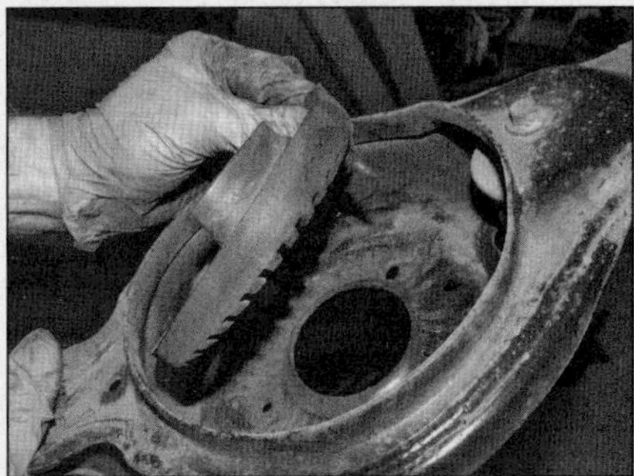
11.7 Refit the lower spring pads

12.3 Remove the lower anti-roll bar link nuts

3 Undo the nut securing the lower ends of the anti-roll bar links **(see illustration)**. Counterhold the balljoint shank with an Allen key/bit. Discard the nut'(s) – new ones must be fitted upon reassembly.
4 Sacken and remove the four subframe mounting bolts. Discard the bolts – new ones must be fitted.
5 Undo the bolts securing the anti-roll bar clamps to the subframe, and manoeuvre the bar from position **(see illustration)**.

Bushes

6 It would appear that the bushes are integral with the anti-roll bar. Check with a Ford dealer or parts specialist.

Links

7 Undo the nuts securing the anti-roll links to the anti-roll bar and trailing arm. Use an Allen key or second spanner to counterhold the balljoint shank as the nut is slackened **(see illustration)**. Discard the nuts – new ones must be fitted.

Refitting

8 Locate the anti-roll bar on the rear subframe, then refit the clamps and tighten the bolts to the specified torque.
9 Lift the subframe and tighten the mounting bolts to the specified torque.
10 The remainder of refitting is a reversal of removal.

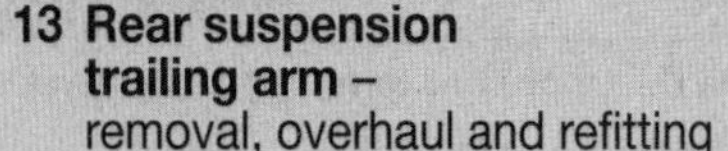

13 Rear suspension trailing arm – removal, overhaul and refitting

Removal

1 Remove the rear coil spring as described in Section 11.
2 Remove the underbody panelling on the relevant side of the vehicle.
3 Unclip any brake hoses, or wiring harnesses from the trailing arm.
4 Slacken and remove the bolts securing the hub carrier to the trailing arm **(see illustration 9.6)**. Note that new bolts will be required.
5 Undo the bolts and manoeuvre the trailing arm from the vehicle. Discard the bolts – new ones must be fitted.

12.5 Undo the bolts for the anti-roll bar clamps

Overhaul

6 To replace the metal/rubber bush on the trailing arm, undo the retaining bolt/nut. Discard the nut – a new one must be fitted.
7 Although the trailing arm bush is available as a separate part, replacement of the bush requires access to several special tools. The bush must be compressed at the same time as being drawn into the trailing arm. Consequently, we recommend that replacement of the bush is entrusted to a Ford dealer or suitably equipped repairer.

Refitting

8 Refitting is a reversal of the removal procedure, noting the following points:
a) *Align the previously made marks prior to tightening the trailing arm bush mounting bracket bolts*
b) *The wheel alignment will also require checking, see Section 21.*

14 Rear suspension control arms – removal and refitting

Removal

Upper arm

1 Slacken the relevant rear roadwheel nuts, then jack up the rear of the vehicle and support it on axle stands (see *Jacking and vehicle support*). Remove the relevant roadwheel.
2 Remove the relevant rear spring, as described in Section 11.

14.6 Make alignment marks between the eccentric nut and the arm

12.7 Undo the anti-roll bar link nuts

3 Support the lower control arm using a floor jack, then undo the upper arm retaining bolts and manoeuvre the arm from place.
4 Refitting is a reversal of removal.

Lower arm

Note: *The bushes in the suspension arms cannot be renewed separately; renew the complete arm if there is any wear or damage.*
5 Slacken the relevant rear roadwheel bolts, then jack up the rear of the vehicle and support it on axle stands (see *Jacking and vehicle support*). Remove the relevant roadwheel.
6 Prior to removing the lower control arm outer retaining bolt, make alignment marks between the serrated eccentric nut and the trailing arm, to preserve the rear wheel alignment upon refitting **(see illustration)**.
7 Slacken and remove the control arm retaining bolts and manoeuvre the arm from under the vehicle. Renew the self-locking nuts.

Refitting

8 Refitting is a reversal of the removal procedure, aligning the previously made marks (lower control arm outer bolt eccentric washer only). Delay fully tightening the control arm mounting bolts, until the vehicle is back on its wheels and normally loaded. Normally loaded is defined as 68 kg on each front seat, 14 kg in the centre of the luggage compartment, and a full tank of fuel.

15 Rear suspension subframe – removal and refitting

Removal

1 Slacken the rear roadwheel nuts, then jack up the rear of the vehicle, and support it securely on axle stands (see *Jacking and vehicle support*). Remove both rear roadwheels.
2 Remove the upper and lower control arms as described in Section 14.
3 Disengage the wheel speed sensor wiring harnesses from the retaining brackets on the subframe.

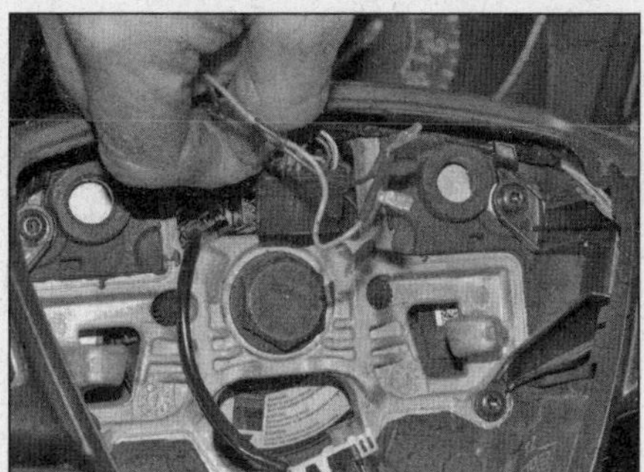
16.2 Disconnect the steering wheel wiring plug

16.3 The end of the steering column shaft has a master spline indicated by the factory-made mark

16.5 Secure the rotary contact unit with tape

4 Slacken the union nut, and disconnect the brake hose each side under the subframe. Be prepared for fluid spillage. Plug the ends of the pipes to prevent fluid loss and dirt/water ingress.
5 Undo the bolts securing the anti-roll bar clamps to the subframe.
6 Place a trolley jack and length of wood under the fuel tank to support it, and undo the two bolts securing the tank retaining straps to the subframe.
7 Undo the four subframe mounting bolts, lower the subframe and manoeuvre it from under the vehicle.

Refitting

8 Refitting is a reversal of the removal procedure, noting the following points:
a) Tighten all bolts to the specified torque.
b) Check, and if necessary have the rear wheel toe setting adjusted.

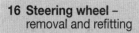

16 Steering wheel – removal and refitting

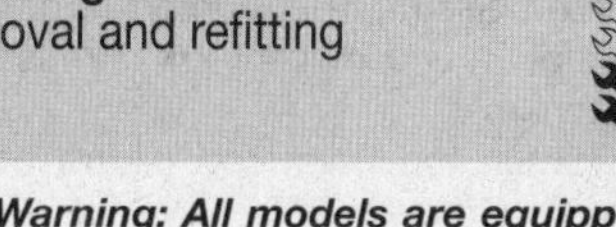

Warning: All models are equipped with an airbag system. Make sure that the safety recommendations given in Chapter 12 Section 24 are followed, to prevent personal injury.

Removal

1 Remove the driver's airbag as described in Chapter 12 Section 24.
2 Ensure the wheel is in the straight-ahead position, then disconnect the steering wheel switch wiring plug **(see illustration)**.
3 Unscrew the retaining bolt from the centre of the steering wheel **(see illustration)**.
4 Remove the steering wheel from the top of the column.
5 Prevent the rotary contact unit from accidentally being rotated by securing it in place with adhesive tape **(see illustration)**.

Refitting

6 Make sure that the front wheels are still facing straight-ahead, then locate the steering wheel on the top of the steering column. Align the master splines of the column shaft and steering wheel boss.
7 Refit the retaining bolt, and tighten it to the specified torque while holding the steering wheel.
8 Reconnect the wiring connector(s) for the horn and other steering wheel switches (where applicable).
9 Refit the airbag as described in Chapter 12 Section 24.

17 Steering column – removal, inspection and refitting

Warning: All models are equipped with an airbag system. Make sure that the safety recommendations given in Chapter 12 Section 24 are followed, to prevent personal injury.

Removal

1 Remove the steering wheel, as described in Section 16.
2 Remove the 2 retaining screws and manoeuvre the lower steering column shroud from place **(see illustration)**.
3 Remove the steering column switch assembly as described in Chapter 12 Section 6.
4 Remove the driver's knee airbag, as described in Chapter 12 Section 24.
5 Undo the pinch bolt at the bottom of the steering column, by the floor **(see illustration)**. Note that a new bolt will be required upon reassembly.
6 Undo the 4 bolts and manoeuvre the column assembly from the vehicle. Note that new bolts will be required upon reassembly.
Note: *The column mounting bolts are different lengths, so take note of which bolt goes where – the shorter bolts go nearest the bulkhead.*

Inspection

7 With the steering lock disengaged, attempt to move the steering wheel up-and-down and also to the left-and-right without turning the wheel, to check for steering column bearing wear, steering column shaft joint play and steering wheel or steering column being loose. The steering column cannot be repaired, if any faults are detected install a new column.
8 Examine the height adjustment lever mechanism for wear and damage.
9 With the steering column removed, check the universal joints for wear, and examine the column upper and lower shafts for any signs of damage or distortion. Where evident, the column should be renewed complete.

Refitting

10 Refitting is a reversal of removal, noting the following points:
a) Make sure the wheels are still in the straight-ahead position when the steering column is installed.
b) Fit new pinch-bolt to the steering column universal joint.
c) Tighten all fasteners to their specified torque where given.
d) Refit the drivers airbag as described in Chapter 12 Section 24.

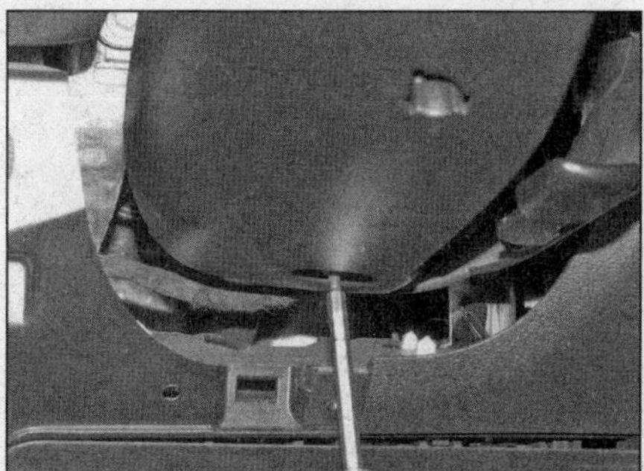
17.2 Undo the screws to remove the shroud

17.5 Remove the steering column pinch bolt

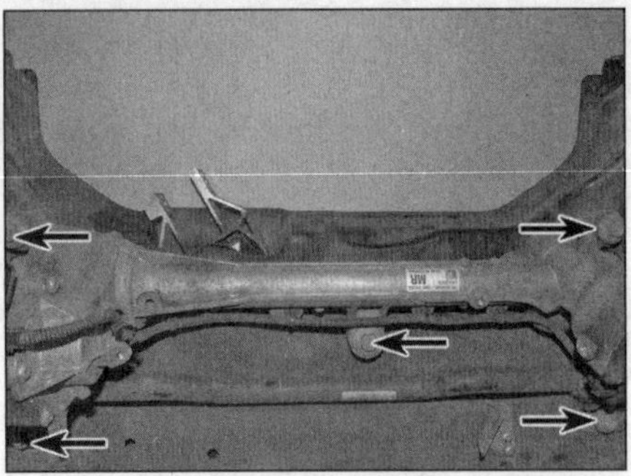

18.5 Remove the steering rack mounting bolts and discard

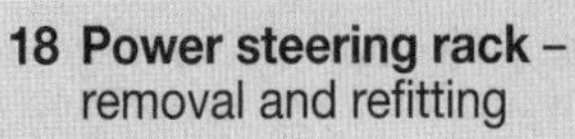

18 Power steering rack – removal and refitting

Removal

1 Centralise the steering wheel so that the front wheels are in the straight-ahead position, then disconnect the battery negative lead as described in Chapter 5 Section 4.

2 Slacken both front roadwheel nuts, then jack up the front of the vehicle and support it securely on axle stands (see *Jacking and vehicle support*). Remove both front roadwheels.

3 Remove the front subframe as described in Section 8.

4 Undo the bolts and remove the heatshield over the steering rack.

5 Undo the bolts securing the rack to the subframe **(see illustration)**. Discard the bolts – new ones must be fitted.

6 With the exception of the rubber gaiters (see Section 19), no further dismantling of the steering rack is recommended. It would appear that replacement steering racks are only available as a complete assembly. Consult a Ford dealer or parts specialist.

Refitting

7 Refitting is a reversal of removal, noting the following points:

a) *Tighten all fasteners to their specified torque where given.*

b) *Renew the steering column lower universal joint pinch bolt.*

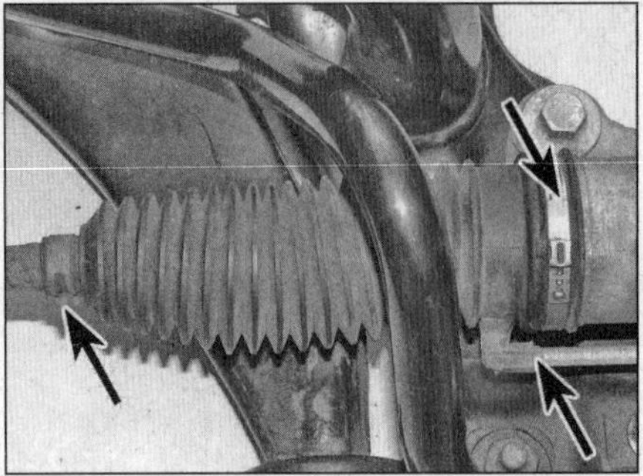

19.3 Undo the clips to remove the gaiters

c) *If a new rack/EPS unit has been fitted, it may need to be programmed using Ford diagnostic equipment. Entrust this task to a Ford dealer or suitably equipped repairer.*

d) *Check the front wheel alignment as described in Section 21.*

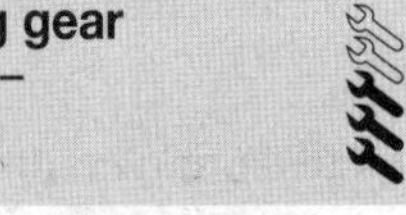

19 Power steering gear rubber gaiters – renewal

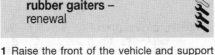

1 Raise the front of the vehicle and support it securely on axle stands (see *Jacking and vehicle support*). Release the fasteners and remove the engine/transmission undershield (where fitted).

2 Remove the track rod end as described in Section 20. Make sure that a note is made of the exact position of the track rod end on the track rod, in order to retain the front wheel alignment setting on refitting.

3 Release the outer and inner retaining clips, and disconnect the gaiter from the steering rack **(see illustration)**.

4 Slide the gaiter off the track rod.

5 Apply grease to the track rod inner joint. Wipe clean the seating areas on the steering rack and track rod.

6 Slide the new gaiter onto the track rod and steering rack.

7 Fit a new inner and outer retaining clips.

8 Refit the track rod end as described in Section 20.

9 Have the front wheel alignment checked, and if necessary adjusted, at the earliest opportunity, as described in Section 21.

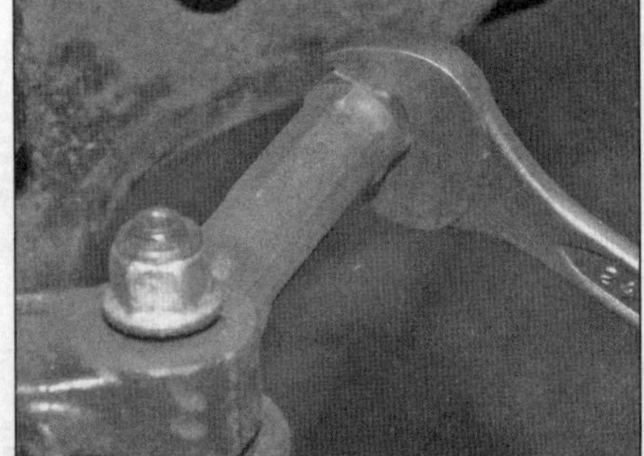

20.2 Slacken the locknut, counterholding with a spanner on the hexagonal section

20.4 Use a separator tool to detach the balljoint from the hub carrier

20 Track rod end – renewal

Removal

1 Slacken the relevant front roadwheel nuts, then jack up the front of the vehicle and support it on axle stands (see *Jacking and vehicle support*). Remove the appropriate front roadwheel.

2 Count the number of threads exposed on the inner section of the track rod to aid refitting, then slacken the locknut securing the track rod end to the track rod **(see illustration)**.

3 Unscrew and remove the track rod end balljoint retaining nut. Discard the nut – a new one must be fitted.

4 To release the tapered shank of the balljoint from the hub carrier, use a balljoint separator tool **(see illustration)**. If the balljoint is to be re-used, take care not to damage the dust cover when using the separator tool.

5 Unscrew the track rod end from the track rod, counting the number of turns necessary to remove it. If necessary, hold the track rod stationary with using the flats provided.

Refitting

6 Screw the track rod end onto the track rod by the number of turns noted during removal.

7 Engage the shank of the balljoint with the hub carrier, and fit the new nut. Tighten the nut to the specified torque. If the balljoint shank turns while the nut is being tightened, use an Allen key to hold the shank or press up on the balljoint. The tapered fit of the shank will lock it, and prevent rotation as the nut is tightened.

8 Tighten the track rod clamp bolt to the specified torque.

9 Refit the roadwheel, and lower the vehicle to the ground. Tighten the roadwheel nuts to the specified torque.

10 Finally check, and if necessary adjust, the front wheel alignment as described in Section 21.

21 Wheel alignment and steering angles – general information

1 Accurate front wheel alignment is essential to provide positive steering, and to prevent excessive tyre wear. Before considering the steering/suspension geometry, check that the tyres are correctly inflated, that the front wheels are not buckled, and that the steering linkage and suspension joints are in good order, without slackness or wear.

2 Wheel alignment consists of four factors **(see illustration)** :

3 *Camber* is the angle at which the front wheels are set from the vertical, when viewed from the front of the vehicle. 'Positive camber'

is the amount (in degrees) that the wheels are tilted outward at the top of the vertical.

4 *Castor* is the angle between the steering axis and a vertical line, when viewed from each side of the car. 'Positive castor' is when the steering axis is inclined rearward at the top.

5 *Steering axis inclination* is the angle (when viewed from the front of the vehicle) between the vertical and an imaginary line drawn through the suspension strut upper mounting and the lower suspension arm balljoint.

6 *Toe setting* is the amount by which the distance between the front inside edges of the roadwheels (measured at hub height) differs from the diametrically-opposite distance measured between the rear inside edges of the roadwheels.

7 With the exception of the toe setting, all other steering angles are set during manufacture, and no adjustment is possible. It can be assumed, therefore, that unless the vehicle has suffered accident damage, all the pre-set steering angles will be correct. Should there be some doubt about their accuracy, it will be necessary to seek the help of a Ford dealer or suitably equipped repairer, as special gauges are needed to check the steering angles.

8 Two methods are available to the home mechanic for checking the toe setting. One method is to use a gauge to measure the distance between the front and rear inside edges of the roadwheels. The other method is to use a scuff plate, in which each front wheel is rolled across a movable plate which records any deviation, or scuff, of the tyre from the straight-ahead position as it moves across the plate. Relatively-inexpensive equipment of both types is available from accessory outlets.

9 Before checking the steering geometry, the vehicle must be loaded to the 'normal' position. To set the vehicle ready for checking, place a 68 kg load on each front seat, a 14 kg load in the luggage compartment, and ensure the fuel tank is full.

10 If, after checking the toe setting using whichever method is preferable, it is found that adjustment is necessary, proceed as follows.

11 Turn the steering wheel onto full-left lock, and record the number of exposed threads on the right-hand track rod. Now turn the steering onto full-right lock, and record the number of threads on the left-hand track rod. If there are the same number of threads visible on both sides, then subsequent adjustment can be made equally on both sides. If there are more threads visible on one side than the other, it will be necessary to compensate for this during adjustment. After adjustment, there should be the same number of threads visible on each track rod. This is most important.

12 To alter the toe setting, slacken the locknut on the track rod end **(see illustration 20.2)**, and turn the track rod using the flats provided to achieve the desired setting. When viewed from the side of the car, turning the rod clockwise will increase the toe-in, turning it anti-clockwise will increase the toe-out. Only turn the track rods by a quarter of a turn each time, and then recheck the setting.

13 After adjustment, tighten the locknuts. Reposition the steering gear rubber gaiters, to remove any twist caused by turning the track rods.

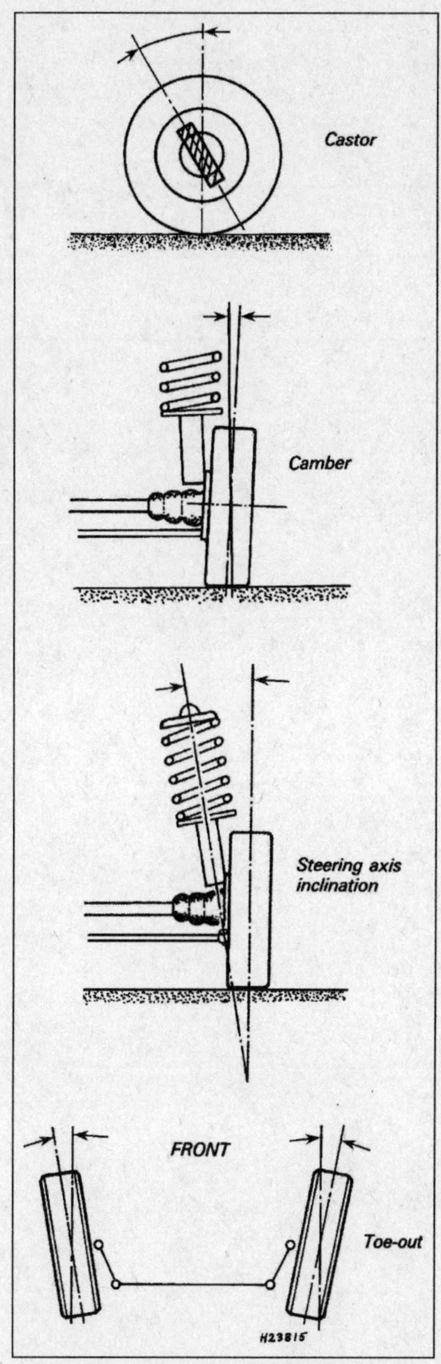

21.2 Wheel alignment and steering angle measurements

Notes

Chapter 11
Bodywork and fittings

Contents

Degrees of difficulty

Easy, suitable for novice with little experience 	Fairly easy, suitable for beginner with some experience 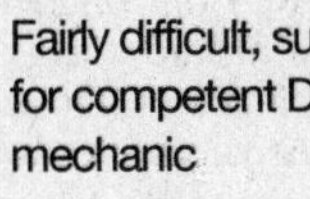	Fairly difficult, suitable for competent DIY mechanic 	Difficult, suitable for experienced DIY mechanic 	Very difficult, suitable for expert DIY or professional 

Specifications

Torque wrench settings	Nm	lb ft
Facia crossmember nuts	25	18
Front seat mounting bolts	55	41
Rear seat mounting bolts	40	30
Seat belt bolts*	40	30
Tailgate-to-hinge nuts	30	22

* *Do not re-use*

1 General information

1 The bodyshell and underframe on all models feature variable thickness steel. Achieved by laser-welded technology, used to join steel panels of different gauges. This gives a stiffer structure, with mounting points being more rigid, which gives an improved crash performance.

2 An additional safety crossmember is incorporated between the A-pillars in the upper area of the bulkhead, and the facia and steering column are secured to it. The lower bulkhead area is reinforced by additional systems of members connected to the front of the vehicle. The body side rocker panels (sills) have been divided along the length of the vehicle by internal reinforcement, this functions like a double tube which increases its strength. All doors are reinforced and incorporate side impact protection, which is secured in the door structure.

3 All sheet metal surfaces which are prone to corrosion are galvanised. The painting process includes a base colour which closely matches the final topcoat, so that any stone damage is not as noticeable. The front wings are of a bolt-on type to ease their replacement if required.

4 Automatic seat belts are fitted to all models, and the front seat safety belts are equipped with a pyrotechnic pretension seat belt stack, which is attached to the seat frame of each front seat. In the event of a serious front impact, the system is triggered and pulls the stalk buckle downwards to tension the seat belt. It is not possible to reset the tensioner once fired, and it must therefore be renewed. The tensioners are fired by an explosive charge similar to that used in the airbag, and are triggered via the airbag control module.

5 In the UK, central locking is standard on all models. In other countries, it is available on certain models only. In the event of a serious accident, a crash sensor unlocks all doors if they were previously locked.

6 Many of the procedures in this Chapter require the battery to be disconnected. Refer to Chapter 5 Section 4, first.

2 Maintenance – bodywork and underframe

1 The general condition of a vehicle's bodywork is the one thing that significantly affects its value. Maintenance is easy, but needs to be regular. Neglect, particularly after minor damage, can lead quickly to further deterioration and costly repair bills. It is important also to keep watch on those parts of the vehicle not immediately visible, for instance the underside, inside all the wheelarches, and the lower part of the engine compartment.

2 The basic maintenance routine for the bodywork is washing – preferably with a lot of water, from a hose. This will remove all the loose solids which may have stuck to the vehicle. It is important to flush these off in such a way as to prevent grit from scratching the finish. The wheelarches and underframe need washing in the same way, to remove any accumulated mud, which will retain moisture and tend to encourage rust. Paradoxically enough, the best time to clean the underframe and wheelarches is in wet weather, when the mud is thoroughly wet and soft. In very wet weather, the underframe is usually cleaned of large accumulations automatically, and this is a good time for inspection.

3 Periodically, except on vehicles with a wax-based underbody protective coating, it is a good idea to have the whole of the underframe of the vehicle steam-cleaned, engine compartment included, so that a thorough inspection can be carried out to see what minor repairs and renovations are necessary. Steam-cleaning is available at many garages, and is necessary for the removal of the accumulation of oily grime, which sometimes is allowed to become thick in certain areas. If steam-cleaning facilities are not available, there are some excellent grease solvents available which can be brush-applied; the dirt can then be simply hosed off. Note that these methods should not be used on vehicles with wax-based underbody protective coating, or the coating will be removed. Such vehicles should be inspected annually, preferably just prior to Winter, when the underbody should be washed down, and any damage to the wax coating repaired. Ideally, a completely fresh coat should be applied. It would also be worth considering the use of such wax-based protection for injection into door panels, sills, box sections, etc, as an additional safeguard against rust damage, where such protection is not provided by the vehicle manufacturer.

4 After washing paintwork, wipe off with a chamois leather to give an unspotted clear finish. A coat of clear protective wax polish will give added protection against chemical pollutants in the air. If the paintwork sheen has dulled or oxidised, use a cleaner/polisher combination to restore the brilliance of the shine. This requires a little effort, but such dulling is usually caused because regular washing has been neglected. Care needs to be taken with metallic paintwork, as special non-abrasive cleaner/polisher is required to avoid damage to the finish. Always check that the door and ventilator opening drain holes and pipes are completely clear, so that water can be drained out. Brightwork should be treated in the same way as paintwork. Windscreens and windows can be kept clear of the smeary film which often appears, by the use of proprietary glass cleaner. Never use any form of wax or other body or chromium polish on glass.

3 Maintenance – upholstery and carpets

1 Mats and carpets should be brushed or vacuum-cleaned regularly, to keep them free of grit. If they are badly stained, remove them from the vehicle for scrubbing or sponging, and make quite sure they are dry before refitting. Seats and interior trim panels can be kept clean by wiping with a damp cloth. If they do become stained (which can be more apparent on light-coloured upholstery), use a little liquid detergent and a soft nail brush to scour the grime out of the grain of the material. Do not forget to keep the headlining clean in the same way as the upholstery. When using liquid cleaners inside the vehicle, do not over-wet the surfaces being cleaned. Excessive damp could get into the seams and padded interior, causing stains, offensive odours or even rot.

Caution: If the inside of the vehicle gets wet accidentally, it is worthwhile taking some trouble to dry it out properly, particularly where carpets are involved. Do not leave oil or electric heaters inside the vehicle for this purpose.

4 Body damage – general information

1 In order to successfully repair damage to the vehicle bodywork, tools, skills and experience are required that are not normally possessed by the occasional DIY'er..

2 Whilst rectifying superficial scratches to the vehicle paintwork can be carried out using touch-up pens etc., it is difficult to achieve repairs of acceptable standard to more serious damage without access to professional equipment, and the necessary skills.

3 Consequently, we recommend that repairs are entrusted to suitably equipped professionals.

4 For minor repairs (scratch/dent removal) it may be worth trying one of the many companies that offer mobile 'smart' repairs. They can offer a convenient service, often with a guaranteed high-level of repair quality.

5 Major bodywork repairs should be carried out by fully equipped automotive bodywork specialist.

5 Bumpers – removal and refitting

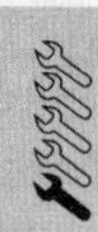

Front bumper cover

1 Raise the front of the vehicle and support it securely on axle stands (see *Jacking and vehicle support*).

5.3 Gently pull the trim away

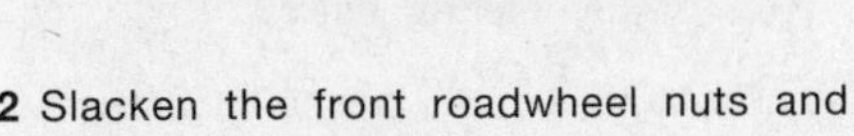

2 Slacken the front roadwheel nuts and remove the front wheels.

3 Carefully release the clips and pull away the wheelarch trim on either side of the vehicle **(see illustration)**.

4 Undo the 7 retaining screws and remove the engine undertray **(see illustration)**.

5 Remove the 3 screws under the front edge of the bumper.

6 Undo the 2 clips at each end of the underside of the bumper **(see illustration)**.

7 Working in the engine bay, detach the cable from the bonnet safety catch release **(see illustrations)**.

8 Undo the 2 retaining bolts and remove the bonnet safety release handle from place **(see illustration)**.

9 Using a trim removal tool, prise out the 9 retaining clips from the upper panel **(see illustration)**.

5.8 Unbolt the bonnet safety catch

5.12 Disconnect the wiring plug behind the left-hand foglight

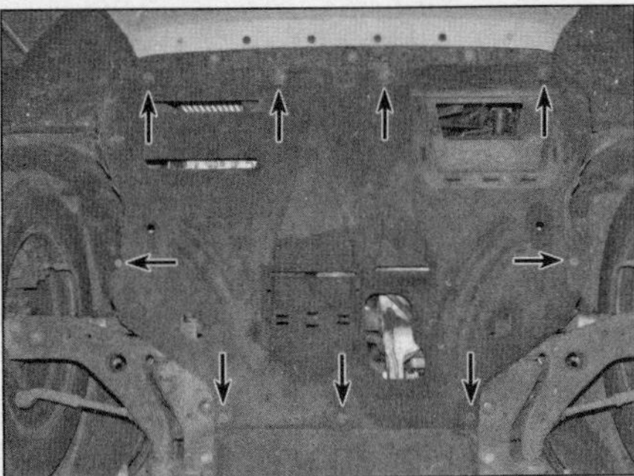

5.4 Undo the screws to remove the undertray

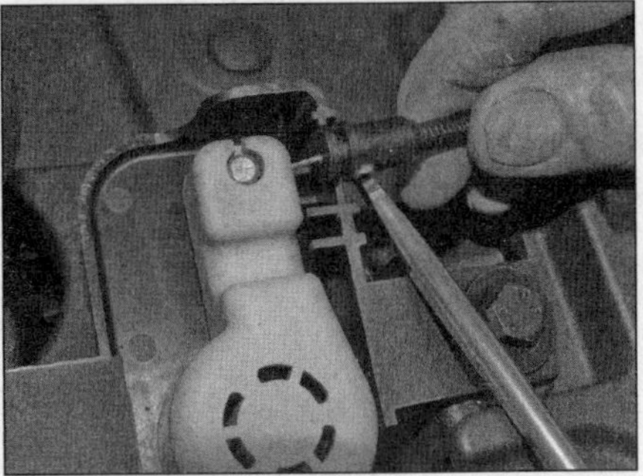

5.7a Detach the safety release cable...

10 Once removed, undo the 7 bolts behind the upper bumper panel **(see illustration)**.

11 Remove the wheelarch liner, as described in Section 39.

12 Disconnect the large grey wiring plug behind the left-hand foglight **(see illustration)**.

5.9 Gently remove the 9 clips from the bumper top panel

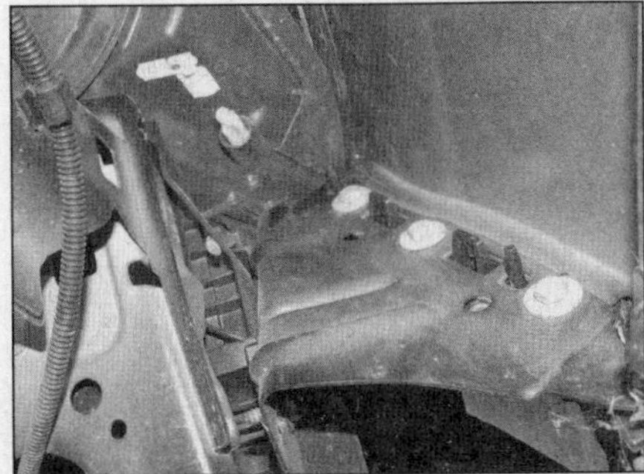

5.13 Undo the 3 retaining bolts at each end of the bumper in the wheelarch area

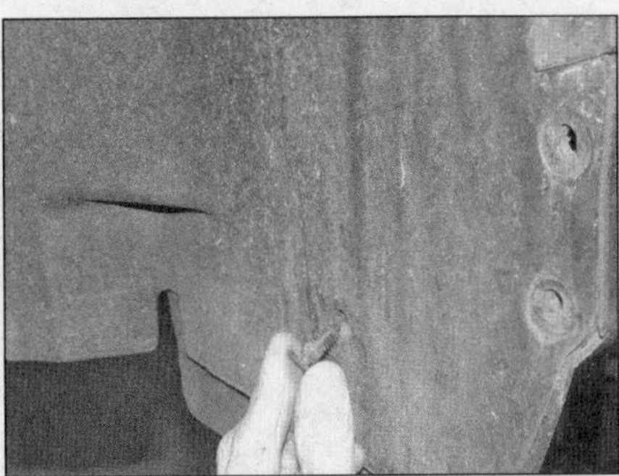

5.6 Remove the 2 clips at each end of the bumper underside

5.7b ...and unclip it from the panel behind

13 Undo the 3 bolts each side in the wheelarch area **(see illustration)**.

14 Press the 2 clips each side rearwards to release the bumper **(see illustration)**.

15 Lift the top of the bumper assembly off the small locating dowel **(see illustration)**.

5.10 Remove the 7 retaining bolts for the upper bumper mounts

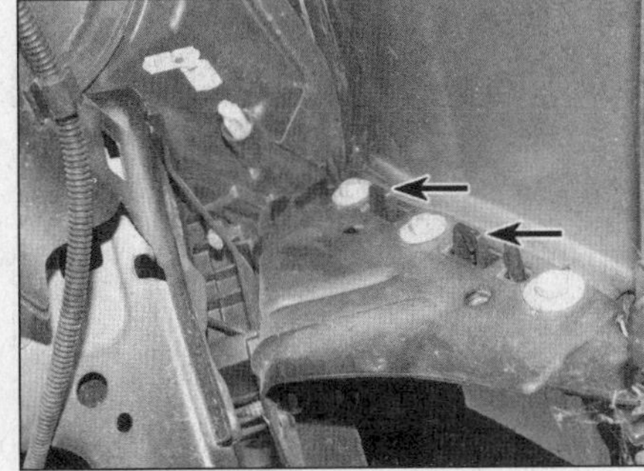

5.14 Press the clips rearwards

5.15 Disengage the bumper assembly from the locating dowel

5.19a Release the wheelarch trim clips...

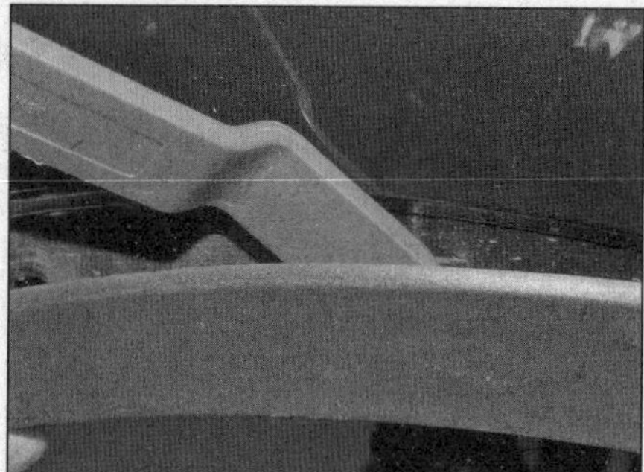

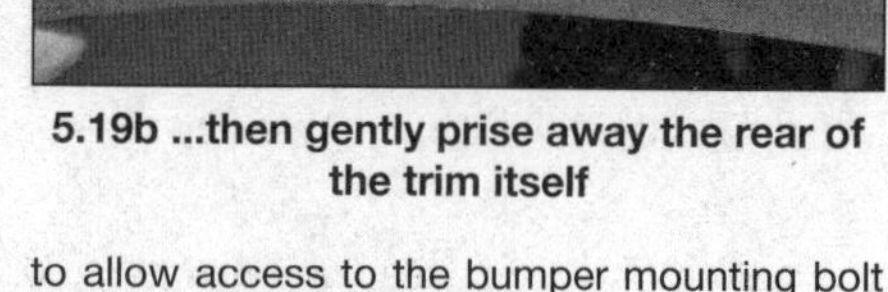

5.19b ...then gently prise away the rear of the trim itself

5.21 Undo the bolt behind the wheelarch trim

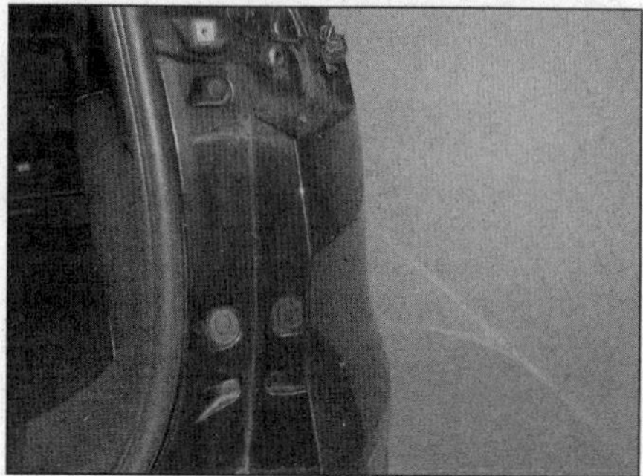

5.22 Remove the 2 bolts by the luggage area

16 With the help of an assistant, pull the bumper forwards and away from the vehicle.

17 Refitting is a reversal of removal.

Rear bumper cover

18 Chock the front wheels, raise the rear of the vehicle and support it securely on axle stands (see *Jacking and vehicle support*).

19 Carefully prise the retaining clips from the rear of the wheelarch trim each side, then gently pull the rear half of the trim from place, to allow access to the bumper mounting bolt behind **(see illustrations)**.

20 Remove the rear lights as described in Chapter 12 Section 9.

21 Undo the bolt at the upper edge of the bumper each side **(see illustration)**.

22 Undo the 2 bolts at each side of the luggage compartment opening **(see illustration)**.

23 Prise out the 3 clips at the bottom rear corner of each wheelarch liner **(see illustration)**.

24 Remove the 4 clips and 3 bolts along the underside rear edge of the bumper cover **(see illustration)**.

25 Disconnect all wiring plugs (for the foglights, rear parking sensors and keyless entry sensor (where fitted) and unclip them from the vehicle frame **(see illustrations)**.

26 With the help of an assistant, manoeuvre the bumper rearwards and withdraw it from the vehicle.

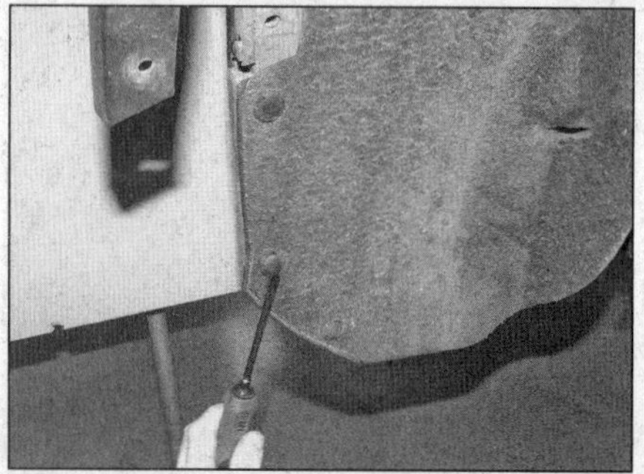

5.23 Remove the wheelarch liner clips

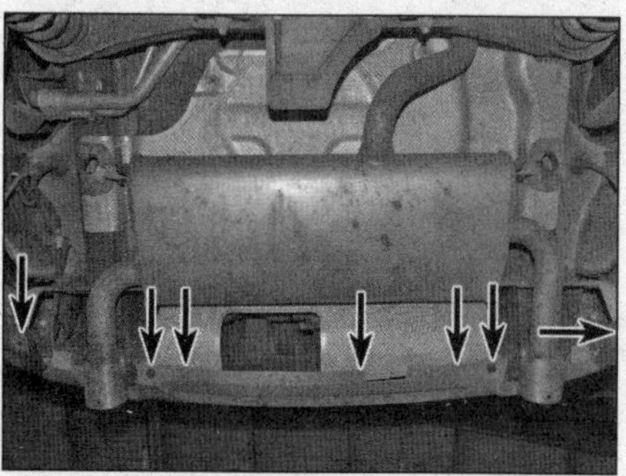

5.24 Remove the lower bolts and retaining clips

5.25a Unplug the rear foglights...

5.25b ...the wiring plugs for the rear parking sensors, and unclip...

5.25c ...and unplug the central wiring plug for the keyless entry sensor (where fitted)

5.29 Remove the bumper frame retaining nuts

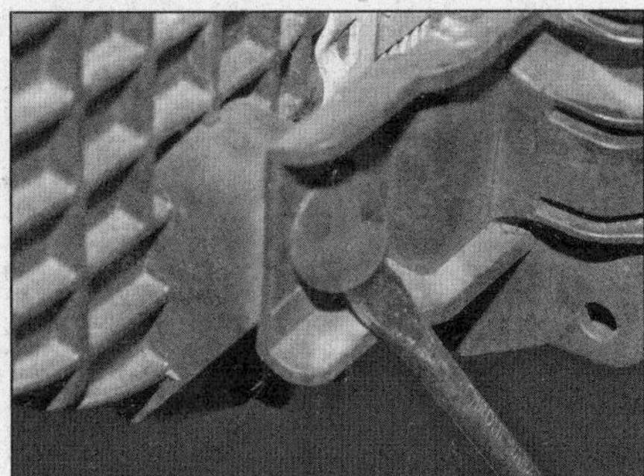
6.3 Remove the clips around the grille panel

6.4 Undo the 2 retaining bolts that hold the active grille to the crossmember

6.5 Rotate the dial to 'ASM'

6.6 Rotate the dial to 'SHIP' to release the grille

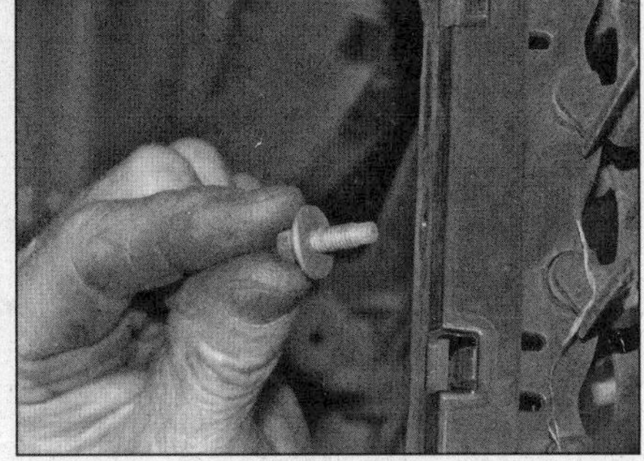
6.8a Remove the lower retaining bolt from the actuator...

6.8b ...then depress the tabs to release the rear of the actuator

27 Refitting is the reverse of the removal procedure.

Rear bumper frame

28 Remove the rear bumper cover as described earlier in this Section.

29 Undo the 4 retaining nuts each side **(see illustration)**.

30 With the aid of an assistant, manoeuvre the bumper frame from place.

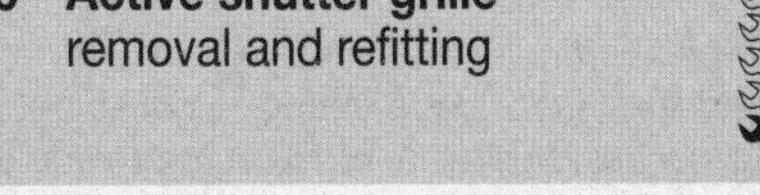
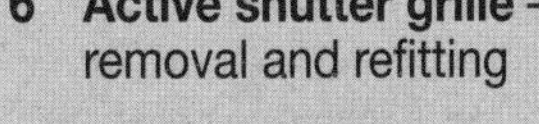

6 Active shutter grille – removal and refitting

Note: *Several models feature a motorised grille, fitted in front of the radiator/condenser assembly. The opening and closing of the slats in the grille is controlled by the Power Control Module (PCM). The position of the slats is calculated from various parameters including vehicle speed, ambient temperature and AC compressor operation. The default position is open. The PCM will open and shut the grille slats at engine start to calibrate the position of the slats. A single stepper motor is used to control the slats in the grille.*

Removal

1 Remove the front bumper cover as described in Section 5.

2 If working on the 1.5-litre petrol model, remove the auxiliary radiator, as described in Chapter 3 Section 5.

3 Use a trim removal tool to remove all the flat plastic clips from around the edge of the active grille **(see illustration)**.

4 Remove the 2 bolts that secure the active grille to the front cross member **(see illustration)**.

5 Rotate the locking locating dials from 'locked' to 'ASM', which will allow the active grille some forward movement **(see illustration)**.

6 Then with the grille pulled forward slightly, rotate the dial again, to 'SHIP', which will release the grille **(see illustration)**.

7 On diesel models, remove the intercooler as described in Chapter 4B Section 20, to allow access behind the active grille.

8 Undo the lower mounting bolt, then depress the tabs to release the bottom rear panel from the active grille actuator **(see illustrations)**.

9 Prise out the 2 retaining clips and remove the air intake pipe **(see illustrations)**.

10 Move to the top of the active grille, reaching down from the engine bay, and undo the retaining bolt at the top of the actuator **(see illustration)**.

6.9a Remove the right hand retaining clip for the air intake pipe...

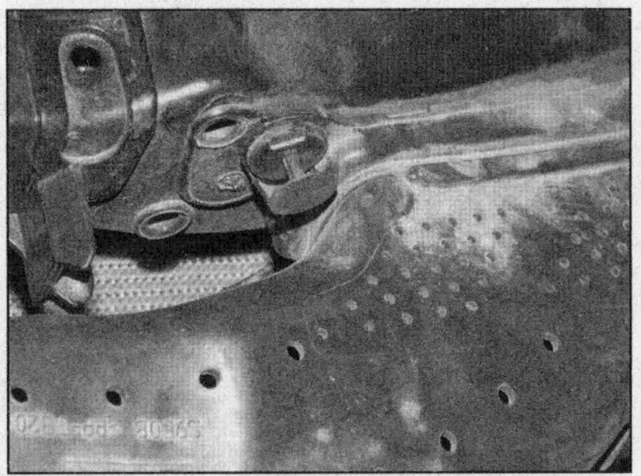
6.9b ...then the left-hand one, and remove the intake pipe

6.10 Slacken the bolt at the top of the actuator

6.11 Depress the tabs to release the top of the actuator rod

6.12 Unclip the wiring connectors

6.13 Disconnect the wiring plug and remove the grille

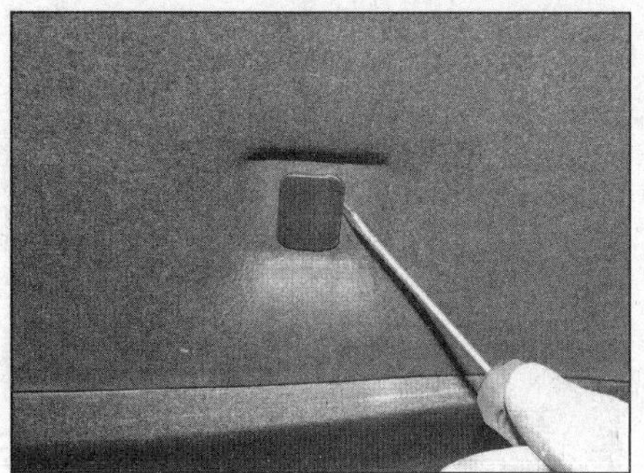

7.1 Squeeze the clips and remove the matting

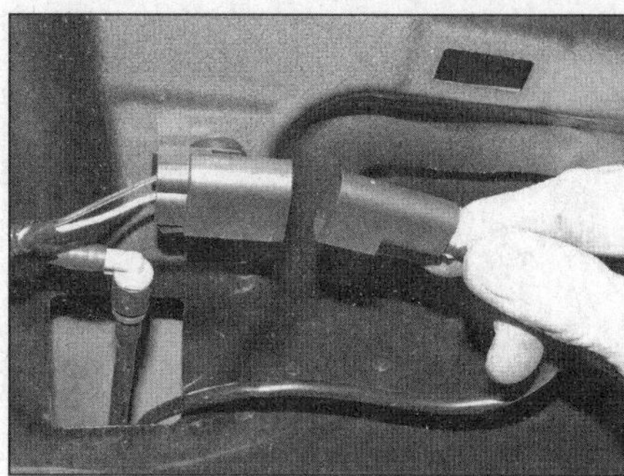

7.2a Disconnect the wiring plugs...

11 Depress the tabs and disengage the top of the actuator rod from the rear of the active grille, then remove **(see illustration)**.

12 Unclip the two wiring loom connectors from the front crossmember **(see illustration)**.

13 Disconnect the wiring plug and manoeuvre the grille assembly from place **(see illustration)**.

14 If required, the stepper motor can be removed from the grille, as described in Chapter 12 Section 14.

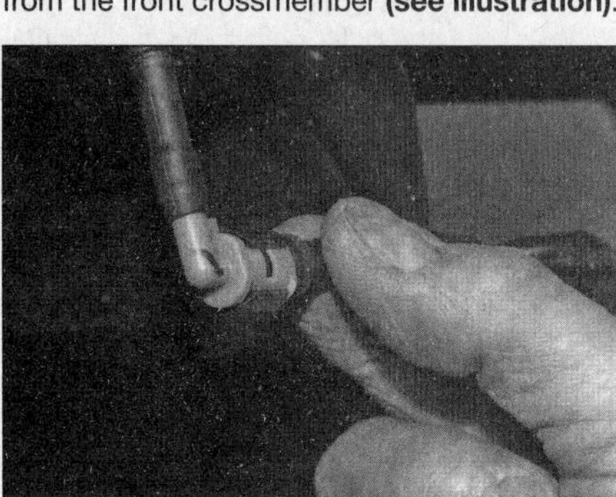

7.2b ... and washer tubing...

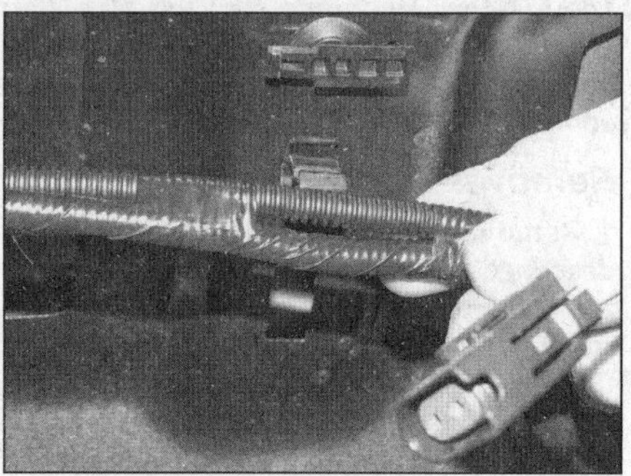

7.2c ...then unclip from the underside of the bonnet

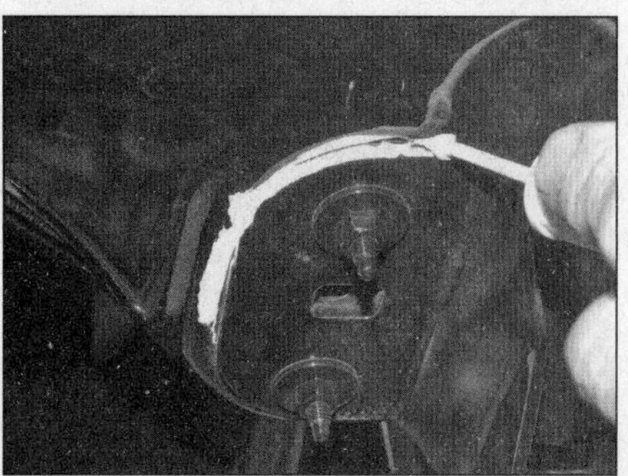

7.3 Make alignment marks on each hinge then undo the nuts

8.2 Squeeze the tabs to release the lever

Refitting

15 Refitting is a reversal of the removal procedure.

7 Bonnet – removal, refitting and adjustment

Removal

1 Open the bonnet, squeeze the clips and remove the under-bonnet matting **(see illustration)**.

2 Disconnect the washer tubing and any wiring plugs then unclip the wiring harness and tubing **(see illustrations)**.

3 Make alignment marks between the hinges and the bonnet to aid refitting. Have an assistant support the bonnet, then undo the nuts and, lift the bonnet from the vehicle **(see illustration)**.

Refitting and adjustment

4 Refitting is a reversal of the removal procedure, noting the following points:

a) *Position the bonnet hinges within the outline marks made during removal, but if necessary alter its position to provide a uniform gap all round.*

b) *Adjust the front height by repositioning the bump stops.*

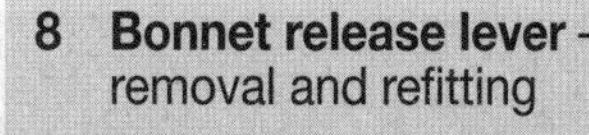

8 Bonnet release lever – removal and refitting

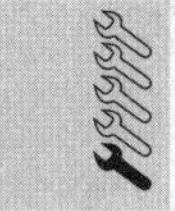

Removal

1 Prise out the cap in the centre of the release lever.

2 Use a small screwdriver to depress the 2 retaining tabs and slide the bonnet lever from place **(see illustration)**.

Refitting

3 Refitting is a reversal of removal.

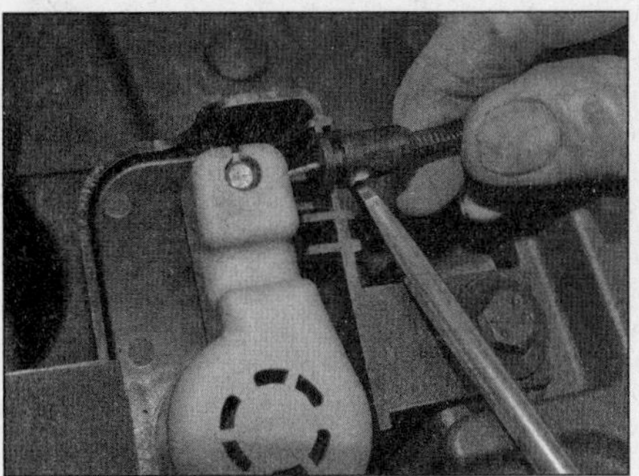
9.1a Use a screwdriver to unclip the cable from the housing...

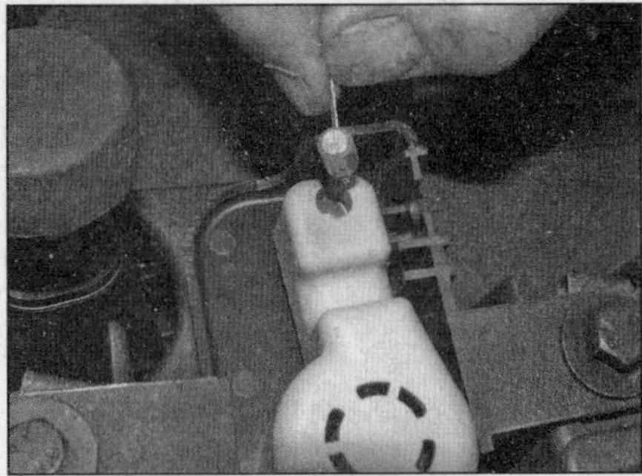
9.1b ...then release it from the lever

9.2 Take out the cable clips from the panel

9.3 Detach the cable from the mechanism

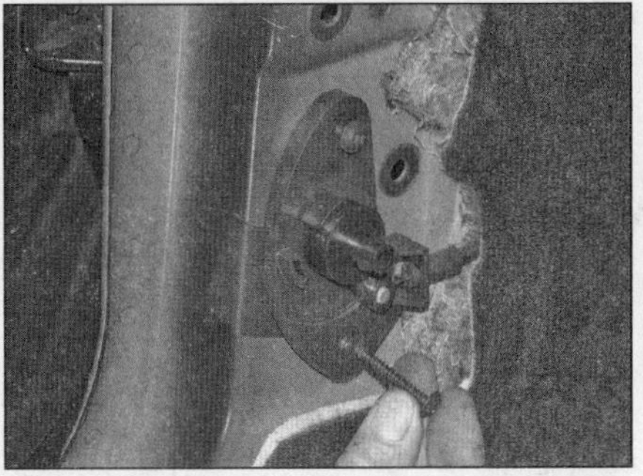
9.7 Unscrew and remove the lever bracket

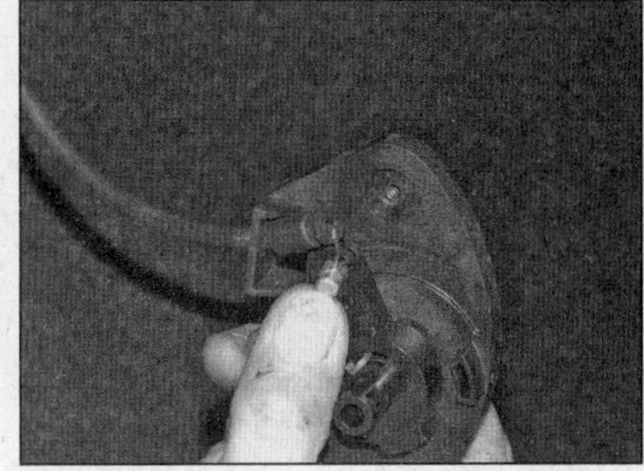
9.8 Pull the outer cable from the bracket

9 Bonnet release cables and mechanism – removal and refitting

Removal

Front cable

1 Unclip the bonnet release cable from the release lever housing, then release the cable from the lever itself **(see illustrations)**.

2 Prise up the cable securing clips from the front slam panel and remove **(see illustration)**.

3 Unhook the cable from the bonnet release mechanism **(see illustration)**.

Rear cable

4 Pull up the rubber weatherstrip from the top of the engine compartment bulkhead.

5 Undo the 3 plastic nuts, rotate the locking clips anti-clockwise and remove the cowl panel from the left-hand end of the windscreen scuttle.

6 Remove the passenger footwell kick panel as described in Section 35.

7 Undo the retaining screw to manoeuvre the lever bracket from place **(see illustration)**.

8 Pull the outer cable from the lever bracket, then disengage the cable end fitting from the release lever **(see illustration)**.

9 Note its routing, then trace the cable(s) forward, and release it from any retaining clips.

10 Unhook the cable from the bonnet release mechanism **(see illustration)**.

11 Pull the cable from place.

Lock mechanism

12 Detach the cable, as previously described in this Section.

13 Disconnect the lock mechanism wiring plug **(see illustration)**.

14 Undo the 2 retaining bolts and manoeuvre the lock from place **(see illustration)**.

Refitting

15 Fit the new cable, and secure it in place with the various retaining clips.

16 Engage the cable end fittings with the release lever and junction box coupling, then push the outer cables into place in the support brackets.

17 Check the operation of the bonnet catch/release lever prior to closing the bonnet. There is no adjustment facility for the cables.

10 Front crossmember and lock carrier – removal and refitting

Removal

Note: *This component is heavy and awkward, so you will require the assistance of a helper.*

1 Jack up the front of the vehicle and support on axle stands (see *Jacking and vehicle support*).

9.10 Detach the cable from the mechanism

9.13 Unplug the bonnet lock wiring connector

9.14 Remove the bolts to release the mechanism

10.7 Remove the front wing bolts

10.8 Remove the front inner wing bolt

2 Disconnect the battery as described in Chapter 5 Section 4.
3 Remove the radiator as described in Chapter 3 Section 6.
4 Remove the front bumper as described in Section 5.
5 Disconnect all wiring and cables from the front crossmember and lock carrier assembly.
6 Unbolt and remove the windscreen washer fluid reservoir, as described in Chapter 12 Section 19.
7 Undo the 2 retaining bolts at the leading edge of each front wing **(see illustration)**.
8 Undo the retaining bolt holding each end of the lock carrier assembly to the front inner wing **(see illustration)**.
9 Mark the position of the front crossmember nuts where it attaches to the chassis leg.
10 Undo the 4 retaining nuts holding the crossmember and lock carrier assembly to the chassis leg on each side of the engine bay.
11 Manoeuvre the whole assembly forward from place.

Refitting

12 Refitting is a reversal of removal, ensuring all fastenings are tighten to the specified torque setting where given.

11 Windscreen upper cowl panel– removal and refitting

Removal

1 Remove the wiper arms, as described in Chapter 12 Section 15.
2 Prise away the metal retaining clips along the front edge of the upper cowl panel **(see illustrations)**.
3 Unclip the rear edge of the panel by pulling it upwards to release the retaining clips, and manoeuvre it from place **(see illustration)**.

Refitting

4 Refitting is a reversal of removal.

12 Windscreen lower cowl panel – removal and refitting

Removal

1 Remove the windscreen upper cowl panel as described in Section 11.
2 Undo the 2 retaining screws and separate the brake fluid reservoir from the lower cowl panel **(see illustration)**.
3 Undo the 4 mounting bolts (2 at each side) and remove the lower cowl panel from place **(see illustration)**.
4 Refitting is a reversal of removal.

13 Front door inner trim panel – removal and refitting

Removal

1 Carefully prise out the cover behind the interior release handle **(see illustration)**.
2 Undo the retaining bolt behind the door release lever **(see illustration)**.

11.2a Prise away the metal clips...

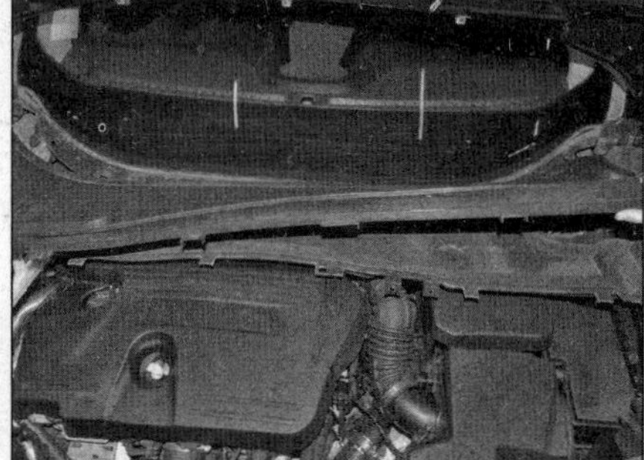
11.2b ....to release the upper cowl panel

11.3 Pull up the rear edge to release the clips

12.2 Undo the screws and release the brake fluid reservoir

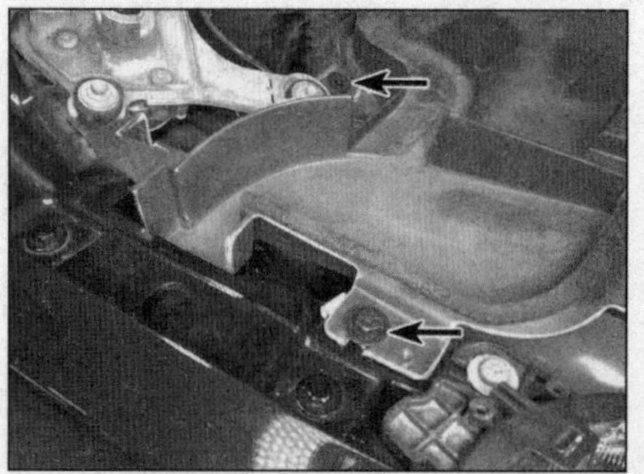
12.3 Undo the 2 bolts each side securing the lower cowl panel

13.1 Prise the cover behind the door release

13.2 Remove the retaining bolt

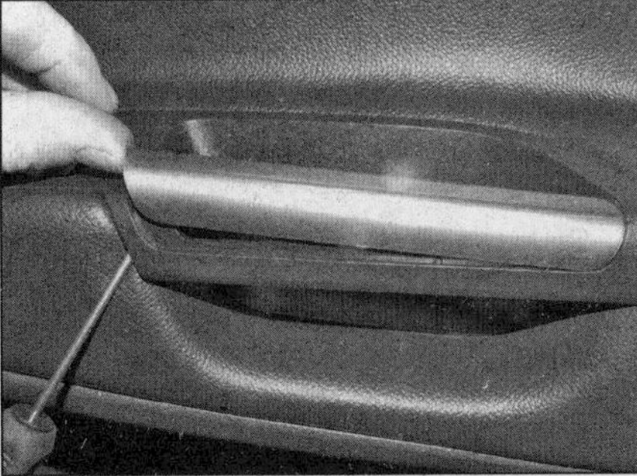

13.3 Lift up the cover for the door handle

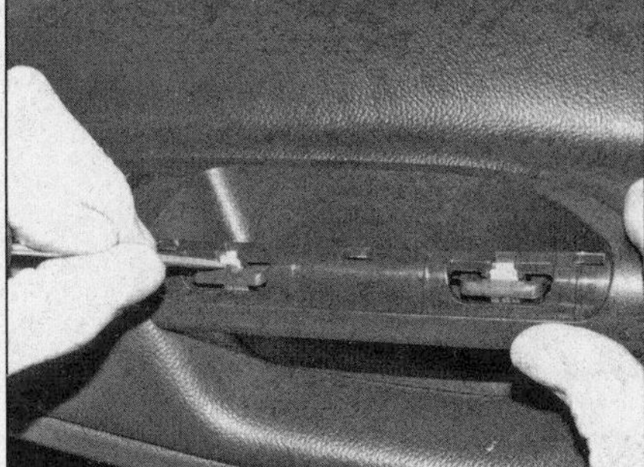

13.4 Depress the plastic tabs inside the door handle

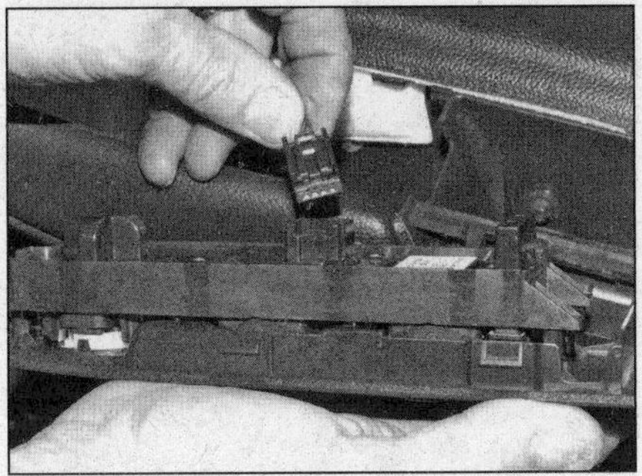

13.5 Lift up the switch and disconnect the wiring plug

13.6a Undo the 2 screws behind the door handle

13.6b And the bolt in the bottom of the door panel

3 Insert a trim removal tool and lift up the cover for the interior door handle **(see illustration)**.

4 Using a trim removal tool, depress the retaining clips inside the interior door handle **(see illustration)**.

5 Carefully prise up the rear of the electric window switch, then slide it rearwards **(see illustration)**. Disconnect the wiring plug as it becomes accessible.

6 Remove the 2 retaining screws behind the door handle and the bolt in the bottom of the door trim panel **(see illustrations)**.

7 Prise out the reflector in the rear of the door panel, and remove the screw behind **(see illustrations)**.

8 Carefully work around the edge of the panel, prise out the retaining clips, and withdraw the panel **(see illustration)**.

Note: *The clips are likely to be reluctant to release. Be prepared for clip breakage.*

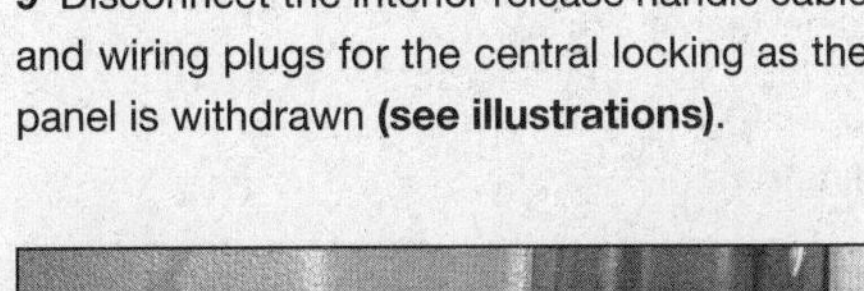

9 Disconnect the interior release handle cable and wiring plugs for the central locking as the panel is withdrawn **(see illustrations)**.

Refitting

10 Refitting is a reversal of the removal procedure.

13.7a Remove the reflector from the panel...

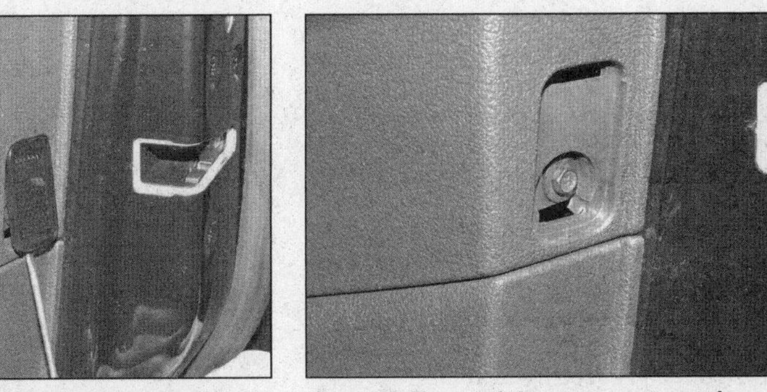

13.7b ...and the screw exposed

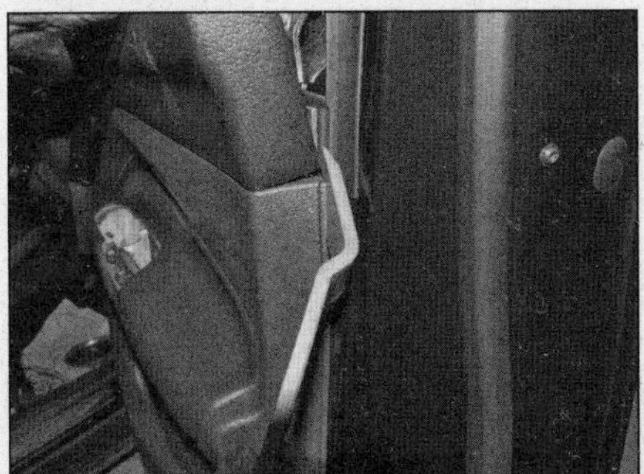

13.8 Use trim tools to remove the door panel

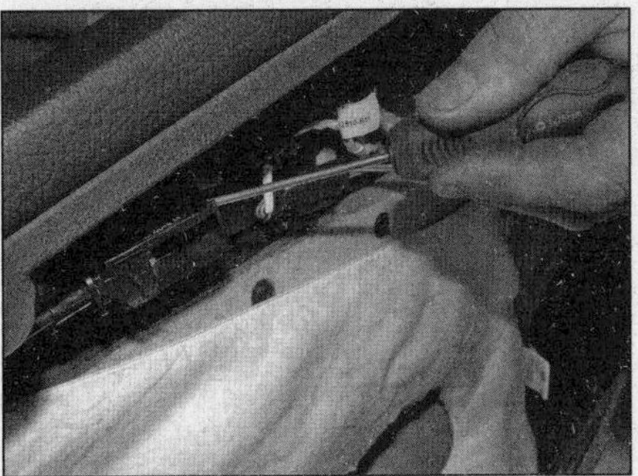

13.9a Disconnect the release cable...

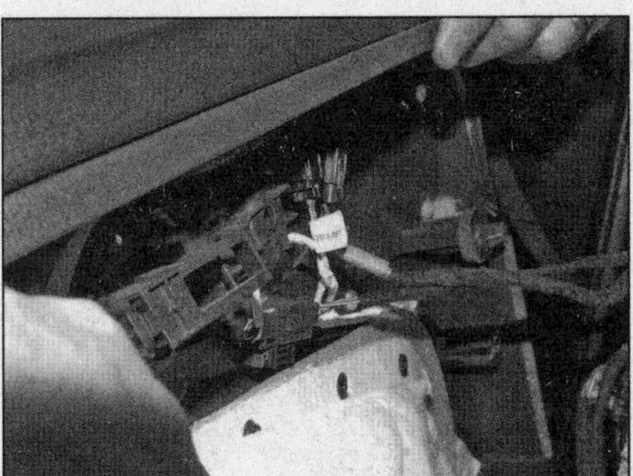

13.9b ...and the wiring plugs for the central locking

14.2 Remove the weatherstrip screw

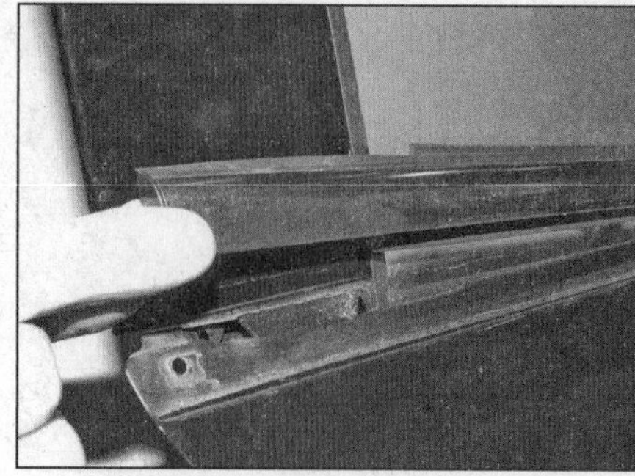
14.3 Carefully lift the weatherstrip

14.4a Disconnect the speaker wiring plug...

14.4b ...then undo the 3 retaining screws and remove

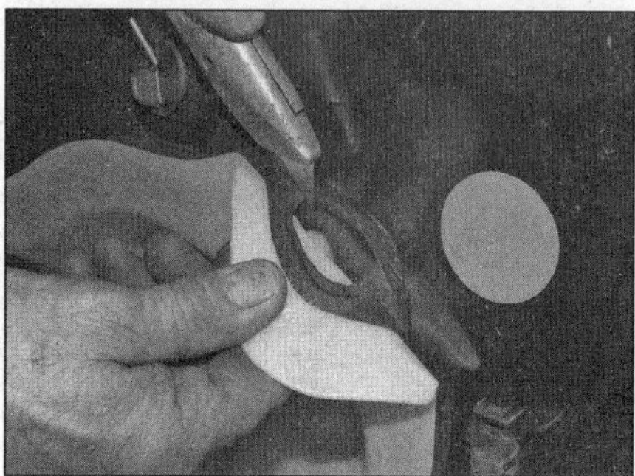
14.5 Cut the door sealant using a sharp knife

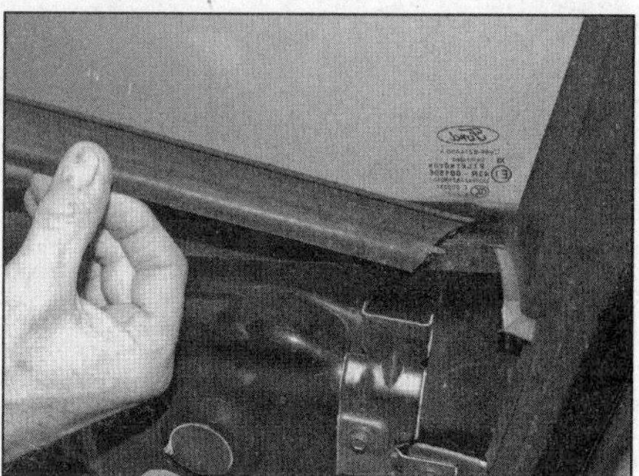
14.6 Remove the interior weatherstrip

14 Front door window glass – removal, refitting and initialisation

Removal

1 Remove the door inner trim panel as described in Section 13.

2 Undo the retaining screw at the rear of the exterior weatherstrip **(see illustration)**.

3 Lift the weatherstrip and manoeuvre from place **(see illustration)**.

4 Disconnect the wiring plug, then undo the 3 screws and remove the door speaker **(see illustrations)**.

5 Using a sharp knife, carefully cut through the sealant securing the waterproof membrane to the door frame **(see illustration)**.

6 Prise up the interior weatherstrip **(see illustration)**.

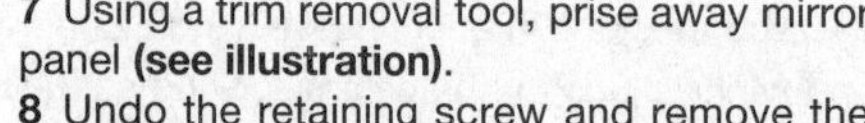

7 Using a trim removal tool, prise away mirror panel **(see illustration)**.

8 Undo the retaining screw and remove the weatherstrip around the window frame **(see illustration)**.

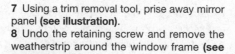

14.7 Remove the mirror panel

9 Reconnect the electric window switch and lower the window glass half way **(see illustration)**.

10 Open the retaining clips holding the glass into the electric window regulator by prising

14.8 Weatherstrip retaining screw

14.9 Reconnect the window switch and lower the window half way

14.10 Open the glass retaining clips

14.11 Pull away the rear window channel rubber

the rear of the clip out through the gap in the window bracket **(see illustration)**.

11 Lower the window glass into the door, then pull the rearmost window channel rubber from place **(see illustration)**.

12 Lifting the rear of the glass first, remove the glass from the door through the window aperture **(see illustration)**.

Refitting

13 Slide the glass into position, ensuring the front and rear clips engage correctly with the regulator clamp(s).

14 The remainder of refitting is a reversal of removal.

Initialisation

15 Upon completion, the window initialisation procedure must be carried out:

a) Move the window to the fully open position. Press and hold the switch in the 'one-touch' open position for 15 to 25 seconds.

b) Fully close the window. Press and hold the switch in the 'one-touch' close position during the entire closing sequence.

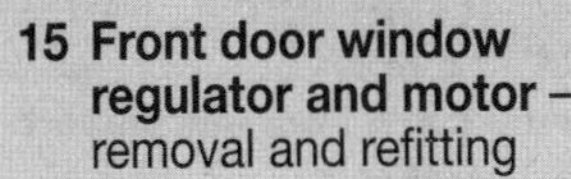

15 Front door window regulator and motor – removal and refitting

Removal

1 Disconnect the window glass from the regulator as described in Section 14.

2 Connect the window electric motor wiring plug and raise the window glass fully.

3 Secure the window glass to the door frame using tape **(see illustration)**.

4 Disconnect the wiring plug for the regulator **(see illustration)**.

5 Undo the 4 retaining nuts and 1 bolt (2 are hidden behind grey sticky pads) and manoeuvre the window regulator assembly from the door **(see illustration)**.

Refitting

6 Refitting is a reversal of the removal procedure. Upon completion, carry out the initialisation procedure as described in Section 14.

16 Front door handle and lock components – removal and refitting

Exterior handle

Removal

1 Remove the interior door trim panel as described in Section 13.

2 Prise out the rubber cap from the rear edge of the door **(see illustration)**.

3 Using a Torx bit/key, slacken the retaining screw until the lock cylinder assembly can be pulled from the door **(see illustrations)**.

14.12 Raise the glass out through the window opening

15.3 Use tape to secure the glass

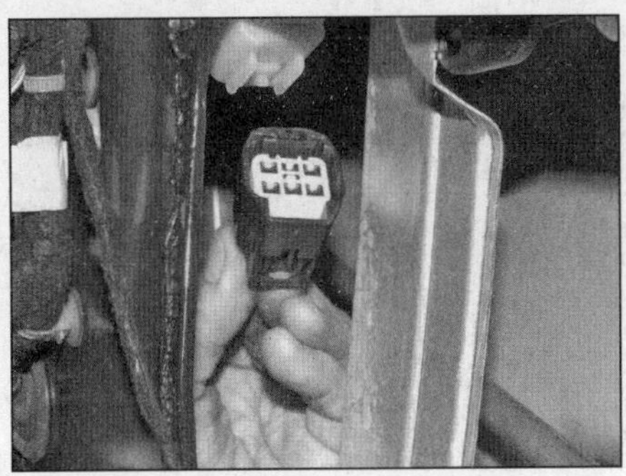

15.4 Disconnect the wiring plug

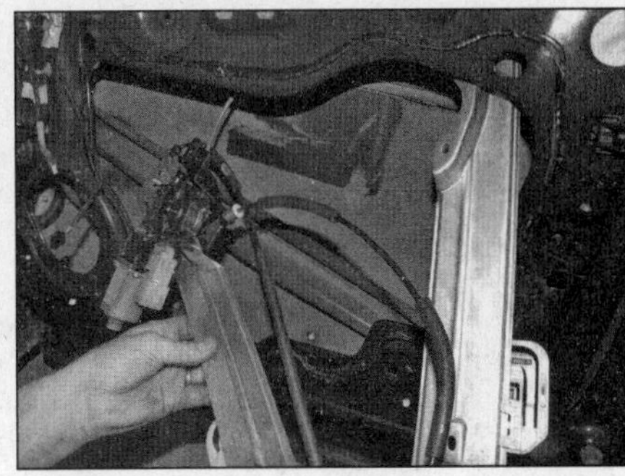

15.5 Manoeuvre the window regulator from the door

4 Pull the exterior handle outwards/rearwards and manoeuvre it from the door **(see illustration)**.

5 Working inside the door, disconnect the door handle wiring plug **(see illustration)**.

Refitting

6 Reconnect the wiring plug, then swivel the connector 90° downwards.

7 Re-engage the front of the handle with the door then push the handle into place.

16.2 Remove the cap from the rear edge of the door

16.3a Undo the retaining screw...

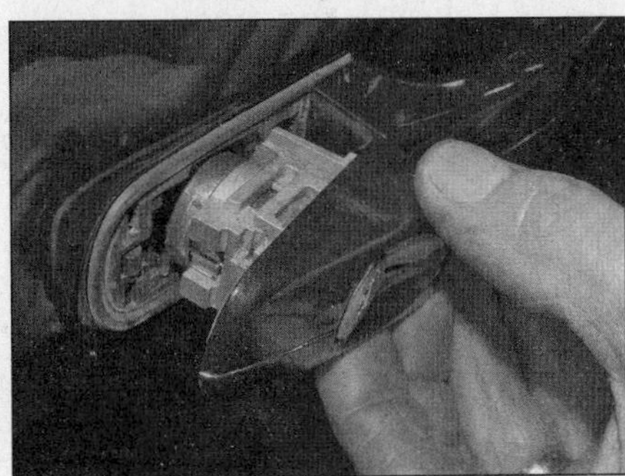

16.3b ...and pull the lock cylinder from the door

16.4 Slide the handle rearwards and outwards

16.5 Disconnect the door handle wiring plug

16.11 Remove the lock retaining screws

16.12 Remove the retaining screw on the frame

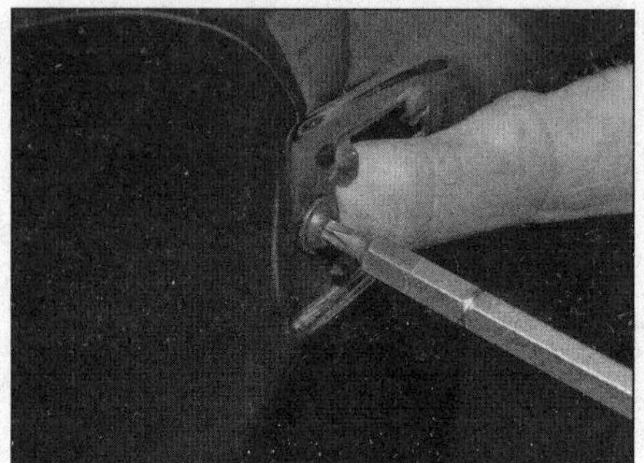
16.13 Undo the handle frame's retaining screw

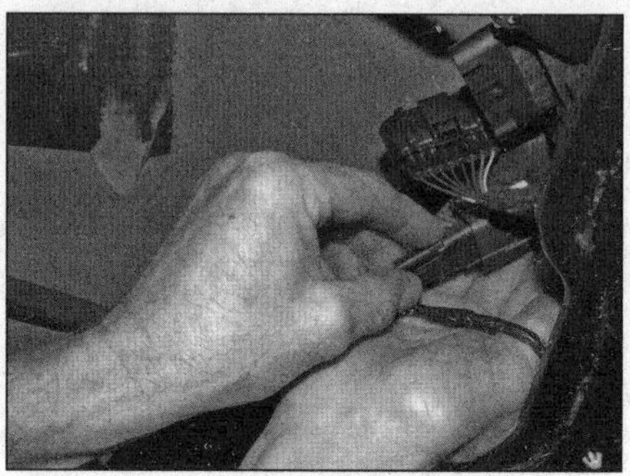
16.14 Disconnect the wiring plugs

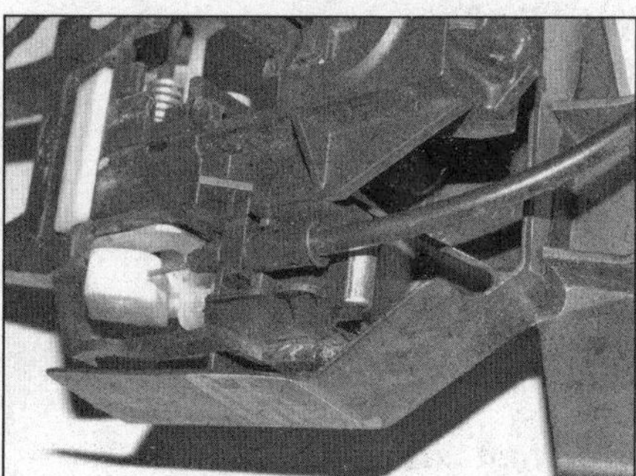
16.15 Detach the cable from the support frame

8 Replace the lock cylinder assembly and retighten the retaining screw.

Lock assembly

9 Remove the window regulator and motor as described in Section 15.

10 Remove the exterior door handle as previously described in this Section.

Note: *The lock and exterior handle frame must be removed as one.*

11 Undo the 3 lock retaining screws at the rear edge of the door **(see illustration)**.

12 Undo the exterior handle frame retaining screw on the door frame **(see illustration)**.

13 Undo the retaining bolt at the front of the exterior handle frame **(see illustration)**.

14 Disconnect the 2 wiring plugs **(see illustration)**.

15 Disconnect the release cable from the exterior handle frame **(see illustration)**.

16 Remove the handle frame and lock assembly from the door, threading the release cable through its opening.

17 If required, disconnect the interior release handle cable from the lock **(see illustration)**.

18 Refitting is a reversal of removal.

Lock cylinder

Note: *The lock cylinder cannot be separated from the lock cylinder frame.*

19 Removal of the lock cylinder assembly is described within the exterior handle removal procedure, described earlier in this Section.

20 Refitting is the reverse of removal.

Striker

21 Using a pencil or correction fluid, mark the position of the striker on the pillar.

22 Undo the Torx bolts, then remove the striker **(see illustration)**.

23 Refitting is a reversal of the removal procedure, but check that the door lock passes over the striker centrally. If necessary, reposition the striker before fully tightening the mounting screws.

17 Front doors – removal and refitting

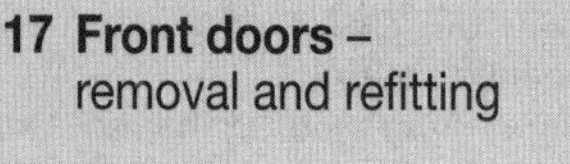

Removal

1 Disconnect the battery negative lead as described in Chapter 5 Section 4.

2 Unscrew the bolt for the door check strap from the door pillar **(see illustration)**.

3 Gently prise off the rubber boot and disconnect the wiring plug **(see illustration)**.

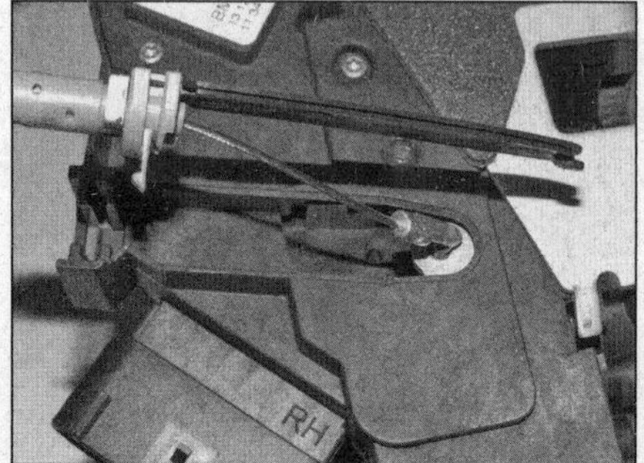

16.17 Separate the release cable from the lock

16.22 Mark the position of the striker, then undo the retaining bolts

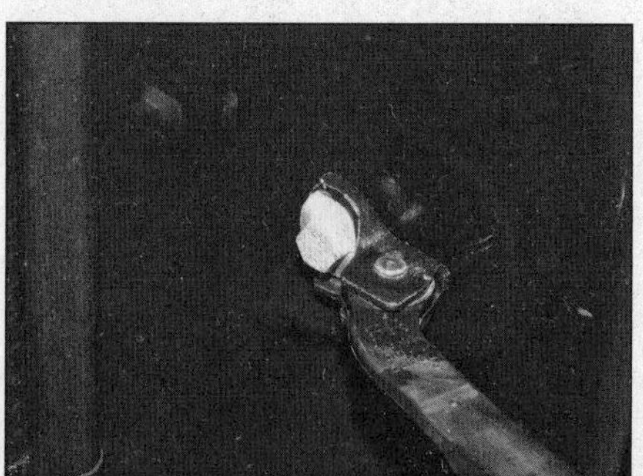
17.2 Remove the door check strap retaining bolt

17.3 Disconnect the wiring plug

17.4 Remove the retaining bolts in the hinges

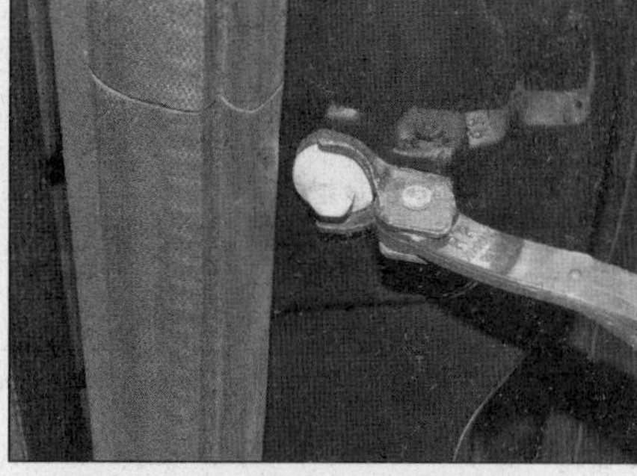

18.2 Remove the door check strap retaining bolt

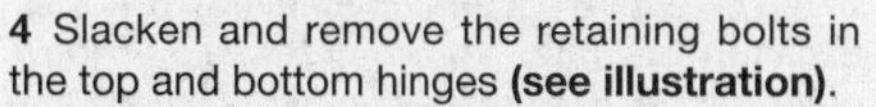

4 Slacken and remove the retaining bolts in the top and bottom hinges **(see illustration)**.
5 Carefully separate the door from the hinges.

Refitting

6 Refitting is a reversal of the removal procedure, but check that the door lock passes over the striker centrally. If necessary, reposition the striker.

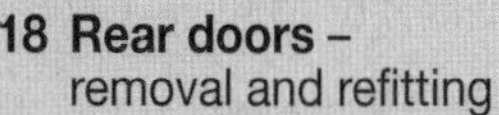

18 Rear doors – removal and refitting

Removal

1 Disconnect the battery negative lead as described in Chapter 5 Section 4.
2 Unscrew the bolt for the door check strap from the door pillar **(see illustration)**.
3 Gently prise off the rubber boot and disconnect the wiring plug **(see illustration)**. **Note:** *There are 3 small tabs that must be depressed to release the connector. The front two can be released with the back door shut to ease access, then the rear one can be accessed with the door open.*
4 Slacken and remove the retaining bolts in the top and bottom hinges **(see illustration)**.
5 Carefully separate the door from the hinges.

Refitting

6 Refitting is a reversal of the removal procedure, but check that the door lock passes over the striker centrally. If necessary, reposition the striker.

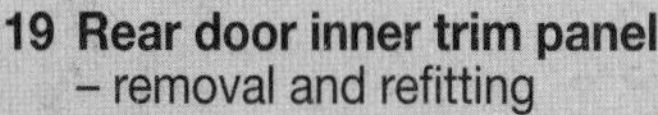

19 Rear door inner trim panel – removal and refitting

Removal

1 Carefully prise out the cover behind the interior release handle **(see illustration)**.
2 Remove the screw behind the interior release handle **(see illustration)**.
3 Insert a trim removal tool and lift up the cover for the interior door handle **(see illustration)**.
4 Disconnect the wiring plug for the electric window switch as it becomes accessible.

18.3 Disconnect the wiring plug

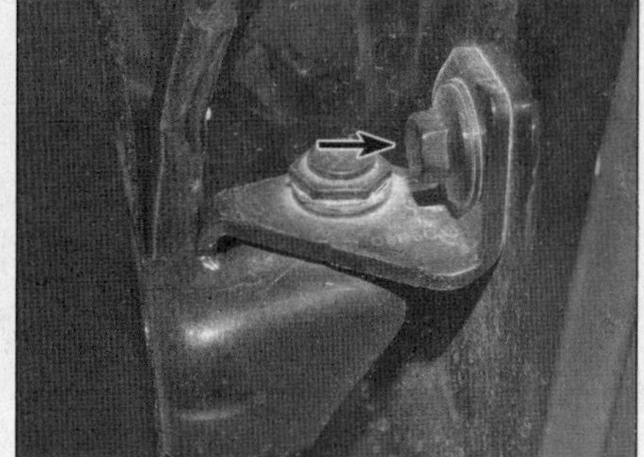

18.4 Remove the retaining bolts in the hinges

5 Remove the 2 retaining screws behind the door handle **(see illustration)**.
6 Remove the screw in the bottom of the door trim panel **(see illustration)**.
7 Using a trim removal tool, and working around the edge of the panel, prise out the 7 door trim clips and remove the panel from place. **Note:** *It is likely that the clips will be reluctant to release. Be prepared for clip breakage.*

19.1 Prise the cover behind the door release handle

19.2 Undo the retaining screw behind the interior release handle

19.3 Lift up the cover for the door handle

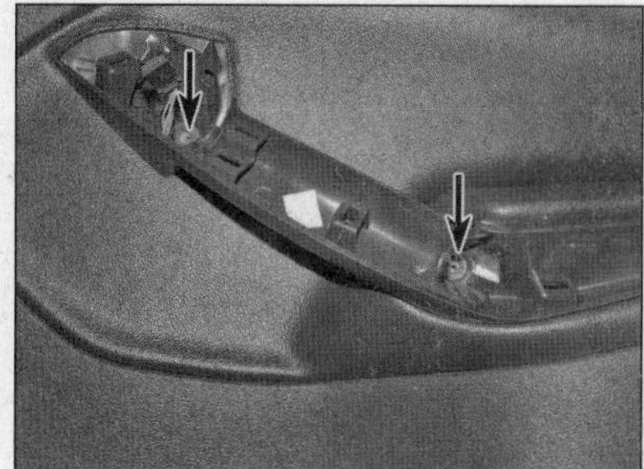

19.5 Undo the 2 screws behind the door handle

19.6 Remove the screw in the bottom of the door panel

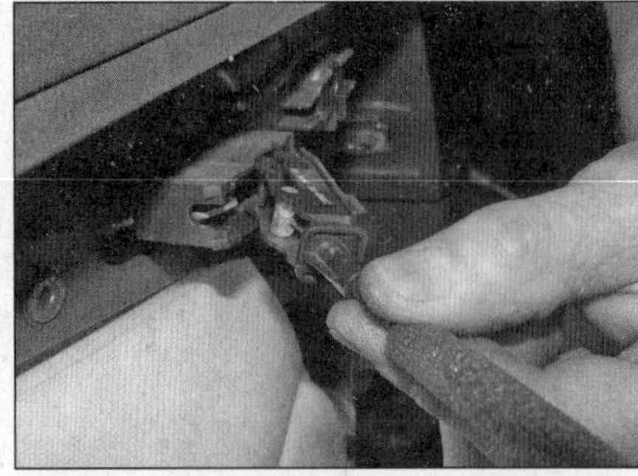
19.8 Disconnect the release cable and the wiring plugs

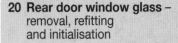

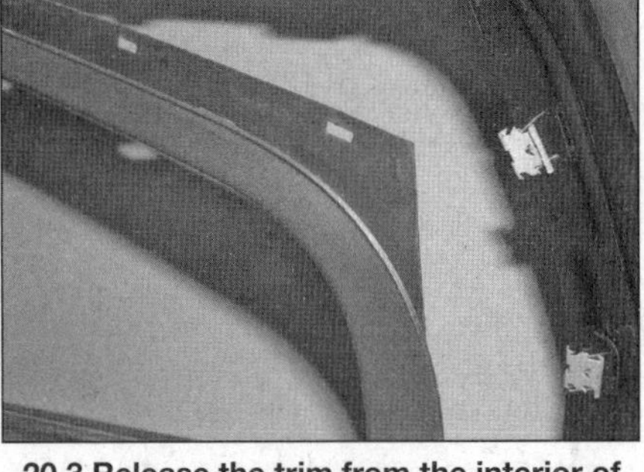
20.3 Release the trim from the interior of the window

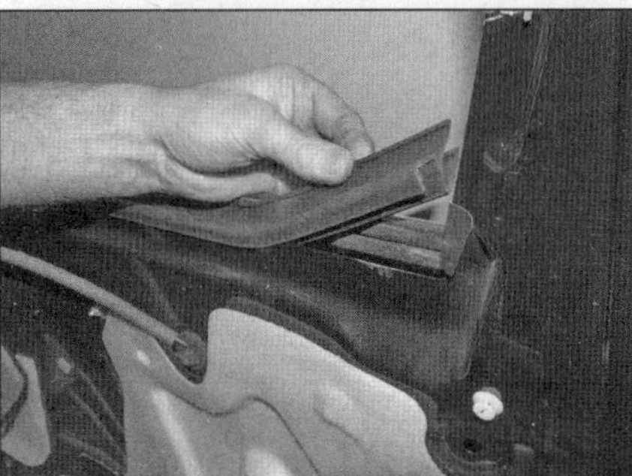
20.4 Lift up the interior weatherstrip

8 Disconnect the interior release handle cable and wiring plugs as the panel is withdrawn **(see illustration)**.

Refitting

9 Refitting is a reversal of the removal procedure.

20 Rear door window glass – removal, refitting and initialisation

Removal

1 Fully lower the window.
2 Remove the door inner trim panel as described in Section 13.
3 Unclip the interior window surround trim and manoeuvre it from place **(see illustration)**.
4 Prise up and remove the interior weather strip **(see illustration)**.
5 Undo the retaining bolts at the front and rear of the exterior weatherstrip **(see illustrations)**.
6 Gently prise the bottom of the rear window guide rubber from place **(see illustration)**.
7 Using a sharp knife, carefully cut through the sealant securing the waterproof membrane to the door frame **(see illustration)**.
8 Fold down the black sticky patch covering the hole in the centre of the door **(see illustration)**.
9 Reconnect the window switch and raise the window a third of the way up, to allow access to the bolts holding the glass to the regulator **(see illustration)**.
10 Undo the 3 screws that retain the rearmost exterior window trim and manoeuvre it from place **(see illustration)**.
11 Gently lift the window out through the window aperture **(see illustration)**.

Refitting

12 Slide the glass into position, ensuring the

20.5a Remove the front weatherstrip bolt...

20.5b ...and the rear bolt

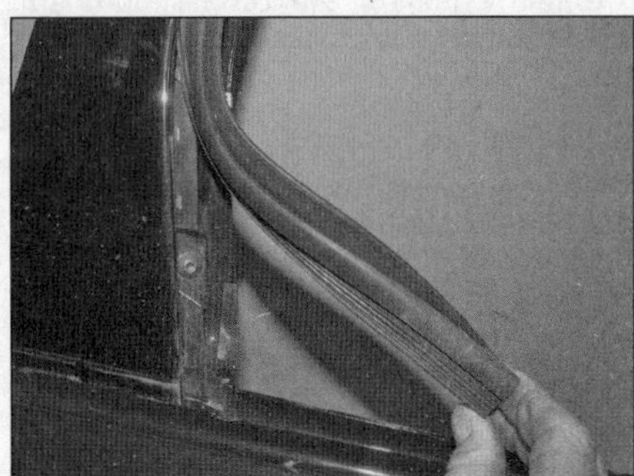

20.6 Prise out the bottom of the rearmost window guide rubber

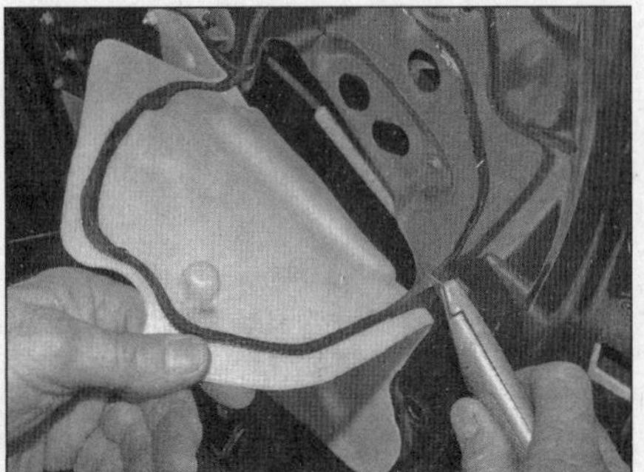
20.7 Gently cut away the waterproof membrane sealant

20.8 Fold the sticky patch out of the way

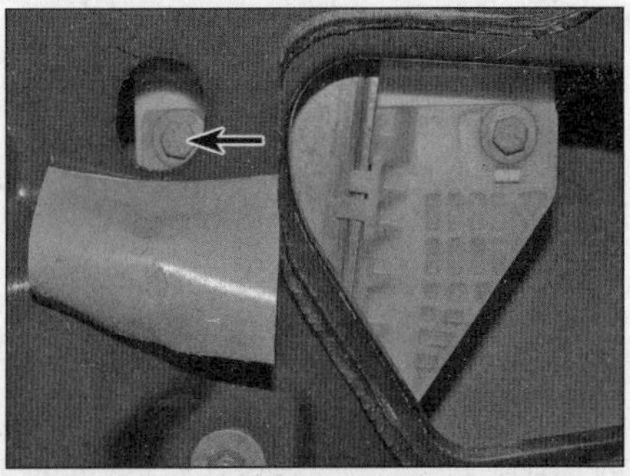

20.9 Raise the window to access the bolts and slacken them

20.10 Undo the screws and remove the outside trim

20.11 Lift the window out through its opening

21.3 Use tape to secure the glass

front and rear clips engage correctly with the regulator clamp(s).

13 The remainder of refitting is a reversal of removal.

Initialisation

14 Upon completion, the window initialisation procedure must be carried out:

a) Move the window to the fully open position. Press and hold the switch in the 'one-touch' open position for 15 to 25 seconds.

b) Fully close the window. Press and hold the switch in the 'one-touch' close position during the entire closing sequence.

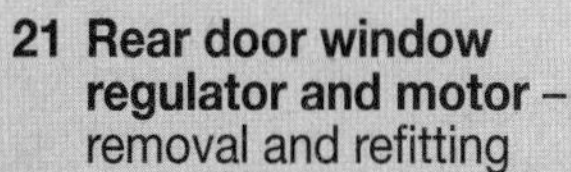

21 Rear door window regulator and motor – removal and refitting

Removal

1 Disconnect the window glass from the regulator as described in Section 14.

2 Connect the window electric motor wiring plug and raise the window glass fully.

3 Secure the window glass to the door frame using tape **(see illustration)**.

4 Remove the door speaker as described in Chapter 12 Section 22.

5 Reaching through the speaker aperture, disconnect the wiring plug for the regulator **(see illustration)**.

6 Undo the 2 retaining nuts and 1 bolt and manoeuvre the window regulator assembly from the door **(see illustration)**.

Refitting

7 Refitting is a reversal of the removal procedure. Upon completion, carry out the initialisation procedure as described in Section 20.

22 Rear door handle and lock components – removal and refitting

Exterior handle

Removal

1 Remove the interior door panel as described in Section 19.

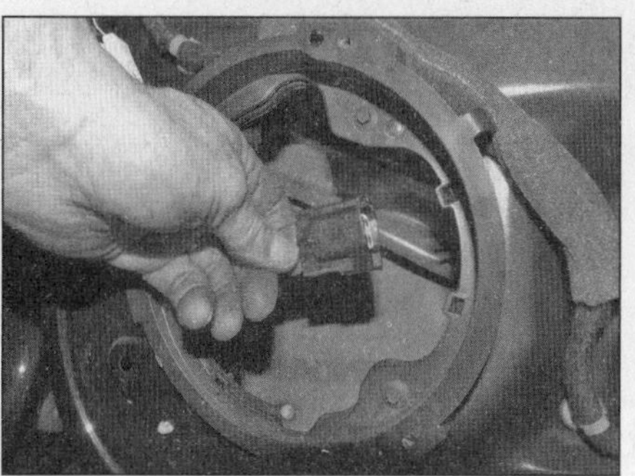
21.5 Disconnect the regulator wiring plug

21.6 Window regulator retaining bolt/nuts

2 Prise out the rubber cap from the rear edge of the door **(see illustration)**.

3 Using a Torx bit/key, slacken the retaining screw until the handle end trim can be pulled out from the door **(see illustrations)**.

4 Pull the exterior handle outwards/rearwards and manoeuvre it from the door **(see illustration)**.

5 Working inside the door, swivel the wiring connector for the door handle upwards and disconnect the plug **(see illustration)**.

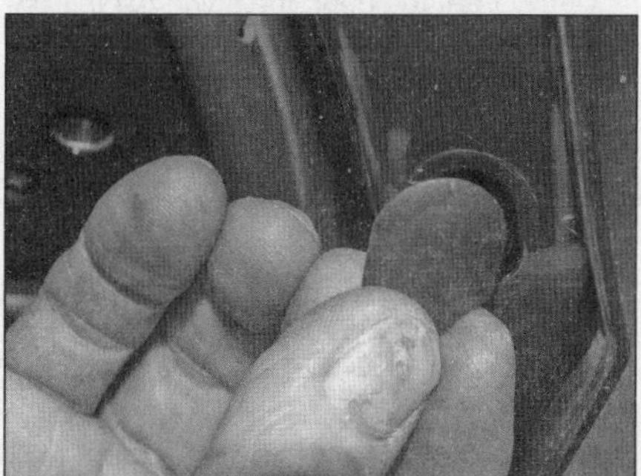
22.2 Remove the rubber cap from the rear edge of the door

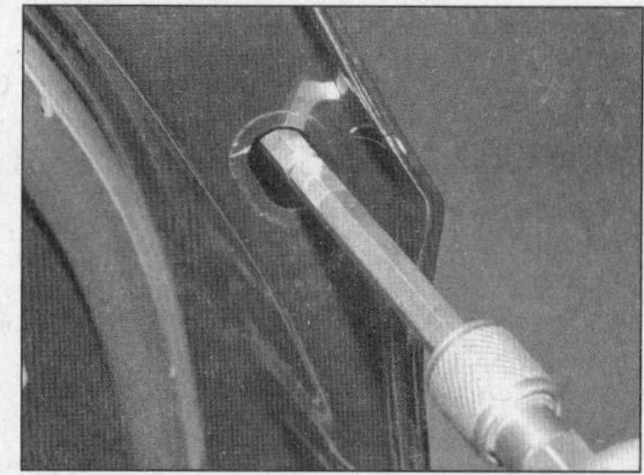
22.3a Slacken the screw...

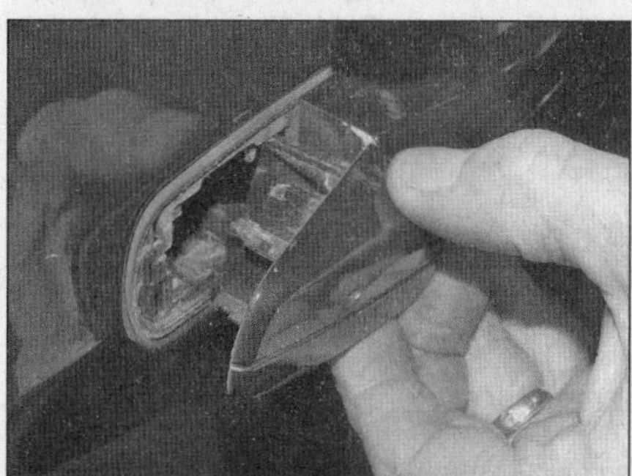
22.3b ...then pull away the end trim

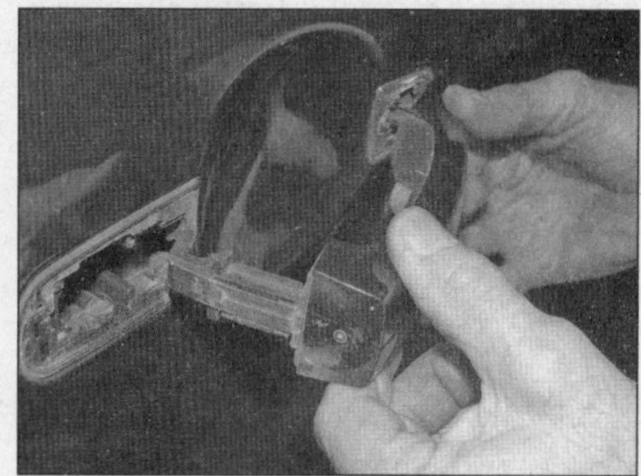
22.4 Slide the handle outwards and rearwards

22.5 Unplug the wiring connector inside the door handle

22.10 Remove the lock retaining screws

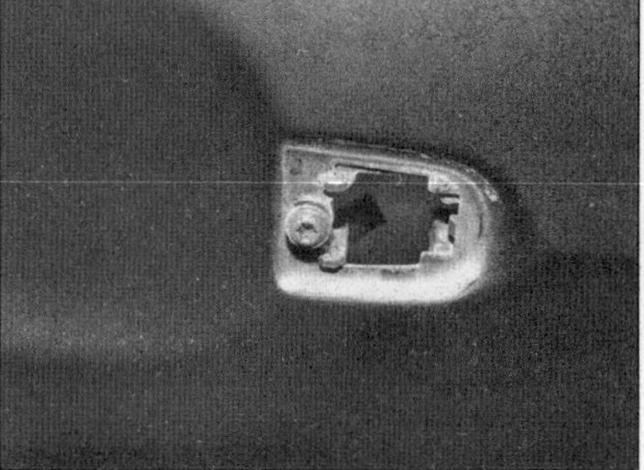

22.11 Remove the retaining screw on the door

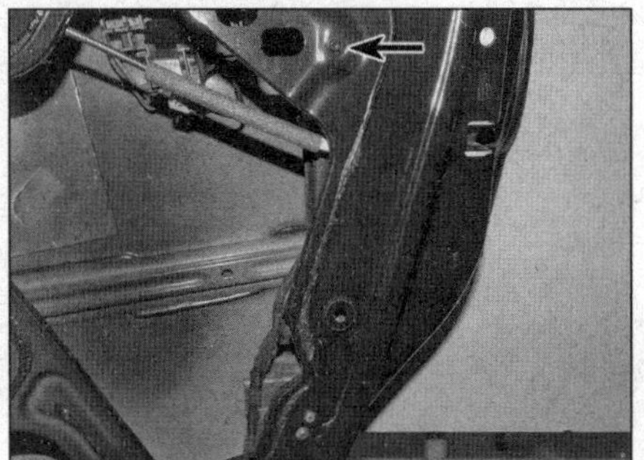

22.12 Remove the lock mechanism retaining bolt on the inside of the door

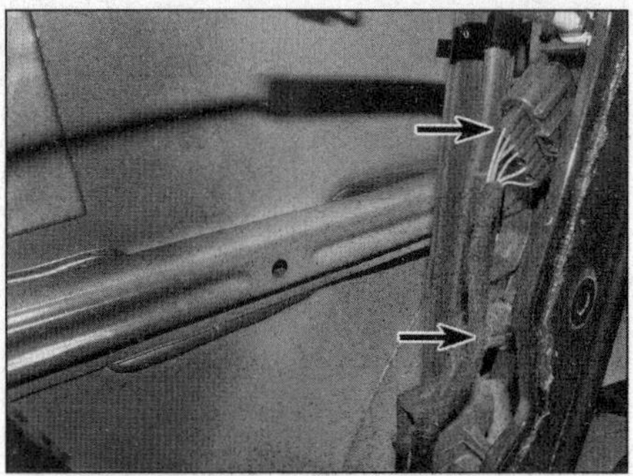

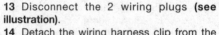

22.13 Disconnect the wiring plugs

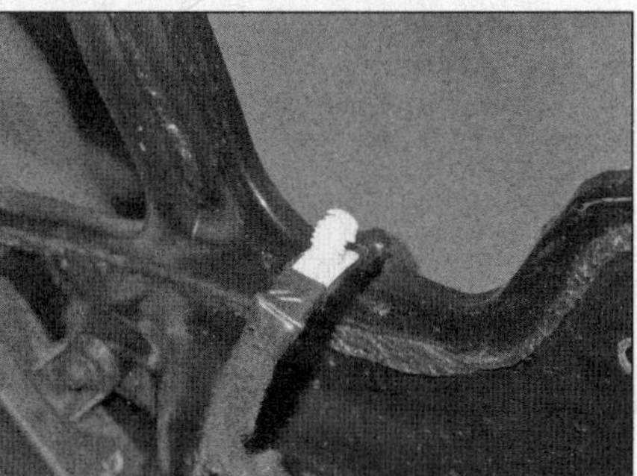

22.14 Unclip the wiring harness

Refitting

6 Reconnect the wiring plug, then swivel the connector 90° downwards.

7 Re-engage the front of the handle with the door then push the handle into place.

8 Replace the end trim and retighten the retaining screw.

Lock assembly

9 Remove the exterior door handle as previously described in this Section.

Note: *The lock and exterior handle frame must be removed as one.*

10 Undo the 3 lock retaining screws **(see illustration)**.

11 Undo the door handle frame retaining screw on the outside of the door **(see illustration)**.

12 Undo the retaining bolt on the inside of the door **(see illustration)**.

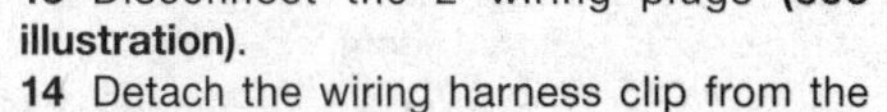

13 Disconnect the 2 wiring plugs **(see illustration)**.

14 Detach the wiring harness clip from the door **(see illustration)**.

15 Remove the handle frame and lock assembly from the door, threading the release cable through its opening.

16 If required, disconnect the interior release handle cable from the lock **(see illustration)**.

17 Refitting is a reversal of removal.

Striker

18 Using a pencil or correction fluid, mark the position of the striker on the pillar.

19 Remove the mounting screws using a Torx key, then remove the striker **(see illustration)**.

20 Refitting is a reversal of the removal procedure, but check that the door lock passes over the striker centrally. If necessary, reposition the striker before fully tightening the mounting screws.

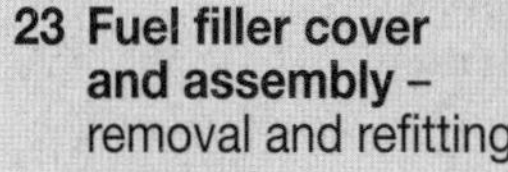

23 Fuel filler cover and assembly – removal and refitting

Filler cover

1 To remove the cover from the fuel filler, insert a screwdriver into the aperture and prise away the fuel filler cover **(see illustration)**.

2 Refitting is a reversal of removal.

Filler assembly

Note: *It is impossible to remove the fuel flap assembly without damaging it.*

3 Remove the fuel filler neck as desribed in Chapter 4B Section 10.

4 Use a knife to cut holes in the four notches indicated on the fuel flap assembly **(see illustration)**.

22.16 Separate the cable from the lock

22.19 Undo the screws and remove the striker

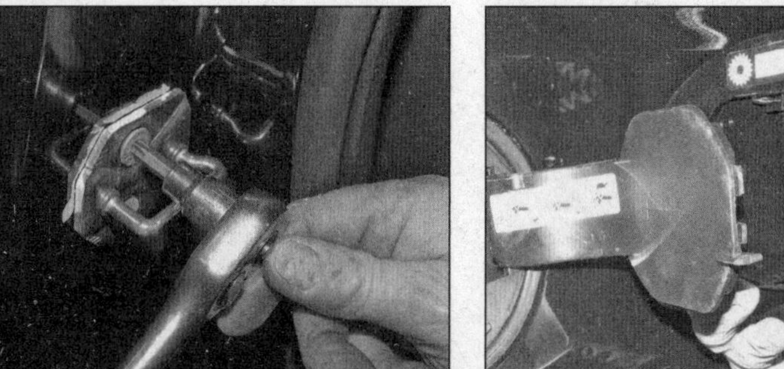

23.1 Use a screwdriver to prise off the filler cover

23.4 Make holes in the 4 notches

24.2 Remove the cover panel for the mirror

24.3 Disconnect the mirror wiring plug

24.4 Remove the 3 screws

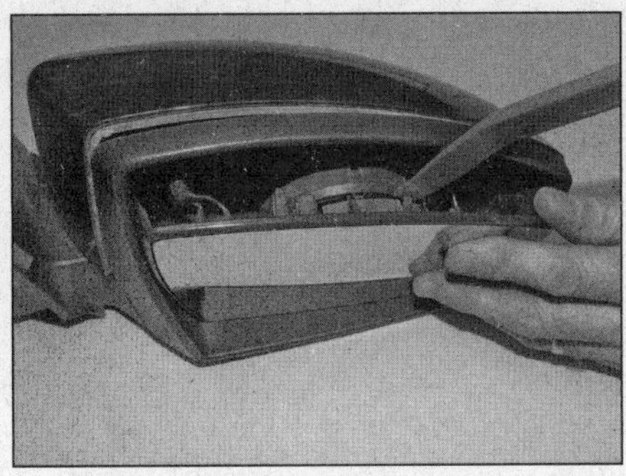
24.6 Prise away the upper edge of the glass

24.7 Disconnect the heated mirror wiring plugs

5 Insert a screwdriver into each hole and prise the fuel flap assembly from place.

6 Rotate the fuel flap assembly to remove it from the car.

24 Exterior mirror and components – removal and refitting

Removal

Complete mirror housing

1 Remove the door inner panel as described in Section 13.

2 Prise off the interior mirror cover panel **(see illustration)**.

3 Disconnect the wiring plug **(see illustration)**.

4 Undo the 3 retaining Torx screws and withdraw the mirror housing **(see illustration)**.

5 Refitting is a reversal of the removal procedure.

Mirror glass

Warning: In case of mirror glass breakage, we recommend gloves and suitable eye protection are worn.

6 Press the inner/lower of the mirror glass into the housing, then use a flat-bladed tool to carefully prise the upper edge of the mirror glass from the retaining clips **(see illustration)**.

7 Withdraw the mirror glass and disconnect the wiring plugs for the heated mirrors **(see illustration)**.

8 Refitting is a reversal of the removal procedure.

Mirror housing cover

9 Remove the mirror glass as previously described in this Section.

10 Using a small flat-bladed screwdriver, release the 2 retaining clips and slide the cover forwards from the housing **(see illustration)**.

11 Refitting is a reversal of the removal procedure.

Puddle light lens

12 Remove the mirror glass as described in this Section.

13 Pull the bulbholder from place **(see illustration)**.

14 Depress the clip and release the light lens **(see illustration)**.

15 Refitting is a reversal of the removal procedure.

Indicator repeater lens

16 Remove the mirror glass and body-coloured mirror shroud as described earlier in this Section.

24.10 Release the clips and slide the housing cover forwards

24.13 Pull the bulbholder from place

24.14 Depress the clip to release the lens

24.18 Remove the bulbholder from place

24.19a Squeeze the tab to free the lens...

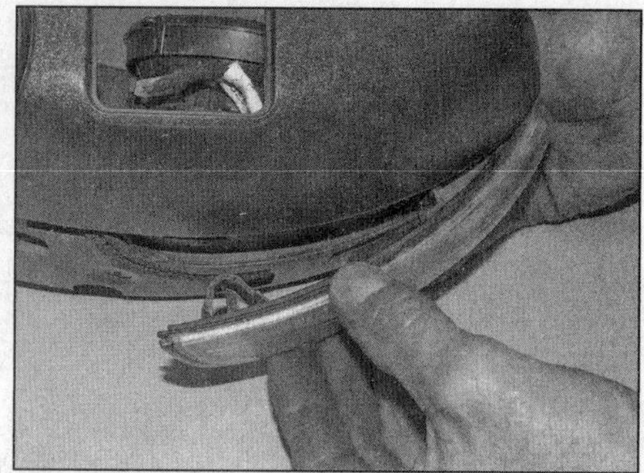
24.19b ...then pull the lens from place

24.22 Unscrew the screw

24.23 Release the tabs to free the motor

24.24 Prise open the clips to release the plug

17 Remove the puddle light glass as described earlier in this Section.

18 Twist and pull the indicator bulbholder from place **(see illustration)**.

19 Reaching up through the puddle light glass area, depress the retaining tab and manoeuvre the repeater lens from place **(see illustrations)**.

20 Refitting is a reversal of the removal procedure.

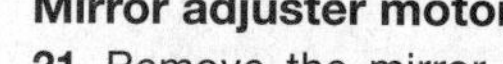

Mirror adjuster motor

21 Remove the mirror glass as described earlier in this Section.

22 Undo the central retaining screw from the mirror motor **(see illustration)**.

23 Squeeze the three tabs around the outside of the motor and pull from place **(see illustration)**.

24 Release the clips and disconnect the wiring plug **(see illustration)**.

25 Refitting is a reversal of the removal procedure.

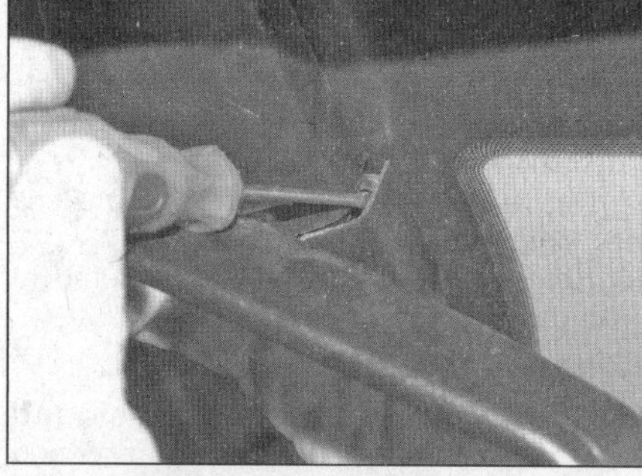
25.1a Prise off the lower half of the interior mirror base cover...

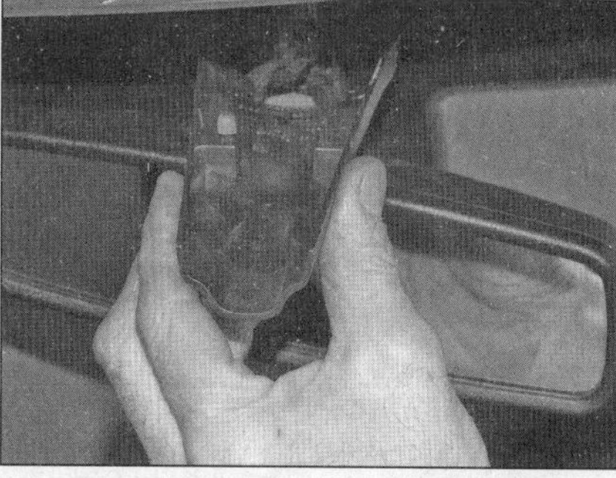

25.1b ...followed by the upper half

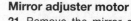

25 Interior mirror – removal and refitting

1 Separate the two halves of the mirror cover **(see illustrations)**.

2 Disconnect the wiring plugs for the mirror dimmer, GPS antenna and rain sensor and move the wires out of the way **(see illustrations)**.

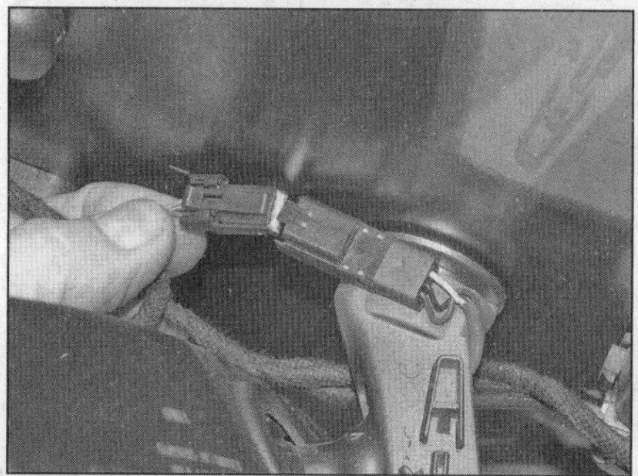
25.2a Disconnect the mirror dimmer...

25.2b ...then the radio antenna...

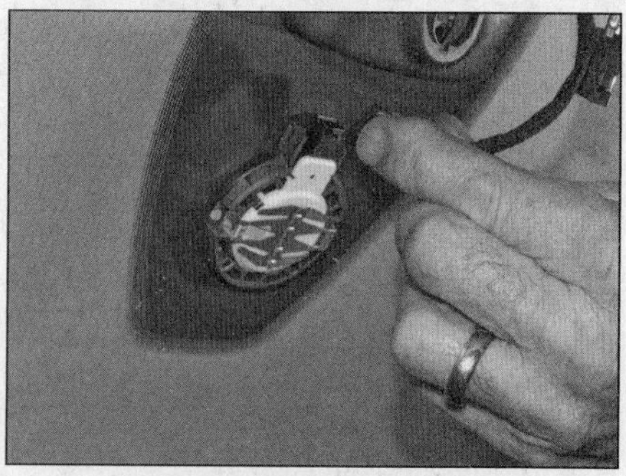
25.2c ...and the rain sensor

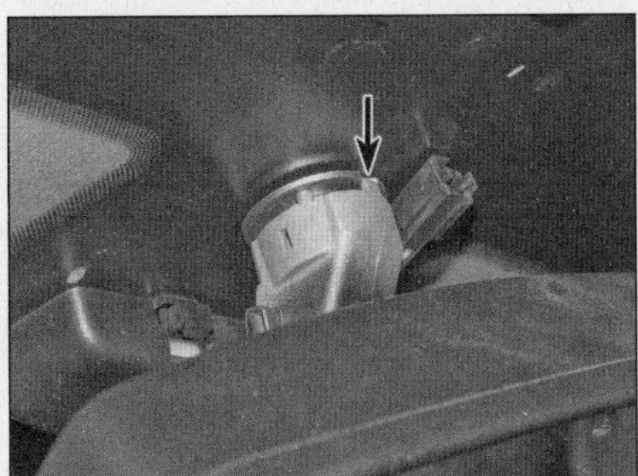
25.3a Carefully prise down the mirror mounting...

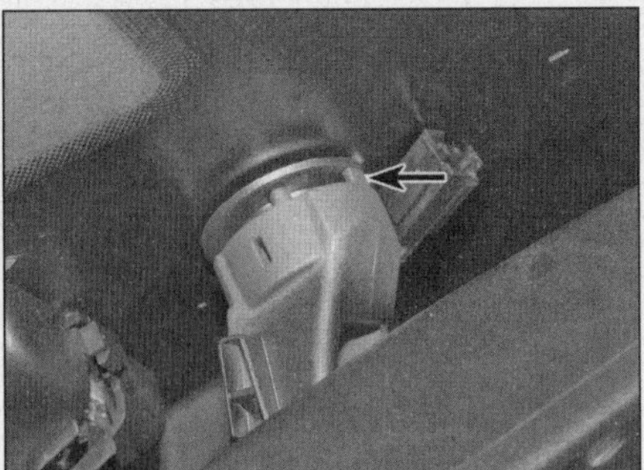
25.3b ...then rotate it anti-clockwise

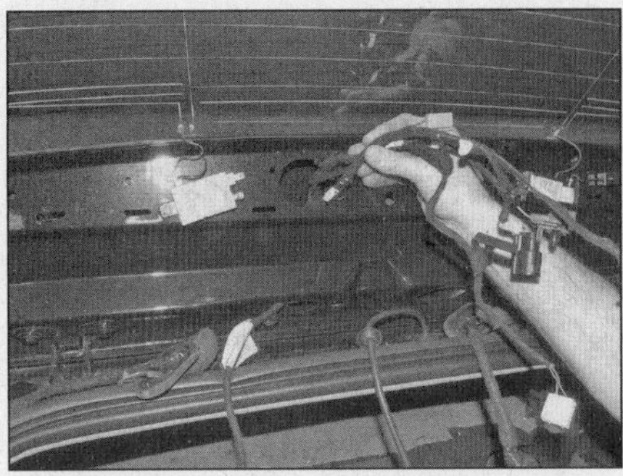
26.3a Disconnect all wiring plugs and unclip the loom...

3 Gently prise down the mirror mounting so that the tab clears the housing, then rotate the whole housing anti-clockwise **(see illustrations)**.

4 Refitting is a reversal of removal.

26 Tailgate – removal and refitting

Removal

1 Remove the interior trim panels as descrtibed in Section 35.

2 Remove the high-level brake light as described in Chapter 12 Section 9.

3 Disconnect all wiring plugs and remove both sides of the wiring loom from place, removing each rubber grommet and threading them through the apertures at the top of the tailgate **(see illustrations)**.

Note: *Do not allow the tailgate to fully close at this point, because the microswitch for the tailgate release is disconnected, so opening the tailgate will be impossible.*

4 Disconnect the hydraulic support struts from the tailgate as described in Section 27.

5 Mark the position of the tailgate hinges, then remove the mounting bolts **(see illustration)**.

Caution: Have an assistant support the tailgate during this procedure.

6 Remove the tailgate, being careful not to damage the paint.

26.3b ...and thread it through the openings at the top of the tailgate

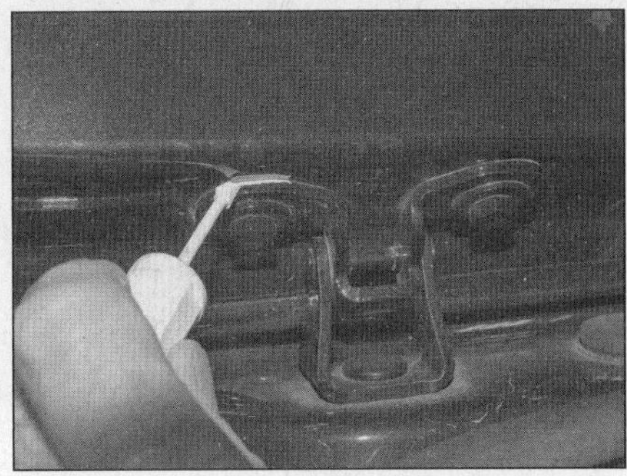
26.5 Mark the tailgate hinge positions, then undo the bolts

Refitting

7 Refitting is a reversal of the removal procedure, but check that the tailgate is located centrally in the body aperture, and that the striker enters the lock centrally. If necessary, loosen the mounting nuts and reposition the tailgate as required.

27 Support struts – removal and refitting

Tailgate

1 Have an assistant support the tailgate in its open position.

2 Slide off the spring clips securing the strut to the tailgate/bonnet/split door, then pull the sockets from the ball-studs **(see illustrations)**.

3 Refitting is a reversal of the removal procedure, making sure that the strut is fitted the same way up as it was removed.

28 Tailgate lock components – removal and refitting

Lock release button

1 Remove the tailgate inner trim panel as described in Section 35.

2 To ease access, undo the retaining bolts and remove the tailgate damper **(see illustration)**.

27.2a Prise off the support strut spring clip

27.2b Lever the strut off the ball-stud

28.2 Unbolt the tailgate damper

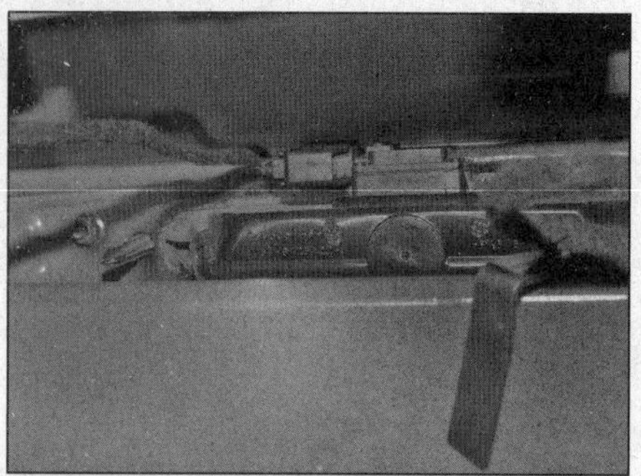
28.3 Disconnect the release switch wiring plug

28.9 Undo the 3 screws and remove the lock assembly

3 Disconnect the wiring plug for the tailgate release button **(see illustration)**.
4 Using a small screwdriver, depress the retaining tabs and manoeuvre the switch from place **(see illustration)**.
5 Gently ease the button from place.
6 Refitting is a reversal of removal.

Lock/latch assembly

7 Remove the tailgate lower trim panel as described in Section 35.
8 To ease access, loosen the 2 retaining bolts and move the tailgate damper assembly to one side **(see illustration 28.2)**.
9 Make alignment marks between the lock bracket and the vehicle body to aid installation, then remove the 3 Torx screws and remove the lock assembly **(see illustration)**.
10 Disconnect the wiring plug from the hatch lock assembly.

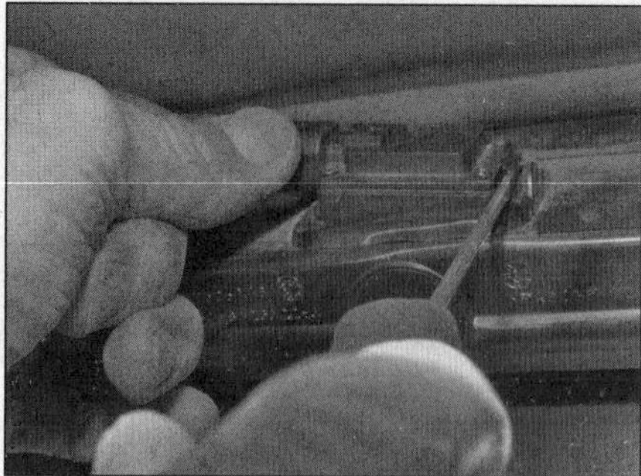
28.4 Depress the tabs and release the switch

11 Refitting is a reversal of the removal procedure.

29 Central locking system components – removal and refitting

Removal

Control unit

1 The central locking function of the vehicle is controlled by the BDC (Body Domain Controller). Removal and refitting of the BDC is described in Chapter 12 Section 28.

Door motors

2 The door lock motor is integral with the door lock. Removal of the door lock is described in Section 16.

Tailgate motor

3 The motor is integral with the tailgate lock. Removal of the lock is described in Section 28.

Refitting

4 In all cases, refitting is a reversal of the removal procedure.

30 Windscreen and fixed windows – removal and refitting

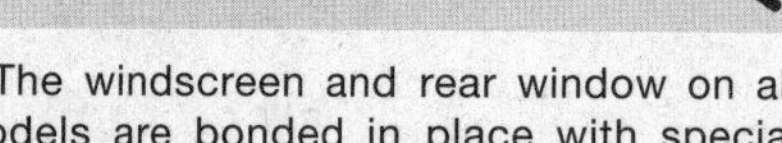

1 The windscreen and rear window on all models are bonded in place with special mastic, as are the rear side windows (where appicable). Special tools are required to cut free the old units and fit replacements; special cleaning solutions and primer are also required. It is therefore recommended that this work is entrusted to a Ford dealer or windscreen replacement specialist.

31 Body exterior fittings – removal and refitting

Front grille

Removal

1 Remove the front bumper cover as described in Section 5.
2 Release the 8 clips at the rear, and the 6 along the top of the grille **(see illustrations)**.
3 Undo the bolt at each end on the top surface of the grille panel **(see illustration)**.
4 Carefully manoeuvre the grille forwards.

Refitting

5 Refitting is a reversal of removal.

32 Sunroof – general information and initialisation

General information

1 Due to the complexity of the sunroof mechanism, considerable expertise is needed to repair, renew or adjust the sunroof components successfully. Removal of the roof first requires the headlining to be removed, which is a complex and tedious operation, and not a task to be undertaken lightly. Therefore, any problems with the sunroof should be referred to a Ford dealer or specialist.
2 The water drain tubes are located at each corner of the sunroof aperture, and are permanently integrated into the vehicle body, and cannot be placed individually.

Initialisation

3 With the battery reconnected, and ignition on, press the sunroof operating switch into the 'tilt' position and hold it there.

31.2a Release the 8 clips behind the grille...

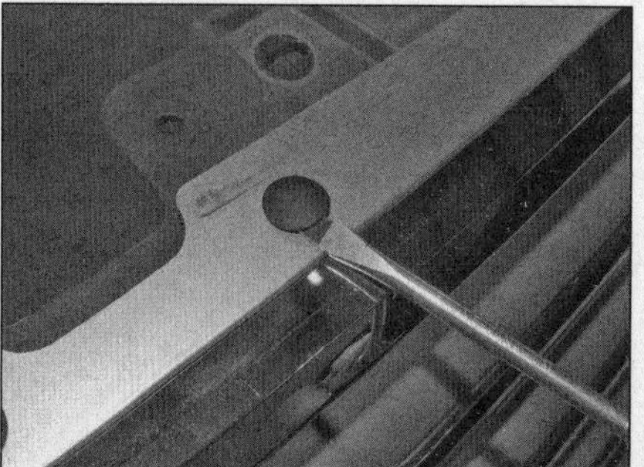
31.2b ...then the 6 along the top surface

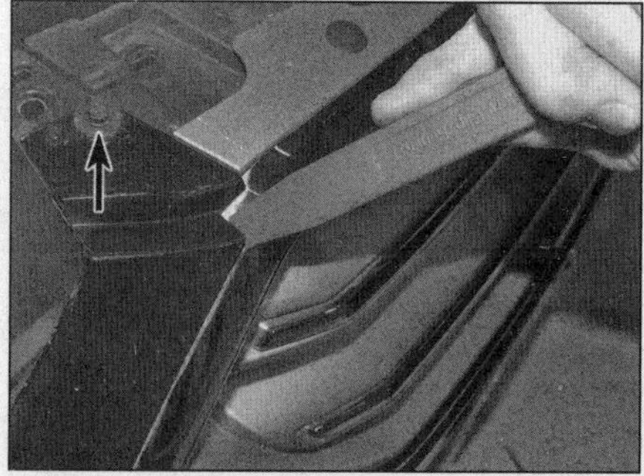
31.3 Remove the 2 bolts on the top of the grille

33.3 Remove the trim caps covering the bolts

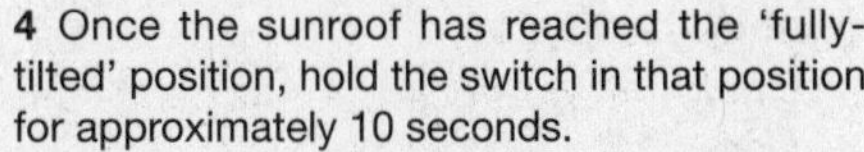

4 Once the sunroof has reached the 'fully-tilted' position, hold the switch in that position for approximately 10 seconds.
5 Close the sunroof and hold the switch in that position for approximately 10 seconds.
6 Check for correct function of the sunroof.

33 Seats – removal and refitting

Removal

Front seat

1 Disconnect the battery, as described in Chapter 5 Section 4.

Warning: Wait a minimum of 5 minutes, as a precaution against accidental firing of the airbag unit. This period ensures that any stored energy is dissipated.

2 Slide the seat fully rearwards.
3 Prise up the caps for the front retaining bolts **(see illustration)**.
4 Undo the two front seat rail bolts **(see illustration)**.
5 Slide the seat fully forwards, then prise off the covers for the two rear seat rail bolts **(see illustration)**.
6 Slacken the 2 rear retaining bolts and remove **(see illustration)**.
7 Tilt the seat backwards, and disconnect the various seat wiring multi-plugs from the seat base, noting their fitted positions **(see illustration)**. Remove the seat from the vehicle.
Note: *The head restraint will have to be fully lowered for the seat to be manoeuvred through the door aperture.*

33.4 Remove the front 2 retaining bolts

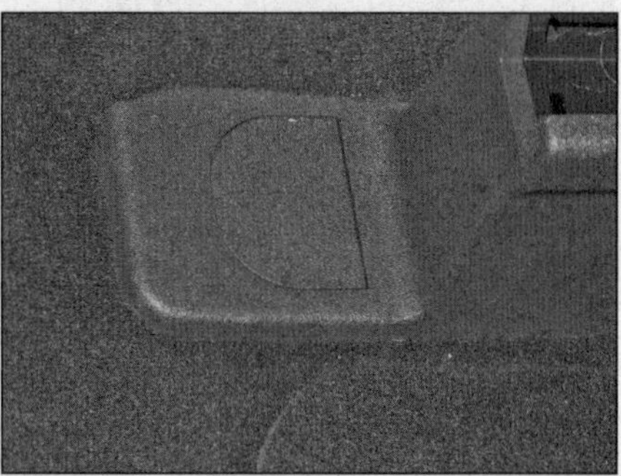

33.5 Prise up the caps for the retaining bolts

Rear seats

8 Remove the parcel shelf.
9 Remove the boot carpet and floor.
10 Prise up the retaining clips for the covers over the lower seat mounting bolts and remove **(see illustration)**.
11 Pull up and remove the folding trim behind the rear seats **(see illustration)**.
12 Undo the rearmost retaining bolts **(see illustration)**.
13 Undo the front retaining bolts **(see illustration)**.
14 Lift up the rear seat cushion, and undo the 2 mounting bolts **(see illustration)**.
15 Disconnect the seatbelt wiring plug **(see illustration)**.
16 Undo the retaining bolts and manoeuvre the seat from place.

33.6 Undo the 2 rear seat retaining bolts

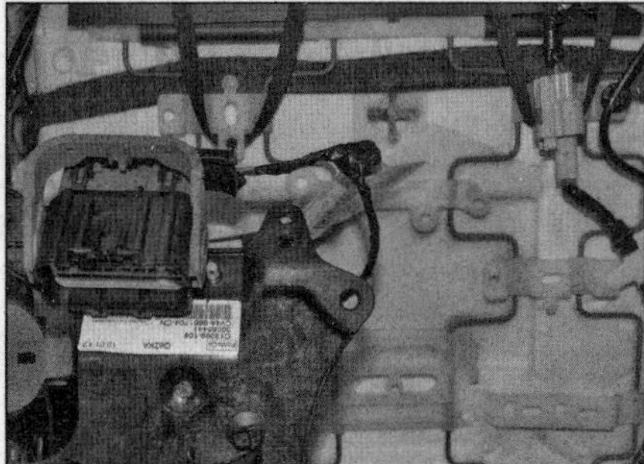

33.7 Disconnect the wiring plugs from the seat

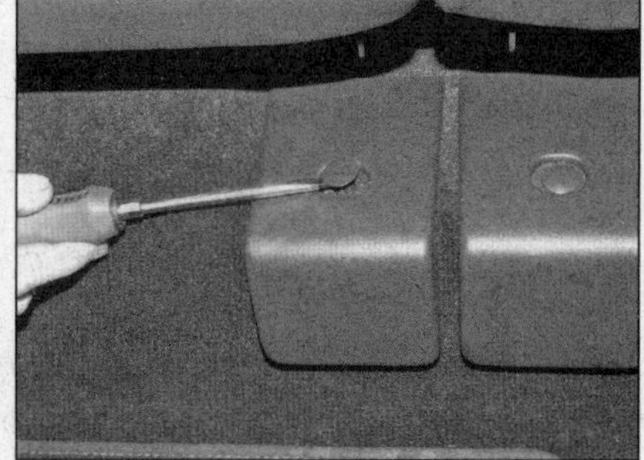

33.10 Remove the mounting bolt cover trims

33.11 Remove the foldable trim

33.12 Undo the front retaining bolts

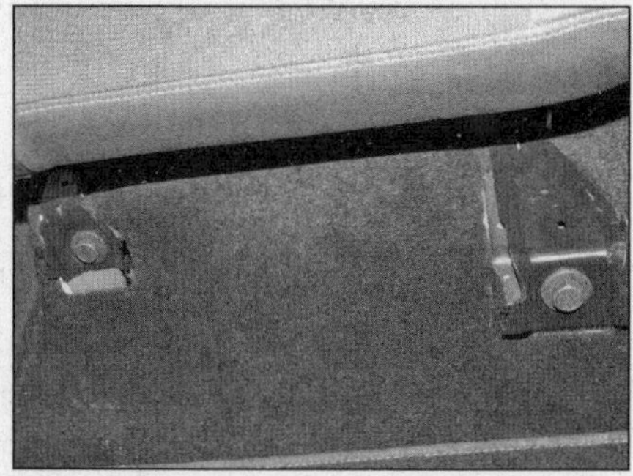

33.13 Remove the rear mounting bolts

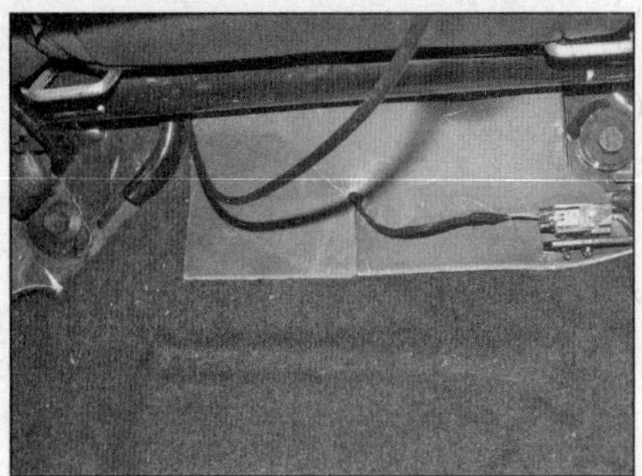

33.14 Undo the mounting bolts

33.15 Disconnect the seatbelt wiring plug

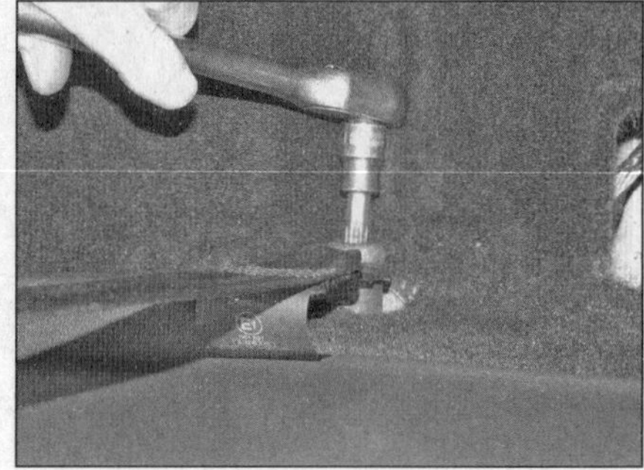

34.4 Remove the lower seat belt anchorage bolt

Refitting

17 Refitting is a reversal of the removal procedure, making sure all bolts are tightened to the required torque, and that the seatbelt stalks are positioned up through the seat where necessary.

34 Seat belts – removal and refitting

Warning: Be careful when handling the seat belt tensioning device, it contains a small explosive charge (pyrotechnic device) similar to the one used to deploy the airbag(s). Clearly, injury could be caused if these are released in an uncontrolled fashion. Once fired, the tensioner cannot be reset, and must be renewed. Note also that seat belts and

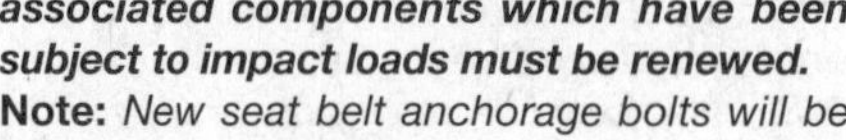

associated components which have been subject to impact loads must be renewed.

Note: *New seat belt anchorage bolts will be required upon reassembly.*

Removal – front seat belt

1 Disconnect the battery negative lead as described in Chapter 5 Section 4.

2 Remove the relevant front seat as described in Section 33.

3 Remove the upper and lower B-pillar trim panels as described in Section 35.

4 Undo the seat belt lower anchorage bolt **(see illustration)**.

5 Undo the bolt and remove the seat belt from the adjuster **(see illustration)**.

6 Undo the retaining bolt, then manoeuvre the inertia reel and seat belt from place **(see illustration)**.

7 Unlock and disconnect the inertia reel wiring plug **(see illustration)**.

Seat belt adjuster

8 Remove the seat belt as described in this Section.

9 Remove the mounting bolt from the top of the adjuster assembly **(see illustration)**.

10 Rotate the entire adjuster 90 degrees anti-clockwise to disengage it from the B-pillar **(see illustration)**.

Removal – rear seat belt

11 Disconnect the battery negative lead as described in Chapter 5 Section 4.

Outer belts

12 Fold forward the rear seat backrest.

13 Remove the luggage compartment side trim panel as described in Section 35.

14 Remove the luggage compartment upper side trim panel as described in Section 35.

15 Undo the lower seat belt anchorage bolt **(see illustration)**.

34.5 Slacken the bolt to remove the seat belt from the adjuster

34.6 Undo the retaining bolt to remove the inertia reel

34.7 Prise up the lock to disconnect the wiring plug

34.9 Undo the mounting bolt and remove

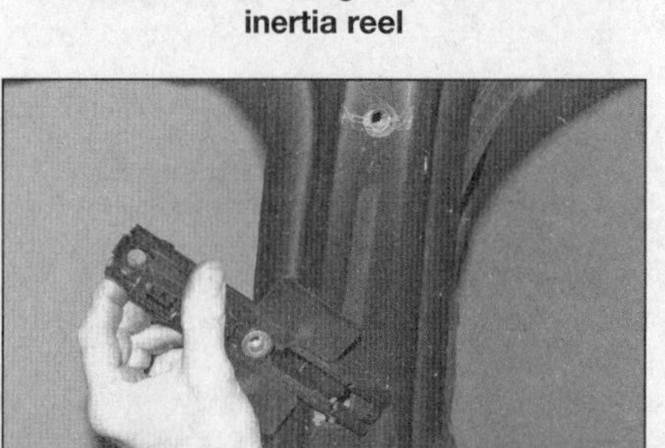

34.10 Turn the adjuster towards the front of the car to release it

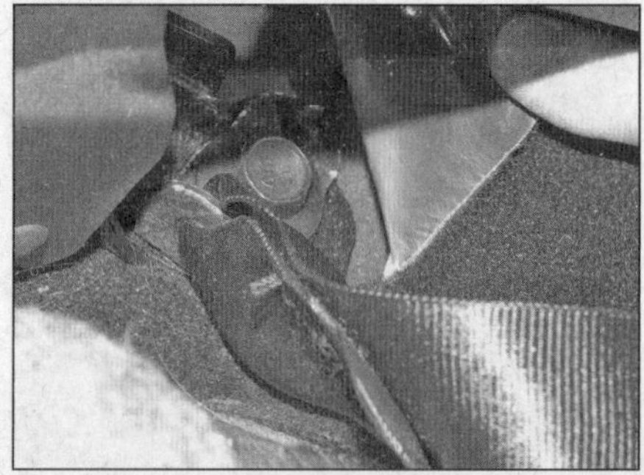

34.15 Undo the seat belt lower anchorage bolt

16 Undo the bolt and remove the inertia reel **(see illustration)**.

Rear centre belt

Caution: Removal of the centre belt involves releasing and refitting a section of the backrest upholstery. We recommend this is left to a Ford dealer or suitable specialist.

Refitting

17 Refitting is a reversal of the removal procedure, noting the following points:

a) *Use a little thread-locking compound, and tighten the new mounting bolts to the specified torque.*

b) *Make sure the seat belt reel locating dowel is correctly positioned.*

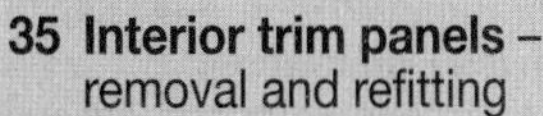

35 Interior trim panels – removal and refitting

Note: *This section covers the removal and installation of the interior trim panels. It may be necessary to remove an overlapping trim before you can remove the one required. For more information on trim removal, look at relevant Chapters and Sections, where the trims may need to be removed to carry out any other procedures (eg, to remove the steering column you will need to remove the shrouds).*

Removal

Sun visor

1 Remove the A-pillar and B-pillar trims, as described later in this Section.

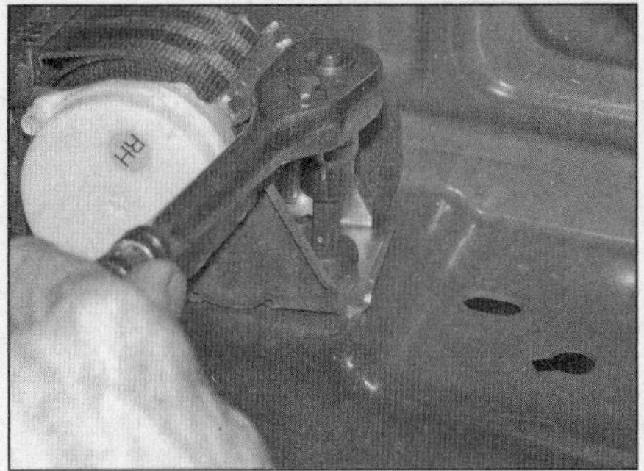

34.16 Undo the bolt to remove the inertia reel

2 Prise down the covers, then unscrew the mounting screws **(see illustrations)**.

3 Lower the corresponding corner of the headlining to allow access to the vanity mirror wiring plug, and disconnect the plug **(see illustration)**.

Grab handle

4 Prise open the covers, then undo the retaining screws and remove the grab handle **(see illustrations)**. **Note:** *The spring to keep the grab handle raised is attached to only the rearmost mount, which will snap shut as it is removed from the rooflining.*

A-pillar trim

5 Disconnect the battery negative lead as described in Chapter 5 Section 4.

6 Carefully pull the trim inwards from place **(see illustrations)**. Disconnect the speaker wiring plug as the trim panel is withdrawn.

B-pillar trim

Lower pillar trim

7 Remove the front and rear door sill trim panels as described later in this Section.

8 Pull the lower B-pillar trim panel inwards to release the retaining clips **(see illustration)**.

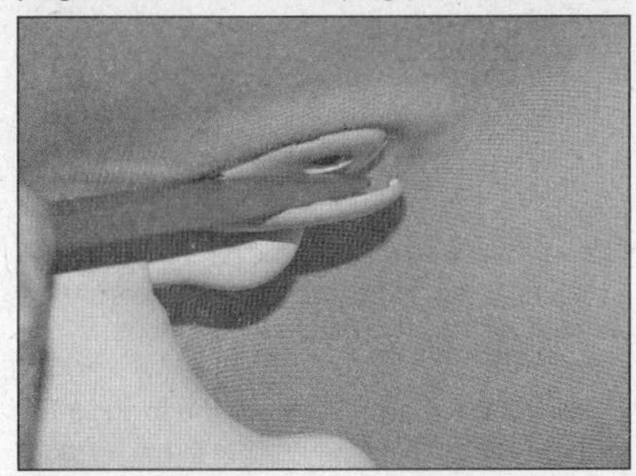

35.2a Prise down the cover to expose the sunvisor mounting screw...

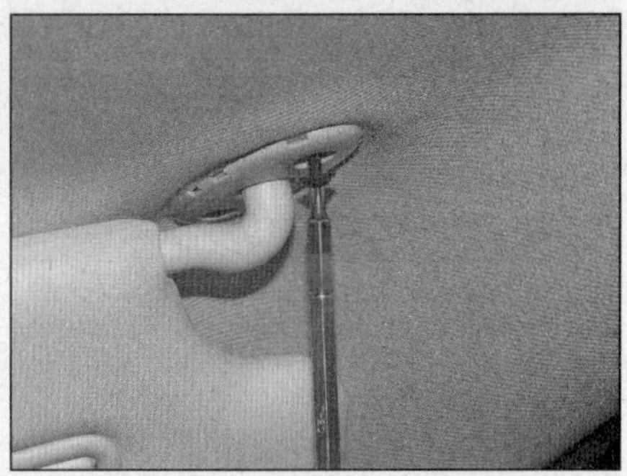

35.2b ...then undo the screw

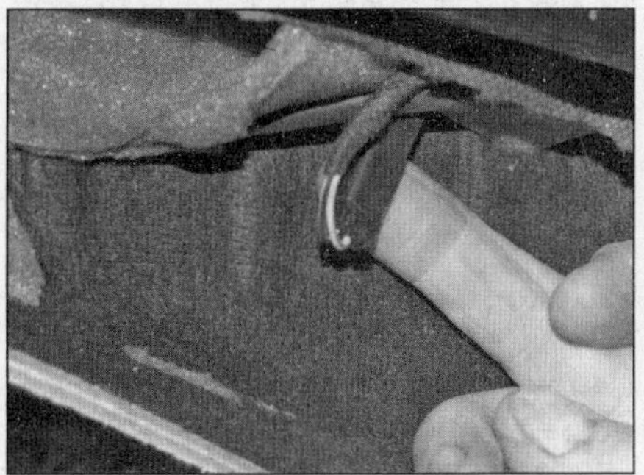

35.3 Lower the headlining and disconnect the wiring plug

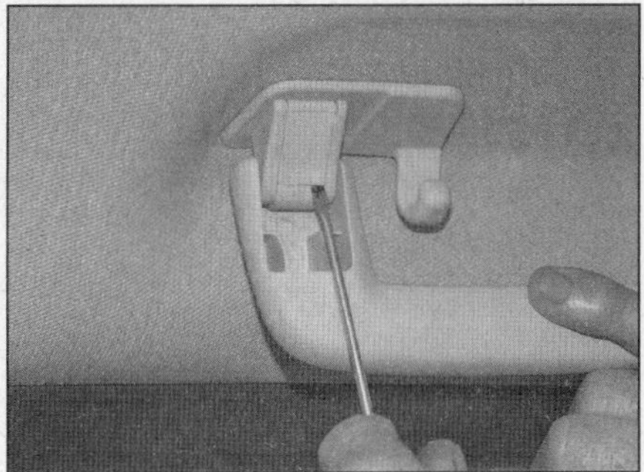

35.4a Prise open the covers...

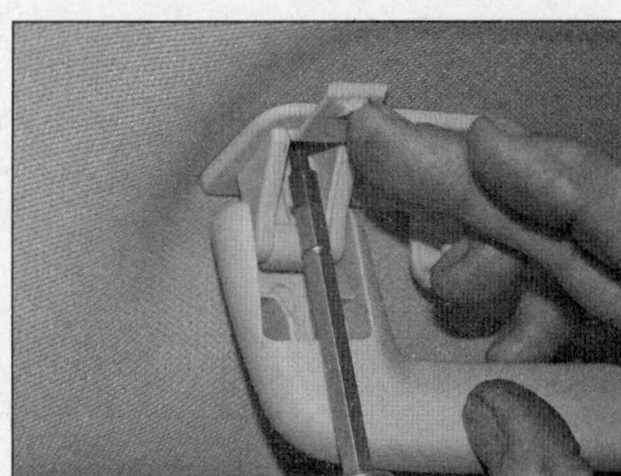

35.4b ...then remove the retaining screws

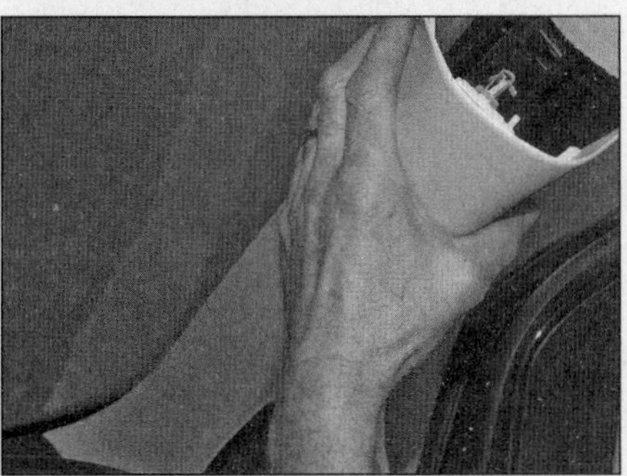

35.6a Pull the panel inwards to release...

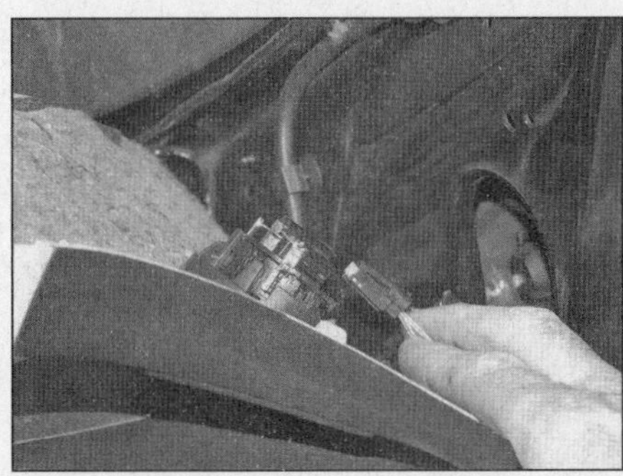

35.6b ...and disconnect the speaker wiring plug

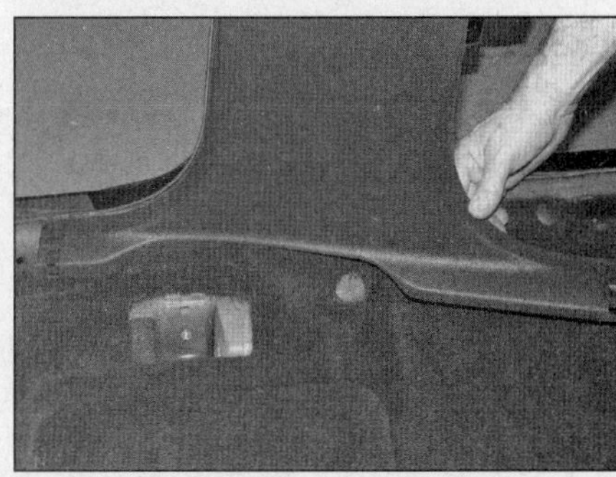

35.8 Pull the trim panel inwards to release it

35.10a Undo the retaining bolt...

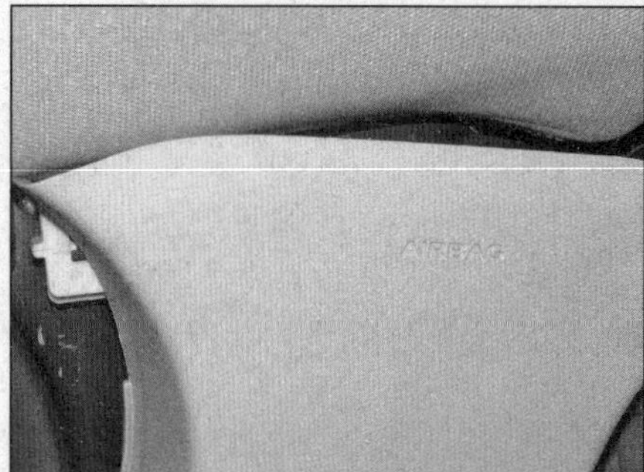

35.10b ...then pull the top of the panel to the rear to disengage

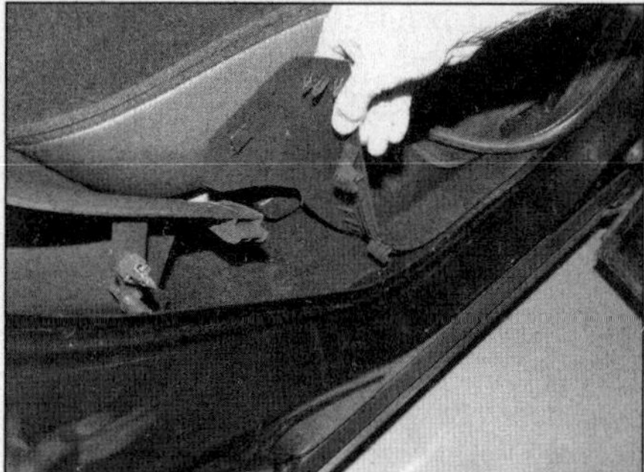

35.11 Prise up the sill trim

35.15 Prise up the tailgate top trim panel

Upper pillar trim

9 Remove the lower B-pillar trim panel as described previously in this Section.

35.16 Prise up and remove the corner panels

10 Undo the retaining bolt at the lower edge of the upper panel, then pull the panel towards the rear of the car to disengage it from the headlining **(see illustrations)**.

C-pillar trim

11 Using a trim removal tool, prise up the rear door sill trim **(see illustration)**.

12 Remove the luggage compartment side trim, as described later in this Section.

13 Remove the luggage compartment upper side trim as described later in this Section.

14 Pull the C-pillar trim inwards to release it from the retaining clips.

Tailgate trim

15 Using a trim removal tool, prise up the trim along the top of the tailgate window **(see illustration)**.

16 Using a trim removal tool, prise up the left and right upper corner panels, depress the tab when it becomes available **(see illustration)**.

17 Use a flat-bladed tool to remove the cover for the tailgate grab handle **(see illustration)**.

18 Undo the 2 retaining screws and remove the handle from place **(see illustrations)**.

19 Using a flat-bladed trim tool prise the main tailgate trim panel away from the tailgate. Disconnect any wiring plugs as they become accessible **(see illustration)**.

20 Remove the high-level brake light assembly as described in Chapter 12 Section 9.

Luggage compartment trim panels

Tailgate striker panel trim

21 Undo the 2 retaining screws and prise out the 2 retaining clips **(see illustrations)**.

22 Manoeuvre the panel from place.

Luggage compartment side panels

23 Lift out the luggage compartment floor

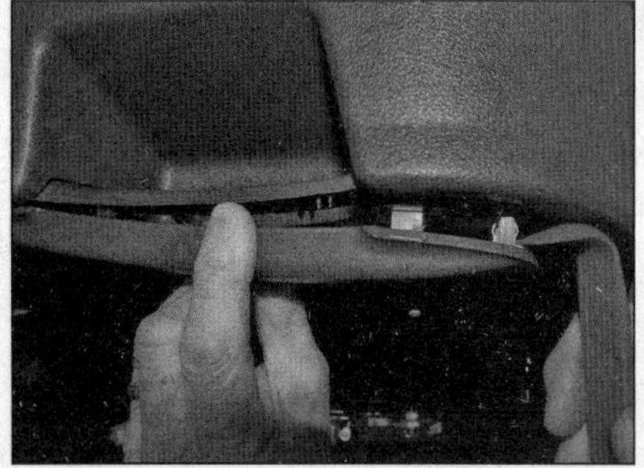

35.17 Remove the grab handle cover

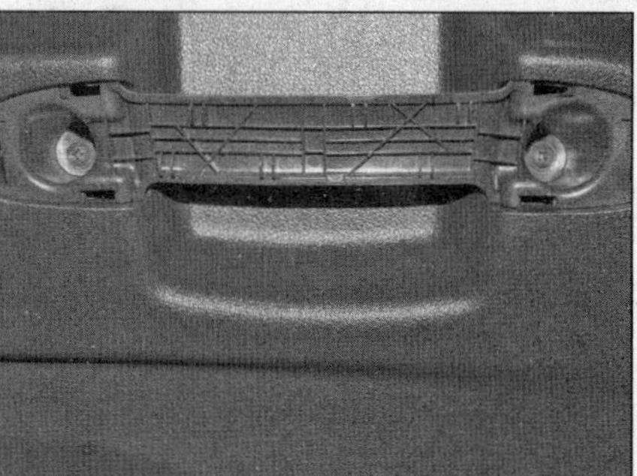

35.18a Undo the screws...

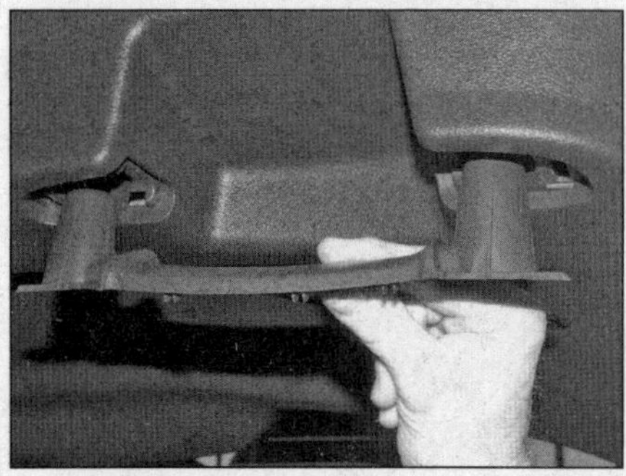

35.18b ...then remove the handle

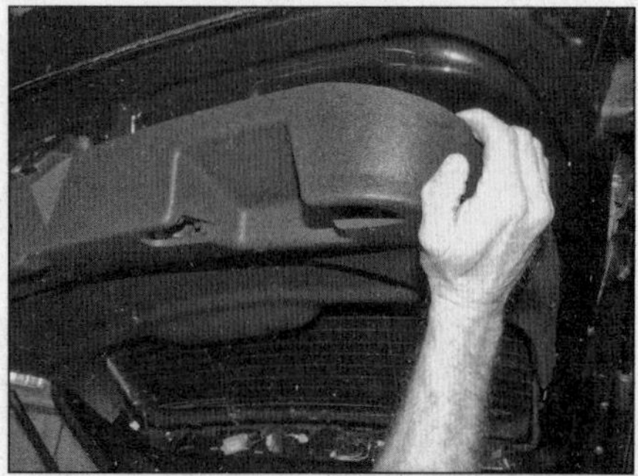

35.19 Gently prise away the panel

35.21a Undo the 2 screws...

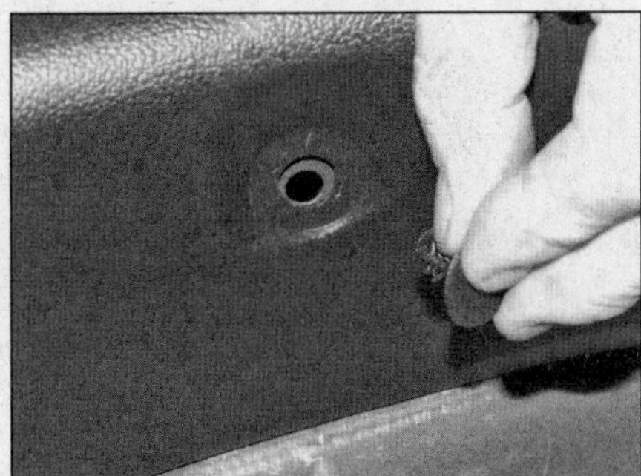

35.21b ...and prise out the clips

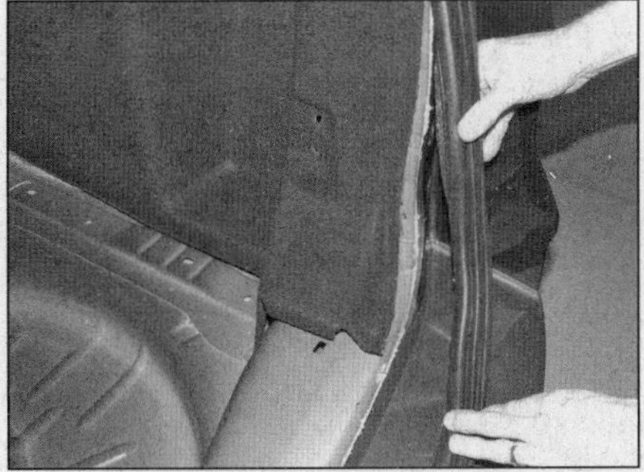

35.25 Remove the weatherstrip around the luggage compartment

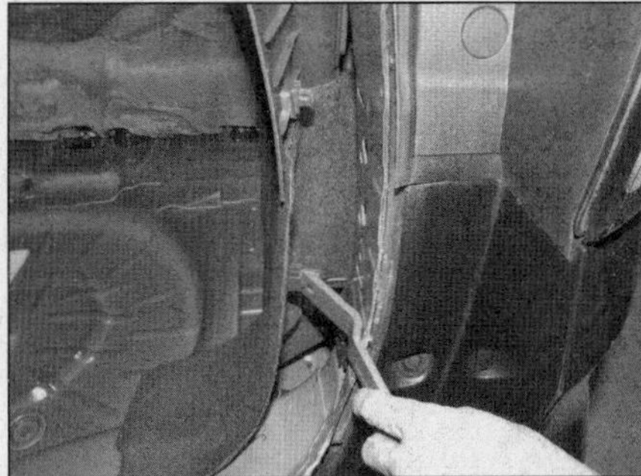

35.26 Prise away the rear of the side panel

35.27 Pull away the weatherstrip

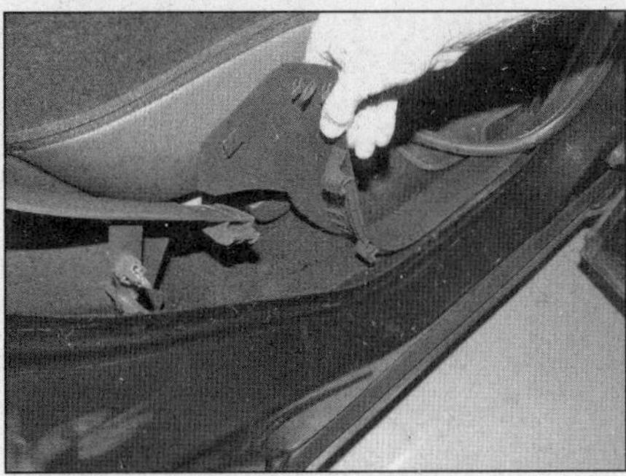

35.28 Lift up the rear of the door sill trim

35.29 Gently ease out the front of the side panel

panel, and fold the rear seat backrests forwards.

24 Remove the tailgate striker panel trim, as described earlier in this Section.

25 Remove the weatherstrip from around the luggage compartment opening **(see illustration)**.

26 Using a trim removal tool, prise away the rear of the side panel **(see illustration)**.

27 Pull the weatherstrip from the C-pillar door aperture **(see illustration)**.

28 Gently prise up the rear of the door sill trim **(see illustration)**.

29 Prise away the front edge of the luggage compartment side panel **(see illustration)**.

30 Undo the lower seatbelt anchorage bolt and manoeuvre the seatbelt through the gap in the side panel **(see illustration)**.

31 Disconnect the wiring pugs for the luggage compartment light and power socket **(see illustration)**.

32 Remove the panel from the vehicle.

Upper side luggage compartment trim panel

33 Remove the side panel as described earlier in this Section.

34 Using a trim removal tool, gently prise the panel from place **(see illustration)**.

Door sill trim panels

Front door

35 Remove the rubber weatherstrip from the door aperture **(see illustration)**.

36 Carefully prise the door sill trim panel upwards to release the retaining clips **(see illustration)**.

Rear door

37 Remove the rubber weatherstrip from the door aperture **(see illustration)**.

38 Gently pull the panel from place **(see illustration)**.

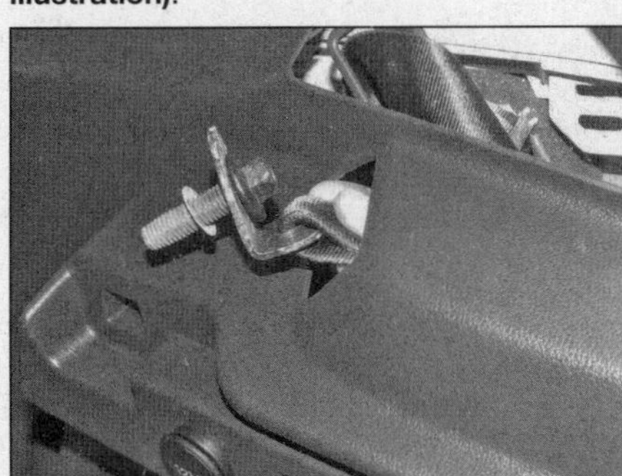

35.30 Undo the lower seat belt anchorage bolt

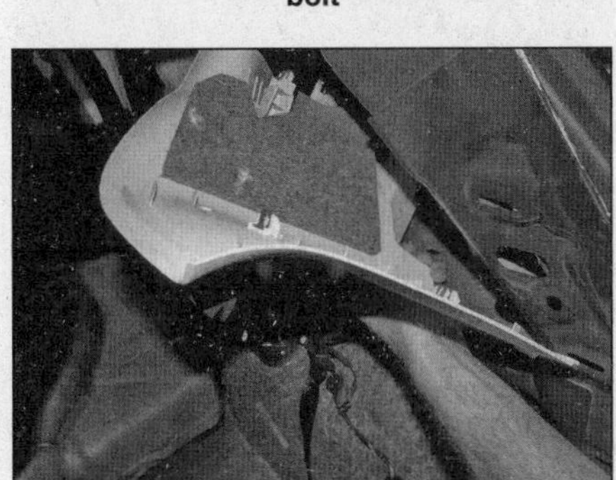

35.34 Pull the upper side panel away

Footwell kick panels

39 Remove the relevant front door sill trim panel as described previously in this Section.

40 Pull away the door rubber weatherstrip at the edge of the footwell kick panel.

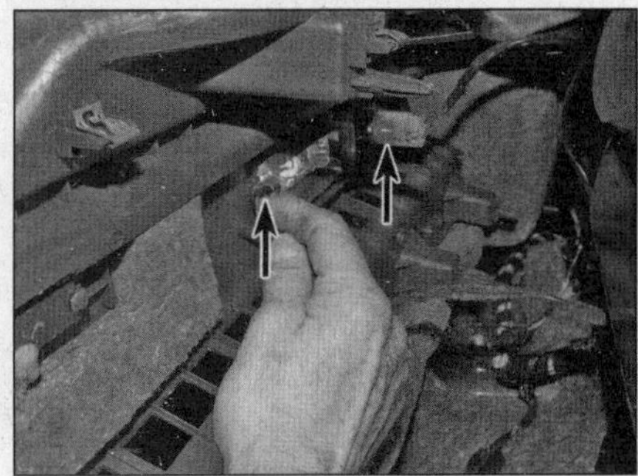

35.31 Disconnect the wiring plugs

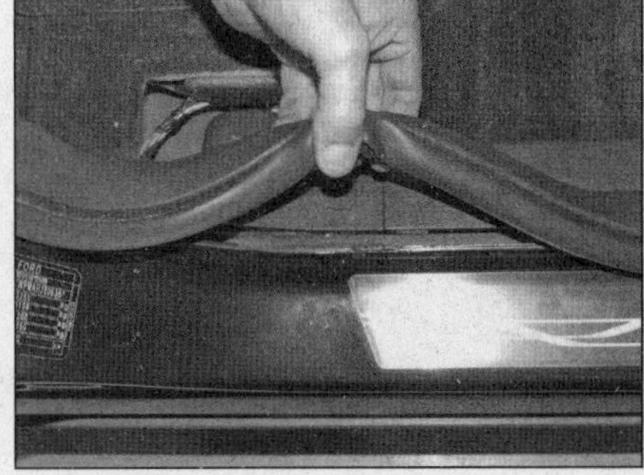

35.35 Pull up the weatherstrip

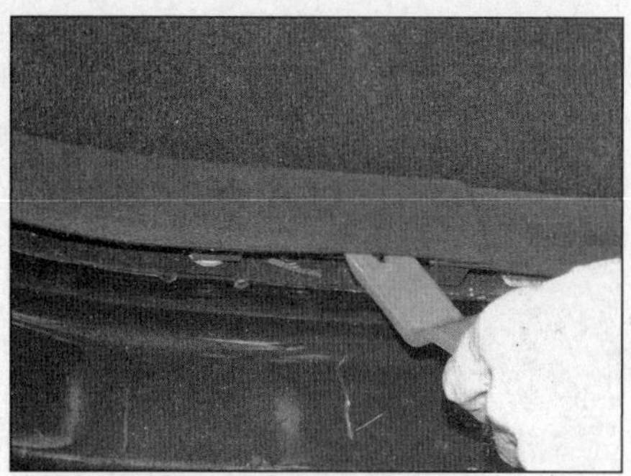
35.36 Prise the sill trim panel upwards

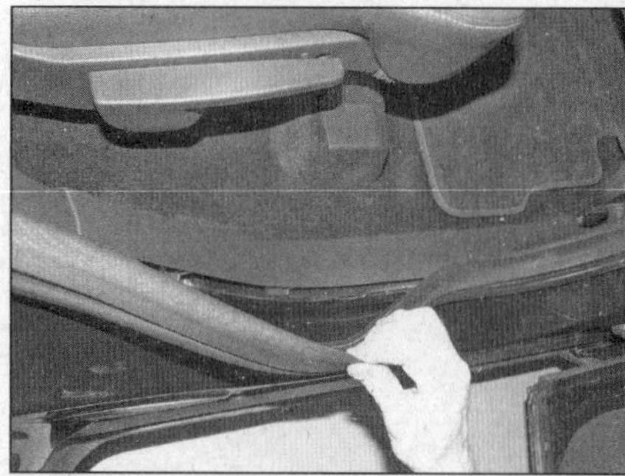
35.37 Pull up the weatherstrip

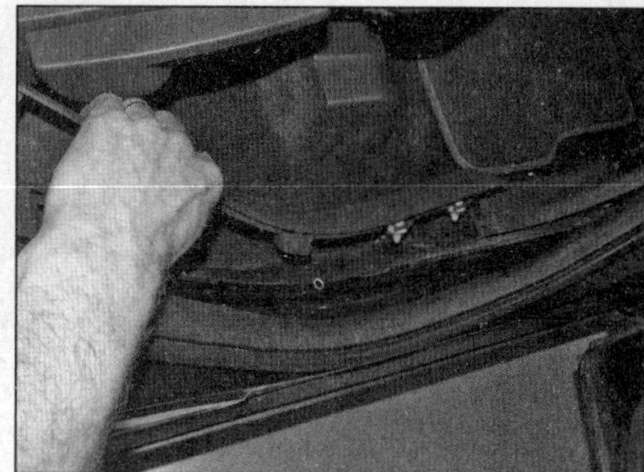
35.38 Pull the panel from place

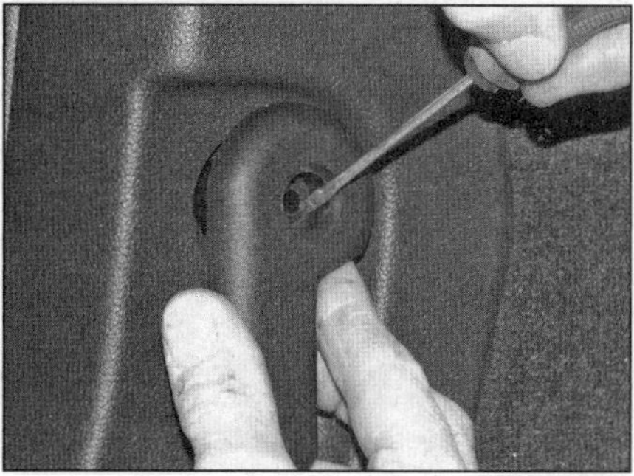
35.41 Remove the centre clip to release the lever

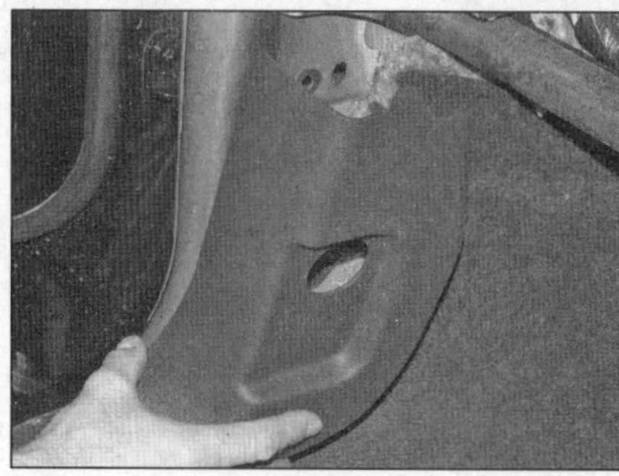
35.42 Gently pull the kick panel inwards

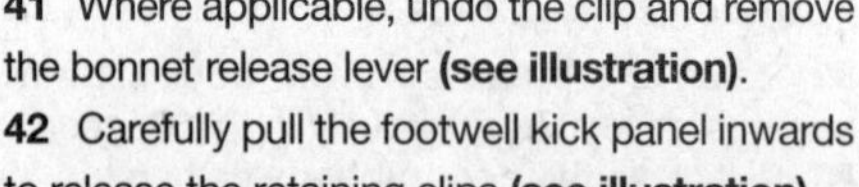
41 Where applicable, undo the clip and remove the bonnet release lever **(see illustration)**.

42 Carefully pull the footwell kick panel inwards to release the retaining clips **(see illustration)**.

Refitting

43 Refitting is a reversal of the removal procedure. Where seat belt fastenings have been disturbed, make sure that they are tightened to the specified torque. Renew any broken clips as required.

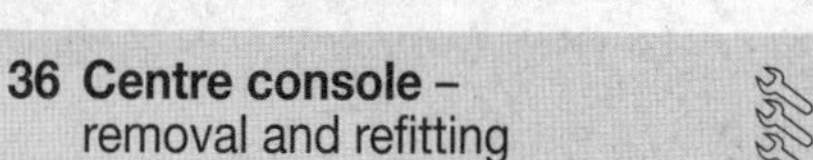

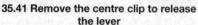

36 Centre console – removal and refitting

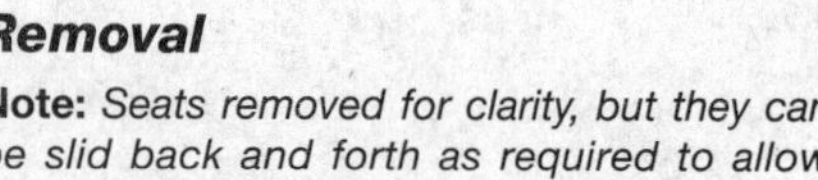

Removal

Note: *Seats removed for clarity, but they can be slid back and forth as required to allow access to the retaining bolts and screws.*

1 Prise up the gear/selector lever gaiter surround **(see illustration)**.

2 Prise away the gear/selector lever surround panel, which extends around the heater controls **(see illustration)**.

3 Undo the 2 retaining screws below the gear/selector lever, then remove the facia trim, which extends across the face of the dashboard and incorporates the ignition button (where fitted) **(see illustrations)**.

4 If your vehicle has a manual handbrake, remove the trim from below the lever **(see illustration)**.

5 Prise up the centre console, which incorporates the cupholders etc **(see illustrations)**. Disconnect the wiring plugs.

6 To remove the cupholder, undo the 2 retaining screws and remove the keyless antenna from place **(see illustration)**.

7 Undo the 4 retaining screws and remove the cupholders assembly from place, taking care not to drop the plastic light ring **(see illustrations)**.

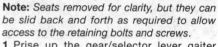

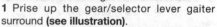

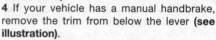

36.1 Lift up the gear/selector lever surround

36.2 Remove the gear/selector lever surround panel

36.3a Unscrew the facia trim...

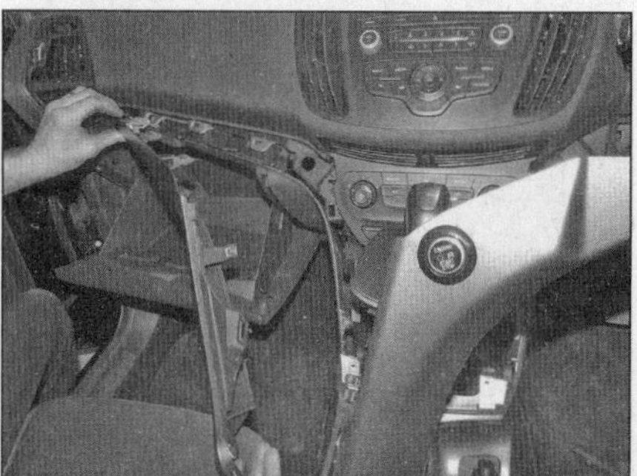
36.3b ...and unclip it from the dashboard...

36.3c ...and disconnect the ignition button wiring plug

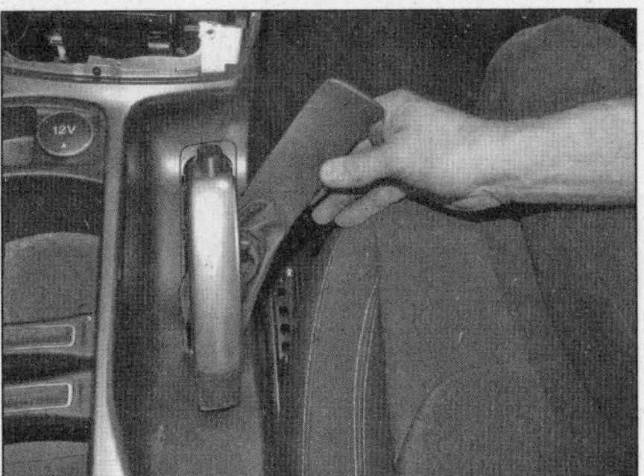

36.4 Prise up the handbrake surround trim

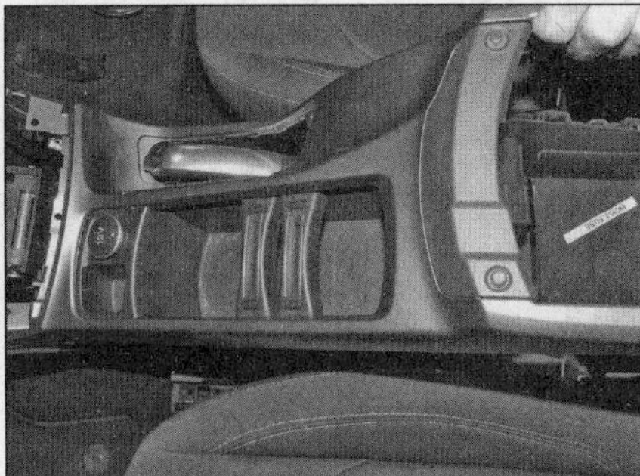

36.5a Prise up the centre console from place...

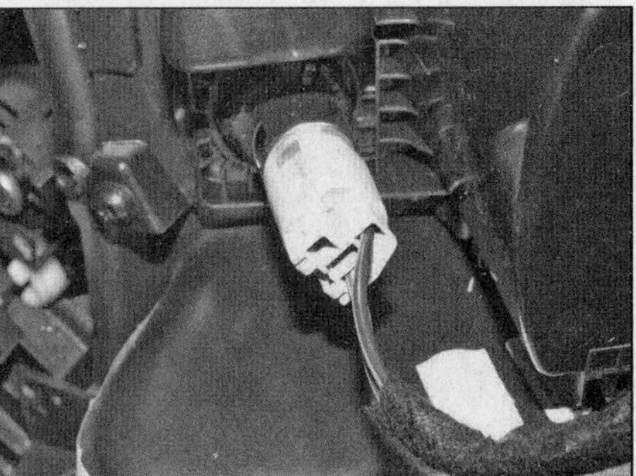

36.5b ...disconnect the power socket wiring plug...

36.5c ...the keyless entry antenna (where fitted)...

36.5d ...and the light ring wiring plug (where fitted)

36.6 Unscrew and remove the keyless antenna

8 Remove the driver and passenger-side kick panels, as described in Section 38.

9 Disconnect the 3 wiring plugs at the front of the centre console on the driver's side **(see illustration)**.

10 Undo the 2 upper retaining screws on each side at the front of the centre console **(see illustration)**.

11 Remove the bolt at the rear of the centre console on either side **(see illustration)**.

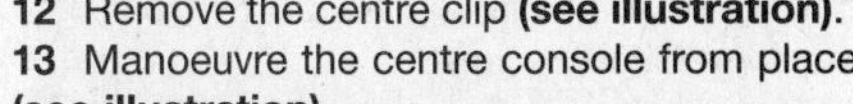

12 Remove the centre clip **(see illustration)**.

13 Manoeuvre the centre console from place **(see illustration)**.

Centre console disassembly

14 Use a trim removal tool to prise out the

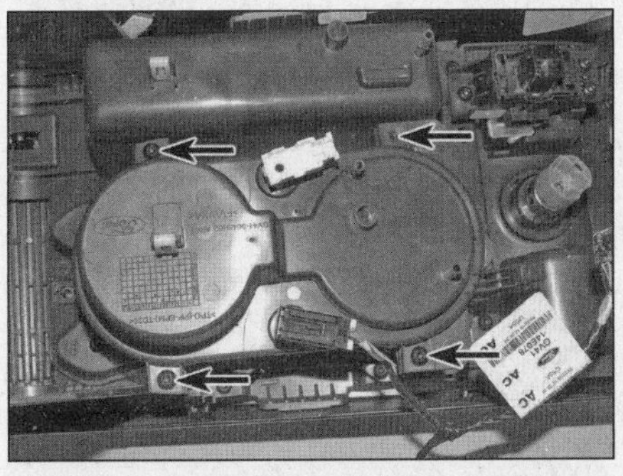

36.7a Unscrew the cupholder assembly...

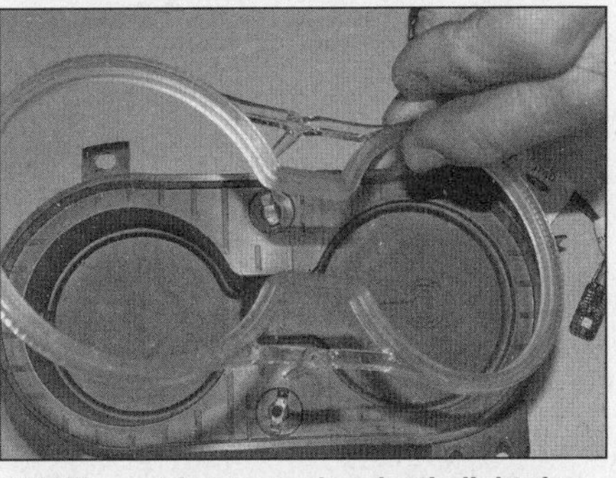

36.7b ...and remove the plastic light ring

36.9 Disconnect the wiring plugs

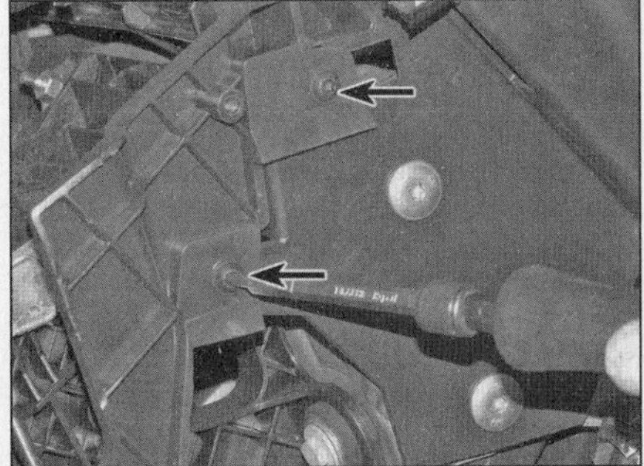

36.10 Remove the 2 upper retaining screws on either side

36.11 Undo the rearmost bolt each side

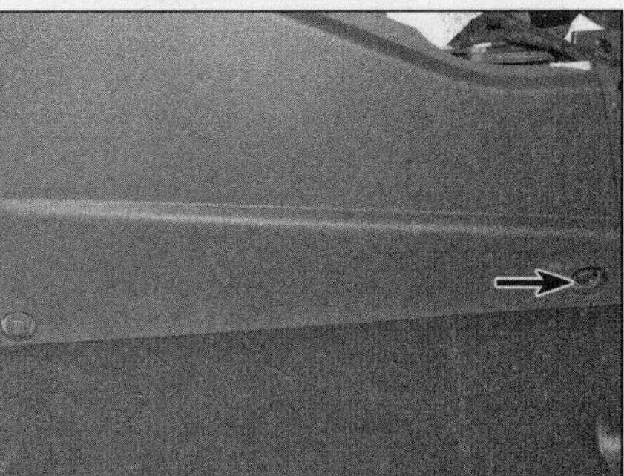

36.12 Detach the central clip on either side

36.13 Pull the console upwards and backwards

36.14 Prise out the bottom of the rear vent to remove

36.15 Undo the 2 mounting screws behind the vent panel

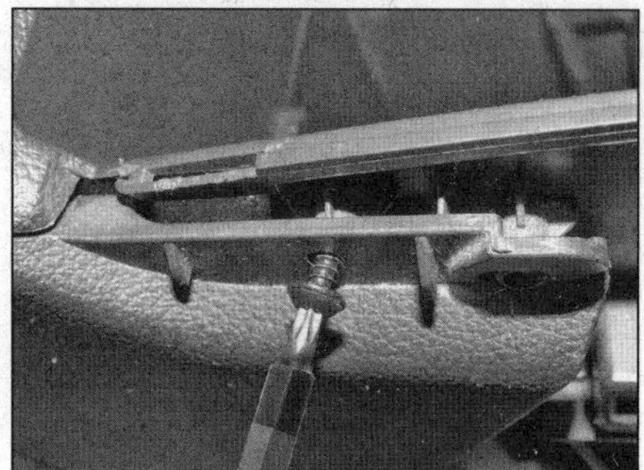

36.16 Remove the top side panel mounting screw

36.17a Remove the front screw at each side of the storage box...

36.17b ...then pull out the side trim and undo the rear screw

bottom edge of the rear centre console vent panel **(see illustration).**

15 Unscrew the 2 mounting screws **(see illustration).**

16 Undo the mounting screw at the top of each side panel **(see illustration).**

17 Remove the 2 screws on each side of the storage box (the second is accessed by pulling out the side panel slightly **(see illustrations).**

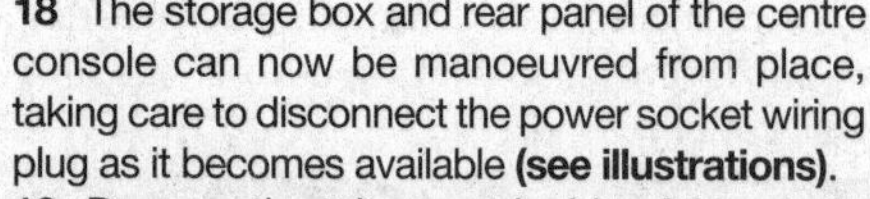

18 The storage box and rear panel of the centre console can now be manoeuvred from place, taking care to disconnect the power socket wiring plug as it becomes available **(see illustrations).**

19 Depress the tab on each side of the power socket, then press from behind to remove it from place **(see illustration).**

20 Make an alignment mark on the power socket and the panel to aid refitting.

Refitting

21 Refitting is a reversal of the removal procedure.

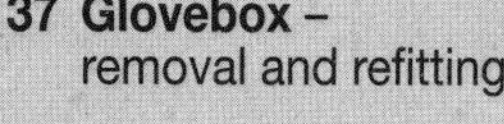

37 Glovebox – removal and refitting

1 Pull away the rubber weatherstrip from the door aperture adjacent to the glovebox.

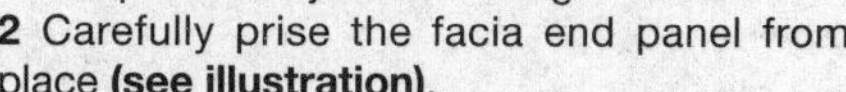

2 Carefully prise the facia end panel from place **(see illustration).**

3 Prise out the covers and remove the 2 screws at the lower edge of the glovebox **(see illustration).**

4 Open the glovebox, undo the 3 screws, and manoeuvre it from place **(see illustration).** Disconnect any wiring plugs as the glovebox is withdrawn.

5 Disconnect the wiring plug for the glovebox light as it becomes accessible **(see illustration).**

6 Refitting is a reversal of the removal procedure, making sure that the glovebox is located correctly before tightening the screws.

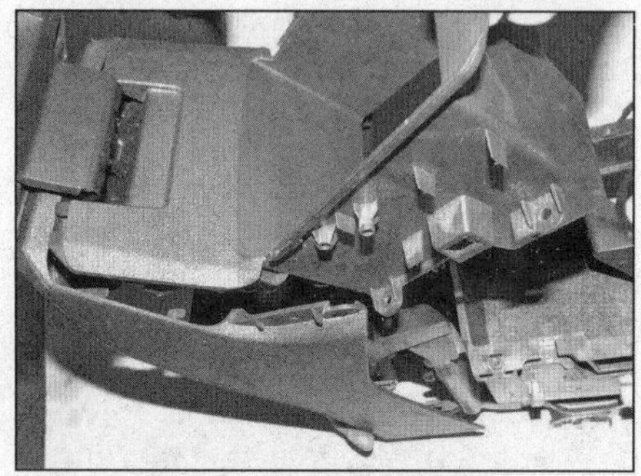

36.18a Separate the rear portion of the centre console from the front...

36.18b ...then disconnect the wiring plug for the power socket

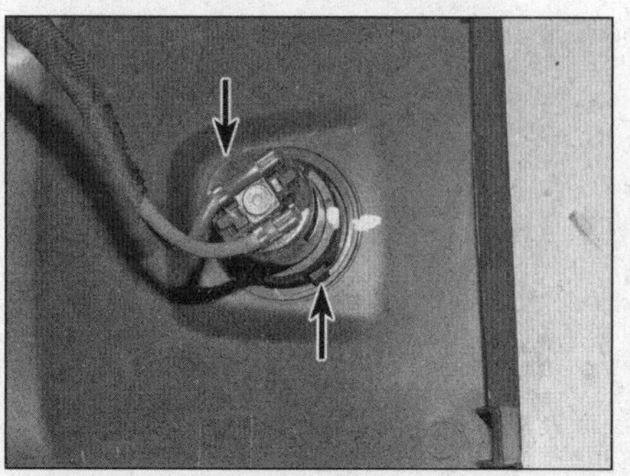

36.19 Depress the tabs and press the power socket out

37.2 Use a trim tool to remove the facia end panel

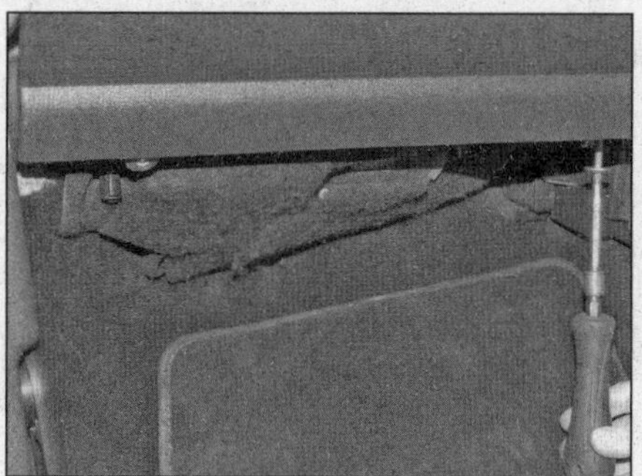

37.3 Remove the 2 screws underneath the glovebox

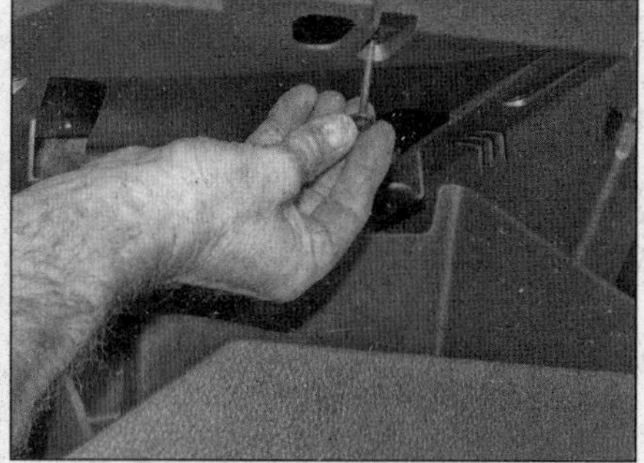

37.4 Undo the 3 screws inside the glovebox

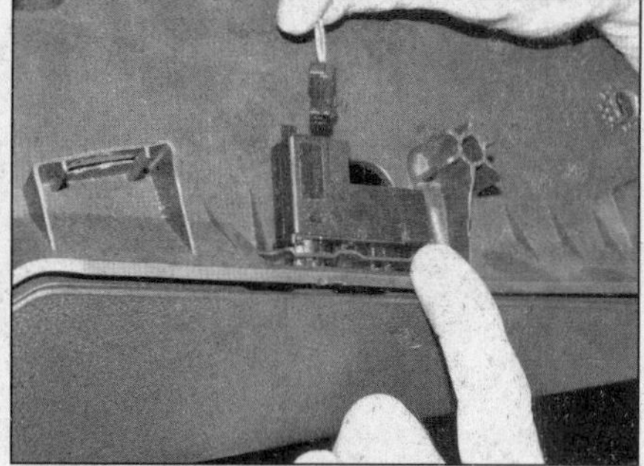

37.5 Disconnect the wiring plug

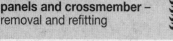

38 Facia, associated panels and crossmember – removal and refitting

Removal

Centre console kick panels

1 Remove the centre console (see Section 36).

2 Using a small screwdriver, prise out the cover, and remove the clip **(see illustrations)**.

3 Remove the retaining screw on the side of the gear/selector lever panel **(see illustration)**.

4 Pull the kick panel rearwards from place.

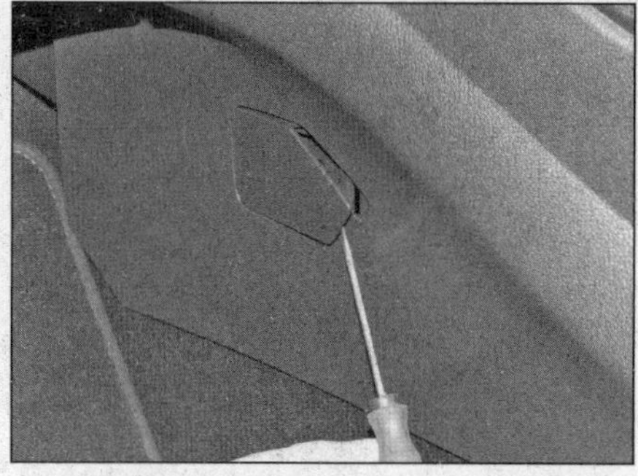

38.2a Remove the cover for the retaining clip...

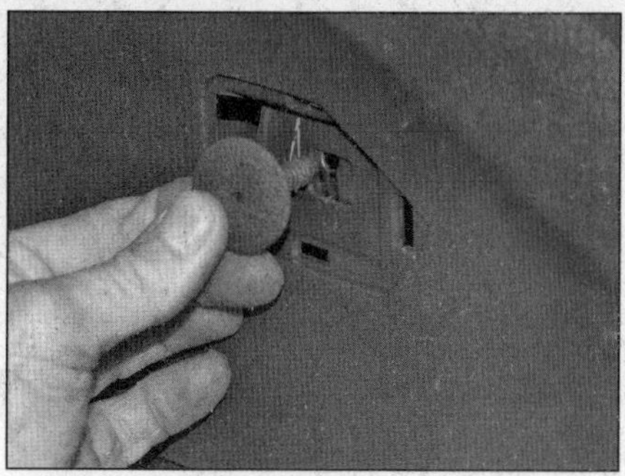

38.2b ...and remove the clip from place

Steering column shrouds

5 Fully extend and lower the steering column.

6 Carefully prise the upper shroud forward from beneath the instruments, and prise the rearmost half up from the top of the steering column **(see illustrations)**.

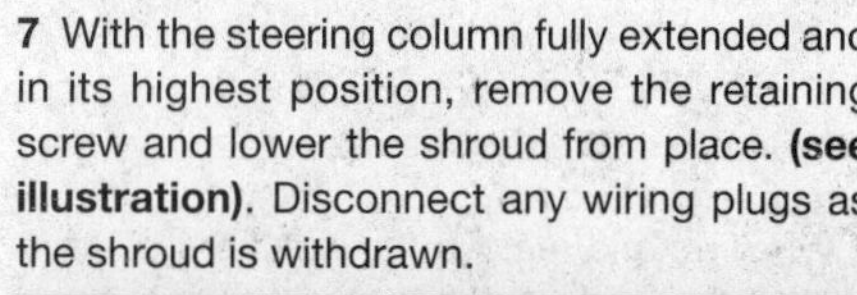

7 With the steering column fully extended and in its highest position, remove the retaining screw and lower the shroud from place. **(see illustration)**. Disconnect any wiring plugs as the shroud is withdrawn.

Lower facia panels – Passenger side

8 Undo the 2 clips at the rear of the panel **(see illustration)**.

9 Pull the panel from place.

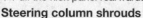

38.3 Undo the retaining screw on the side of the gear/selector lever panel

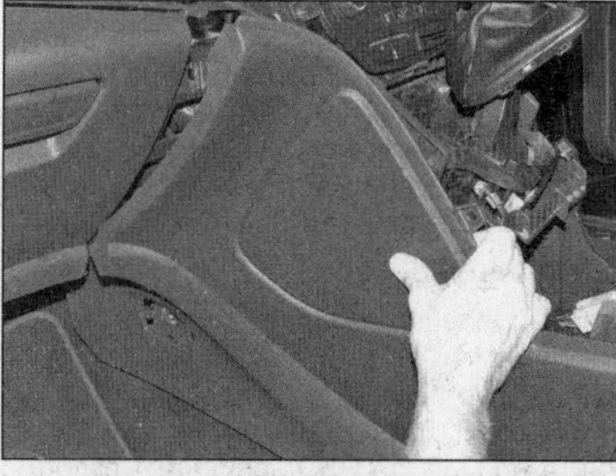

38.4 Pull the panel rearwards to remove it

38.6a Pull forward to shroud from the instruments...

38.6b ...and pull it up from the steering column

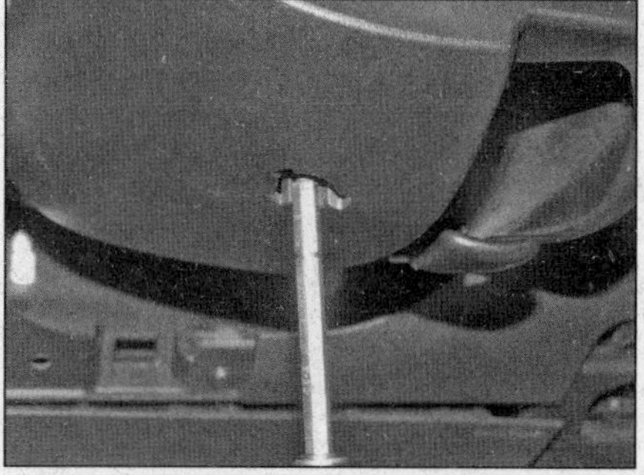

38.7 Undo the retaining bolt and lower the shroud

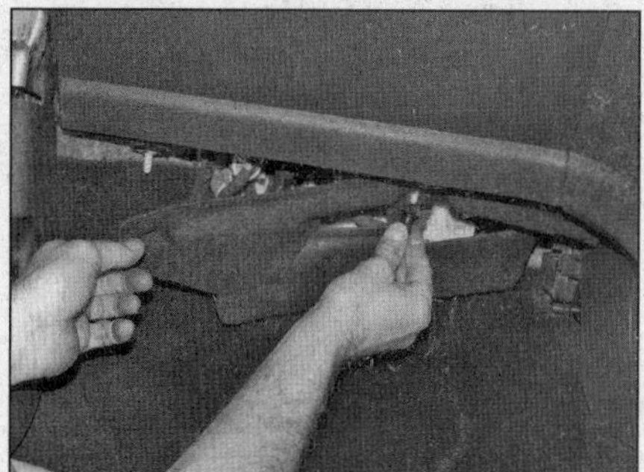

38.8 Undo the 2 retaining clips

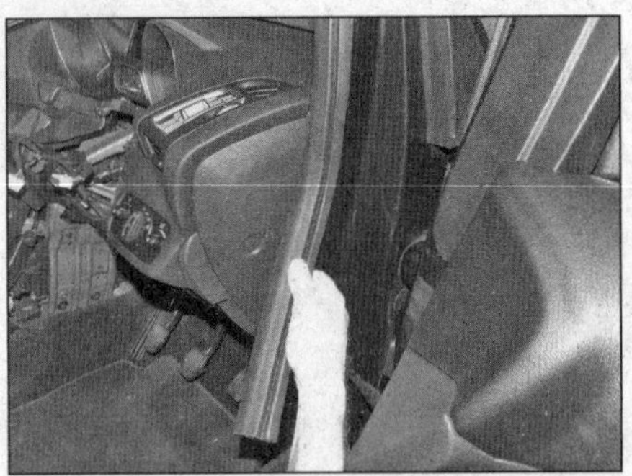
38.10a Pull away the weather strip from the door aperture...

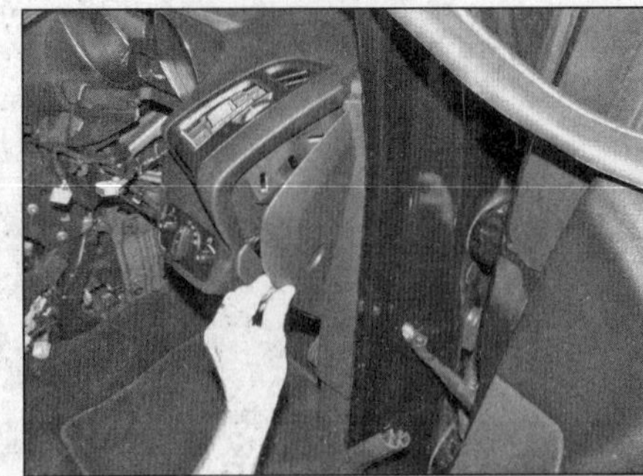
38.10b ...then remove the facia end panel

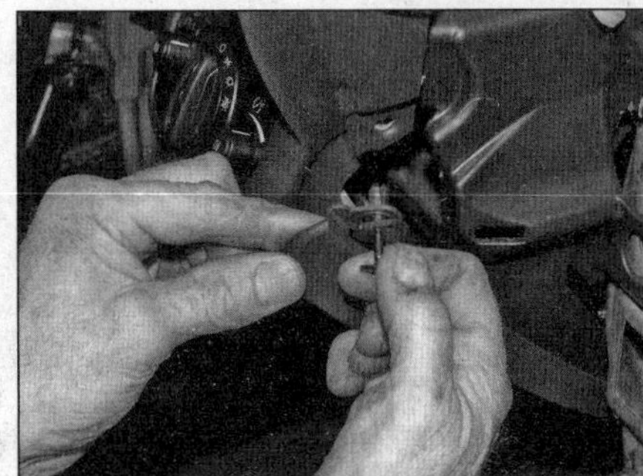
38.12 Remove the 2 clips and 3 screws to free the panel

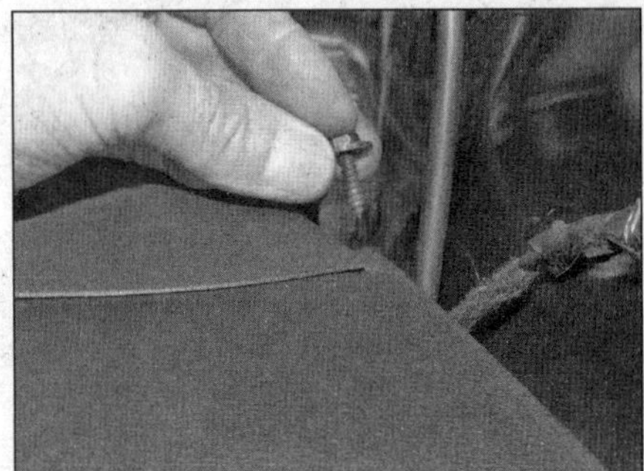
38.14 Remove the facia end panel retaining screws

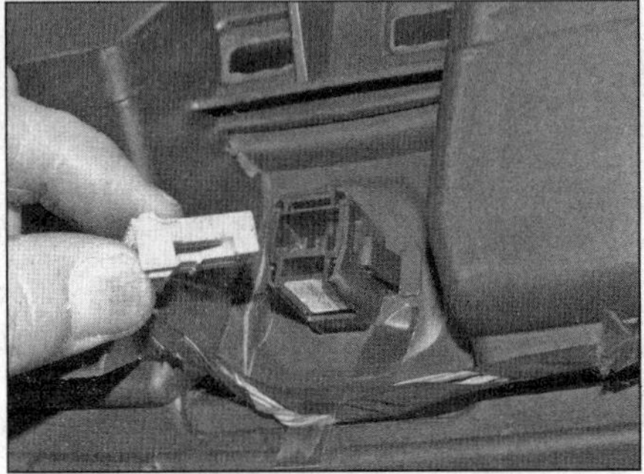
38.15 Disconnect any wiring plugs from the facia panel

38.18 Prise up the door sill trim

Lower facia panels – Driver's side

10 Pull away the rubber weatherstrip from the door aperture adjacent to the panel, then carefully prise the facia end panel from place **(see illustrations)**.

11 Fold down the cover for the OBD socket to expose the panel mounting screws.

12 Undo the 3 retaining screws and 2 clips to release the lower facia panel **(see illustration)**.

Upper facia panel

13 Remove both A-pillar trims, as described in Section 35.

14 Undo the retaining screw at either end of the upper facia panel **(see illustration)**.

15 Prise up the panel from place, disconnecting the wiring plugs as they become available **(see illustration)**.

Passenger side kick panel

16 Remove the bonnet release lever as described in Section 8.

17 Pull up and remove the weatherstrip from around the front door aperture.

18 Use a trim removal tool to prise up the door sill trim **(see illustration)**.

19 Remove the facia end panel as described earlier in this Section.

20 Use a trim removal tool to prise the kick panel from its locating clips **(see illustration)**.

Facia panel assembly

21 Disconnect the battery negative lead as described in Chapter 5 Section 4.

22 Remove the steering wheel as described in Chapter 10 Section 16.

23 Disengage the OBD socket as described in Chapter 12 Section 29.

24 Remove the instrument panel, and the central instrument display panel as described in Chapter 12 Section 12.

25 Remove both A-pillar trim panels as described in Section 35.

26 Use a trim removal tool to prise out the panel from each end of the main facia **(see illustration)**.

27 Prise up and remove the speaker cover from the centre of the facia **(see illustration)**.

28 Undo the retaining screws and remove the disc player surround from place **(see illustration)**.

29 Undo the screw and pull the fresh air vent each side of the central instrument display panel rearwards **(see illustration)**.

30 Remove the heating/air conditioning control panel as described in Chapter 3 Section 13.

38.20 Gently prise the panel from its mounting clips

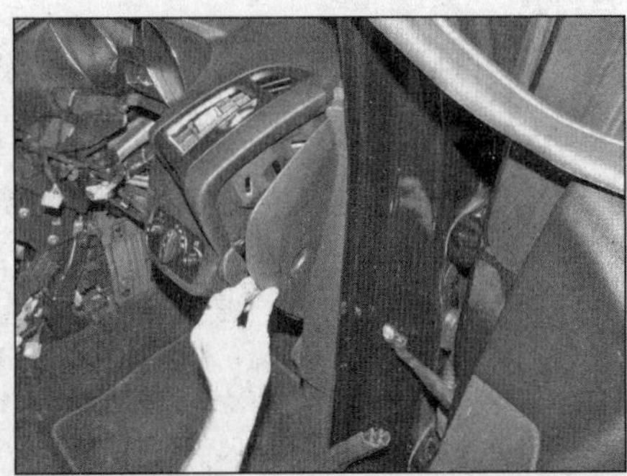
38.26 Gently ease the facia end panel from place

38.27 Lift and remove the speaker cover

38.28 Unscrew the disc player surround screws

38.29 Undo the vent retaining screw each side

38.35a There is one screw at either end...

38.35b ...one through the glovebox aperture...

38.35c ...2 below the passenger side...

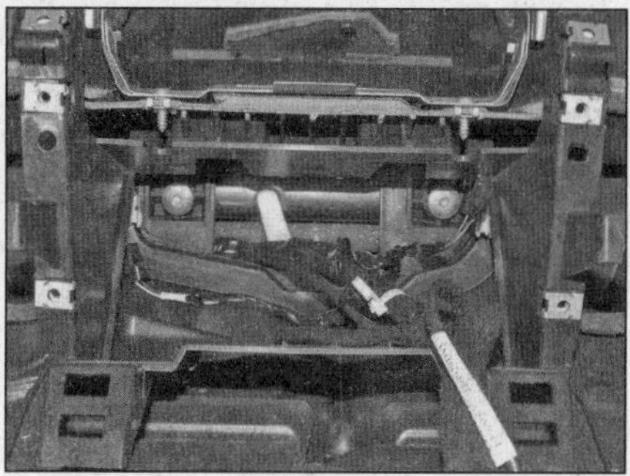

38.35d ...2 in the central aperture...

31 Remove the passenger glovebox as described in Section 37.

32 Remove the central facia switch panel as described in Chapter 12 Section 6.

33 Remove the driver and passenger side lower facia panels as described earlier in this Section.

34 Remove the steering column combination switch assembly as described in Chapter 12 Section 6.

35 The facia is now secured by 2 screws in the central aperture, 1 screw each side at the top/outer edge, 1 screw behind the glovebox aperture, 2 screw either side of the gear/ selector lever aperture, 2 screws under the passengers side, 2 screws under the drivers side and 2 screws behind the instrument panel **(see illustrations)** Undo the screws and, with the help of an assistant, raise the facia panel, then disconnect the passengers airbag wiring plug, and manoeuvre it from the cabin. Feed any wiring harnesses through the apertures as the panel is withdrawn (where applicable).

Crossmember

36 If required, the facia crossmember is removed as follows:

37 Remove the facia as described in this Section 38(where applicable).

38 Remove the footwell vents and centre console vents as described in Chapter 3 Section 13.

39 Undo the 4 bolts and 1 screw to remove the bracing bracket to the right-hand side of the heater assembly **(see illustration)**.

40 Undo the retaining screws and remove the central mounting frame **(see illustration)**.

38.35e ...2 either side of the centre console...

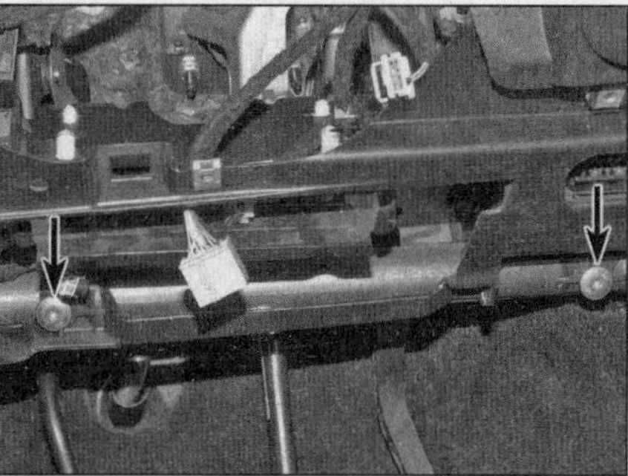

38.35g ...and 2 under the driver's side

41 Pull the two vent ducts from place **(see illustration)**.

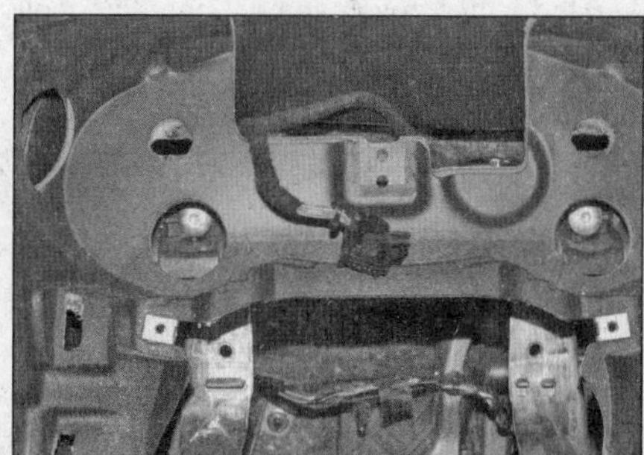

38.35f 2 behind the instrument panel...

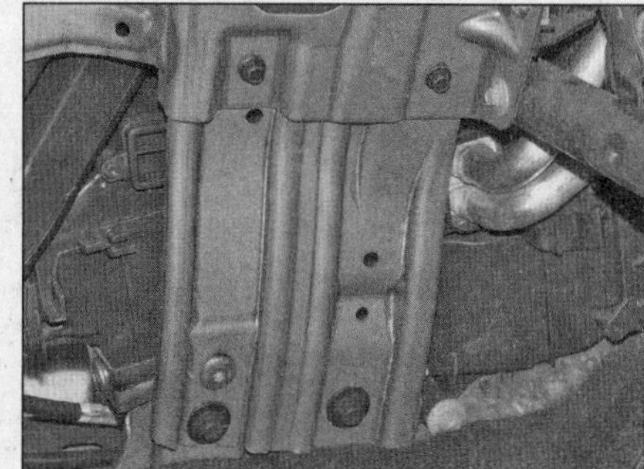

38.39 Undo the bolts and remove the bracing bracket

38.40 Remove the 8 screws to detach the frame

38.41 Pull away the ventilation ducts

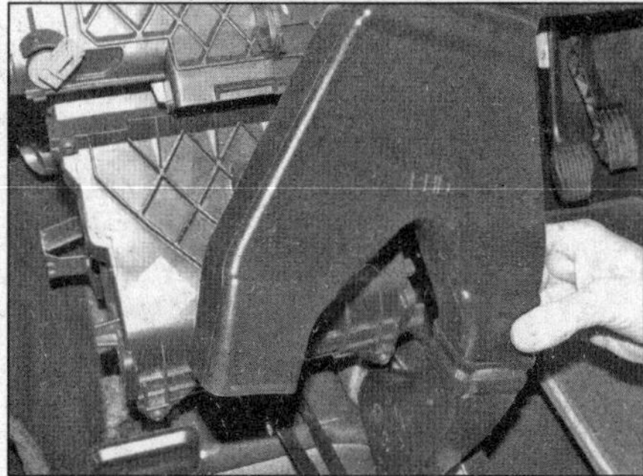
38.42 Remove the central vent duct

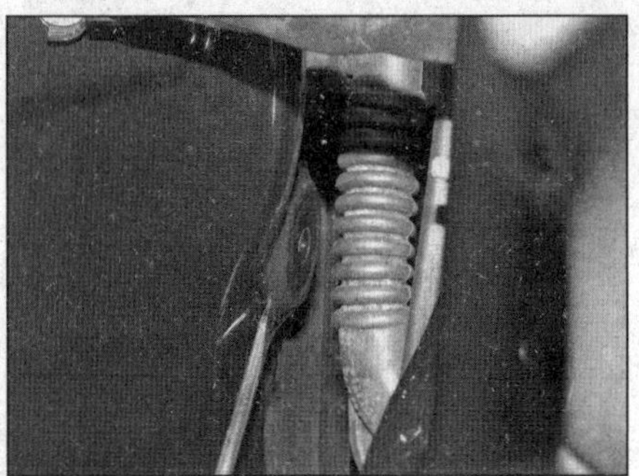
38.43 Prise out the grommet in the door pillar

38.44 Undo the crossmember mounting bolts

38.45 Undo the remaining 8 mounting bolts to remove the crossmember

42 Pull away the central ventilation junction duct **(see illustration)**.

43 Remove the grommet in each A-pillar that corresponds with the lower crossmember spar **(see illustration)**.

44 Undo the crossmember mounting bolt each side **(see illustration)**.

Note: *As more of the bolt becomes visible, remove the socket before it fouls against the door, and continue the slackening process with a spanner.*

45 Undo the 8 mounting bolts around the crossmember frame and manoeuvre the crossmember from place, ensuring all wiring plugs are as it is withdrawn **(see illustration)**. **Note:** *An assistant will be required to manoeuvre the crossmember from the cabin.*

Refitting

46 Essentially, refitting is a reversal of removal. As the lower crossmember mounting bolts are refitted through the A-pillar, ensure that the tensioner bolts on the inside of the A-pillar are tightened sufficiently so that they contact the inside of the pillar when the bolts are fully tightened. Ensure all wiring harnesses are correctly routed, securely reconnected, and check for correct operation before venturing out onto the roads.

Facia ventilation components

Driver's side end ventilation grille

47 Use a trim removal tool to release the retaining tab through the grille at the bottom of the vent **(see illustration)**.

48 Whilst the tab is released, use a trim tool to ease out the side of the vent and pull it rearwards from place **(see illustration)**.

49 Unscrew the retaining strap and remove the vent from place (side panel removed for clarity) **(see illustration)**.

50 Refitting is a reversal of removal, except the facia side panel will have to be prised out from place to allow reattachment of the retaining strap.

Central ventilation grille

51 Remove the heater control panel as described in Chapter 3 Section 13.

52 Using trim removal tools, release the 4 top clips, and 2 at the bottom of the vent and manoeuvre it from place **(see illustrations)**.

39 Wheelarch liner – removal and refitting

Removal

Front

1 Slacken the relevant front roadwheel bolts,

38.47 Release the tab through the vent

38.48 Prise out the side of the vent

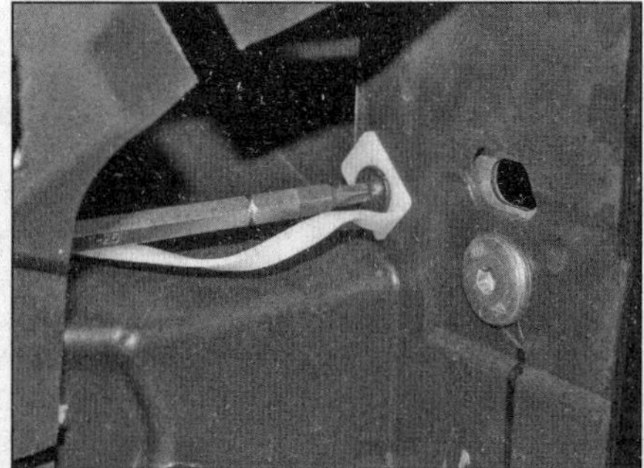
38.49 Detach the vent retaining strap

38.52a Use trim tools to release the clips...

38.52b ...then pull the vent from place

39.2a Prise up the centre pins, lever out the plastic expansion rivets...

raise the front of the vehicle and support it securely on axle stands (see *Jacking and vehicle support*). Remove the roadwheel.

2 Remove the expansion rivets around the edge and manoeuvre the wheelarch trim from place **(see illustrations)**.

Note: *Be prepared for clip breakage*.

3 Remove the fasteners and manoeuvre the wheelarch liner from place **(see illustration)**.

Rear

4 Chock the front wheels, and engage 1st gear. If the wheel is to be removed (to improve access), loosen the wheel nuts. Jack up the rear of the vehicle and support it on axle stands (see *Jacking and vehicle support*). Remove the rear wheel (where applicable).

5 Undo the 2 nuts for the deflector at the front of the wheelarch, remove the deflector, then remove the expansion rivets, prise off the circular retaining clips and manoeuvre the wheelarch liner from place.

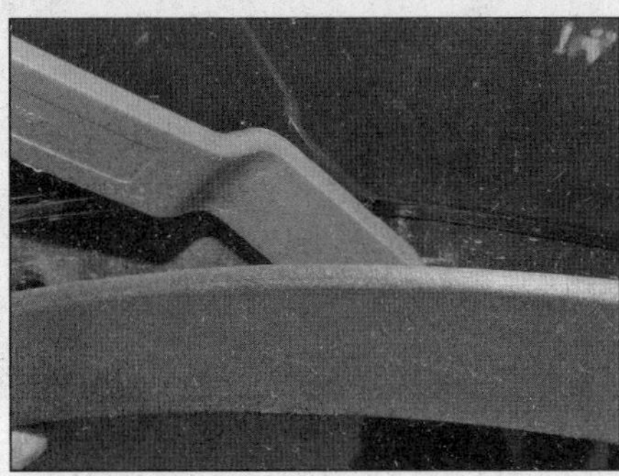
39.2b ...and gently remove the wheelarch trim

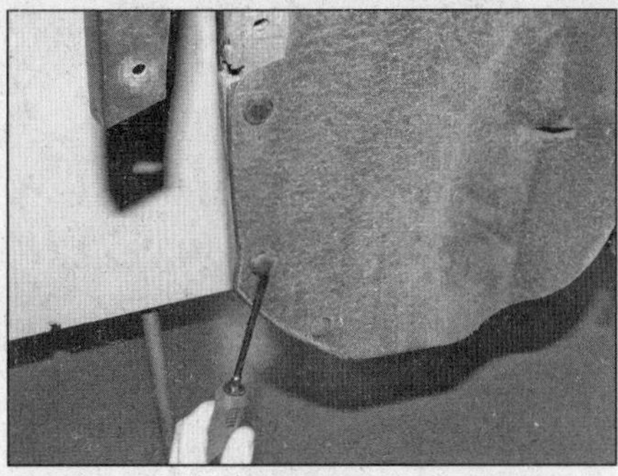
39.3 The wheelarch liners are secured by various fasteners

Refitting

6 Refitting is a reversal of the removal procedure. Where applicable, tighten the wheel nuts to the specified torque.

Chapter 12
Body electrical systems

Contents

Degrees of difficulty

Easy, suitable for novice with little experience 	Fairly easy, suitable for beginner with some experience 	Fairly difficult, suitable for competent DIY mechanic 	Difficult, suitable for experienced DIY mechanic	Very difficult, suitable for expert DIY or professional 

Specifications

Fuses and relays

Refer to the wiring diagrams at the end of this Chapter, and the information given on the fuse box lid inner.

Note: *Fuse and relay ratings and circuits are liable to change from year to year. Consult the handbook supplied with the vehicle, or consult a Ford specialist, for the latest information.*

Bulbs	**Wattage**	**Type**
Daytime running lights	24	PSX
Directional indicator lights:		
Front	24	Bayonet
Rear	21	Bayonet
Door entry light LED	N/A	N/A
Footwell light LED	N/A	N/A
Front foglight	35	H8 Halogen
Headlight LED	N/A	N/A
Headlight Halogen	60/55	H4
High-level stop-light LED	N/A	
Glovebox	5	Wedge
Ceiling light:		
Basic version	6	Wedge
All other versions LED	N/A	N/A
Luggage compartment	8	Wedge
Number plate lights LED	N/A	N/A
Rear foglight	16	Wedge
Stop light	21	Bayonet
Reversing lights	21	Bayonet
Side repeater direction indicator lights	5	Wedge
Sidelights	5 or LED	Wedge
Vanity light	1.2	Festoon
Tail light:		
Basic version	21	Bayonet
All other versions LED	N/A	

Torque wrench settings

	Nm	lbf ft
Airbag control unit nuts	11	8
Crash sensor screw/nut*	8	6
Knee airbag nuts	9	7
Passengers' airbag screws	2.3	1.7

** Do not re-use*

1 General information

Warning: Before carrying out any work on the electrical system, read through the precautions given in Safety first! at the beginning of this manual.

1 The electrical system is of 12-volt negative earth type. Power for the lights and all electrical accessories is supplied by a silver-calcium battery which is charged by the alternator.

2 This Chapter covers repair and service procedures for the various electrical components not associated with the engine. Information on the battery, alternator and starter motor can be found in Chapter 5 ; the ignition system is covered in Chapter 6A.

3 All models are fitted with a driver's airbag, which is designed to prevent serious chest and head injuries to the driver during an accident. A similar bag for the front seat passenger is also fitted. The electronic control module for the airbag is located under the centre console inside the vehicle. It contains two frontal impact micro machine sensors, a crash sensor, and a safety sensor. The crash sensor and safety sensor are connected in series, and if they both sense a deceleration in excess of a predetermined limit, the electronic airbag control module will operate the airbag. The airbag is inflated by a gas generator, which forces the bag out of the module cover in the centre of the steering wheel. A sliding contact ring ensures that a good electrical connection is maintained with the airbag at all times as the steering wheel is turned in each direction. There is also a coiled spring, that is able to 'wind-up' and 'unwind' as the steering wheel is turned, maintaining the electronic contact at all times.

4 Some models have side airbags built into the sides of the front seats. The intention of the side airbags is principally to offer greater passenger protection in a side impact. The side airbags are linked to the 'front' airbags, and are also controlled by the electronic control module under the centre console. The side air bags are also controlled by the sensors located under the carpet and sill trims inside the vehicle. Side airbags incorporated into the headlining are also available.

5 All models are fitted with an ignition immobiliser, which is built into the key and ignition lock.

6 It should be noted that, when portions of the electrical system are serviced, the lead should be disconnected from the battery negative terminal, to prevent electrical shorts and fires.

Caution: When disconnecting the battery for work described in the following Sections, refer to Chapter 5 Section 4.

2 Electrical fault finding – general information

Note: *Refer to the precautions given in 'Safety first!' before starting work. The following tests relate to testing of the main electrical circuits, and should not be used to test delicate electronic circuits (such as engine management systems, anti-lock braking systems, etc), particularly where an electronic control module is used. Also refer to the precautions given in Chapter 5.*

General

1 A typical electrical circuit consists of an electrical component, any switches, relays, motors, fuses, fusible links or circuit breakers related to that component, and the wiring and connectors which link the component to both the battery and the chassis. To help to pinpoint a problem in an electrical circuit, wiring diagrams are included at the end of this Chapter.

2 Before attempting to diagnose an electrical fault, first study the appropriate wiring diagram, to obtain a complete understanding of the components included in the particular circuit concerned. The possible sources of a fault can be narrowed down by noting if other components related to the circuit are operating properly. If several components or circuits fail at one time, the problem is likely to be related to a shared fuse or earth connection.

3 Electrical problems usually stem from simple causes, such as loose or corroded connections, a faulty earth connection, a blown fuse, a melted fusible link, or a faulty relay (refer to Section 3 for details of testing relays). Visually inspect the condition of all fuses, wires and connections in a problem circuit before testing the components. Use the wiring diagrams to determine which terminal connections will need to be checked in order to pinpoint the trouble-spot.

4 The basic tools required for electrical fault finding include a circuit tester or voltmeter (a 12-volt bulb with a set of test leads can also be used for certain tests); an ohmmeter (to measure resistance and check for continuity); a battery and set of test leads; and a jumper wire, preferably with a circuit breaker or fuse incorporated, which can be used to bypass suspect wires or electrical components. Before attempting to locate a problem with test instruments, use the wiring diagram to determine where to make the connections.

5 To find the source of an intermittent wiring fault (usually due to a poor or dirty connection, or damaged wiring insulation), a 'wiggle' test can be performed on the wiring. This involves wiggling the wiring by hand to see if the fault occurs as the wiring is moved. It should be possible to narrow down the source of the fault to a particular section of wiring. This method of testing can be used in conjunction with any of the tests described in the following sub-Sections.

6 Apart from problems due to poor connections, two basic types of fault can occur in an electrical circuit – open-circuit, or short-circuit.

7 Open-circuit faults are caused by a break somewhere in the circuit, which prevents current from flowing. An open-circuit fault will prevent a component from working.

8 Short-circuit faults are caused by a 'short' somewhere in the circuit, which allows the current flowing in the circuit to 'escape' along an alternative route, usually to earth. Short-circuit faults are normally caused by a breakdown in wiring insulation, which allows a feed wire to touch either another wire, or an earthed component such as the bodyshell. A short-circuit fault will normally cause the relevant circuit fuse to blow.

Finding an open-circuit

9 To check for an open-circuit, connect one lead of a circuit tester or the negative lead of a voltmeter either to the battery negative terminal or to a known good earth.

10 Connect the other lead to a connector in the circuit being tested, preferably nearest to the battery or fuse. At this point, battery voltage should be present, unless the lead from the battery or the fuse itself is faulty (bearing in mind that some circuits are live only when the ignition switch is moved to a particular position).

11 Switch on the circuit, then connect the tester lead to the connector nearest the circuit switch on the component side.

12 If voltage is present (indicated either by the tester bulb lighting or a voltmeter reading, as applicable), this means that the section of the circuit between the relevant connector and the switch is problem-free.

13 Continue to check the remainder of the circuit in the same fashion.

14 When a point is reached at which no voltage is present, the problem must lie between that point and the previous test point with voltage. Most problems can be traced to a broken, corroded or loose connection.

Finding a short-circuit

15 To check for a short-circuit, first disconnect the load(s) from the circuit (loads are the components which draw current from a circuit, such as bulbs, motors, heating elements, etc).

16 Remove the relevant fuse from the circuit, and connect a circuit tester or voltmeter to the fuse connections.

17 Switch on the circuit, bearing in mind that some circuits are live only when the ignition switch is moved to a particular position.

18 If voltage is present (indicated either by the tester bulb lighting or a voltmeter reading, as applicable), this means that there is a short-circuit.

19 If no voltage is present during this test, but the fuse still blows with the load(s) reconnected, this indicates an internal fault in the load(s).

Finding an earth fault

20 The battery negative terminal is connected to 'earth' – the metal of the engine/transmission unit and the vehicle body – and many systems are wired so that they only receive a positive feed, the current returning via the metal of the car body. This means that the component mounting and the body form part of that circuit.

21 Loose or corroded mountings can therefore cause a range of electrical faults, ranging from total failure of a circuit, to a puzzling partial failure. In particular, lights may shine dimly (especially when another circuit sharing the same earth point is in operation), motors (eg, wiper motors or the radiator cooling fan motor) may run slowly, and the operation of one circuit may have an apparently-unrelated effect on another.

22 Note that on many vehicles, earth straps are used between certain components, such as the engine/transmission and the body, usually where there is no metal-to-metal contact between components, due to flexible rubber mountings, etc. **(see illustration)**.

23 To check whether a component is properly earthed, disconnect the battery as described in Chapter 5 Section 4, and connect one lead of an ohmmeter to a known good earth point. Connect the other lead to the wire or earth connection being tested. The resistance reading should be zero; if not, check the connection as follows.

24 If an earth connection is thought to be faulty, dismantle the connection, and clean both the bodyshell and the wire terminal (or the component earth connection mating surface) back to bare metal. Be careful to remove all traces of dirt and corrosion, then use a knife to trim away any paint, so that a clean metal-to-metal joint is made.

25 On reassembly, tighten the joint fasteners securely; if a wire terminal is being refitted, use serrated washers between the terminal and the bodyshell, to ensure a clean and secure connection.

26 When the connection is remade, prevent the onset of corrosion in the future by applying a coat of petroleum jelly or silicone-based grease, or by spraying on (at regular intervals) a proprietary water-dispersant lubricant.

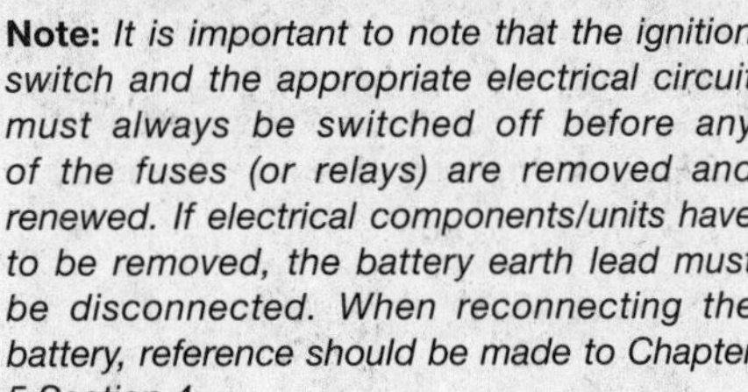

3 Fuses and relays – testing and renewal

Note: *It is important to note that the ignition switch and the appropriate electrical circuit must always be switched off before any of the fuses (or relays) are removed and renewed. If electrical components/units have to be removed, the battery earth lead must be disconnected. When reconnecting the battery, reference should be made to Chapter 5 Section 4.*

1 Fuses are designed to break a circuit when a predetermined current is reached, in order to protect components and wiring which could be damaged by excessive current flow. Any excessive current flow will be due to a fault in the circuit, usually a short-circuit (see Section 2). The main power distribution boxes, which also carry some relays, are located in the engine compartment and under the passenger's side of the facia, whilst an additional fusebox is located on the right-hand side of the luggage compartment **(see illustrations)**.

2 Each circuit is identified by numbers on the main fusebox. Reference to the wiring diagrams at the end of this Chapter will indicate the circuits protected by each fuse.

3.1a Fuses are under the dashboard...

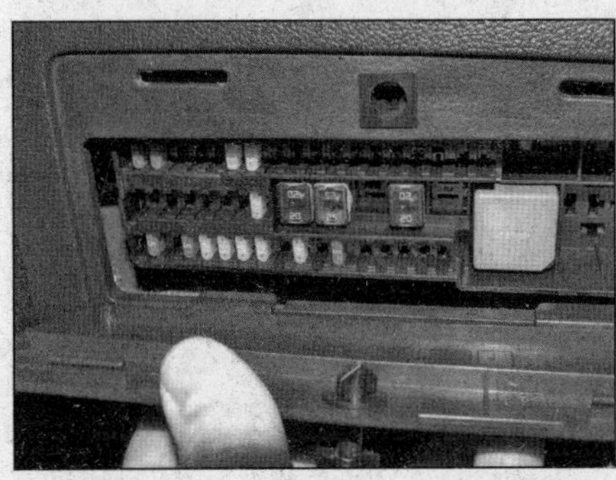

3.1c ...and in the luggage compartment

2.22 The main engine earth strap is attached to the engine compartment bulkhead

Plastic tweezers are attached to the auxiliary fusebox to remove and refit the fuses and relays. To remove a fuse, use the tweezers provided to pull it out of the holder, then slide the fuse sideways from the tweezers. The wire within the fuse is clearly visible, and it will be broken if the fuse is blown **(see illustration)**.

3 Always renew a fuse with one of an identical rating. Never substitute a fuse of a higher rating, or make temporary repairs using wire or metal foil; more serious damage, or even fire, could result. The fuse rating is stamped on top of the fuse. Never renew a fuse more than once without tracing the source of the trouble.

4 Relays are electrically-operated switches, which are used in certain circuits. The various relays can be removed from their respective locations by carefully pulling them from the sockets. Some of the relays in the fuseboxes

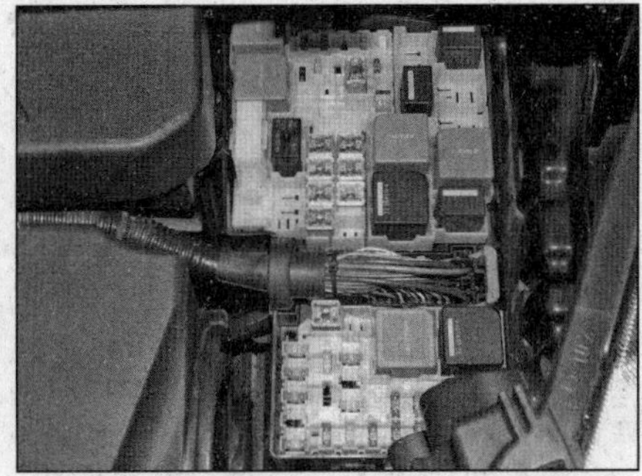

3.1b ...in the left-hand corner of the engine compartment...

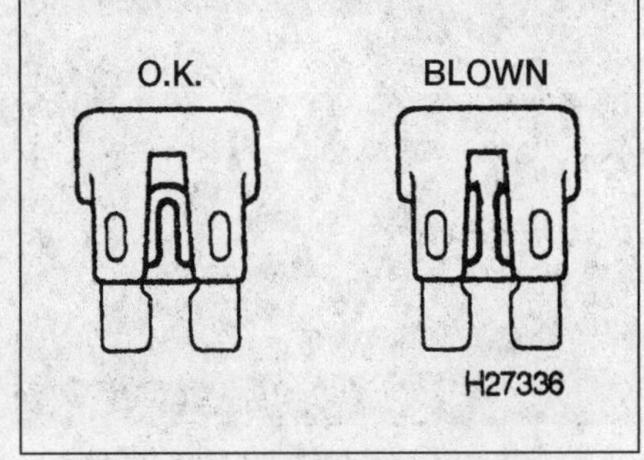

3.2 When a fuse blows, the element between the terminals melts

have a plastic bar on its upper surface to enable the use of the tweezers.

5 If a component controlled by a relay becomes inoperative and the relay is suspect, listen to the relay as the circuit is operated. If the relay is functioning, it should be possible to hear it click as it is energised. If the relay proves satisfactory, the fault lies with the components or wiring of the system. If the relay is not being energised, then either the relay is not receiving a switching voltage, or the relay itself is faulty (do not overlook the relay socket terminals when tracing faults.) Testing is by the substitution of a known good unit, but be careful; while some relays are identical in appearance and in operation, others look similar, but perform different functions.

4 Fuse box – removal and refitting

Removal

1 Remove the right-hand luggage compartment trim panel, as described in Chapter 11 Section 35.

2 Release the two lower tabs on the fusebox and manoeuvre from place, disconnecting the wiring plugs as they become available **(see illustration)**.

Refitting

3 Refitting is a reversal of removal.

4.2 Release the tabs to remove the fusebox

5 Electrical connectors – general information

1 Most electrical connections on these vehicles are made with multiwire plastic connectors. The mating halves of many connectors are secured with locking clips molded into the plastic connector shells. The mating halves of some large connectors, such as some of those under the instrument panel, are held together by a bolt through the center of the connector.

2 To separate a connector with locking clips, use a small screwdriver to pry the clips apart carefully, then separate the connector halves. Pull only on the shell, never pull on the wiring harness, as you may damage the individual wires and terminals inside the connectors. Look at the connector closely before trying to separate the halves. Often the locking clips are engaged in a way that is not immediately clear. Additionally, many connectors have more than one set of clips.

3 Each pair of connector terminals has a male half and a female half. When you look at the end view of a connector in a diagram, be sure to understand whether the view shows the harness side or the component side of the connector. Connector halves are mirror images of each other, and a terminal shown on the right side end-view of one half will be on the left side end-view of the other half.

4 It is often necessary to take circuit voltage measurements with a connector connected. Whenever possible, carefully insert a small straight pin (not your meter probe) into the rear of the connector shell to contact the terminal inside, then clip your meter lead to the pin. This kind of connection is called "backprobing." When inserting a test probe into a terminal, be careful not to distort the terminal opening. Doing so can lead to a poor connection and corrosion at that terminal later. Using the small straight pin instead of a meter probe results in less chance of deforming the terminal connector. "T" pins are a good choice as temporary meter connections. They allow for a larger surface area to attach the meter leads too.

Electrical connectors

5 Typical electrical connectors **(see illustrations)**:

5.5a Most electrical connectors have a single release tab that you depress to release the connector

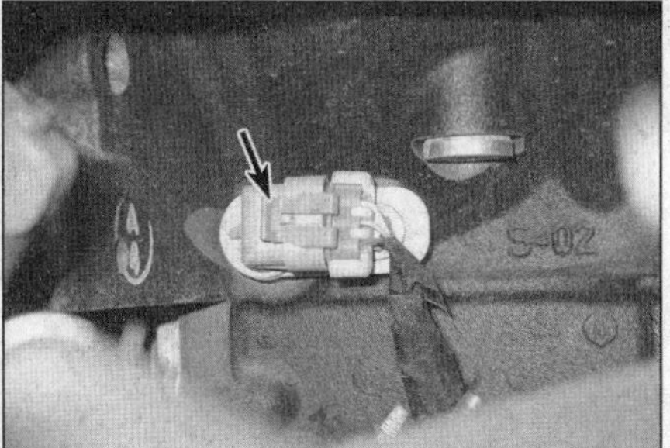

5.5b Some electrical connectors have a retaining tab which must be pried up to free the connector

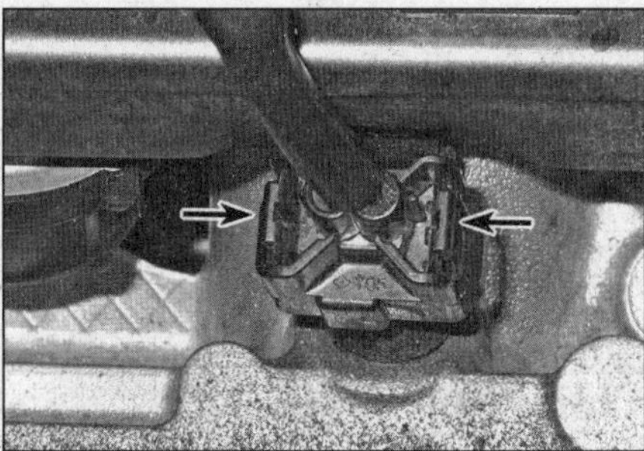

5.5c Some connectors have two release tabs that you must squeeze to release the connector

5.5d Some connectors use wire retainers that you squeeze to release the connector

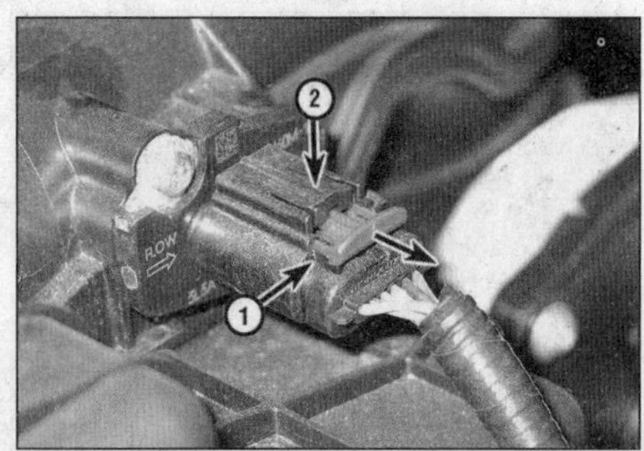

5.5e Critical connectors often employ a sliding lock (1) that you must pull out before you can depress the release tab (2)

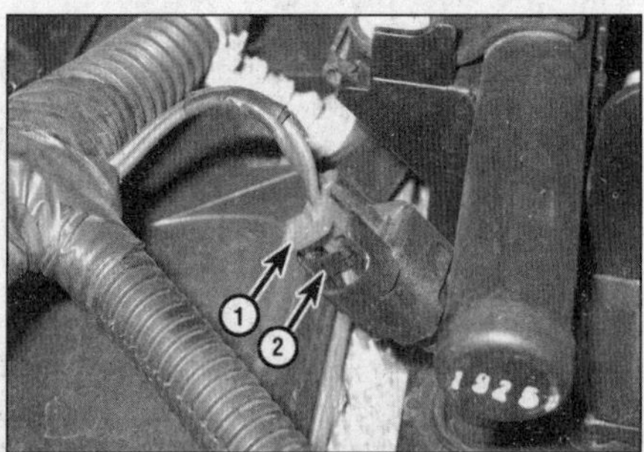

5.5f Here's another sliding-lock style connector, with the lock (1) and the release tab (2) on the side of the connector

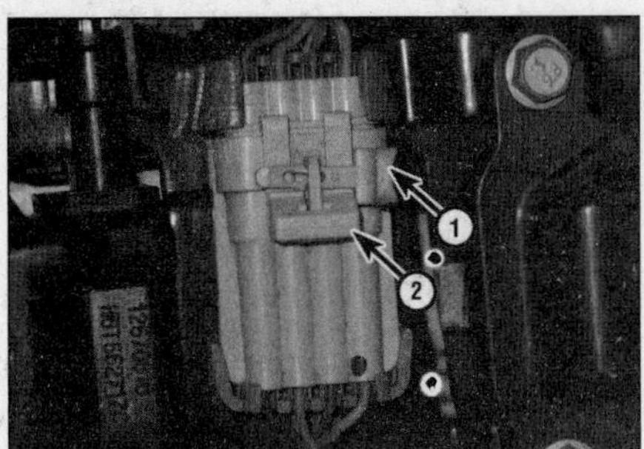

5.5g On some connectors the lock (1) must be pulled out to the side and removed before you can lift the release tab (2)

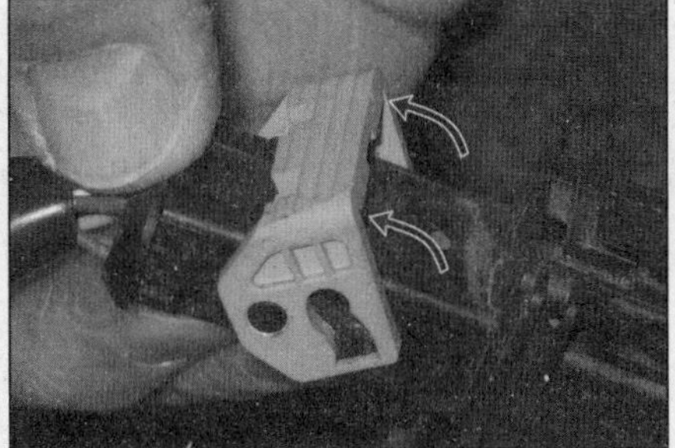

5.5h Some critical connectors, like the multi-pin connectors at the Electronic Control Module employ pivoting locks that must be flipped open

6.2 Disconnect the ignition switch wiring plug

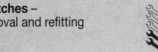

6 Switches – removal and refitting

Note: *Before removing any electrical switches, disconnect the battery negative (earth) lead as described in Chapter 5 Section 4.*

Removal

Ignition switch

1 Remove the central facia trim panel, as described in Chapter 11 Section 36.

2 Disconnect the ignition switch wiring plug **(see illustration)**.

3 Using a small screwdriver, depress the locating tabs and manoeuvre the ignition button from place **(see illustration)**.

Centre console power socket

4 Remove the centre console as described in Chapter 11 Section 36.

5 Disconnect the wiring plug for the power socket **(see illustration)**.

6 Using a small screwdriver, depress the 2 retaining tabs on the rear of the socket, and press it out from the rear **(see illustrations)**.

Handbrake switch

7 Remove the centre console panel from place, as described in Chapter 11 Section 36

8 Disconnect the handbrake switch wiring plug **(see illustration)**.

9 Undo the 3 retaining screws and manoeuvre from place **(see illustration)**.

Electric window switch

10 Remove the switch from the door as described in Chapter 11 Section 13.

11 Undo the retaining screws and separate the electric window switch panel from the door handle trim.

12 Refitting is a reversal of removal.

Central locking switch

13 This procedure is described in Chapter 11 Section 13.

Steering wheel switches

14 Remove the driver's airbag unit as described in Section 24.

15 Undo the relevant retaining screw and manoeuvre the switch from place **(see illustration)**.

6.3 Press in the tabs to release the button

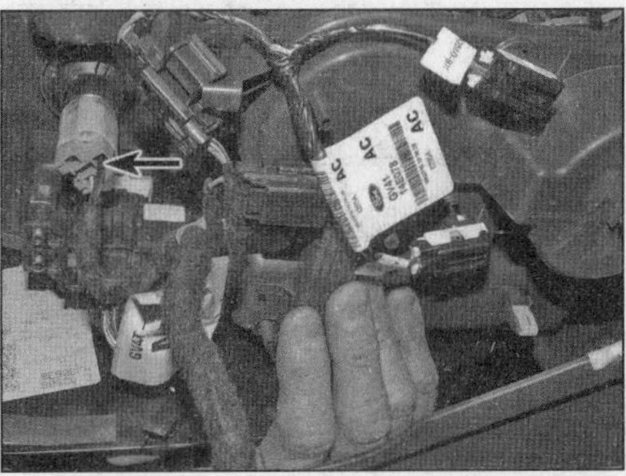

6.5 Disconnect the power socket wiring plug

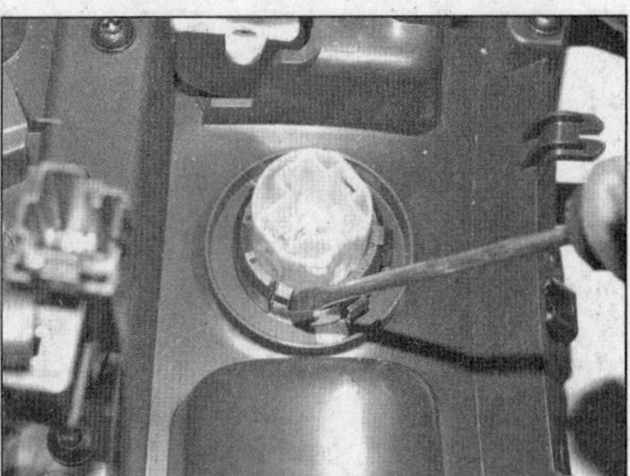

6.6a Use a screwdriver to activate the tabs...

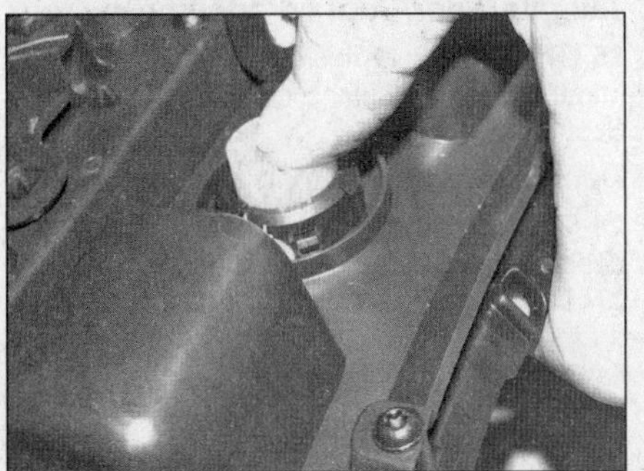

6.6b ...then press the socket from place

6.8 Disconnect the wiring plug

6.9 Unscrew the retaining fasteners and remove the switch

6.15 Unscrew the screw and remove the switch

6.16 Depress the tab and disconnect the wiring plug

6.17 Prise up the switch surround

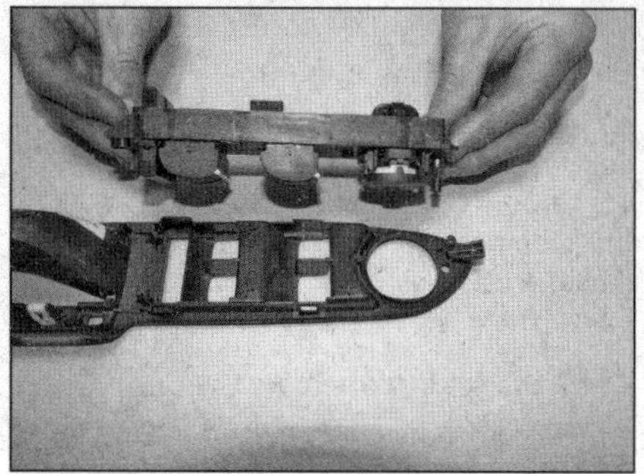
6.19 Undo the screws and detach the switch cluster

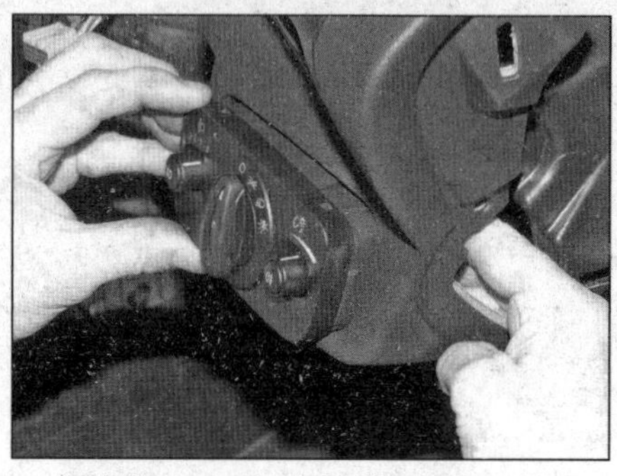
6.22 Depress the tabs then press the switch assembly rearwards

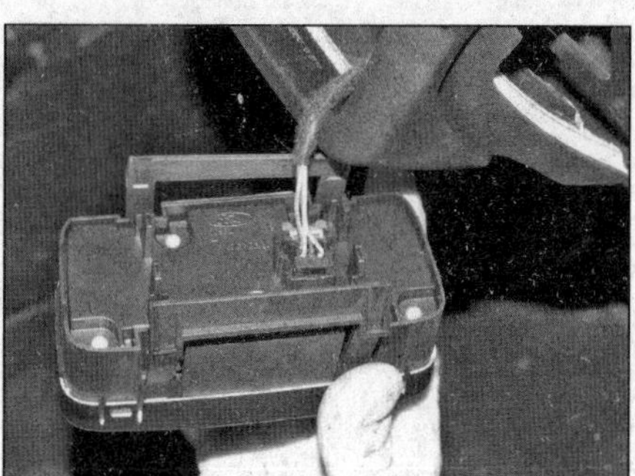
6.23 Disconnect the wiring plug

16 Using a small screwdriver, depress the tab and remove the wiring plug **(see illustration)**.

Electric window/ Door mirror control switches

17 Starting at the rear, carefully prise the trim and switch surround from the door trim **(see illustration)**.

18 Disconnect the wiring plug.

19 Undo the retaining screws and withdraw the switch cluster from the plastic trim **(see illustration)**.

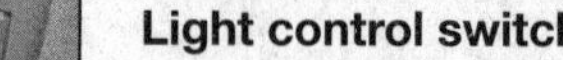

Light control switch

20 Remove the driver's side facia end panel as described in Chapter 11 Section 38.

21 Remove the driver's side lower facia panel as described in Chapter 11 Section 38.

22 Reach behind the facia panel and depress the upper and lower tabs, then press the switch assembly rearwards **(see illustration)**.

23 Disconnect the wiring plug **(see illustration)**.

Courtesy light door switch

24 The function of this switch is incorporated into the door lock assembly. See Chapter 11 Section 16.

Tailgate/door/boot lid opening switch

25 The function of this switch is incorporated into the tailgate lock assembly. See Chapter 11 Section 28.

Handbrake-on warning switch

26 Remove the rear centre console as described in Chapter 11 Section 36.

27 Disconnect the wiring, undo the screw and remove the switch from the handbrake lever bracket **(see illustration)**.

Roof console

28 Carefully prise the panel from the front of the console **(see illustrations)**. Disconnect any wiring plugs as the panel is withdrawn.

6.27 Disconnect the wiring plug, and undo the switch retaining screw

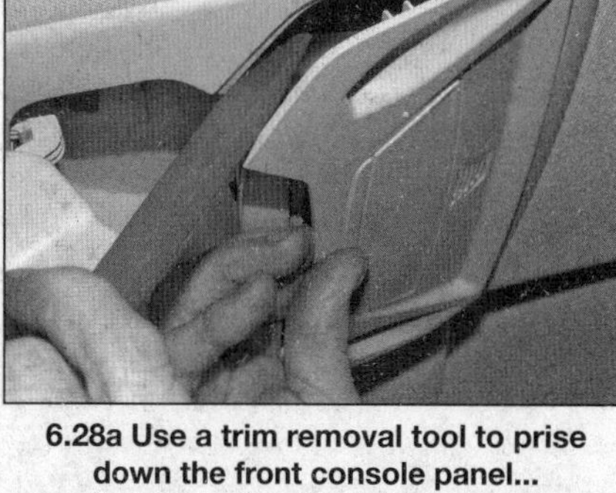
6.28a Use a trim removal tool to prise down the front console panel...

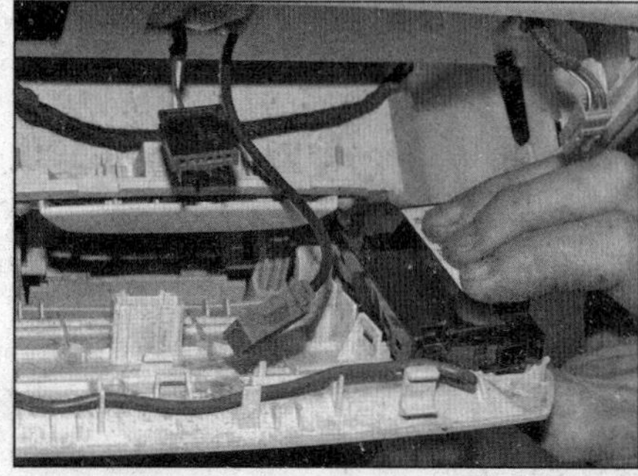
6.28b ...then disconnect any wiring plugs

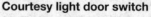

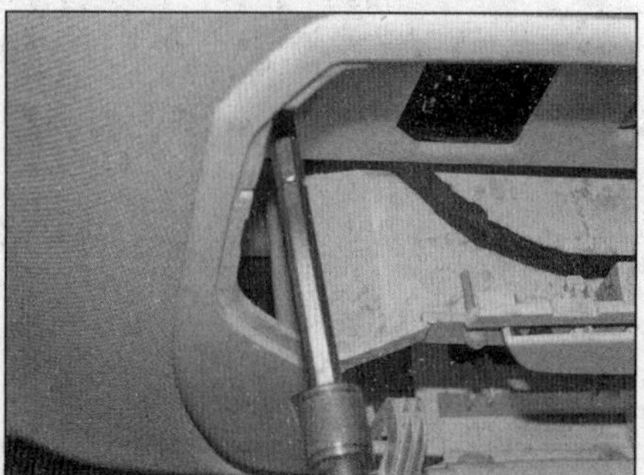
6.29a Remove the retaining screws...

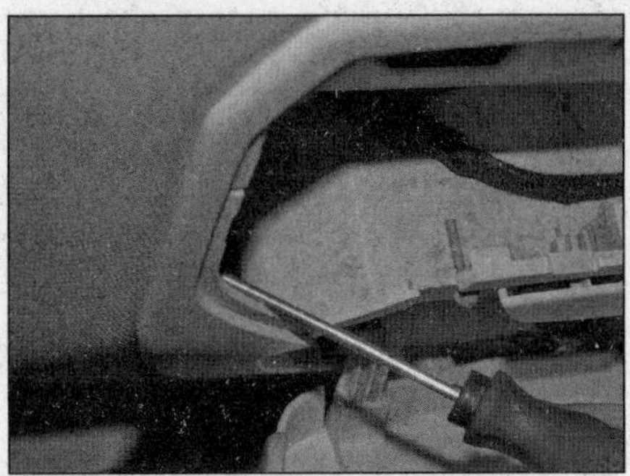

6.29b ...then release the clips

7.2 Prise away the light's protective cap

7.4 Gently pull the bulb from the holder

29 Undo the retaining screws and release the retaining tabs at each side of the panel **(see illustrations)**. Lower the panel from place.

Refitting

30 Refitting of all switches is a reversal of the removal procedure.

7 Bulbs (exterior lights) – renewal

1 Whenever a bulb is renewed, note the following points:

a) *Remember that if the light has just been in use, the bulb may be extremely hot.*

b) *Always check the bulb contacts and holder, ensuring that there is clean metal-to-metal contact between the bulb and its live(s) and earth. Clean off any corrosion or dirt before fitting a new bulb.*

c) *Wherever bayonet-type bulbs are fitted, ensure that the live contact(s) bear firmly against the bulb contact.*

d) *Always ensure that the new bulb is of the correct rating and that it is completely clean before fitting it; this applies particularly to headlight/foglight bulbs.*

e) *Do not touch the glass of halogen-type bulbs (headlights, front foglights) with the fingers, as this may lead to rapid blackening and failure of the new bulb; if the glass is accidentally touched, clean it with methylated spirit.*

f) *If renewing the bulb does not cure the problem, check the relevant fuse and relay with reference to the Specifications, and to the wiring diagrams at the end of this Chapter.*

Headlight dipped and main beam

2 At the rear of the headlight unit, prise the relevant rubber cap from place **(see illustration)**.

Dipped-beam bulb

3 Rotate the plastic bulb-holder anti-clockwise and remove it from the rear of the headlamp.

4 Pull the bulb from the bulbholder **(see illustration)**.

Main-beam bulb

5 Press the retaining clip to one side and withdraw the bulb **(see illustrations)**.

Front direction indicator

6 Using a trim removal tool, prise out the plastic surround of the indicator/foglight unit **(see illustration)**.

7 Undo the 2 retaining bolts and gently pull the unit from place, disconnecting the wiring plugs as they become available **(see illustrations)**.

8 Twist the bulbholder anti-clockwise and withdraw it **(see illustration)**.

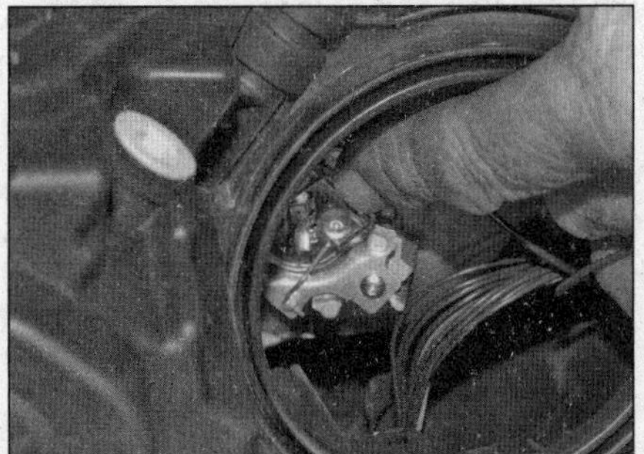

7.5a Squeeze the clip...

7.5b ...and remove the bulb

7.6 Prise out the light unit surround

7.7a Undo the 2 bolts...

7.7b ...and remove the light unit

7.8 Rotate the bulbholder anti-clockwise

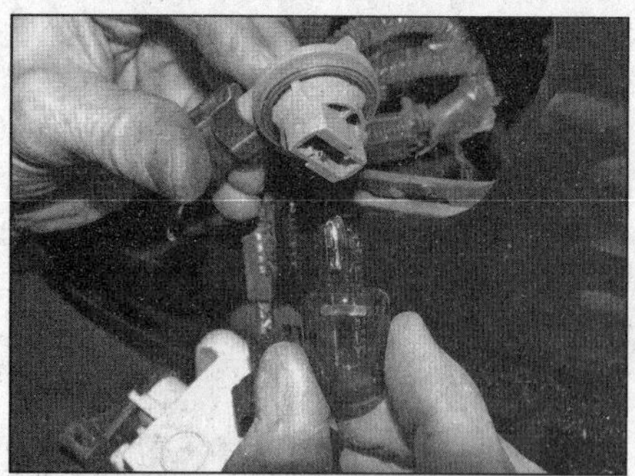
7.9 Pull the bulb from the holder

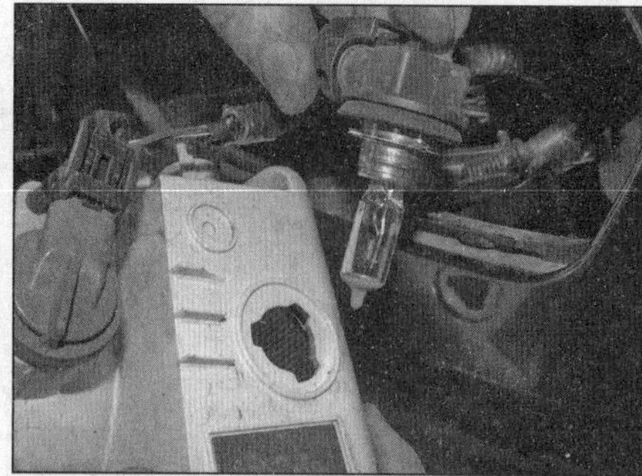
7.14 The foglight bulb is integral with the holder

7.16 Rotate the rear foglight bulbholder anti-clockwise

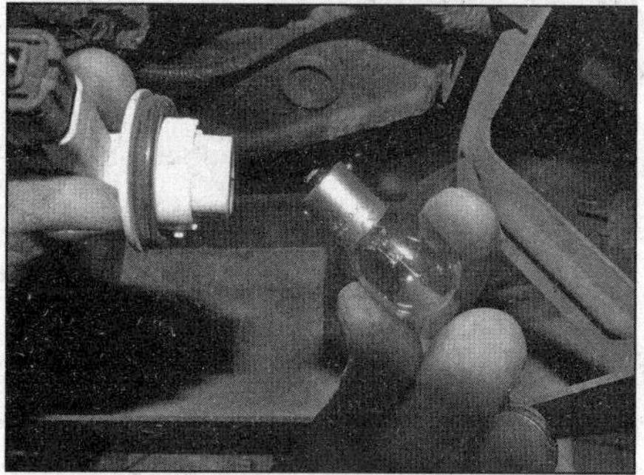
7.17 Twist and push the bulb to remove

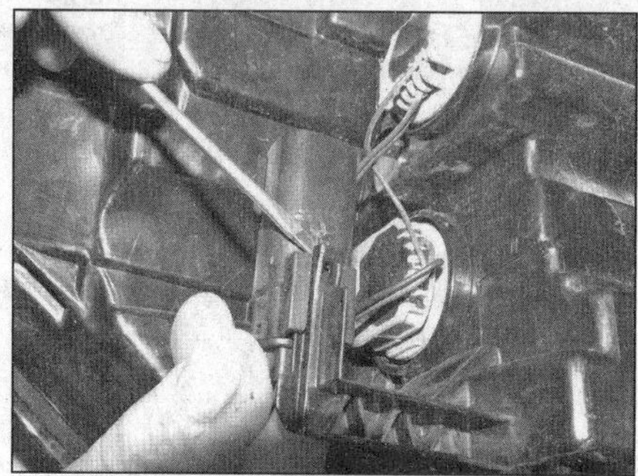
7.20 Separate the wiring plug holder from the unit

7.21 Depress and twist the lower bulbholder anti-clockwise

9 Pull the capless bulb from the holder **(see illustration)**.

10 Refitting is reversal of removal.

Direction indicator side repeaters

11 This procedure is described in Chapter 11 Section 24.

Daytime driving lights

12 These are part of the main headlight assembly, which is described in Section 9.

Front foglights

13 Remove the front indicator assembly as described earlier in this Section.

14 Rotate the bulbholder anti-clockwise, withdraw it from the light unit **(see illustration)**.

15 Refitting is reversal of removal.

Rear foglights

16 Reach up behind the relevant side of the bumper, turn the bulbholder anti-clockwise to remove it from the light unit **(see illustration)**.

17 Press and twist the bulb anti-clockwise to remove it from the bulbholder **(see illustration)**.

18 Fit the new bulb using a reversal of the removal procedure. Make sure that the light unit is located correctly.

Rear direction indicator

19 Remove the light cluster from the vehicle as described in Section 9.

20 Use a small screwdriver to disengage the retaining tab and detach the wiring plug holder from the rear of the light unit **(see illustration)**.

21 To replace the indicator bulb, depress and twist the lower of the two bulbholders anti-clockwise to remove it from the unit **(see illustration)**.

22 Pull the capless indicator bulb from the bulbholder **(see illustration)**.

23 Fit the new bulb using a reversal of the removal procedure.

Reversing light bulb

24 Remove the rear light cluster as described in Section 9.

25 Twist the bulbholder anti-clockwise to remove from place **(see illustration)**.

26 Press and twist the bulb anti-clockwise to remove.

27 Refitting is a reversal of removal.

Number plate light

28 Using a small screwdriver, gently prise the number plate light unit from the tailgate **(see illustration)**.

7.22 Pull the bulb straight out of the holder

7.25 Twist and remove the reversing light bulbholder

7.28 Gently prise the light unit from place

29 Twist the bulbholder anti-clockwise and remove it **(see illustration)**.
30 Pull the capless bulb from the bulbholder.
31 Refitting is a reversal of removal.

High-level stop-light

32 The high-level stop light is an LED unit. If defective, the complete assembly must be replaced as described in Section 9.

Puddle lights

33 Removal of the puddle lights is described in Chapter 11 Section 24.

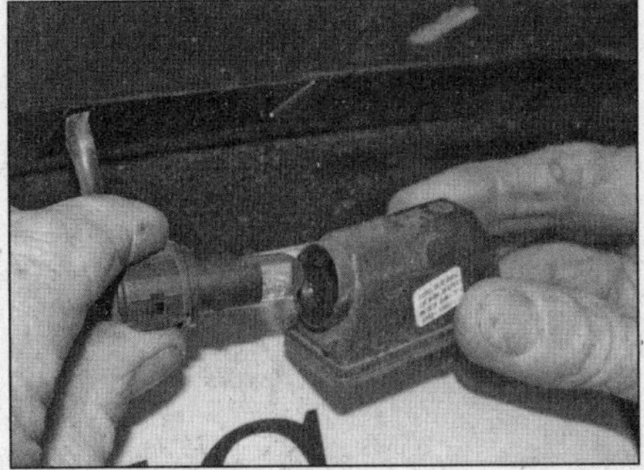

7.29 Twist and remove the bulbholder

8 Bulbs (interior lights) – renewal

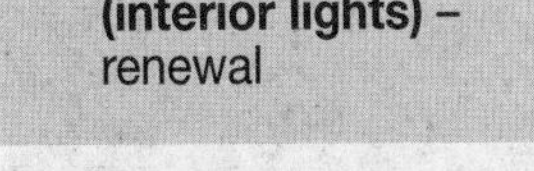

1 Whenever a bulb is renewed, note the following points:

a) *Remember that if the light has just been in use, the bulb may be extremely hot.*
b) *Always check the bulb contacts and holder, ensuring that there is clean metal-to-metal contact between the bulb and its live(s) and earth. Clean off any corrosion or dirt before fitting a new bulb.*
c) *Wherever bayonet-type bulbs are fitted, ensure that the live contact(s) bear firmly against the bulb contact.*
d) *Always ensure that the new bulb is of the correct rating and that it is completely clean before fitting it.*

Ceiling lights

Front

High-spec models

Note: *The ceiling lights are LEDs (Light Emitting Diodes). It is not possible to replace the internal components. If faulty, the complete light unit may require replacement.*

Front

2 Using a trim removal tool, prise down the rear edge of the light unit to release it from the headlining **(see illustration)**.
3 Disconnect the wiring plug from the light unit **(see illustration)**.
4 Refitting is a reversal of removal.

Rear

5 Carefully prise the light unit from place.
6 Disconnect the wiring plug.
7 Refitting is a reversal of removal.

Front door trim panel illumination

8 These are illuminated by LEDs. In order to remove them, remove the door inner trim panel as described in Chapter 11 Section 13.
9 Disconnect the wiring plug, release the clips and slide the LED from place **(see illustration)**.
10 Refitting is a reversal of removal.

Instrument panel illumination and warning lights

11 The instrument panel and warning light are illuminated by LEDs. No provision is made for the replacement of these LEDs.

Heater control/fan switch illumination

12 The control panel and switches are illuminated by LEDs. No provision is made for the replacement of these LEDs.

Glovebox lights

13 Remove the glovebox as described in Chapter 11 Section 37.
14 Disconnect the wiring plug and carefully prise the light unit from place **(see illustration)**.
15 Rotate the bulbholder anti-clockwise and pull it from the light unit.
16 Pull the wedge type bulb out to remove.
17 Fit the new bulb using a reversal of the removal procedure.

Luggage compartment lights

18 Insert a blunt, flat-bladed tool at the marked position, and carefully prise the light unit from place **(see illustration)**.
19 Pull the capless bulb from place.
20 Refitting is a reversal of removal.

Vanity lights

21 Fold down the sun visor, and carefully prise the light lens from place, levering at its edge as shown **(see illustration)**.
22 Prise the festoon bulb from the holder **(see illustration)**.
23 Refitting is a reversal of removal.

Front footwell lights

24 Undo the 2 retaining clips and remove the lower trim panel **(see illustration)**.

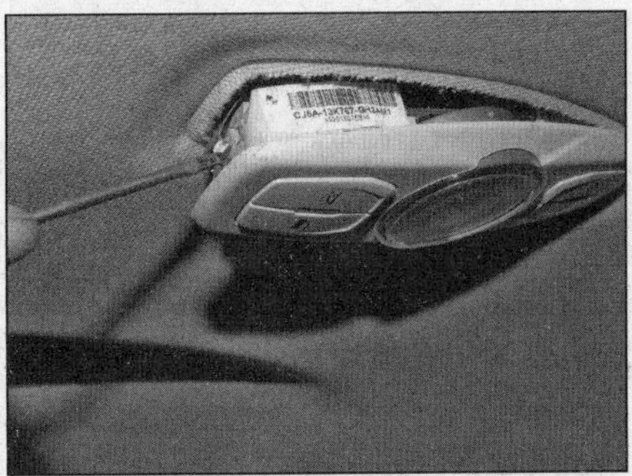

8.2 Lever down the rear of the light unit to release it

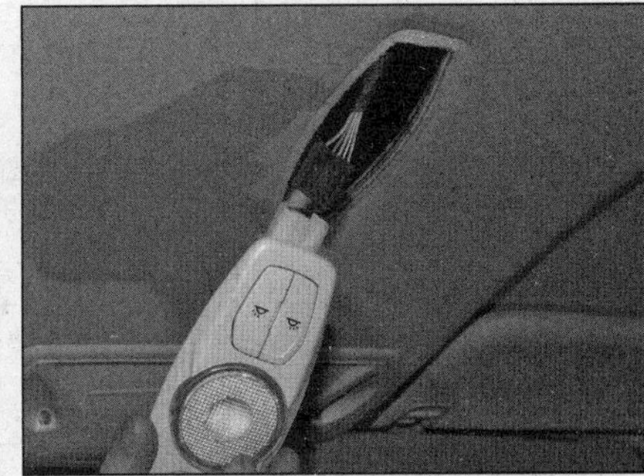

8.3 Disconnect the wiring plug

8.9 Disconnect the wiring plug and release the LED clips

8.14 Carefully prise out the light unit

8.18 Use a flat-bladed tool to gently prise out the light unit

8.21 Use a small screwdriver to prise away the vanity light bulb cover

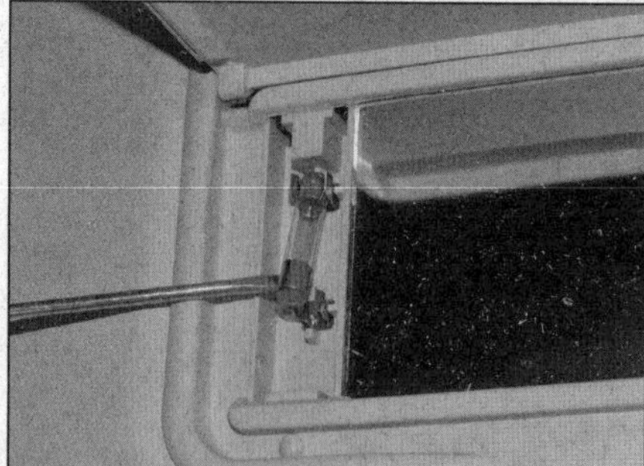
8.22 Prise the bulb from the holder

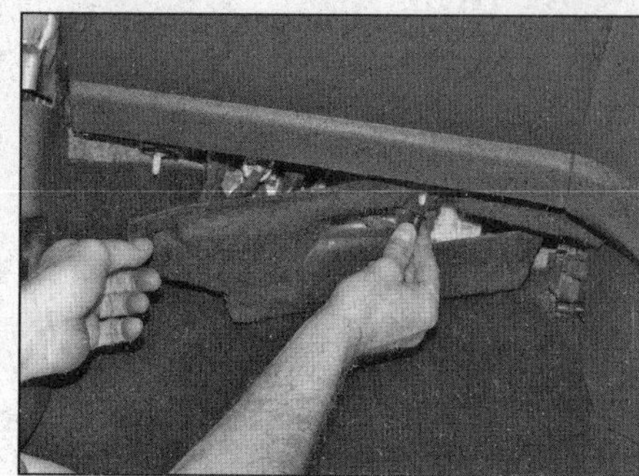
8.24 Release the clips and lower the panel

25 Using a small screwdriver, gently prise out the footwell light from its retaining bracket and unplug **(see illustrations).**

Note: *The light is an LED unit. If defective, the complete assembly must be replaced.*

9 Exterior light units – removal and refitting

1 Before removing any light unit, note the following points:

a) *Ensure that the light is switched off before starting work.*

b) *Remember that if the light has just been in use, the bulb and lens may be extremely hot.*

Headlight unit

2 Remove the front bumper cover as described in Chapter 11 Section 5.

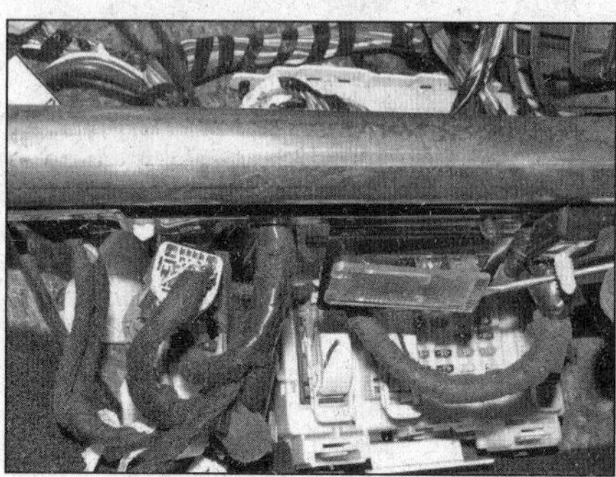
8.25a Prise out the footwell light...

8.25b ...and disconnect the wiring plug

3 Undo the 3 mounting screws **(see illustrations).**

4 Disconnect the wiring plug **(see illustration).**

5 Undo the plastic grille top mounting panel retaining bolt **(see illustration).**

6 Lift up the plastic mounting to disengage the headlight locating tab, then pull the headlight forward **(see illustrations).**

7 Refitting is a reversal of removal. Check the gap between the headlight and bonnet –

9.3a Undo the top front screw...

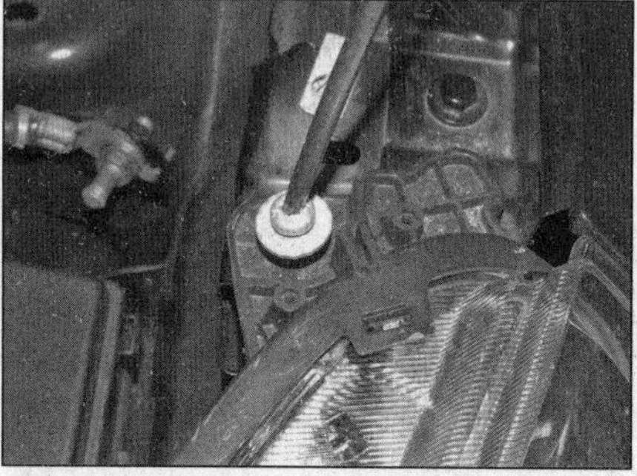
9.3b ...then the rear top mounting screw...

9.3c ...and finally the side mounting screw

9.4 Disconnect the headlight wiring plug

9.5 Undo the grille top mounting retaining bolt

9.6a Disengage the locating tab...

9.6b ...then pull forward the headlight

9.9 Undo the 3 retaining screws and remove the control unit

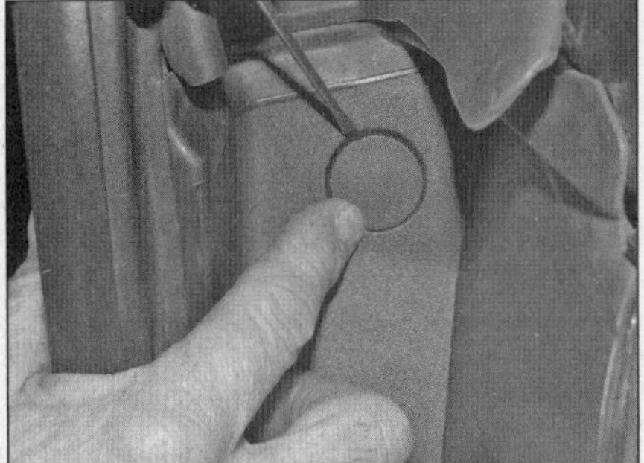
9.13 Gently prise the bolt covers away

9.14 Rear light retaining bolts

9.15a Remove the light unit from the body of the vehicle...

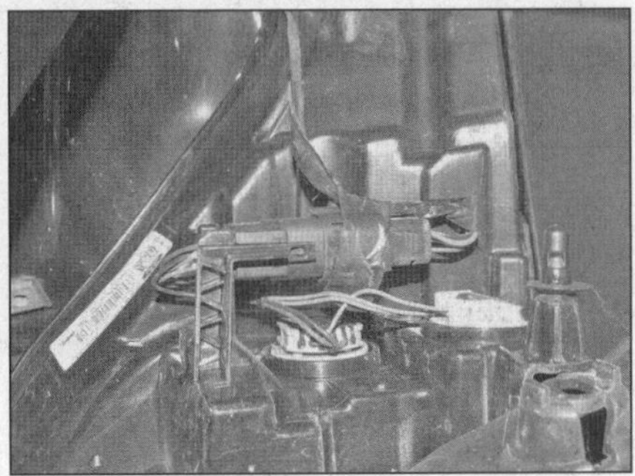
9.15b ...and disconnect the wiring plug

reposition the headlight as necessary. Have the headlight alignment checked as described in the Section 10.

Front light electronics control unit – LED headlights

Note: *If a new control unit is to be fitted, it must be programmed using Ford diagnostic equipment (or equivalent). Entrust this task to a Ford dealer or suitably equipped repairer.*

8 Remove the relevant headlight as described previously in this Section.

9 Undo the 3 retaining screws and detach the control unit from the headlight **(see illustration)**. The wiring plug is automatically disconnected as the control unit is detached from the headlight.

10 Refitting is a reversal of removal. Ensure the rubber seal between the control unit and the headlight is clean and free from damage or deterioration.

Direction indicator side repeaters

11 Removal and refitting the side repeaters is described in Section 7.

Front fog lights

12 Removal and refitting the foglights is described in Section 7.

Rear light cluster

13 Using a flat-bladed tool, carefully prise the covers for the light unit retaining bolts from place **(see illustration)**.

14 Undo the 2 retaining bolts **(see illustration)**.

15 Carefully prise the light unit from the vehicle body. Disconnect the wiring plug as the unit is withdrawn **(see illustrations)**.

16 Refit the light unit using a reversal of the removal procedure. Make sure that the light unit is located correctly.

Reversing light cluster

17 Remove the tailgate inner trim as described in Chapter 11 Section 35.

18 Unscrew the 2 retaining bolts and manoeuvre the cluster from place **(see illustrations)**.

High-level stop light

19 Remove the tailgate upper trim as described in Chapter 11 Section 35.

20 Working through the apertures in the tailgate, prise off the clips from the rear of the stop light **(see illustration)**.

21 Close the tailgate and pull the stop light

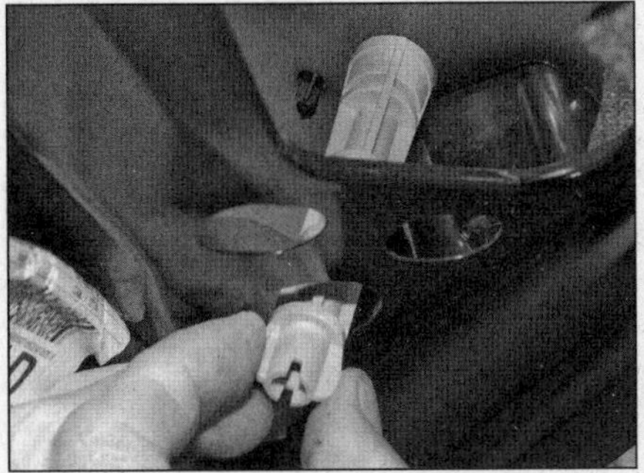
9.18a Undo the retaining bolts...

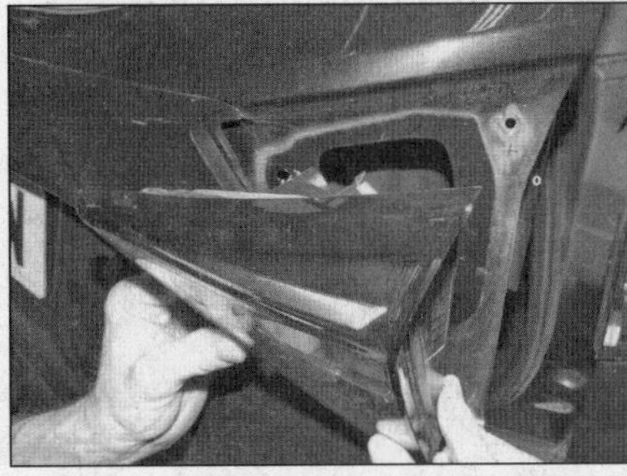
9.18b ...and pull the cluster rearwards

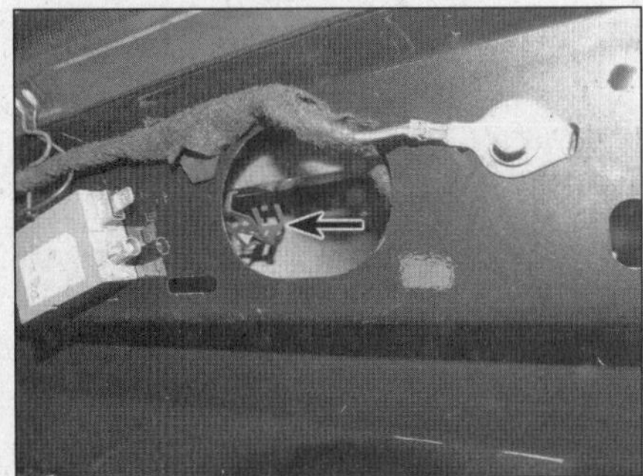
9.20 Remove the clips from the light unit

9.21a Pull the light rearward...

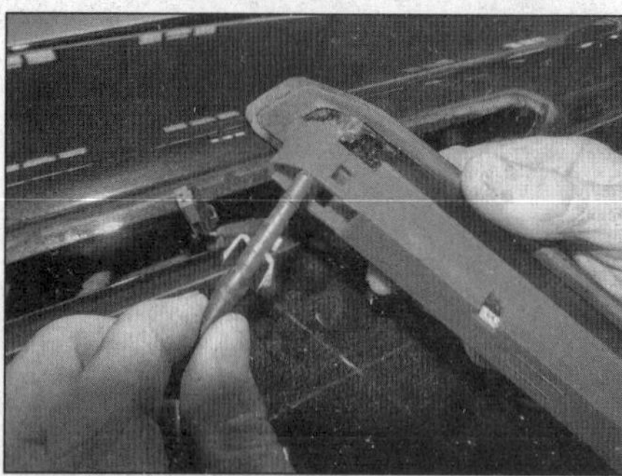
9.21b ...then disconnect the washer jet...

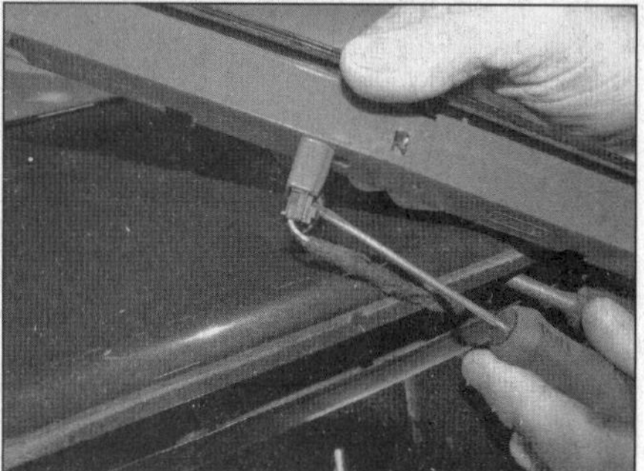

9.21c ...and wiring plug

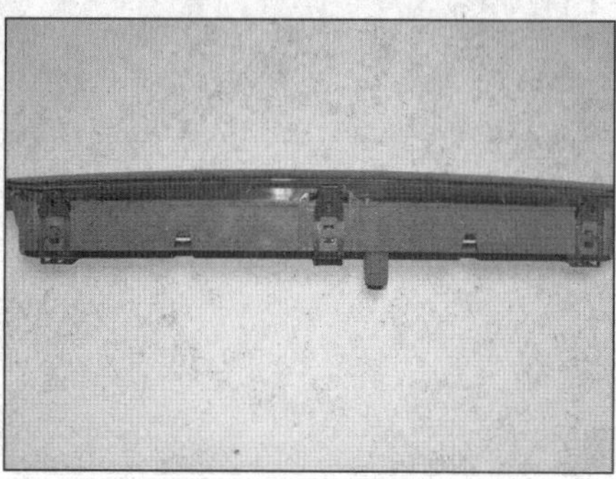
9.22 Make sure the clips fit to the tabs on the light unit

from place, disconnecting the washer jet and wiring plug as they become available **(see illustrations)**.

22 If any of the clips have fallen off, retrieve them from the tailgate and fit to the stop light unit **(see illustration)**.

23 Fit the new light unit using a reversal of the removal procedure.

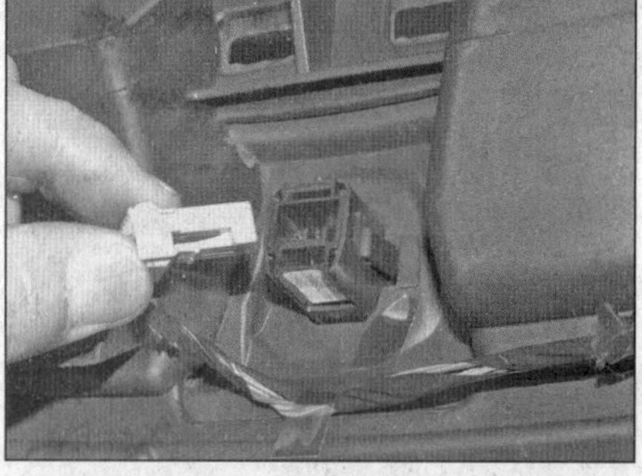
11.2 Disconnect the wiring plug for the light sensor

11.3 Squeeze together the tabs and remove the light sensor

10 Headlight levelling motor – removal and refitting

1 It's not possible to dismantle the headlight unit and renew the levelling motor. In the event of a fault the complete headlight unit must be replaced as described in Section 9.

11 Front light sensor – removal and refitting

Removal

1 Remove the facia top panel as described in Chapter 11 Section 38.

2 Disconnect the light sensor wiring plug **(see illustration)**.

3 Squeeze the tabs and remove the light sensor from place **(see illustration)**.

Refitting

4 Refitting is a reversal of removal.

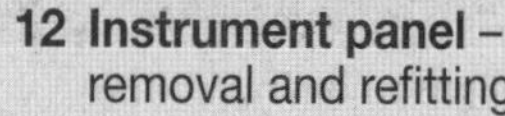

12 Instrument panel – removal and refitting

Caution: If the instrument panel is being renewed, the stored configuration data must be loaded into Ford's diagnostic system, and download into the new instrument panel once fitted. Refer to your local Ford authorised repairer or suitably equipped specialist.

Removal

1 Disconnect the battery negative lead as described in Chapter 5 Section 4.

Main instrument panel

2 Prise out the steering column upper shroud **(see illustration)**.

3 Undo the 2 retaining screws below the instrument panel **(see illustration)**.

4 Manoeuvre the instrument panel rearwards and disconnect the wiring plug as it becomes accessible **(see illustrations)**.

12.2 Unclip the steering column upper shroud

12.3 Remove the 2 instrument panel screws

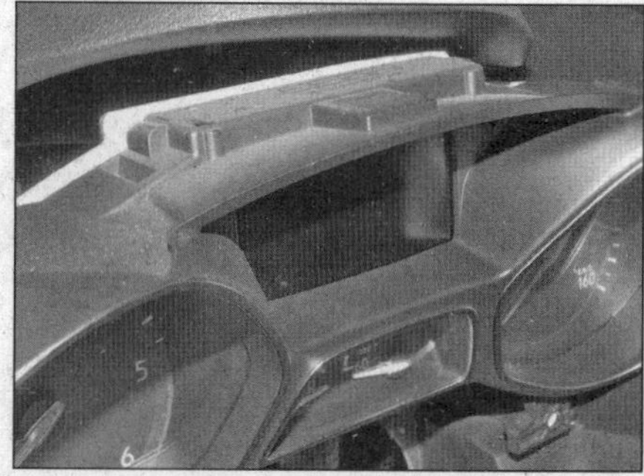
12.4a Pull the panel rearwards...

12.4b ...and disconnect the wiring plug

13.2 Horn retaining nut

13.3 Disconnect the horn wiring plug

Refitting

5 Refitting is a reversal of the removal procedure.

13 Horns – removal and refitting

1 Remove the panel across the top of the front grille as described in Chapter 11 Section 5.

2 Undo the retaining nut on each horn and manoeuvre the horn from place **(see illustration)**.

3 Disconnect the horn wiring plug **(see illustration)**.

4 Refitting is a reversal of the removal procedure.

14 Active shutter grille motor – removal and refitting

Removal

1 Remove the active shutter grille from the vehicle, as described in Chapter 11 Section 6.

2 Working on the right-hand side of the shutter motor, remove all the slats, including the controlling slat (second one down from the top, with a flat cut-out in it) **(see illustration)**.

3 Remove the cover from the rear of the motor, disengaging it from the slats on the left-hand side of the motor **(see illustration)**.

4 Turn over the active grille, and prise out the panel next to the motor using a small screwdriver **(see illustration)**. This panel contains a small locating rod that holds the motor in place.

5 Lift the motor from its mounting **(see illustration)**.

Refitting

6 Refitting is reversal of removal, making sure to replace the control slat in the correct place, attached to the motor.

15 Wiper arms – removal and refitting

Removal

1 Ensure the wipers are parked in the normal at-rest position. If necessary, mark the positions of the blade(s) on the windshield, using a wax crayon or strips of masking tape, although there are marks printed on the screen already.

2 Open the bonnet and secure it.

3 Remove the plastic cap from the bottom of the wiper arm, and slacken the nut one or two turns **(see illustration)**.

4 Lift the wiper arm, and carefully release it from the taper on the spindle by moving it from side-to-side. If the wiper arm is stubborn to remove, use a puller **(see illustration)**.

5 Completely remove the nut, and withdraw the wiper arm from the spindle **(see illustrations)**. Mark each arm to identify it's fitted position.

Refitting

6 Switch on the ignition and operate the

14.2 The control slat has a flat cut-out in it

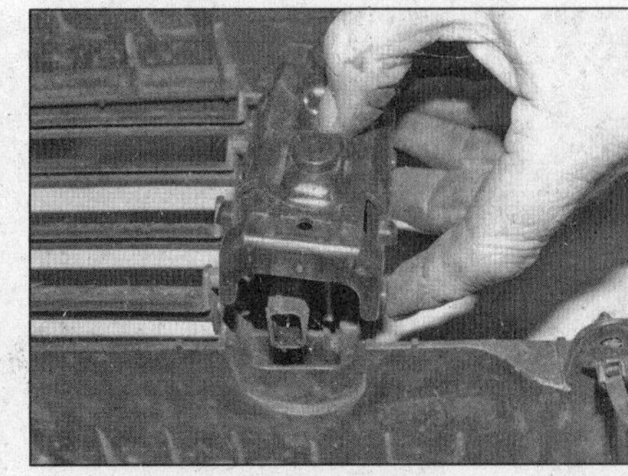
14.3 Disengage the motor cover from all the slats

14.4 Prise the motor panel from place

14.5 The motor can now be removed

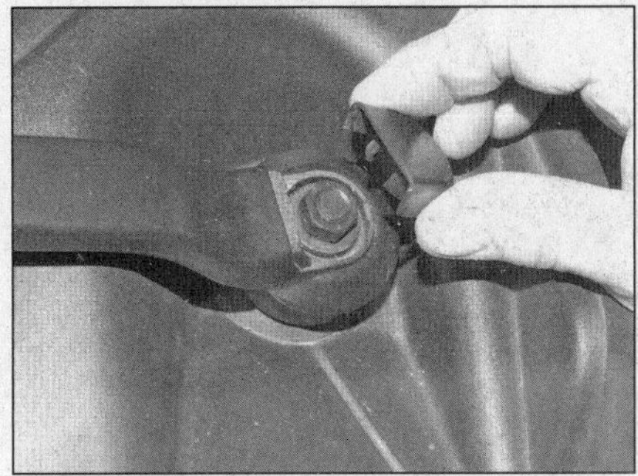
15.3 Lift up the cap and slacken the spindle nut

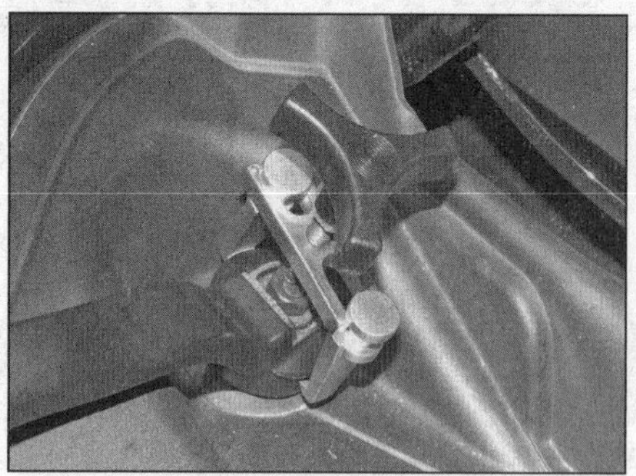
15.4 If necessary, use a puller to remove the wiper arm

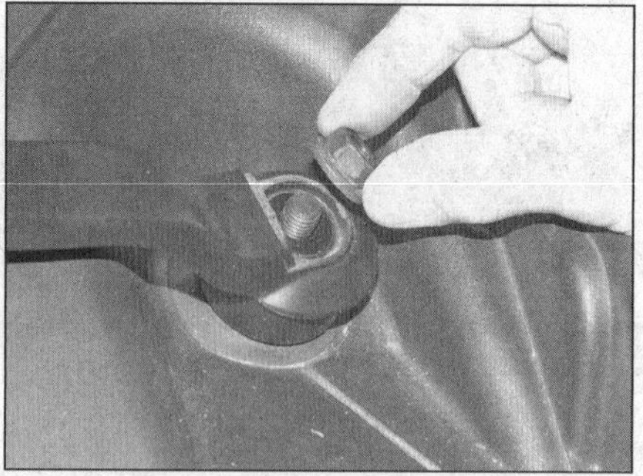
15.5a Undo the nut and withdraw the arm

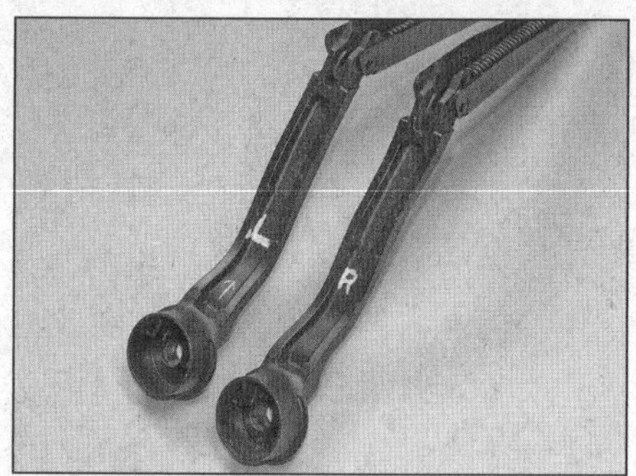

15.5b Mark the arms to aid refitting

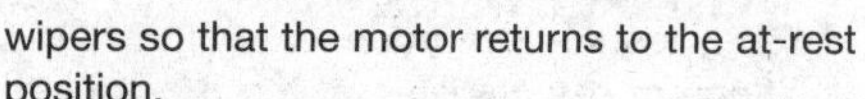

wipers so that the motor returns to the at-rest position.

7 Installation is a reversal of the removal procedure. Make sure that the arm is installed in the previously noted position before tightening the nut.

16 Windscreen wiper motor and linkage – removal and refitting

Removal

Note: *There are two wiper motors, one at each side of the engine bay below the windscreen. Each is embossed with 'LH' or 'RH' on its upper cover, to signify left-hand or right-hand motor.*

1 Remove the windscreen lower trim panel as described in Chapter 11 Section 12.

2 Disconnect the wiring plug for the heated windscreen **(see illustration)**.

3 Undo the mounting bolt and withdraw the relevant motor **(see illustration)**.

4 Disconnect the wiring plug and manoeuvre the motor and linkage assembly from place.

5 To separate the motor from the bracket, first place an alignment mark between the bracket and motor **(see illustration)**.

6 Undo the 3 mounting screws and separate the motor from the bracket **(see illustration)**.

Refitting

7 Refitting is a reversal of the removal procedure, noting the following points:

a) *Tighten the wiper motor mounting bolts securely.*

b) *Use grease to lubricate the wiper spindle and linkages when re-assembling.*

17 Tailgate wiper arm – removal and refitting

Removal

1 With the wiper parked (in the normal at-rest position), mark the positions of the blade(s) on the rear screen, using a wax crayon or strips of masking tape **(see illustration)**.

2 Lift up the plastic cap from the bottom of the wiper arm, and slacken the nut one or two turns **(see illustration)**.

3 Lift the wiper arm, and carefully release it from the taper on the spindle by moving it from side-to-side. If the wiper arm is reluctant to release, use a puller **(see illustration)**.

4 Completely remove the nut, and withdraw the wiper arm from the spindle.

16.2 Disconnect the heated screen wiring plug

16.3 Undo the motor mounting bolts

16.5 Mark the motor and bracket to aid realignment

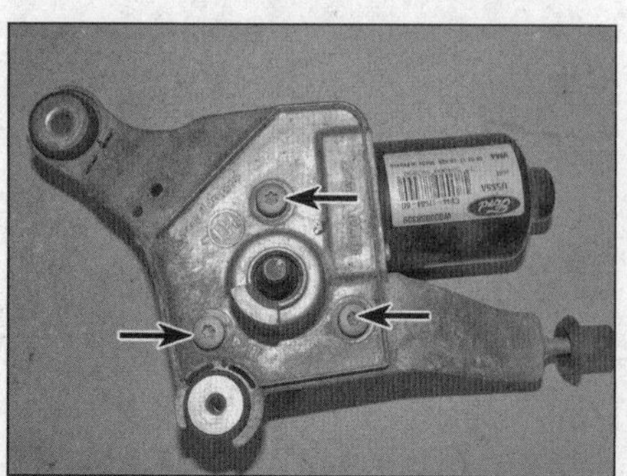
16.6 Undo the 3 mounting screws and separate the bracket from the motor

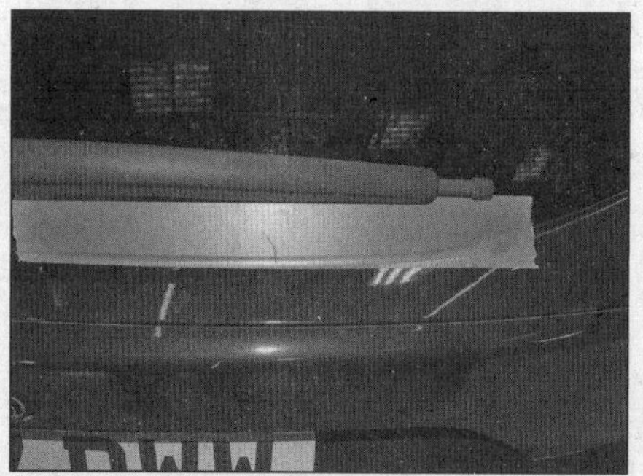
17.1 Mark where the wiper should rest

17.2 Lift up the arm cover and slacken the spindle nut

17.3 If necessary, use a puller to remove the wiper arm

18.3 Disconnect the wiring plug

18.4 Tailgate wiper motor mounting bolts

Refitting

5 Installation is a reversal of the removal procedure. Make sure that the arm is installed in the previously noted position before tightening the nut.

18 Tailgate wiper motor assembly – removal and refitting

Removal

1 Remove the tailgate wiper arm as described in Section 15.

2 Remove the tailgate inner trim panel as described in Chapter 11 Section 35.

3 Disconnect the wiring plug from the wiper motor **(see illustration)**.

4 Unscrew the 3 mounting bolts, and remove the wiper motor from inside the tailgate **(see illustration)**.

Refitting

5 Refitting is a reversal of the removal procedure. Make sure that the wiper motor is in its 'parked' position before fitting the wiper arm.

19 Windscreen/tailgate washer system components – removal and refitting

Removal

Windscreeen/tailgate washer reservoir

1 Detach the front of the right-hand front wheelarch liner as described in Chapter 11 Section 39 and move it out of the way.

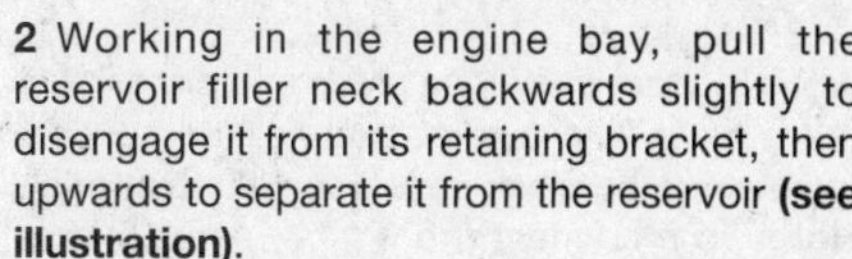

2 Working in the engine bay, pull the reservoir filler neck backwards slightly to disengage it from its retaining bracket, then upwards to separate it from the reservoir **(see illustration)**.

3 Disconnect the wiring plugs for the fluid level sensor and washer pump, then disconnect the hoses from the pump **(see illustrations)**.

4 Undo the retaining bolt at the each side of the reservoir **(see illustration)**.

5 Carefully prise the bottom of the reservoir up to detach it from its lower mounting and withdraw it.

6 Refitting is the reverse of removal.

Washer jet (windscreen)

7 Open the bonnet and secure it.

8 Use a screwdriver to release the 14 retaining clips and remove the under-bonnet acoustic matting **(see illustrations)**.

19.2 Pull the reservoir neck backwards and upwards to remove

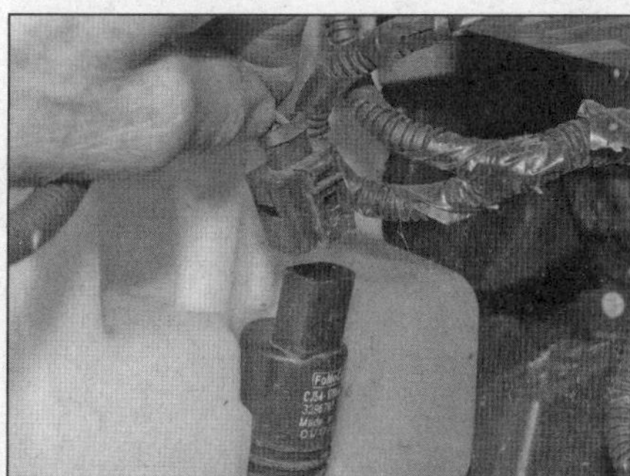

19.3a Disconnect the wiring plug...

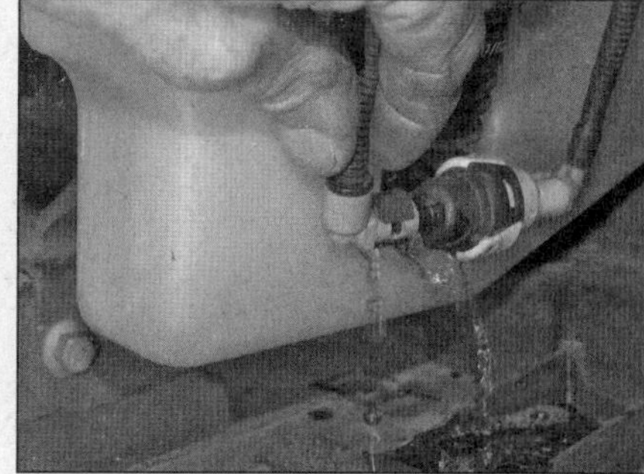

19.3b ...rotate the collar and disconnect the hoses

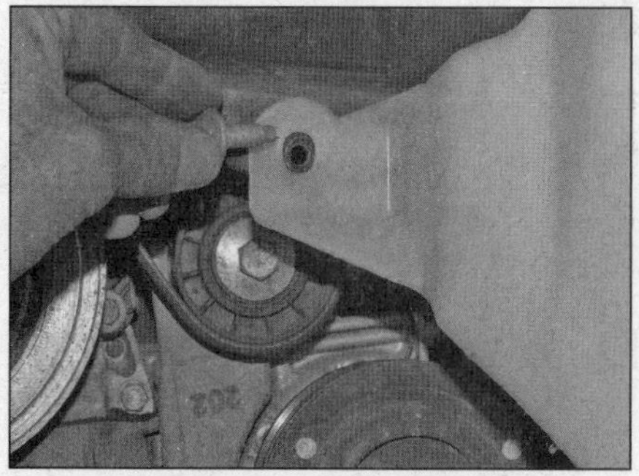

19.4 Remove the 2 retaining bolts

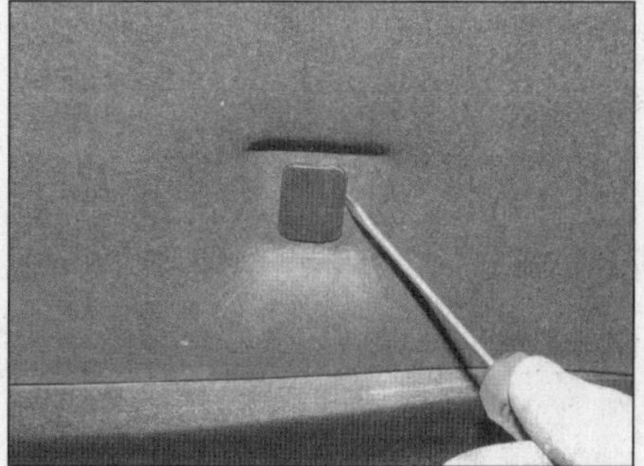

19.8a Remove the 14 clips...

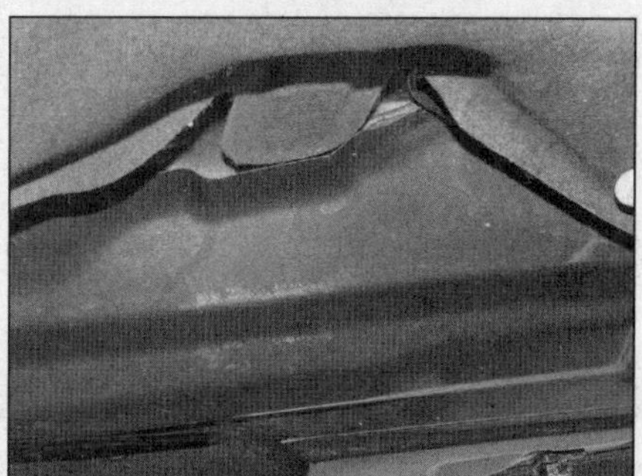

19.8b and remove the under-bonnet matting

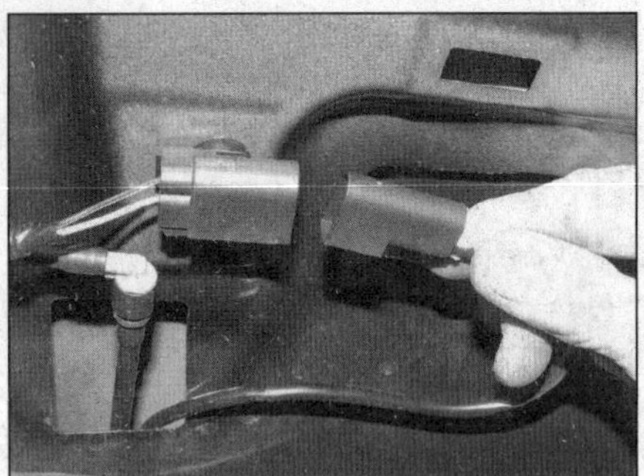
19.9a Disconnect the plugs...

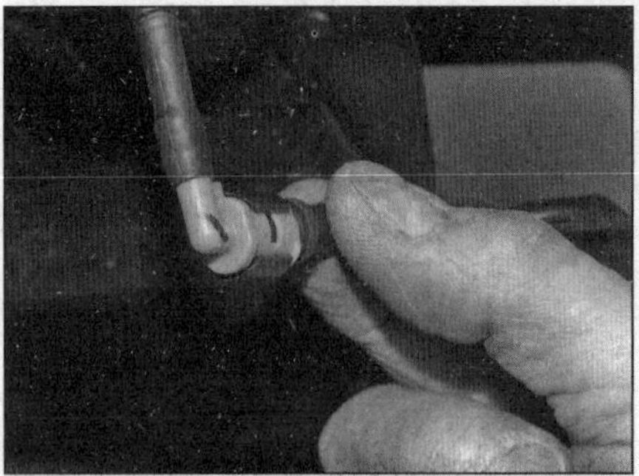
19.9b ..and then the washer connections by rotating the black collar and separating the pipes

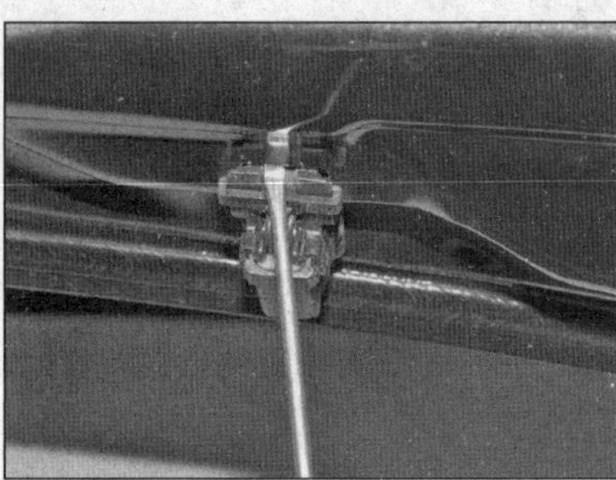
19.10 Release the jet and pull from place

9 Disconnect the wiring plugs and disconnect the washer fluid pipe at each joining section, by rotating the black collar **(see illustrations)**. **Note:** *To reconnect the washer pipes, rotate the collar back into the 'locked' position, and the pipe will snap into its fixing when pressed home.*

10 Use a small screwdriver to depress the retaining clip and pull the washer jet from place, taking care to feed the wire and plug through the aperture **(see illustration)**.

Washer jet (rear window)

11 The jet is integral with the high-level stoplight assembly. The removal and refitting procedures are covered in Section 9.

Refitting

12 Refitting is a reversal of the removal procedure, noting the following points:

a) *In the case of the screen washer jets, press them in firmly until they are fully engaged.*

b) *If necessary, the aim of the windscreen jets can be adjusted using a fine needle or pin. Take care not to inadvertently increase the diameter of the jet hole with an oversize pin/needle.*

20 Audio Unit, Car Communication Computer and Head unit – removal and refitting

1 Disconnect the battery negative lead as described in Chapter 5 Section 4.

SYNC screen and disc player

2 Prise up the mesh grille on top of the facia **(see illustration)**.

3 Undo the 2 retaining screws that secure the disc-player housing panel **(see illustration)**.

4 Prise up the panel by the light sensor (on some models this may contain a speaker) **(see illustration)**.

5 Use a trim removal tool to gently prise up the disc-player surround panel **(see illustration)**.

6 Disconnect the wiring plug for the light units **(see illustration)**.

7 Remove the 2 retaining screws at the top of the screen surround panel **(see illustration)**.

8 Using a trim removal tool, prise up the bottom of the screen surround panel, and withdraw it **(see illustration)**.

9 Disconnect the wiring plug for the audio controls **(see illustration)**.

10 Undo the 4 mounting screws and remove the central display screen from place **(see illustration)**.

20.2 Gently prise up the facia mesh grille

20.3 Remove the disc-player panel securing screws

20.4 Use a trim removal tool to lever up the panel by the light sensor

20.5 Carefully prise up the disc-player surround panel

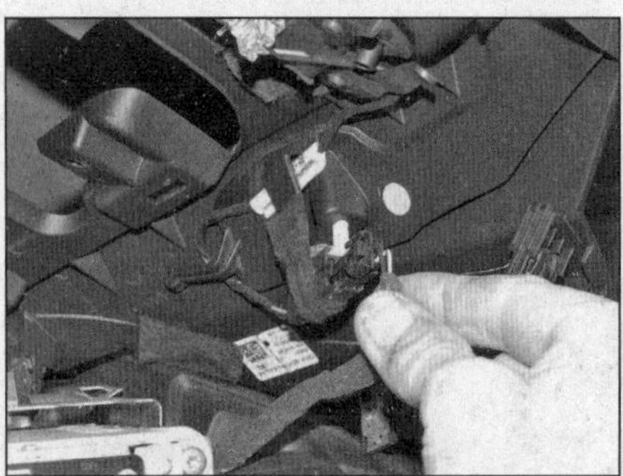
20.6 Disconnect the wiring plug

20.7 Undo the screen surround panel retaining screws

20.8 Prise up the panel

20.9 Disconnect the wiring plug for the audio controls

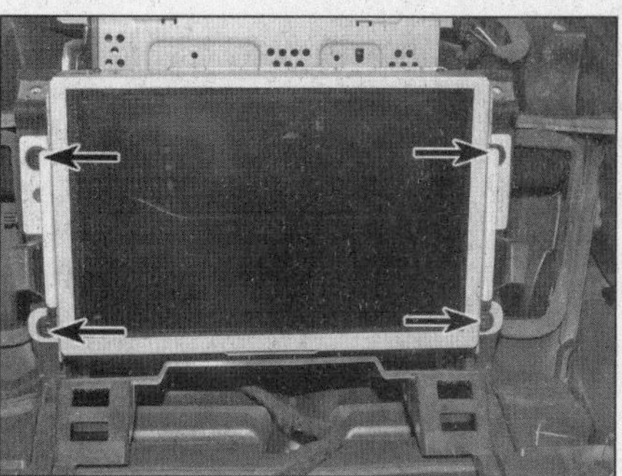
20.10 Undo the screws and remove the screen

11 Disconnect the wiring plugs from the rear of the unit as they become available.
12 To remove the disc player, undo the 2 mounting screws **(see illustration)**.
13 Disconnect the wiring plugs **(see illustration)**.
14 Refitting is a reversal of removal.

21 USB sockets – removal and refitting

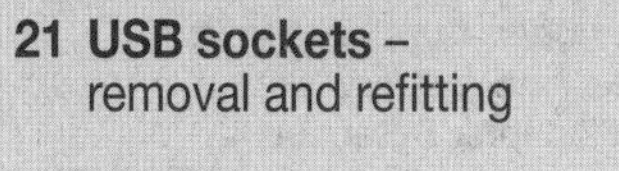

Removal

1 The USB sockets are located in the storage compartment at the rear of the centre console.
2 Use a hook-shaped trim removal tool to depress the tab behind each side of the USB socket panel and prise up **(see illustration)**.
3 Disconnect the wiring plugs as they become available **(see illustration)**.

Refitting

4 Reconnect the wiring plugs and press the USB panel back into place.

22 Speakers – removal and refitting

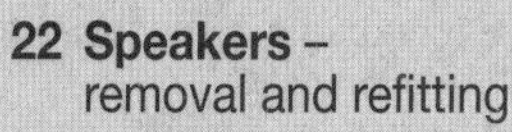

Removal

Front and rear door speakers

1 Remove the door inner trim panel as described in Chapter 11 Sections 13 or 19.

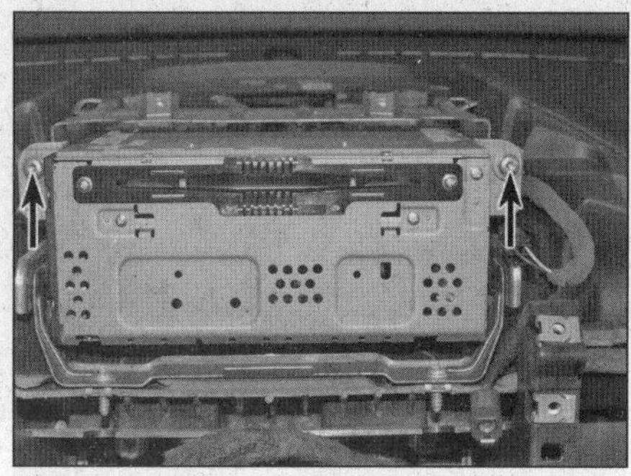
20.12 Undo the 2 mounting screws to remove

20.13 Disconnect the wiring plugs

2 Disconnect the wiring plug **(see illustration)**.
3 Unscrew the 3 screws, and withdraw the speaker **(see illustration)**.

Facia speaker

4 Carefully prise the speaker cover from the centre of the facia **(see illustration)**.
5 Undo the 2 retaining screws and remove

21.2 Use a hook to depress the tab and lift up the USB panel

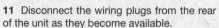

21.3 Disconnect the wiring plugs

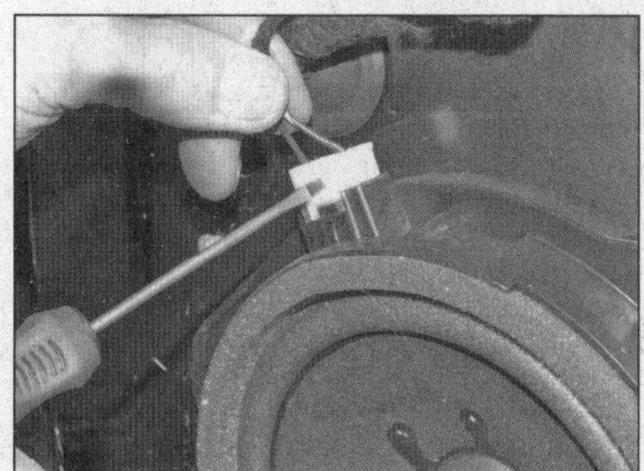
22.2 Disconnect the wiring plug

22.3 Undo the screws and remove the speaker

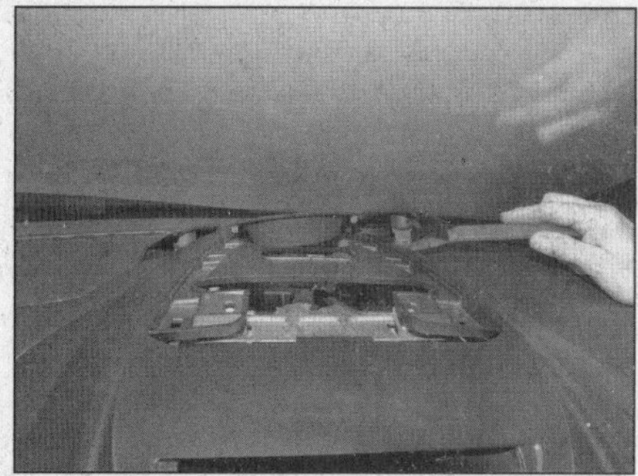
22.4 Prise up the plastic cover from the centre of the facia

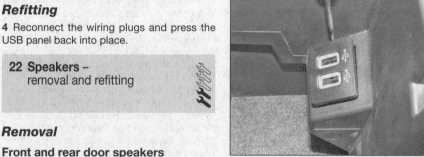

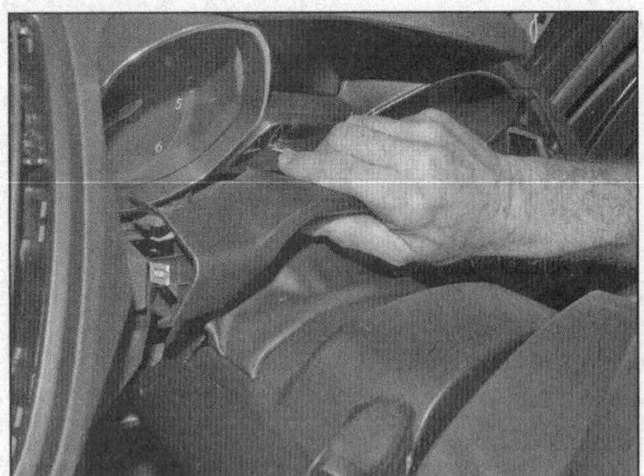

24.2a Pull the trim below the instruments rearwards...

24.2b ...then prise the upper steering column shroud upwards

24.3 Turn the wheel 90° then use a screwdriver to release the clip

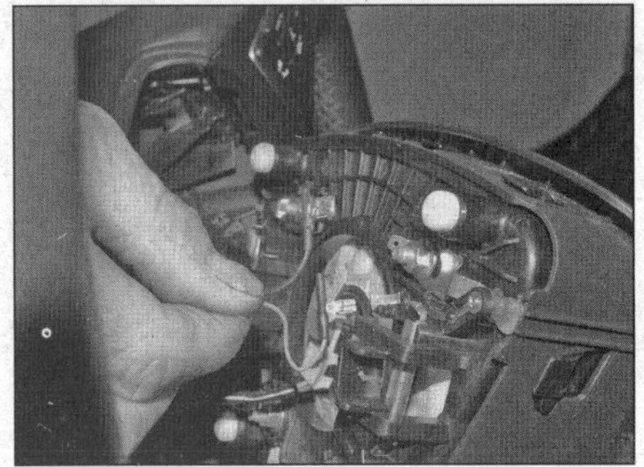
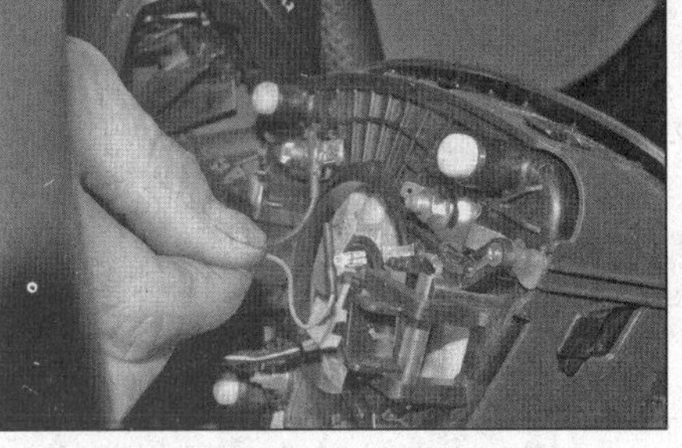

24.5a Unplug the small wiring plugs...

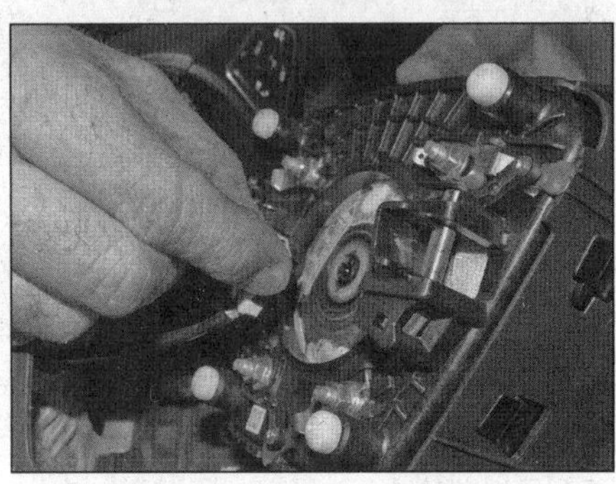
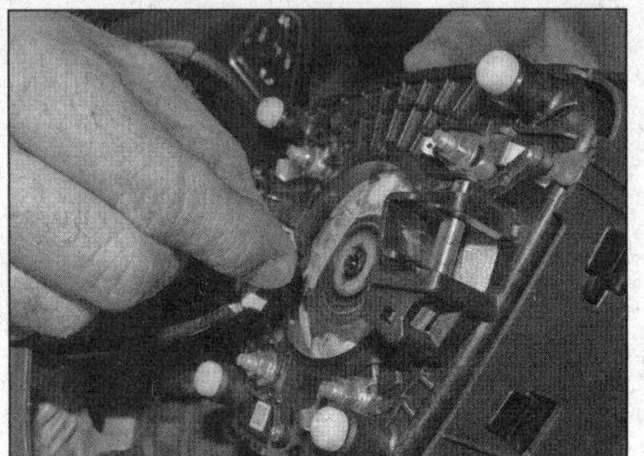

24.5b ...and the main airbag plug

the speaker. Disconnect the wiring plug as the speaker is withdrawn.

Refitting

6 Refitting is a reversal of the removal procedure.

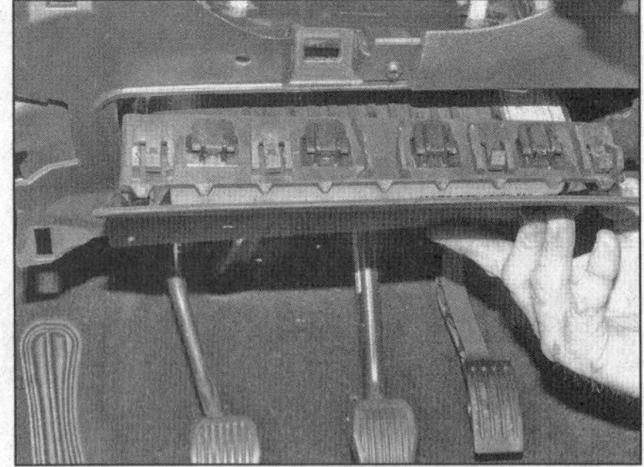

24.7 Undo 2 nuts and pull the airbag unit rearwards

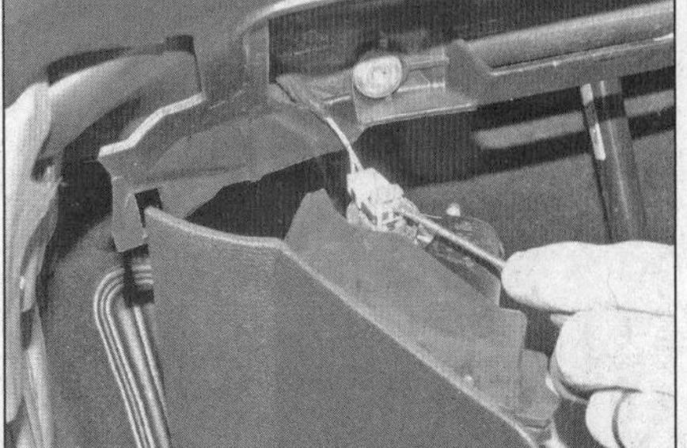

24.8 Disconnect the airbag wiring plug

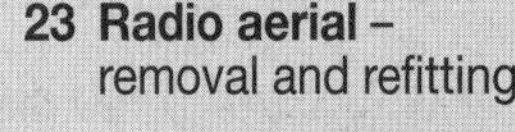

23 Radio aerial – removal and refitting

1 The aerial is integral with the heated rear window and cannot be removed separately.

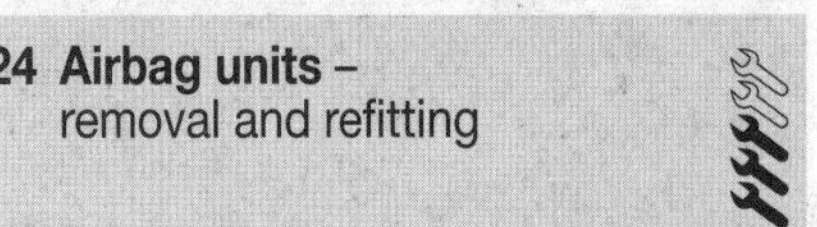

24 Airbag units – removal and refitting

Warning: Handle any airbag unit with extreme care, as a precaution against personal injury, and always hold it with the cover facing away from the body. If in doubt concerning any proposed work involving an airbag unit or its control circuitry, consult a Ford authorised repairer or other experienced specialist.

24.11 Disconnect the airbag wiring plug

Warning: Stand any airbag in a safe place with the cover uppermost, and do not expose it to heat sources in excess of 100°C.

Warning: Do not attempt to open or repair an airbag unit, or apply any electrical current to it. Do not use any airbag unit which is visibly damaged or which has been tampered with.

1 Disconnect the battery negative lead as described in Chapter 5 Section 4.

Warning: Before proceeding, wait a minimum of 5 minutes, as a precaution against accidental firing of the airbag unit. This period ensures that any stored energy in the back-up capacitor is dissipated.

Driver's airbag

2 With the steering wheel in the straight-ahead position, remove the steering column upper shroud **(see illustrations)**.

3 Turn the steering wheel 90°, to allow access to 1 of the 2 airbag retaining clips on the rear of the steering wheel, then insert a screwdriver to release the retaining clip **(see illustration)**.

4 Rotate the steering wheel 180° in the opposite direction, then use a screwdriver to release the second retaining clip.

5 Turn the wheel back to the straight-ahead position, then manoeuvre the airbag from place, disconnecting all wiring plugs as they become available **(see illustrations)**.

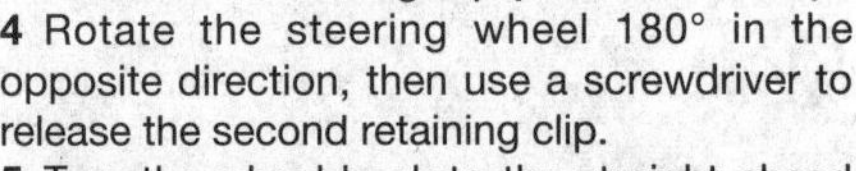

6 Place the airbag in a safe location with the cover facing up as soon as possible. Refitting is the reverse of removal, pushing the airbag unit into place until the retaining spring clips engage with the airbag.

Knee airbag

7 Working behind the facia and reaching up behind the airbag unit from the pedal area, undo the 2 retaining nuts then pull the knee airbag rearwards **(see illustration)**.

8 Unlock and disconnect the airbag wiring plug **(see illustration)**.

9 Refitting is a reversal of removal. Tighten the airbag retaining nuts to the specified torque.

Passenger's airbag

10 Remove the glovebox as described in Chapter 11 Section 37.

11 Disconnect the airbag wiring plug **(see illustration)**.

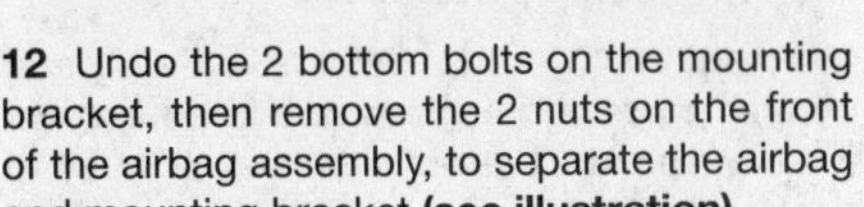

24.12 Remove the 2 bolts on the bracket and 2 nuts on the front of the airbag unit

24.15a Remove the airbag mounting bracket...

24.15b ...followed by the airbag unit

12 Undo the 2 bottom bolts on the mounting bracket, then remove the 2 nuts on the front of the airbag assembly, to separate the airbag and mounting bracket **(see illustration)**.

13 This allows access to the retaining nut on the airbag unit that's sited behind the mounting bracket.

14 Undo the 3 nuts on the back of the airbag assembly.

15 Manoeuvre the mounting bracket downwards from place, then the airbag unit **(see illustrations)**.

16 Refitting is a reversal of removal. Tighten the retaining screws to the specified torque setting.

Side and side curtain airbags

17 These are not considered to be DIY operations, and should be referred to a Ford authorised repairer or specialist.

25 Airbag control module and crash sensors – removal and refitting

Removal

1 Disconnect the battery negative lead as described in Chapter 5 Section 4.

Warning: Before proceeding, wait a minimum of 5 minutes, as a precaution against accidental firing of the airbag unit. This period ensures that any stored energy is dissipated.

Airbag control module

2 Remove the centre console as described in Chapter 11 Section 36.

3 Unclip the wiring harness, then undo the nut and bolt and remove the holder from above the control module.

4 Undo the 3 retaining bolts and remove the control module **(see illustration)**. Disconnect the wiring plugs as the module is withdrawn.

Side impact sensors – B-pillar

5 Remove the B-pillar lower trim panel as described in Chapter 11 Section 35.

6 Disconnect the sensor wiring plug **(see illustration)**.

7 Undo the retaining bolt and remove the sensor. Discard the bolt because a new one must be fitted.

Side impact sensors – Front door

8 Remove the door inner trim panel as described in Chapter 11 Section 13.

9 Using a sharp knife, carefully cut through the sealant and partially remove the waterproof membrane from the door.

10 Disconnect the sensor wiring plug **(see illustration)**.

11 Undo the retaining nuts and remove the sensor.

Refitting

12 Refitting is a reversal of the removal procedure, noting the following points:

a) If a new control module has been fitted, it must be coded/reprogrammed using Ford diagnostic equipment (or equivalent) prior to use. Entrust this task to a Ford dealer or suitably equipped specialist.

b) Tighten all fasteners to their specified torque where given.

26 Airbag rotary contact – removal and refitting

1 The airbag rotary contact unit is integral with the steering column switch assembly. Removal, refitting and re-centreing is described in Section 6.

27 Parking sensor system – component renewal

Control unit

1 Remove the right-hand luggage compartment rear side panel, as described in Chapter 11 Section 35.

2 Disconnect the wiring plugs from the control unit.

3 Prise out the retaining clips and slide the control unit from place **(see illustration)**.

4 Refitting is a reversal of removal. If a new control unit is fitted, it may need to be programmed using Ford diagnostic equipment (or equivalent). Entrust this task to a Ford dealer or suitably equipped repairer.

Ultrasonic sensors

5 Remove the relevant bumper as described in Chapter 11 Section 5.

6 Unclip the sensor from the bumper then disconnect the wiring plug **(see illustrations)**.

7 Refitting is a reversal of removal.

25.4 Remove the 3 retaining bolts to manoeuvre the unit from place

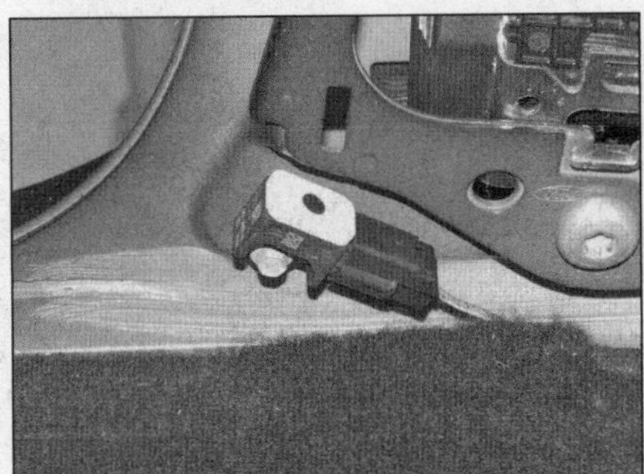

25.6 Disconnect the sensor wiring plug

25.10 Disconnect the sensor wiring plug

27.3 Use a trim tool to remove the clips and manoeuvre the unit from place

27.6a Unclip the sensor...

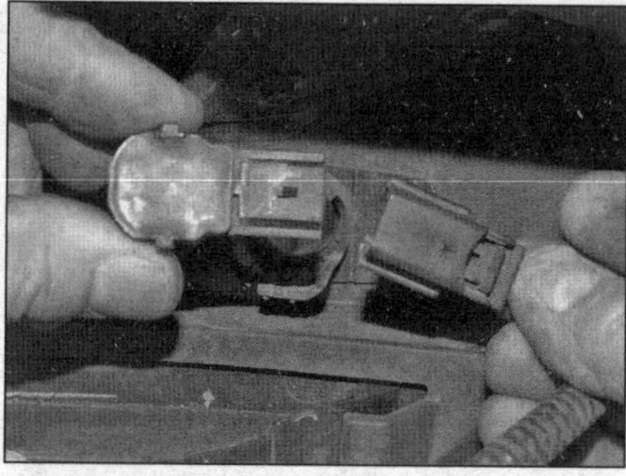
27.6b ...then disconnect the wiring plug

Reversing camera

8 Remove the tailgate interior trim as described in Chapter 11 Section 35.

9 Undo the retaining screw, and detach the camera from place.

10 Refitting is a reversal of removal. If a new camera has been fitted, it may need to be programmed using Ford diagnostic equipment (or equivalent). Entrust this task to a Ford dealer or suitably equipped repairer.

28 Electronic control units – removal and refitting

Body domain controller

1 The Body Domain Controller (BDC) is the vehicle body electronics central control unit.

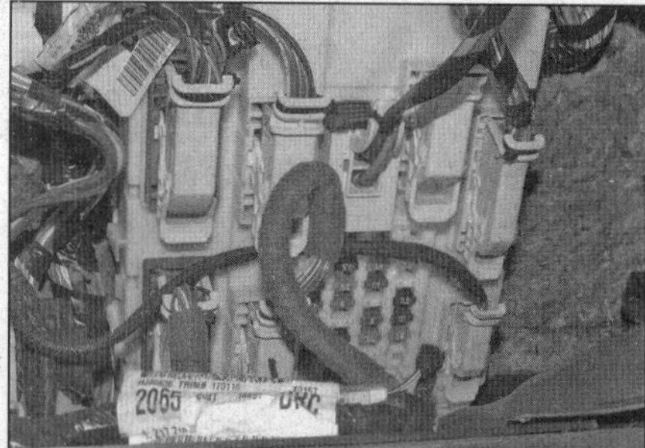
28.6 Unplug the various wiring plugs

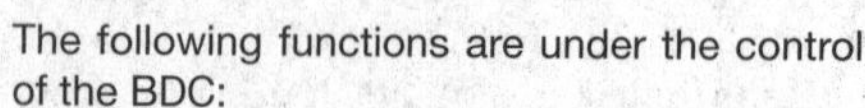
The following functions are under the control of the BDC:

a) Electronic immobiliser
b) Central locking
c) Comfort access (Eg. contactless tailgate opening)
d) Steering column combination switch assembly
e) Front and rear exterior lights
f) Interior lighting
g) Power windows
h) Exterior mirrors
i) Wash/wipe system
j) Seat heating
k) Air recirculation
l) Fuel tank level sensing
m) Vehicle network control – gateway control module (ZGM) is incorporated into the BDC

2 Should a fault with the BDC be suspected, have the controllers self-diagnosis system interrogated via the vehicles diagnostic connector using Ford diagnostic equipment (or equivalent). Entrust this task to a Ford dealer or suitably equipped repairer.

28.7 Release the catches and lower the BDC from place

Removal

3 Disconnect the battery negative lead as described in Chapter 5 Section 4.

4 Remove the glovebox as described in Chapter 11 Section 36.

5 Remove the passenger-side lower dashboard panel as described in Chapter 11 Section 38.

6 Note their fitted positions, then disconnect the various wiring plugs from the BDC **(see illustration)**.

7 Release the catches at the side and lower the BDC from the holder **(see illustration)**.

Refitting

8 Refitting is a reversal of removal. If a new BDC is being fitted, it must be programmed using Ford diagnostic equipment (or equivalent). Entrust this task to a Ford dealer or suitably equipped repairer.

Engine stop-start control unit

Removal

9 Remove the glovebox as described in Chapter 11 Section 37.

10 Remove the passenger airbag unit, as described in Section 24.

11 Slacken the 2 retaining screws that hold the control unit to its mounting bracket, but do not remove them completely at this stage **(see illustration)**.

12 Remove the control units mounting bracket screws **(see illustrations)**.

28.11 Loosen the 2 control unit retaining screws

28.12a Undo the 2 front screws...

28.12b ...followed by the 3rd mounting screw

28.13 Manoeuvre the control unit downwards

28.14 Unplug the control unit wiring plug

28.17 Unplug the keyless module wiring plug

13 Fully remove the 2 screws holding the control unit to the bracket, then remove the bracket and unit downwards **(see illustration)**.
14 Disconnect the wiring plug as it becomes available **(see illustration)**.

Refitting

15 Refitting is a reversal of removal.

Keyless entry control module

Removal

16 These are sited all around the vehicle, behind the rear bumper, behind the luggage compartment trim, behind the facia, beneath the centre console, all of which are covered in Chapter 11.
17 In every case, disconnect the wiring plug **(see illustration)**.
18 Undo the 3 mounting screws and remove the module from place **(see illustration)**.

Refitting

19 Refitting is a reversal of removal.

All-wheel-drive control module

20 Remove the right-hand side panel from the luggage compartment, as described in Chapter 11 Section 35.
21 Undo the 2 retaining bolts for the all-wheel-drive control module and manoeuvre from place, disconnecting the wiring plug as it becomes available **(see illustration)**.
22 Refitting is a reversal of removal.

Fuel pump driver module

Removal

23 Remove the plastic trim from the right-hand rear door aperture, as described in Chapter 11 Section 35.
24 Prise up the covers for the rear seat retaining bolts in the footwell (the left-hand one is held down by a plastic rivet **(see illustration)**.
25 Undo the 2 lower retaining bolts and fold up the right-hand rear seat cushion **(see illustration)**.
26 Prise up the carpet from the rear door aperture, to gain access to the fuel pump driver module underneath.
27 Disconnect the wiring plug and undo the 2 retaining bolts to manoeuvre the unit from place **(see illustration)**.

28.18 Undo the screws and remove the module

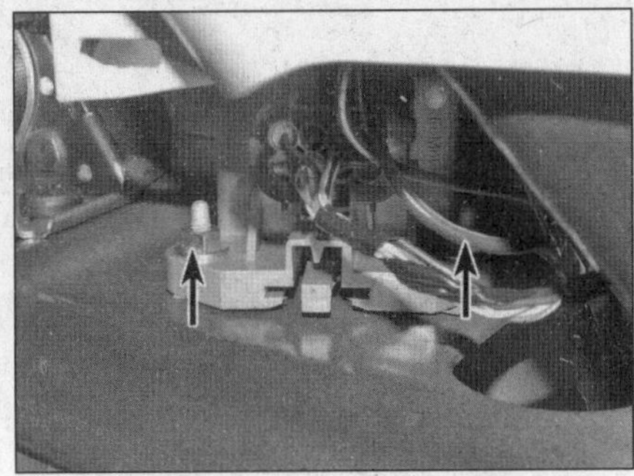
28.21 Remove the retaining bolts and disconnect the unit

Refitting

28 Refitting is a reversal of removal.

Door control module

29 Remove the front or rear door trim as applicable, as described in Chapter 11 Section 13 and Chapter 11 Section 19.
30 Disconnect the 3 wiring plugs from the door control module **(see illustration)**.
31 Undo the 3 retaining bolts and manoeuvre

28.24 Remove the bolt covers

28.25 Undo the bolts to lift the cushion

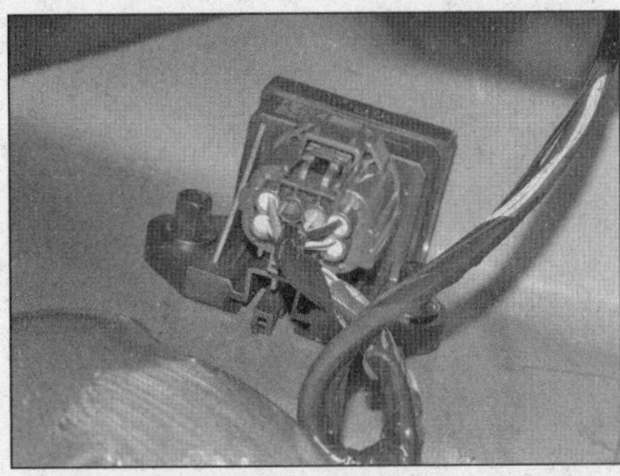
28.27 Undo the 2 bolts and disconnect the control unit

28.30 Disconnect the door control module

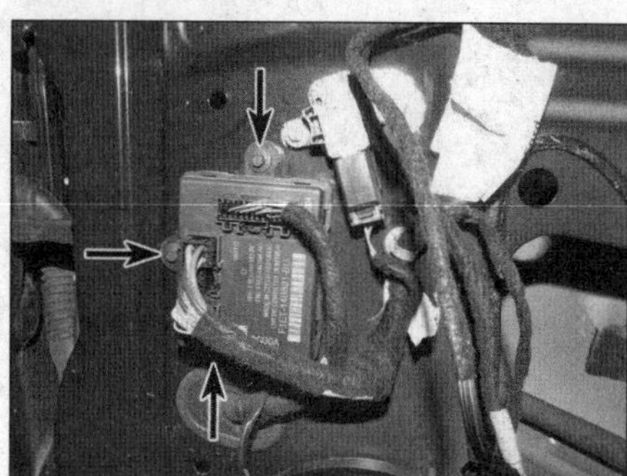
28.31 Remove the bolts to release the control unit

29.2 Prise up the OBD socket locking tab

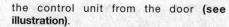

30.4 Remove the 2 securing bolts to take out the siren

30.5 Disconnect the siren wiring plug

the control unit from the door **(see illustration)**.

29 OBD socket – removal and refitting

Removal

1 Fold down the OBD (On-Board Diagnostic) socket cover.

2 Using a screwdriver, prise the tab on top of the OBD socket upwards **(see illustration)**.

3 Press the OBD socket forwards to remove it.

Refitting

4 Refitting is a reversal of removal.

30 Alarm siren – removal and refitting

Removal

1 Disconnect the battery as described in Chapter 5 Section 4.

2 Support the car as described in *Jacking and vehicle support* and remove the right front roadwheel.

3 Remove the front wheelarch liner as described in Chapter 11 Section 39.

4 Undo the 2 mounting bolts and manoeuvre the alarm siren from place **(see illustration)**.

5 Disconnect the wiring plug as it becomes available **(see illustration)**.

Refitting

6 Refitting is a reversal of removal.

FUSE BOX ON THE BATTERY - HIGH CURRENT BATTERY JUNCTION BOX (BJB)

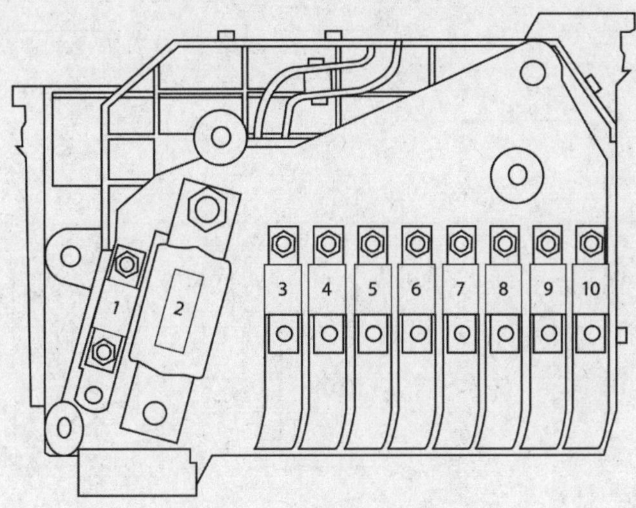

FUSE	VALUE	DESCRIPTION	OEM NAME
1	80A	Power steering control module	MEGA 1
2	150A	Starter motor, Generator	MEGA 2
3	100A	Fuse box in engine compartment – Battery Junction Box (BJB)	MEGA 3
4	50A	Body control module (BCM)	MEGA 4
5	80A	Electric booster heater	MEGA 5
6	70A	Fuse box in luggage compartment – Rear Junction Box (RJB)	MEGA 6
7	60A	Accessory relay (up to Model Year 2016)	MEGA 7
		Fuse box in luggage compartment – Rear Junction Box (RJB), Accessory relay (from Model Year 2017)	
8	50A	Engine cooling fan relay (up to Model Year 2016)	MEGA 8
	70A	Fuse box in engine compartment – Battery Junction Box (BJB), Front window defrost relay, 40A also used (from Model Year 2017)	
9	50A	Body control module (BCM)	MEGA 9
10	60A	Glow plug module or Glow plug relay	MEGA 10

FUSE AND RELAY BOX IN ENGINE COMPARTMENT - BATTERY JUNCTION BOX (BJB)

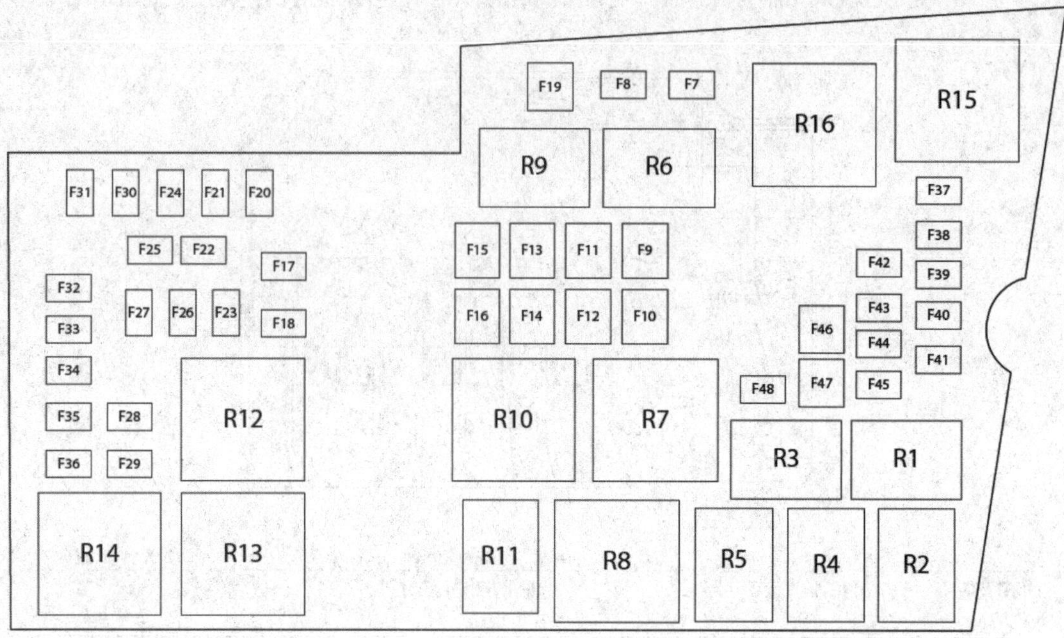

FUSE/ RELAY	VALUE	DESCRIPTION	OEM NAME
1	-	Not used	F1
2	-	Not used	F2
3	-	Not used	F3
4	-	Not used	F4
5	-	Not used	F5
6	-	Not used	F6
7	50A	Anti-lock Brake System (ABS) module, 40A also used	F7
8	30A	Anti-lock Brake System (ABS) module	F8
9	20A	Headlamp washer relay (up to Model Year 2016)	F9
	50A	Fan control 1 (FC1) relay, 40A also used (from Model Year 2017)	
10	40A	Blower motor relay	F10
11	30A	Low voltage direct current/direct current (DC/DC) converter or Body control module (BCM)	F11
12	30A	PCM power relay	F12
13	30A	Starter relay	F13
14	25A	Heated windshield element RH (up to Model Year 2016)	F14
		Cooling fan motor 2 (from Model Year 2017)	
15	20A	Auxiliary power point or Front power outlet socket	F15
16	25A	Heated windshield element LH (up to Model Year 2016)	F16

	-	Not used (from Model Year 2017)	
17	20A	Fuel fired booster heater module (up to Model Year 2016)	F17
	50A	Fan control 2 (FC2) relay, 40A also used (from Model Year 2017)	
18	-	Not used (up to Model Year 2016)	F18
	20A	Headlamp washer relay (from Model Year 2017)	
19	5A	Anti-lock Brake System (ABS) module	F19
20	15A	Horn relay	F20
21	5A	Brake pedal position (BPP) switch	F21
22	15A	Battery monitoring sensor	F22
23	5A	Ignition relay, Blower motor relay, Horn relay, A/C clutch relay, Front window defrost relay, Rear window defrost relay (up to Model Year 2016)	F23
		Ignition relay, Blower motor relay, Horn relay, Front window defrost relay (from Model Year 2017)	
24	5A	Headlamp switch	F24
25	-	Not used	F25
26	5A	PCM power relay (Petrol engines up to Model Year 2016)	F26
	15A	PCM power relay, Transmission control module (TCM) (Diesel engines up to Model Year 2016)	
	15A	Transmission control module (TCM) (from Model Year 2017 with MPS6 transmission)	
	25A	Transmission fluid pump (from Model Year 2017 with 6F35 transmission)	
27	15A	A/C clutch relay	F27
28	7.5A	Proximity warning radar unit (up to Model Year 2016 with Start-Stop)	F28
	10A	Fuel injectors (up to Model Year 2016 Without Start-Stop)	
	7.5A	Proximity warning radar unit, Side obstacle detection control modules, Rear parking aid camera or Fuel injectors (from Model Year 2017)	
29	25A	Rear window defrost relay (up to Model Year 2016)	F29
	5A	Headlamps (from Model Year 2017)	
30	-	Not used (up to Model Year 2016)	F30
	20A	Fuel fired booster heater module (from Model Year 2017)	
31	-	Not used (up to Model Year 2016)	F31
	5A	PCM power relay (from Model Year 2017)	
32	15A	Powertrain Control Module (PCM) (up to Model Year 2016)	F32
		Powertrain Control Module (PCM), Fan control 1 (FC1) relay, 10A also used (from Model Year 2017)	
33	10A	Powertrain Control Module (PCM) (up to Model Year 2016)	F33
	15A	Coil on plugs (petrol engines from Model Year 2017)	

	15A	Oxygen sensors, Fuel volume control valve, Exhaust gas recirculation (EGR) cooler bypass valve, Turbocharger variable vane actuator (1.5L), Variable oil pump, Wastegate control valve (2.0L), Fuel heater (diesel engines from Model Year 2017)	
34	10A	Vaporizer relay, Four Wheel Drive (FWD) control module, Engine cooling fan relay, Mass air flow meter, Fuel metering valve, Fuel vaporizer system fuel pump, Water in fuel sensor (up to Model Year 2016)	F34
		Fan control relays, Four Wheel Drive (FWD) control module, A/C compressor control solenoid, Turbocharger bypass valve, Transmission fluid temperature control valve 2, A/C clutch relay, Charge air cooler pump, Turbocharger wastegate regulating valve solenoid (petrol engines from Model Year 2017)	
		Fan control relays, Four Wheel Drive (FWD) control module, A/C compressor control solenoid, A/C clutch relay, Vaporizer relay, Variable oil pump, Fuel metering valve (diesel engines from Model Year 2017)	
35	15A	Fuel heater (diesel engines up to Model Year 2016)	F35
	-	Not used (petrol engines up to Model Year 2016)	
	10A	Water in fuel sensor, Particulate matter bank 1, sensor 1 (diesel engines from Model Year 2017)	
	15A	Variable camshaft timing solenoids, Evaporative emission canister purge valve, Oxygen sensors (petrol engines from Model Year 2017)	
36	5A	Active grille shutter	F36
37	5A	Overhead console, Passenger airbag deactivated (PAD) indicator	F37
38	5A	Powertrain control module (PCM), Transmission control module (only for diesel engines) (up to Model Year 2016)	F38
		Powertrain control module (PCM), Glow plug relay, Transmission control module (TCM) (diesel engines from Model Year 2017)	
		Transmission fluid pump (TFP) (petrol engines from Model Year 2017)	
39	5A	Adaptive front lighting module, Headlamps (up to Model Year 2016)	F39
	15A	Adaptive front lighting module (from Model Year 2017)	
40	5A	Power steering control module (PSCM)	F40
41	20A	Fuses 85 and 86 in Fuse and relay box in passenger compartment (Body control module – BCM)	F41
42	15A	Rear window wiper motor	F42
43	15A	Adaptive front lighting module (up to Model Year 2016)	F43
	-	Not used (from Model Year 2017)	
44	5A	Proximity warning radar unit	F44
45	10A	Windshield heated washer jets	F45
46	40A	Windshield wiper motors	F46
47	-	Not used	F47
48	15A	Vaporizer relay	F48

R1	-	Fan control 4 (FC4) relay	-
R2	-	Horn relay	-
R3	-	Vaporizer relay	-
R4	-	Not used	-
R5	-	Fan control 5 (FC5) relay	-
R6	-	Fan control 3 (FC3) relay	-
R7	-	Front window defrost relay	-
R8	-	Glow plug relay	-
R9	-	Headlamp washer relay	-
R10	-	Starter relay	-
R11	-	A/C Clutch relay	-
R12	-	Fan control 1 (FC1) relay	-
R13	-	Blower motor relay	-
R14	-	PCM power relay	-
R15	-	Rear window defrost relay or Fan control 2 (FC2) relay	-
R16	-	Ignition relay	-

FUSE BOX IN PASSENGER COMPARTMENT - PART OF BODY CONTROL MODULE (BCM)

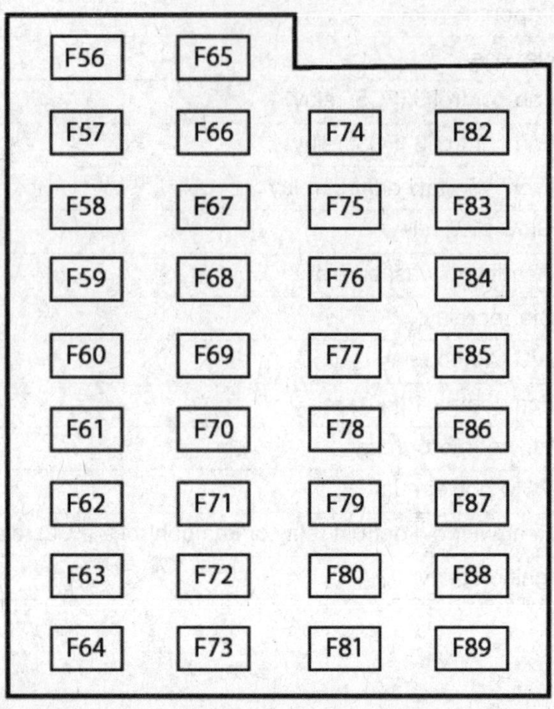

FUSE	VALUE	DESCRIPTION	OEM NAME
F56	20A	Fuel pump relay, Fuel pump driver module (FPDM)	F56
F57	-	Not used	F57
F58	-	Not used	F58
F59	5A	Passive anti-theft system (PATS) transceiver or Not used	F59
F60	10A	Luggage compartment lamp, Courtesy lamps, Footwell lamps, Glove compartment lamp, Driver door window control switch, Vanity mirror lamps, Front interior lamps, Rear interior lamps, Overhead console	F60
F61	-	Not used	F61
F62	5A	Auto-dimming interior mirror, Rain sensor	F62
F63	10A	Proximity warning radar unit	F63
F64	-	Not used	F64
F65	10A	Liftgate/luggage compartment lid latch, Liftgate/decklid release relay	F65
F66	20A	Driver door unlock relay, Spare relay	F66
F67	7.5A	Accessory protocol information module (APIM), Front control/ display interface module (FCDIM), Global positioning system module (GPSM)	F67
F68	15A	Steering column lock relay, Steering column control module (SCCM)	F68
F69	5A	Instrument panel cluster (IPC) module	F69

F70	20A	Passenger door unlock relay, All lock relay	F70
F71	10A	Heating, ventilation and air conditioning (HVAC) module, Electronic automatic temperature control (EATC) module	F71
F72	7.5A	Steering column control module (SCCM) (up to Model Year 2016)	F72
		Data link connector (DLC) (from Model Year 2017)	
F73	5A	Data link connector (DLC), Anti-theft alarm horn with integral battery – RHD (up to Model Year 2016)	F73
	7.5A	Anti-theft alarm horn with integral battery, Steering column control module (SCCM) (from Model Year 2017)	
F74	15A	High beam relay, Headlamps	F74
F75	15A	Fog lamp relay, Fog lamps	F75
F76	10A	Reversing lamp relay, Auto-dimming interior mirror, Reversing lamps	F76
F77	20A	Front washer relay, Rear washer relay, Windshield washer pump	F77
F78	5A	Ignition switch, Remote function actuator (RFA) module	F78
F79	15A	Audio unit, Front controls interface module (FCIM)	F79
F80	-	Not used (up to Model Year 2016)	F80
	20A	Roof opening panel module (from Model Year 2017)	
F81	5A	Remote Frequency (RF) receiver, Intrusion sensor	F81
F82	20A	Front washer relay, Rear washer relay (up to Model Year 2016)	F82
		Front washer relay, Rear washer relay, Windshield wiper pump (from Model Year 2017)	
F83	20A	Passenger door unlock relay, All lock relay	F83
F84	20A	Driver door unlock relay, Spare relay	F84
F85	7.5A	Audio unit, Seat heater switches, In-vehicle temperature sensor, Electric booster heater, Heated seat modules, Low voltage direct current/direct current (DC/DC) converter (up to Model Year 2016)	F85
		Electronic automatic temperature control (EATC) module, Heating, ventilation and air conditioning (HVAC) control module, Electric booster heater, Heated seat modules, Image processing module A (IPMA), , Low voltage direct current/ direct current (DC/DC) converter, Front distance sensing module (FDSM), USB charge port (from Model Year 2017)	
F86	10A	Restraints control module (RCM)	F86
F87	-	Not used (up to Model Year 2016)	F87
	15A	Steering column control module (SCCM) (from Model Year 2017)	
F88	-	Not used	F88
F89	-	Not used	F89

FUSE AND RELAY BOX IN LUGGAGE COMPARTMENT - REAR JUNCTION BOX (RJB)

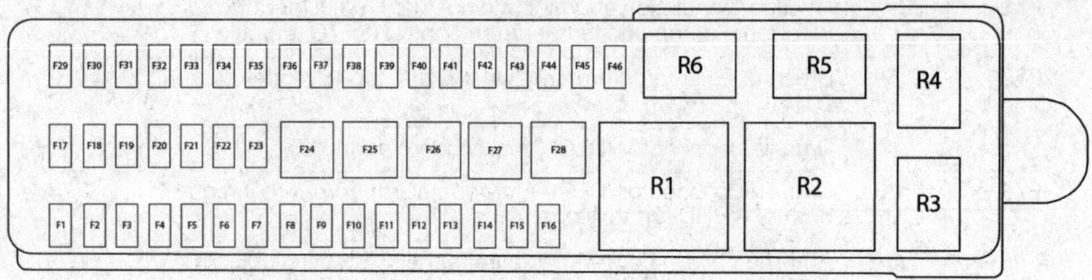

FUSE/ RELAY	VALUE	DESCRIPTION	OEM NAME
F1	5A	Handsfree activation module	F1
F2	10A	Remote function actuator (RFA) module or Heated wiper park relay, 5A also used	F2
F3	5A	Exterior door handles	F3
F4	25A	Driver door module (DDM)	F4
F5	25A	Passenger door module (PDM)	F5
F6	25A	Door module, left rear	F6
F7	25A	Door module, right rear	F7
F8	-	Not used	F8
F9	25A	Seat control switch, driver side front	F9
F10	5A	Driver seat module (DSM) or Not used	F10
F11	5A	Accessory relay, Rear window defrost relay	F11
F12	-	Not used	F12
F13	-	Not used	F13
F14	-	Not used	F14
F15	-	Not used	F15
F16	-	Not used	F16
F17	-	Not used	F17
F18	-	Not used	F18
F19	-	Not used	F19
F20	-	Not used	F20
F21	-	Not used	F21
F22	-	Not used	F22
F23	25A	Rear window defrost relay	F23
F24	30A	Direct current/alternating current (DC/AC) inverter	F24
	20A	Rear passenger power outlet socket	
F25	25A	Rear gate trunk module (RGTM)	F25

F26	40A	Trailer module, Trailer socket, Retractable tow bar release module	F26
F27	20A	Luggage compartment power outlet socket	F27
F28	-	Not used	F28
F29	5A	Front distance sensing module (FDSM), Image processing module A (IPMA), Image processing module B (IPMB), Side obstacle detection control modules (SOD-L) (SOD-R) (up to Model Year 2016)	F29
		Front distance sensing module (FDSM), Image processing module A (IPMA), Image processing module B (IPMB), Side obstacle detection control modules (SOD-L) (SOD-R), Low voltage direct current/direct current (DC/DC) converter (from Model Year 2017)	
F30	5A	Parking aid module (PAM)	F30
F31	-	Not used	F31
F32	5A	Direct current/alternating current (DC/AC) inverter	F32
F33	-	Not used	F33
F34	20A	Heated seat module, left front	F34
F35	20A	Heated seat module, right front	F35
F36	-	Not used	F36
F37	-	Not used	F37
F39	-	Not used	F39
F40	-	Not used	F40
F41	-	Not used	F41
F42	-	Not used	F42
F43	-	Not used	F43
F44	-	Not used	F44
F45	-	Not used	F45
F46	-	Not used	F46
R1	-	Accessory relay	-
R2	-	Rear window defrost relay or Not used	-
R3	-	Rear window defrost relay	-
R4	-	Not used	-
R5	-	Not used	-
R6	-	Not used	-

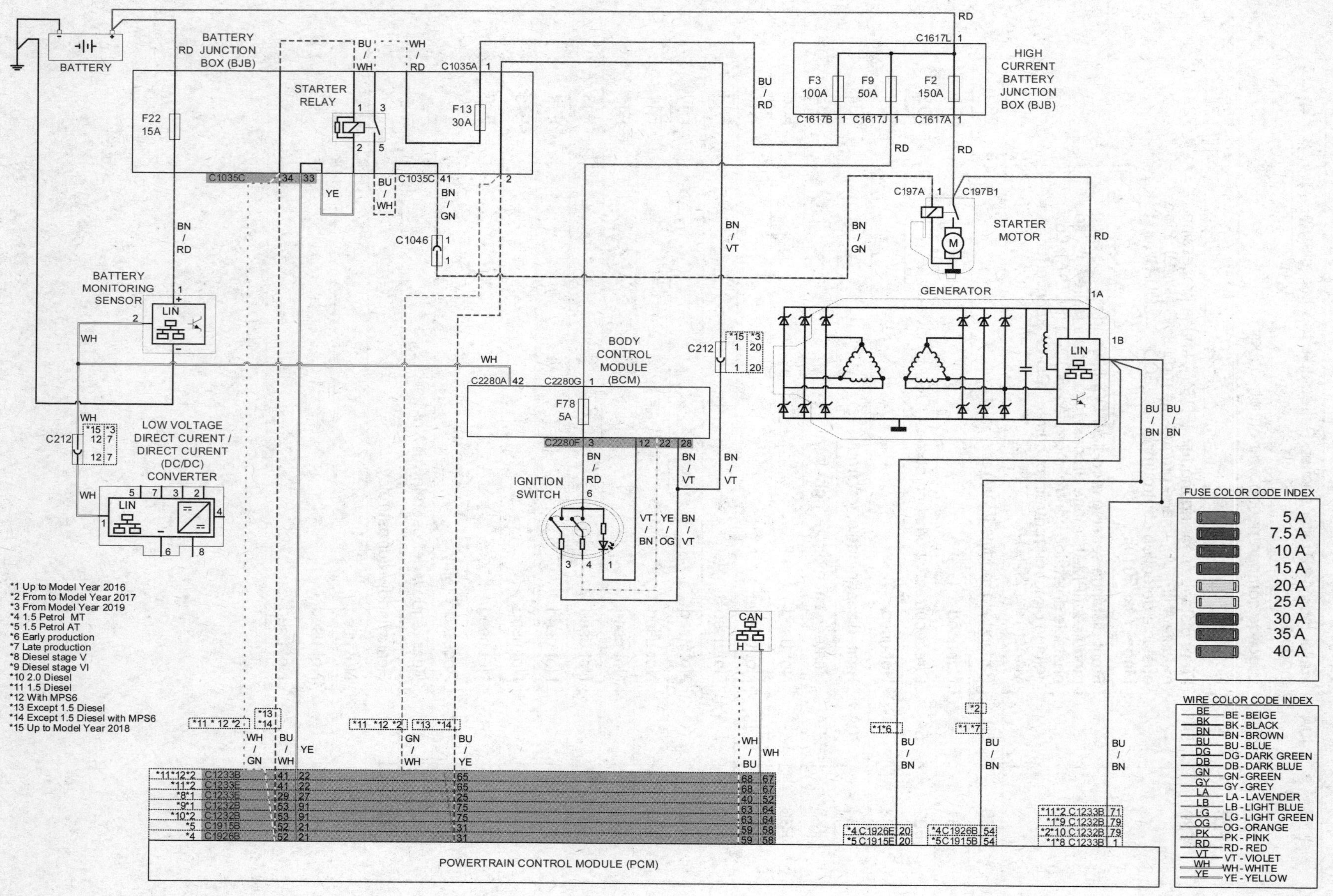

Diagram 1 – Starting and charging

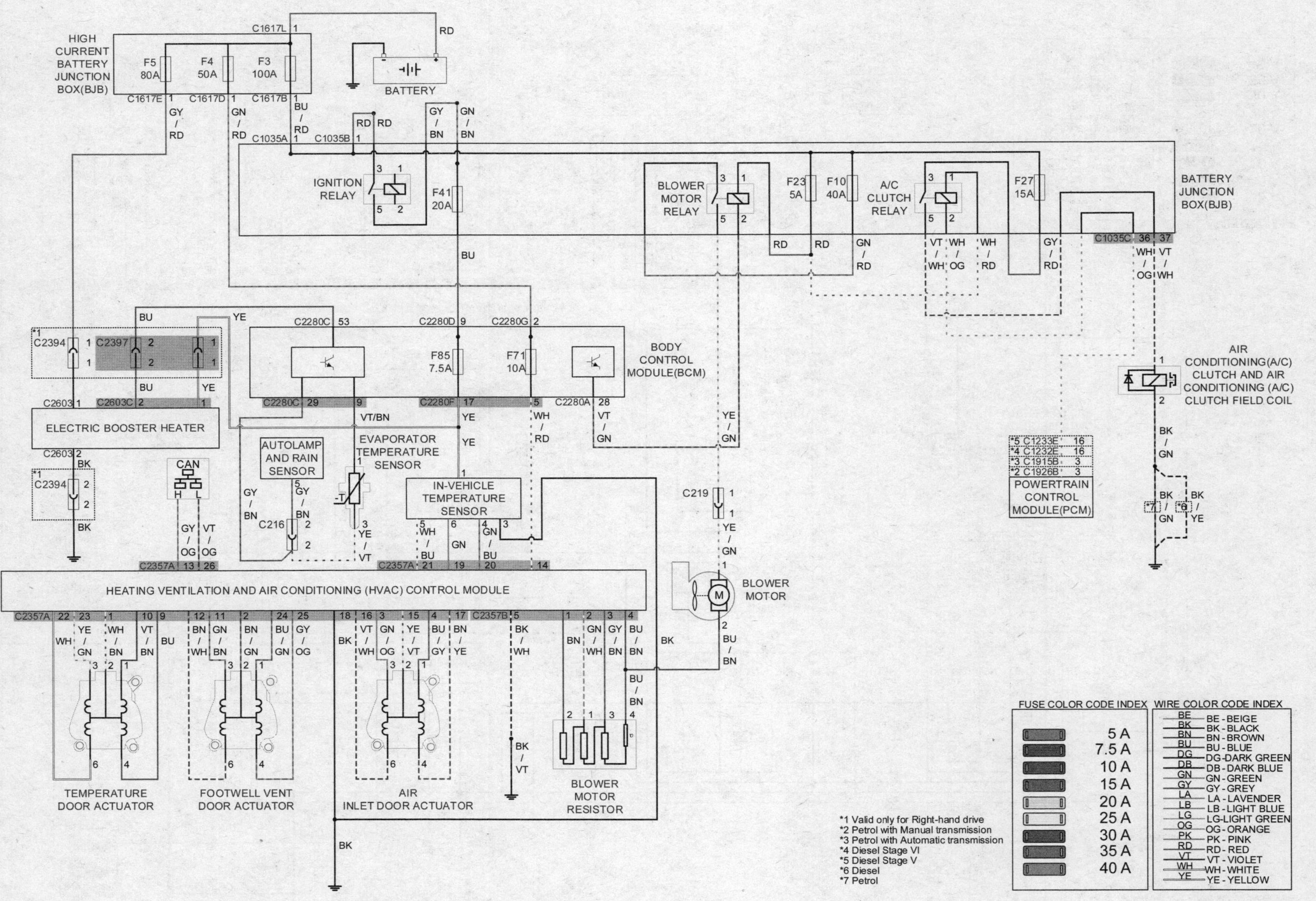

Diagram 2 – Heating and cooling – Manual air conditioning up to 2016 model year

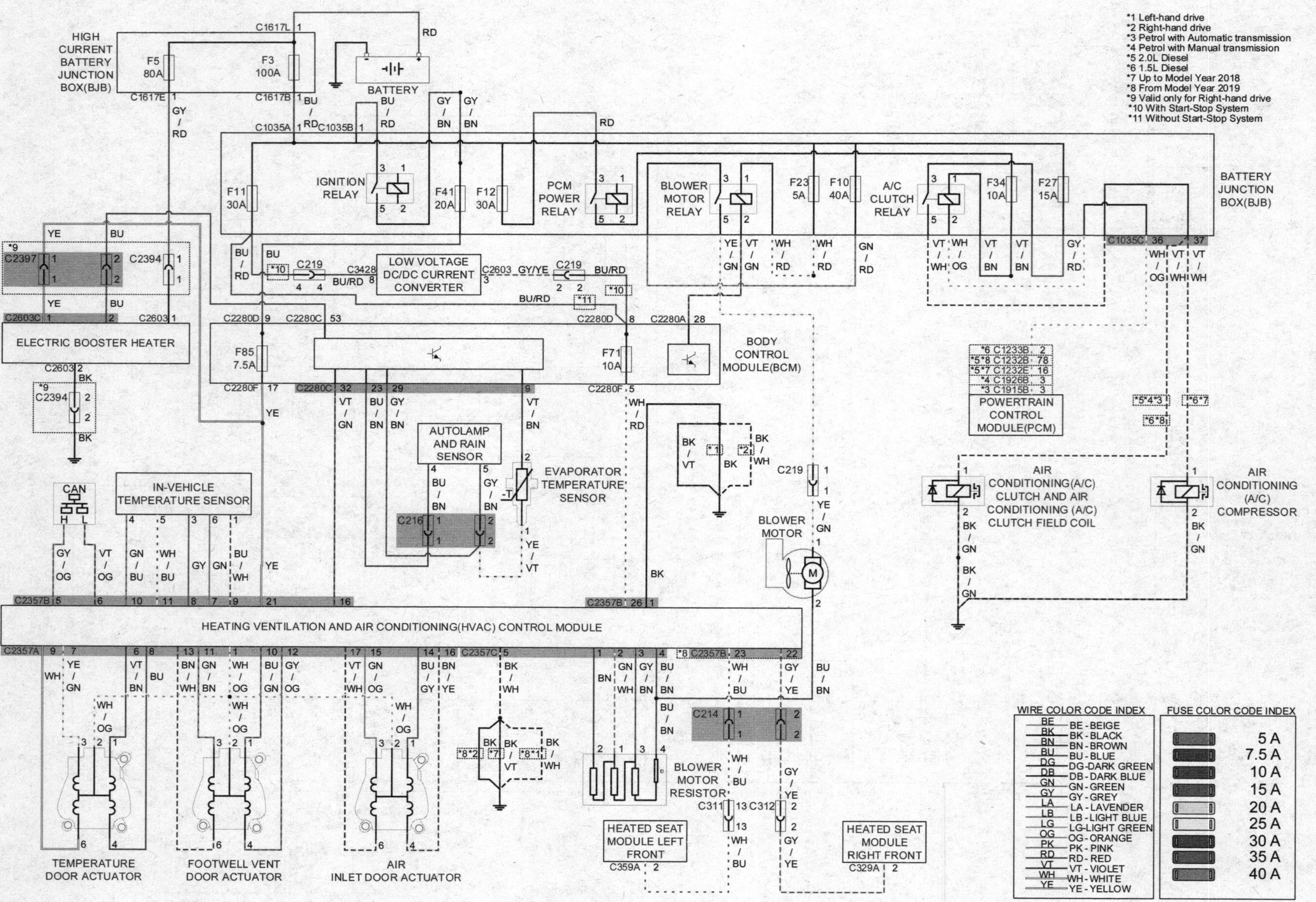

Diagram 3 – Heating and cooling – Manual air conditioning from 2017 model year

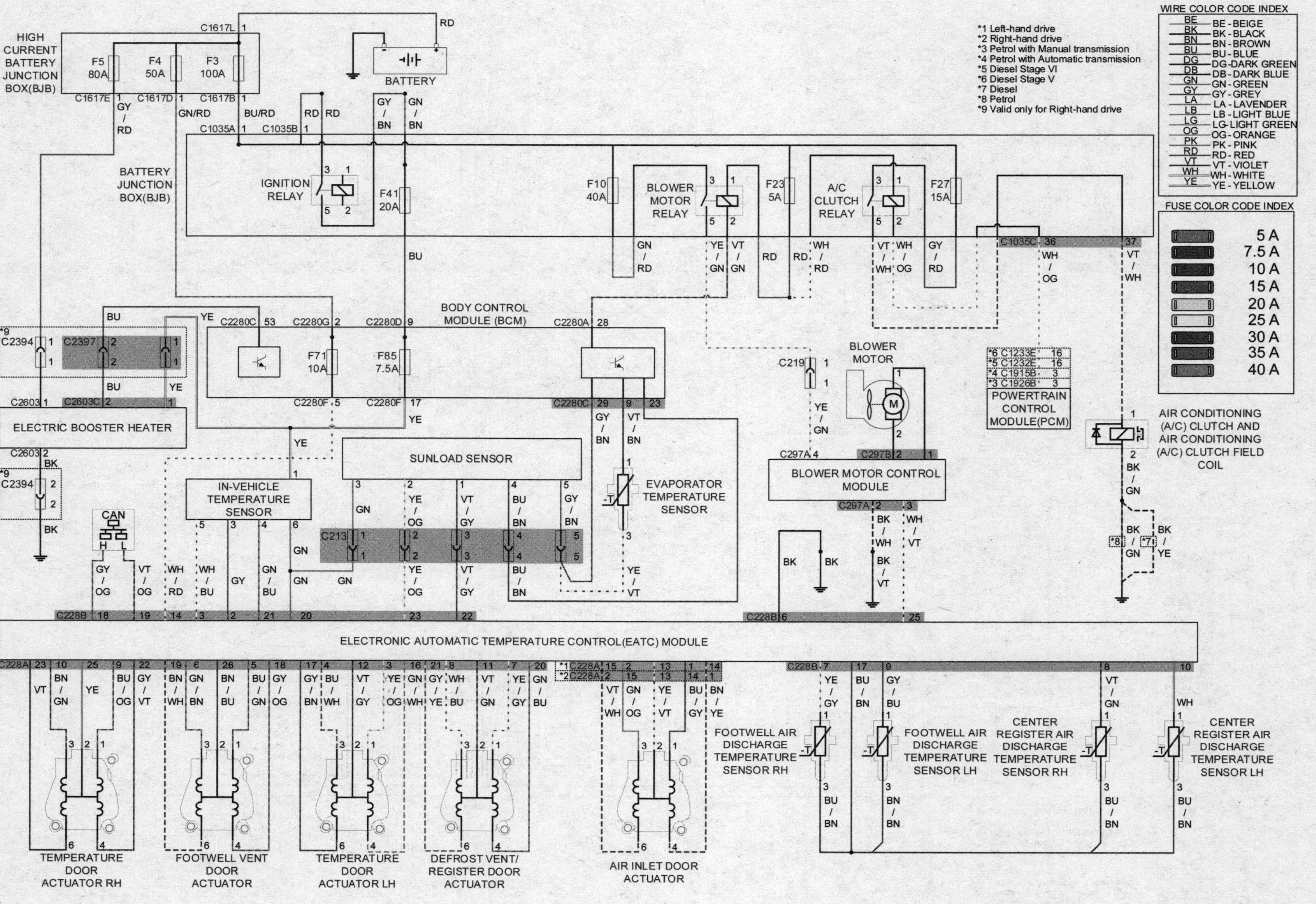

Diagram 4 – Heating and cooling – Automatic air conditioning up to 2016 model year

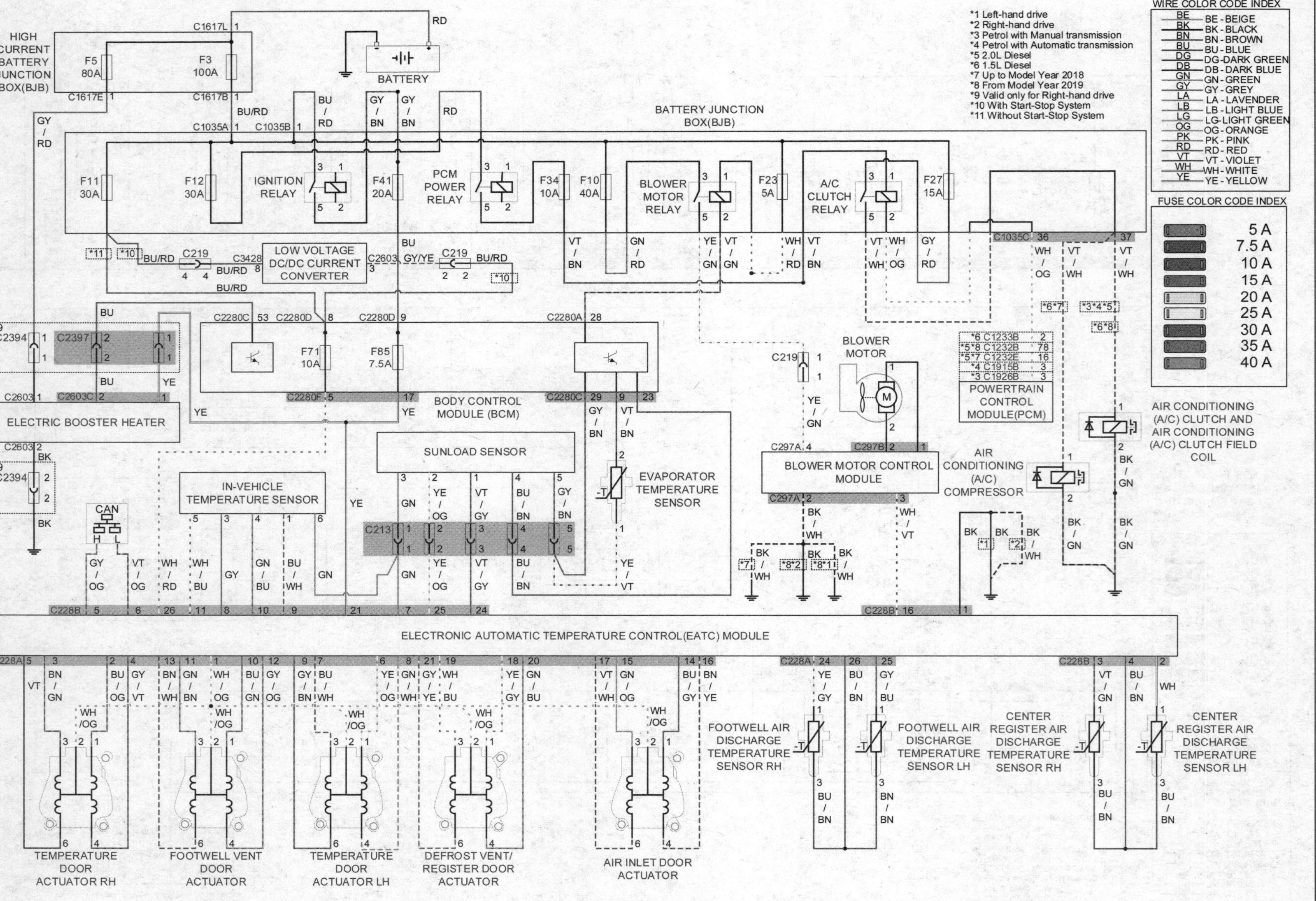

Diagram 5 – Heating and cooling – Automatic air conditioning from 2017 model year

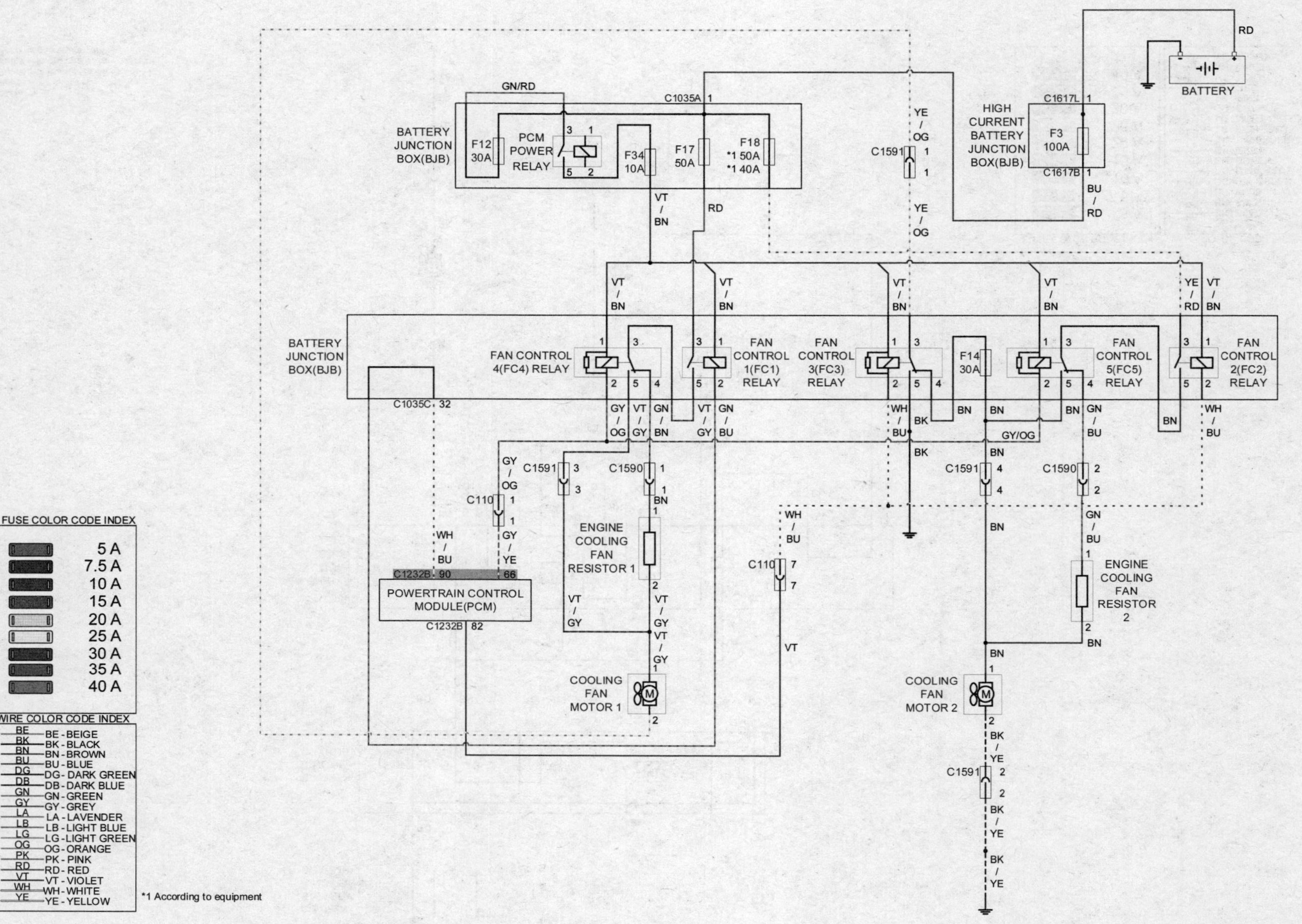

Diagram 6 – Cooling fan – up to 2016 model year (Diesel 2WD)

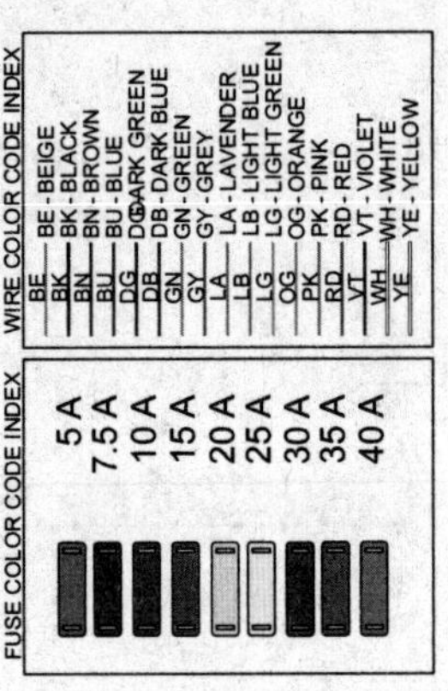

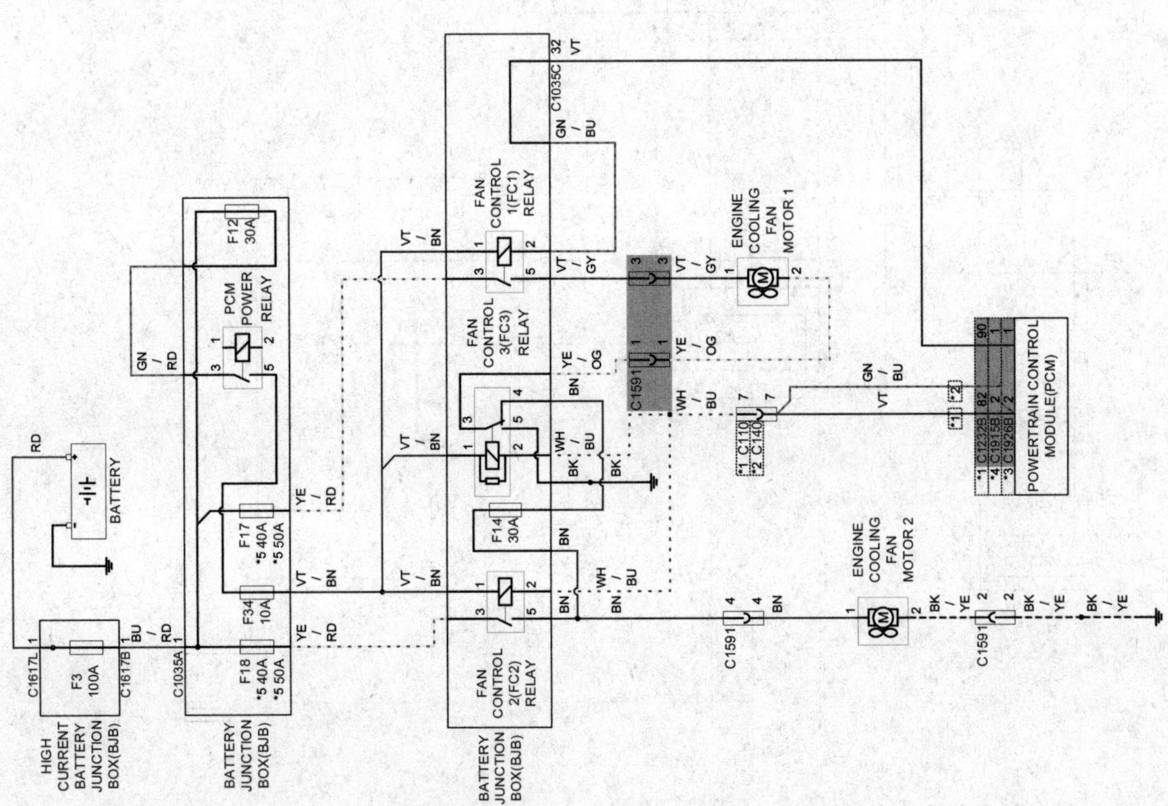

*1 Diesel
*2 Petrol
*3 Petrol with manual transmission
*4 Petrol with automatic transmission
*5 According to equipment

Diagram 7 – Cooling fan – up to 2016 model year (Diesel 4WD and petrol)

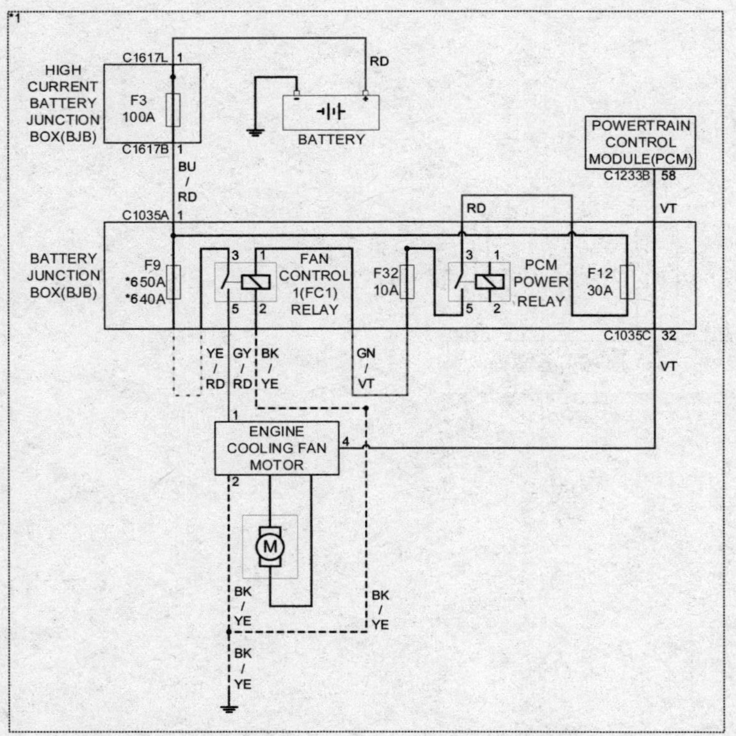

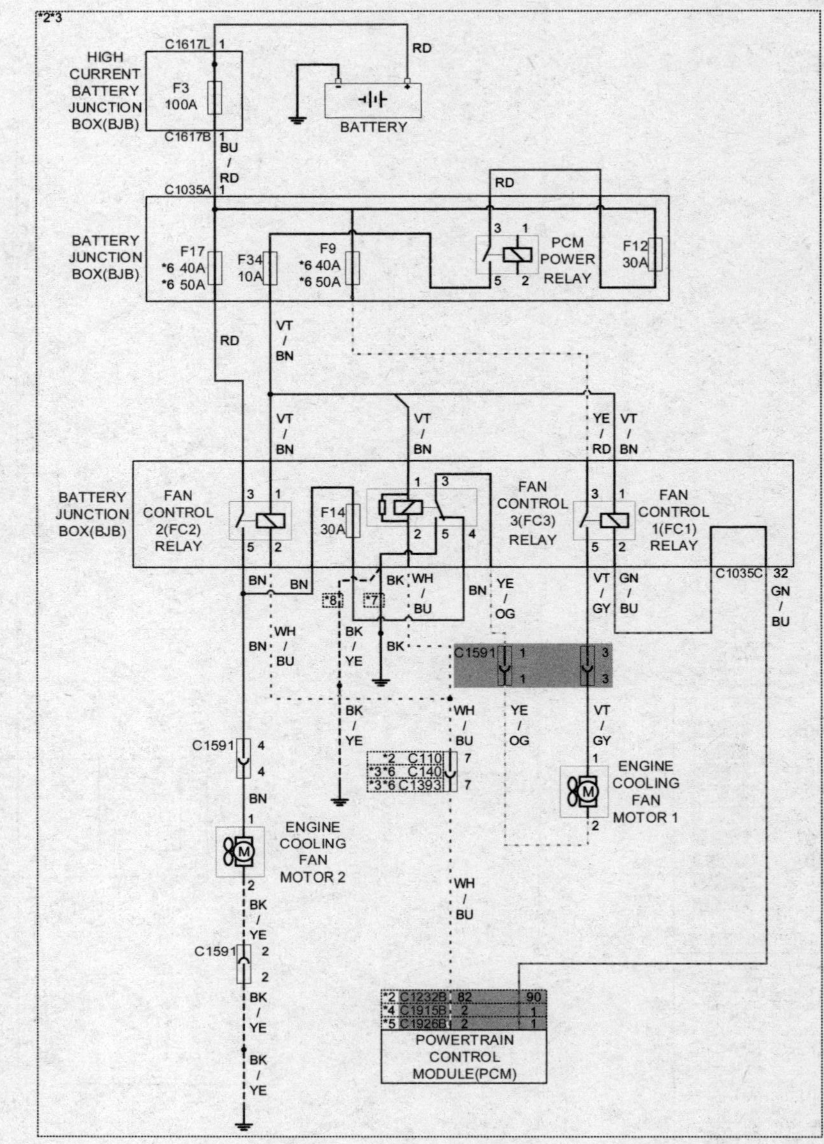

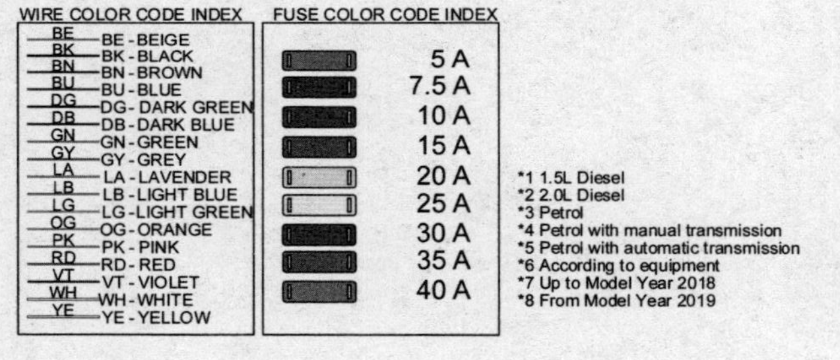

Diagram 8 – Cooling fan – from 2017 model year

WIRE COLOR CODE INDEX

BE	BE - BEIGE
BK	BK - BLACK
BN	BN - BROWN
BU	BU - BLUE
DG	DG - DARK GREEN
DB	DB - DARK BLUE
GN	GN - GREEN
GY	GY - GREY
LA	LA - LAVENDER
LB	LB - LIGHT BLUE
LG	LG - LIGHT GREEN
OG	OG - ORANGE
PK	PK - PINK
RD	RD - RED
VT	VT - VIOLET
WH	WH - WHITE
YE	YE - YELLOW

FUSE COLOR CODE INDEX

5 A
7.5 A
10 A
15 A
20 A
25 A
30 A
35 A
40 A

*1 Early production
*2 Late production
*3 Up to Model Year 2016
*4 From Model Year 2017

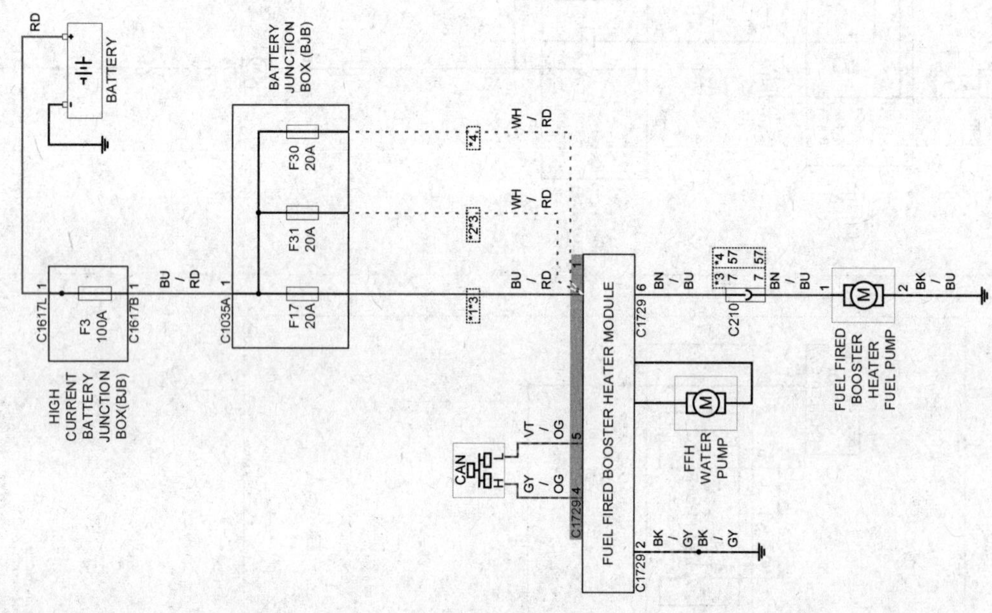

Diagram 9 – Fuel burning heater

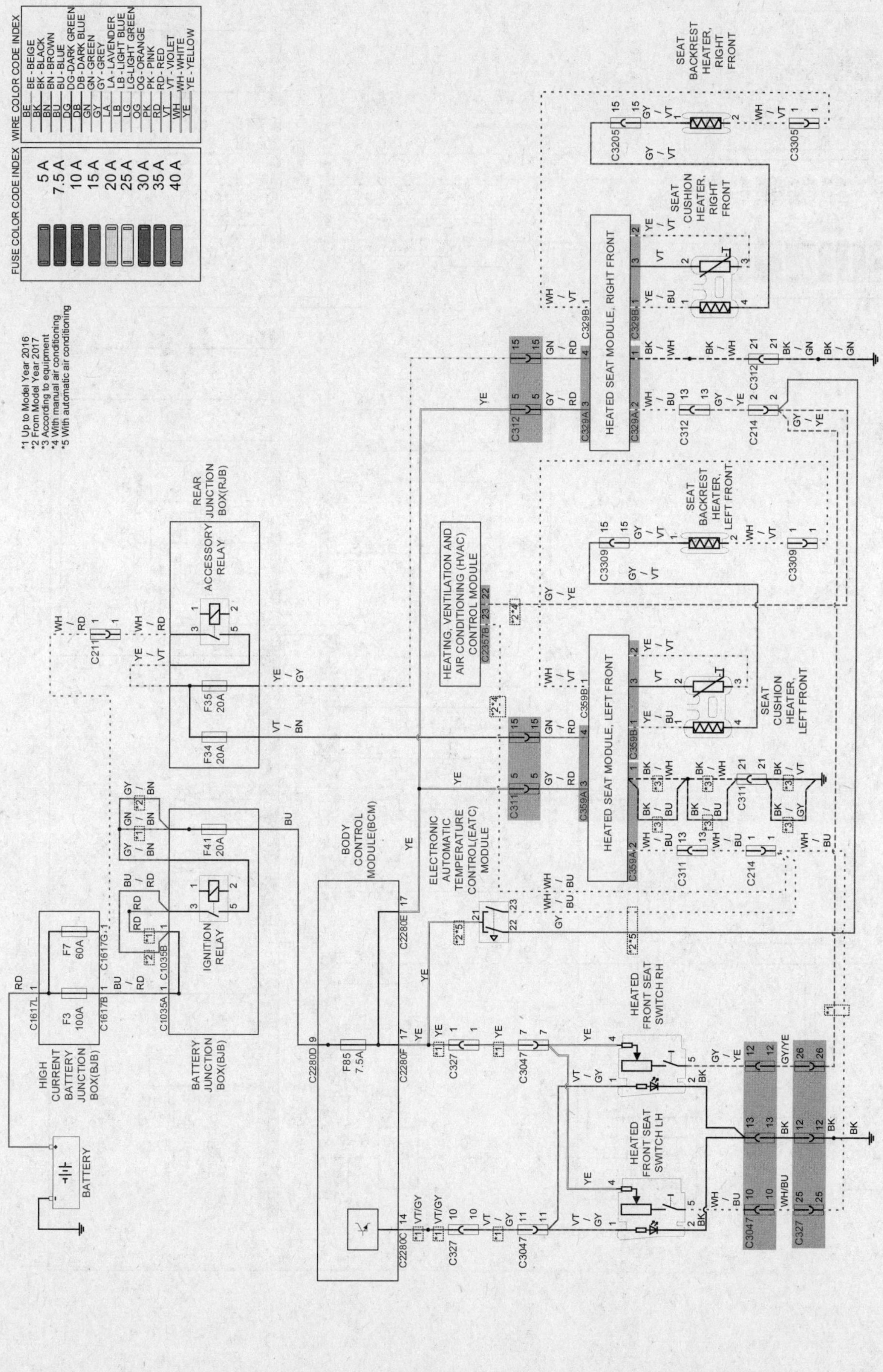

*1 Up to Model Year 2016
*2 From Model Year 2017
*3 According to equipment
*4 With manual air conditioning
*5 With automatic air conditioning

FUSE COLOR CODE INDEX
5 A
7.5 A
10 A
15 A
20 A
25 A
30 A
35 A
40 A

WIRE COLOR CODE INDEX	
BE	BE - BEIGE
BK	BK - BLACK
BN	BN - BROWN
BU	BU - BLUE
DG	DG - DARK GREEN
DB	DB - DARK BLUE
GN	GN - GREEN
GY	GY - GREY
LA	LA - LAVENDER
LB	LB - LIGHT BLUE
LG	LG - LIGHT GREEN
OG	OG - ORANGE
PK	PK - PINK
RD	RD - RED
VT	VT - VIOLET
WH	WH - WHITE
YE	YE - YELLOW

BATTERY

HIGH CURRENT BATTERY JUNCTION BOX(BJB)

F3 100A

F7 60A

BATTERY JUNCTION BOX(BJB)

IGNITION RELAY

F41 20A

F34 20A

F35 20A

ACCESSORY RELAY

REAR JUNCTION BOX(RJB)

BODY CONTROL MODULE(BCM)

F85 7.5A

ELECTRONIC AUTOMATIC TEMPERATURE CONTROL(EATC) MODULE

HEATING, VENTILATION AND AIR CONDITIONING (HVAC) CONTROL MODULE

HEATED FRONT SEAT SWITCH LH

HEATED FRONT SEAT SWITCH RH

HEATED SEAT MODULE, LEFT FRONT

SEAT CUSHION HEATER, LEFT FRONT

SEAT BACKREST HEATER, LEFT FRONT

HEATED SEAT MODULE, RIGHT FRONT

SEAT CUSHION HEATER, RIGHT FRONT

SEAT BACKREST HEATER, RIGHT FRONT

Diagram 10 – Heated seats

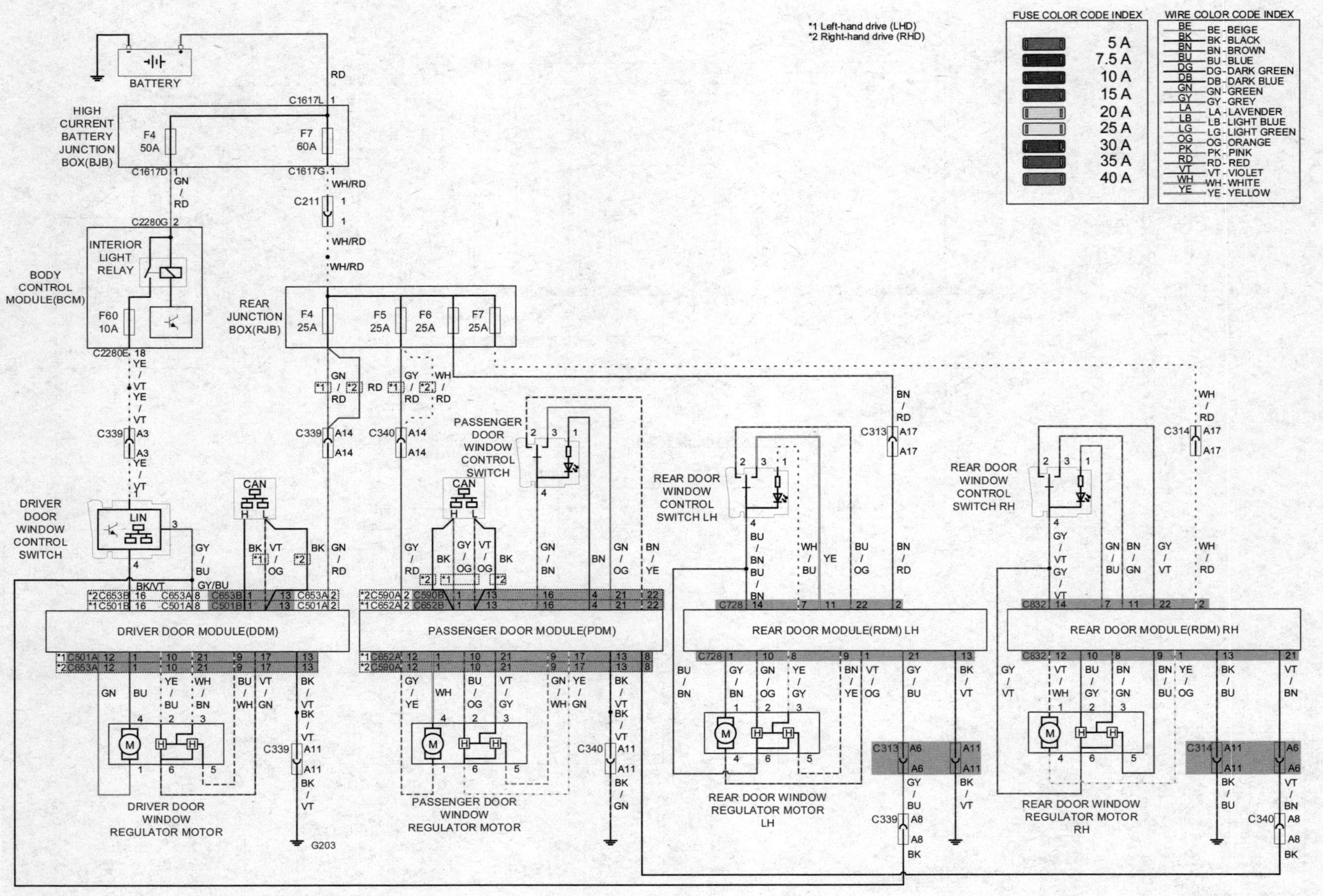

Diagram 11 – Power windows – up to 2016 model year

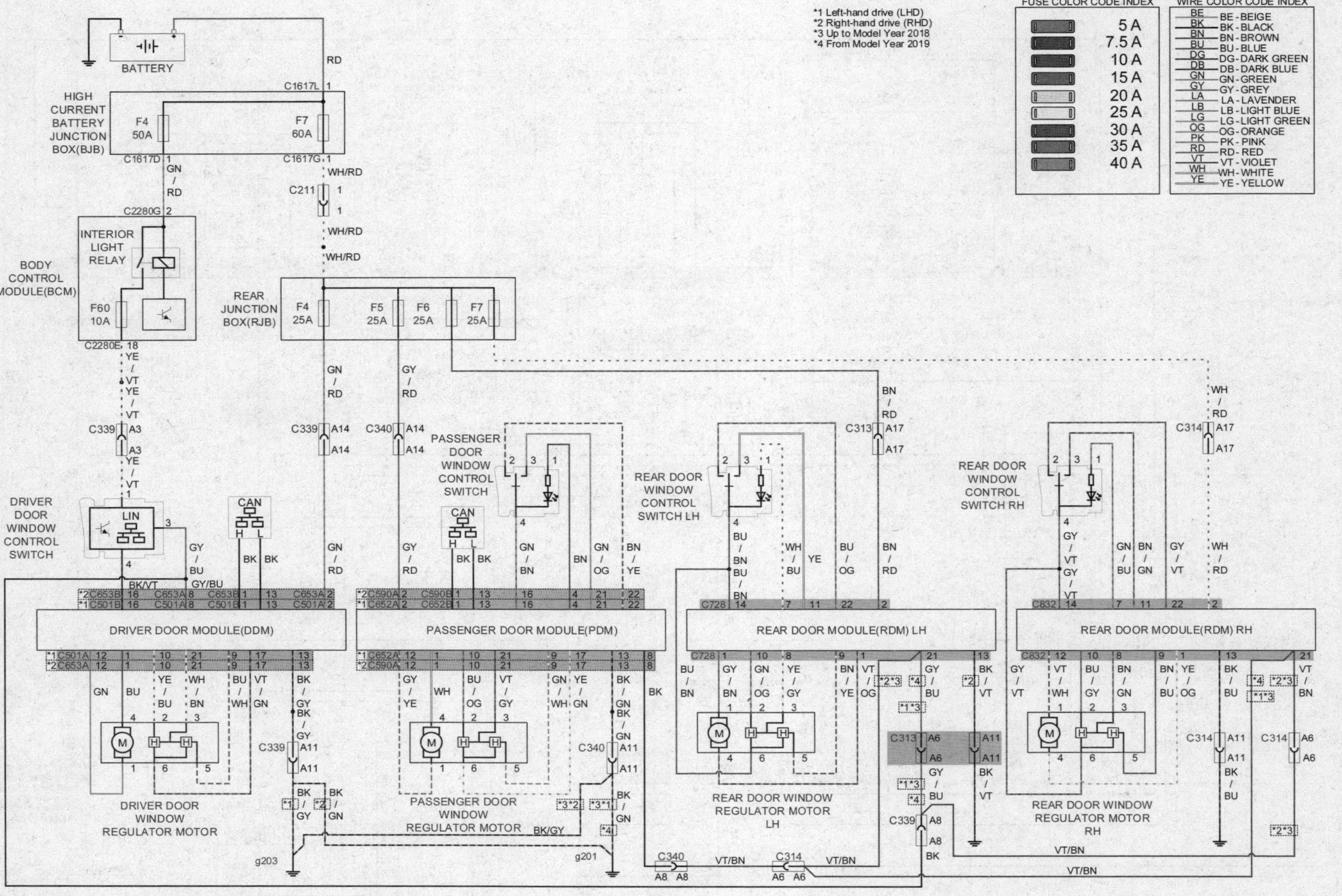

Diagram 12 – Power windows – from 2017 model year

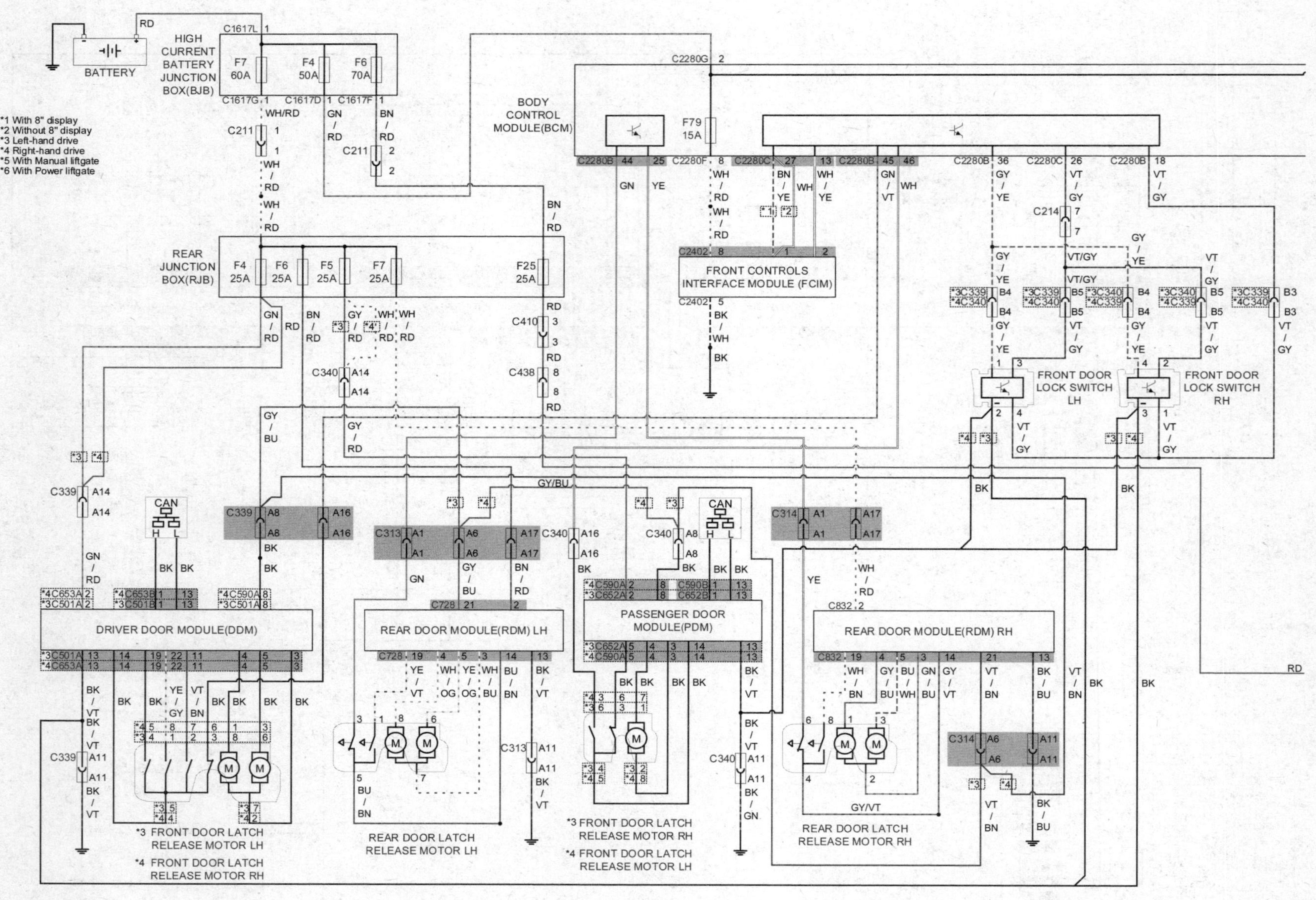

Diagram 13 – Central locking – up to 2016 model year (early production - Part 1)

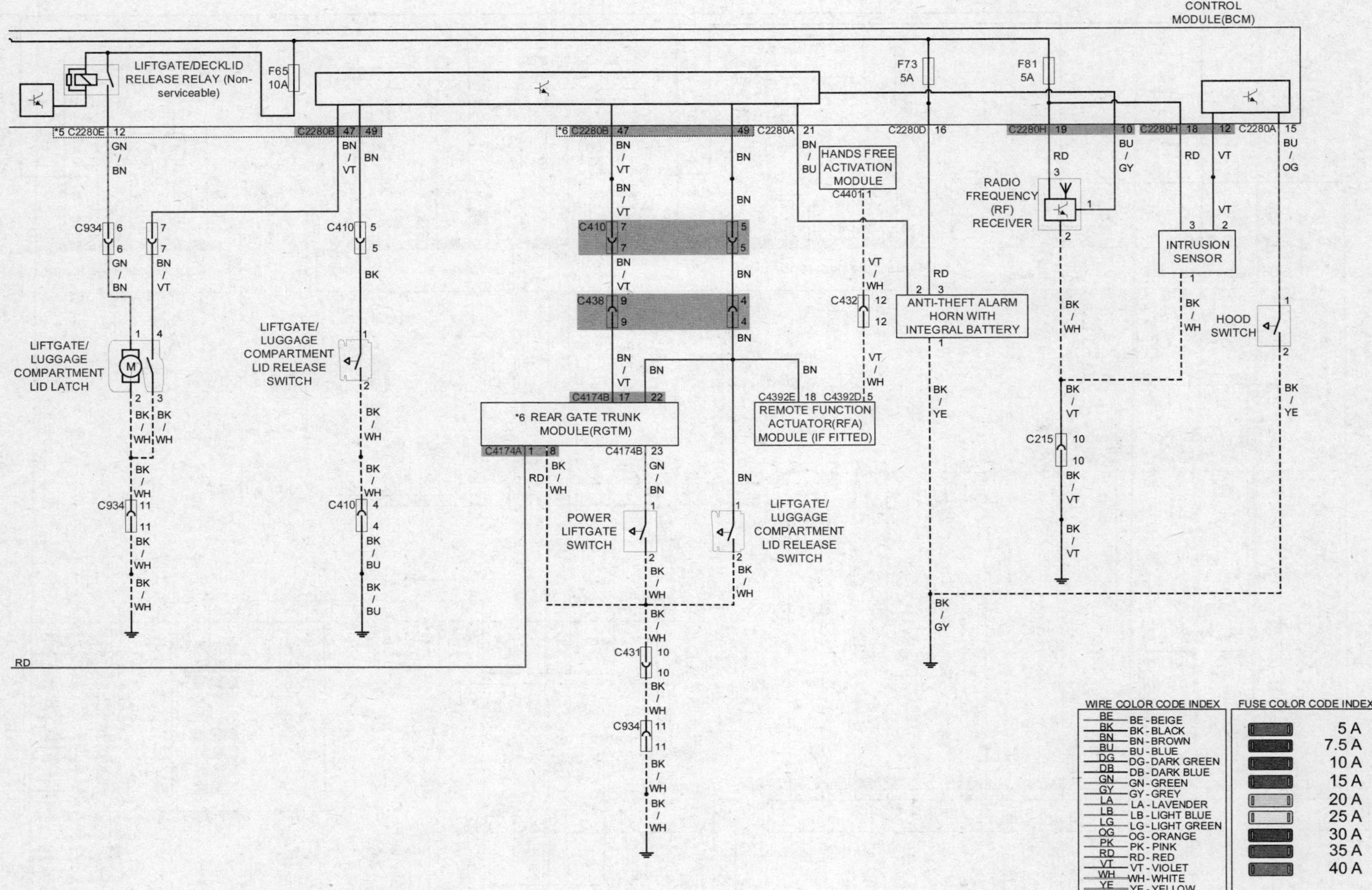

Diagram 14 – Central locking – up to 2016 model year (early production - Part 2)

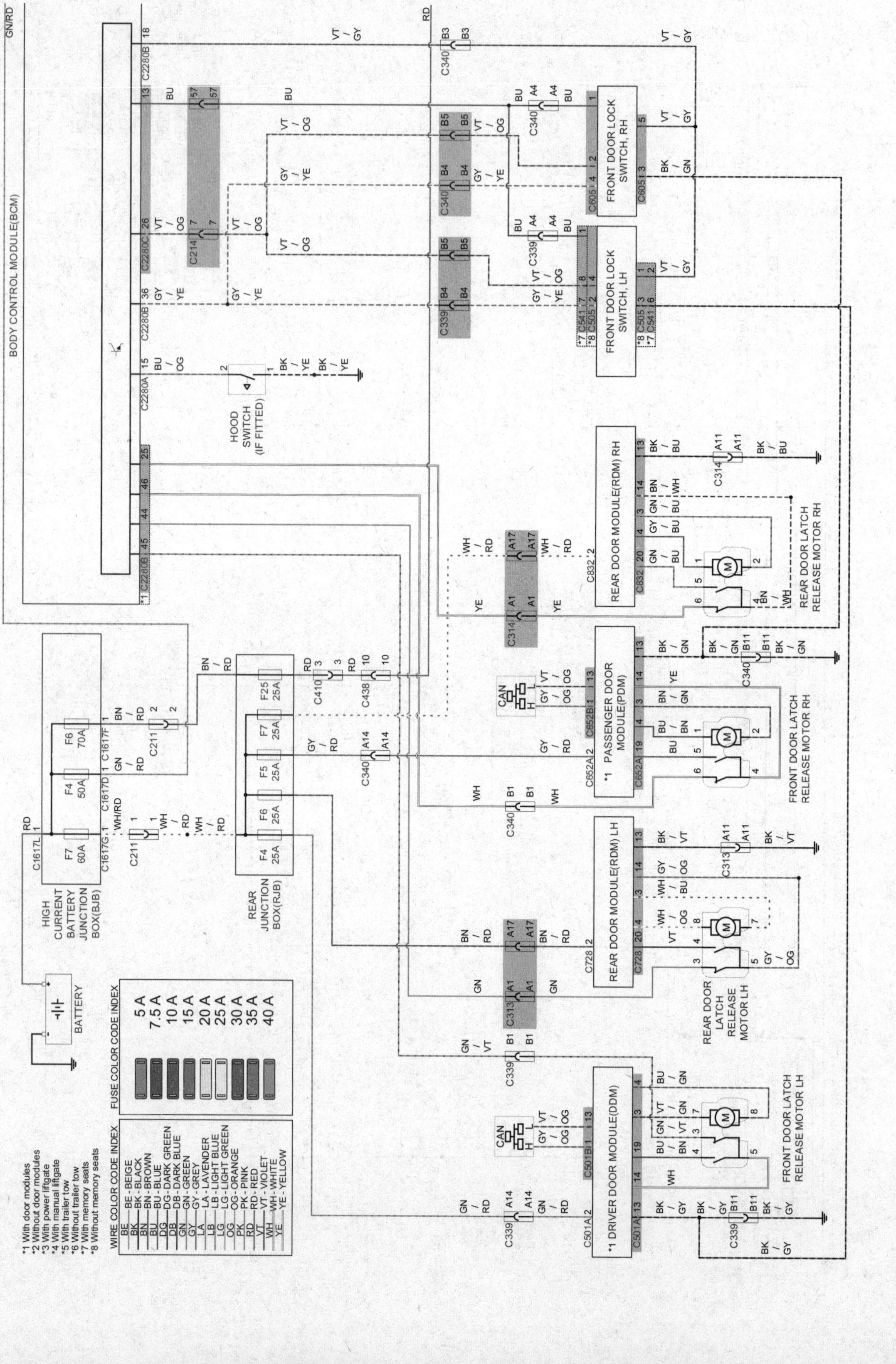

*1 With door modules
*2 Without door modules
*3 With power liftgate
*4 With manual liftgate
*5 With trailer tow
*6 Without trailer tow
*7 With memory seats
*8 Without memory seats
WIRE COLOR CODE INDEX
BE - BEIGE
BK - BLACK
BN - BROWN
BU - BLUE
DG - DARK GREEN
DB - DARK BLUE
GN - GREEN
GY - GREY
LA - LAVENDER
LB - LIGHT BLUE
LG - LIGHT GREEN
OG - ORANGE
PK - PINK
RD - RED
VT - VIOLET
WH - WHITE
YE - YELLOW
FUSE COLOR CODE INDEX
5 A
7.5 A
10 A
15 A
20 A
25 A
30 A
35 A
40 A
BATTERY
HIGH CURRENT BATTERY JUNCTION BOX(BJB)
F7 60A
F4 50A
F6 70A
REAR JUNCTION BOX(RJB)
F4 25A
F6 25A
F5 25A
F7 25A
F25 25A
BODY CONTROL MODULE(BCM)
HOOD SWITCH (IF FITTED)
*1 DRIVER DOOR MODULE(DDM)
FRONT DOOR LATCH RELEASE MOTOR LH
REAR DOOR MODULE(RDM) LH
REAR DOOR LATCH RELEASE MOTOR LH
*1 PASSENGER DOOR MODULE(PDM)
FRONT DOOR LATCH RELEASE MOTOR RH
REAR DOOR MODULE(RDM) RH
REAR DOOR LATCH RELEASE MOTOR RH
FRONT DOOR LOCK SWITCH, LH
FRONT DOOR LOCK SWITCH, RH
CAN

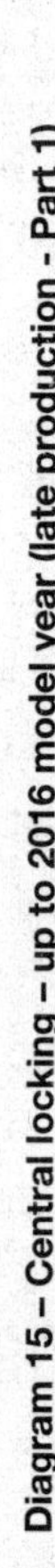

Diagram 15 – Central locking – up to 2016 model year (late production - Part 1)

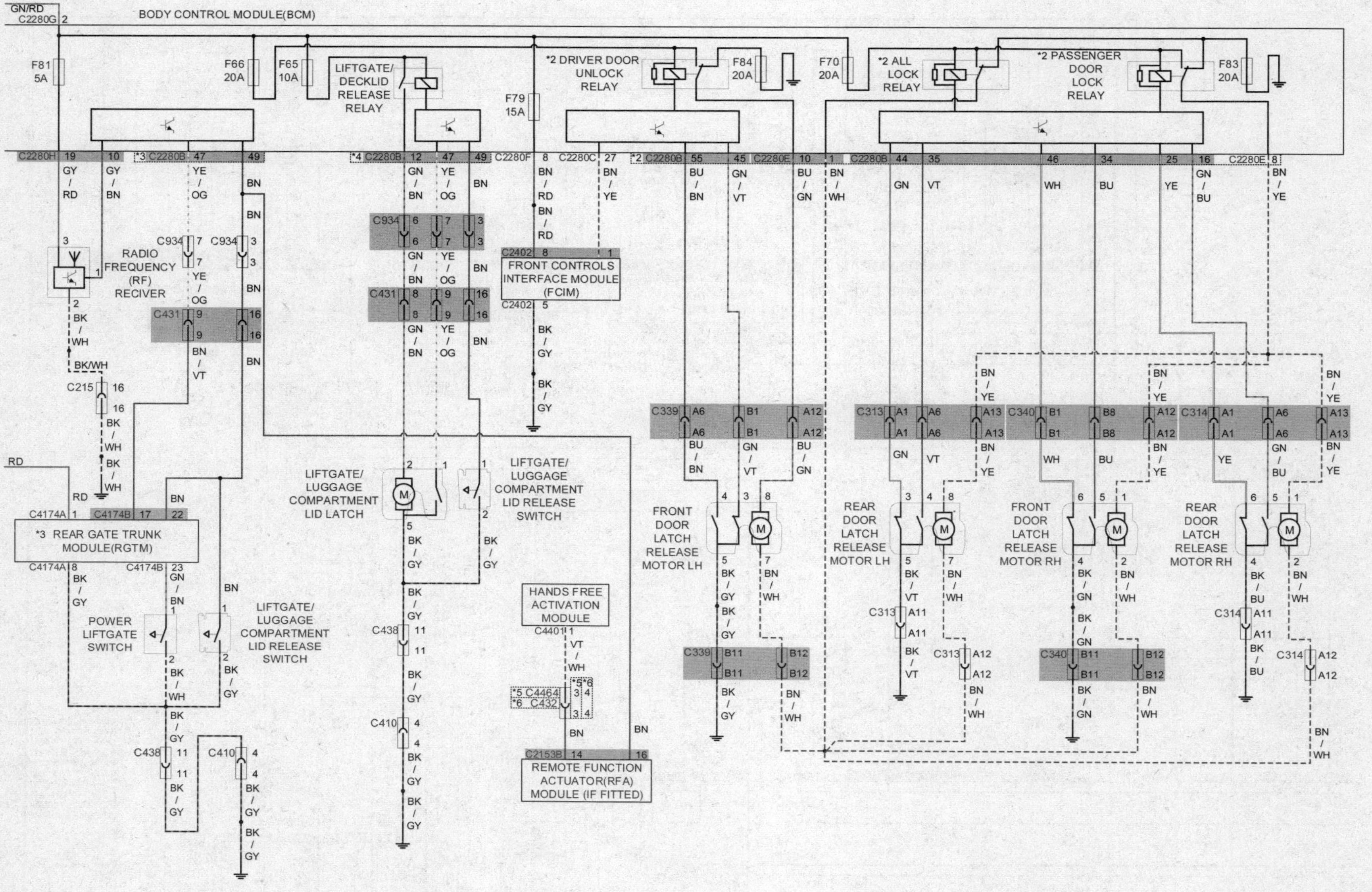

Diagram 16 – Central locking – up to 2016 model year (late production - Part 2)

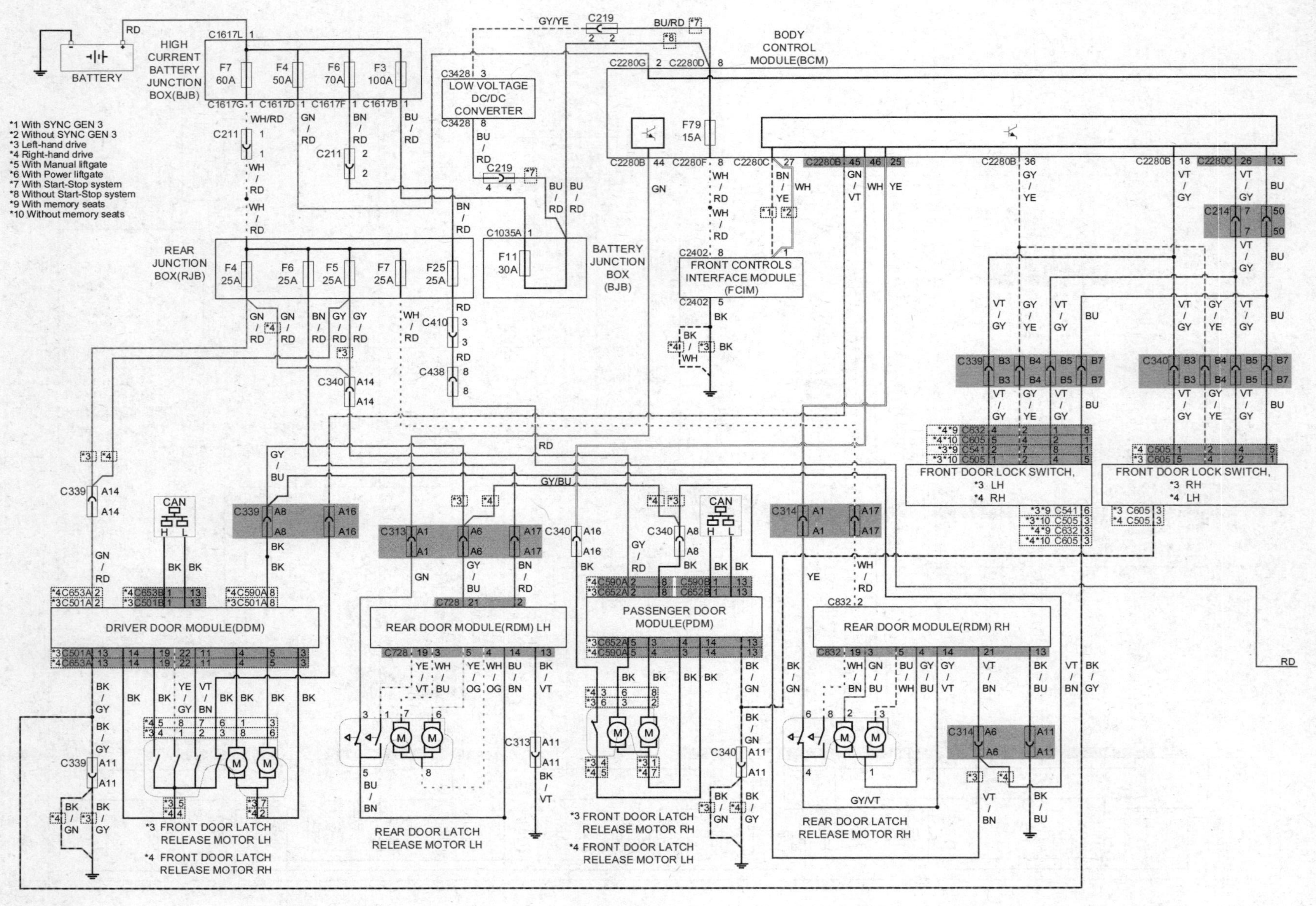

Diagram 17 – Central locking – 2017 to 2018 model year (Part 1)

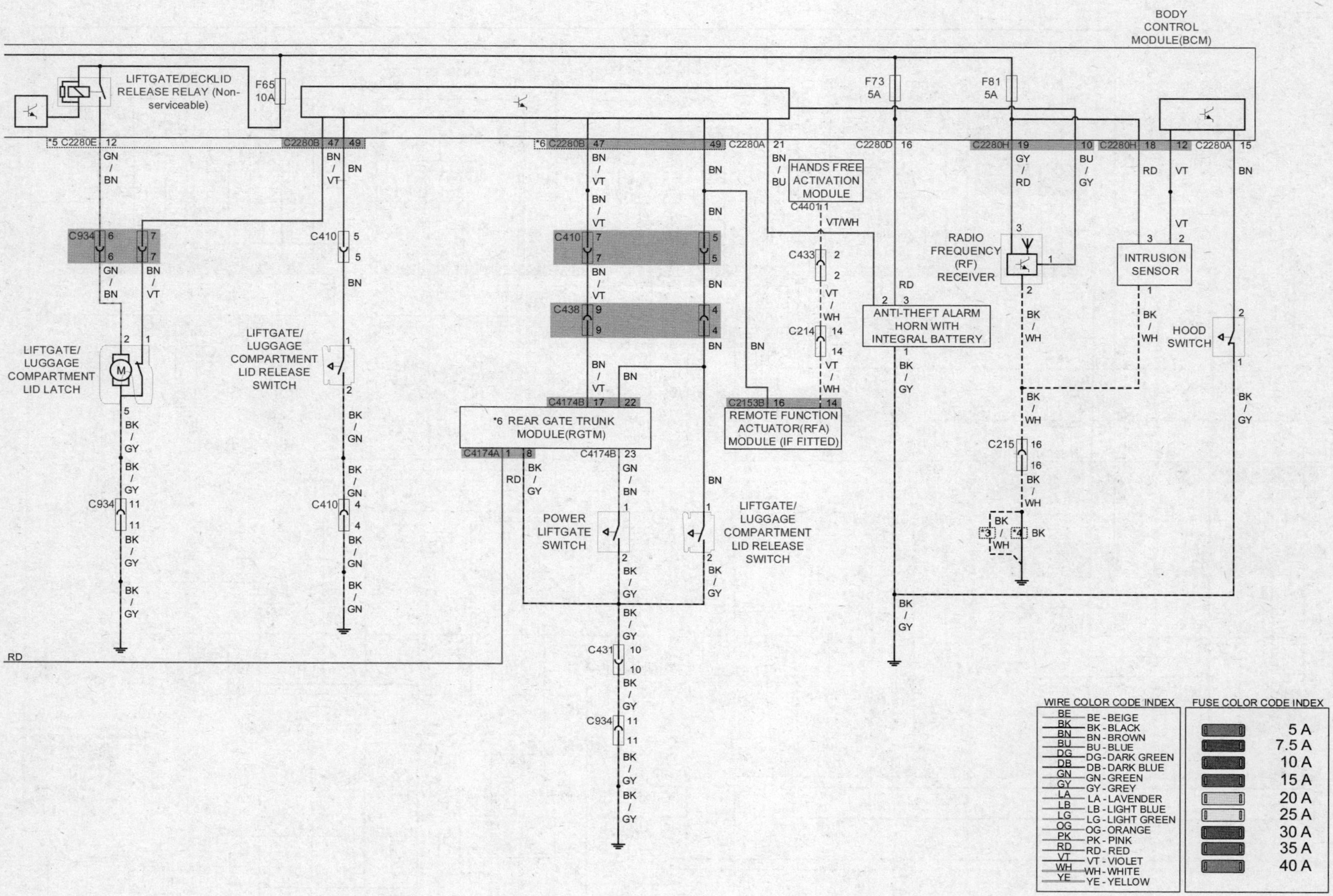

Diagram 18 – Central locking – 2017 to 2018 model year (Part 2)

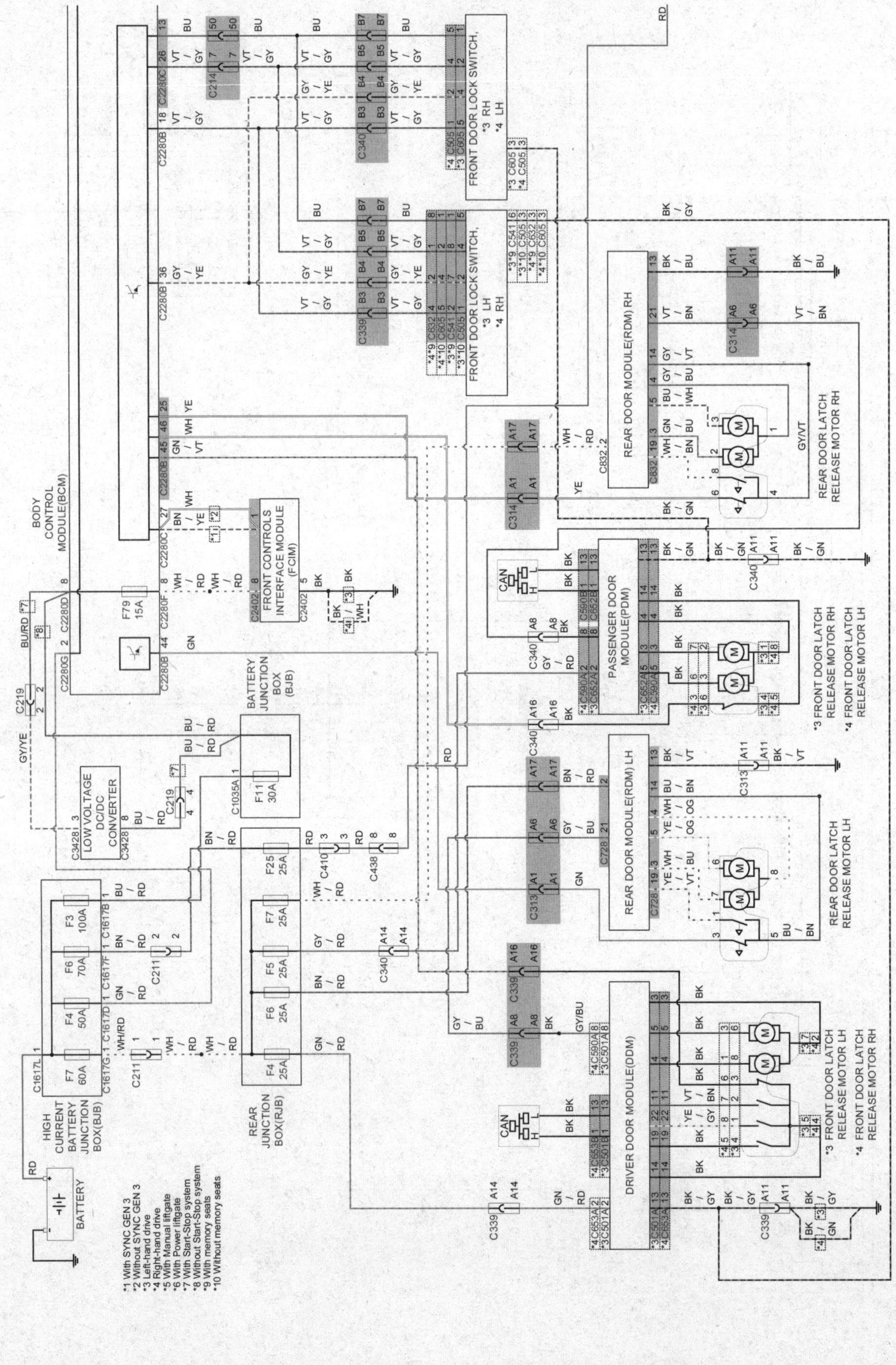

*1 With SYNC GEN 3
*2 Without SYNC GEN 3
*3 Left-hand drive
*4 Right-hand drive
*5 With Manual liftgate
*6 With Power liftgate
*7 With Start-Stop system
*8 Without Start-Stop system
*9 With memory seats
*10 Without memory seats

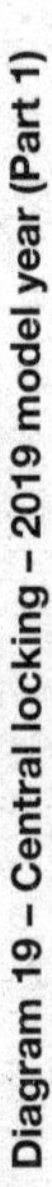

Diagram 19 – Central locking – 2019 model year (Part 1)

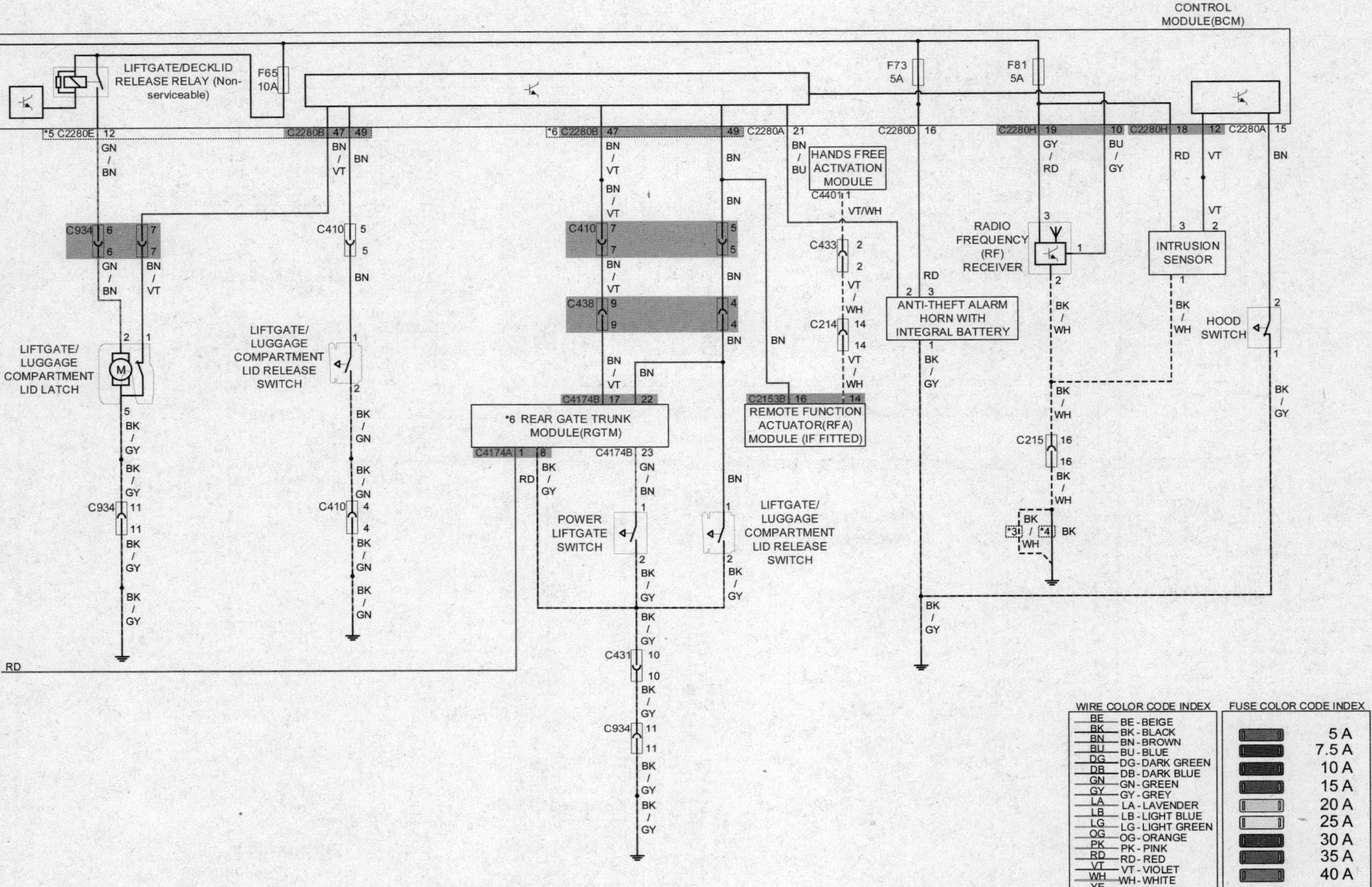

Diagram 20 – Central locking – 2019 model year (Part 2)

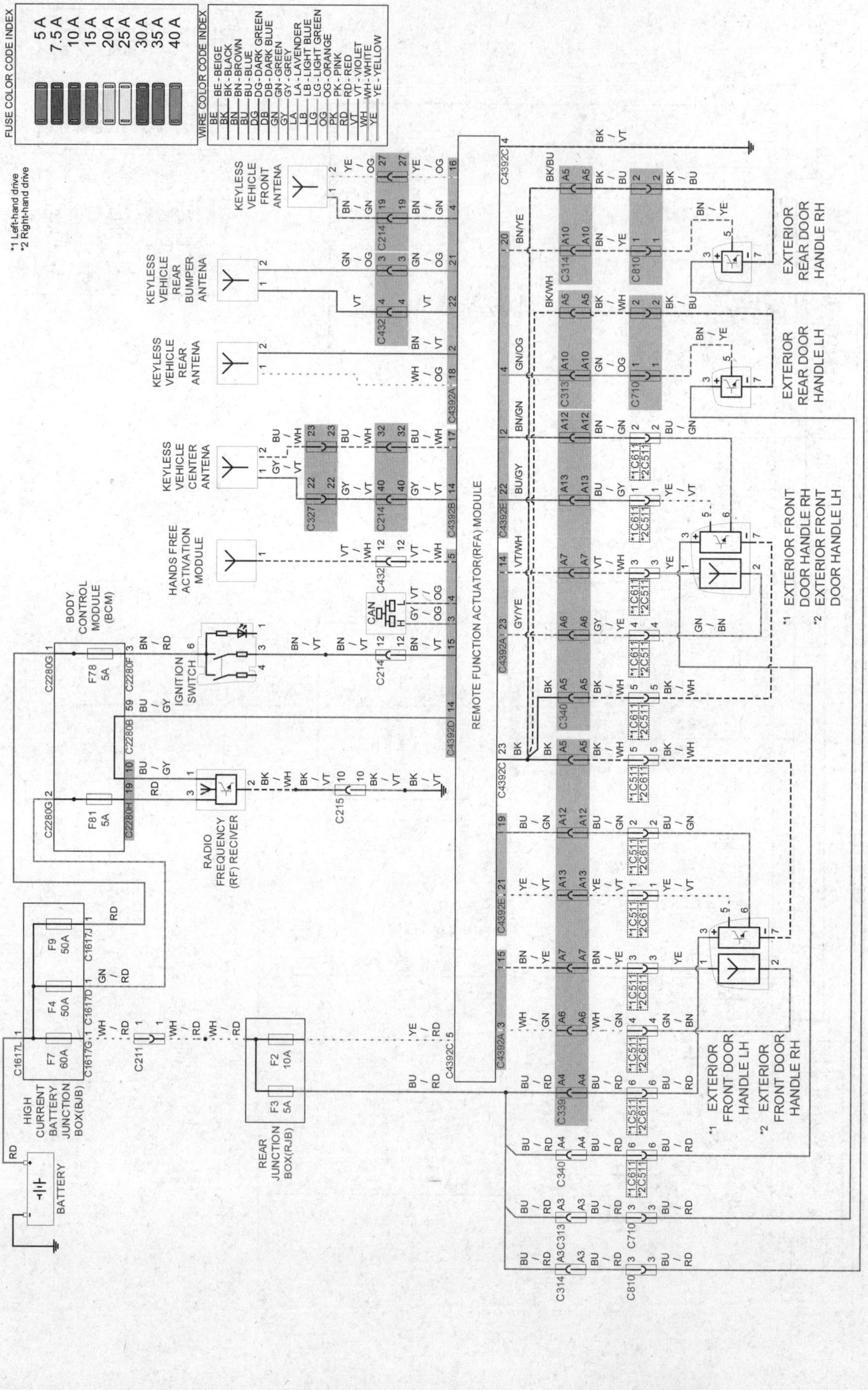

Diagram 21 – Keyless entry and start – up to 2016 model year (early production)

*1 Left-hand drive
*2 Right-hand drive

FUSE COLOR CODE INDEX

5 A
7.5 A
10 A
15 A
20 A
25 A
30 A
35 A
40 A

WIRE COLOR CODE INDEX

BE	BE-BEIGE
BK	BK-BLACK
BN	BN-BROWN
BU	BU-BLUE
DG	DG-DARK GREEN
DB	DB-DARK BLUE
GN	GN-GREEN
GY	GY-GREY
LA	LA-LAVENDER
LB	LB-LIGHT BLUE
LG	LG-LIGHT GREEN
OG	OG-ORANGE
PK	PK-PINK
RD	RD-RED
VT	VT-VIOLET
WH	WH-WHITE
YE	YE-YELLOW

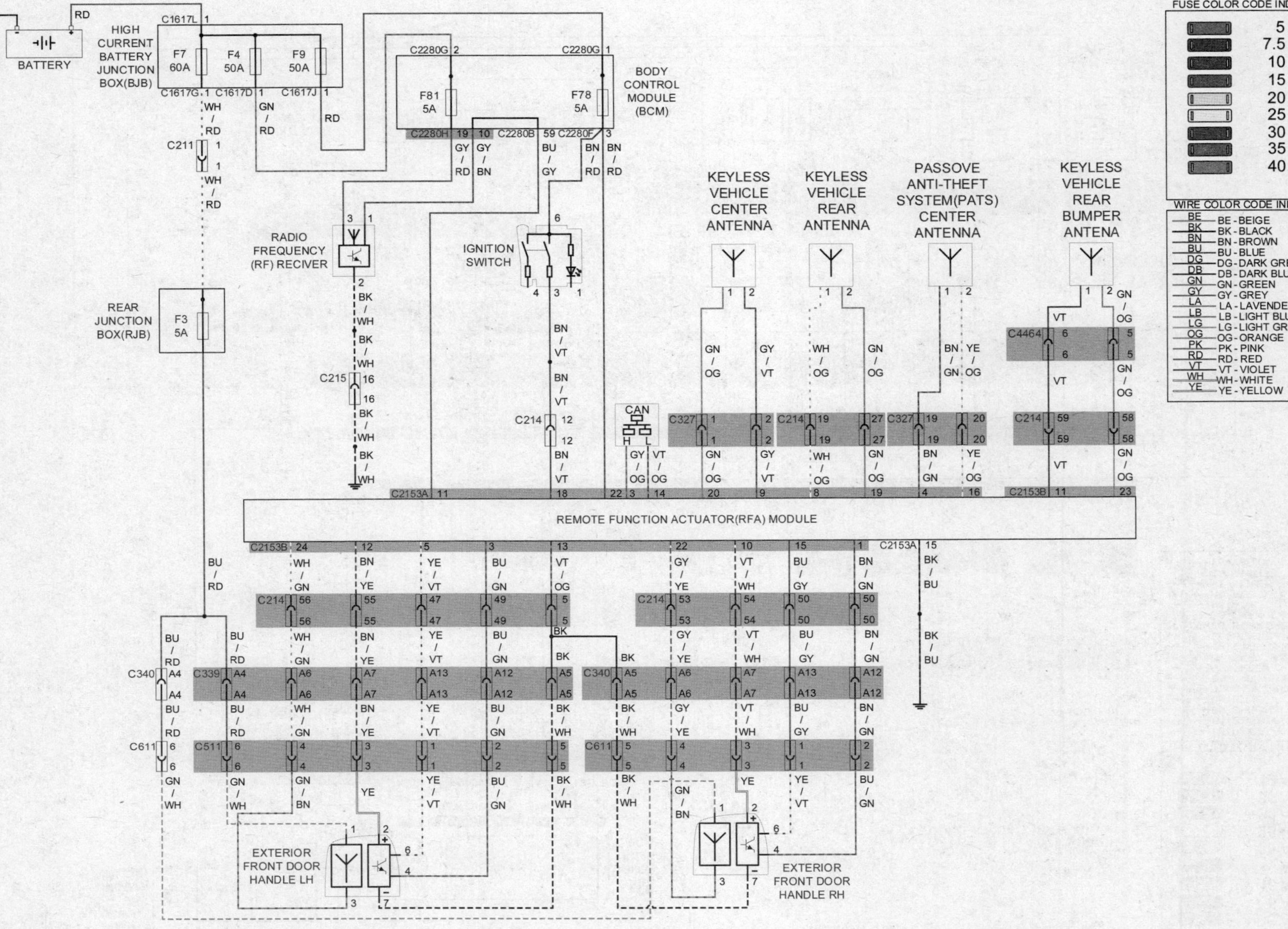

Diagram 22 – Keyless entry and start – up to 2016 model year (late production)

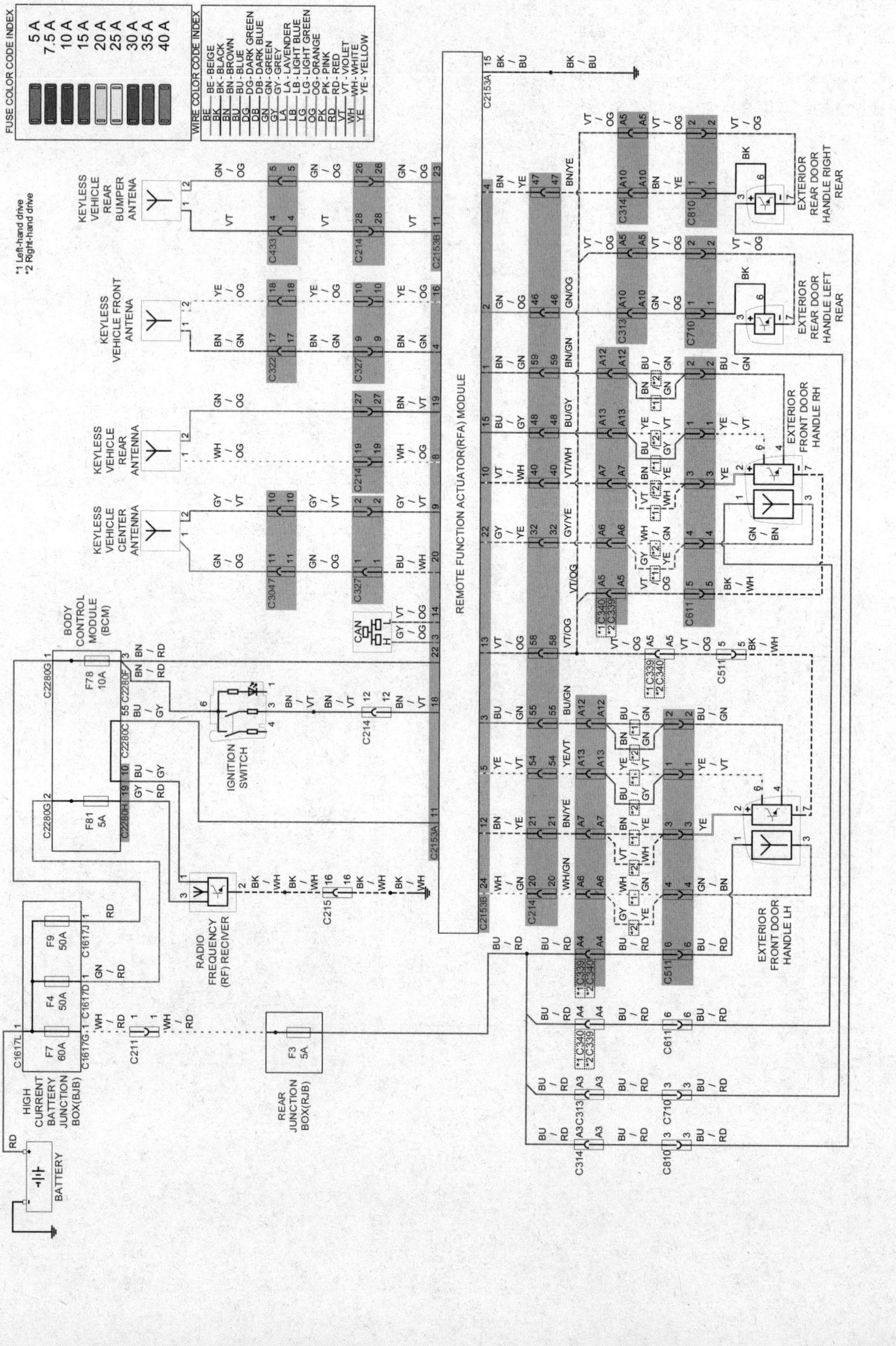

FUSE COLOR CODE INDEX

5 A
7.5 A
10 A
15 A
20 A
25 A
30 A
35 A
40 A

WIRE COLOR CODE INDEX

BE	BE - BEIGE
BK	BK - BLACK
BN	BN - BROWN
BU	BU - BLUE
DG	DG - DARK GREEN
DB	DB - DARK BLUE
GN	GN - GREEN
GY	GY - GREY
LA	LA - LAVENDER
LB	LB - LIGHT BLUE
LG	LG - LIGHT GREEN
OG	OG - ORANGE
PK	PK - PINK
RD	RD - RED
VT	VT - VIOLET
WH	WH - WHITE
YE	YE - YELLOW

*1 Left-hand drive
*2 Right-hand drive

BATTERY

HIGH CURRENT BATTERY JUNCTION BOX(BJB)

REAR JUNCTION BOX(RJB)

RADIO FREQUENCY (RF) RECIVER

IGNITION SWITCH

BODY CONTROL MODULE (BCM)

KEYLESS VEHICLE CENTER ANTENNA

KEYLESS VEHICLE REAR ANTENNA

KEYLESS VEHICLE FRONT ANTENNA

KEYLESS VEHICLE REAR BUMPER ANTENNA

REMOTE FUNCTION ACTUATOR(RFA) MODULE

EXTERIOR FRONT DOOR HANDLE LH

EXTERIOR FRONT DOOR HANDLE RH

EXTERIOR REAR DOOR HANDLE LEFT REAR

EXTERIOR REAR DOOR HANDLE RIGHT REAR

Diagram 23 – Keyless entry and start – 2017 to 2018 model year

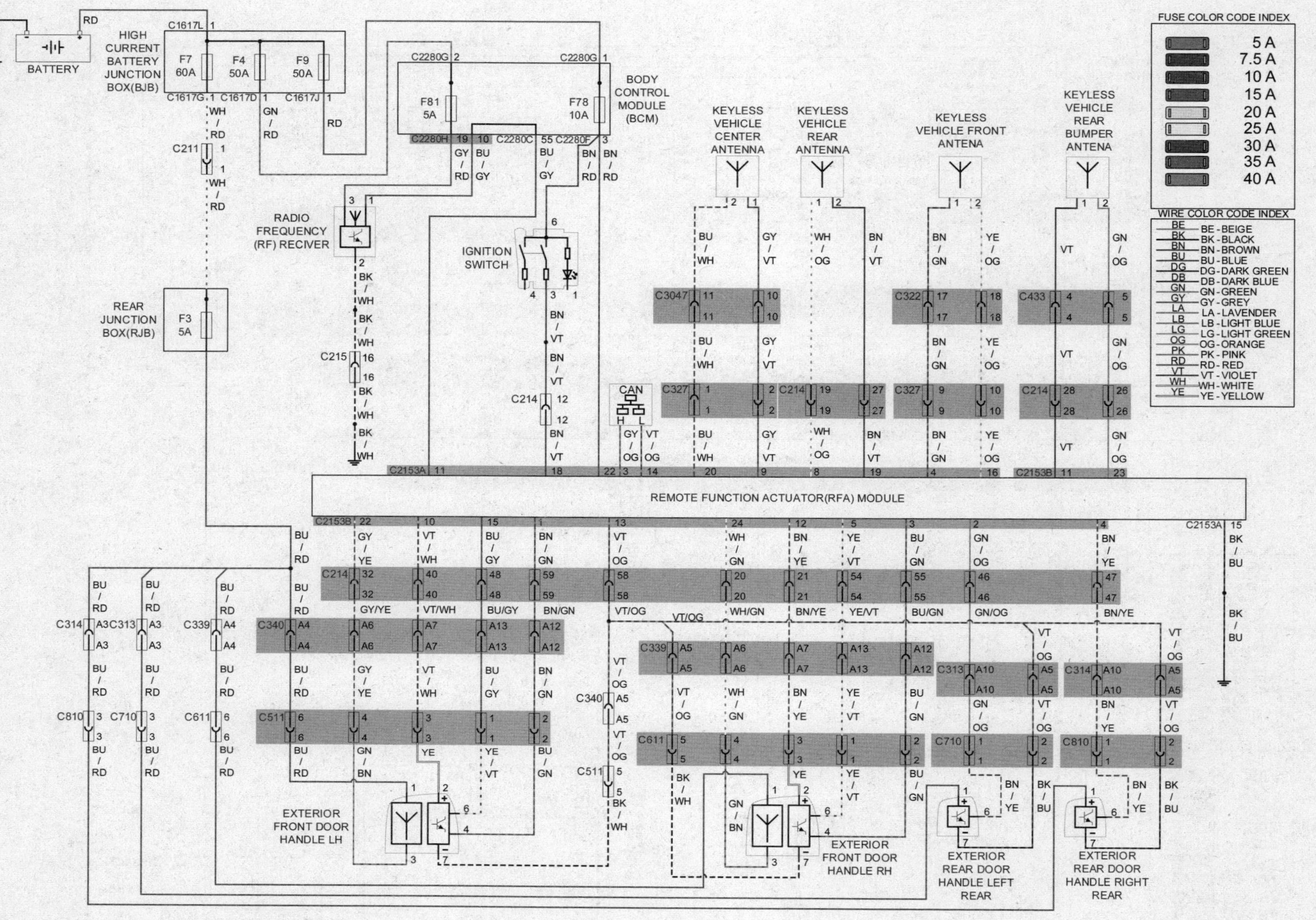

Diagram 24 – Keyless entry and start – RHD from 2019 model year

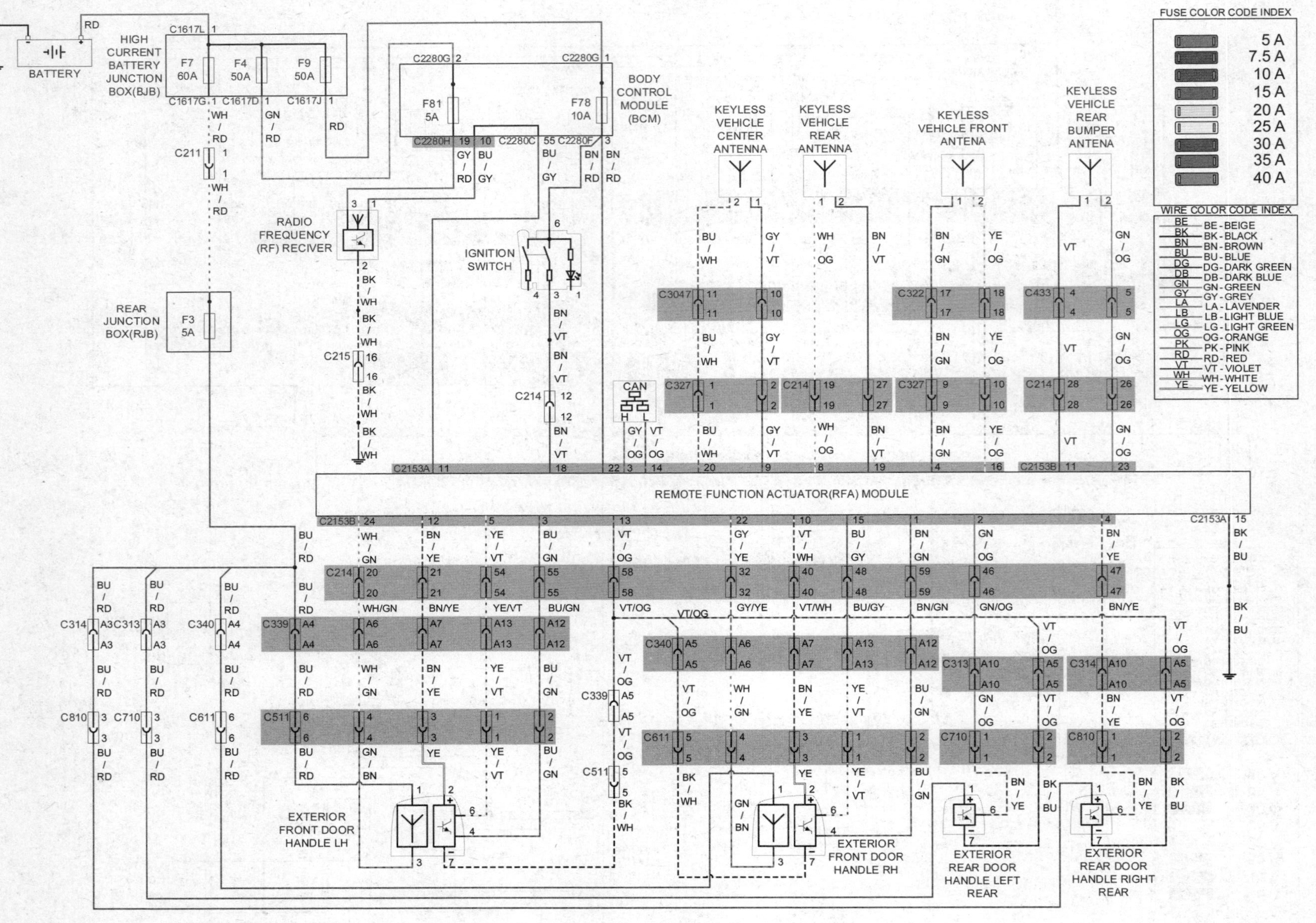

Diagram 25 – Keyless entry and start – LHD from 2019 model year

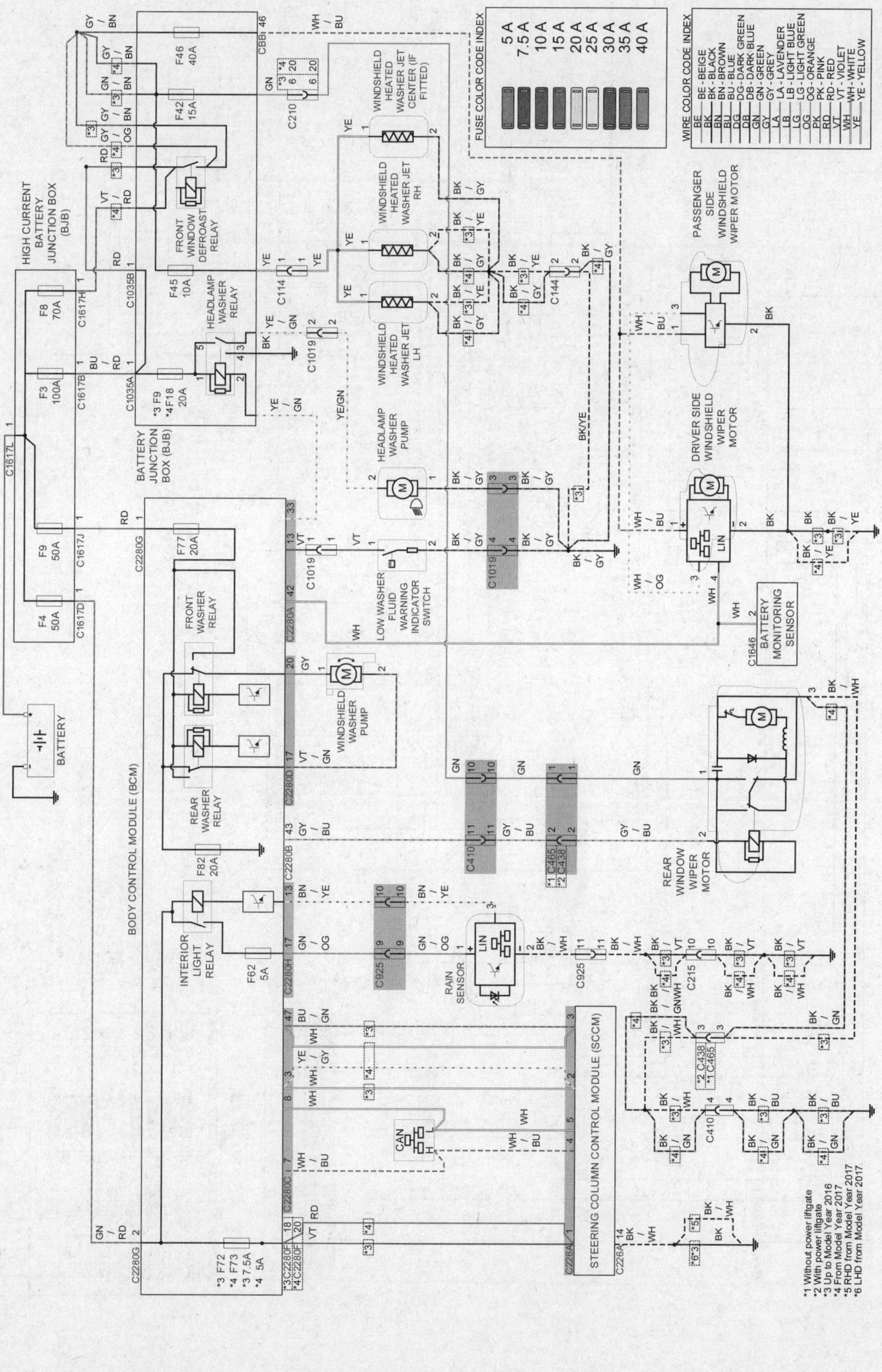

BATTERY

HIGH CURRENT BATTERY JUNCTION BOX (BJB)

F4 50A
F9 50A
F3 100A
F8 70A

BODY CONTROL MODULE (BCM)

BATTERY JUNCTION BOX (BJB)

INTERIOR LIGHT RELAY

REAR WASHER RELAY

FRONT WASHER RELAY

F82 20A
F77 20A
F62 5A
*3 F72
*4 F73
*3 7.5A
*4 5A

*3 F9
*4 F18
20A

F45 10A
F42 15A
F46 40A

HEADLAMP WASHER RELAY

FRONT WINDOW DEFROAST RELAY

WINDSHIELD WASHER PUMP

LOW WASHER FLUID WARNING INDICATOR SWITCH

HEADLAMP WASHER PUMP

WINDSHIELD HEATED WASHER JET LH

WINDSHIELD HEATED WASHER JET RH

WINDSHIELD HEATED WASHER JET CENTER (IF FITTED)

CAN

RAIN SENSOR

STEERING COLUMN CONTROL MODULE (SCCM)

REAR WINDOW WIPER MOTOR

DRIVER SIDE WINDSHIELD WIPER MOTOR

PASSENGER SIDE WINDSHIELD WIPER MOTOR

BATTERY MONITORING SENSOR

*1 Without power liftgate
*2 With power liftgate
*3 Up to Model Year 2016
*4 From Model Year 2017
*5 RHD from Model Year 2017
*6 LHD from Model Year 2017

FUSE COLOR CODE INDEX

5 A
7.5 A
10 A
15 A
20 A
25 A
30 A
35 A
40 A

WIRE COLOR CODE INDEX

BE	BE - BEIGE
BK	BK - BLACK
BN	BN - BROWN
BU	BU - BLUE
DG	DG - DARK GREEN
DB	DB - DARK BLUE
GN	GN - GREEN
GY	GY - GREY
LA	LA - LAVENDER
LB	LB - LIGHT BLUE
LG	LG - LIGHT GREEN
OG	OG - ORANGE
PK	PK - PINK
RD	RD - RED
VT	VT - VIOLET
WH	WH - WHITE
YE	YE - YELLOW

Diagram 26 – Washers and wipers

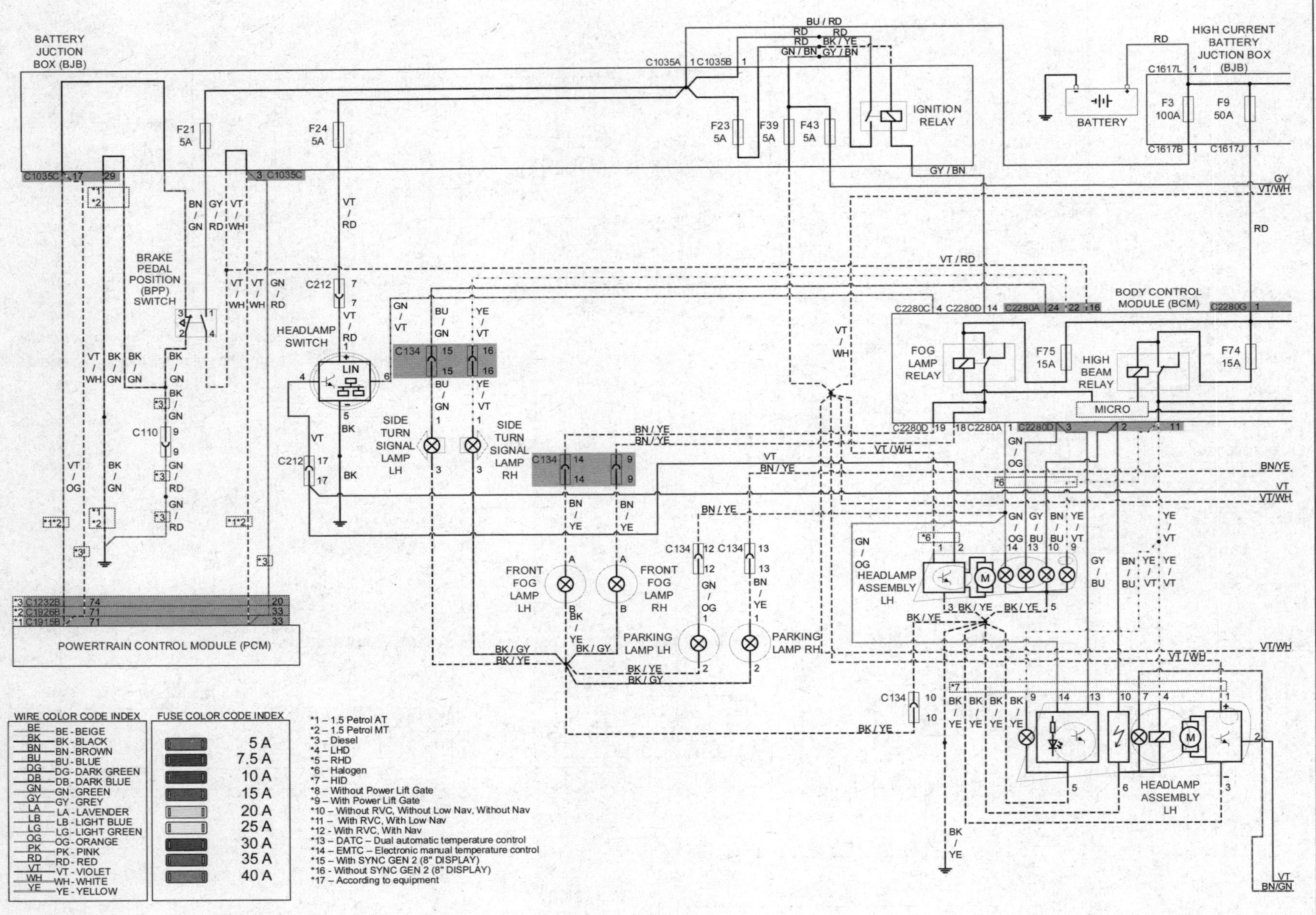

Diagram 27 – Exterior lights – up to 2016 model year (Part 1)

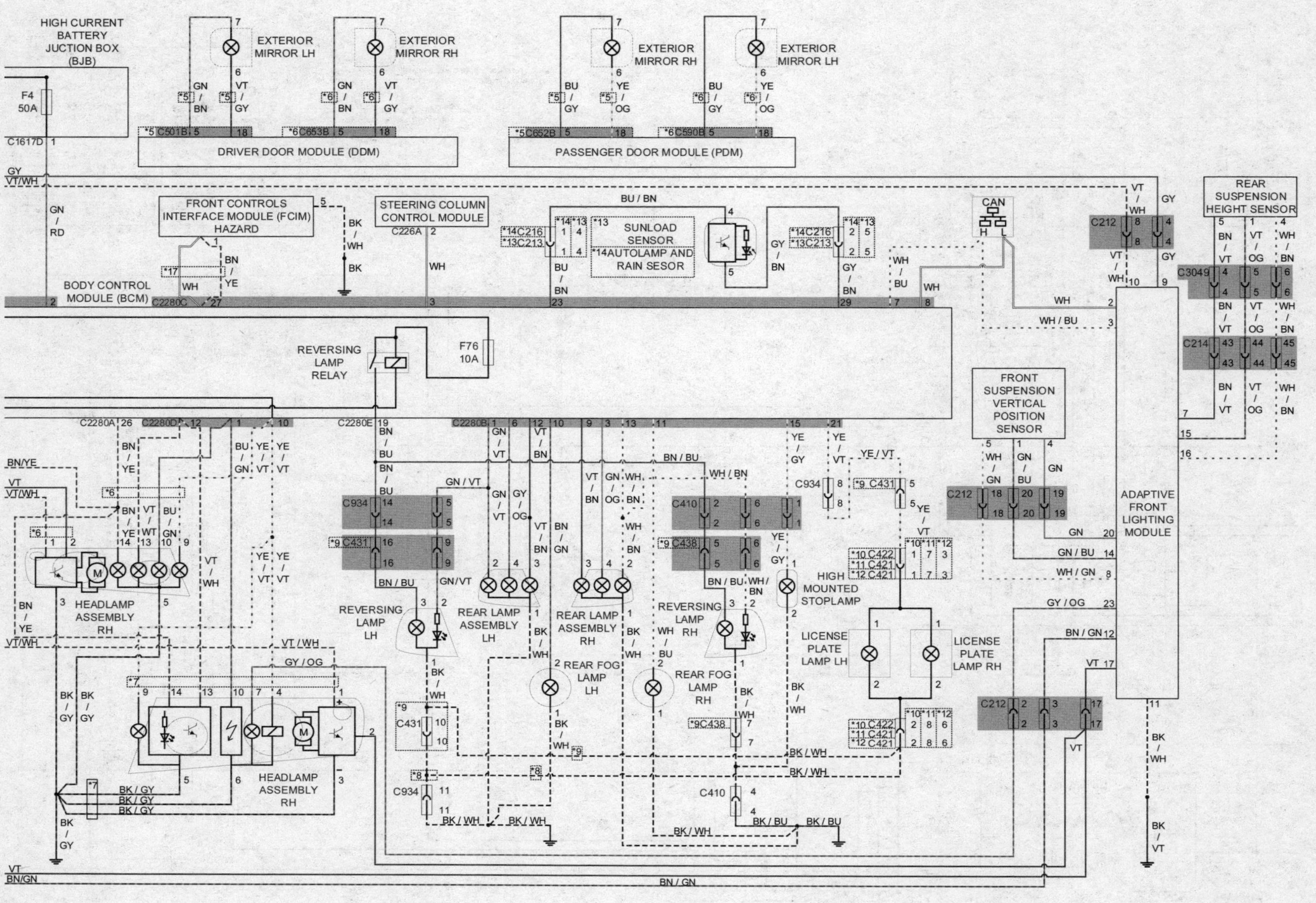

Diagram 28 – Exterior lights – up to 2016 model year (Part 2)

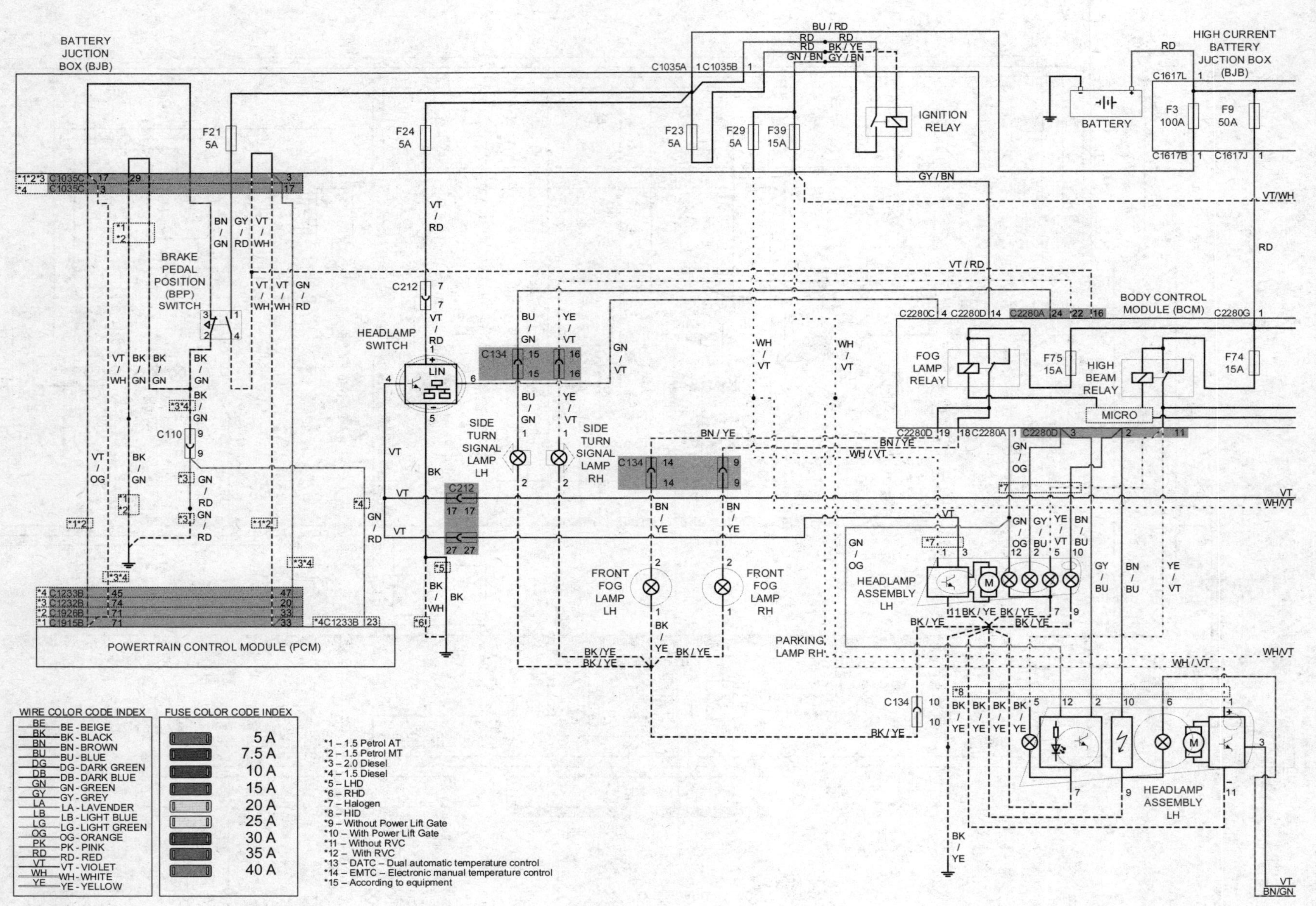

Diagram 29 – Exterior lights – 2017 to 2018 model year (Part 1)

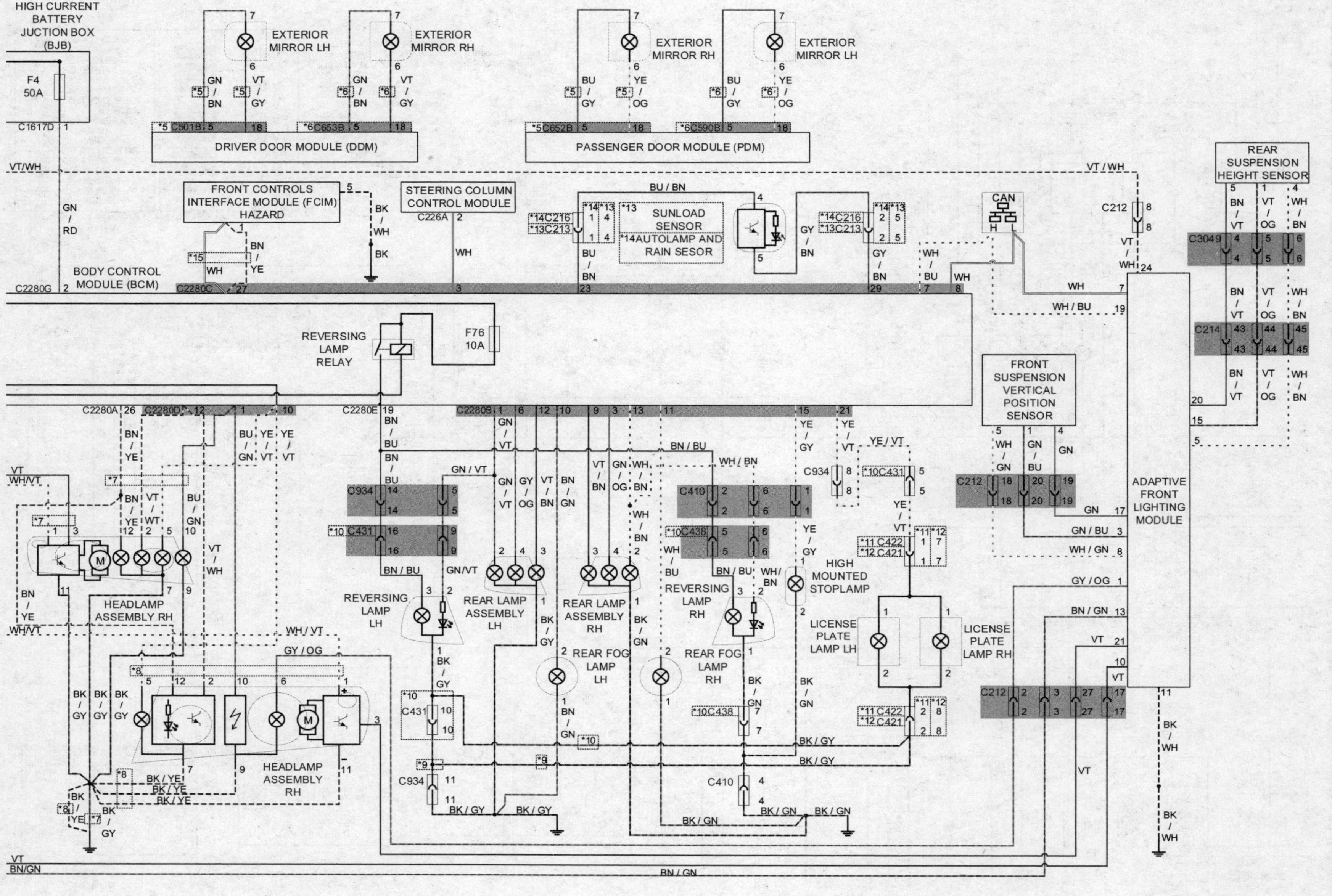

Diagram 30 – Exterior lights – 2017 to 2018 model year (Part 2)

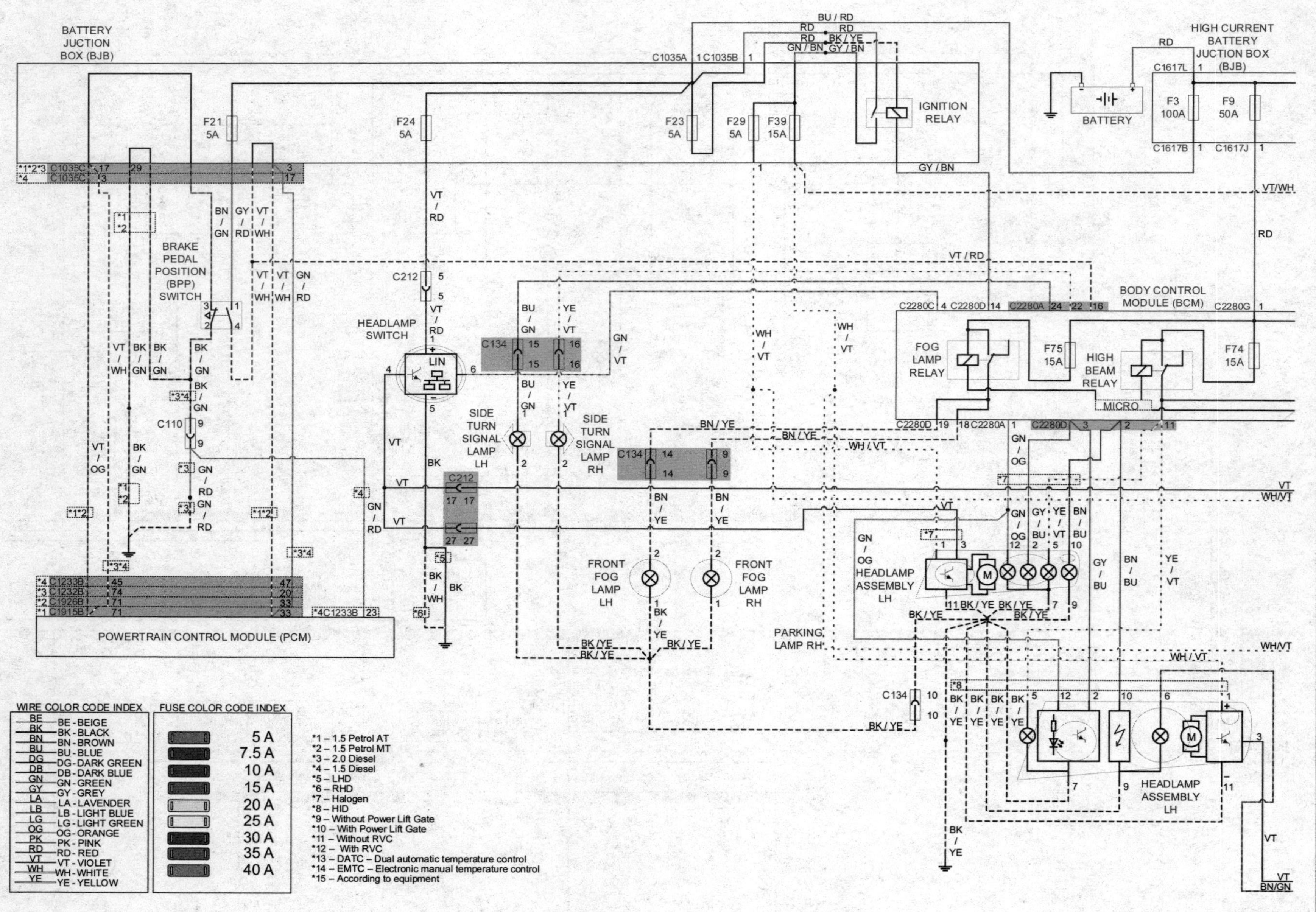

Diagram 31 – Exterior lights – from 2019 model year (Part 1)

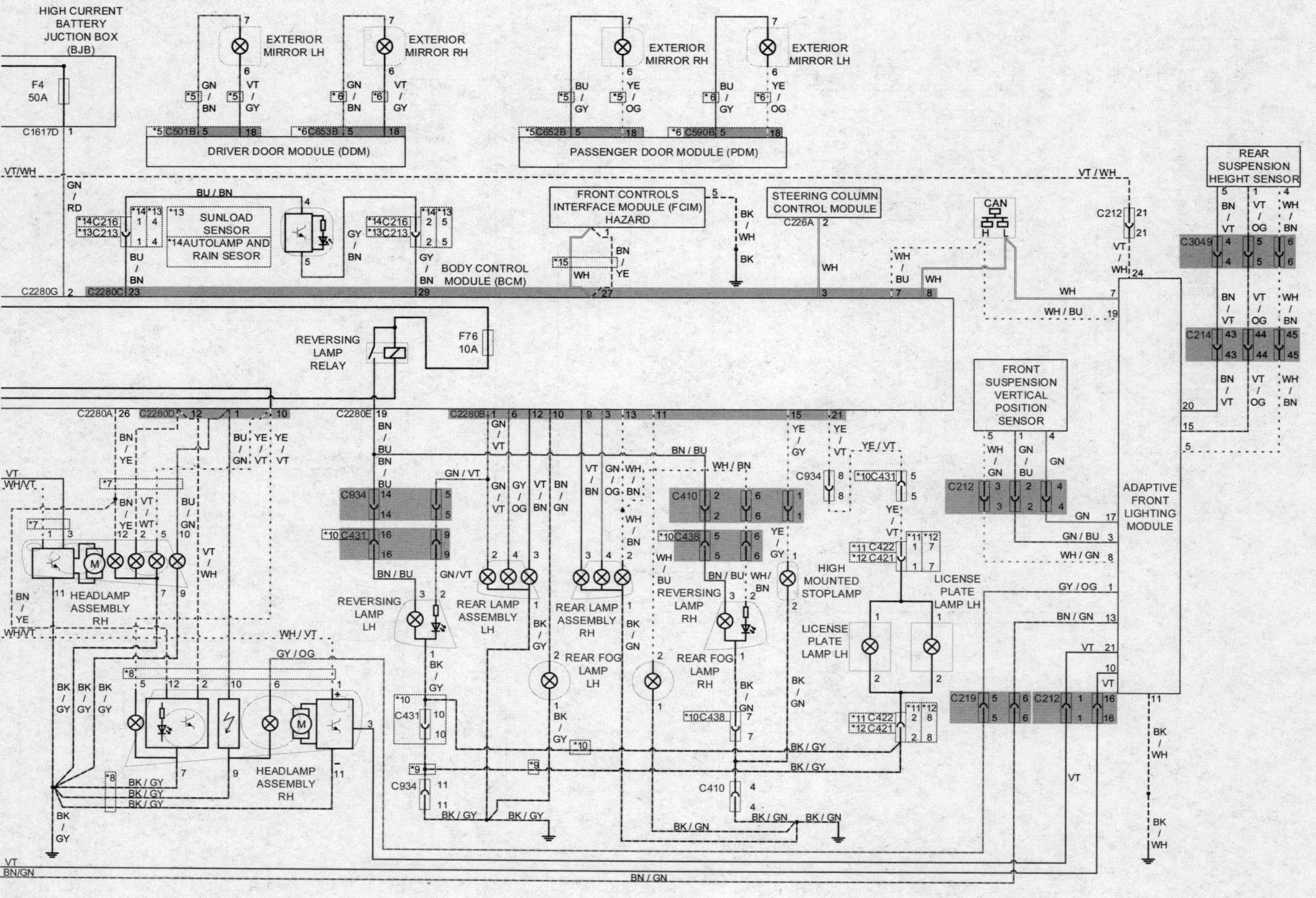

Diagram 32 – Exterior lights – from 2019 model year (Part 2)

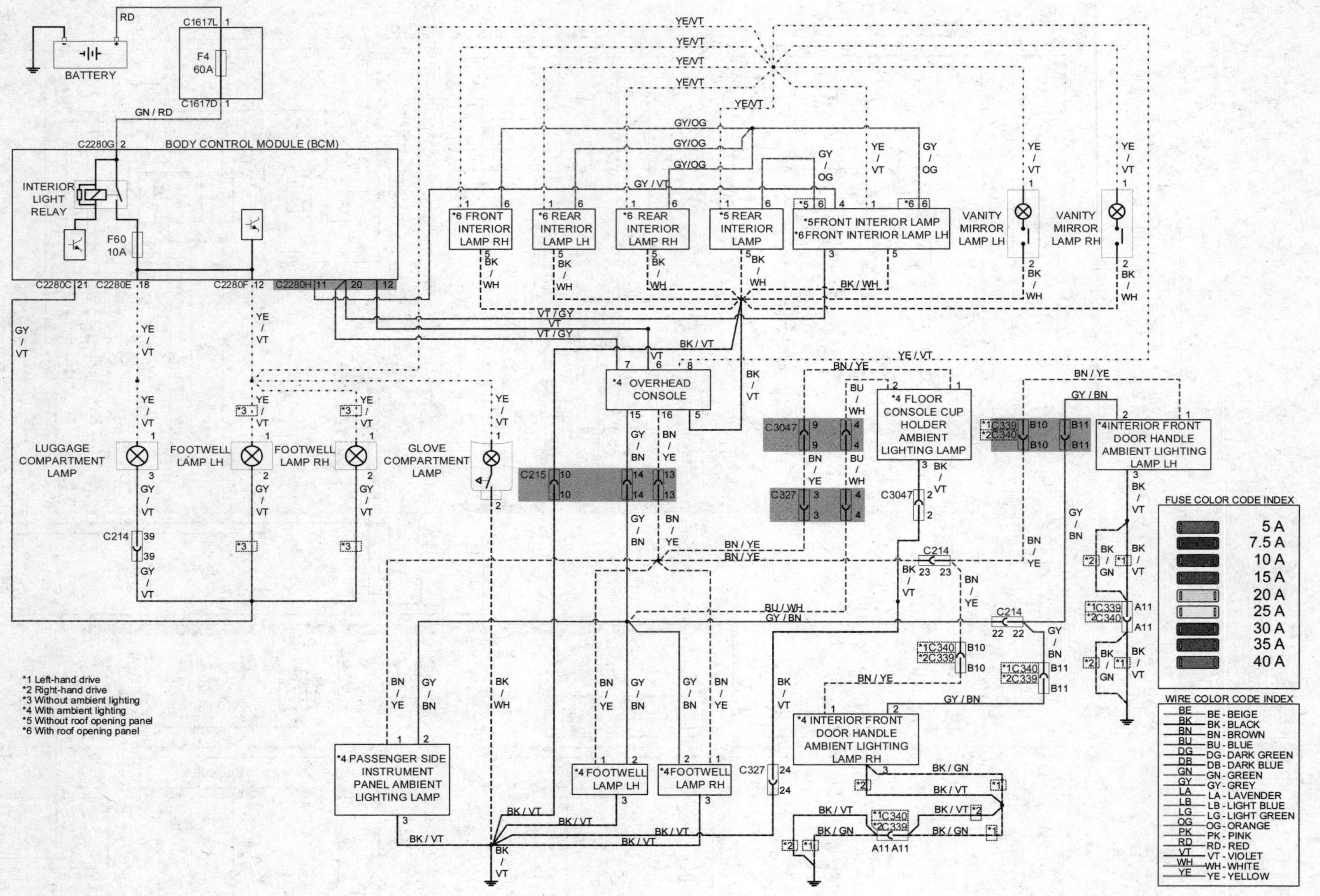

Diagram 33 – Interior lights – up to 2016 model year

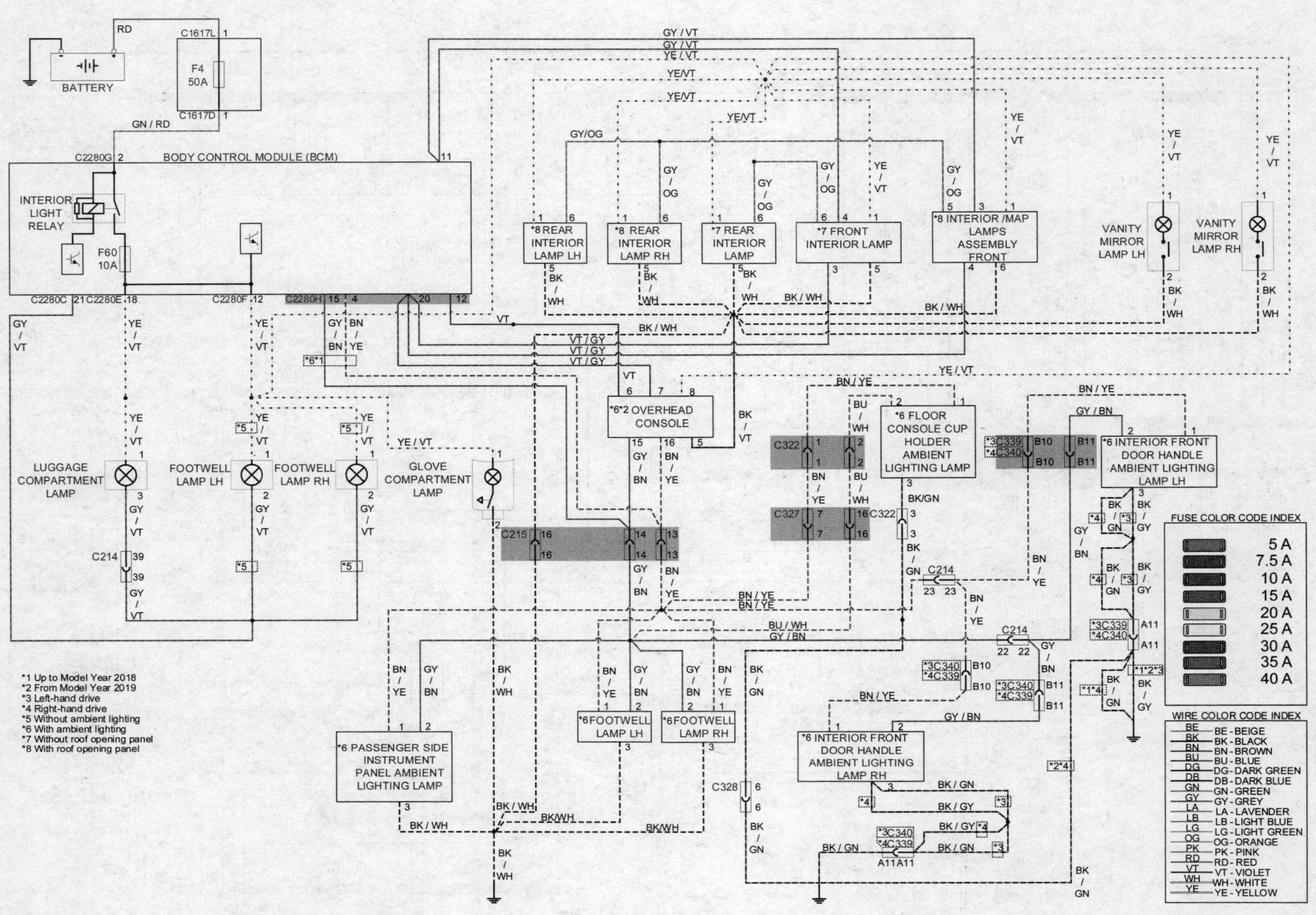

Diagram 34 – Interior lights – from 2017 model year

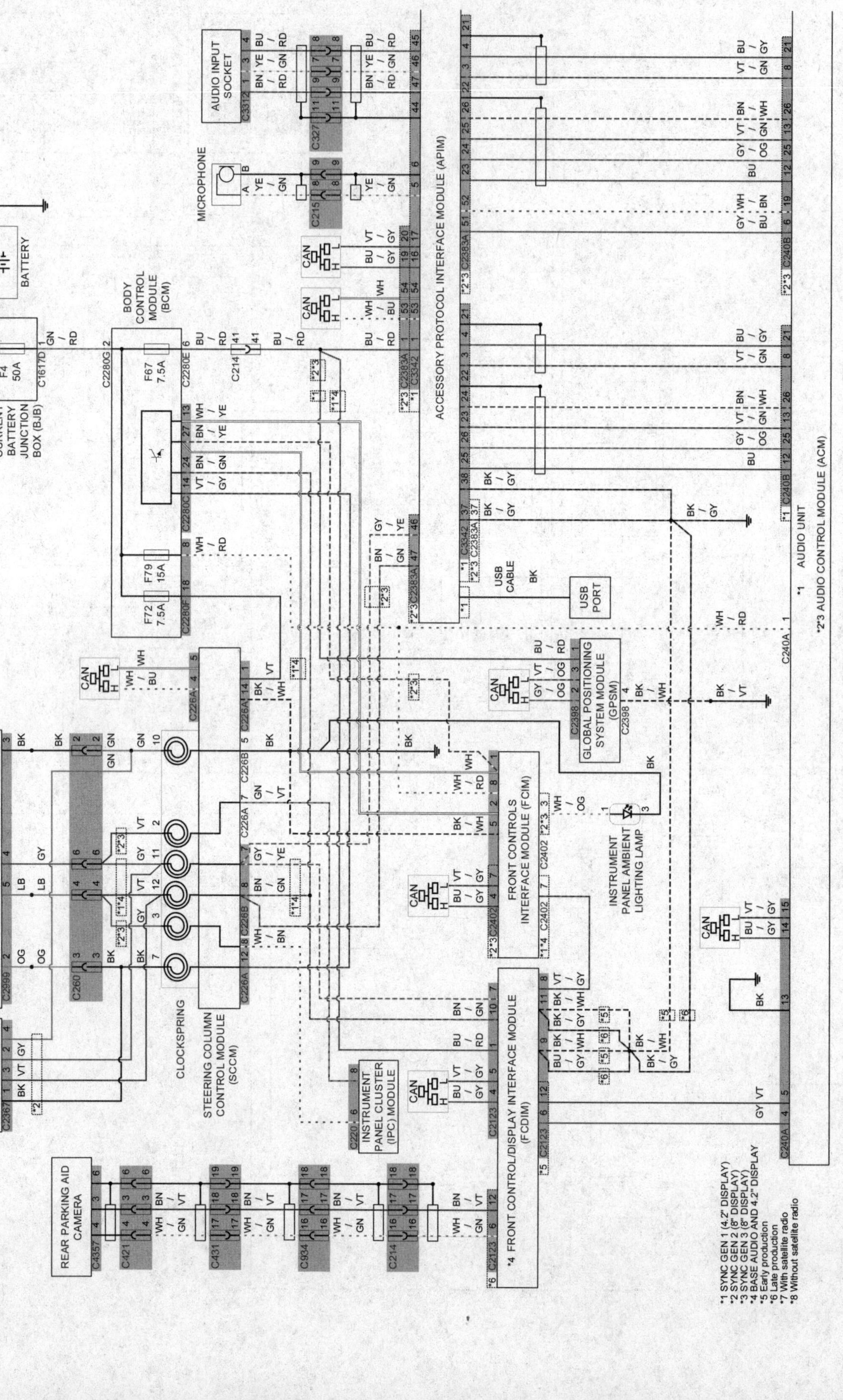

STEERING WHEEL SWITCH, RH LOWER

STEERING WHEEL SWITCH, RH UPPER

REAR PARKING AID CAMERA

CLOCKSPRING

STEERING COLUMN CONTROL MODULE (SCCM)

INSTRUMENT PANEL CLUSTER (IPC) MODULE

HIGH CURRENT BATTERY JUNCTION BOX (BJB)

BATTERY

BODY CONTROL MODULE (BCM)

MICROPHONE

AUDIO INPUT SOCKET

ACCESSORY PROTOCOL INTERFACE MODULE (APIM)

USB CABLE

USB PORT

*4 FRONT CONTROL/DISPLAY INTERFACE MODULE (FCDIM)

FRONT CONTROLS INTERFACE MODULE (FCIM)

GLOBAL POSITIONING SYSTEM MODULE (GPSM)

INSTRUMENT PANEL AMBIENT LIGHTING LAMP

*1 AUDIO UNIT

*2*3 AUDIO CONTROL MODULE (ACM)

*1 SYNC GEN 1 (4.2" DISPLAY)
*2 SYNC GEN 2 (8" DISPLAY)
*3 SYNC GEN 3 (8" DISPLAY)
*4 BASE AUDIO AND 4.2" DISPLAY
*5 Early production
*6 Late production
*7 With satellite radio
*8 Without satellite radio

Diagram 35 – Sound system – up to 2016 model year (Part 1)

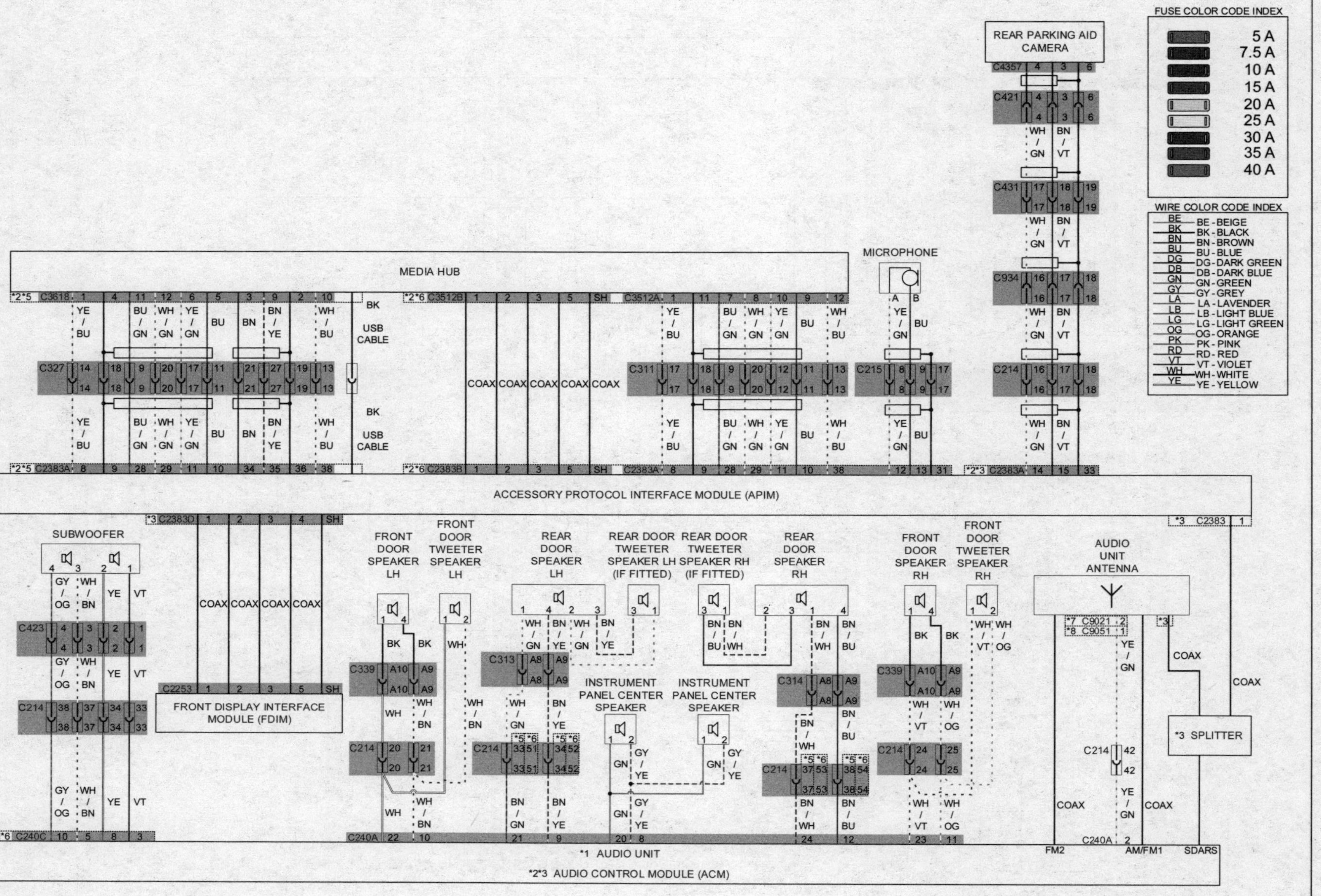

Diagram 36 – Sound system – up to 2016 model year (Part 2)

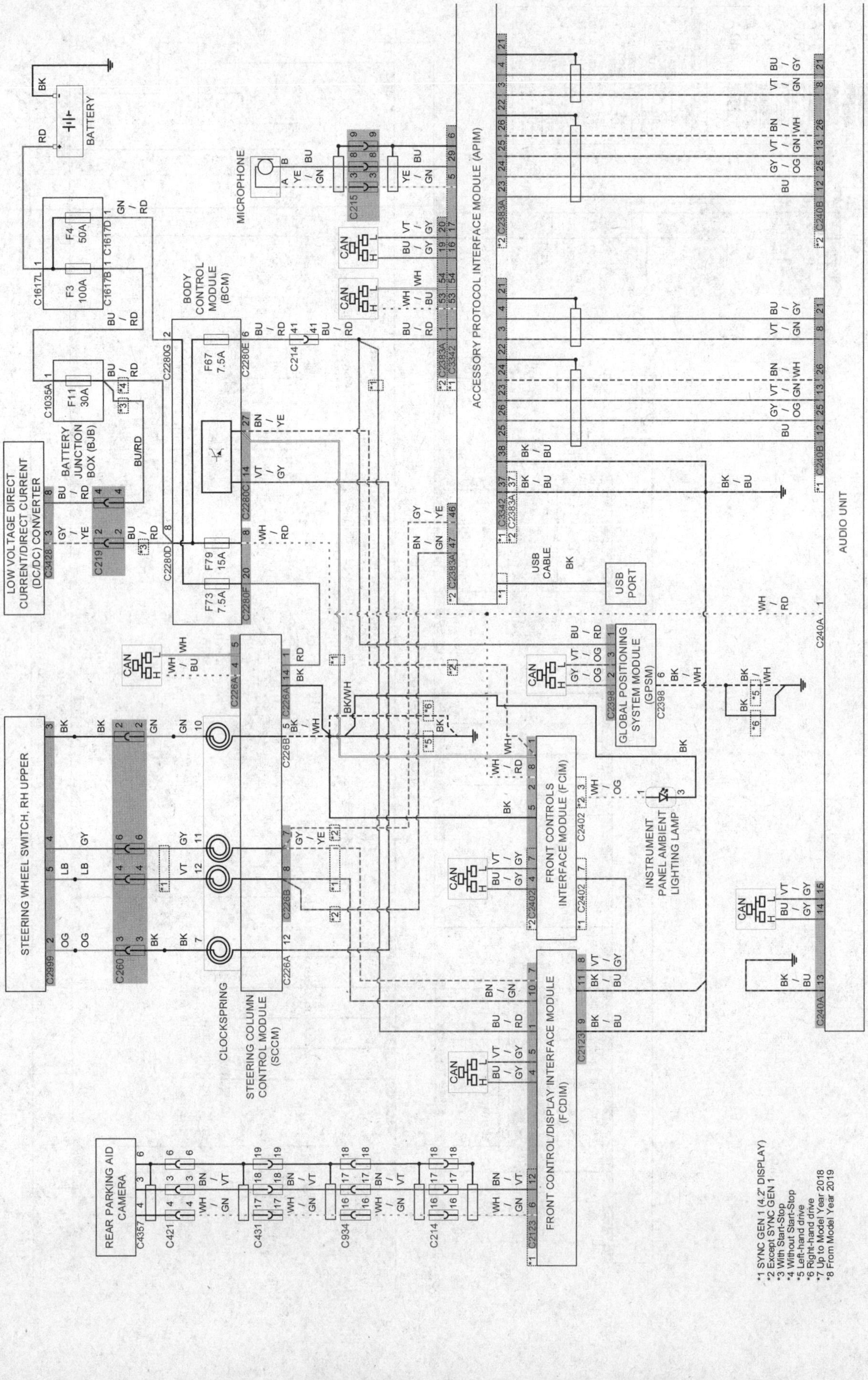

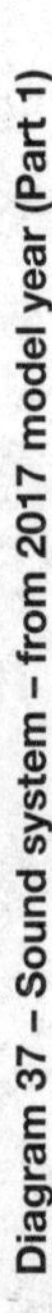

Diagram 37 – Sound system – from 2017 model year (Part 1)

*1 SYNC GEN 1 (4.2" DISPLAY)
*2 Except SYNC GEN 1
*3 With Start-Stop
*4 Without Start-Stop
*5 Left-hand drive
*6 Right-hand drive
*7 Up to Model Year 2018
*8 From Model Year 2019

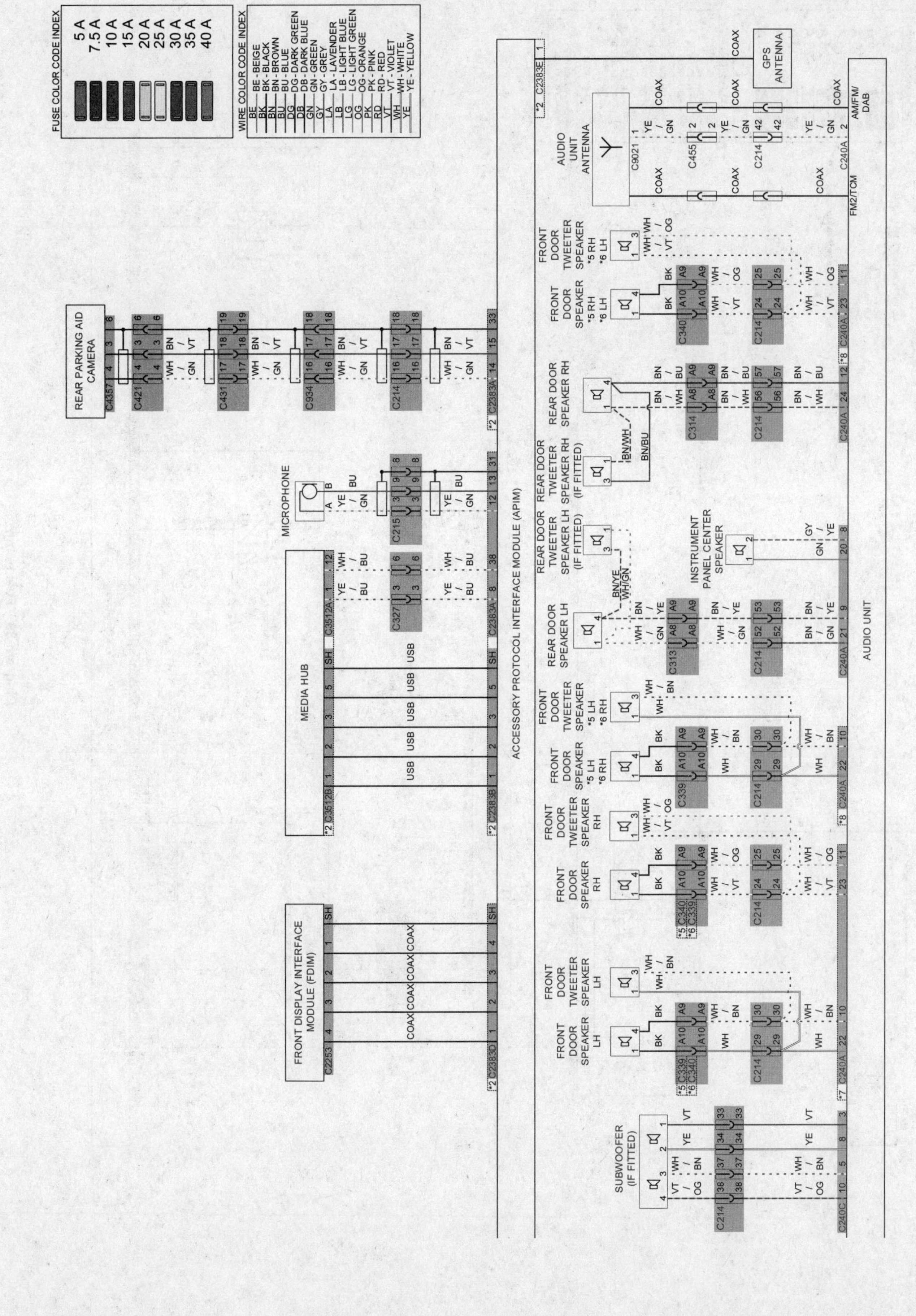

FUSE COLOR CODE INDEX

- 5 A
- 7.5 A
- 10 A
- 15 A
- 20 A
- 25 A
- 30 A
- 35 A
- 40 A

WIRE COLOR CODE INDEX

BE	BE - BEIGE
BK	BK - BLACK
BN	BN - BROWN
BU	BU - BLUE
DG	DG - DARK GREEN
DB	DB - DARK BLUE
GN	GN - GREEN
GY	GY - GREY
LA	LA - LAVENDER
LB	LB - LIGHT BLUE
LG	LG - LIGHT GREEN
OG	OG - ORANGE
PK	PK - PINK
RD	RD - RED
VT	VT - VIOLET
WH	WH - WHITE
YE	YE - YELLOW

FRONT DISPLAY INTERFACE MODULE (FDIM)

MEDIA HUB

MICROPHONE

REAR PARKING AID CAMERA

ACCESSORY PROTOCOL INTERFACE MODULE (APIM)

SUBWOOFER (IF FITTED)

FRONT DOOR SPEAKER LH

FRONT DOOR TWEETER SPEAKER LH

FRONT DOOR SPEAKER RH

FRONT DOOR TWEETER SPEAKER RH

FRONT DOOR SPEAKER *5 LH *6 RH

FRONT DOOR TWEETER SPEAKER *5 LH *6 RH

REAR DOOR SPEAKER LH

REAR DOOR TWEETER SPEAKER LH (IF FITTED)

REAR DOOR TWEETER SPEAKER RH (IF FITTED)

REAR DOOR SPEAKER RH

INSTRUMENT PANEL CENTER SPEAKER

FRONT DOOR SPEAKER *5 RH *6 LH

FRONT DOOR TWEETER SPEAKER *5 RH *6 LH

AUDIO UNIT ANTENNA

GPS ANTENNA

AUDIO UNIT

Diagram 38 – Sound system – from 2017 model year (Part 2)

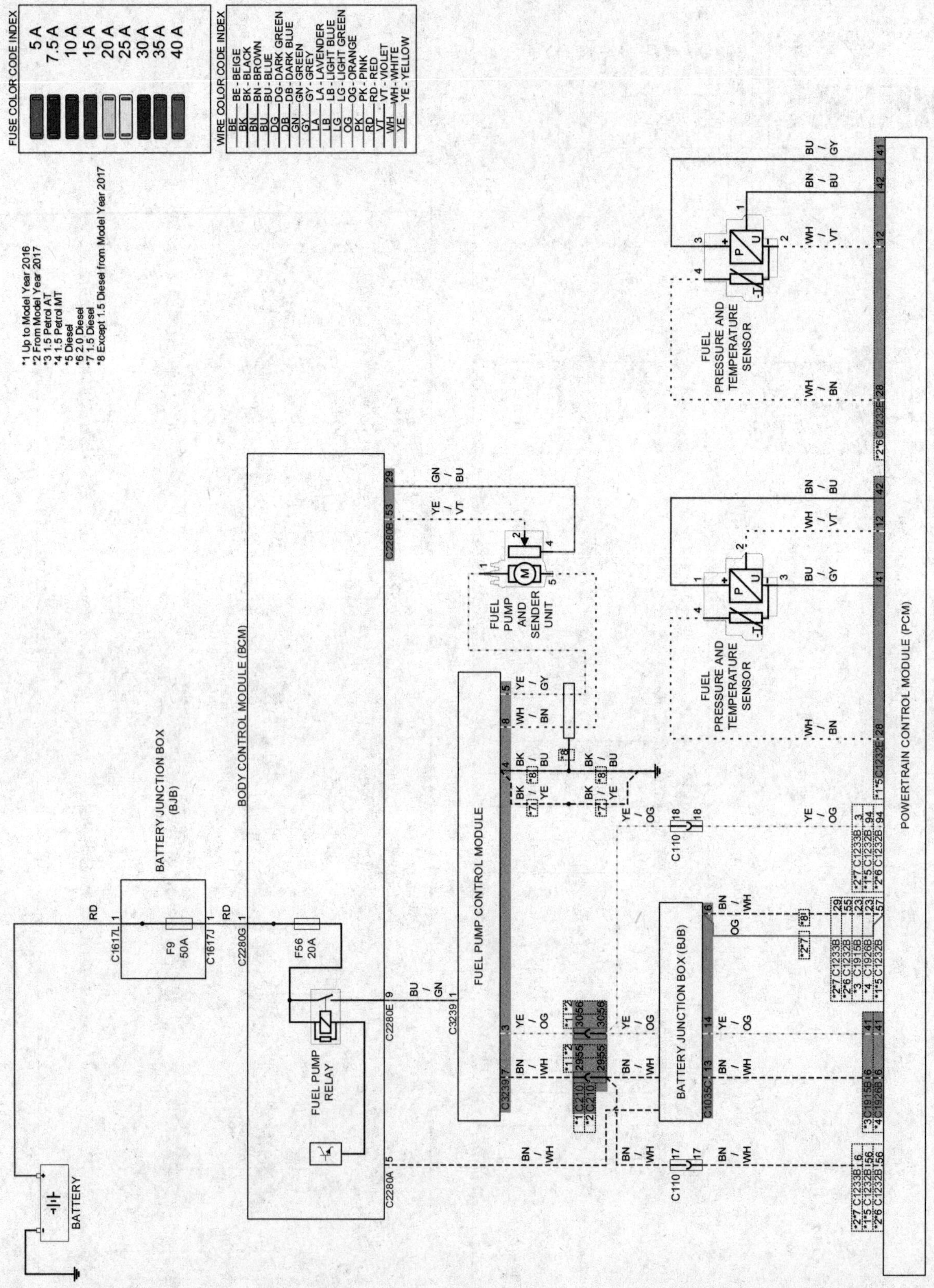

Diagram 39 – Fuel pump

Note: *References throughout this index are in the form "Chapter number" • "Page number". So, for example, 2C•15 refers to page 15 of Chapter 2C.*

A

B

C

Note: *References throughout this index are in the form "Chapter number" • "Page number". So, for example, 2C•15 refers to page 15 of Chapter 2C.*

Note: *References throughout this index are in the form "Chapter number" • "Page number". So, for example, 2C•15 refers to page 15 of Chapter 2C.*

Note: *References throughout this index are in the form "Chapter number" • "Page number". So, for example, 2C•15 refers to page 15 of Chapter 2C.*

14.1 Squeeze the tangs and pull away the panel

14.2 Unclip the pollen filter housing cover

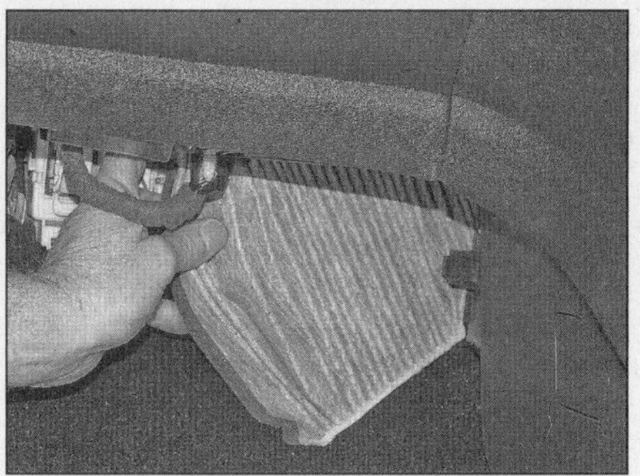

14.3 Slide out the pollen filter, into the passenger's footwell, and remove it

under the vehicle, refit the undershield, then lower the vehicle to the ground.

33 Remove the old oil and all tools from under the car, then lower the car to the ground.

34 Remove the dipstick, then unscrew the oil filler cap. Fill the engine, using the correct grade and type of oil (see *Lubricants and fluids*). An oil can spout or funnel may help to reduce spillage. Pour in half the specified quantity of oil first, then wait a few minutes for the oil to run to the sump. Continue adding oil a small quantity at a time until the level is up to the lower mark on the dipstick. Adding approximately 1.0 litre will bring the level up to the upper mark on the dipstick. Refit the filler cap.

35 Start the engine and run it for a few minutes; check for leaks around the oil filter seal and the sump drain plug. Note that there may be a delay of a few seconds before the oil pressure warning light goes out when the engine is first started, as the oil circulates through the engine oil galleries and the new oil filter (where fitted) before the pressure builds-up.

36 Switch off the engine, and wait a few minutes for the oil to settle in the sump once more. With the new oil circulated and the filter completely full, recheck the level on the dipstick, and add more oil as necessary.

37 Refit the engine undertray.

38 Dispose of the used engine oil and filter safely, with reference to *General repair procedures*. Do not discard the old filter with domestic household waste. The facility for waste oil disposal provided by many local council refuse tips and/or recycling centres generally has a filter receptacle alongside.

14 Pollen filter renewal

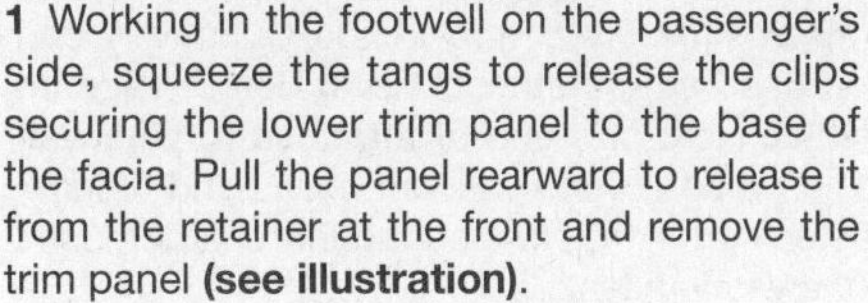

1 Working in the footwell on the passenger's side, squeeze the tangs to release the clips securing the lower trim panel to the base of the facia. Pull the panel rearward to release it from the retainer at the front and remove the trim panel **(see illustration)**.

2 Squeeze open the retaining clips and remove the pollen filter cover **(see illustration)**.

3 Slide out the pollen filter, into the passenger's footwell, and remove it **(see illustration)**.

4 When fitting the new filter, note the direction-of-airflow arrow marked on its top edge – the arrow should point rearwards.

5 Slide the filter fully into position and clip the cover into place, then refit the facia lower trim panel pushing the clips onto the pins to retain panel in place.

15 Fuel filter water draining

Note: *Various types of fuel filters are fitted to these engines depending on model year and territory. The following procedures depict a typical example. Not all filters are fitted with a drain facility.*

1 On the 2.0 litre (both to emissions level Stage V and Stage VI), the fuel filter is located on the top right of the engine, towards the front. On the 1.5 litre, it is on the top of the engine at the left-hand rear corner.

2 Remove the engine undertray.

3 Pull up the plastic cover from the top of the engine.

4 On the 2.0 litre engines, undo the three retaining bolts for the fuel filter cover and manoeuvre from place. On the 1.5 litre engine, undo the 3 studs and manoeuvre the cover from place **(see illustrations)**.

5 Use a Torx screwdriver to open the drain tap, and allow the fuel/water to drain from the filter **(see illustration)**. As soon as water-free fuel emerges from the pipe below the engine, retighten the drain screw.

6 Start the engine. If difficulty is experienced, bleed the fuel system as described in Chapter 4B Section 5.

Caution: Operate the starter motor in short bursts of no more that 10 seconds, allowing it cool in between attempts.

16 Hose and fluid leak check

General

1 Visually inspect the engine joint faces, gaskets and seals for any signs of water or oil leaks. Pay particular attention to the areas around the cylinder head cover, cylinder head, oil filter and sump joint faces. Bear in mind that, over a period of time, some very slight seepage from these areas is to be expected – what you are really looking for is any

15.4a On 2.0 litre engines, remove the filter cover retaining bolts

15.4b On 1.5 litre engines, remove the 3 retaining studs

15.5 Use a Torx screwdriver to undo the drain screw

indication of a serious leak. Should a leak be found, renew the offending gasket or oil seal by referring to the appropriate Chapters in this manual.

2 High temperatures in the engine compartment can cause the deterioration of the rubber and plastic hoses used for engine, accessory and emission systems operation. Periodic inspection should be made for cracks, loose clamps, material hardening and leaks.

3 When checking the hoses, ensure that all the cable-ties or clips used to retain the hoses are in place, and in good condition. Clips which are broken or missing can lead to chafing of the hoses, pipes or wiring, which could cause more serious problems in the future.

4 Carefully check the large top and bottom radiator hoses, along with the other smaller-diameter cooling system hoses and metal pipes; do not forget the heater hoses/pipes which run from the engine to the bulkhead. Inspect each hose along its entire length, renewing any that are cracked, swollen or shows signs of deterioration. Cracks may become more apparent if the hose is squeezed, and may often be apparent at the hose ends.

5 Make sure that all hose connections are tight. If the large-diameter air hoses from the air cleaner are loose, they will leak air, and upset the engine idle quality. If the spring clamps that are used to secure some of the hoses appear to be slackening, they should be updated with worm-drive clips to prevent the possibility of leaks.

6 Some other hoses are secured to their fittings with clamps. Where clamps are used, check to be sure they haven't lost their tension, allowing the hose to leak. If clamps aren't used, make sure the hose has not expanded and/or hardened where it slips over the fitting, allowing it to leak.

7 Check all fluid reservoirs, filler caps, drain plugs and fittings, etc, looking for any signs of leakage of oil, transmission and/or brake hydraulic fluid and coolant. Also check the clutch hydraulic fluid lines which lead from the fluid reservoir, master cylinder, and the slave cylinder (on the transmission).

8 Remember that some leaks will only occur with the engine running, or when the engine is hot or cold. Remove the engine undertray. Check that the handbrake is fully on, start the engine from cold, and let the engine idle while you examine the underside of the engine compartment for signs of leakage.

9 If an unusual smell is noticed inside or around the car, especially when the engine is thoroughly hot, this may point to the presence of a leak.

10 As soon as a leak is detected, its source must be traced and rectified. Where oil has been leaking for some time, clean away the accumulated dirt so that the exact source of the leak can be identified.

Vacuum hoses

11 It's quite common for vacuum hoses, especially those in the emissions system, to be colour-coded, or to be identified by coloured stripes moulded into them. Various systems require hoses with different wall thicknesses, collapse resistance and temperature resistance. When renewing hoses, be sure the new ones are made of the same material.

12 Often the only effective way to check a hose is to remove it completely from the vehicle. If more than one hose is removed, be sure to label the hoses and fittings to ensure correct installation.

13 When checking vacuum hoses, be sure to include any plastic T-fittings in the check. Inspect the fittings for cracks, and check the hose where it fits over the fitting for distortion, which could cause leakage.

14 A small piece of vacuum hose (approximately 6 mm inside diameter) can be used as a stethoscope to detect vacuum leaks. Hold one end of the hose to your ear, and probe around vacuum hoses and fittings, listening for the 'hissing' sound characteristic of a vacuum leak.

Warning: When probing with the vacuum hose stethoscope, be very careful not to come into contact with moving engine components such as the auxiliary drivebelt, radiator electric cooling fan, etc.

Fuel pipes/hoses

Warning: Refer to the safety information given in 'Safety first!' and Chapter 4B Section 3 before disturbing any of the fuel system components.

15 Check all fuel lines at their connections to the injection pump, accumulator rail, injectors and fuel filter housing.

16 Examine each fuel hose/pipe along its length for splits or cracks. Check for leakage from the union nuts and examine the unions between the fuel lines and the fuel filter housing. Also check the area around the fuel injectors for signs of leakage.

17 To identify fuel leaks between the fuel tank and the engine bay, the vehicle should raised and securely supported on axle stands. Inspect the fuel tank and filler neck for punctures, cracks and other damage. The connection between the filler neck and tank is especially critical. Sometimes a rubber filler neck or connecting hose will leak due to loose retaining clamps or deteriorated rubber.

18 Carefully check all rubber hoses and metal fuel lines leading away from the fuel tank. Check for loose connections, deteriorated hoses, kinked lines, and other damage. Pay particular attention to the vent pipes and hoses, which often loop up around the filler neck and can become blocked or kinked, making tank filling difficult. Follow the fuel supply and return lines to the front of the vehicle, carefully inspecting them all the way for signs of damage or corrosion. Renew damaged sections as necessary.

Air conditioning refrigerant

Warning: Refer to the safety information given in 'Safety first!' and Chapter 3 Section 14, regarding the dangers of disturbing any of the air conditioning system components.

19 The air conditioning system is filled with a liquid refrigerant, which is retained under high pressure. If the air conditioning system is opened and depressurised without the aid of specialised equipment, the refrigerant will immediately turn into gas and escape into the atmosphere. If the liquid comes into contact with your skin, it can cause severe frostbite. In addition, the refrigerant contains substances which are environmentally damaging; for this reason, it should not be allowed to escape into the atmosphere.

20 Any suspected air conditioning system leaks should be immediately referred to a Ford dealer or air conditioning specialist. Leakage will be shown up as a steady drop in the level of refrigerant in the system.

21 Note that water may drip from the evaporator drain pipe, underneath the car, immediately after the air conditioning system has been in use. This is normal, and should not be cause for concern.

17 Auxiliary drivebelt check

1 A single auxiliary drivebelt is fitted at the right-hand side of all diesel engines. The length of the drivebelt varies according to whether air conditioning is fitted. An automatic tensioner is fitted, so setting the drivebelt tension is unnecessary.

2 Due to their function and material makeup, drivebelts are prone to failure after a long period of time, and should therefore be inspected regularly.

3 Since the drivebelt is located very close to the right-hand side of the engine compartment, it is possible to gain better access by raising the front of the car and removing the right-hand wheel and wheelarch liner.

4 With the engine stopped, inspect the full length of the drivebelt for cracks and separation of the belt plies. It will be necessary to turn the engine (using a spanner or socket and bar on the crankshaft pulley bolt) in order to move the belt from the pulleys so that the belt can be inspected thoroughly. Twist the belt between the pulleys so that both sides can be viewed. Also check for fraying, and glazing which gives the belt a shiny appearance. Check the pulleys for nicks, cracks, distortion and corrosion.

5 Small cracks in the belt ribs are not usually serious, but look closely to see whether the crack has extended into the belt plies. If the belt is in any way suspect, or is known to have seen long service, renew it as described in Section 32.

6 If the belt appears to be too slack (or has actually been slipping in service), this may indicate a problem with the belt tensioner, or external contamination of the belt (eg, by oil or water).

18 Seat belt check

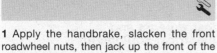

1 Check the seat belts for satisfactory operation and condition. Pull sharply on the belt to check that the locking mechanism engages correctly. Inspect the webbing for fraying and cuts. Check that they retract smoothly and without binding into their reels.

2 Check the accessible seat belt mountings, ensuring that all bolts are securely tightened.

19 Front brake pad and disc wear check

1 Apply the handbrake, slacken the front roadwheel nuts, then jack up the front of the car and support it securely on axle stands (see *Jacking and vehicle support*). Remove the front roadwheels.

2 The brake pad thickness, and the condition of the disc, can be assessed roughly with just the wheels removed **(see illustration)**. For a comprehensive check, the brake pads should be removed and cleaned. The operation of the caliper can then also be checked, and the condition of the brake disc itself can be fully examined on both sides. Refer to Chapter 9 for further information.

3 On completion, refit the roadwheels and lower the car to the ground. Tighten the roadwheel nuts to the specified torque.

20 Driveshaft gaiter check

1 With the car raised and securely supported on stands, turn the steering onto full lock, then slowly rotate the roadwheel. Inspect the condition of the outer constant velocity (CV) joint rubber gaiters while squeezing the gaiters to open out the folds. Check for signs of cracking, splits or deterioration of the rubber which may allow the grease to escape and lead to water and grit entry into the joint. Also check the security and condition of the retaining clips. Repeat these checks on the inner CV joints **(see illustration)**. If any damage or deterioration is found, the gaiters should be renewed as described in Chapter 8.

2 At the same time, check the general condition of the CV joints themselves by first holding the driveshaft and attempting to rotate the wheel. Repeat this check by holding the inner joint and attempting to rotate the driveshaft. Any appreciable movement indicates wear in the joints, wear in the driveshaft splines, or a loose driveshaft retaining nut.

21 Steering and suspension check

Front suspension and steering

1 Raise the front of the car, and securely support it on axle stands (see *Jacking and vehicle support*).

2 Visually inspect the balljoint dust covers and the steering rack-and-pinion gaiters for splits, chafing or deterioration **(see illustration)**. Any wear of these components will cause loss of lubricant, together with dirt and water entry, resulting in rapid deterioration of the balljoints or steering gear.

3 Grasp the roadwheel at the 12 o'clock and 6 o'clock positions, and try to rock it **(see illustration)**. Very slight free play may be felt, but if the movement is appreciable, further investigation is necessary to determine the source. Continue rocking the wheel while an assistant depresses the footbrake. If the movement is now eliminated or significantly reduced, it is likely that the hub bearings are at fault. If the free play is still evident with the footbrake depressed, then there is wear in the suspension joints or mountings.

4 Now grasp the wheel at the 9 o'clock and 3 o'clock positions, and try to rock it as before. Any movement felt now may again be caused by wear in the hub bearings or the steering track rod balljoints. If the outer balljoint is worn, the visual movement will be obvious. If the inner joint is suspect, it can be felt by placing a hand over the rack-and-pinion rubber gaiter and gripping the track rod. If the wheel is now rocked, movement will be felt at the inner joint if wear has taken place.

19.2 With the wheel removed, the pad thickness can be seen through the front of the caliper

5 Using a large screwdriver or flat bar, check for wear in the suspension mounting bushes by levering between the relevant suspension component and its attachment point. Some movement is to be expected, as the mountings are made of rubber, but excessive wear should be obvious. Also check the condition of any visible rubber bushes, looking for splits, cracks or contamination of the rubber.

6 With the car standing on its wheels, have an assistant turn the steering wheel back-and-forth, about an eighth of a turn each way. There should be very little, if any, lost movement between the steering wheel and roadwheels. If this is not the case, closely observe the joints and mountings previously described. In addition, check the steering column universal joints for wear, and also check the rack-and-pinion steering gear itself.

Rear suspension

7 Chock the front wheels, then jack up the rear of the car and support securely on axle stands (see *Jacking and vehicle support*).

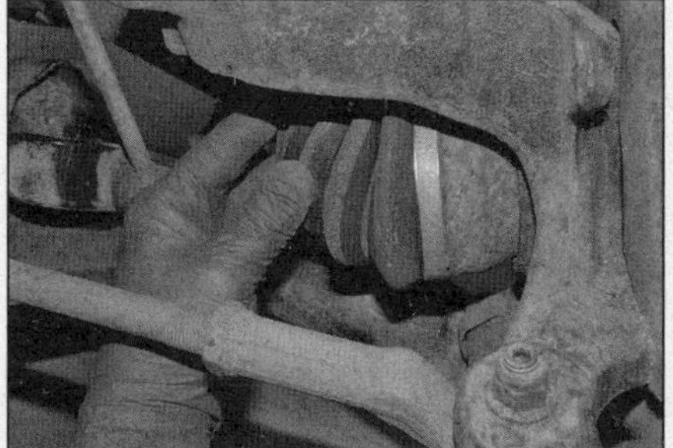

20.1 Check the outer constant velocity (CV) joint gaiters and, though less prone to wear, check the inner gaiters too

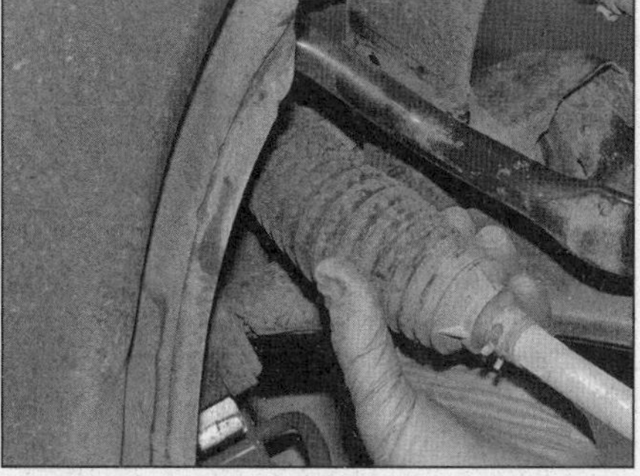

21.2 Check the steering gaiters for signs of splitting

21.3 Check for wear in the front suspension and hub bearings

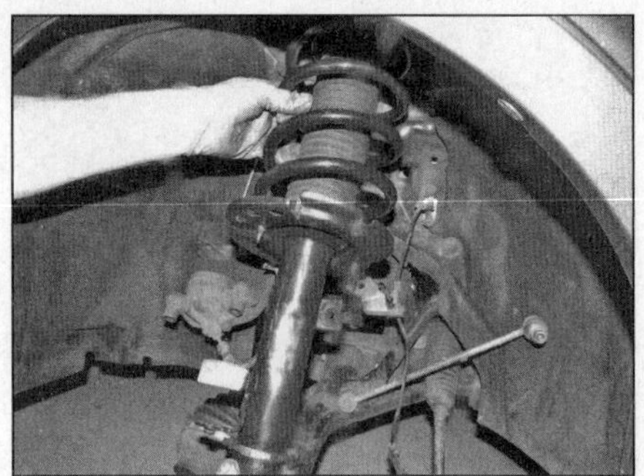

21.9 Check for signs of fluid leakage from the shock absorbers

8 Working as described previously for the front suspension, check the rear hub bearings, the suspension bushes and the shock absorber mountings for wear.

Shock absorber

9 Check for any signs of fluid leakage around the shock absorber body, or from the rubber gaiter around the piston rod **(see illustration)**. Should any fluid be noticed, the shock absorber is defective internally, and should be renewed. **Note:** *Shock absorbers should always be renewed in pairs on the same axle.*

10 The efficiency of the shock absorber may be checked by bouncing the car at each corner. Generally speaking, the body will return to its normal position and stop after being depressed. If it rises and returns on a rebound, the shock absorber is probably suspect. Also examine the shock absorber upper and lower mountings for any signs of wear.

22 Handbrake check and adjustment

1 The handbrake should be fully applied (and capable of holding the car on a slope) after approximately 3 to 5 clicks of the ratchet. Should adjustment be necessary, refer to Chapter 9 Section 14 for the full adjustment procedure.

23 Exhaust system check

1 With the engine cold (at least three hours after the vehicle has been driven), check the complete exhaust system, from its starting point at the engine to the end of the tailpipe. Ideally, this should be done on a hoist, where unrestricted access is available; if a hoist is not available, raise and support the vehicle on axle stands (see *Jacking and vehicle support*).

2 Make sure that all brackets and rubber mountings are in good condition, and tight; f any of the mountings are to be renewed, sure that the new ones are of the correct e – in the case of the rubber mountings, colour is a good guide. Those nearest to

23.2 Check the condition of the exhaust rubber mountings

the catalytic converter are more heat-resistant than the others **(see illustration)**.

3 Check the pipes and connections for evidence of leaks, severe corrosion, or damage. One of the most common points for a leak to develop is around the welded joints between the pipes and silencers. Leakage at any of the joints or in other parts of the system will usually show up as a black sooty stain in the vicinity of the leak. **Note:** *Exhaust sealants should not be used on any part of the exhaust system upstream of the catalytic converter (between the converter and engine) – even if the sealant does not contain additives harmful to the converter, pieces of it may break off and foul the element, causing local overheating.*

4 At the same time, inspect the underside of the body for holes, corrosion, open seams, etc, which may allow exhaust gases to enter the passenger compartment. Seal all body openings with silicone or body putty.

5 Rattles and other noises can often be traced to the exhaust system, especially the rubber mountings. Try to move the system, silencer(s), heat shields and catalytic converter. If any components can touch the body or suspension parts, secure the exhaust system with new mountings.

24 Roadwheel nut tightness check

1 Remove the wheel trims or alloy wheel centre covers where necessary, and slacken the roadwheel nuts slightly.

2 Tighten the nuts evenly in a diagonal pattern to the specified torque.

25 Hinge and lock lubrication

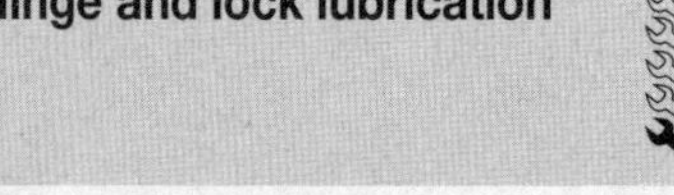

1 Work around the car and lubricate the hinges of the bonnet, doors and tailgate with light oil.

2 Lightly lubricate the bonnet release mechanism with a smear of grease.

3 Check carefully the security and operation of all hinges, latches and locks, adjusting them where required. Check the operation of the central locking system.

4 Check the condition and operation of the tailgate struts, renewing them both if either is leaking or no longer able to support the tailgate securely when raised.

26 Electrical systems check

1 Check the operation of all the electrical equipment, ie, lights, direction indicators, horn, etc. Refer to the appropriate sections of Chapter 12 for details if any of the circuits are found to be inoperative.

2 Note that the brake light switch is described in Chapter 9 Section 17.

3 Check all accessible wiring connectors, harnesses and retaining clips for security, and for signs of chafing or damage. Rectify any faults found.

27 Road test

Instruments and electrical equipment

1 Check the operation of all instruments and electrical equipment.

2 Make sure that all instruments read correctly, and switch on all electrical equipment in turn, to check that it functions properly.

Steering and suspension

3 Check for any abnormalities in the steering, suspension, handling or road 'feel'.

4 Drive the car, and check that there are no unusual vibrations or noises.

5 Check that the steering feels positive, with no excessive 'sloppiness', or roughness, and check for any suspension noises when cornering and driving over bumps.

Drivetrain

6 Check the performance of the engine, clutch, transmission and driveshafts.

7 Listen for any unusual noises from the engine, clutch and transmission.

8 Make sure that the engine runs smoothly when idling, and that there is no hesitation when accelerating.

9 Check that the clutch action is smooth and progressive, that the drive is taken up smoothly, and that the pedal travel is not excessive. Also listen for any noises when the clutch pedal is depressed.

10 Check that all gears can be engaged smoothly without noise, and that the gear lever action is smooth and not abnormally vague or 'notchy'.

11 Listen for a metallic clicking sound from the front of the car, as the car is driven slowly in a circle with the steering on full-lock. Carry out this check in both directions. If a clicking noise is heard, this indicates wear in a driveshaft joint (see Chapter 8).